Readings in Canadian History
Pre-Confederation

Second Edition

Readings in Canadian History

Pre-Confederation

Second Edition

R. Douglas Francis
Donald B. Smith

Holt, Rinehart and Winston of Canada, Limited

Canadian Cataloguing in Publication Data

Main entry under title:
Readings in Canadian history

Contents: [v. 1.] Pre-Confederation — [v. 2.] Post Confederation.
ISBN 0-03-921876-7 ([v. 1]). — ISBN 0-03-921877-5 ([v. 2])

1. Canada — History — Addresses, essays, lectures.
I.   Francis, R. D. (R. Douglas), 1944-
II. Smith, Donald B., 1946—

FC164.R42 1986   971   C85-098585-4
F1026.R42 1986

Cover: *Behind Bonsecours Market, Montreal,* 1866, by William Raphael.
Reprinted by permission of the National Gallery of Canada, Ottawa.
Publisher: Anthony Luengo
Developmental Editor: Tessa McWatt
Managing Editor: Mary Lynn Mulroney
Copy Editor: Warren Laws
Cover Design: John Zehethofer
Typesetting and Assembly: Cundari Group Ltd.

Printed in Canada

1 2 3 4 5 90 89 88 87 86

Contents

Preface

In this edition of our two volume *Readings in Canadian History*, as in the first edition, our concern is to provide a collection of articles suitable for introductory Canadian history tutorials. This has meant selecting topics related to the major issues dealt with in such history courses, and providing useful readings of a general nature. We have once again included material that deals with the various regions of the country, and selected, whenever possible, readings that reflect new research interests among Canadian historians. Consequently, we have changed some of the topics, and many of the readings. Unfortunately, these new additions have necessitated the elimination of worthwhile readings in the first edition due to a limitation of space. Still, we hope that this edition will continue to meet the needs of introductory students in Canadian history.

This volume includes two or three selections on each of fifteen topics thus providing instructors flexibility in choosing readings. Short introductions to each topic set the readings in an historical context and offer suggestions for further readings. It is our hope that this reader will contribute to increased discussion in tutorials, as well as complement course lectures and, where applicable, textbooks.

In preparing the reader, we and the publisher have both sought advice from a number of Canadian historians. Their comments have been generously given and have greatly improved the original outline. We would like once again to thank Douglas Baldwin of the University of Prince Edward Island and Neil Semple of the United Church Archives, Toronto, who helped us with selections for the first edition. In addition we would like to thank, for the first volume, Olive Dickason of the University of Alberta, Douglas Leighton of Huron College, University of Western Ontario, Richard Reid of the University of Guelph, Hugh Tuck of Memorial University, St. John's Newfoundland, and Christon Archer of the University of Calgary; for the second volume, David Mills of the University of Alberta, and Thomas P. Socknat of Queen's University. All made constructive suggestions for improvement in this second edition. As well, appreciation is extended to the tutorial assistants and students at the University of Calgary, from 1982 to 1984, who offered valuable comments, based on their use of the first edition. Heartfelt thanks also go to Tony Luengo, Brian Henderson and Tessa McWatt of Holt, Rinehart and Winston for their constant encouragement towards the completion of this second edition. Finally we wish to thank those Canadian historians who consented to let their writings be included in this reader. Their ideas and viewpoints will greatly enrich the study and appreciation of Canadian history among first- and second-year university students.

Douglas Francis
Donald Smith
Department of History
University of Calgary

Topic One

The Native Peoples and Early European Contact

The Europeans who came to North America looked upon it as an empty continent, completely open for settlement. In reality Indian tribal groups claimed and inhabited almost every part of the "New World," from the Gulf of Mexico to the Arctic coast, from the Atlantic to the Pacific. There were over fifty such groups in Canada alone.

In the pre-European period there existed no common designation for the whole country, nor even a single name for the native inhabitants. The "Indians" of Canada owed their allegiance to their family, their band, their village, their tribe, and — in case of several tribes — to their confederacy. But they had no concept of a pan-Indian identity. Each tribe spoke its own language and regarded its own members as "the people." This lack of a perceived common identity contributed to their failure to resist the Europeans. But certainly other factors contributed as well: the reliance of some native groups on European manufactured trade goods, fur trade rivalries, colonial wars, and the catastrophic drop in population due to exposure to European diseases.

In their article, "The Indians of Northeastern North America," Jacques Rousseau and George W. Brown present a sketch of the native groups of Eastern Canada at the time of white contact, showing how the Europeans' arrival both improved, and at the same time fatally weakened, the native societies. Anthropologist Bruce Trigger, in "The French Presence in Huronia: the Structure of Franco-Huron Relations in the First Half of the Seventeenth Century," follows the fortunes of the Hurons, one of the native groups that came into the closest contact with French fur traders in the seventeenth century.

One of the great difficulties of writing Canadian Indian history arises from the absence of Indian-produced accounts. What was the North American Indians' view of the world, immediately before the Europeans' arrival? Chief John Snow of the Wesley band of the Stoney Indians (the band lives in the foothills of southern Alberta) reviews his peoples' oral traditions in "The Oral History of the Stoneys," the first chapter in his recent (1977) history

1

of his people, *These Mountains Are Our Sacred Places: The Story of the Stoney People.*

How did the Europeans' view of land and nature differ from that of the Indians? In what ways would their attitudes lead to misunderstandings with the Indians? The questions of Indian sovereignty, and the right to self-determination, are an important issue today.

The Europeans' early attitudes toward Indian sovereignty are reviewed in: Brian Slattery's "French Claims in North America, 1500-59," *Canadian Historical Review*, 59 (1978): 139-169; Olive Patricia Dickason's "Renaissance Europe's View of Amerindian Sovereignty and Territoriality," *Plural Societies*, 8, 3-4 (1977): 97-107; and W.J. Eccles, "Sovereignty-Association, 1500-1783," *Canadian Historical Review*, 65 (1984): 475-510.

The best summary of Canada's native peoples still remains Diamond Jenness's, now dated, *Indians of Canada* (Ottawa: King's Printer, 1932, numerous editions since). Anthropologist Alice B. Kehoe provides an overview in her *North American Indians: A Comprehensive Account* (Englewood Cliffs, N.J.: Prentice-Hall, 1981). Thomas Y. Canby's "The Search for the First Americans," *National Georgraphic*, 156, 3 (September, 1979): 330-363 is an interesting acount of recent archaeological work in the Americas. J.V. Wright's *Six Chapters of Canada's Prehistory* (Ottawa: National Museums of Canada, 1976), reviews what is currently known of the Canadian Indian before the arrival of the European.

A very good introduction to the subject of early French-Indian relations in the Americas is Olive Patricia Dickason's *The Myth of the Savage and the Beginnings of French Colonialism in the Americas* (Edmonton: University of Alberta Press, 1984). Other introductory texts are Alfred G. Bailey's *The Conflict of European and Eastern Algonkian Cultures, 1504-1700* (1937, 2nd edition published by the University of Toronto Press, 1969); the short booklet by Bruce Trigger, *The Indians and the Heroic Age of New France* (Canadian Historical Association Booklet No. 30, 1977); and George F.G. Stanley's "The Indian Background of Canadian History," *Canadian Historical Association Report*, (1952), pp. 14-21.

Students interested in pursuing the subject further should consult James Axtell, ed., *The Indian Peoples of Eastern America: A Documentary History of the Sexes* (New York: Oxford, 1981); Cornelius Jaenen, *Friend and Foe: Aspects of French-Amerindian Cultural Contact in Sixteenth and Seventeenth Centuries* (Toronto: McClelland and Stewart, 1976); Bruce Trigger, *The Children of Aataentsic: A History of the Huron People to 1660*, 2 volumes (Montreal: McGill-Queen's, 1976); and Basil Johnston, *Ojibway Heritage* (Toronto: McClelland and Stewart, 1976).

Two interesting books on the early fur trade have recently appeared. Calvin Martin's *Keepers of the Game: Indian-Animal Relationships and the Fur Trade* (Berkeley, California: University of California Press, 1978), should be supplemented by Shepard Krech's edited work, *Indians, Animals and the Fur Trade: A Critique of Keepers of the Game* (Athens, Georgia: University of Georgia Press, 1981).

The Indians of Northeastern North America*
JACQUES ROUSSEAU and
GEORGE W. BROWN

This volume of the Dictionary contains the biographies of 65 Indians. In many ways they are a group apart. For almost all of them the information is fragmentary. Like fireflies they glimmer for a moment before disappearing again into the dark forest of unrecorded history. More important, their stories must be extracted almost entirely from records which are not their own. The history of the Americas as we know it is the white man's history, written of necessity from his own records. The Indians' oral tradition has added a little, but not a great deal; archaeology in recent years has added much, but most significantly on the pre-white period. We can now begin, however, to understand more fully the tremendous drama of interracial and intercultural conflict, with all its tragic consequences, which followed the white man's "discovery" of the Americas. Here biography can help us, since the stories of individual Indians often give us clearer glimpses of these conflicts and tensions than we might otherwise have, for they are revealed to us in human terms and not as impersonal forces. For this reason the number of Indians included in this volume has on the whole leaned to the generous side.

Of the first natives met by Europeans in what is now Canada we have no individual records, though there are numerous references to such meetings in explorers' accounts. Amongst the Amerinds the Eskimos belong to a distinct linguistic and cultural family and were mainly encountered in the explorations of Hudson Bay, though they are mentioned also in the Norse sagas. Contacts with them were, however, brief and sporadic.

At the beginning of the historical period the Eskimos had penetrated as far south as Havre-Saint-Pierre (formerly Pointe-aux-Esquimaux), on the north shore of the St. Lawrence. The first Indians of the Gulf region encountered by the early explorers were the Beothuks. Probably belonging to a distinct linguistic family, with a population of about 500 persons at the time of their discovery, they were entirely confined to Newfoundland. Their treatment by the whites in the early period was deplorable, members of the tribe being regarded as little better than animals by the Newfoundland fishermen who hunted them down. No missionaries were ever sent to the Beothuks and no colonist of the island ever learned their language. The tribe finally disappeared about the middle of the 19th century (*see* J. P. Howley, *The Beothuks or Red Indians, the aboriginal inhabitants of Newfoundland* (Cambridge, 1915); Jacques Rousseau, "Le dernier des Peaux-rouges," *Cahiers des Dix*, XXVII (1962), 47–76).

3

* From *Dictionary of Canadian Biography*, Vol. I (1000–1700). Copyright 1966 by University of Toronto Press. Reprinted by permission.

It is when we come to the Amerinds of the mainland that we find records of large numbers of identifiable persons from whom a representative selection for a volume such as this can be made. Northeastern North America was, however, a very large area stretching from Acadia westward through the entire region of the St. Lawrence and Great Lakes; and it is essential, as a background for the Indian biographies, that we recall that in the 17th century the Indians of this region present an often confusing mosaic of shifting tribes and bands at various levels of culture and with great differences in their ways of life. Beyond this also, if we are to have any true appreciation of the tension and tragedy in which both the Indian and the white man became involved, we must have some understanding of the basic rhythms and patterns of life which affected Indian thought and action.

In the northeastern region there were, broadly speaking, two linguistic groupings of Indian tribes: the Algonkian, migratory and primarily dependent on hunting and fishing; and the Iroquoian, semi-sedentary and semi-agricultural. Occupying the northern, and by far the larger, part of the region, were the many tribes of the Algonkian family. Farthest to the east were the Micmacs and the Malecites, inhabiting at the time of their discovery what is now the province of Nova Scotia, including Cape Breton Island, northern New Brunswick, and Prince Edward Island. The boundary between them was the height of land separating the waters that flow into the Saint John River from those that enter the Gulf of St. Lawrence; the Malecite territory extended to the shore of the St. Lawrence opposite present-day Tadoussac, and included also part of the state of Maine. The Malecites and several Algonkian tribes to the southward formed the Abenaki Confederacy (including, among others, the Passamaquoddy, Penobscot, and possibly the Sokoki Indians), which allied itself in the 17th century with the French against the Iroquois Confederacy and the English colonists of the Atlantic seaboard.

North of the St. Lawrence and east of the St. Maurice were the Montagnais; while further east along the north shore of the Gulf and stretching north into Labrador over a very great area were the roving bands of the closely related, and at times almost indistinguishable, Naskapis. West of the St. Maurice and occupying the Ottawa River basin were the Algonkians. Still further west were the Ottawas, on the route toward Georgian Bay; the Nipissings in the vicinity of Lake Nipissing; and the Chippewas or Ojibwas to the north around Lake Superior. North also of the Algonkians and Ojibwas, occupying the watershed of James Bay and stretching westward into present-day Saskatchewan, were the many roving bands of Crees.

The Algonkian peoples are usually described as migratory because so many individual tribes ranged more or less continually over wide expanses in search of game — moose, deer, caribou, smaller animals which were trapped — and fish. They also used wild plants to augment their diet and in certain places they gathered wild rice and made maple syrup in season. A few tribes also practised horticulture on a small scale, planting maize,

4

beans, and squash. Food was generally plentiful during the summer months but many of the tribes experienced severe food shortages in the winter.

Because the Algonkians were migratory, their material possessions were, of necessity, portable. Baskets and other containers were woven or made out of bark or wood. The single-family peaked or dome-shaped lodge or wigwam, as it is called, was the basic form of shelter used throughout the area. With its covering of birch-bark rolls, woven rush mats, or skins, this type of house was easy to assemble and dismantle. For winter travel, the Algonkians used the toboggan and snow-shoes and for summer expeditions, the graceful birch-bark canoe, one of the great Indian contributions to water transportation in North America.

The important socio-economic unit was the band, although there were tribal divisions which were known and recognized. Bands varied in size from a few families to several hundred individuals. In many ways, the Algonkian peoples inclined to individualism — so much so that they have been described by many authorities as "atomistic." The recognized leader of the band was usually an experienced hunter, noted for his astuteness and good judgement. In some instances, these positions were hereditary in a powerful family (descent among these people was through the male line). A particularly gifted man might become chief of the tribe when a number of bands joined in the conduct of war, in negotiations with other tribes, or with the white men's governments. At the local level, however, it was more often the shaman who exerted the greatest influence.

5

With the rise of the fur trade, the Algonkians found their knowledge of the forest and the habits of the fur-bearing animals most valuable, as trapping became their major occupation. It was the European traders who introduced them to iron tools, guns, kettles, brandy, and other facets of white culture. In exchange, the traders received the pelts of lynx, otter, marten, fox, and, most important of all, beaver. In becoming trappers, the Algonkians had to relinquish much of their traditional woodland economy as they settled around the trading-posts. Thus they became dependent on the fur market, with all its vicissitudes, and were exposed to many evil aspects of European civilization, alcoholism in particular. Their participation in the fur trade as allies of the French involved them in conflicts with the Iroquois and, ultimately, dragged them into the struggle between England and France for North America itself.

In considerable contrast to the life of the Algonkians was that of the Iroquoian tribes, most prominent among whom in the early 17th century were the Hurons located south of Georgian Bay, and the Iroquois of the Five Nations Confederacy occupying the territory south of the St. Lawrence and Lake Ontario from the Richelieu River almost to Lake Erie. Situated in these well-watered and fertile regions of present-day southern Ontario and western New York, they had an hospitable environment for an extensive agricultural economy. Here they were able to grow maize, their principal crop, as well as beans, squash, pumpkins, tobacco, and other vegetable products, some in considerable quantity. The surrounding woodlands furnished them with a number of wild plants, game animals (deer in particular), and fish.

A rich, well-documented ethnohistorical literature describes the role of these peoples in the 17th century but their history before contact with the white man evokes considerable debate among archaeologists. It is now believed that the Hurons and the Iroquois shared a common origin in the south, having pushed into the region of the Great Lakes from the southwest, following the line of the Ohio and splitting on lakes Erie and Ontario, some going to the north side of these lakes, some to the south. In 1534 Cartier found Iroquois on the lower St. Lawrence; but, in the interval between then and the coming of Champlain in 1608, they went back to the position south of the river which in the 17th century became a "buffer zone" between New France and the English colonies on the Atlantic seaboard.

6   Leagued in the Huron or Wyandot Confederacy were four tribes: Attignaouantan (Bear), Attingneenougnahak (Cord), Ahrendarrhonon (Rock), and Tahontaenrat (Deer). Adjoining the Hurons were other Iroquoian tribes: the Tobacco Nation or Petuns to the west, and the Neutrals to the south along the north shore of Lake Erie. The famous Iroquois Confederacy consisted in the 17th century of five tribes: the Mohawks farthest east toward the Richelieu River, and westward from them the Oneidas, Onondagas, Cayugas, and Senecas. South and west of the Senecas were the Eries, another Iroquoian tribe.

All these Iroquoian peoples lived in rather permanent villages which were abandoned after an occupancy of 10 to 15 years. These villages were usually situated on high ground near some source of water and were fairly large, attaining populations of several hundreds or more. Most were protected by a log palisade. The houses were multiple-family units, appropriately called "long-houses" because of their rectangular shape, and usually accommodated eight to ten families each, although some have been reported to house from 20 to 30 families.

The household was the basic unit of Iroquoian social organization, which may be described technically as a maternal lineage, with descent reckoned through the female line. The core of any household consisted of a number of females descended from a common ancestress. When a man married, he occupied his wife's house. Authority in these households was vested in an old woman. While not constituting a true matriarchate, these older women did exert a great deal of influence, particularly in the political sphere.

The clan, a larger kin group, consisted of a number of households and resembled somewhat a great family. Clansmen considered themselves siblings, intermarriage between them was prohibited, custom dictated that they aid one another in time of need, they held property as a corporate group, they redressed injuries to one another and avenged deaths. Most of the clans bore animal names, Bear, Wolf, and Turtle being almost universal.

The significant political unit was the tribe. It had a name, occupied a defined territory, and possessed a council of chiefs or sachems. Linguistic affinity and a common way of life did not, however, necessarily imply friendly intercourse. The Hurons, who became the irreconcilable enemies of the Iroquois, their linguistic and cultural kin, were on much better terms with the Algonkians, originally migratory hunters, speaking an alien dialect. Thus it was that by the time the white man arrived confederacies had been founded, the purpose of which was to maintain peace among the member tribes. The Five Nations referred to their confederacy as the "League of the Iroquois" or "the great peace." Its founders were the half-legendary Dekanahwideh and Hiawatha. In this system those tribes which were not members of the League were theoretically considered at war with it.

The institutional structure of the League of the Iroquois was described in symbolic terms derived from the long-house, certain tribes being "keepers of the door," etc. The kinship bonds of the maternal line, representing the household, were extended across the member tribes, which were themselves divided into clans. Since certain clans extended across various tribes, it then followed that quarrelling between clan "brothers" would theoretically be unthinkable.

7

The decisions of the league were made by a federal council composed of 50 sachems, whose positions were hereditary in the female line. It was the old women who decided which eligible male relative would actually inherit. Indeed the older women, the heads of the households, made most of the decisions, while the men holding the titles of authority carried them out. The five tribes comprising the league did not, it might be noted, enjoy equal representation. The Senecas, for example, were represented by 8 sachems and the Onondagas by 14, with the three remaining tribes ranging in between. The requirement that decisions be unanimous offset this unequal representation, however. Sachems enjoyed high repute. Indeed, aside from warfare, the office of sachem was the only means whereby a man might gain prestige.

Eloquence was one of the prime qualifications for a great sachem. Oratory and the recitation from memory of the great legends surrounding the founding of the league were outstanding attractions at the annual meeting of the Federal Council held at Onondaga, New York. As an aid to memory, wampum belts were used, combinations of black and white beads (made from clam and other shells), signifying important ideas and events. At times wampum was also used as a form of currency.

Although members of the league did, on occasion, join one another to wage concerted war (the destruction of the Hurons is a case in point), the greater part of their military activities smacked of the vendetta. A few warriors would combine to conduct a raid, making the most of surprise attack. Scalps were taken and prisoners brought back to the village, where they were either killed or adopted. Each household which had lost a member had the right to select a captive to fill the vacancy. Death by torture was the fate of the remainder. To die without showing the slightest indication of pain was considered ideal behaviour and victims were supposed to exhibit contempt for their captors by presuming to enjoy the tortures they received. Whatever their warfare, small- or large-scale, during the historic period, the Iroquois suffered great losses, witness a passage in the Jesuit *Relations* to the effect that Huron and Algonkian captives made up two-thirds of the Oneida tribe in 1668 (*JR* (Thwaites), LI, 123).

Such in sketchiest outline are a few suggestions about the nature of Indian society at the time of the white man's arrival, but even these will help us to understand why the impact of the 17th-century European culture on that of the Indian profoundly altered every aspect of Indian life and thought. That any remnants of Indian culture survived is a tribute to its strength and to the loyalty of the Indians to their traditions. The nature and devastating effects of this clash of cultures can be understood better now than by any observer at the time, though there are many penetrating recorded observations by both Indians and whites, especially by persons like Marie de l'Incarnation and some of the Jesuits, for example, in their letters, relations, and journals.

8

For the Indians of northeastern North America there were three vital areas where they suffered the full impact of the culture clash: first, the ideological, in which their religious beliefs and tribal organization were shaken to their very roots and the authority and influence of chiefs and medicine-men were gravely weakened; second, the economic, in which the fur trade caused a revolution affecting every aspect of daily life, sowing discord among the tribes, and finally erupting into the fur-trade wars; and third, political, where the imperial rivalries of French and English relentlessly dragged the Indians into the white men's struggles for military supremacy. In each of these areas the results were inevitably far more profound and tragic for the Indians than for the whites. From the first limited contacts with the early explorers, subsequently multiplied a thousand-fold across the whole continent, the Indians found their ancient ways completely disrupted, and social and moral disintegration, aggravated by brandy and disease, began to haunt them. M. André Vachon in his "L'eau-de-vie dans la société indienne," *CHA Report* (1960–61), 26–27, has vividly described this revolution:

"Indian society, which was extremely primitive, was in no way prepared for contact with Europeans. The Indian's first meeting with the white man was a brutal shock for him. Suddenly he discovered a world, the dimensions of which bore no relation to his own: the iron blades of the white men had more cutting power than the Indian's flint knives; their canoes were immense; their fire-arms killed from a distance with a noise like thunder. Surely the spirits on the side of the white men were infinitely more powerful than any others the Indian had ever encountered. Accustomed as he was to explaining natural phenomena in supernatural terms, the Indian recoiled from this first clash with western and Christian civilization, profoundly shaken in the very core of his existence — his religion.

"As these contacts with the white man became more frequent and prolonged, the Indian soul suffered a corresponding attrition. At first the French gave knives, axes, and kettles to the Indians in order to win their friendship. But this contact with European goods completely upset the Indian way of life. They could not resist the metal tools, so superior to their own in utility and convenience, which were, in their minds, imbued with power and strength, and they adopted them immediately. In consequence, they forsook their traditional crafts, they ceased to make their own weapons and utensils, they modified their methods of hunting to suit the new weapons. The French traded clothing, as well, in return for furs, also food and brandy. Each time the Indians accepted a European product, they abandoned a portion of their own culture. Little time elapsed before they became the slaves of the fur traders, for they were forced to bring more and more furs to the company stores in order to get all the new goods they needed. The Indian who, hitherto, had hunted only to satisfy his own limited needs, faced the brutal fact that he now lived in a competitive society which already had completely altered his life pattern . . . little by little, certain fundamental traditions were forgotten; and the demoralized Indian, conscious of his decline, gradually lost the will to live.

9

"Brandy, without question, played its part in this disintegration of the Indian culture. But we must guard against the temptation to isolate this element and to exaggerate its importance. Brandy was only one of the many factors which combined to bring about the physical and spiritual deterioration of the Indian."

The predominant influence in the ideological sphere was the impact made by the missions, initiated by the Recollets and later taken over by the Jesuits. The primitive Indians found it well-nigh impossible to reconcile the two dominant motives for the white man's penetration of their continent: the search for material wealth and the conversion of pagan souls. Neither motive seemed reasonable to men who provided merely for the material needs of the moment and who possessed an integrated system of belief peculiarly adapted to the natural environment in which it had evolved. Moreover, the Indians were further confused by a secular authority which revealed its will to them, sometimes through the black-robes, sometimes through Onontio (the governor), and sometimes through the traders. This multiple standard in the ideologies and behaviour of the white men was to make an indelible impression on the Indian. The ensuing clash of interests and cultural values was to beget a fatal violence at the very foot of the altar and does much to explain the obstacles encountered by both the missionaries and those whom they sincerely wished to aid in bridging the gulf separating the palaeolithic from the modern age. Many persons, both Indians and whites, whose lives are described in this volume found themselves struggling, often helplessly, with complex and almost insoluble problems created by this pioneer phase of Canadian history.

The Hurons and their fate, as allies of the French, provide perhaps the best and most tragic example of the results which followed the deep penetration of a primitive, indigenous culture by a European one, so far removed from it by centuries of civilization. Coming in a spirit of the utmost devotion and willing to suffer every hardship, even torture and death, the missionaries found themselves facing the baffling problem of bringing new concepts, religious and secular, to a people whose ways and language, in the beginning at least, they did not understand. And, an added difficulty, they soon found themselves, as important representatives of the small, educated minority in the colony, inextricably and often unwillingly involved in civil and commercial policy; in the disputes over the fur trade and the sale of brandy; and in the bitter Indian military conflicts which destroyed the Huron country and, for a time, threatened even the existence of New France itself.

Despite a high mortality rate, the native population had maintained its equilibrium before the arrival of the white men. Infectious diseases, hitherto unknown, were introduced by the Europeans, causing a catastrophic drop in population.

A too hasty judgement might attribute to warfare the numerical decline of the Indians. The majority succumbed first of all to these new diseases carried by the whites. When the Huron nation first allied itself with the French, its population numbered 30 000 in contrast with the Iroquois total of 15 000. Measles raged among the Hurons in 1634, which was soon followed by smallpox and some other unnamed epidemic. In 1640 the Hurons numbered no more than 12 000, while the Iroquois population remained substantially the same. This epidemiological disparity has its own explanation. The Huron and Algonkian allies, with their families, paid regular visits to the trading-posts of New France, camping there for weeks at a time, in contact with the colonists and thus exposed to fresh contagion. The French missionaries and traders, on their part, freely frequented the Indian villages, whereas the Dutch and English more rarely penetrated to the Iroquois country. The Mohawks lived in the forest heart and many a long portage was necessary before their emissaries arrived to complete their brief transactions at Fort Orange (Albany, N.Y.). Solitary and on foot, in a hurry to return home, they were better able to avoid contagion than were entire households, travelling in canoes and prepared to stay for an extended period. The Iroquois family was not welcome at Fort Orange, a fact which saved it. The Dutch supplied fire-arms to the Iroquois after 1643 but the French, fearing revolt, refused to arm their non-Christian Indian allies. In 1649, when the Five Nations gave the final blow to the Hurons, disease had already conquered them. History often overwhelms its victims. The Hurons and the Iroquois had been equal, both belonging to the same race, speaking the same language, with the same characteristics and social structure (*see* Jacques Rousseau, "Les premiers Canadiens," *Cahiers des Dix,* XXV (1960), 9–64).

The geographical location of the Iroquois in the western part of what is now the state of New York gave them an important military advantage, enabling them to attack from the south, with relative impunity, the routes along the St. Lawrence and Lake Ontario, both vital links in the French communications with the *pays d'en haut* (the up-country), their major fur supply, to which the Iroquois also sought access. Thus the Iroquois had a motive for aggression and the base from which to launch it, whereas the Hurons had no interest in attacking their neighbours to the south.

Unlike the Hurons, the Iroquois were in a strategic position for diplomatic bargaining with more than one European government. Although the Iroquois were caught, against their will, in the conflicts and rivalries between the French on the St. Lawrence and the Dutch (after 1664 the English) of the Hudson River valley and New York, their strong military position (though it proved vulnerable in the long run) allowed them through most of the 17th century to play off the Dutch or the English against the French and thus to gamble for high stakes in the fur trade, with all the diplomatic and oratorical arts in which their leaders excelled.

"Are there practical persons who believe that Champlain would have done better to form an alliance with the Iroquois? Others maintain that his idealism led him to take the side of the Hurons and Algonkins, exposed as they were to the foul deeds of the cruel Iroquois. Neither of these views *11* is well founded. Champlain wanted to explore west from New France, to discover the route to China, and to create an agriculturally self-sufficient colony; but in the beginning he favoured the fur trade, the economic base for the young nation and the justification for the existence of the Compagnie des Cent-Associés, at that time masters of Canada. The north country harboured the finest furs — and the water routes leading into it were controlled by the Algonkins and the Hurons. The latter were, therefore, much more useful to the colony than were the Iroquois. The Hurons, moreover, profited from the same social structure as the Iroquois and they exceeded them by 10,000 to 15,000 men. The facts of the situation dictated Champlain's choice. But these tribes also had their problems. To participate in the fur trade they needed military aid against the Iroquois, with whom they had been at war for a half-century. Their enemies wanted to force them to join the Confederacy of the Five Nations. Independence is a prize for which a high price must be paid" (Rousseau, "Les premiers Canadiens," *ibid.*, 50).

For the fur trade the geographical location of the Iroquois during the 17th century was less favourable than that of the Hurons. They could not fall back on the rich resources to the west when their own fur supply became exhausted, and occupying the coveted Indian position of middleman between the hunting tribes or bands and the European purchasers, French, Dutch, or English, was thus beyond their reach. From the 1620's on, the European demand for furs was insatiable and the Hurons controlled access to the northern and western fur supply. They carefully prevented even the French from contacts at first hand with the Tobacco and Neutral nations which were their trading partners and with the Nipissings to the north who provided them with furs. For a brief period, the Allumette Island tribe (Algonkian), which inhabited an island in the Ottawa River, athwart the Huron-French trade route, cherished commercial ambitions, in spite of its numerical inferiority, but it was never successful in supplanting the Hurons, although its members were sufficiently powerful to exact tribute from the river traffic. Indian manoeuvres to control the fur trade are well illustrated by the career of the infamous Oumasasikweie.

In the 1630's and 1640's, however, it was the Hurons who demonstrated, collectively and most strikingly, the powerful position of the middleman. Located just south of the Precambrian Shield they were able to build up a trading empire among the Algonkian tribes stretching from the Great Lakes to the St. Maurice River, and even beyond it to the Saguenay, and northward to Hudson Bay. Their trading canoes loaded with their own and European goods, they threaded their way through the lakes and rivers of this great area, bartering for furs which would then be carried down to Montreal and Quebec, the Ottawa being the principal convoy route. From their neighbours, the Neutral and Tobacco nations, who were jealously guarded against contact with the French, the Hurons obtained native products such as corn and tobacco to supplement their own articles of barter with the Algonkian tribes.

It was this Huron trading empire, already weakened by disease, which, along with the Jesuit missions, the Iroquois destroyed in 1649–50, so completely indeed that the Hurons ceased to exist as a people, their remnants being dispersed among the tribes north and west with some seeking refuge on the île d'Orléans, later moving into Quebec itself and then, after ten years, to Notre-Dame-de-Foy, three or four miles west of Quebec.

"Of the 50 000 Hurons, Neutrals, and Eries who were in existence at the time the colony was founded, there remained only a remnant; in Oklahoma the Wyandots, their descendants, numbered scarcely 378 in 1905 and at Lorette, in the neighbourhood of Quebec, there were 835 Hurons in 1953. The majority of the fugitives merged with the Iroquois; Father Le Moyne encountered 1,000 among the Onondagas in 1653. Three years later, the Iroquois presented an ultimatum to the vanquished in the vicinity of Quebec: assimilation or war to the death? The majority of Hurons bowed before this threat" (Rousseau, "Les premiers Canadiens," *ibid.*, 51). So completely did they lose their identity that the Iroquois fighting against Dollard at the Long Sault in 1660 could include adopted Hurons in their ranks. The dialogue between Dollard's Hurons and those of the enemy, as reported by Louis Taondechoren, an Indian who escaped from the massacre, would tend to confirm this.

After 1650 the Iroquois never fully reaped the reward of replacing the Hurons in the fur trade, for the Ottawas fell heir to much of the Huron trade. The fierce forays of the Iroquois continued, however, far to the north and east, with ambuscades which at times closed the Ottawa to the fur convoys and with attacks on the settlements along the St. Lawrence which threatened the very existence of New France. Not until the arrival and campaign (1665–66) of the Carignan-Salières regiment under the Marquis de Tracy did the colony gain even a partial security in the military sense. Even then the long record of negotiations, treaty-making, and alternate intervals of war and peace did not end. It spanned, in fact, the entire 17th century, and spilled over into the 18th, for the Iroquois were then no less deeply involved in the Anglo-French wars and in the campaigns of the American Revolution. Thus the Iroquois provide the most striking example of the impact made on the Indians of north-eastern North America by the white man's imperial rivalries, which dominated the new continent as well as the old.

What part geographical location and the fur trade played in the 17th century Iroquois history is impossible to determine exactly. That both had a very great influence there is no question, even if one cannot accept the too rigidly deterministic explanation put forward, for example, by George T. Hunt in *The wars of the Iroquois* (Madison, 1940). Between Hurons and Iroquois, even though they were linguistically and culturally closely related, there were important contrasts in ideologies and institutions. The Iroquois, for example, never responded as deeply to Christianity as did the Hurons. Missionary projects were not attempted by the Dutch and English, while French efforts, religious as well as secular, were centred north of the St. Lawrence and from this base expanded into the Mississippi regions. The devoted but tragic and unsuccessful attempt of Father Jogues to found a mission in the Mohawk country was too slight and temporary an episode to affect the course of Iroquois cultural development. Whatever the explanation, the Iroquois were successful in defending themselves to some extent against catastrophic cultural changes, so that even today their descendants form a distinct cultural entity. Doubtless geographical location, leadership, the internal strength of Iroquois tradition and institutions, and other less tangible factors all played a part in their survival as a people. Of particular institutional significance was the famous Confederacy of the Five Nations. Although it was a voluntary association and its members acted with great freedom both in war and in peace, it undoubtedly had a cohesive influence, especially, it would appear, after 1660.

13

The clash of cultures, while affecting the Indian more drastically, also had its impact on the European, a stranger at first in the unfamiliar environment of the New World. Indeed, he owed to the Indian his own survival in these harsh surroundings. Cartier's description of his voyage of 1534 is our first authentic account of Indian-European contacts in north-eastern North America. In it he described the Iroquoians whom he met in Gaspé Bay, explained their customs, and mentioned maize, a plant under cultivation there. The two young Indians, Domagaya and Taignoagny, taken to France with the reluctant permission of their father, Donnacona, became in the next year the first Canadian interpreters at Stadacona. Through their good offices Cartier was able to learn something of the Great River of Canada, notably that it was *not* a strait leading into the Sea of Cathay. The cartographers of the Old World, drawing the first maps of Canada, were greatly indebted to the invaluable information collected from the Indians. From the Indians also, Cartier learned the spectacular cure for scurvy which beset his men in the winter of 1535–36 (Jacques Rousseau, "L'annedda et l'arbre de vie," *RHAF*, VIII (1954), 171–212).

The first and probably the most important contribution of the Indian to the white man was in exploration. It was the Indian, his canoe, his snow-shoes, and his interpreters (many of them children of the first unions between the French and Indian women) that enabled Champlain, Jolliet, La Vérendrye, and many others to thread their way towards *les pays d'en haut*, sometimes by streams which were little more than a trickle, and thus to discover a continent. It was also through the lore of the Indian and his knowledge of the fur-bearing animals that the *coureurs-de-bois* were able to make themselves at home in the forest and ultimately to build a commercial venture of world-wide importance, the development of which forms a dominant theme in early Canadian history.

The Indians' knowledge of native plants became of great importance to the European. Tobacco, maize, all types of squash or pumpkin, and beans, were unknown in Europe before Columbus. The Hurons made oil from the sunflower which they used to grease their hair. Champlain discovered the Jerusalem artichoke in eastern Canada but it was the historian, Marc Lescarbot, who introduced it into Europe. The Canadian Indians were familiar with maple syrup though maple sugar, the *sucre du pays* was unknown to them. Some Indian foods have been incorporated into the European-American cuisine, such as corn cooked on the cob and in other ways, for example, as succotash (a mixture of Indian corn and boiled beans, a favourite dish in New England); game cooked with wild rice; and, finally, certain methods of making bread stuffs which have been perfected in the northern forests, much to the benefit of the modern explorers. The native peoples of Central and South America alone have given more than 100 plants to world agriculture and thus transformed the commerce and cuisine of the Old World. The potato, called *patate* in French-Canada and in several provinces of France, comes from Peru. Carib Indians contributed the manioc and the sweet potato. The pimento provided the principal condiment in Mexico and was highly esteemed there as a vegetable. Some species of cotton were cultivated in New Mexico. And among other species which came from the recently discovered continent, were the tomato, cocoa, peanuts, the pineapple, the avocado, and arrow root.

The French and English languages have also borrowed from the Indian dialects; in English, for example, *pow-wow, canoe, tepee, chipmunk, moose, hominy, squash, tamarack*, etc. In French no less than 100 words have been adopted, among them *canot, tobagane, wigwam*, and more than 25 names of plants and animals in the province of Quebec alone.

Thus the 65 Indian biographies in this volume are only a slight reminder of the part played by the Indians in Canada's early development, a token tribute to a host of other unnamed Indians. Unknown contributors to today's culture, obscure heroes who fell in many battles, interpreters and canoe-men, they helped literally to haul half a continent into the modern

age. It is to this anonymous multitude that Canadian history owes some
of its most striking pages.

The French Presence in Huronia:
The Structure of Franco-Huron
Relations in the First Half
of the Seventeenth Century*
BRUCE G. TRIGGER

Few studies of Canadian history in the first half of the seventeenth century
credit sufficiently the decisive role played at that time by the country's
native peoples. The success of European colonizers, traders, and missionaries
depended to a greater degree than most of them cared to admit on their
ability to understand and accommodate themselves not only to native
customs but also to a network of political and economic relationships that
was not of their own making. Traders and missionaries often were forced
to treat Algonkians and Iroquoians as their equals and sometimes they had
to acknowledge that the Indians had the upper hand. If the Europeans
were astonished and revolted by many of the customs of these Indians
(often, however, no more barbarous than their own), they also admired
their political and economic sagacity.[1] Indeed, one Jesuit was of the
opinion that the Huron were more intelligent than the rural inhabitants of
his own country.[2] If the missionary or fur trader felt compelled to understand the customs of the Indians, the modern historian should feel no less
obliged to do so.

In order to appreciate the role that the Indians played in the history of
Canada in the first half of the seventeenth century, it is necessary to study
their customs and behaviour and the things they valued. Because their way
of life differed from that of the Europeans, the fur traders and missionaries
who interacted with them frequently became amateur anthropologists,
and some of them became very good ones. For some tribes the documentation amassed by these early contacts is extensive and of high quality.
For no tribe is this truer than for the Huron.[3] From the detailed picture
of Huronia that emerges from these studies, it is possible to ascertain
the motives that prompted the behaviour of particular Indians, or groups
of Indians, in a manner no less detailed than our explanations of those
which governed the behaviour of their European contemporaries. I might
add, parenthetically, that historians are not alone to blame for the failure
to utilize anthropological insights in the study of early Canadian history.
Iroquoian ethnologists and archaeologists have tended to avoid historical

15

*From *The Canadian Historical Review*, 49 (1968): 107–141. Reprinted by permission.

or historiographic problems. Only a few individuals, such as George T. Hunt, have attempted to work in the no man's land between history and anthropology.

Two explanations have been used by anthropologists and historians to justify the existing cleavage between their respective studies. One of these maintains that when the Europeans arrived in eastern North America, the native tribes were engaged in a struggle, the origins and significance of which are lost in the mists of time and therefore wholly the concern of ethnohistorians. Because of this, there is no reason for the historian to try to work out in detail the causes of the conflicts and alliances that existed at that time.[4] Very often, however, the struggle between different groups is painted in crude, almost racist, terms (and in complete contradiction to the facts) as one between Algonkian- and Iroquoian-speaking peoples, the former being an indigenous population, mainly hunters, the latter a series of invading tribes growing corn and living in large villages. It should be noted that such a simplistic explanation of European history, even for the earliest periods, would now be laughed out of court by any competent historian. The alternative hypothesis suggests that European contact altered the life of the Indian, and above all the relationships among the different tribes, so quickly and completely that a knowledge of aboriginal conditions is not necessary to understand events after 1600.[5] From an *a priori* point of view, this theory seems most unlikely. Old relationships have a habit of influencing events, even when economic and political conditions are being rapidly altered. Future studies must describe in detail how aboriginal cultures were disrupted or altered by their contact with the Europeans, rather than assume that interaction between Indians and Europeans can be explained as a set of relationships that has little or no reference to the native culture.

We will begin by considering developments in Huronia prior to the start of the fur trade.

The Huron

When the Huron tribes were described for the first time in 1615,[6] they were living in the Penetanguishene Peninsula and the part of Simcoe County that runs along Matchedash Bay between Wasaga Beach and Lake Simcoe. The Huron probably numbered twenty to thirty thousand, and, according to the most reliable of the descriptions from the Jesuit missionaries,[7] they were divided into four tribes that formed a confederacy similar in its structure to the league of the Iroquois.[8] The Attignaouantan or Bear tribe, which included about half of the people in the confederacy, lived on the western extremity of Huronia. Next to them lived the Attingueenougnahak, or Cord tribe, and the Tahontaenrat or Deer tribe. Farthest east, near Lake Simcoe, were the Ahrendarrhonon or Rock nation. The Tionnontate, or Petun, who spoke the same language as the Huron and were very similar to them, inhabited the country west of Huronia near the Blue

Mountain. The Petun, however, were not members of the Huron confederacy and prior to the arrival of the French, they and the Huron had been at war. Another Iroquoian confederacy, the Neutral, lived farther south between the Grand River and the Niagara frontier. Except for a few Algonkian bands that lived west of the Petun, there do not appear to have been any other Indians living in southern Ontario, except in the Ottawa Valley. The uninhabited portions of the province were the hunting territories of the Huron, Neutral, and Petun and also served as a buffer zone between these tribes and the Iroquois who lived south of Lake Ontario.

The Huron, like other Iroquoian tribes, grew corn, beans, and squash. These crops were planted and looked after by the women, who also gathered the firewood used for cooking and heating the houses. Contrary to popular notions the men also made an important contribution to the tribal economy, inasmuch as it was they who cleared the fields for planting (no small task when only stone axes were available) and who caught the fish which were an important source of nutrition. Because of the high *17* population density, the areas close to Huronia appear to have been depleted of game and expeditions in search of deer had to travel far to the south and east.[9] In general, hunting appears to have been of little economic importance among the Huron.

Huron villages had up to several thousand inhabitants and the main ones were protected by palisades made of posts woven together with smaller branches. Inside large villages there were fifty or more longhouses, often 100 feet or more in length, made of bark attached to a light wooden frame. These houses were inhabited by eight to ten very closely related families. Families that traced themselves back to a common female ancestor formed a clan which was a political unit having its own civil chief and war leader. Each tribe in turn was made up of a number of such clans and the clan leaders served on the tribal and confederal councils.[10]

The events that led to the formation of the Huron confederacy are not well understood. The Huron themselves said that it began around AD 1400 with the union of the Bear and Cord tribes and grew thereafter through the addition of further lineages and tribes. Archaeologically it appears that, although one or more of the Huron tribes was indigenous to Simcoe County, other groups moved into historic Huronia from as far away as the Trent Valley, the Toronto region, and Huron and Grey counties to the west.[11] Two tribes, the Rock and the Deer, had been admitted to the confederacy not long before the arrival of the French.

Historians frequently have asserted that it was fear of the Iroquois that prompted the Huron to seek refuge in this remote and sheltered portion of Ontario.[12] While this may be why some groups moved into Huronia, it is clear that in prehistoric times the Huron outnumbered the Iroquois and probably were not at any military disadvantage. For this reason ethnologists have begun to seek other explanations to account for the heavy concentration of population in Huronia in historic times. An abundance of light, easily workable soil may be part of the answer. Since the Huron lacked the tools to work heavier soils, this advantage may have outweighed the tendency towards drought and the absence of certain trace minerals in the soil which now trouble farmers in that area.[13] Huronia also lay at the south end of the main canoe route that ran along the shores of Georgian Bay. North of there the soil was poor and the growing season short, so that none of the tribes depended on agriculture. They engaged mainly in hunting and fishing and tribes from at least as far away as Lake Nipissing traded surplus skins, dried fish, and meat with the Huron in return for corn which they ate in the winter when other food was scarce.[14]

As early as 1615 the French noted that Huronia was the centre of a well-developed system of trade. Hunt, however, seems to have seriously overestimated both the extent of this network and the degree to which the Huron were dependent on it.[15] The main trade appears to have been with the hunting peoples to the north who happened to be Algonkian-speaking. The other Iroquoian tribes had economies similar to that of the Huron, so that with the exception of a few items, such as black squirrel skins, which came from the Neutral country, and tobacco from the Petun, trade with the other Iroquoian tribes was of little importance. Trade with the north, however, brought in supplies of dried meat, fish, skins, clothing, native copper, and "luxury items" such as charms which were obtained in exchange for corn, tobacco, fishing nets, Indian hemp, wampum, and squirrel skins.[16] Although manufactured goods, as well as natural products, flowed in both directions, the most important item the Huron had for export undoubtedly was corn. In 1635 Father Le Jeune described Huronia as the "granary of most of the Algonkians."[17]

18

Whole bands of northerners spent the winters living outside Huron villages, trading furs and dried meat with their hosts in return for corn. The Huron assumed a dominant position in these trading relationships and the Jesuits record that when the Algonkians had dealings with them, they did so in the Huron language since the latter did not bother to learn Algonkian.[18] The social implications of such linguistic behaviour cannot be lost on anyone living in present-day Quebec. In the French accounts the Algonkians appear to have been better friends of the Rock tribe than they were of the Bear.[19]

Considerable quantities of European trade goods that are believed to date between 1550 and 1575 have been found in Seneca sites in New York State.[20] Since both archaeological and historical evidence suggests that there was contact between the Huron and the tribes that lived along the St. Lawrence River in the sixteenth century,[21] it is possible that trade goods were arriving in Huronia in limited quantities at this time as well. In any such trade the Algonkin tribes along the Ottawa River would almost certainly have been intermediaries. It is thus necessary to consider the possibility that trade between the Huron and the northern Algonkians originally developed as a result of the Huron desire to obtain European trade goods.

There are a number of reasons for doubting that trade with the northern tribes had a recent origin. For one thing, the rules governing trade were exceedingly elaborate. A particular trade route was recognized as the property of the Huron tribe or family that had pioneered it, and other people were authorized to trade along this route only if they had obtained permission from the group to which it belonged.[22] Thus, since the Rock were the first Huron tribe to establish relations with the French on the St. Lawrence, they alone were entitled by Huron law to trade with them.[23] Because of the importance of this trade, however, the Rock soon "shared" it with the more numerous and influential Bear, and with the other tribes of Huronia.[24] The control of trade was vested in a small number of chiefs, and other men had to have their permission before they were allowed to engage in it.[25] An even more important indication of the antiquity of Huron contact with the north is the archaeological evidence of the Huron influence on the native cultures of that region, which can be dated as early as AD 900 and is especially evident in pottery styles.[26] Taken together, these two lines of evidence provide considerable support for the hypothesis of an early trade.

19

In the historic period the Huron men left their villages to visit other tribes in the summers, while their women were working in the fields. Profit was not the only reason for undertaking long voyages. The Jesuits report that many travelled into distant regions to gamble or to see new sights — in short for adventure. Trading expeditions, like war, were a challenge for young men.[27] Trading between different tribes was not always a safe and uncomplicated business and, for all they had to gain from trade during the historic period, the Huron frequently were hesitant to initiate trade with tribes of whom they had only slight acquaintance.

The dangers that beset intertribal contacts were largely products of another institution, as old, if not older than trade — the blood feud. If a man was slain by someone who was not his kinsman, his family, clan, or tribe (depending on how far removed the murderer was) felt obliged to avenge his death by slaying the killer or one of the killer's relatives. Such action could be averted only by reparations in the form of gifts paid by the group to which the murderer belonged to that of the murdered man. When an act of blood revenge actually was carried out, the injured group usually regarded it as a fresh injury; thus any killing, even an accidental one, might generate feuds that would go on for generations. This was especially true of intertribal feuds.[28]

The Huron and Five Nations had both suppressed blood feuds within their respective confederacies, but only with great difficulty. When quarrels arose between individuals from tribes not so united, they frequently gave rise to bloodshed and war. The chances of war were also increased because skill in raiding was a source of prestige for young men who therefore desired to pursue this activity.[29] If it were possible, prisoners captured in war were taken back to their captors' villages to be tortured to death, partly as an act of revenge, but also as a sacrifice to the sun or "god of war."[30] These three motives — revenge, individual prestige, and sacrifice — were common to all the Iroquoian-speaking peoples of the northeast and to many of their neighbours and generated and sustained intertribal wars over long periods of time. Indeed, where no close political ties existed, such as those within the Huron confederacy, and where there were no mutually profitable trading relationships, war between tribes appears to have been the rule. The Huron were almost invariably at war with one or more of the Five Nations, and prior to the development of the fur trade (when they started to carry French goods to the south and west) they appear to have been at war with the Neutral and Petun as well.[31]

On the other hand, when a trading relationship developed between the Huron and some neighbouring tribe, every effort was made to control feuds that might lead to war between them. The payment that was made to settle a blood feud with the Algonkians was greater than that made to settle a feud inside the confederacy,[32] and the dearest payment on record was made to the French in 1648 to compensate them for a Jesuit *donné* murdered by some Huron chiefs.[33]

A second method of promoting stable relations between tribes that wished to be trading partners appears to have been the exchange of a few people both as a token of friendship and to assure each group that the other intended to behave properly. Very often, these hostages appear to have been children. Although this custom is never explicitly described by the early French writers, the evidence for its existence is clear-cut. A Huron, whose sons or nephews (sister's sons and therefore close relatives) were sent to the Jesuit seminary in Quebec, boasted that they were relatives of the French and for this reason hoped for preferential treatment when they went to trade on the St. Lawrence.[34] Others said they had "relatives" among the Neutral and Petun and one man is reported as leaving his daughter with these relatives.[35] The priests and lay visitors who came to Huronia in early times were treated as kinsmen by the Huron, and families and individuals were anxious to have them live with them,[36] no doubt because the Huron regarded these visitors as pledges of good faith whose association with a particular family would establish good relations between that family and the French officials and traders downriver. The presentation of young children to Jacques Cartier at a number of villages along the St. Lawrence suggests, moreover, that this custom may have been an old one.[37]

The Huron thus not only traded with other tribes prior to the start of the fur trade, but also, in common with other tribes in the northeast, had developed a code or set of conventions that governed the manner in which this trade was conducted. Being a product of Indian culture, this code was designed to deal with specifically Indian problems. We will now turn to the French attempts to adapt themselves to the native trading patterns after Champlain's first encounter with the Indians in 1608.

Early Franco-Huron Relations

In 1608, the year Champlain established a trading post at Quebec, he was visited by the representatives of some Algonkin tribes from the Ottawa Valley and, in order to win their respect for him as a warrior and to secure their goodwill, he agreed to accompany them the following year on a raid against their chief enemy, the Iroquois.[38] The regions to the north gave promise of more pelts and ones of better quality than did the Iroquois country to the south and fighting with a tribe alongside its enemies was an effective way of confirming an alliance.[39] Thus Champlain's actions seem to have been almost inevitable. At the same time he probably also hoped to drive Iroquois raiders from the St. Lawrence Valley and to open the river as a valuable trade artery.[40]

When the Ottawa River Algonkin returned the next year, they were accompanied by a party of Huron warriors from the Rock tribe. In later times the Huron informed the Jesuits that they had first heard of the French from the Algonkians early in the seventeenth century, and as a result of this had decided to go downriver to meet these newcomers for themselves.[41] Very likely Champlain's account and the Huron one refer to the same event. Some of the Ottawa River Algonkin, who were already probably in the habit of wintering in Huronia, may have tried to recruit Huron warriors for their forthcoming expedition against the Iroquois, and the Huron, prompted by curiosity and a desire for adventure, may have agreed to accompany them to Quebec.

Champlain was keenly interested at this time both in exploring the interior and in making contacts with the people who lived there. Learning the size of the Huron confederacy and their good relations with the hunting (and potentially trapping) peoples to the north, Champlain realized their importance for the development of the fur trade and set out to win their friendship. The Huron, on the contrary, were at first extremely hesitant in their dealings with the French,[42] in part because they had no treaty with them and also because they regarded the French as allies of the Algonkin, who might become hostile if they saw the Hurons trying to establish an independent relationship with them.

The ambiguity of the Huron position can be seen in the exchange of children that was arranged in 1610. At that time the Huron gave Champlain custody of a boy, who was to go to France with him, and in exchange they received a young Frenchman. When the Huron departed, however, the French boy (probably Etienne Brûlé) did not leave with them, but stayed with Iroquet, an Algonkin chief from the lower Ottawa.[43] Iroquet, however, seems to have been one of the Algonkin who was in the habit of wintering in Huronia. Thus a three-sided exchange seems to have been arranged in which the Huron laid the basis for a friendly relationship with the French, but one that was subordinate to, and dependent upon, their relationship with the Algonkin.

As trade with the French increased, the Huron began to appreciate

French goods and to want more of them. Metal awls and needles were superior to native bone ones, and iron arrowheads could penetrate the traditional shields and body armour of their enemies. Metal kettles were easier to cook in than clay pots and metal knives were much more efficient than stone ones. Clearing fields and cutting wood was easier when stone axes were replaced by iron hatchets. Luxury items, such as cloth and European beads, were soon sought after as well.[44]

The growing demand for these products in a population that numbered between twenty and thirty thousand no doubt made the Huron anxious to establish closer relations with the French, without, if possible, having to recognize the Ottawa River Algonkin as middlemen or to pay them tolls to pass through their lands.[45] Since the principal item that the French wanted was beaver pelts,[46] the Huron probably also began to expand their trade with the north at this time in order to secure these furs in larger quantities. In return for these furs, they carried not only corn and tobacco but also French trade goods to their northern trading partners. The tribes north of Lake Huron seem to have continued to trade exclusively with the Huron rather than seeking to obtain goods from the French. No doubt this was in part because Huronia was nearby and reaching it did not require a long and hazardous journey down the Ottawa River. Such a journey would have been time-consuming, if not impossible, for a small tribe. More importantly, however, they wanted corn for winter consumption which the Huron, but not the French, were able to provide. Although there is no documentary evidence to support this suggestion, it seems likely that increasing supplies of corn permitted these hunters to devote more time to trapping and relieved them of some of their day-to-day worries about survival.[47] Thus the growth of the fur trade may have led the northern groups to concentrate on trapping and the Huron to devote more of their energy to producing agricultural surpluses to trade with the north.[48] On at least one occasion, the Huron were providing even the French at Quebec with needed supplies of food.[49] In the 1640s their close friends and trading partners, the Nipissing, were travelling as far north as James Bay each year in order to collect the furs which they passed on to the Huron.[50]

In spite of the Huron desire for French goods and their ability to gather furs from the interior, the development of direct trade between Huronia and the St. Lawrence required the formation of a partnership that was expressed in terms the Indian could understand. Without continual assurances of goodwill passing between Huron and French leaders and without the exchange of gifts and people, no Huron would have travelled to Quebec without fear and trepidation. Even after many years of trade, Hurons going to Quebec felt safer if they were travelling with a Frenchman whom they knew and who could be trusted to protect their interests while they were trading.[51] Champlain understood clearly that treaties of friendship were necessary for successful trading partnerships with the Indians. For this reason he had been willing to support the Algonkin and Montagnais in their wars with the Mohawk and, since it was impossible to be friendly with both sides, had maintained his alliance with these northern tribes in spite of Iroquois overtures for peace.[52] The cementing of a treaty with the various Huron tribes was clearly the main reason he visited Huronia in 1615, a visit made in the face of considerable opposition from the Ottawa River Algonkin.[53]

Quite properly in Huron eyes, Champlain spent most of his time in Huronia with the Rock tribe. This had been the first of the Huron tribes to contact him on the St. Lawrence and therefore had a special relationship with the French according to Huron law. When he accompanied a Huron war party on a traditional, and what appeared to him as an ill-fated raid against the central Iroquois, Champlain was resorting to a now-familiar technique for winning the friendship of particular tribes.[54] What Champlain apparently still did not realize was that the aim of these expeditions was adventure and taking prisoners, rather than the destruction of enemy villages.[55] The Huron were undoubtedly far more pleased with the results of the expedition than Champlain was.

23

From 1615 on, a number of Frenchmen were living in Huronia; their main purpose in being there was to encourage the Huron to trade.[56] Many of these young men, like the coureurs de bois of later times, enjoyed their life among the Indians and, to the horror of the Catholic clergy, made love to Huron women and probably married them according to local custom. The rough and tumble ways of individuals like Etienne Brûlé endeared them to their Huron hosts and this, in turn, allowed them to inspire confidence in the Indians who came to trade. It has been suggested that the main reason these men remained in Huronia was to persuade the Huron to trade in New France rather than to take their furs south to the Dutch who had begun to trade in the Hudson Valley after 1609.[57] This explanation seems unlikely, however. Until 1629 most of the Dutch trade appears to have been confined to the Mahican.[58] Although the Dutch were apparently anxious to trade with the "French Indians" as early as 1633, the Mohawk were not willing to allow them to do so unless they were in some way able to profit from the trade themselves.[59] This the Huron, who had a long-standing feud with the Iroquois, were unwilling to let them do.

The main job of the early coureurs de bois appears to have been to live in Huronia as visible evidence of French goodwill and as exchanges for the Huron youths who were sent to live with the French.[60] In this capacity they were able to encourage the Indians to engage in trade. Each year some of them travelled downriver with the Huron to see that the Algonkin did not prevent the passage of their canoes or scare the Huron off with stories of disasters or plots against them in Quebec.[61] They also acted as interpreters for the Huron and aided them in their dealings with the traders.[62] Except for the years when the Mohawk blockaded the Ottawa River, the Huron sent an annual "fleet" or series of fleets to Quebec bearing the furs they had collected.[63] It is unfortunate that the records do not supply more information on these fleets, particularly about who organized them and what was their tribal composition. The fleets left Huronia in the spring and returned several months later. When the St. Lawrence was blocked by the Iroquois, the Hurons made their way to Quebec over the smaller waterways that led through the Laurentians.[64]

The Recollet and Jesuit missionaries who worked in Huronia between 1615 and 1629 were accepted by the Huron as part of the Franco-Huron trading alliance and as individuals whose goodwill was potentially advantageous in dealing with the traders and authorities in Quebec. That they lacked interest except as shamans is evident from Gabriel Sagard's statement that it was hard to work among any tribe that was not engaged in trade (i.e. bound by the Franco-Huron alliance).[65] The priests appear to have restricted their missionary activities to caring for the needs of the French traders in Huronia and trying to make some converts among the Indians. Their preaching, as far as it was understood, did not appear to present a challenge or affront to the Huron way of life, although the customs of the priests were strange to the Indians, who found these men austere and far less appealing than the easy-going coureurs de bois.[66] For obvious reasons, relations between the priests and local traders were not good and Sagard claims that among other things the latter often refused to help the missionaries learn native languages.[67] The most serious charge that the priests levelled at these traders was that their behaviour sowed confusion and doubt among the Huron and impeded the spread of the Christian faith among them.[68] These early experiences convinced the Jesuits that to run a mission in Huronia properly the priests must control those Europeans who were allowed to enter the country.

In the early part of the seventeenth century the colony of New France was nothing more than a trading post and its day-to-day existence depended upon securing an annual supply of furs.[69] Not understanding the long-standing hostility between the Huron and the Iroquois, the French were apprehensive of any move that seemed likely to divert furs from the St. Lawrence to the Hudson Valley. The French made peace with the Mohawk in 1624 and French traders did business with them, an arrangement that no doubt pleased the Mohawk as it made them for a time less dependent on the Dutch and therefore gave them more bargaining power in their dealings with Albany.[70] Nevertheless, the French became extremely alarmed about a peace treaty that the Huron negotiated with the Seneca in 1623. This appears to have been one of the periodic treaties that the Huron and Iroquois negotiated in order to get back members of their respective tribes who had been taken prisoner, but not yet killed, by the enemy.[71] As such, it was probably perfectly harmless to French interest. Nevertheless the situation was judged sufficiently serious for a delegation of eleven Frenchmen, including three clerics, to be sent to the Huron country.[72] Various writers have followed Jean Charlevoix in saying that this delegation was instructed to disrupt the new treaty. Charlevoix, however, wrote long after the event took place and is not an unbiased witness.[73] It seems more likely that the expedition had as its main purpose simply the reaffirming of the alliances made between Champlain and the various Huron chiefs in 1615. In actual fact the Huron probably had no thought of trading with the Iroquois at this time. To the chagrin of the Dutch, the Mohawk were firm in their refusal to allow the northern tribes to pass through their country to trade on the Hudson. The Huron undoubtedly felt that direct trade with the French, even if they were farther from Huronia than the Dutch,[74] was preferable to trade via the Mohawk with the Europeans in New York State.

The very great importance that the Huron attached to their trade with the French even at this time is shown by their efforts to prevent potential rivals, such as the Petun or Neutral, from concluding any sort of formal alliance with the French. Neither group seems to have constituted much of a threat, since the Petun had to pass through Huron territory in order to paddle north along the shore of Georgian Bay[75] and the Neutral, who do not seem to have had adequate boats, would have had to travel down the St. Lawrence River to Quebec — en route the Mohawk would have either stolen their furs or forced them to divert most of the trade to the south.[76] The Huron do not seem to have minded well-known coureurs de bois occasionally visiting the Neutral or other tribes with whom they traded, but when, on his visit to the Neutral in 1626, Father de La Roche Daillon proposed an alliance between them and the French, the Huron spread rumours about the French that brought an end to the proposed treaty.[77] The ease with which the Huron did this, and repeated the manoeuvre in 1640–41,[78] is an indication both of the insecurity that tribes felt in the absence of a proper treaty with foreigners and of the importance that the Huron placed on their privileged relationship with the French. These observations reinforce our conclusion that coureurs de bois did not live in Huronia simply to dissuade the Huron from going to trade with either the Mohawk or the Dutch, but instead were a vital link in the Franco-Huron alliance and necessary intermediaries between the Huron and the French fur traders in Quebec. Such were the services for which Brûlé received a hundred pistoles each year from his employers.[79]

Franco-Huron trade increased in the years prior to 1629. Undoubtedly the Huron were growing increasing reliant on European goods, but it is unlikely that they were ever completely dependent on trade during this period. There is no evidence that the British occupation of Quebec led them to trade with New Holland or with the Iroquois. Several renegade Frenchmen, including Brûlé, remained in Huronia and probably encouraged the Huron to trade with the British.[80] It was during this period that Brûlé was murdered by the Huron living in Toanché. Since he was given a proper burial it is unlikely that he was tortured to death and eaten as Sagard reports.[81] More likely, he was killed in a brawl with the Huron among whom he lived. That he was killed during the British occupation of New France does not, however, seem to be without significance. Until the French withdrawal he had been protected not only by his popularity but more importantly by the Franco-Huron alliance. Once the French had departed, he was on his own.

The Jesuits Take Control

The Compagnie des Cent-Associés, which took effective control of the affairs of New France after the colony was retroceded to France in 1632, was different from earlier trading companies in that its members were more interested in missionary work than their predecessors had been. At this time the Society of Jesus also managed to obtain the *de facto* monopoly over missionary activities in New France that it was to hold for many years.[82] The Jesuits brought about a number of changes in policy with regard to Huronia. In particular, they were much more anxious to evangelize the Huron *as a people*, than the Recollets had been.[83] As their prime goal they sought to lead the entire confederacy toward the Christian religion, rather than to convert individuals. Moreover, as a result of the strong influence they wielded at the French court, they were in a better position to command the support of officials and fur traders.[84] For the first while after they returned to the Huron country, the Jesuits continued many of the mission practices that had been current prior to 1629, such as sending Indian children to their seminary at Quebec.[85] As their knowledge of the Huron language and of the country improved (in both cases as a result of systematic study) they gradually began to modify their work along lines that were more in keeping with their general policy.[86]

A major *bête noire* of the missionaries prior to 1629 was the French traders who lived in Huronia and set a bad example for the natives. In order to assure unity of purpose for their work, the duties that formerly had been carried out by these coureurs de bois were taken over by lay brothers, workmen, and *donnés* directly subject to Jesuit supervision.[87] Later accusations that the Jesuits were engaged in the fur trade seem to have sprung largely from this action. The oft-repeated claim that priests were vital to the fur trade in Huronia is obviously without foundation. The coureurs de bois, who had lived in Huronia for many years, not only had functioned effectively during this period without missionary support but also appear to have been substantially more popular and more effective in their dealings with the Huron than the priests had been. The Jesuits wished to be rid of this group principally to assure that the French living in Huronia would not be working at cross-purposes. The trading companies apparently were willing to allow the Jesuits to have their own way in this matter, but in return it was necessary that the laymen attached to the Jesuit mission discharge at least the most vital functions of organizing the annual trade which the coureurs de bois had done heretofore.[88] The reasons that the Jesuits had for wanting to be rid of the coureurs de bois were clearly religious, not economic.

The Jesuits' connections with the fur trade did not arise, however, simply from their desire to be rid of the coureurs de bois; they also depended on it not only to get into Huronia but also for their personal safety so long as they remained there. The Huron were obviously not at all interested in what the Jesuits had to teach, and on several occasions after 1634 they made it clear that they preferred the former coureurs de bois to the Jesuits and their assistants.[89] In 1633, and again in 1634, they offered a whole series of excuses, including the hostility of the Algonkin from Allumette Island, as reasons for not taking the Jesuits home with them.[90] Moreover, fearing revenge for the death of Brûlé, they were unwilling to allow their children to remain as seminarians at Quebec.[91] In 1634 Champlain made the official French position clear when he informed the Huron that he regarded the Jesuits' presence in their country as a vital part of a renewed Franco-Huron alliance, at the same time expressing the hope that they would someday agree to become Christians.[92] Since the Huron wanted to renew their former trading relationship with the French, they agreed to accept the priests as a token of this alliance. Henceforth they were bound by treaty to allow the Jesuits to live among them and to protect the priests from harm. The thought of having these individuals who were so respected by the French in Huronia and under their control must also have given the Huron confidence in their dealings with the French who remained in Quebec.

27

Although the Jesuits travelled to Huronia in 1635 in canoes that belonged to members of the Cord and Rock tribes, they were put ashore rather unceremoniously in the territory of the Bear tribe, where Brébeuf had worked previously and where Brûlé had been murdered.[93] It is not clear whether the Jesuits had wanted to go to this region or were left there by their Rock and Cord hosts who did not want to take them to their own villages. It is possible that the Bear, who were the most powerful of the Huron tribes, exerted their influence to have the Jesuits left among them. In this regard it is perhaps not without meaning that the Jesuits previously had discussed with the Indians the possibility of their settling in Ossossané, the chief town of the Bear nation.[94] Brébeuf was welcomed by the villagers of Ihonitiria, among whom he had lived before, and the Jesuits decided to settle in that village both because it was close to the canoe route to New France and also in order to persuade the villagers that they bore them no ill will for having murdered Brûlé. The latter, the Jesuits said, was regarded by the French as a traitor and debauched renegade.[95] Nevertheless, his murder haunted the Huron, and even some neighbouring tribes,[96] who feared that it might lead to war with the French. Such fears may have been responsible for the dispute that the Jesuits observed between certain villages of the Bear tribe shortly after their arrival in Huronia.[97]

It would appear that according to native custom the Jesuits coming to Huronia had a right to expect they would receive free food and lodgings. This would have been in return for similar care given by the French to the young seminarists in Quebec.[98] In Huron eyes the latter had been exchanged as tokens of good faith in return for the Jesuits and their assistants.[99] In fact, the Huron provided food and shelter for the Jesuits only rarely. The missionaries had to purchase or provide these things for themselves and found the Huron demanding payment of some sort for most of their services.[100]

For a time after their return to Huronia the Jesuits were the objects of friendly public interest and their presence and goodwill were sought after, in part because individual Hurons sought to obtain favours in Quebec through their commendation, in part because the services people performed for the Jesuits, and even attendance at religious instruction, were rewarded with presents of trade goods and tobacco. The latter, although a native product, was scarce in Huronia at the time.[101] Since all of the priests (except perhaps Brébeuf) were struggling to learn the Huron language, most of the missionary activities during the first few years were confined to the Bear country. Only a few trips were made into more distant areas of Huronia.[102]

28

The Epidemics of 1635 to 1640

The first serious trial for the Jesuits, and for the Franco-Huron alliance, occurred between the years 1635 and 1640. An unspecified disease, either measles or smallpox, was present in Quebec the year the Jesuits returned to Huronia and it followed the Huron fleet upriver. This was the beginning of a series of epidemics which swept away more than half the Huron population in the next six years.[103] These new maladies were especially fatal to children and old people. Because they were fatal to the latter group, many of the most skilful Huron leaders and craftsmen, as well as the people most familiar with native religious lore, perished.[104] The loss of children may well have meant that the proportion of men of fighting age in the Huron population was below normal by the end of the next decade.

The Jesuits, who wished to save the souls of dying children, frequently baptized them, both with and without their parents' permission. The Huron, being unclear about the Jesuits' intention in doing this, observed that children tended to die soon after baptism and came to suspect that the Jesuits were practising a deadly form of witchcraft.[105] The rumour revived that the Jesuits had been sent to Huronia to seek revenge for Brûlé's murder,[106] a rumour which gained credence from pictures of the torments of hell that the Jesuits displayed in their chapel and from the ritual of the mass (which the Huron understood had something to do with eating a corpse).[107] According to Huron law, sorcerers could be killed without a trial, and in times of crisis extensive pogroms appear to have been unleashed against persons suspected of this crime.[108] Nevertheless, while individuals threatened to murder the Jesuits and on one occasion a council of the confederacy met to try the Jesuits on a charge of witchcraft,[109] none of the Frenchmen in Huronia was killed.

Although the majority of the people were frightened of the Jesuits and believed that they were working to destroy the country, their leaders repeatedly stressed that they could not afford to rupture the Franco-Huron alliance by killing the French priests.[110] One well-placed chief said that if the Huron did not go downriver to trade with the French for even two years, they would be lucky if they found themselves as well off as the [despised] Algonkians.[111] While this statement was a bit of rhetoric, it stresses the importance of the fur trade to the Huron at this time and their growing reliance on French trade goods. During the entire course of the epidemics only one village, apparently a small one, was willing to give up the use of trade goods, and hence presumably to sever relations with the French.[112] Instead, the Huron resorted to indirect means to persuade the Jesuits to leave Huronia *voluntarily*. Children were encouraged to annoy them, their religious objects were befouled, and occasionally they were personally threatened or mistreated.[113] The Jesuits noted, rather significantly, that these persecutions diminished before the annual trip downriver or after the return of a successful fleet.[114] The French officials in Quebec were aware of the dangerous situation in which the Jesuits found themselves, but as long as feelings ran high in Huronia, these authorities could do no more than to try to spare them from the worst excesses of Huron anger. They did this by threatening to cut off trade if the Jesuits were killed.

29

By 1640 the serious epidemics in Huronia were over. That summer, the new governor of Canada, Charles Huault de Montmagny, took action to "punish" the Huron who came to Quebec for their bad treatment of the Jesuits.[115] It is not clear what form this punishment took, but it appears that in the course of his dealings with them he made it clear that he considered their bad treatment of the Jesuits had terminated the existing alliance. At the same time he offered to renew the alliance, but only on the clear understanding that the Jesuits would continue to live in Huronia and work there unmolested. This is the first time, to our knowledge, that French officials had injected a positive element of threat into their dealings with the Huron. Presumably, the great losses in manpower and skills that the Huron had suffered and their consequent increasing dependence on trade and French support made such action possible. The Huron were in good health and expecting an abundant harvest; hence, many of the anxieties that had plagued them in recent years were dispelled. Because of this they were once more in a good mood and, hence, under the protection of a renewed Franco-Huron alliance the Jesuits found themselves free not only to continue the mission work among them but also to intensify their efforts.[116]

Already during the final crisis of 1639, the Jesuits had decided to establish a permanent centre for their missionary work in the Huron area. This centre was foreseen as serving various functions. Not only would it provide a refuge in time of danger (such as they lacked in 1639), but it also would allow them to put up buildings of European design. It had not been economical to construct these in the Huron villages which shifted their location about once every decade. The Jesuits' centre was thus designed to be a further example of European culture in the heart of Huronia, a focus from which new ideas could diffuse to the local population. Gradually, pigs, fowl, and young cattle were brought upriver from Quebec and European crops were grown in the fields nearby.[117] The residence of Ste Marie acquired a hospital and a burial ground and became a place where Christian Indians could come for spiritual retreats and assembly on feast days.[118] Being located apart from any one village, and near the geographical centre of the confederacy, it was better able, both from a political and a geographical point of view, to serve as a mission centre for all Huronia. (During the worst years of the epidemics the Jesuits had remained for the most part in the northwest corner of Huronia.) In 1639 the Jesuits also made a survey and census of the country prior to setting up a system of missions that would carry the Christian message to all of the Huron tribes and, as far as possible, to other tribes as well.[110]

The Jesuits had thus weathered a difficult period. It is clear that they had been allowed to enter Huronia and to continue there only because of the Franco-Huron alliance. That they were not killed or expelled from Huronia at the height of the epidemics is an indication of how dependent the Hurons were becoming on the fur trade and how much the alliance with the French meant to them. It also indicates that the Huron leaders were able to restrain their unruly followers in order to preserve good relations with New France.[120] Evidence of lingering malice towards the priests can be seen in the events that came to light on the visit of Fathers Brébeuf and Chaumonot to the Neutral country in the winter of 1640–41. There the priests learned that the Huron had offered the Neutral rich presents, if they would kill the missionaries.[121] In this way the Huron hoped to destroy two of the "sorcerers" who had been tormenting their nation without endangering the French alliance. They also had other motives, however. The proposed murder, so long as it was not traced back to the Huron, would put the Neutral in a bad light and would prevent Brébeuf from pursuing any dealings with the Seneca. Although there is no evidence that Brébeuf planned to visit the Seneca, a rumour had spread that having failed to kill the Huron with witchcraft he now was seeking to turn their enemies loose upon them.[122]

A Crisis in Huron-Iroquois Relations

If the year 1640 marked the end of the persecution of the Jesuits in Huronia, unknown to them and to their Huron hosts, it also marked the beginning of a crisis that was to destroy Huronia. Beaver had become rare in the Huron country and most of the skins they traded with the French came from neighbouring tribes to the north.[123] A similar decline in the beaver population of New York State seems to have reached a point of crisis by 1640. That year the number of pelts traded at Fort Orange is reported to have dropped sharply.[124] While it is possible that at least part of the decline was the result of clandestine traders cutting into official trade, most commentators agree that it was basically related to the exhaustion of the supply of beaver in the Iroquois' home territory.[125]

While this hypothesis is not well enough documented that it can be regarded as certain, it seems a useful one for explaining Iroquois behaviour during the next few years. There is little doubt that after 1640 the Iroquois were preoccupied with securing new sources of pelts. The main controversy concerning their relations with their neighbours during this period centres on whether they were seeking to obtain furs by forcing the Huron to share their trade with them[126] or were attacking their neighbours in order to secure new hunting territories. Although Trelease[127] supports the latter theory, the data he uses apply for the most part to a later period and come mainly from sources in New York State and New England. Contemporary Canadian evidence definitely seems to rule out his claims; indeed if his hypothesis were true, the events leading to the destruction of Huronia would make little sense at all.

Trelease's theory finds its main support in claims made by the Iroquois *31* in the early part of the eighteenth century that they had conquered Ontario and adjacent regions as beaver hunting grounds. In the treaty of 1701, in which the Iroquois placed their "Beaver ground" under the protection of the King of England, the Iroquois said explicitly that they had driven the indigenous tribes from this area in order to hunt there.[128] Trelease errs, however, in assuming that the reasons the Iroquois gave for conquering this territory in 1701 were the same as those they actually had for doing so half a century earlier. There is no doubt that in 1701 the Iroquois (mainly the Seneca) were hunting beaver in Ontario, but since the Huron country was reported in the 1630s to be as hunted out as their own it is illogical to assume that they attacked this region in 1649 in order to secure more hunting territory. The Huron beaver supplies they sought to capture were those coming by trade from the north. Only after their attacks failed to capture the western fur trade and after Ontario was deserted for a time allowing the restoration of the local beaver population did the Iroquois begin to hunt there. Since they lacked historical records, it is not surprising that by 1701 the Iroquois believed the use that they were making of Ontario at the present time was the same reason they had for attacking the tribes there long before. The attacks the Iroquois launched against the Petun and Neutral, following their attack on the Huron, offer no opposition to this theory. Although these groups had not participated in the fur trade prior to 1649, there was considerable danger that with the Huron gone they would attempt to do so. Hence, their dispersal was also necessary.

Trelease's theory thus fails to provide an acceptable explanation of events in Canada in the middle of the seventeenth century. It seems much more likely that the Iroquois, and mainly the Mohawk, began by trying to force the Huron to trade with them and that only latterly, when their efforts in this direction were unsuccessful, did they decide to destroy the Huron (and their neighbours) as an intermediary group.

The Mohawk began to intimidate the Huron by harassing those travelling along the Ottawa River — a tactic that had the additional advantage of providing a supply of captured furs. In 1642 Iroquois raiders spread fear and terror throughout all of the Huron villages,[129] and in 1644 they succeeded in preventing contact between Quebec and Huronia.[130] The increasing number of guns that the Iroquois were acquiring from the Dutch, English, and Swedish colonies along the Atlantic seaboard gradually gave them military superiority over the Huron, among whom the French had limited and controlled the sale of guns.[131] In 1644 the French despatched more than twenty soldiers to Huronia to protect the Huron over the winter and assure the arrival of their furs in Quebec the next spring.[132] The Mohawk were also harassing the French in the St. Lawrence Valley who were moved the next spring to discuss peace, both to assure their own safety and to re-open the river to trade. Although the subsequent treaty of 1645 was with the French, the Mohawk seem to have interpreted it as involving a commitment that in the future the Huron would trade with them as well as with the French.[133] The Huron, however, had no intention of doing this, and the French, who may not have perceived clearly what the Mohawk wanted, did not want to encourage them to divert trade. The main French reason for the treaty with the Mohawk was the short-term one of opening the river. The French had little to offer the Iroquois in return and refused to sell them guns, the one item they wanted.[134] When it became clear to the Mohawk that the Huron did not intend to trade with them, they renewed their attack on Huronia and on the Huron fleet.

32

The Development of a Christian Faction

While this dangerous crisis in intertribal relations was boiling up, a situation was developing in Huronia that put a new strain on the Franco-Huron alliance.

Prior to 1640, most Christian converts were Hurons on the point of death, many of whom knew nothing about Christian theology but who hoped that baptism would save their lives.[135] At one point during the epidemics a Huron version of the rite of baptism became part of a native healing cult that was said to be inspired by a native deity who had revealed himself as the real Jesus.[136] In these rites the sick were sprinkled with water as part of an orgiastic ceremony typical of traditional Huron healing rituals. After 1640, however, the Jesuits began to convert increasing numbers of people who were in good health. Many were men of importance, whose conversions made that of their families, friends, and tribesmen easier.[137] In order to prevent backsliding, the Jesuits at first made it a policy to baptise (except in cases of extreme ill health) only adults who had provided substantial proof of their devotion to Christianity and whose family life seemed to be stable.[138]

Many factors seem to have induced people to convert: some admired the bravery of the Jesuits, others wished to be able to follow a Christian friend to heaven, still others noted in their names a theological term that the Jesuits were using.[139]

Although economic motives were not the only ones involved in conversion, it is noteworthy that at least a few Huron became Christians to avoid participation in pagan feasts, which required them to give away considerable amounts of property in the form of presents and entertainment.[140] A far larger number of people hoped through conversion to receive preferential treatment in their dealings with traders and officials in New France.[141] In 1648, when only 15 per cent of the Huron were Christian, half of the men in the Huron fleet were either converts or were preparing for baptism.[142] Those who traded with the French in Quebec not only were more exposed to French culture and to Christianity than were those who remained at home but also had more to gain from good relations with the French. Commercial considerations may also explain why the Jesuits generally found it easier to convert men than women.

While stressing the practical economic motives that certainly motivated many conversions, personal and cultural factors should not be ignored. The Huron were increasingly dependent on French culture and in the eyes of many, but (as we shall see) certainly not all, of the Huron the priest was coming to replace the native sorcerer as an object of awe and respect. This did not, however, lead the Huron to lose faith in themselves or in their culture, as it did in many other tribes.[143] Supported by the respect shown by the Jesuits for the Huron people and for much of their culture, many Huron converts appear to have been imbued with a sincere zeal to change and reform their own culture. No doubt the size of the Huron confederacy and its isolation from unsupervised contact with the Europeans did much to prevent the deterioration in self-confidence that is obvious among many weaker tribes. Had other circumstances not been adverse, I think it would have been possible for the Jesuits to have transformed Huronia successfully into a nation that was both Christian and Indian.

For a time the growing number of Huron converts posed no serious problems for the rest of society, although individual converts were frequently taunted and sometimes expelled from their longhouses with much resulting personal hardship.[144] (A woman who had been a member of a pagan healing society was threatened with death when after conversion she refused to perform in the society.[145]) Threats and assassination no doubt were the fate of other converts. The Jesuits and their assistants, however, were no longer attacked or molested in any way.[146] It appears that at least some headmen surrendered their political office on becoming Christians, since they felt that the obligation to participate in Huron festivals which these offices entailed was contrary to their new faith.[147] In this and in other ways the nascent Christian community avoided for a time the possibility of an open clash with the large pagan majority.

Gradually, however, a rift began. Some Christians refused, for example, to be buried in their tribal ossuaries, which in effect was to deny membership

33

in their village or tribe.[148] They also refused to fight alongside pagans in the war parties but instead formed their own detachments, no doubt because of the religious implications of traditional Iroquoian warfare.[149] As the number of converts grew, men retained their political offices after conversion, but appointed deputies to handle the religious functions traditionally associated with them.[150] As the number of Christians who held these important offices continued to grow, the split between pagans and Christians became increasingly a political issue.

The Jesuits, for their part, now set as their immediate goal the Christianizing of an entire village.[151] Significantly the most promising town was Ossossané where the Jesuits had been working for a long time. This town, belonging to the Bear tribe, was also the political centre of the Huron confederacy.[152] In 1648 they achieved their objective. By then the majority of people in Ossossané were converts. And that winter the chiefs of the village refused to allow the people who remained pagan to celebrate the traditional festivals, and they appointed a Jesuit as the chief headman of the village, with the right to act as a censor of public morals.[153]

The Pagan Reaction and the Destruction of Huronia

Although in 1645 such social revolutions were still several years in the future, many of the pagans had already begun to fear for the survival of their traditional customs and beliefs.[154] Undoubtedly a large number of these people were genuinely attached to the old ways and for this reason alone resented the growth of Christianity. It is also possible that many chiefs who wished to remain pagan began to fear a decline in their own influence as Christians began to play a stronger role in the life of the country. They probably resented the closer contacts that Christian chiefs had with the French and feared that these contacts would be used as a source of power. As a result of these fears and rivalries, pagan and Christian factions began to develop within the various tribes and villages throughout Huronia.[155]

Although the documentation in the Jesuit Relations is scanty, there appears to have been a considerable variation in attitude towards the Jesuits and Christianity among the different Huron tribes. The Bear, among whom the Jesuits had lived for the longest time and whose main town, Ossossané, had a large and rapidly growing Christian community, seem to have been the most pro-Christian and pro-French.[156] The Cord probably had much the same sort of attitude.[157] The Rock and Deer tribes, however, seem to have been considerably less friendly. The Jesuits report that the former tribe, being the easternmost, had suffered most from the attacks of the Iroquois and was therefore the most inclined to seek peace with their traditional enemies. The Rock were also described, however, as a tribe with a strong aversion to the faith who never had been converted.[158] The Deer had a reputation among the Jesuits for being sorcerers,[159] and one assumes from this that they gave the missionaries a bad time. Both of these tribes joined the Iroquois of their own free will after the break-up of Huronia in 1649.[160] Despite this variation, however, there were people in all the Huron tribes who were starting to have misgivings about the future of Huronia and who resented the changes that the French alliance was bringing about.

After 1645 these sentiments seem to have led to the formation of a sizable anti-French party, which apparently found a certain amount of support everywhere in Huronia, except perhaps in Ossossané. This marked a new development in French-Huron relations, all previous opposition having been to the priests resident in Huronia rather than to the French in general. Supporters of this party seem to have reasoned that Christianity was a threat to Huronia, that Christianity flourished because the Jesuits were able to work there under the terms of the Franco-Huron alliance, and that the best way to save the country (and enhance the power of the pagan chiefs at the expense of their Christian rivals) was therefore to expel the Jesuits, break off the alliance, and begin trading with the Iroquois. In this way, not only would the traditional culture of Huronia be saved, but the attacks of the Iroquois, which had been growing in intensity,[161] could be brought to an end. Thus for the first time a respectable body of opinion in Huronia came to believe that an alliance with enemies who shared similar beliefs and culture was preferable to one with strangers seeking to change the Huron way of life. The threat that was facing the traditionalists made the thought of trading with their old enemies and rivals seem much less unpleasant than it had been a few years previously.

The first plan for a rapprochement with the Iroquois was well conceived and sought to exploit internal differences within the Iroquois confederacy for the Hurons' own advantage. Since the treaty of 1645 had failed to obtain the furs they wanted, the Mohawk were likely to be suspicious of, if not hostile to, further Huron blandishments. The Seneca likewise were unfriendly because of recent Huron attacks on them.[162] The Onondaga, however, had long enjoyed the position of being the chief tribe in the confederacy and were increasingly jealous of the Mohawk, who were exploiting their close contacts with the Dutch and the English in an effort to dominate the league.[163] It is therefore no surprise that it was through the Onondaga that the Huron attempted to make peace with the Iroquois.

The Jesuits did not record, and may not be have known, the exact nature of the treaty that the Huron were trying to negotiate. The presence of a clause promising that the Huron would trade furs with the Iroquois is suggested by a remark, attributed to the Andaste or Susquehannock (who were allies of the Huron and sent ambassadors to the Onondaga to argue on their behalf), that such a treaty would promote the trade of all these tribes with one another.[164] It is also significant that among the Huron the Bear tribe was the one most opposed to this treaty.[165] The Jesuits said this was because the Bear had suffered less from Iroquois raids than had the other Huron tribes, but a second reason could be that the Christians who were more numerous in this tribe than in the others, saw in these negotia-

35

tions a clear threat to the Franco-Huron alliance and to their own power and well-being. Negotiations continued for some time, but were terminated in January 1648, when a party of Mohawk warriors slew a Huron embassy on its way to the chief Onondaga town to arrange the final terms of the treaty.[166] A distinguished Onondaga chief, who had remained in Huronia as a hostage, committed suicide when he learned what the Mohawk had done.[167]

There seems little reason to doubt the honesty of the Onondaga in these negotiations. The Mohawk probably attacked the Huron embassy because they were angry that negotiations were being conducted with the Onondaga rather than with them. The Mohawk may also have believed that the Huron were trying to deceive the Onondaga and that the only way of dealing with the Huron confederacy was to destroy it. In any case, the Mohawk managed to bring the first major political offensive of the anti-French faction in Huronia to an ignominious conclusion.

36   Even though this first effort had failed, at least some Huron apparently believed that a rapprochement with the Iroquois still was possible. Indeed, either because they were totally convinced of the necessity of appeasing the Iroquois or because of their extreme hatred of the Christians, a minority seems to have become convinced that a break with the French was a precondition for further negotiation. The group responsible for the next move was led by six, apparently distinguished, chiefs from three villages.[168] Unfortunately, these village are unnamed. The chiefs decided to make a public issue of the question of a continued Franco-Huron alliance through the simple expedient of killing a Frenchman. They do not appear to have designated any particular victim and their henchmen slew Jacques Douart, a *donné* whom they encountered not far from Ste Marie. Once Douart was slain, the conspirators issued a proclamation calling for the banishment from Huronia of the French and all of the Huron who insisted on remaining Christian.[169] An emergency council was convened (apparently from all over the country) and for several days these proposals were debated. On the one side were the Christians and those pagans who felt that the Franco-Huron alliance should continue; on the other the traditionalists who had stirred up the trouble and no doubt some other Hurons who hated neither Christianity nor the French, but who felt that a peace treaty with the Iroquois was important enough to be worth the termination of the French alliance. Among the latter must have been many refugees from the Rock tribe which had been forced to abandon its villages as a result of Iroquois attacks only a short time before.[170] The pro-French party finally won the debate and the Jesuits in turn agreed to accept the traditional Huron compensation for a murder, in this case one hundred beaver skins.[171] The ritual presentation of this settlement made clear that it was designed to reaffirm and protect the Franco-Huron alliance which the unprecedented actions of these chiefs had endangered. Thus ended what appears to have been the last attempt to rupture the Franco-Huron alliance.

During the summer of 1648 the Seneca attacked and destroyed the large town of St. Joseph. As the situation grew more serious the Huron turned increasingly to the French for help and the number of conversions increased sharply.[172] As in 1644, a few French soldiers were sent to winter in Huronia. These soldiers, so long as they remained in Huronia, were believed sufficient to hold off the Iroquois, but they had been instructed to return to Quebec with the Huron fleet in the spring.[173] As the military situation in Huronia grew more desperate, the French in Quebec became increasingly anxious to profit as much as possible while they still could. In the summer of 1649, a party of over thirty coureurs de bois made a flying trip to Huronia and returned to Quebec bringing with them 5000 pounds of beaver.[174]

In the spring of 1649 the Iroquois unleashed the attack that resulted in the death of Fathers Lalemant and Brébeuf and brought about the dispersal of the Huron confederacy. Many factors contributed to the Iroquois victory, but their superior number of guns was undoubtedly the most important.[175] Hunt has suggested that the Huron were so given over to trading by 1649 that virtually all of their food was imported from the Neutral and Petun tribes and that the main factor in their defeat was therefore the cutting of their supply routes.[176] This suggestion is entirely without foundation. Agriculture was a woman's occupation and little affected by increasing trade. While men may have spent more time trading, the importation of iron axes made it easier to cut trees and hence there was no problem clearing the forests for agriculture. There are frequent references to the Huron as engaged in agricultural activities in the years prior to 1649 and one of the reasons the Iroquois returned to Huronia in the spring of 1650 was to prevent the planting of crops.[177] Driven from their homes and deprived of food, the Hurons scattered and their trading monopoly came to an end. It is interesting that large numbers of Huron, particularly from the Rock and Deer tribes, migrated to the Iroquois country and settled there. The latter tribe settled *en masse* among the Seneca, where they lived in their own village and retained their separate customs for a long time.[178] Their tribal affiliations suggest that these refugees were for the most part traditionalists and probably among them were many of the people who had been the most hostile to the French during the last years of the Jesuit mission. This hostility explains how these groups were so easily adopted by the people who had destroyed their homeland.

For the Jesuits the destruction of Huronia was the end of their first dream of leading a nation to Christianity in the heart of the Canadian forest. At least once in the Relations they mentioned the work their colleagues were accomplishing in Paraguay and compared this work with their own.[179] The chance had been lost of converting a people to Christianity while allowing them to retain their language and those institutions and customs that were not incompatible with their new faith. Because they were writing

37

for a patriotic French audience, the Jesuits have little to say about the constitutional status of the Huronia they wished to create. Nevertheless, it seems clear that what they aimed at was not so much a French colony as an Indian state, which under Jesuit leadership could blend the good things of Europe with those already in the native culture. A Catholic Huronia would of necessity have been allied with France, the only Catholic power in eastern North America. Years later Louis de Buade de Frontenac probably came closer to a basic truth than he realized when he accused the Jesuits at Quebec of disloyalty because they kept the Indians apart from the French and taught them in their own language.[180]

The fur trade was the one means by which the Jesuits could gain admittance to Huronia and the only protection they had while working there. Ties with fur traders and government officials in Quebec were thus vital for the success of the Huron mission, but these ties do not seem to have prevented the Jesuits from seeking to serve the best interests of their Huron converts and Huronia at large — as they perceived these interests. To reverse the equation and say that the Jesuits were in Huronia mainly *for the purpose* of serving either the fur trade or the French government does not accord with anything we know about their activities.

In the short run the destruction of Huronia was a serious setback for New France. For a time the fur trade, on which the well-being of the colony depended, was cut to practically nothing. The Iroquois, on the other hand, seem to have achieved less than they hoped for from the destruction of Huronia. The western tribes soon became involved in a protracted war with the Erie[181] and tribal jealousies rent the confederacy. As a result of these jealousies the four western tribes began to trade with the French to avoid travelling through Mohawk towns to reach the Dutch.[182] By 1654 the French were starting to put together the rudiments of a new trading network north of the Great Lakes.[183] The remnants of the Huron and Petun who had remained in this area, and more importantly the Ottawa, an Algonkian tribe, played a major role in pushing this trading network to the west in the years that followed.[184] As the population of New France increased, the young men of the colony, with or without official permission, joined in this trade. Thus the destruction of Huronia was neither a total nor a permanent disaster for New France and certainly it did not help to save North America for Protestantism and the Anglo-Saxons as at least one eminent historian has suggested.[185]

A more serious question is what would have happened had the anti-French party in Huronia been successful. Had they been able to organize an effective resistance to the Huron Christians and conclude a treaty with the Iroquois, the trade from the north might have been diverted permanently from the St. Lawrence into the Hudson Valley. Had that happened (and as Sagard and Le Clercq indicate the people in Quebec knew it well[186]) the chances of the infant French colony surviving even for a short time would have been slim. Instead of the destruction of Huronia tipping the balance of power in favour of the English, its survival might well have led to a Huron-Iroquois alliance that would have resulted in the destruction of New France and the end of the French presence in North America.

Notes

This paper is based in part on research carried out with the assistance of Miss A. Elaine Clark during the academic year 1965–66. Miss Clark's assistance was made possible through a research grant provided by the French Canada Studies Programme of McGill University.

1. See, e.g., Samuel de Champlain's comment on the sagacity of the Indians in trade (H. P. Biggar, ed., *The Works of Samuel de Champlain* (6 vols.; Toronto, 1922–36), II, 171), and Jean de Brébeuf, Gabriel Lalemant, and Francesco Bressani on the efficacy of Huron law (R. G. Thwaites, ed., *The Jesuit Relations and Allied Documents* (73 vols.; Cleveland, 1896–1901), X, 215; XXVIII, 49–51; XXXVIII, 277).
2. Thwaites, ed., *Relations* XVIII, 21. A similar statement is made by Paul Ragueneau (XXIX, 281).
3. Invariably, however, these early witnesses of Indian culture were interested in rather limited aspects of Indian life and tended to interpret Indian culture in terms of their own. Because of this, a valid assessment of these early records requires a comparative knowledge of Indian culture in later times. The groundwork for our understanding of seventeenth-century Huron culture is thus the work of several generations of ethnologists and ethnohistorians in Canada and the United States. The best résumé of Huron culture is Elisabeth Tooker, *An Ethnography of the Huron Indians, 1615–1649* (Washington, 1964). For a shorter and less complete synopsis see W. V. Kinietz, *The Indians of the Western Great Lakes, 1615–1760* (Ann Arbor, 1940).
4. F. Parkman, *The Jesuits in North America in the Seventeenth Century* (Centenary Edition, Boston, 1927), pp. 3, 4, 435, 436; G. E. Ellis, "Indians of North America," in J. Winsor, ed. *Narrative and Critical History of America* (8 vols.; Boston and New York, 1884–89), I, 283.
5. G. T. Hunt, *The Wars of the Iroquois: A Study in Intertribal Relations* (Madison, 1940), pp. 4, 19.
6. Biggar, ed., *Works of Champlain*, III, 49–51; IV, 238–44.
7. Thwaites, ed., *Relations*, XVI, 227.
8. L. H. Morgan, *League of the Ho-de-no-sau-nee, or Iroquois* (Rochester, 1851; reprinted New Haven, 1954). For a briefer description, see Morgan's *Houses and House-life of the Indian Aborigines* (Washington, 1881; reprinted with original pagination Chicago, 1965), pp. 23–41.
9. Meat remained largely a festive dish, commonest in winter and spring (G. M. Wrong, ed., *Sagard's Long Journey to the Country of the Hurons* (Toronto, 1939), p. 82; Thwaites, ed., *Relations*, XVII, 141–3).
10. Thwaites, ed., *Relations*, XVI, 227–9. See also Elisabeth Tooker, "The Iroquois Defeat of the Huron: A Review of Causes," *Pennsylvania Archaeologist*, XXXIII (1963), 115–23, especially 119, 120.
11. J. V. Wright, *The Ontario Iroquois Tradition* (Ottawa, 1966), 68–83. For information concerning the movements from the west I am indebted to a personal communication from Dr. Wright.
12. See, for example, D. Jenness, *The Indians of Canada* (5th ed.; Ottawa, 1960), p. 280.
13. B. G. Trigger, "The Historic Location of the Hurons," *Ontario History*, LIV (1962), 137–48. For physiographic conditions, see L. J. Chapman and D. F. Putnam, *The Physiography of Southern Ontario* (2nd ed.; Toronto, 1966), pp. 299–312.
14. Biggar, ed., *Works of Champlain*, III, 52, 53. On the importance of corn meal among the northern hunters see Wrong, ed., *Sagard's Long Journey*, p. 268.
15. Hunt, *Wars of the Iroquois*, pp. 53–65.
16. For the reference to squirrel skins see Thwaites, ed., *Relations*, VII, 13; to nets, VI, 309.
17. *Ibid.*, VIII, 15.
18. Wrong, ed., *Sagard's Long Journey*, p. 86.
19. For a hostile statement about the Bear by the Algonkins, see Thwaites, ed., *Relations*, X, 145.
20. C. F. Wray and H. L. Schoff, "A Preliminary Report on the Seneca Sequence in Western New York State, 1550–1687," *Pennsylvania Archaeologist*, XXIII (1953), 53–63.
21. Colonel James F. Pendergast (personal communication) reports finding considerable evidence of Huron influence in late Iroquoian sites along the St. Lawrence River. These probably date from the sixteenth century or only a little earlier. For the historical evidence of contacts between the St. Lawrence Iroquoians and the interior of Ontario, see H. P. Biggar, ed., *The Voyages of Jacques Cartier* (Ottawa, 1924), 170–1, 200–2.
22. Thwaites, ed., *Relations*, X, 225.
23. *Ibid.*, XX, 19.
24. *Ibid.* In 1640 Lalemant reported that the Rock still considered themselves the special allies of the French and were inclined to protect them. This attitude changed after the Jesuits became more active in the interior of Huronia.
25. Wrong, ed., *Sagard's Long Journey*, p. 99. Sagard says that a special council decided each year the number of men who could go out from each village. For more on the control of trade by old and

influential men, see Thwaites, ed., *Relations*, XIV, 39.

26. J. V. Wright, "A Regional Examination of Ojibwa Culture History," *Anthropologica*, N.S., VII (1965), 189–227.

27. Thwaites, ed., *Relations*, V, 241.

28. The Huron claimed that their feud with the Iroquois had been going on fifty years prior to 1615 (Biggar, ed., *Works of Champlain*, V. 78).

29. Thwaites, ed., *Relations*, XXIII, 91.

30. Wrong, ed., *Sagard's Long Journey*, pp. 159–61. For comparative discussions of Iroquoian warfare see Nathaniel Knowles, "The Torture of Captives by the Indians of Eastern North America," *Proceedings of the American Philosophical Society*, LXXXII (1940), 151–225; R. L. Rands and C. L. Riley, "Diffusion and Discontinuous Distribution," *American Anthropologist*, LVIII (1958), 274–97.

31. For the wars with the Petun, see Thwaites, ed., *Relations*, XX, 43. Even at the time of Sagard's visit, there was a threat of war with the Neutral (Wrong, ed., *Sagard's Long Journey*, pp. 151, 156, 157).

32. Thwaites, ed., *Relations*, XXXIII, 243.

33. *Ibid.*, XXXIII, 239–49.

34. *Ibid.*, XIII, 125. The Bear Tribe wanted the French to participate in their Feast of the Dead so that they could thereby claim them as relatives (X, 311).

35. *Ibid.*, XXVII, 25; XX, 59.

36. Chretien Le Clercq, *First Establishment of the Faith in New France*, trans. J. G. Shea (2 vols.; New York, 1881), I, 97; Wrong, ed., *Sagard's Long Journey*, p. 71.

37. Biggar, ed., *Voyages of Cartier*, pp. 132–3, 143. The custom of giving children to Cartier may have arisen, on the other hand, as a result of the Indians observing Cartier's predilection for kidnapping Indians. In 1534 he had seized the two sons of Donnaconna, the chief of Stadacona.

38. The fact that the Huron and Algonkians both were at war with the Five Nations naturally pitted the French against these latter tribes. Presumably Champlain's decision to side with the Huron and Algonkians was based on his conviction that it was impossible to maintain satisfactory relations with both sides, as well as on the economic factors mentioned in the text. For a discussion of the origins of the hostility between the Algonkians and Five Nations, see B. G. Trigger, "Trade and Tribal Warfare on the St. Lawrence in the Sixteenth Century," *Ethnohistory*, IX (1962), 240–56.

39. For Champlain's own comment on Indian expectations in this regard, see Biggar, ed., *Works of Champlain*, II, 70, 71, 110.

40. H. A. Innis, *The Fur Trade in Canada* (2nd ed.; Toronto, 1956), pp. 23–6.

41. Thwaites, ed., *Relations*, XV, 229. The first Huron chief to have dealings with the French was Atironta of the Rock tribe.

42. Biggar, ed., *Works of Champlain* II, 188, 189, 193. For a more general reference see II, 254.

43. *Ibid.*, II, 141; IV, 118, 119. This interpretation is reinforced by Champlain's statement that the boy was brought back by 200 Huron on June 13, 1611 (II, 186; IV, 136).

44. For comments on the Indians' desire for European manufactured goods, see Innis, *Fur Trade*, pp. 16–19; Hunt, *Wars of the Iroquois*, pp. 4, 5.

45. For examples of Algonkin harassment of Huron trade along the Ottawa River and various Algonkin attempts to imperil French-Huron relations (particularly by the Algonkin from Allumette Island) see Biggar, ed., *Works of Champlain*, V, 102; Wrong, ed., *Sagard's Long Journey*, p. 262; Thwaites, ed., *Relations*, V, 239; VII, 213; VIII, 83, 99; IX, 271; X, 77; XIV, 53. The Montagnais also tried to intimidate the Huron, mainly to get free corn (Wrong, ed., *Sagard's Long Journey*, pp. 265–8).

46. Innis, *Fur Trade*, pp. 3–6, 11–15.

47. This is essentially the kind of relationship that existed between trading companies and Indian trappers in the north in more recent times.

48. Champlain reports that the Huron produced large food surpluses which he says were meant to carry them over years of poor crops (Biggar, ed., *Works of Champlain*, III, 155–6). At least a part of these surpluses was used for trade.

49. Le Clercq, *Establishment*, I, 298.

50. Thwaites, ed., *Relations* XXXV, 201. There is good evidence, however, that the Nipissing were travelling north even earlier (Biggar, ed., *Works of Champlain*, II, 255–6).

51. Le Clercq, *Establishment*, I, 211; Wrong, ed., *Sagard's Long Journey*, p. 244.

52. Biggar, ed., *Works of Champlain*, V, 73–80; Hunt, *Wars of the Iroquois*, p. 69.

53. The Huron had invited Champlain to visit their country as early as 1609 (Biggar, ed., *Works of Champlain*, II, 105). His attempt to travel up the Ottawa River in 1613 was brought to an end by the opposition of the Algonkin, among other things. Marcel Trudel (*Histoire de la Nouvelle-France*. II. *Le Comptoir, 1604–1627* (Montreal, 1966), 198–201) may be correct when he suggests that the Algonkin stirred up trouble between Champlain and Vignau in order to protect their trading interests in the interior.

54. Although Champlain visited all the major Huron villages, he returned repeatedly to Cahiague, a Rock village. He also spent more time there than anywhere else. Lalemant reports that in 1640 his reputation was still very much alive among the Rock (Thwaites, ed., *Relations*, XX, 19).

40

55. Biggar, ed., *Works of Champlain*, III, 66, 69,73; IV, 254–66; also Hunt, *Wars of the Iroquois*, p. 20.
56. Since most of the available data about this period was recorded by priests, we have little information about these men, and practically none from a friendly source. For what there is see, Biggar, ed., *Works of Champlain*, V, 101, 108, 129, 131, 132, 207; Le Clercq, *Establishment*, I, 205; Wrong, ed., *Sagard's Long Journey*, pp. 194–5; Thwaites, ed., *Relations*, V, 133; VI, 83; XIV, 17, 19; XVIII, 45; XX, 19; XXV, 85.
57. A. W. Trelease, *Indian Affairs in Colonial New York: The Seventeenth Century* (Ithaca, 1960), p. 30.
58. *Ibid.*, p. 46. Intermittent hostilities between the Mahican and Mohawk kept the latter from Fort Orange prior to the stunning defeat of the Mahican in 1628 or 1629 (p. 48).
59. *Ibid.*, pp. 52–4; Thwaites, ed., *Relations*, VIII, 59–61; Hunt, *Wars of the Iroquois*, p. 34. In 1638 the Huron told the Jesuits that "Englishmen" had come as far as Montreal telling the Indians that the Jesuits were the cause of sickness in Huronia (and no doubt attempting to trade with them or divert trade to the south) (Thwaites, ed., *Relations*, XV, 31.)
60. See, e.g., Biggar, ed., *Works of Champlain*, V, 101, 207.
61. *Ibid.*, V, 108. On the usefulness of having Frenchmen accompany the fleet see Wrong, ed., *Sagard's Long Journey*, p. 262. Sagard reports that in the 1620s the Iroquois refrained from attacking Huron flotillas when they knew Frenchmen were travelling with the Indians (p. 261).
62. These were at least the functions that the Huron expected Frenchmen who had lived in Huronia would perform. The coureurs de bois are frequently referred to as interpreters (Biggar, ed., *Works of Champlain*, III, 168–72).
63. Wrong, ed., *Sagard's Long Journey*, pp. 249–56.
64. This route apparently had been used in prehistoric times as well (Biggar, ed., *Voyages of Cartier*, pp. 200–1, as interpreted by Innis, *Fur Trade*, p. 22).
65. Edwin Tross, ed., *Histoire du Canada et voyages que les Frères mineurs Recollets y ont faicts pour la conversion des infidèles depuis l'an 1615 . . .*, by G. Sagard (4 vols.; Paris, 1866), I, 42. This statement refers to the visit Le Caron made with Champlain. On the Huron desire to have the priests act as go-betweens in their trade with the French see Wrong, ed., *Sagard's Long Journey*, 244; Le Clercq, *Establishment*, I, 211.
66. The Indians often were reluctant to take missionaries back to Huronia with them (Thwaites, ed., *Relations*, IV, 221). Some priests, however, became personally popular with the Huron. The popularity of Father Brébeuf during his initial stay in Huronia is evident from the welcome he received when he returned in 1634.
67. This claim appears in the *Dictionary of Canadian Biography*. I. *1000 to 1700* (Toronto, 1966), 133. It appears to be based on Sagard's comments on the behaviour of an interpreter named Nicolas Marsolet. Although Marsolet refused to teach the Montagnais language to the Recollets, he later agreed to instruct the Jesuits (Tross, éd., *Histoire du Canada*, II, 333).
68. It is perhaps significant that the main complaint was about the sexual behaviour of these men rather than the sale of alcohol to the Indians (cf. André Vachon, "L'Eau-de vie dans la société indienne," Canadian Historical Association, *Report*, 1960, pp. 22–32). Alcohol does not appear to have been a serious problem in Huronia, no doubt because the Huron did not at this time feel their culture threatened by European contacts. The Jesuits' distaste for these men is reiterated in the Jesuit Relations, particularly when they are compared with the *donnés* and other men who served in Huronia under Jesuit supervision after 1634. See Thwaites, ed., *Relations*, VI, 83; XIV, 19; XV, 85; XVII, 45.
69. Trudel, *Histoire de la Nouvelle-France*, II, 405–34.
70. Trelease, *Indian Affairs*, p. 52; Hunt, *Wars of the Iroquois*, pp. 69–70.
71. Thwaites, ed., *Relations*, XXXIII, 121.
72. Le Clercq, *Establishment*, I, 204; Tross, éd., *Histoire du Canada*.
73. There is nothing in Sagard or Le Clercq that implies that the priests were instructed to disrupt this treaty, as Hunt implies. Trudel (*Histoire de la Nouvelle-France*, II, 370) says that it was necessary to send Father Le Caron and the other Frenchmen to Huronia to prevent a commercial treaty between the Huron and the Iroquois. It is my opinion that the prospect of this treaty was a figment of the imagination of the French in Quebec and never a real possibility (see text below).
74. On the Mohawk refusal to let the French Indians pass through their country to trade with the Dutch see Trelease, *Indian Affairs*, pp. 52–3; Hunt, *Wars of the Iroquois*, p. 34. Trudel's (*Histoire de la Nouvelle-France*, II, 364–6) suggestion that the Huron were about to trade with the Dutch and that the French who stayed in Huronia did so to prevent this seems unlikely in view of the traditional enmity between the Huron and the Iroquois. To reach Albany the latter would have had to travel through the tribal territory of the three eastern Iroquois tribes. Mohawk opposition to this seems to have effectively discouraged the Huron from attempting such trade.
75. Sagard says that the Huron did not permit other tribes to pass through their territory without special permission (Wrong, ed., *Sagard's Long Journey*, p. 99). The Jesuits say categorically that the Huron did not permit the Petun to trade with the French (Thwaites, ed., *Relations*, XXI, 177).
76. For a reference about canoes see Hunt, *Wars of the Iroquois*, p. 51.
77. Le Clercq, *Establishment*, I, 267. The Huron spread evil rumours about the Jesuits among the Petun when the Jesuits tried to do mission work there in 1640 (Thwaites, ed., *Relations*, XX, 47–51).

41

78. Thwaites, ed., *Relations*, XXI, 207–15. At first the priests pretended to be traders. This pretence, however, failed.

79. Biggar, ed., *Works of Champlain*, V, 131.

80. The French later describe him as a traitor (Thwaites, ed., *Relations*, V, 241).

81. Tross, éd., *Histoire du Canada*, II, 431. For a description of his proposed reburial see Thwaites, ed., *Relations*, X, 307–9.

82. G. Lanctot, *A History of Canada*, I (Toronto, 1963), 148–9.

83. It appears that one reason the Recollets received little support from the trading companies was that their policy of settling migratory Indians and of wanting Huron converts to settle in Quebec conflicted with the traders' own interests (Le Clercq, *Establishment*, I, 111).

84. The support of Governor Montmagny appears to have been particularly effective (Thwaites, ed., *Relations*, XXI, 143; XXII, 309, 311).

85. Thwaites, ed., *Relations*, X, 33; XI, 97, 109, 111, 113; XIII, 9; XIV, 125 161, 231, 235, 255. On the discontinuation of the seminary, see XXIV, 103. During the first two years the Jesuits were back in Huronia they were struggling to orient themselves and to understand the nature of Huron society better. At first they tended to be rather patronizing. They gave advice on military matters (X, 53) and, failing to understand the nature of Huron politics, felt that their intervention was needed to mediate disputes among the different tribes (IX, 273; XIV, 17, 21). Later, when they realized how the Huron did things and that intervention was unnecessary, these efforts ceased.

86. One example is the decision to seek to baptize older men — and especially influential ones (Thwaites, ed., *Relations*, XV, 109).

87. For Jesuit policy regarding lay assistants in Huronia, see Thwaites, ed., *Relations*, XXI, 293–303. See also VI, 81, 83; XV, 157; XVII, 45; XX, 99; XXV, 85; XXVII, 91.

88. Parkman, *Jesuits in North America*, pp. 465–7. Concerning early charges of Jesuit participation in the fur trade and a declaration by the directors of the Company of New France concerning their innocence, see Thwaites, ed., *Relations*, XXV, 75.

89. Thwaites, ed., *Relations*, XIV, 17–19. For a clear statement that the Jesuits were aware that their presence in Huronia depended on the traders' ability to coerce the Huron to let them stay, see XXXIV, 205. Soon after the Jesuits returned to Huronia, Brébeuf wrote that they won the esteem of the Indians by giving them arrowheads and helping them to defend their forts (XXXIV, 53). He hoped that the confidence won by these actions would permit the Jesuits eventually to "advance the glory of God."

90. The main reason seems to have been that the French had detained a Huron who was implicated in killing a Frenchman in Huronia (*ibid.*, VI, 19). It is interesting to note that the Huron also made it clear they wanted Frenchmen with guns instead of, or at least alongside, the priests (VII, 217).

91. *Ibid.*, IX, 287.

92. *Ibid.*, VII, 47. The officials in Quebec continued to exhort the Huron to become Christians (XVII, 171).

93. *Ibid.*, VIII, 71, 91, 99.

94. That was in July 1633 (*ibid.*, V, 259). The people of Ossossané continued to press the Jesuits to move there.

95. *Ibid.*, VIII, 99, 103–5. They also stayed at Ihonitiria because they felt it better to start work in a small village rather than a large and important one (VIII, 103). Ossossané was also unsatisfactory as its inhabitants were planning to relocate the village the next spring (VIII, 101).

96. *Ibid.*, V, 239, VIII, 99; X, 309; XIV, 99–103.

97. For an account of this dispute and the Jesuits attempts to resolve it, see *ibid.*, X, 279–81, 307; XIV, 21. No mention is made of the dispute after 1637, so presumably it was patched up. Brébeuf mentions elsewhere that, as a result of Brûlé's murder, other Huron were threatening the people of Toanché (the village where he was killed) with death (VIII, 99). The bad relations between Ossossané and the village of Ihonitiria (which was inhabited by Toanchéans) were exacerbated in 1633 when the latter became angry at the efforts of the chiefs of Ossossané to persuade all the Jesuits to settle in their village (V, 263).

98. Presents were also given to the Huron both as tokens of goodwill and to ensure the good treatment of the Jesuits.

99. For a discussion of the financial help the Jesuits expected to receive from the trading company see Thwaites, ed., *Relations*, VI, 81–3. The financial support of the mission is discussed in Parkman, *Jesuits in North America*, pp. 465–7.

100. Thwaites, ed., *Relations*, X, 249; XIII, 141; XVII, 95; XVIII, 19, 97.

101. *Ibid.*, X, 301.

102. One of these trips was to visit the father of a young convert named Amantacha who lived at St. Joseph (*ibid.*, VIII, 139). A careful tabulation by Miss Clark of the places the Jesuits mention visiting each year and the amount of attention given to each village in Huronia shows clearly that prior to 1640 their activities were confined to the Bear nation and particularly to the Penetang Peninsula. After that time their mission work spread into all parts of Huronia.

103. To less than twelve thousand.

104. Thwaites, ed., *Relations*, XIX, 123, 127; VIII, 145-7. The high mortality rate among children is an over-all impression gained from reading the relations of the years 1636-40. It also corresponds with what is known about similar epidemics among other Indian groups.

105. *Ibid.*, XIX, 223.

106. *Ibid.*, XIV, 17, 53, 99-103.

107. *Ibid.*, XXXIX, 129.

108. *Ibid.*, XIX, 179.

109. *Ibid.*, XV, 59-67.

110. At all times the Huron leaders appear to have been convinced that killing a priest or one of their assistants would terminate the Franco-Huron alliance.

111. Thwaites, ed., *Relations*, XIII, 215, 217. For a French statement emphasizing the Huron dependence on trade goods see XXXII, 179 (1647-48).

112. *Ibid.*, XV, 21.

113. *Ibid.*, XV, 51.

114. *Ibid.*, XV, 55; XVII, 115.

115. *Ibid.*, XXI, 143; XXII, 310.

116. *Ibid.*, XXI, 131.

117. One heifer and a small cannon arrived in 1648 (*ibid.*, XXXII, 99).

118. *Ibid.*, XXVI, 201.

119. Concerning the establishment of Ste Marie and the mission system see *ibid.*, XIX, 123-65.

120. There is a considerable amount of other evidence concerning the coercive power of Huron chiefs. See B. G. Trigger, "Order and Freedom in Huron Society," *Anthropologica*, N.S., V (1963), 151-69.

121. Thwaites, ed., *Relations*, XXI, 213. About the same time the Huron were spreading bad reports concerning the Jesuits among the Petun (XX, 54) with whom they had recently made a new treaty of friendship (XX, 43). These rumours were spread by Huron traders.

122. *Ibid.*, XXX, 75-7. So bitter was the Huron opposition to Brébeuf after he returned to Huronia that the Huron mission was compelled to send him down to Quebec until the situation quieted down (XXIII, 35).

123. The Jesuit Relation of 1635 records that the beaver was already totally extinct in the Huron country and that all the skins they traded with the French were obtained elsewhere (*ibid.*, VIII, 57).

124. Trelease, *Indian Affairs*, pp. 118-20; Hunt, *Wars of the Iroquois*, pp. 32-4. For a later source see Jean Talon cited in Hunt, *Wars of the Iroquois*, 137.

125. Hunt, *Wars of the Iroquois*, pp. 32-4; Trelease, *Indian Affairs*, p. 118.

126. This theory was first advanced by C. H. McIlwain in 1915. It was taken up in Innis, *Fur Trade*, pp. 34-6 and Hunt, *Wars of the Iroquois*, pp. 32-7, 74.

127. Trelease, *Indian Affairs*, p. 120.

128. E. B. O'Callaghan, ed., *Documents Relative to the Colonial History of the State of New York* . . . (15 vols.; Albany, 1853-87), IV, 908.

129. Thwaites, ed., *Relations*, XXIII, 105.

130. Hunt, *Wars of the Iroquois*, p. 76.

131. Tooker, "Defeat of the Huron," pp. 117-18.

132. Thwaites, ed., *Relations*, XXVI, 71; XXVII, 89, 277. Brébeuf returned to Huronia at this time.

133. Hunt, *Wars of the Iroquois*, pp. 77-8.

134. For the Iroquois desire to obtain French guns, see the evidence presented in Hunt, *Wars of the Iroquois*, p. 74.

135. Thwaites, ed., *Relations*, X, 13; XIII, 171.

136. *Ibid.*, XX, 27-31.

137. *Ibid.*, XX, 225; XXVI, 275.

138. *Ibid.*, XV, 109. For the later relaxation of these requirements see XXXIII, 145-7.

139. *Ibid.*, XIX, 191.

140. *Ibid.*, XVII, 111; XXIII, 129.

141. Concerning this preferential treatment see *ibid.*, XX, 225, 227.

142. *Ibid.*, XXXII, 179.

143. Vachon, "L'Eau-de-vie."

144. Thwaites, ed., *Relations*, XXIII, 67, 127; XXVI, 229. Pagan women also attempted to seduce Christian men to persuade them to give up their faith (XXX, 33). The Relation of 1643 mentions that some converts lived for six months at Quebec to avoid facing temptation in their homeland (XXIV, 121).

145. *Ibid.*, XXX, 23.

146. *Ibid.*, XXI, 131.

147. *Ibid.*, XXIII, 185.

148. *Ibid.*, XXIII, 31.

149. For another reference to the Huron-pagan rift see *ibid.*, XXIII, 267.

150. *Ibid.*, XXVIII, 89. For other acts of Christian assertiveness around this time see XXIX, 263-9; XXX, 63.

43

151. *Ibid.*, XXV, 85.
152. Tross, éd., *Histoire du Canada*, I, 200; *ibid.*, V, 259.
153. Thwaites, ed., *Relations*, XXXIV, 105, 217.
154. For one incident see *ibid.*, XXX, 61–3. Various cults also arose that appear to have been aimed at organizing ideological resistance to Christianity. One was the cult of a forest monster (XXX, 27); the second was more explicitly anti-Christian (XXX, 29–31).
155. As one Huron put it, "I am more attached to the church than to my country or relatives" (*ibid.*, XXIII, 137). The Jesuits also observed that it was hard to be a good Christian and a good Huron (XXVIII, 53).
156. *Ibid.*, XXVI, 217. The Jesuits had noted the special inclination of the Bear tribe to receive Christianity as early as 1636 (X, 31).
157. After the destruction of Huronia the Cord were very loyal to the French. They were the only Huron tribe that refused to leave Quebec to go and live with the Iroquois (*ibid.*, XLIII, 191). Prior to 1640, the Cord were not at all friendly with the Jesuits (XVII, 59); their change in attitude seems to have come about soon after (XXI, 285; XXIII, 151; XXVI, 265).
158. *Ibid.*, XLII, 73. Concerning their early desire for peace with the Iroquois see XXXIII, 119–121.
159. *Ibid.*, XVII, 89.
160. *Ibid.*, XXXVI, 179. The Deer lived among the Seneca in their own village and on good terms with their hosts (XLIV, 21). Many Rock people including the Indians of Contarea, lived among the Onondaga (XLII, 73).
161. For evidence of incipient deterioration in morale and the beginning of the abandonment of Huronia in the face of Iroquois attack, see *ibid.*, XXX, 87; XXXIII, 83–9.
162. *Ibid.*, XXXIII, 125. Hunt (*Wars of the Iroquois*, p. 72) notes that in 1637 the Huron had broken a peace treaty with the Seneca.
163. Thwaites, ed., *Relations*, XXXIII, 71, 123.
164. *Ibid.*, XXXIII, 131.
165. *Ibid.*, XXXIII, 119–21.
166. *Ibid.*, XXXIII, 125.
167. *Ibid.*, XXXIII, 125–7. He probably did this through anger at his allies and to show the innocence of the Onondaga. He might also have committed suicide to avoid Huron vengeance directed against his person, but this would have been construed as an act of cowardice. It is unlikely that the Onondaga would have exposed an important chief to almost certain death had they not been negotiating in good faith.
168. *Ibid.*, XXXIII, 229.
169. *Ibid.*, XXXIII, 231.
170. *Ibid.*, XXXIII, 81.
171. *Ibid.*, XXXIII, 233–49.
172. *Ibid.*, XXXIV, 227.
173. *Ibid.*, XXXIV, 83.
174. Lanctot, *History of Canada*, I, 194, based on *ibid.*, XXXIV, 59–61.
175. Tooker, "Defeat of the Hurons," pp. 117–18; Innis, *Fur Trade*, pp. 35–6. For the effective use of firearms by the Iroquois see Thwaites, ed., *Relations*, XXII, 307. The Jesuits saw the danger of growing Iroquois firepower as early as 1642 (XXII, 307) but the French officials in Quebec never developed a policy to counteract it. The restiveness of the Huron pagans may be one reason why the French did not want too many guns in Huron hands, even if they were being sold only to Christians.
176. Hunt, *Wars of the Iroquois*, p. 59.
177. Thwaites, ed., *Relations*, XXXV, 191.
178. *Ibid.*, XXXVI, 179; XLIV, 21; XLV, 243. Many of the Rock nation, particularly from Contarea, were later found living with the Onondaga (XLII, 73).
179. *Ibid.*, XII, 221. The work in Paraguay is also mentioned in XV, 127.
180. G. Lanctot, *A History of Canada*, II (Toronto, 1964), 63.
181. Hunt, *Wars of the Iroquois*, pp. 100–2.
182. Thwaites, ed., *Relations*, XLI, 201–3, and XLIV, 151; Hunt, *Wars of the Iroquois*, pp. 99, 100.
183. Thwaites, ed., *Relations*, XL, 215; Lanctot, *History of Canada*, I, 212–13. On the lack of furs in Montreal in 1652–53 see Thwaites, ed., *Relations*, XL, 211.
184. Hunt, *Wars of the Iroquois*, pp. 102–3.
185. Parkman, *Jesuits in North America*, pp. 550–3.
186. Tross, éd., *Histoire du Canada*, III, 811; Le Clercq, *Establishment*, I, 204.

44

The Oral History of the Stoneys*
CHIEF JOHN SNOW

Long ago my ancestors used to go to the mountain tops to pray. They were a deeply religious, sincere, and tradition-oriented people who followed, observed, and upheld the teachings, customs, and beliefs of our forefathers, respected the creations of the Great Spirit, and lived in harmony with nature. They were Stoneys — members of the Great Sioux Nation who spoke a dialect of the Nakota branch of the Siouan language family. Today we, their descendants, speak the same tongue.

The word Sioux conjures up the whole of the rich history and culture of the Plains — Sitting Bull, the Custer battle, great buffalo hunts, magnificent eagle-plume headdresses, and beautiful quill-decorated, buckskin clothing. This is the heritage we share with the Dakota and the Assiniboine and the Oglala through our language-family connections. Our other neighbours were the Algonkian-speaking people — the Ojibway, the Cree, and the Blackfoot — with whom blood feuds were a continual fact. Nearby, too, were smaller groups, such as the Athapascan-speaking Sarcee. To the west our contacts were with the people of the mountains, the Kootenay, the Shuswap, and occasionally the Flathead; our relations with these were somewhat more cordial, but not always peaceful.

45

Indian traditions and oral history say that my people were always present in this part of the Great Island (the native name for the North American continent), roaming along the foothills out onto the prairies to the east and deep into the Rocky Mountain country to the west. Our traditional hunting territory seems to have extended north to the Brazeau River-Jasper area, south a little past what is now the international border, east beyond the present-day city of Calgary, and west into the Rockies beyond what would become the British Columbia border.

In order to understand the vital importance the mountains had — and still have — to my people, it is necessary to know something of our way of life before the coming of the whiteman. It is not enough to say the mountains were the Stoneys' traditional place of prayer because our life was not a fragmented one with a compartment for religion. Rather, our life was one in which religion (and reverence for nature, which revealed religious truth) was woven throughout all parts of the social structure and observed in conjunction with every activity. Our forefathers were a proud people because they knew they had been selected by the Creator to receive a precious gift of special understanding and they have handed that gift down to us as a sacred trust.

*From *These Mountains are our Sacred Places: The Story of the Stoney Indians.* ©1977 by Samuel-Stevens, Publishers, Toronto. Reprinted by Permission.

In the days prior to the coming of the whiteman, we lived a nomadic way of life, hunting, fishing, and gathering from the abundance of this good land. There were literally millions of buffalo roaming on the western prairies, along the foothills, and even into the Rocky Mountains themselves. There were game animals of all kinds — moose, elk, deer, wild sheep, and goats — readily available for us to hunt and to enjoy. The land was vast, beautiful, and rich in abundant resources. Our Mother Earth called us from the forests, the prairies, the valleys, the mountainous areas, the lakes, rivers, and springs: "Come, my children, anyone who is hungry, come and eat from the fruits and gather from the abundance of this land. Come, everyone who thirsts, come and drink pure spring waters that are especially provided for you." Everywhere the spirits of all living things were alive.

We talked to the rocks, the streams, the trees, the plants, the herbs, and all nature's creations. We called the animals our brothers. They understood

46

Brazeau District

Chief Mountain

Stoney country prior to the 1800s, along the eastern slopes and foothills of the Rocky Mountains, ranging from the Athabaska River to Chief Mountain.

our language; we, too, understood theirs. Sometimes they talked to us in dreams and visions. At times they revealed important events or visited us on our vision quests to the mountain tops. Truly, we were part of and related to the universe, and these animals were a very special part of the Great Spirit's creation.

Our livelihood, our very culture were based on the necessity for hunting animals, but the hunt was never for the sake of killing them. We did not hunt for head trophies and kill off the game in the process. When we were in need of meat, when we were hungry, the medicine man of the tribe performed sacred ceremonies before the hunters went out. When the game was killed, the hunters observed a Stoney ritual of eating certain parts of the animal and thanking the Creator for providing us with food. We even shared some of the game with our brothers, the wild animals of the forest and the prairies. We would leave a special part of the animal for the birds of the air and other small animals. After the meat was brought back to the encampment, the medicine man held a special ceremony and made a humble offering of incense, sweet grass, and a special part of the meat to thank the Creator for His providence.

47

We made use of the whole animal for our livelihood. The buffalo's head was (and is) sacred to us; we used its skull in the sacred Sun Dance. From the game animals we received ribs and other bones for making knives, needles, and other needed tools. From the hides we made clothing, moccasins, teepees, and robes for bedding in the cold winter months.

The eagle held a very sacred place in our society. Ceremonies, prayers, and fasting took place and visions had to appear before an eagle was killed. The hunters were taught that the eagle is a sacred messenger created by the Great Spirit. Therefore, no Indian hunter was to kill the eagle unless the feathers were required for a ceremonial occasion. So even the feathers of the birds were used in our way of life.

Truly, our people respected the Creator's beings, and as a result, in our long history of dominance on this continent, none of the animals we hunted ever became extinct.

Later summer and fall were the main hunting seasons in this harsh climate. But except during the winter we spent most of our time migrating along the foothills in search of food, preparing for the cold months ahead.

The tribe did not travel as a unit, but lived in several bands, usually breaking off into smaller, extended-family groups as we moved about. The elderly and sick were left at a base camp, with a few men to provide daily food. The rest of the band or family group moved for several days or weeks along the foothills or into the mountains. If the hunt was good, we might stay in one place for some time, preparing the meat for storage. If the hunt was less successful, we kept moving.

There was one band of Stoneys, divided in two main groups, who usually traveled north of what is now Morley. These groups migrated along the foothills north to the Brazeau River area. Another band of two groups roamed around the Morley area and west past what is now the British Columbia border. A third band of three groups migrated south of Morley in the Chief Mountain area and on beyond the present international border.

During the hunting season there might be several or no returns to the base camp depending on the distance traveled. During the winter the band came together in protected winter camp grounds. For ceremonial and other occasions the entire tribe gathered.

Such a migratory people required many types of shelter. Some of them were seasonal and portable; others were permanent.

Our seasonal dwellings, generally used during the summer, were spruce bark teepees. The spruce bark was taken usually in the month of June when the bark was easiest to peel off. The spruce trees were not cut down but only the bark at the bottom of the tree was taken. The sap is rich at that time, so it was a good time to take it. Also, we made shelters from poles and fir, pine, or spruce branches. In the hot summer, such shelters were made from poplar branches with their leaves left on to make shades and arbours. There were also portable dwellings, used as my people traveled from place to place. These were, of course, teepees made from the tanned hides of buffalo, moose, and elk.

48

The permanent shelters were pole and moss dwellings of two kinds. One was a teepee, about ten feet across at the base, constructed with poles twelve to sixteen feet high. The poles were set in a circular teepee style, all very close together. Then green moss was stuffed between the poles. Another layer of poles was set around them, and additional moss put over them, making a double layer of poles and moss. A fire was made in the centre to heat the dwelling.

The other type of pole and moss dwelling was larger and resembled a roofed modern-day house. It was about fourteen feet high, twelve feet wide, and eighteen to twenty feet long. Again a double layer of poles and moss and clay or mud was used to build it. The fire was made at one end.

These pole and moss dwellings, cool in summer and warm in winter, served somewhat as communal tourist lodges. Their locations were known to all tribal families — they were the property of no one, yet belonged to everybody, and were available for those traveling light and staying in the locality but briefly. Like everything we possessed they were designed to meet a need — and they did, for we were a migratory people.

But a migratory people are not necessarily a people who lack civilization, not if "civilization" is taken in the sense of a law-abiding and caring society. My people were a proud and noble race, a great prehistoric society. We did not have written laws — we did not have a written language. Neither did we have one type of home for the rich and another for the poor in those days — there were no rich families and no poor families. If one member of a band went hungry, everyone went hungry. If one family had meat cooked on the campfire, everyone had meat. The whole tribe shared and lived as one big family. We had no old people's homes where we placed the aged to die "out of sight, out of mind." Old people were a very important part of the tribal society. They were the wise elders with a lifetime of rich experience that was valued by all. They taught our children, tutored our youth, advised younger adults and Tribal Councils. We did not have mental institutions. We did not have jails. Locks and keys were unnecessary in our communities because we were taught honesty and integrity, and we respected the creations of the Great Spirit. We were taught to respect other people's belongings, just as we were taught to respect their religions and traditions.

Human kindness was imprinted in our hearts, and the law of the Great Spirit, the Creator, was the only law that we observed. Our society was built around the concept that the Creator is the Supreme Being, the Great Mystery; recognizing Him as the One who provides all things was the very first step and beginning of our tribal society. The recognition of the Creator in all of life was essential for our survival here on earth and in the hereafter.

In this society there was no need to convince anyone that there was a Creator who made all things. In our long history there was never a story of a Stoney atheist. The theory of atheism was foreign and unknown in our society. (I am sure that this was generally true of all tribal societies on this Great Island before the coming of the whiteman.) When a child began to talk and understand things, one of the very first lessons he or she received was about the Great Spirit. A child would grow up learning about nature and the importance of respecting all things in creation.

There was no formal education as such, but education was interwoven into the life of the tribal society. A very important responsibility of the tribal members was to pass on valuable information to the next generation by the spoken word. Parents, grandparents, and elders told and retold stories and legends to the childen by the campfires, in the teepees, on the hillsides, in the forest, and at special gatherings during the day and at night. It was an ongoing educational process about religion, life, hunting, and so on. Other topics were bravery, courage, kindness, sharing, survival, and foot tracks of animals, so it was a very extensive study of many things.

With such an education based on religion, the child was established in Stoney tribal society. He or she was one of the Great Spirit's people.

A very special religious education was in Indian medicine. This was usually taught by experienced medicine men and women, although knowledge was sometimes received in dreams and visions.

I cannot discuss my people's medicine in detail here because it is sacred to us. But I can describe our general approach to healing, although it may be difficult for the modern reader to understand it.

Our philosophy of life sees the Great Spirit's creation as a whole piece. If something in the environment harms man, it is reasonable that the Creator has provided a specific herb to cure the sickness or has given some person the wisdom to heal it. Man is a complex being of body, mind, and spirit. We have always known that a sick mind or spirit can cause the body to show symptoms of physical sickness. (Western medicine today partially recognizes this interrelationship and speaks of psychosomatic illness.)

In the traditional times, we were basically a healthy people. Our diet was mainly meat and fish, supplemented by wild vegetables and fruit. Because of this, we were lean and hard. We were outdoor people and developed high tolerance to cold. Our lifestyle was probably responsible for a low incidence of heart disease and other diseases of the main organs. The diet assisted in good dental health. Herbal remedies (by which I include mineral and animal remedies) were available for all the common ailments.

Some of these herbal remedies were known to all, but many were known only to one person and regarded as closely guarded secrets. As in any society, a person's reputation in herbal medicine grew as cures were made and talked about. Among the Stoney people, both men and women became respected practitioners in herbal medicine. The collecting and preserving of herbs was an important activity of these medicine people during the warm months of the year.

The sacred waters of the mountains — the mineral hot springs — were also important to maintaining our health and curing illness. A person would journey to the sacred waters at the direction of a medicine man or woman and use them with suitable preparation and prayer.

Prayer was the essential part of all medicine; it put the person troubled by illness into a proper relationship with the Great Spirit and His creation. The medicine man who understood the relationship of the body, the mind, and the spirit of man to the Great Spirit could be a great healer. The counselling skills of the modern psychiatrist were well known in our culture. Combining these with a full awareness of unity of the Great Spirit's creation, gained through fasting and prayer, the medicine men and women were able to heal the whole person.

Such wisdom was acquired through a lifetime of study, experience, and prayer. The candidate for such knowledge had to be touched by the Great Spirit Himself. He learned of his selection by a sign which could not be misunderstood or denied. With this vision came much understanding, a direction for the future, and a change in the individual's personality, which made it clear to all that this individual had been touched by the Creator's hand. None recognized the new candidate better than the old men of wisdom. He then began his studies at their feet.

The medical skills of my people reinforced our belief that the Creator's teachings and lessons could be learned by observing the universe around us. So we studied the laws of nature and we lived by them. The creations of the Great Spirit have revealed many mysteries to us.

For example, there was no fear of death in our society because there was no concept of "Hell." Death was part of life. The elders interpreted it as entering another life beyond in the beautiful land of the spirits, the Happy Hunting Grounds. This was not difficult to understand when we watched the sunset. Each sunset was unique and glorious, foretelling of a land beyond. But the land that awaited us was far more beautiful than all the sunsets.

Again, the little crocus reminded us that there was a second life after death. Along the Rocky Mountain foothills the crocus is the first wild flower to blossom in the spring. It blooms beautifully for a while, then fades away. But in the autumn, when all the summer flowers have bloomed and gone, the little crocus comes out again. It appears and fades once more, as though to say: "So long for this summer, but I'll be the first one to return next spring." The appearance of the crocus twice in one summer revealed to us that there is more than one life.

So, too, from nature did my people garner much symbolism, which they used in formulating their principles, theories, philosophies and religion. For instance, the number four is a complete number in our tribal society, like the four winds of the earth and the four seasons that complete a year's cycle. A circle was interpreted in theory as a whole or something complete. The sun comes to a complete circle in a year. The moon is round like a circle. Therefore, the religion of the Great Spirit is based on a circle. There is no beginning and end to the creation and creating powers of the Great Spirit. All things in creation are related to his huge circle and all have a part to play in the universe. We held our Tribal Council and conducted our meetings sitting in a circle. Indian teepees are set in a circular formation, and there is the closely knit family circle. So using this symbolism of a circle, religion could be seen as the heart and the centre of Stoney tribal society.

51

Being members of such a complete society, the Stoneys were always a proud people. I will try to explain what I mean by being a proud people. I am not thinking of a foolish man's arrogance. The pride that I am thinking of is a native pride in being part of this Great Island. It is something the Creator instilled in every member of His Creation.

The bald eagle soars to great heights and takes pride in the strength of his wings. He does not pretend to be something else. He takes pride in the realization that the Creator has allowed him to share the bird kingdom's unique ability to fly. The mountain lion is also proud of what he is. He will climb the tallest mountain, not to show off foolishly but to proclaim his pride in being one of the Great Spirit's unique creations.

Likewise we, the Stoney Indians, are a proud people. We walk in beauty and in dignity. Whenever we stand to speak or to dance in a pow-wow, we do it with pride and dignity. This is a pride we must never lose because it was a gift the Great Spirit instilled in our being at the same time of Creation. Each of us must stand erect and tall and say: "I am an Indian. I am proud to know who I am and where I originated. I am proud to be a unique creation of the Great Spirit. We were the first human beings on the Great Island. We are part of Mother Earth."

Pride and bravery were the marks of the great warriors of our tribe. To be brave was to be a true Stoney warrior. It was the bravest warriors and the most successful hunters who became the tribal leaders.

Our world was not without perils for our people, so bravery was a survival factor for the individual, the family, and the tribe. Food might be in short supply for long periods. The freezing temperatures of winter were a constant threat. Blizzards and avalanches killed in those days as surely as they kill today. Many animals — bears, mountain lions and others — might kill the unwary hunter. Warriors from other tribes, particularly the Blackfoot and Cree, were a day-to-day danger. Occasionally tribal wars were fought over hunting areas or in retaliation for the killing of a chief's son by another tribe. The Stoney warriors were not called *Wapamâthe* (throat-cutters) for nothing. The *Wapamâthe* won more than their share of the battles.

Since bravery was a treasured quality in our society, every warrior instructed his son in it, even at a very early age. He would say: "My son, when you go to war, be brave, be like a true Stoney-Sioux warrior, and never turn back in defeat from your enemies. You must never run away from the enemy, because the survival of your tribe rests with you as you go to war. If you are defeated, that means we are all defeated as a tribe. If you are victorious, then we as Stoneys are victors and will retain our hunting territories. My son, perhaps some day you might be killed in battle, and if your wound was in the back I, your brave warrior father, would be embarassed and sad because it would look as if you had been running away from the enemy. But if the arrow mark or wound was on your chest or on the front, then I would be proud of you, my son, for it would show that you were facing your enemy bravely when you were killed. I would know that you died as a true warrior because you were protecting your people and defending your beautiful country with its animals of all kinds, birds of all colours, its beautiful lakes, rivers, and streams."

Having been so instructed from boyhood, warriors faced their enemies courageously, and many tales are told about the deeds of bravery performed by our forefathers. Indeed, much of what we know of the past is preserved for us in the Indian oral tradition. Much of the wisdom acquired by our people throughout the ages is passed on to us by our elders through the legends that tell of Stoney courage, history, and religious life. These legends are like parables; they convey social teachings and religious truths.

There are many Stoney legends of warriors, braves, and medicine men and women, who, when in difficult situations, changed into animals and birds. Such stories usually praise some virtue while reflecting our concept of the unity of nature.

George Ear, a present-day Stoney elder, tells a favorite legend about a Stoney warrior named Wolf-Come-Into-View. His father was a great warrior named Ear; he had been loved as a champion of justice and feared as a fighter, but he was killed by cowardly enemies who did not have the courage to face him in open battle.

During his own life, Wolf-Come-Into-View was approached by a spirit of wolf guise, who imparted a gift to him. Wolf-Come-Into-View often relied on this gift to help him out of difficult situations, as was the case one time at Cochrane Hill, east of Morley.

On that day he was hunting buffalo and he climbed Cochrane Hill in order to look over the valleys below. Upon reaching the summit he spotted enemy warriors; they too were viewing the land below for buffalo herds and saw him before he could duck out of sight. They immediately gave a loud whoop and came after him, but Wolf-Come-Into-View ducked into the nearby bushes and called upon his guardian wolf-spirit to deliver him.

The enemy warriors scoured the bushes attempting to find him, but to no avail. Finally one of them pointed northward toward the next hill and said, "Look over there." The others looked and saw a wolf loping away. The enemy leader said, "Do not bother. That man has turned into a wolf. He must be spiritually gifted. He must be a great warrior." From that time on, Wolf-Come-Into-View was respected by all enemy warriors.

This was only one of many feats that he performed in his lifetime.

When the missionaries first came to this part of the country, Wolf-Come-Into-View himself elected to change his name to Mark because it was more appealing to him. Today all who go by the surname of Mark are his descendants. They have every reason to be proud of him because he was a brave man in every true sense of the word.

Some of the most exciting and unusual legends and stories in the history of the Stoneys concern Iktûmnî, a great medicine man, a wise teacher, a prophet.

When I speak to whitemen of Iktûmnî I find I run into one of the great problems of dealing with another social group: language. Different cultures produce different value systems, which in turn produce diverse vocabularies. Sometimes I find it almost impossible to translate certain Stoney words into English and keep the true meaning or give the correct connotation.

The name *Iktûmnî* offers such a problem. Literally the word in the Stoney language means one who is out of his mind or crazy; but this English translation doesn't really convey the proper meaning. However, Iktûmnî had two names, and when both interpretations are combined they may better describe his character in English. This other name was *Thichâ-Yuski,* meaning one who outwits others or a person with deep understanding and extraordinary wisdom.

Iktûmnî had deep understanding of the ways of the animal world. There was a legend told of a race between Iktûmnî and a fox. One day Iktûmnî was walking along a lake when he found several duck eggs. He gathered the eggs very carefully, made a fire, and cooked them. Before he ate the eggs he continued his walk and met a fox. Iktûmnî challenged the fox to a race around the lake. Iktûmnî told the fox that he had cooked some eggs at the other end of the lake and whoever got there first could eat the eggs.

The fox was limping and said he could not run. So Iktûmnî said, "In order to make a fair race, I'll tie a rawhide around my ankle and drag a big stone while I run. That would make the race more fair to you since obviously you are lame."

Along one side of the lake were trees; the other side was flat and open. The fox said, "I will run along the side where there are trees."

The race started. The fox limped until he was out of sight in the trees. Then he ran like the wind. He was not lame at all. Iktûmnî ran dragging the big stone behind him. All the forest could hear the big stone thumping as he ran.

When the fox got to Iktûmnî's fire, he ate all the eggs, then put the shells back together so they looked as if they were not eaten, and then left. Iktûmnî came to the fire at last. He sat down beside the fire and said to himself, "Poor old lame fox." He started to open the eggs and found that they had all been eaten.

He was very angry when he found out the fox had tricked him. He said to himself "Wait till I see that fox again."

The animals took similar advantage of Iktûmnî on many occasions but as he got to know them and learned their ways, he eventually came out as the hero.

Iktûmnî was wise because he was able to talk and commune with both the natural and the spiritual world. He was able to interpret the animal world in human terms and understanding to the tribal members. The animals and the birds were his brothers and he lived with them, so he was able to talk with them in their own language. The rocks and trees were also his brothers, so he communed with them and learned the secrets and ways of nature. He communicated and talked with the spirits of the mountains, who revealed ancient truth, philosophies, and prophecies to him. In turn, he taught these things to the Stoney people.

We believe that Iktûmnî was sent to us by the Great Spirit to teach us the laws of the Creator — laws about medicine, about religion, and about life. To this day during the medicine ceremonial songs, prayers, and dances, Iktûmnî's name is mentioned as the keeper of medicine. When the medicine bundles are opened, Iktûmnî's name is mentioned in a respectful way as the one who taught the secrets of various healing herbs and medicine to our tribe.

Iktûmnî was perhaps the most famous of all the Stoneys in finding truth in nature, but he was by no means the only such seeker or even the only successful one. Indeed all the Stoney people were continually searching for the truth by observing the universe around them.

The most sacred search was a special religious journey into the rugged mountains, seeking wisdom and divine guidance. This was known as the vision quest, a tradition handed down through the centuries and practised by us as a means of approaching the Great Spirit. If the seekers were favoured, the Great Spirit would deliver a revelation and thus give direction and guidance to our tribe.

Sacred ceremonies and rituals were observed by these seekers of truth before they journeyed into the rugged mountainous country. In this preparation they were guided and aided by many members of the tribe who spent much time fasting and praying in the sweat lodge.

The sacred lodge was erected by a chosen few who were appointed by the elders; its construction was vigilantly and prayerfully observed by everyone. The lodge's frame was usually made from willow wood and branches shaped into a dome-roofed, circular building about eight or ten feet across and about five feet high; this was usually covered over with animal skins and hides, although sometimes spruce bark and branches and poplar leaves were used. A man or men were appointed by the medicine men to make the lodge ready for the ceremony. One of their chief tasks was to gather choice rocks to be heated in the sacred fire.

When the sacred lodge was completed one of the medicine men would, in traditional style, rub two sticks together to create the spark that would start the sacred fire. The old wise men or elders, the medicine men or holy men, the ceremonial leaders, and the brave warriors would take part in this religious ceremony. Upon this sacred fire they would burn sweet grass, cedar branch needles and boughs, and other incense that ascended to the Great Spirit, the Creator. (Similar fires were used during various other ceremonial observances.)

The sacred pipe was brought in next. The peace pipe and its rituals were handed down to us by our forefathers for use in religious ceremonies and prayers. The holy men would offer the pipe of peace to the Sun, Mother Earth, the four winds, and the spirits that the Creator appointed to be our guardians here on earth. One of the leaders would offer a prayer using the sacred pipe and offer it in a circular manner beginning from the east (from where the sun rises), then to the south, then to the west, and concluding by holding the stem of the pipe toward the north.

55

After the purification ceremonies were prayerfully observed in the sacred lodge, the seeker of truth and insight into religious thought would be prepared to set off on the vision quest. There in the mountainous wilderness he would be alone; he would live close to nature and perchance he would receive a special revelation. It might come through a dream or a vision, through the voice of nature, or by an unusual sign. It might be that the wild animals or birds would convey the message of his calling to him.

Many a brave has sojourned to these sacred mountains of ours in search of his calling — the purpose for which he was born. He searched in hope that the Great Spirit would make known to him his future task so that he could take his place in the tribal society, and help his people.

Even if no specific vision was granted the seeker, the Great Spirit's presence was never doubted. In times past He appeared and revealed Himself in various ways. He appeared in dreams, visions, and sometimes He spoke to us through the wild animals, the birds, the winds, the thunder, or the changing seasons. The Great Spirit was always present in the Stoney Indian history — He was everywhere.

In our migrations, as in our vision quests, my people continued to observe the animals, plants, rocks, trees, streams, winds, sun, moon, stars, and all things. Our teaching has always been that everything was created for a purpose by the Great Spirit. We must, therefore, respect all things of creation and learn as much as we can. There are lessons hidden in creation that we must learn in order to live a good life and walk the straight path. Behind these lessons and teachings is the Creator. These things can only be understood through the Great Spirit.

Century after century the rugged Rocky Mountains sat there in majesty, and nature seemed to say: "Your thoughts must be as firm as these mountains, if you are to walk the straight path. Your patience and kindness must be as solid as these mountains, if you are to acquire understanding and wisdom.''

The old Stoney medicine man had said: "You must continue to go to the sacred mountains. You must fast and pray for many days and nights, and perchance you will see a vision upon the mountains." Before he went to the beautiful land of the spirits beyond the sunset, the old man with a century of experience spoke these words: "You must search and search and you will find ancient truths and wisdom that shall guide you in the future." He continued: "My grandfathers told me these things when I was just a little boy and in my youth it was told to me over and over again by the campfire and in the tribal encampment, so it has been imprinted in my heart ever since that time."

And the medicine man stated further: "My grandchildren, you must search and continue to search in order to find them. When a revelation is open to you, you will become a special person to our tribe. It may be that you will gain courage and bravery and become a hero in many battles. It may be that you will be given understanding and wisdom and become a Chief amongst Chiefs. It may be that you will become a great hunter, knowing the paths and circling of the four winds, knowing where the animals roam and birds migrate at the seasons appointed for them by the Creator. It may be that you will be given the gift of prophecy, see into the future, and will advise and guide your people along the straight path."

Upon these lofty heights, the Great Spirit revealed many things to us. Some of my people received powers to heal. They could heal the physical body with herbs, roots, leaves, plants, and mineral spring waters. They could also heal the broken and weary soul with unseen spiritual powers. Others received powers over the weather. These gifted religious men and women could call for a great storm or calm the weather; they could call on the winds, rain, hail, snow, or sleet, and they would come. From these mountain-top experiences my fellow tribesmen and women were given unique tasks to perform to help the tribe prepare for things to come.

Therefore the Rocky Mountains are precious and sacred to us. We knew every trail and mountain pass in this area. We had special ceremonial and religious areas in the mountains. In the olden days some of the neighbouring tribes called us the "People of the Shining Mountains." These mountains are our temples, our sanctuaries, and our resting places. They are a place of hope, a place of vision, a place of refuge, a very special and holy place where the Great Spirit speaks with us. *Therefore, these mountains are our sacred places.*

56

Topic Two

Seasonal and Permanent Settlements in Atlantic Canada

During the fifteenth century, Europe began an age of great expansion, one marked by the development of overseas commerce and the establishment of colonies. The English, the Portuguese, the Basques, and the French were among the earliest Europeans to harvest the rich Newfoundland fishery, and to travel to Northeastern North America. Only one European group, as far as we know, had previously visited North America — the Norse around 1000 A.D. The archaeologist Robert McGhee examines the evidence of Norse contacts with the original inhabitants of the far north in "Possible Norse-Eskimo Contacts in the Eastern Arctic."

Five centuries after the Norse voyages, European fishermen established a number of seasonal settlements on the Atlantic coast to prepare and dry their fish. One group, the Basques, from what is now the border country on the Bay of Biscay between Spain and France, arrived in the 1520s and 30s. Selma Barkham discusses the research pertaining to the Basque summer settlement sites on the Strait of Belle Isle — separating Newfoundland from Labrador — in "The Basques: Filling a Gap in Our History Between Jacques Cartier and Champlain."

The origins of English-speaking Canada date back to 1583 when Sir Humphrey Gilbert laid claim to Newfoundland. England's fishery off the island soon grew to rival that of France, Spain, and Portugal. Keith Matthews summarizes the first two centuries of English and French settlement in Newfoundland (and their struggle to control the fishery) in his two lectures, "The Nature of Newfoundland History," and "The Framework of Newfoundland History."

For an overview of European exploration in the North Atlantic, consult Samuel Eliot Morison, *The European Discovery of America: The Northern Voyages, A.D. 500-1600* (New York: Oxford University Press, 1971). The context of the Europeans' journeys around the world is given by Daniel J. Boorstin in *The Discoverers: A History of Man's Search to Know His World and Himself* (New York: Random House, 1983). A beautifully illustrated account of the Norse and their arrival in Northeastern North America is *The Vikings and their Predecessors,* by Kate Gordon, with a contribution by Robert McGhee (Ottawa: National Museum of Man, 1981). Three popular accounts of the Basques on the southern Labrador coast are: James A. Tuck and Robert Grenier, "A 16th Century Basque Whaling Station in Labrador," *Scientific American,* 245, 5 (November, 1981): 180-190; and Selma Barkham, "From Biscay to the Grand Bay," *Horizon Canada,* 1,1 (1984): 14-19; and the series of articles in the *National Geographic,* 168,1 (July 1985): 40-71, entitled, "Discovery in Labrador: A 16th Century Basque Whaling Port and its sunken Fleet," with contributions by archaeologists James A. Tuck and Robert Grenier. D.W. Prowse, *A History of Newfoundland* (London: Macmillan, 1895), and Frederick W. Rowe, *A History of Newfoundland and Labrador* (Toronto: McGraw-Hill, 1980) deal with early settlement in Newfoundland. Several specialized articles on the early history of Newfoundland appear in G.M. Story, ed. *Early European Settlement and Exploitation in Atlantic Canada* (St. John's, Newfoundland: Memorial University, 1982). A short summary of Newfoundland's history is given by Gordon Rothney in his booklet in the Canadian Historical Association series, *Newfoundland: A History* (Ottawa: Canadian Historical Association, 1964; booklet no. 10).

58

Possible Norse-Eskimo Contacts in the Eastern Arctic*
ROBERT McGHEE

Approximately 1000 years ago, at a time when the Arctic climate was becoming considerably warmer than it is today, there were two major migrations of people into Arctic North America. From the west came Alaskan Eskimos, the ancestors of the present Eskimos of Arctic Canada and Greenland. These Thule culture people, travelling in large skin boats and living primarily on sea mammals, spread rapidly across Arctic Canada and may have reached northwestern Greenland by 1000 AD. From the east came the Icelandic Norse, who established colonies in southwestern Greenland during the late 10th century, and continued to occupy that area for approximately the following 500 years. According to interpretations of Norse sagas and historical accounts, the Norse also explored and built briefly occupied settlements on the eastern coasts of North America. The only North American archaeological site, accepted by a majority of archaeologists as evidence of Norse occupation, is that at L'Anse aux Meadows on the northern tip of Newfoundland. Recently, however, scattered archaeological finds of Norse objects in Canadian Arctic Eskimo sites allow us to speculate on the possibility of contact between the Norse and the Eskimo occupants of the area.

*From *Early European Settlement and Exploitation in Atlantic Canada,* ed. by G.M. Story. ©1982 by Memorial University of Newfoundland. Reprinted by permission.

Documentary sources may also provide some information on the nature of the contact between these two populations. These documentary sources are extremely rare, and are of a quite different form than those used by most historical studies. Here we are not dealing with the journals and account books of explorers, traders or missionaries, but primarily with stories which were passed from generation to generation as oral tradition for several generations before they were committed to writing. Most of the Norse traditions were written at least two to three centuries after the events which they describe, while the few Eskimo traditions relating to these events were not written until the 19th century. Both sets of traditions must have been distorted over the centuries of oral transmission; we can expect, for example, that the incidence of dramatic events, usually including violence, may have become exaggerated over time. Let us first look briefly at the Norse traditions, which set the historical stage, and then at the archaeological evidence and Eskimo traditions which allow us to speculate further on the relationships between the two groups.   *59*

According to the Norse sagas, Greenland was discovered by Erik the Red in 982 AD.[1] When Erik landed on the southwestern coast of this new country he found no human occupants, but the archaeological remains of former occupations. These fragments of boats and stone tools cannot have been the remains of Eskimo settlement, since the Eskimos had not, in all likelihood, reached southwestern Greenland by this time. They are more likely the remains left by an earlier population known in Eskimo tradition as the "tunit" and known archaeologically as the Dorset culture, an Eskimo or Eskimo-like race which had occupied Arctic North America since approximately 2000 BC, and who seem to have been exterminated by the invading Eskimos. There is one brief saga account[2] which suggests a possible meeting between Norse and Dorset people. About 1000 AD an Icelander named Thorgils Orrabeinsfostre was shipwrecked on the southeastern coast of Greenland, and was trapped for three years by the notoriously bad ice conditions of the area. Here, among other strange and terrible adventures, he and his men are said to have seen two "witches" cutting up a sea mammal beside a hole in the ice; they cut off the hand of one witch, the witches fled, and the Norse claimed the sea mammal. The early Norse name for the east coast of Greenland, *Trolbugterne* or "Troll Bays" suggests that they knew this area to be occupied by strange beings.[3] These hints suggest that brief contacts may have occurred between the Norse and an aboriginal population, perhaps Dorset culture people, on the east coast of Greenland.

The next contacts between Norse and aboriginal peoples occurred not in Greenland, but on the expeditions to Vinland and Markland which occurred between approximately 1000 and 1030 AD. In Markland, the forested coast which can probably be identified as Labrador, they met people who slept under their boats, and one of whom killed the leader of the Norse expedition with an arrow. In Vinland, probably the Northern Peninsula of Newfoundland, they met people who travelled in boats; at first contact these people traded furs for red cloth, but the second contact produced a battle which may have influenced the Norse to abandon their colonies in the new land. There has been a great deal of debate as to whether these "Skraelings" were Indians or Eskimos, perhaps southern relatives of the Dorset culture trolls of eastern Greenland. The saga descriptions are too vague to allow us to make any decision on the matter. Archaeological evidence from Newfoundland and Labrador suggests that these areas were occupied by Indians during this period, probably the Algonkian ancestors of the Beothuck and Montagnais, but it is not impossible that remnant Dorset populations may have remained in some coastal areas. Until the archaeological record is more clearly known, it is not useful to speculate on the racial affinities of the "Skraelings" of the traditional Norse accounts.

When Skraelings are next mentioned, they obviously refer to Eskimos in western Greenland. None of these few brief statements come from traditional sagas, but from letters and other accounts. The first contact between Norse and Eskimos appears to have occurred in the *Nordsetur*, the northern hunting ground probably in the region of Disco Bay. One account states that in 1266 AD the hunters ventured farther north than usual, perhaps as far as Melville Bay, and found traces of Skraeling occupation.[4] The *History of Norway*, a manuscript which probably dates to a 13th century source, states that "...further to the north, hunters have come across small people, whom they call Skraelings; when they are hit their wounds turn white and they do not bleed, but when they die there is no end to their bleeding. They possess no iron, but use walrus tusk for missiles and sharpened stones instead of knives."[5]

The next account of contact occurs in the Western Settlement, the Norse settlement in the area around modern Godthab. Around 1350 AD a man named Ivar Bardson was sent on a relief expedition to the Western Settlement, which he found to be abandoned. His account states that "...now the Skraelings have the entire Western Settlement; but there are horses, goats, cows and sheep, all wild. There are no people, neither Christians nor heathens."[6] Although no Eskimos were met on the expedition, the implication is that Eskimos may have had a hand in the extinction of the Western Settlement. Some 30 years later, in 1379, the Icelandic chronicles tell of a Skraeling attack on the Eastern Settlement, in which the Eskimos killed 18 men and captured two boys and a woman.[7] The last mention of possible contact comes in a rather dubious papal letter of 1448, stating that the Greenland settlement had been attacked 30 years previously "from the nearby shores of the heathens," and that most of the churches had been destroyed.[8]

These few brief statements, all that exist in the contemporary or traditional accounts of the Greenland colonies, suggest that contacts between Eskimos and Norse were few and violent, and the idea that the Norse colonists were exterminated by the Eskimos has become entrenched in writings on the subject. Archaeology tells a somewhat different story. In the Norse settlements there is no evidence of massacres, nor of destruction of farmsteads or re-occupation by Eskimos. In Eskimo settlements throughout Greenland there is evidence of acquisition of Norse materials throughout the period between the 13th and 16th centuries, but no indication as to whether or not this material was acquired through trading, warfare or looting of abandoned sites. McGovern suggests that the Eskimos acquired Norse material in four stages: (1) between roughly 1050 and 1300 AD through contact with hunters in the *Nordsetur,* perhaps by limited trading but more likely by raiding small hunting parties or looting abandoned camps; (2) between roughly 1300 and 1350 AD by raids on the Western Settlement; (3) between 1350 and 1500 by looting the abandoned Western Settlement and attacking Eastern Settlement farms; and (4) after approximately 1500 by looting the farms and churches of the Eastern Settlement. Again in this scheme, the emphasis is on violent contact between the two populations.

If this general scheme of Norse-Eskimo contact is correct, one would expect that items of European origin would only become common in Eskimo archaeological sites dating to the period after 1300. And indeed, this appears to be generally true in the 14th to 16th century Inugsuk period settlements of Greenland. Far to the north, however, in the Thule district of northwestern Greenland, several items are found in the probably 11th to 13th century Inuarfigssuak and Ruin Island sites;[9] these include a fragment of chain mail, the leg of a metal cooking pot, a comb, a draughtsman, and a fragment of woolen cloth. Across Smith Sound to the west of the Thule district, in the vicinity of Alexandra Fiord on the east coast of Ellesmere Island, an Eskimo site which has been dated to 1270 + 110 A.D. (GX-6069) has recently yielded another fragment of chain mail, woolen cloth, a metal clinch nail of the type used in Norse boats, and a piece of oak wood.[10]

61

Objects of probably Norse origin are found in early contexts in other regions of Arctic Canada. At the site of Silumiut located near Chesterfield Inlet on the west coast of Hudson Bay, dated relatively securely by radiocarbon dating to the period around 1200 AD (one-half century earlier than any mention of Eskimos in the Norse records) three fragments of iron tools were analyzed. Two of these appeared to be of meteoric iron, but one was of smelted iron.[11] Iron fragments, iron oxide stains left by iron blades mounted in bone tools, and bone cut with metal tools, are found in practically all Thule culture archaeological sites across Arctic Canada, and are particularly common in High Arctic sites. Indeed, the Thule culture from the 12th century on can be suitably thought of as an iron-age culture. Although most of this iron was probably obtained from meteoric sources (largely or entirely from the Cape York meteorites of northwestern Greenland) some of the iron, as well perhaps as the techniques of working iron by cold-hammering, may have originated in the Norse colonies.

The Eskimos of Arctic Canada were acquiring other metals as well. Recent analysis of metal fragments recovered 30 years ago from an early Thule site at Resolute Bay, Cornwallis Island, has shown that some of these fragments are of bronze rather than native copper, as had previously been assumed (Brian Yorga, personal communication 1979). A few small metal fragments excavated this past summer from a 12th century Thule village on Bathurst Island appear to be of smelted bronze.

All of the finds previously mentioned appear to date from a period prior to the abandonment of the Norse colonies, and therefore prior to a period in which such goods could have been obtained by raiding or looting by the Greenlandic Eskimos. They all date to McGovern's first period of contact, in which contact can only have occurred with small groups of Norse hunters in the *Nordsetur* region of Disco Bay or regions farther north. Although we must agree with McGovern that all of the European material so far found in Eskimo sites of northern Greenland and Arctic Canada could have been obtained from one Greenlandic Eskimo raid on a small Norse hunting party, and thence traded widely across the area, we should perhaps question the likelihood of such an interpretation. First, the number of archaeological sites which have been excavated is an extremely small proportion of sites dating to this period which exist across Arctic Canada. If we consider the excavated sites to be representative of the total population of sites, we should expect that the amount of European material imported at this time must have been much larger than that so far recovered. Secondly, the Greenlandic Norse were chronically short of metal, most of which had to be imported from Europe, and we would not expect that hunting parties going to the *Nordsetur* region would have been equipped with large numbers of tools of iron, bronze and copper, unless such items were carried as goods to be traded to the Eskimo populations of the region. The wide distribution of such goods throughout Arctic Canada suggests that metal was an extremely valuable trade commodity to the Eskimos of the period.

It would seem likely that such trading would have been very beneficial to the Norse. The Greenland colonies depended on trade with Europe for many of their requirements — grain, metal, timber, and various luxury goods. In addition, after 1261 they had to pay an annual tribute and fines to the Norwegian king,[12] as well as tithes and crusade taxes to the Roman church. These payments were made in materials of the country, primarily walrus and narwhal ivory, but also walrus skin and the hides of polar bears and other animals. In 1327 the Greenland see paid tithes in the form of 687 kg of walrus ivory, which must represent the tusks of approximately 200 animals.[13] Assuming that this represents a year's kill, and if we consider that walrus ivory may also have been used to pay European traders in return for imported goods, the take of walrus in that year must have been larger than that of the take for the entire west coast of Greenland during the early part of this century prior to the introduction of schooner-hunting (rarely more than 150 animals.)

Walrus do not occur today in the area of the Norse colonies, and almost certainly did not occur there at the time that the colonies were occupied when the climate appears to have been warmer than at present. In order to obtain ivory, hunters had to travel to the *Nordsetur*, probably the Disco Bay region 400 km. to the north of the Western Settlement. McGovern has emphasized the strain which such hunting trips must have put on the Norse economy, in that extended hunting trips to the *Nordsetur* deprived the colonies of much of the manpower required to undertake subsistence activities such as fishing, sealing, caribou hunting and farming. If ivory and other materials could be obtained by trade from the Eskimo populations of Disco Bay and the regions to the north, in return for small pieces of metal or worn-out tools, it would seem profitable for the Norse to exploit this trade. Such a trading relationship would be more likely to result in the widespread scatter of Norse objects among 12th and 13th century Eskimos in Arctic Canada than would one or a few Eskimo raids on small Norse hunting parties.

Traditional Eskimo accounts suggest that such trading did take place at a later period. According to legends recorded by Niels Egede during the 18th century, when the Eskimos moved south to the area of the Eastern Settlement and wished to settle close to the Norse farmsteads the Norse would not allow it but were willing to trade.[14] Legends written by Aron of Kangek, a 19th century Greenlandic hunter, picture relationships between the Norse and Eskimo populations which would have been conducive to trade. These legends also probably relate to the 14th and 15th century period when Eskimos were living in the region of the Norse settlements. Among the tales of murder and massacre, there are indications of a somewhat different relationship between the two populations. They tell, for example, of friendly meetings, of an individual Eskimo and an individual Norseman who were best friends, of an Eskimo woman working as a servant on a Norse farm, and they also recall recognizable Norse names.[15] People who know each other's names are certainly in a position to trade, and if that trade was profitable on both sides, as it would appear to have been in medieval Greenland, we should expect that trading activities would have been extensive.

If such a trade did take place, especially during the 12th to 14th century *Nordsetur* expeditions, would it have been limited to West Greenland, or would the Norse have been likely to send trading expeditions farther north and west? The nature of the European materials recovered from Thule period houses in northwestern Greenland and Ellesmere Island, may hint that a hunting or trading expedition had reached that area. Articles such as chain mail, boat nails, or oak wood could have been traded from hand to hand through the Eskimo settlements of western Greenland and eastern Ellesmere Island, but in view of their rarity, it would seem likely that they would have been reworked into useful artifacts by the time that they reached Ellesmere Island. Perhaps we may speculate that such articles may have been obtained either by trading, or by raiding a small boat party in this area far to the north of the Norse settlements, as suggested by Schledermann.[16]

An even more interesting artifact was recently recovered (Patricia Sutherland, personal communication 1977) from a Thule period site on the west coast of Ellesmere Island. This small bronze bar is a part of a folding balance, very similar to those used by medieval Norse traders for weighing coins and other small objects.[17] Although these items are well known from northern Europe, none have been found in the Norse colonies of Greenland.

63

The presence of this trader's artifact in an Eskimo site some 2000 km to the northwest of the Norse colonies allows us to again speculate on the possibility of Norse traders having penetrated this most northeasterly part of Arctic Canada.

A final archaeological specimen suggesting Norse visits to the eastern Arctic was found in a 13th century Eskimo house on southern Baffin Island.[18] This is a small wooden carving, typical in many of its attributes of Thule carvings of the time, but this figure represents a person in a long robe with what appears to be a cross upon the chest. The clothing is consistent with European clothing of the day, and suggests that the carver had seen someone dressed in this fashion. It seems unlikely that the Baffin Island Eskimos could have crossed Davis Strait to Greenland. It is also unlikely that the carving was traded through the Eskimo communities from Greenland to southern Baffin Island; several Greenlandic Eskimo carvings of Norsemen have been found on archaeological sites in Greenland, and these are all in a conventional style emphasizing the hood and cape of the Norse costume (Mathiassen 1930: Figs. 41,42; Pl. 223,4). Since the Baffin Island carving is not in this style, we may suspect that it was carved by a local artist who was unfamiliar with the stylistic conventions of the Greenland Eskimo.

From the saga evidence, it seems almost certain that the Norse knew of Baffin Island, the Helluland described as a stony and barren country located to the north of Markland and Vinland. The sailing route from Greenland to Markland and Vinland appears to have taken ships north along the Greenland coast, then across Davis Strait at its narrowest point to make a landfall on the Cumberland Peninsula of Baffin Island.[19] Voyages to Markland (Labrador), probably in order to cut timber, continued to be made until at least 1347 when a ship bound from Markland to Greenland is recorded as having been driven to Iceland.[20] Thus the Norse must have sailed along the eastern coast of Baffin Island at least occasionally for over three centuries, and it seems likely that some landings may have been made. The area was occupied at the time by Thule culture Eskimos, and if we speculate that trading relationships had been established with Greenlandic Eskimos, it would seem natural to suggest that such relationships could have been profitably extended to the Eskimos of Baffin Island.

On the northern coast of Ungava, directly across Hudson Strait from the Thule site which produced the carving, Lee has reported structures, stone cairns, an iron axe and human skeletons which he claims to be related to a Norse occupation of the region.[21] This claim is not accepted by the majority of archaeologists. The stone-walled "longhouses" resemble similar structures built by Dorset culture people elsewhere in Arctic Canada, and are associated with Dorset artifacts; the cairns appear to be unique, having counterparts neither elsewhere in Arctic Canada nor in the medieval Norse world; the iron axe, found out of context in a modern Eskimo tent site, may well relate to the fur-trade period; and the skeletons are generally considered to be those of Eskimos. Unfortunately, due to an acrimonious relationship between Lee and most other scholars working in the area, there has never

64

been an open debate on this material. It appears likely that the Ungava coast was occupied by Dorset culture people at the time of the Norse voyages to Markland and Vinland, and it is possible that the contact did occur between the Norse and the Dorset population of the area. A Dorset amulet found on the eastern coast of Hudson Bay and dating to around 1000 A.D. appears to have been made of smelted copper, and may have originated in such contact.[22]

In summary, the reader will obviously be aware that the above argument, based on a few historical accounts, most of which were written long after the events which they describe, and on a few specimens found in widely scattered archaeological sites, must be treated as extremely speculative. All contacts between Norse and Eskimos may have been brief and violent, as suggested by the Norse accounts. All of the iron and bronze and copper and cloth artifacts found in Canadian Arctic Eskimo sites may have been obtained by a few raids on Greenlandic farms or hunting parties and traded northward through Eskimo communities to the Thule district and then west and south across Arctic Canada. Such trade obviously did exist, as is witnessed by the occurrence of meteoric iron from the Thule district in many Canadian Thule sites, and by the bronze bowl fragment found in a Devon Island Thule village which was probably occupied during the 15th century, long after the Norse expeditions to the north had ceased.[23]

On the other hand, traditional Eskimo accounts suggest that the Norse may have been more eager to trade than to fight with the Eskimos whom they encountered and, given the economic realities of medieval Greenland, these accounts have a certain ring of truth. It seems doubtful that the relationship between Eskimo and Norse can be seen as one of occasional brief and violent encounter. Rather, it would seem possible that these people engaged in mutually beneficial trading activities over a period of several centuries, and that these activities may have encouraged Norse penetration of parts of the eastern Canadian Arctic.

65

Notes

1. Gwyn Jones, *The Norse Atlantic Saga* (New York: Oxford University Press, 1964).
2. Eigil Knuth, *K'avdlunatsianik* (Godthab: Det Gronlandske Forlag, 1969), p. 14.
3. Ibid., p. 16
4. Fin Gad, *The History of Greenland: I* (Montreal: McGill-Queen's University Press, 1971), p. 138.
5. Ibid., p. 88.
6. Ibid., p. 141.
7. Ibid., p. 147.
8. Ibid. p. 157.
9. Eric Holtved, *Archeological Investigations in the Thule District: I and II* (Copenhagen, 1944), p. 108.
10. Peter Schledermann, "Preliminary Results of Archaeological Investigations in the Bache Peninsula Region, Ellesmere Island, N. W. T." *Arctic* 31 (4): 459-474.
11. A.P. McCartney, and D.J. Mack, "Iron Utilization by Thule Eskimos of Central Canada." *American Antiquity* 38 (3): 328-339.
12. Gad, *The History of Greenland: I*, p. 120.
13. Ibid, p. 136.
14. Ibid., p. 258.
15. Knuth, *K'avdlunatsianik*, pp. 74, 76, 80.

16. Schledermann, "Preliminary Results...," p. 472.

17. The National Gallery of Canada, *The Vikings Exhibition*, (Ottawa: 1968).

18. Deborah Sabo and George Sabo III, "A Possible Thule Carving of a Viking from Baffin Island, N.W.T." *Canadian Journal of Archaeology* 2: 33-42.

19. Jones, *The Norse Atlantic Saga*, p. 88.

20. Gad, *The History of Greenland: I*, p. 123.

21. Thomas E. Lee, *Archaeological Investigations of a Longhouse on Pamiok Island, Ungava, 1970* (Quebec: Centre d'Etudes Nordiques, 1971), p. 71.

22. Elmer Harp, "A Lake Dorset Copper Amulet from Southeastern Hudson Bay." *Folk* 16-17 (1974): 33-45.

23. Robert McGhee, "Paleoeskimo Occupations of Central and High Arctic Canada." *In Eastern Arctic Prehistory: Paleoeskimo Problems*, Moreau S. Maxwell ed. *Memoirs of the Society for American Archaeology*, 31 (1976), p. 25.

66

The Basques: Filling a Gap in Our History Between Jacques Cartier and Champlain*

SELMA BARKHAM

Tiles — literally thousands of large, curved, red, roof tiles, narrower at one end for a well-fitted overlap — these are the calling cards left up and down the southern coast of Labrador by 16th Century Spanish Basques. It is in many ways miraculous that so much tangible evidence should be left from a fairly brief period of occupation, beginning in the 1540s and at its peak about 400 years ago.

Recent settlements like Carrol Cove (referred to locally as "Carrol's Cove") and Semadet (East St. Modeste), which were thriving only 30 or 40 years ago, have now disappeared leaving scarcely a trace ...a cellar or two and a few stone foundations but, luckily, Basque roof tiles are remarkably indestructible; even if they have been crushed into crumbs they help distinguish Basque sites from all other places of early occupation along the northern shore of the Strait of Belle Isle.

Generations of Labrador children living in former Basque ports have apparently been in the habit of grinding up tile to make red ochre for the painting of model boats, and have used whole pieces of tile as chalk to write their names on rocks. In dozens of potato patches there is a constant turning over of old ceramic tile in the soil while small bits also are found mixed with beach gravel. However, more satisfactorily, enough large pieces still remain under relatively undisturbed sod to please the probing eyes of archaeologists and to confirm the findings of historians.

The historical importance of these tiles is that they corroborate the mounds of documentary evidence that have been turning up in Spanish archives since

*From *The Canadian Geographic Journal*, 96, 1 (February/March 1978). pp. 1-15. Copyright by Selma Barkham. Reprinted by permission.

1972 as a result of work done for the Public Archives of Canada. Several insurance policies written for galleons going to Red Bay, a 1547 agreement with coopers (barrel-makers) for the Blanc Sablon area, wills actually written in 1577 and 1584 for dying Basques in Red Bay and Carrol Cove (probably the earliest surviving wills written north of Mexico), and several hundred ship and cargo charters and other preparatory contracts for voyages are the sort of documents that have helped to fill in the 60-year gap between the Cartier and Roberval expeditions of 1541 and 1542 and Champlain's explorations at the beginning of the 1600s.

The Basque presence in Canada has been acknowledged for a long time in a general way, just as the visits of Portuguese and Spanish codfishers throughout the 1500s are often mentioned, but until recently there has been no detailed knowledge of Basque activities from year to year.

Many undocumented assertions have been published, but no definite answers to queries about names of ships and their owners and which Canadian ports they went to, or how many whales would have to be killed in order that a 500- or 600-ton ship could return with a full cargo of train oil (oil obtained by boiling whale blubber), how many men died on these whaling expeditions, or which ports on the Basque coast sent out the most ships.

67

Those are the types of questions that are now gradually being answered, very often because of information recorded during the course of a lawsuit over some problem that arose on a Terranova* voyage. We know, for instance, that not more than 20 or 30 ships at the most were employed in any Labrador season. However, some of these ships could carry up to 1,800 or 2,000 barrels of oil, each regular barrel weighing 400 lbs. Though not all the galleons were in the 500 to 750 ton category, in an average year as many as 20,000 barrels of whale oil could have been sent back to Europe. This figure would help explain the colossal quantity of whale bone that can still be seen emerging from the grass on the western side of Red Bay below Tracey Hill.

Indeed, the Basque whaling industry (with the concomittant ship building industry) was second only to the Basque iron industry in size and importance. It was a prime source of wealth for early Basque capitalists and inspired endless litigation. No wonder that the judicial archives of the Corregimiento in Guipúzcoa, and the archives of the appeal court, the Real Chancillería, at Valladolid, are rich with law suits directly or indirectly concerned with Canada, since Canada provided the raw material for a product that was prized up and down the Atlantic coast of Europe. There are references as early as 1547 to Basques taking whale oil directly from ports in Labrador to Bristol, Southampton, London and Flanders. From about 1580 onwards, baleen too became a valuable item on the European market and was also shipped back from Labrador. The abundant lawsuits arising from this thriving commerce throw considerable light on the way Basque merchant sailors fitted out their ships and divided up profits, on whaling procedure during their

---

*Terranova, i.e. La Provincia de Terranova, was "New Found Land" of the 1500s. It included the coasts and islands of the Gulf of St. Lawrence.

stay in Canada, and on their difficulties when winter arrived too soon, ensnaring their ships in ice.

It was precisely because of some legal hearings about an insurance claim that had been filed as a result of an early freeze-up in Puerto Nuevo, a whaling station at the northeastern end of the Strait of Belle Isle, that we first became aware of the enormous quantity of tiles that had gone to Labrador in Basque whaling galleons.

In 1566, a young man called Miguel de Cerain, from the port of Deva in the province of Guipúzcoa, was captain of *Nuestra Señora de Guadalupe,* a galleon of 425 tons burden (i.e. cargo capacity according to her registration), belonging to three men from Bilbao, one of whom was the ship's master, Martin de Sertucha. Unfortunately Miguel de Cerain and Martin de Sertucha did not see eye to eye on the running of the ship, and Sertucha blamed Cerain when the ship got into trouble.

When trying to recover some of his losses from the Burgos merchants who had underwritten his insurance policy, Cerain and the witnesses who testified for him mentioned on several occasions 6,000 tiles that had been left on land in Puerto Nuevo towards the end of the whaling season, when the sea suddenly "froze like curds" and the anchor cables had to be cut so that the ship could get clear of the encroaching ice.

At no point during the legal hearings about *Nuestra Señora de Guadalupe* is there any mention of how the 6,000 tiles were to be used, but a document written a few years earlier, in 1563, specified that "a sufficient quantity of tiles and other materials for *the repair of the cabins*" was to be taken aboard the ship of Francisco de Elorriaga when she sailed for the Province of Terranova, while in 1564 Simon de Azcoitia from Guetaria, a harpooner on another of Elorriaga's ships, accidentally told posterity what at least one of the cabins was used for. He mentioned that he had been talking to Francisco de Jauregieta of Orio when he was standing *"beside the cabin that they had made for the boiling down of the whales they kill."*

It would appear that a sturdy covering was needed to keep rain and snow out of the great copper cauldrons where blubber was boiled over the "ovens" or furnaces and, certainly, an amazing amount of charcoal slag is now found in combination with broken tile and rotting baleen precisely in the places where whaling "ovens" are very likely to have been located.

Unlike codfishers who, in the 16th Century, only inhabited the coast of Canada during summer months, Basque whalers commonly stayed on in Labrador well into winter; they rarely returned to Europe before the middle of January. They required, therefore, rather more solid buildings than the transient codfishers, particularly workshops for the coopers who were responsible for putting together anywhere between 1,000 and 2,000 barrels for each galleon* and making sure that the barrels were tight enough so that no leakages of valuable whale oil would occur on the voyage home.

Smithies, even if on a minor scale with small forges and anvils, would

*French Basque galleons, of lesser tonnage, carried a much smaller cargo.

have been needed for these cooper's shops, and enough storage room for barrel staves, hoops, and tools. It is quite logical that remnants of these tiled shelters should cover an extensive area around harbours that the Basques frequented.

The question may well be asked as to how we know which harbours were most in use during the period of Basque predominance on the Labrador coast. The twofold answer is reasonably simple: first, there are not many good whaling harbours to choose from; and, second, though relatively few documents state *the exact place* in Terranova where a ship was going or had gone to, those that do mention the nine ports where Basque whalers normally anchored leave no doubt whatever that Red Bay and Chateau Bay were statistically the most important.

In other words, while piles of documents are being sifted, Red Bay and Chateau Bay turn up with regularity, seven other Labrador ports appear with less regularity, and absolutely no whaling documents written prior to 1580 have appeared *as yet* for a port farther west than Rivière St. Paul, about 45 km west of Blanc Sablon, or farther east than the end of the Strait of Belle Isle.

69

In 1590, when a change in Basque whaling habits seems to have taken place there was a lawsuit about the voyage of *Nuestra Señora de la Esperanza,* a small ship fresh from the shipyards of Motrico, that says Captain Sebastian de Sorarte of Deva was unable to load all the oil from the whales he had caught in a harbour called Babaçulo. This is the first reference found up to now in Spanish documents for a port to the west of Rivière St. Paul. It is shown both on the Plancius map published in Antwerp about 1592, and on later Basque maps, but unfortunately the location is so inexact that Babaçulo could be anywhere between Baie de Jacques Cartier and the Little Mecatina River. I think wherever it was located, Babaçulo was certainly not as well known as Red Bay.

Red Bay is still described by fishermen as the best harbour on the coast; red bluffs of granite are at the origin of both the modern name and the old French name Havre des Buttes; the latter was corrupted in Spanish documents to Butus, Buytes, Buitres and several other variants. Now it is a hospitable community of about 500 inhabitants whose main source of income is herring, cod and salmon fishing. Older inhabitants remember when some 23 sailing schooners would drop anchor on a Saturday afternoon and remain quietly in the harbour all Sunday before continuing up the coast to other fishing grounds.

During the last war six corvettes and a larger mother ship were moored in the basin, but that was not the first time the harbour had been used as a wartime base. It was recorded in 1554, during a Franco-Spanish war, that 13 French Basque ships after a tough battle near Los Hornos brought four captive Spanish Basque ships into the harbour, eventually allowing 180 of the Spanish Basques to return from there to Spain all crowded into one vessel.

Normally there appear to have been nine or ten galleons arriving in Red Bay every summer and using the harbour for a joint whaling operation. Basques, on the whole, were strongly in favour of private enterprise, usually operating on a very individual basis; their ships could not be considered as a commercial fleet however often their king tried to persuade them to voyage together.

Nevertheless, once moored in the same port, it was simpler for them to work in a co-operative rather than a competitive way. There were frequent remarks in one lawsuit about shallops (small whaling boats with oars and sails) from several ships combining to tow in a whale that had been killed in the Strait. It took at least five shallops to tow a really large dead whale, and very often two or three shallops were needed for the kill.

While shallops, each manned by half-a-dozen men, would roam over a wide area of the Strait, particularly in places "where the whales were in the habit of passing," the galleons stayed in the most sheltered parts of the harbours and acted as floating warehouses to store processed whale oil. Occasionally there were fierce disputes between captains in different ports over the ownership of whales.

70

In 1575, Nicolas de la Torre in Carrol Cove was said to have let his men boil up a whale that had been killed by harpooners from Joan Lopez de Reçu's galleon which was in Red Bay. De la Torre's men were accused of having cut loose this large female whale from a little cove called Antongoçulo where the whale had been temporarily tied up because of adverse tide and wind. The resulting lawsuit continued in the court of appeal at Valladolid for nearly 20 years until both captains were dead and the widows had to finish the case.

Carrol Cove appears as "P. Bertan" on the Plancius map, and was called Puerto Breton in Spanish documents, probably because this excellent little harbour is formed by a curved cape which used to be known as Cabo Breton. The Bretons had a strong influence on the nomenclature of the southern Labrador coast and may have been fishing in that region for as much as three decades before Basque whalers started to monopolize the best ports.

Another well-used anchorage was in the "Tickle" at West St. Modeste, which runs between the island and the mainland. An odd historical puzzle has been bequeathed to us due to the contraction of St. Modeste to "Semadet." The name Semadet is applied by modern fishermen to *East* St. Modeste, but that name seems to have slipped over to the east side of Pinware Bay in comparatively recent times; old maps and rutters* show Semadat or Saumaudet to the *west* of the Pinware River. In Captain Cook's day the two St. Modestes appear to have been known as Grand St. Modeste to the west and Little St. Modeste to the east of what Cook calls the St. Modeste River (the Pinware).

It is possible that Little or East St. Modeste was the site of the 16th Century port called Los Hornos, but it is also possible that Los Hornos was on the Pinware River estuary. Unfortunately the location of Los Hornos

*Rutter (ruttier): a captain's or pilot's set of instructions or notes for finding a course at sea; a guide to sea routes, tides, hazards, etc.

remains up to now unresolved, in spite of the very generous grant provided by The Royal Canadian Geographical Society for a 1977 expedition which hoped to clarify many points to do with ancient and modern toponymy. Some points have indeed been clarified but the exact locations of Los Hornos and of Puerto Nuevo are still unclear, and will have to be established either by the fortuitous appearance of a contemporary lawsuit which describes the area in some detail or, possibly, by a future expedition.

There is definite evidence to show that the sandy coastline has changed quite considerably around Pinware Bay. Not only has the end of the spit at the mouth of the river altered several times during the lives of some of Pinware's older inhabitants, but there also has been a great deal of erosion on the east bank of the river, where a settlement existed not long ago. At the moment it is hard to imagine a galleon being able to negotiate the narrow entrance between shoals at the river's mouth, even if it were being towed in by shallops, as it would have been in similar river estuaries on the Basque coast, but there is a reasonable likelihood that the bar is now much *71* worse than it used to be.

The tidal lagoon formed by the spit at the mouth of the Pinware is shown clearly as a large river entrance quite unlike the harbours marked on two copies of a Basque map in the Bibliothèque Nationale in Paris. The name *Les Fours* is placed beside the river entrance by Pierre Detcheverry Dorre, who drew the map in Placentia for Monseigneur Parat, the then French governor of Newfoundland, in 1689. The same place is called *Los Fornos* on the Plancius map drawn about 1592, *Furx* in Martin de Hoyarsabal's 1579 rutter, and *Labeeta* in the 1677 Basque version of the rutter, translated by Detcheverry Dorre. All of these names mean "the ovens" in English.

Two islands and a shoal marked to the east of Les Fours on the Detcheverry Dorre map are referred to as *Las Islas de Los Hornos* in Spanish documents and are the equivalent of Lily and Nelly islands on modern maps (in reality there also is a third small island). But all this information still leaves us unable as yet to pinpoint exactly where this whaling station, which was in production prior to 1554, was situated.

Luckily the clear-cut geographical features which enhance the attractiveness of Chateau Bay, Red Bay, Carrol Cove and West St. Modeste do not seem to have altered significantly in four centuries. Either islands or headlands to give sufficient protection from the prevailing winds were essential from a Basque point of view. Open bays only provided safe anchorage in fine weather, and it is unlikely that Basques would have had establishments at the heads of the wide bays where the settlements of L'Anse-au-Loup, English Point and Forteau are now situated. Though Forteau Bay is mentioned in the Hoyarsabal rutter, only the very smallest cod-fishing ships could find shelter in shallow water behind the points where Forteau Brook emerges.

Schooner Cove is an exception to the general rule. It is an open bay but affords good shelter since it is protected by the headland at the southwest corner of L'Anse-au-Loup. In spite of the fact that no 16th Century documents as yet can be said to apply to this small bay, a sufficient quantity of tile was found along the shore last summer to make Basque use of this cove seem indisputable. There was a whale factory functioning in the cove at the beginning of this century, and there is a possibility that the name *Baye de Balene* or *Baleabaya* (on the Basque maps) was given to this cove, where an extraordinarily genuine-looking Basque harpoon head was found by one member of our 1977 expedition.

The headlands along the southern Labrador coast give the Strait a very similar appearance to Basque whaling grounds along the Cantabrian coast, except that the Basque coast of northern Spain faces the open Atlantic whereas the Strait of Belle Isle is in fact a relatively narrow funnel, a funnel which the Basques called *Granbaya* and which appeared on old English maps as *The Grand Bay*. Through this funnel huge numbers of migrating whales used to pass each year on their way in and out of the Gulf. It was, therefore, the ideal place for the Basques to lie in wait for their prey.

Some galleons certainly sailed farther into the Gulf, but whether Spanish Basques bothered to go up as far as Anticosti before the 1580s is a moot point. While tiles have been reported as far up as Mingan, these could have been brought at a later date, although Basques were definitely at Brest on the Rivière St-Paul by 1551. In that year a French Basque from St. Jean de Luz, Esteban de Arriçaga, nicknamed "Chartico," said he sold a shallop there to Joan de Aguirre of Orio for eight ducats.

It is an interesting fact that the 1579 Hoyarsabal rutter does not go farther than Brest in its description of the coast, while the 1677 version describes a much more extensive area of the Gulf including the west coast of Newfoundland and the Gaspé peninsula. This would imply that prior to the 1580s the average seaman was not passionately interested in exploring the Gulf, and that the Strait's area was not overpopulated in spite of the very large crews brought by most Spanish ships.

Sizes of ships and crews are vital statistics in the sensitive area of differentiation between Spanish and French Basques. There were no French Basque ports to compare with the deep water port of Pasajes, a few miles over the Spanish border, and this discouraged French Basques from building larger ships, while their easy access to salt in Breton ports was an incentive to specialize more in cod-fishing than whaling. Sixteenth Century Basques were, of course, quite unaware of 20th Century Canadian boundaries, but they were well aware of the boundary between France and Spain; during periods of war when they were unable to benefit from shared facilities like the Breton salt supply or the renowned winter haven of Pasajes, they cheerfully compensated for this lack by capturing each other's ships.

In times of peace, however, their use of a common language, almost unquestionably the oldest language in Europe, and their identical methods of fishing and whaling meant that fraternal co-operation in French and Spanish ports was normal, particularly in business dealings. Merchants from both sides of the border often were partners in the joint outfitting of cod and whaling voyages, and the first known ship to winter in Labrador was a French ship that had been fitted out by a Spanish Basque of San Sebastian for the 1574 whaling season. The captain and owner of the ship was Martin Sanz de Aguirre, nicknamed "Amuros;" when he had failed to return by April, 1575, the outfitter, Sebastian de la Bastida, became thoroughly worried about his investment in the victuals and equipment of Aguirre's ship, and dashed off to Red Bay in another ship to recover his share of the whale oil. Presumably he also took a fresh supply of victuals with him to comfort the suffering crew.

One of the main reasons that Spanish Basques were often the outfitters for French Basque ships was because there appears to have been a larger supply of capital on the Spanish side of the border up until the disastrous Armada of 1588. During the second half of the 16th Century Spanish galleons were, on the whole, larger and better armed than French Basque ships, but when there were not enough Spanish ships available, due to a royal embargo, then smaller French ships were chartered by Spanish Basque merchants.

Spanish merchant vessels were constantly being embargoed (forbidden to leave port and held for service of the state) for royal purposes, much to the annoyance of shipowners who preferred sending their ships to Terranova than having them destroyed in their king's service. Joan Lopez de Reçu was accused of deliberately allowing his new galleon to drift onto some rocks when she was being launched in order to avoid an embargo for the fleet that was being prepared to attack the Azores in 1582.   *73*

In spite of embargoes, however, and other problems at home, there was a period of at least 30 years when Spanish Basque ships definitely dominated the scene in Labrador. There were crews of up to 130 men on the larger galleons and, in a port like Red Bay, that could have meant a maximum of about 900 men and a minimum of about 600 every season. The average for the whole Labrador coast would have probably been as many as 2,000 Basques per year, of all ages and sizes, some as young as 11 or 12 years old.

Priests frequently accompanied the crews, and Labrador harbours must have often resounded to the rhythms of txistu (a wind instrument) and drum and the stirring sound of Basques singing. The only people who were automatically left behind were the women, who had to do many of the toughest jobs in the small coastal towns as a result of an almost total drainage of able-bodied men to *La Provincia de Terranova*.

With such a large yearly exodus to Newfoundland and Labrador for the cod and whaling, it is not surprising to find the Basques referring to this part of the New World as if it were a Spanish province, just as much a Spanish possession as *La Provincia de Peru*. The only surprising thing is that Spain officially never made any real effort to appropriate any part of the Labrador or Newfoundland coast. Perhaps there were enough administrative headaches for the Spanish crown to cope with from Florida southwards, and possibly the Portuguese claims in the north were still being respected.

Whatever the reasons for the lack of official support for such a booming commercial success, the two Basque wills written in Labrador point out the nuisance of not having an official royal notary in the province of Terranova. It may seem absurd but there is a plaintive note in the depositions of witnesses during the authentication of both wills, in the town of Orio, about the lack of legal amenities in that "country of savages," but at least both wills were considered authentic and accepted in the notarial files of Orio.

More than five decades later, Champlain was not so lucky. When he was dying in Quebec, in 1635, he dictated a will in the presence of seven adult witnesses which the parliament in Paris first confirmed but later judged null and void on the petition of a cousin. (The will ignored his wife and made the Virgin Mary his heiress.)

Why did this well-organized and highly remunerative Basque whaling industry begin to fade before the end of the 16th Century and finally peter out soon after the 1620s? Biologists have suggested that the Basques' intensive destruction of whales may have reduced the seasonal catch to an uneconomic level, but this does not appear to be the entire answer. There were still a few large Basque galleons going out to the Grand Bay at the turn of the century, and 38 Basques wintered in Red Bay in 1604. The basic problem seems to have been lack of private capital after the unhappy 1588 expedition to England which drained Basque resources — money, ships and men.

This lack of capital at a moment when there was growing Dutch and English competition in the New World, plus the loss of the traditional trade route to Flanders (where much of the Terranova whale oil had formerly been disposed of at very satisfactory prices) tended to make Basque merchants concentrate on other traditional and safer areas of trade — with Seville and the Indies.

During the 16th Century a combined Spanish and French Basque monopoly of the whale oil trade had been maintained, because of the simple fact that there were no other European experts on large scale whaling. Unfortunately the Basques played straight into Dutch and English hands when the Spitsbergen whaling was opened up in the second decade of the 17th Century. Shipowners like Joanes de Cigarroa of Fuenterrabia, who normally sent his ships to Terranova, helped to fit out the *Santiago* in 1615 for "parts of the north in Norway." He was only one of many Basques who gave Dutch and English seamen a chance to pick up Basque whaling skills. From then on the Basque monopoly was broken.

Gradually the tiled cabins on the Labrador coast fell into disrepair and collapsed, but shores piled high with while skeletons of whales were dramatic monuments to mark where Basques had been. Later, French and English visitors to the former Basque ports remarked on these enormous quantities of bone. In 1766, Sir Joseph Banks attributed a combination of tile and baleen that had been found on an island in Chateau Bay to the Vikings or "Danes" from Greenland. Apparently it did not strike Sir Joseph as odd that Vikings should bring quantities of Iberian tile in their longships.

The Portuguese would have been more likely candidates for bringing Iberian tile, but no records are known to suggest that Portuguese fishermen used ports in the Strait of Belle Isle. Subsequently, French settlers normally used slate for permanent buildings, and wooden slats or bark to roof their huts. It is not clear what the early 19th Century Jersey sealers and English fishermen used on their roofs, but they certainly did not use Iberian tile, whereas the Basques as well as using the tile recorded the fact in their documents.

Perhaps the most curious thing about our Canadian Basques is that they were not only the first large scale *exporters* of Canadian produce to London, Rouen, Antwerp and Seville, but they were also the first large scale *importers* for the construction of buildings in Canada.

The Nature and the Framework of Newfoundland History*
KEITH MATTHEWS

75

The Nature of Newfoundland History

The basic factor in Newfoundland history is that which underlies many events in modern times — the expansion of Western Europe, which in the fifteenth century began to emerge from self-containment and comparative isolation to seek out and eventually to dominate vast areas in other parts of the world. This expansion took the form of overseas commerce and the establishment of colonies beyond the seas. From the very earliest days the Newfoundland fishery formed an important element in the development of European trans-oceanic commerce, and while the establishment of a settlement upon the Island occurred comparatively late when compared with those of the Spanish and Portuguese in South America, it was one of the first settlements to be attempted by the English who eventually possessed Newfoundland. Even more, it was through the "migratory" fishery wherein men from the west of England came annually to fish here that the English first acquired the seaman-ship interest in and knowledge of the North American world which enabled them to develop what eventually became a world-wide empire.

This brings us to a seeming paradox. This was the first part of North America to be visited by Englishmen and amongst the first areas to receive English settlers, and yet the Island's economic, social and political development was painfully slow when compared to the West Indian colonies, or the thirteen British colonies in what is now the United States of America. This is one of the greatest puzzles of Newfoundland history, and in the lectures following we will try to find answers to it. We know that Newfoundland was not neglected because it was thought unimportant, for the Newfoundland fishery, the Grand Cod Fishery of the Universe as Pitt the Elder described it, was considered to be one of the most important foreign trades carried

*From *Lectures on the History of Newfoundland: 1500-1830.* Copyright 1973 by the Maritime History Group, Memorial University of Newfoundland. Reprinted by permission.

on from Western Europe. As early as 1620 it was said that without New-foundland dried cod, Spain and Italy could hardly live while France and England quarrelled, competed and often fought over the right to control the fishery. If one thinks of the importance of the Grand Bank fishery to the fleets of many nations today, it is hardly surprising that ever since the discovery of the New World, it has been eagerly sought after by Europeans.

We can say therefore that the history of Newfoundland has been shaped by its fishery and by the international competition which arose around it.

The fishery alone attracted men to Newfoundland and in the competi-tion for the fishery, the Island fell almost as a by-product into the hands of the English who won the struggle. The old west country fishermen of the seventeenth century had a rhyme; "If it were not for wood, water and fish, Newfoundland were not worth a rush," and for the fishermen and for the nations they came from, that saying expressed almost all that was valued here. As can be seen today, the fishery could be carried on without necessarily occupying the land, but if you wanted to make the light salted "shore" fish for which Newfoundland became famous, then you needed "fishing rooms" in the harbours along the coast, and the first struggles over the Island, as distinct from the fishery, occurred as men quarrelled about who should take possession of the best fishing rooms. Yet the fact remained, the hopes and dreams of the first settlers notwithstanding, Newfoundland was valued only as a fishery and the Island as a great ship moored near the banks.

We know that the English won control over the Island of Newfoundland, but we should not assume that this was inevitable. Indeed until the last twenty years of the sixteenth century, her fishery at Newfoundland was puny when compared to that of France, Spain or even Portugal. Why then did she emerge as the dominant nation? We will discuss this question quite often during the course of the series.

Newfoundland depended upon the fishery for its very life and that was established long before the first settlers came out to plant. The international fishery had developed its own rough laws and customs which took no ac-count of the possibility of permanent settlement. In the rest of the New World, European settlers came out to virgin territory, unpopulated and un-visited by other Europeans, so that, able to ignore the native peoples as savages, they could do what they pleased. This was not true of Newfoundland for the first English settlers arrived to find thousands of English fishermen and many more of France, Portugal and Spain who also claimed the right to use the Island for making fish. England claimed to own Newfoundland but France also laid claim to it and Spain could at least claim that she had anciently used the land for her fishing. Thus from the outset, colonisation in Newfoundland was radically different from that of the rest of the New World. Four nations claimed rights, thousands of men from different coun-tries were established here, and settlement had to take account of this.

The experiences of the first settlers soon showed that they, as much as the visiting fishermen, must go a-fishing if they wanted to make a living for the land was infertile and our mining industry did not develop until the nineteenth century. Thus the settlers became completely dependent upon an uncertain industry which not even the merchants who bought their fish could control, for the fish had to be sold in foreign countries in Southern Europe. Unlike the settlers of the English mainland colonies, those in New-foundland could not even hope to become self-sufficient, for the infertility of the soil, the shortness of the growing season, and (until the mid-eighteenth century) the lack of a hardy crop like the potato meant that almost all of the food they consumed had to be imported from abroad. If you kept a cow here in the seventeenth century, you might have to import hay from Boston to keep it alive during the winter. The fishing season lasted only during the summer so that a settler had to make enough money in three or four months to buy all that he needed to live for twelve and almost everything that he ate, wore, or used had to be imported and paid for with fish. It was a hard life and not many people wanted to emigrate here. However, for anyone who knew how to fish, a good living could be made, so that most of the early settlers were men from the west of England who, bred up to the trade by coming here annually to fish, decided for various reasons to settle down for a while at least and try the life of a "planter".

77

The origins of these early colonists made Newfoundland rather different from the English mainland colonies. There, men had come out from many different regions of Europe and for many different reasons, but most of them expected to "make a new life" and to leave the Old World behind forever. Those who came to Newfoundland, however, came out to fish and having relatives and friends back in the west of England (or later in Southern Ireland), could always return to their homes on a fishing ship anytime they wanted to. Many of our settlers were indeed indentured servants hired to come out and work here for two or three years before returning to Britain. This was in marked contrast to the rest of North America.

By 1800 the mainland colonies contained settlers from many different regions of Europe for the need to develop the land created a great demand for labour and called for skills which were widespread through much of Western Europe. In Newfoundland the demand was for skilled fishermen only — no one came to Newfoundland to go farming, and commerce and industry were only just beginning to develop. Only the French and the English knew anything about fishing in Newfoundland, and the French, after 1713, were not allowed to live here. This left the English and Irish as the only possible colonisers of our Province. In England, only the peo-ple living in the "West Country" counties of Devonshire, Dorset, Somerset and Hampshire knew anything about the fishery, and most of the Irishmen came out via Waterford and Cork; two ports on the south coast of Ireland which had much contact with Newfoundland. They were drawn mainly from four counties around those cities. Thus our population was remarkably homogeneous compared with North America as a whole, and of course it has largely remained so.

The fishery first drew men to Newfoundland; the fishery shaped the policies of the nations concerned in it; the fishery both created and limited the way of life of the colonists and the fishery, though its fluctuating prosperity, its assumed value to Europe and the conflicts it caused determined when, where, in what numbers, and under what conditions the colonists should settle. By 1670 English settlement in Newfoundland had become firmly established, but England did not possess the entire Island. France had established settlements in Placentia Bay and at St. Mary's, and she and the Spanish monopolised the fishery north of Bonavista Bay. The English fishery in Newfoundland was confined to what is in some places still referred to as the "Old English Shore", a region stretching from Trepassey to Greenspond. Only in this area could English colonists find protection and here English settlement was confined until 1713. This was not a great handicap at the time for the area contained excellent fishing grounds and harbours for shipping and for making fish, but as the first region of English settlement, it continued to be the major region of population on the Island until the present century and contains the oldest settler families here. Expansion of settlement to the rest of Newfoundland had to wait the evacuation of other nations, and a growth in the population and fishery of Newfoundland which would make men want to exploit the other fishing areas, while the development of inland communities had to await this present century, for the population lived only by fishing. As a result, Newfoundland lacked a natural "centre" which could link together the many communities and regions into one whole "community". All communications were by sea, and each bay had its own major commercial centres which were independent of the others, importing and exporting goods and people directly from and to the outside world. The towns of the west of England which controlled the fishery at Newfoundland "divided up" the English shore, with particular parts of the west of England, fishing only along particular parts of the Newfoundland coast. Thus the settlers who came to the various communities and bays chose their place of residence from the ports which their ship came to. Since the merchants of Poole, for example, controlled all the trade of Trinity and Bonavista Bays, most of the English settlers there came from the counties of Dorset, Hampshire and Somerset. The "Southern Shore" from Torbay to Trepassey was fished by the fishermen and merchants of South Devon, so that most of the English settlers there came from the same region. It might be said that until the nineteenth century there was no "community" of Newfoundland, but a series of separate cultural and economic bays independent of and relatively indifferent to each other. This feeling exists even today in some forms. Only with the rise of St. John's as the commercial and political capital of the Island did the feeling of distinctness and independence between the bays begin to decline, and this did not begin to happen until late in the eighteenth century.

78

These are some of the themes in Newfoundland history. Beginning as an international fishery, the Island became a largely British fishery carried on by a mixture of settlers and visiting fishermen; then an English colony and finally a distinctive "community" with an identity and culture of its own.

The Framework of Newfoundland History

In the last lecture I mentioned that the main theme of our history was the manner in which Newfoundland changed from an international fishery to a largely British fishery and finally to a distinctive community on its own. This change took over 300 years and was caused by the ever changing pressures of events and the decisions and conflicts of men. To enable you to understand how these changes occurred I am devoting this lecture to a breakdown of that long period of time into seven distinct periods. With this chronology in mind the lectures which follow can be more easily understood.

The first period we will call the period of anarchy. It begins with the rediscovery of the Island by Europeans in the fifteenth century and ends in 1610 with the establishment of an English colony in Newfoundland. John Cabot claimed the Island for England by right of discovery, but his meant little, for England at this time was weak and backward, her naval and commercial strength were undeveloped and she was absorbed in the aftermath of the Wars of the Roses. Although English fishermen soon followed Cabot, they were few in number and the French and Portuguese nations soon outstripped the English in the Newfoundland fishery. By 1640 Spain, with her enormous wealth and power, had also become important in the fishery and all nations were soon competing to develop their interests at the expense of their neighbours. In Europe the shifting alliances of nations saw many wars and the fighting inevitably spread to the Newfoundland fishing fleets. Obsessed with these conflicts no nation attempted to establish a colony on the Island, although in the second half of the sixteenth century individuals in both France and England began to think of doing so. While Europe quarrelled, the international fishery in Newfoundland grew chaotically with no one to keep the peace either between the national groups or even within them. To solve this problem the fishermen gradually evolved a code of customs which, unrecognised by any government, at least attempted to control the anarchy and violence amongst the fishing fleets. As late as 1570 the English still lagged far behind their competitors in the size of their fishery, yet the complex changes which occurred in Western Europe between then and 1600 created conditions in the Newfoundland trade which by 1700 had made England equal in importance to France while the fisheries of Spain and Portugal were in irreversible decline.

The next period in Newfoundland's history lasted between 1610 and 1660 and may be called the era of English settlement. With the end of the European conflict in 1604 nations turned to trade and colonisation, and both the French and English fisheries prospered well. By 1620 a de facto division of the land was taking place, each nation gradually confining its fishing operations to separate parts of the coast. The English fished along what became known as the "Old English Shore" stretching from Trepassey to Greenspond, while the French used the south coast and the area North of Bonavista Bay. This process was not the result of any international agreement and occurred only gradually and for a time; the Spanish and Portuguese

79

continued to fish wherever they could find harbour room. England laid claim to most of Newfoundland but France too claimed sovereignty, and in practice each contented itself with what it could control. The English domination of the Avalon Peninsula turned men's thoughts towards the possibility of establishing colonies here which paying their way by fishing, logging, agriculture, mining and even manufacturing might become profitable to their promoters and help to secure the fishery for England. However, repeated attempts ended in failure for the settlements could not be made to return a profit. There was also conflict between the proprietors of some colonies and the already established English migratory fishery. The English Civil War brought chaos and ruin to the fishery, but although the Proprietory Colonies failed, groups of settlers had become firmly established on the Island.

The third period lasted from 1660 to 1713 and was the period of Anglo-French rivalry within the Island itself. Until 1659 France claimed sovereignty over parts of Newfoundland but developing her colonies on the mainland and in the West Indies, did not formally plant here. In 1662 however she established a settlement in her main fishing area at Placentia and for a few years energetically promoted schemes to increase settlement. Simultaneously, the end of war in Europe saw a great revival in the French fishery which by 1675 was seriously affecting the fortunes of that of the English. The latter were in a state of decline for the long wars and a series of disastrous fishing seasons in the 1660s had ruined the west of England merchants and captains. The old methods of fishing no longer sufficed and new ones were required. Both the settlers and visiting fishermen were ruined by the declining fishery and the latter attempted to have the settlers removed. The British government alone could decide upon this, and at first they agreed that settlement should be ended. However, they quickly changed their mind, but were unable to decide whether the Island should be formally recognised as a colony. For twenty years after 1680 the government followed a policy of having no policy and the Island was left to develop as best it could. In 1689 King William's War broke out and with an intermission between 1697 and 1701 the conflict lasted until 1713. The fighting both here and in Europe had drastic effects upon Newfoundland, and the government was forced to formulate some kind of policy towards her. That policy was unworkable, but the war obscured this to some degree. In 1713 by the Treaty of Utrecht France ceded her colony on the south coast to England and admitted English sovereignty over the entire Island. However, she obtained certain fishing rights along parts of the coast and the "French shore" problem began its wearying course. The war had also obscured fundamental changes within the fishery which were changing the old division between "settlers" and "migratory" fishermen, bringing them together under the west country merchants.

Newfoundland underwent a new series of adaptations in what I will call the era of integration within the English fishery between 1713 and 1763. English settlement expanded into the south coast and as far up as Fogo and

Twillingate. The fishery continued to be poor until the late 1720s but the need for men to move into the newly ceded south coast resulted in the beginnings of large scale Irish emigration to Newfoundland with enormous effects upon its future history. Men found that the attempt to divide the Island into an area monopolised by the English and another shared between them and the French created much friction, but the French had lost their best fishing grounds, their competition in Europe gradually diminished and from 1730 onwards the English fishery began to prosper well. The English soon developed a thriving bank fishery which together with the bye boat keepers formed the backbone of the migratory English fishery causing not only its revival but a steady expansion by 1750.

It was an era when the merchants of London withdrew from the fishery which was now almost monopolised by merchants and fishermen of the west of England. After 1748 the population began to rise steadily and during the Seven Years' War (1756-1763) English fishermen for the first time learned of the rich fishing grounds along the Northern Peninsula and even more important on the Labrador. The British government was forced by increasing population to introduce a rudimentary civil government, and there was an end to discord between the settlers and the visiting fishermen. The Seven Years' War resulted in the English conquest of Canada and laid the conditions for an even larger expansion in Newfoundland after 1763. *81*

Period five was short, lasting only from 1763 until 1775 when the outbreak of the American Revolution portended great changes for Newfoundland. However, it was a period of great prosperity and growth both in settlement and in the fortunes of the fishery. The Treaty of Paris in 1763, amongst other things, ceded the French possessions in Canada to Britain, and the English government decided to attach Labrador and the Magdalen Islands to Newfoundland. Thus began the Labrador fishery. In Europe the markets for Newfoundland fish continued to grow and for almost the entire period the fishery proved unusually successful. This created a great demand for ships, seamen and fishermen so that both the migratory and the sedentary fishery grew quickly and the population rose. However, after a long period of neglect the British government again looked at the question of how Newfoundland should be governed. Their first thought was to create a formal colony, but a change of government and the advent of Governor Palliser caused an abrupt change of mind. Alarmed by the growth of settlement the government sought to discourage it and to promote the migratory fishery. This policy was first adapted for the new fishery at Labrador where it failed. The government persisted and in 1775 Palliser's Act was passed. It signalled a renewal of official hostility towards the settlers, but was viewed with intense hostility by the merchants, and the outbreak of the American Revolution delayed its enforcement.

The sixth period lasted from the beginning of the American Revolution in 1775 to the outbreak of the French Revolutionary Wars in 1793. Before 1775 America had been a great competitor to Newfoundland in the fishery, but it had also become almost the only supplier of shipping, foodstuffs and rum without which the settlers could not live. The outbreak of war abruptly severed the supply routes between America and Newfoundland and caused great but temporary problems. The war itself had great effects on the fishery but even more important was the result. American independence took the United States out of the British Empire and her vessels could no longer bring supplies. Neither could fishermen and merchants buy American shipping and America could not longer supply the British West Indies with fish. In the years before 1775 anyone who wanted to leave Newfoundland during a time of depression could easily find a ship to take him to Boston. Now this was no longer possible and he would be forced to remain on the Island if he could not return to England or Ireland. The supply links with the American colonies were slowly replaced by links with the Maritimes of Canada and with Quebec. Newfoundland built its own ships and took over the West Indian markets for fish. From 1783 to 1789 there was a great post-war boom in the fishery which again caused a rapid increase in settlement. In 1789 the boom collapsed, but the population did not decline greatly as had been the case in past depressions. The migratory fishery began to decline and by 1793 it was becoming clear that Newfoundland now had a population which was too large to be moved, which could not even be discouraged from growing, and which was in desperate need of better government and laws. The British government was forced to abandon its policy of discouraging settlement and the future of the Island was assured.

Our last period commences with the outbreak of war in 1793 and lasts until 1832. It may be called the "era of Newfoundland's emergence as an independent community." The long and difficult wars killed the migratory fishery and made all dependent upon the resident fishermen. Until 1810 it was difficult to obtain labour from England or Ireland, but natural increase amongst the Newfoundland population kept it growing and restricted wartime markets meant that no more labour was required. From 1811 to 1815 the gradual re-opening of the European markets together with the temporary extinction of every fishing competitor with the exception of Canada created one of the greatest booms that Newfoundland had ever known. In response thousands of men poured into Newfoundland, especially from Southern Ireland. The Labrador seal and cod fisheries gave additional sources of employment, and there was a great boom in shipbuilding for the Labrador and the coastal trades. St. John's became truly the capital of Newfoundland, and the growth of a large more or less resident middle class led to the development of social and political consciousness which led to the formation of groups and institutions devoted to charitable, social and eventually political ends. This middle class became the ruling elite of the Island and took the lead in the definition of a distinct Newfoundland consciousness, first expressed in the desire for internal self-government.

Topic Three
The Societies of New France and Acadia

The population of New France grew extremely slowly, due to the dominance of the fur trade which required little manpower. In the autumn of 1608 only twenty-eight people lived at Quebec, and over thirty years later the population of New France still stood at less than three hundred. Only after the establishment of direct royal government in 1663 did the colony finally begin to expand.

Royal government helped the colony's growth in three specific ways. The Crown first established an effective political system. Secondly, the dispatch of a sizeable military force against the Iroquois led to an effective truce with the Confederacy, securing twenty years of peaceful development for the colony. Finally the French government sponsored the emigration of several thousand settlers, men and women, who helped to build a more diversified economy in New France. From 1663 to 1700 the colony's population rose from 2,500 to 15,000. By the late seventeenth century the society of New France had taken on a definite form. Who were these French Canadians of the New World? What was the nature of this new North American society? In what respects, if any, did New France differ from France? W.J. Eccles outlines the general characteristics of the French Canadian in New France in his chapter, "Society and the Frontier," in *The Canadian Frontier, 1534-1760*. John F. Bosher reviews an important institution in the colony in "The Family in New France."

The French began their first permanent settlement of Acadia (later Nova Scotia) on the Atlantic Coast in 1604. Its strategic location near the Gulf of St. Lawrence meant that England and France fought continually for its possession. The region changed hands frequently, until 1713 when France ceded Acadia to England in the Treaty of Utrecht. For the next half-century Britain ruled over the colony with its predominantly French-speaking and Roman Catholic population.

The Acadians sought to remain neutral in conflicts between England and France. Initially this was possible, but with the construction of the large French fortress of Louisbourg during the 1720s on Cape Breton Island, and the founding of Halifax in 1749, the situation changed. With the revival of hostility between France and England in 1755, Nova Scotia's Lieutenant-Governor, Charles Lawrence, and his council at Halifax, insisted that the Acadians take an unconditional oath of allegiance to the British Crown. When they refused, Lawrence expelled approximately 10,000 French Acadians. Naomi Griffiths in "The Golden Age: Acadian Life 1713-1748," reviews Acadian society before the expulsion.

A number of excellent studies exist of the society of New France. One of the best, Louise Dechêne's study of Montreal in the late seventeenth century, *Habitants et Marchands de Montréal au XVII siècle* (Paris: Librairie Plon, 1974), is available only in French. In *The Beginnings of New France, 1524-1663* (Toronto: McClelland and Stewart, 1973), Marcel Trudel reviews several aspects of the society of New France in its early years. An overview of the seigneurial system is provided by the geographer Richard Colebrook Harris in *The Seigneurial System in Early Canada* (Madison: University of Wisconsin Press, 1966). Cornelius Jaenen's *The Role of the Church in New France* (Toronto: McGraw-Hill Ryerson, 1976), reviews the work of this important institution. W.J. Eccles has also written a short book on *Canadian Society During the French Regime* (Montreal: Harvest House, 1968). Three important articles by G. Frégault, J. Hamelin, and W.J. Eccles are reprinted in *Society and Conquest*, edited by Dale Miquelon (Toronto: Copp Clark, 1977), in the section "The Debate on the Economy and Society of New France," pp. 85-131. Frégault's Canadian Historical Association booklet, *Canadian Society in the French Regime* appears as one of the selections in Topic Four. Peter N. Moogk has written on an aspect of the popular culture of New France, "'Thieving Buggers' and 'Stupid Sluts': Insults and Popular Culture in New France," *William and Mary Quarterly*, 3rd series, 36 (1979): 524-547. As there were no newspapers in New France, historians have often underestimated the extent of popular discontent under the French Regime. Terence Crowley presents the surviving evidence in "'Thunder Gusts': Popular Disturbances in Early French Canada," *Historical Papers*, 1982, pp. 11-32.

For a first-hand account of New France in 1750, students might consult the English translation of Peter Kalm's *Travels in North America* (2 vols., New York: Dover Publications, 1964).

An abundant literature exists on the Acadians; in fact, by the end of the nineteenth century two hundred books and pamphlets had been written on the subject of the Acadian expulsion alone. A short review of the major issues appears in C. Bruce Fergusson's "The Expulsion of the Acadians," *Dalhousie Review*, 35 (1955): 127-135. The best guides to the subject of Acadian society are Griffith's *The Acadians: Creation of a People* (Toronto: McGraw-Hill Ryerson, 1973); J.B. Brebner's, earlier *New England's Outpost: Acadia Before the British Conquest of Canada* (New York: Columbia University Press, 1927); and Andrew H. Clark's *Acadia: The Geography of Early Nova Scotia to 1760* (Madison: University of Wisconsin Press, 1968). For an award-winning

84

account of life at Louisbourg, consult: Christopher Moore's *Louisbourg Portraits: Five Dramatic True Tales of People who Lived in an Eighteenth Century Garrison Town,* (Toronto, Macmillan, 1982).

Society and the Frontier*
W. J. ECCLES

Of the more tangible factors that influenced Canadian society there can be no doubt that geography was very important. The St. Lawrence River and certain of its tributaries dominated life in the colony. The land suitable for agricultural settlement stretched in a narrow band along the St. Lawrence, wider on the south shore than on the north. Near Quebec the Laurentian Shield, scraped nearly bare long ago by an advancing ice age, meets the river. Below this point only small pockets of land at river mouths were suitable for agriculture. Above Quebec, on the north shore, the Shield draws away from the river to a distance of some forty miles at Montreal. On the south shore the belt of fertile land is quite wide between Quebec and Montreal but becomes a narrow ribbon along the river toward Gaspé. West of Montreal there is also good land but on both the St. Lawrence and Ottawa rivers, rapids make communications difficult. Consequently throughout the French regime land settlement was concentrated in the St. Lawrence Valley from a point a few miles west of Montreal to a little below Quebec, with pockets of settlement on both sides lower down the river.

85

   Prior to 1663 the number of settlers and the amount of land cleared grew very slowly. In 1634 the first seigneurial grant was made to Robert Giffard by Richelieu's Company of New France. During the ensuing thirty years some seventy other seigneuries were granted. The company sent a few settlers to the colony but in the main let this responsibility fall to the seigneurs who, for the most part, lacked the means to engage in a large-scale immigration program. The religious orders did bring out a goodly number of servants, laborers, and settlers; and the crown from time to time sent detachments of soldiers to aid in the colony's defense. By these means the population slowly grew, and stretches of forest near the three areas of settlement, Quebec, Trois-Rivières, and Montreal, were cleared back from the shores of the river. In 1640 the total French population in the colony — settlers, soldiers, clergy, fur trade company employees — numbered only about 240; by 1663, largely as a result of the efforts of the religious orders, this number had increased to some 2500. After the latter date, under the stimulus of the crown, settlement increased very rapidly; by 1669 the population had increased by two thirds,

*Chapter 5 of *The Canadian Frontier, 1534–1760*, by W. J. Eccles. Copyright 1965 by University of New Mexico Press. Reprinted by permission.

and by the end of the century it was at approximately the 15,000 mark, doubling thereafter each generation to a total of some 70,000 at the Conquest.[1]

The St. Lawrence dictated the pattern of settlement in another way. It was the main means of communication in the colony, in summer by canoe or sailing barque, in winter by sleigh on the ice. The need for roads was thus obviated until the eighteenth century. Every settler desired land on the river, and the land holdings early took on the peculiar pattern that has endured to the present day, that of narrow strips running back from the river. Survey lines separating seigneuries ran at right angles to the river and as the generations succeeded each other the individual holdings became increasingly narrow. According to the law of the land, the *Coutume de Paris*, a seigneur's eldest son inherited the manor house and half the domain land; the rest was divided among the remaining children. The children of the humbler settlers, the *censitaires*, inherited equal parts of the parental land. After a few generations many of the individual holdings became too narrow to be worked efficiently, and in 1745 the intendant forbade anyone to build a house or barn on land narrower than one and a half arpents (approximately 100 yards) by thirty or forty linear arpents in depth. Those who contravened the *ordonnance* were fined 100 *livres* and their buildings were torn down at their expense.

By the eighteenth century the pattern was well established. Along both banks of the St. Lawrence from Quebec to Montreal the farms stretched back from the river, the houses and barns on the river bank spaced a few hundred yards apart. Every few miles there was a seigneurial manor house and a mill, and eventually a steep-roofed stone church. Later in the century concessions were taken up in the second range and another row of narrow strip farms stretched back from the rear of the first, with a roadway between the two. To anyone traveling by river up to Montreal nearly all of New France passed in review.

This pattern of land settlement was not without its disadvantages. Until the end of the seventeenth century the Iroquois were an almost constant menace, and with the homes spaced in this fashion mutual aid in times of attack was almost impossible. Individual farms and their occupants could be destroyed all too easily before aid could be mustered. While the Iroquois assaults were at their height stockaded forts had to be built in the exposed seigneuries where the people could take refuge with their livestock, abandoning their homes to the depredations of the enemy. Attempts by some of the royal officials to have the settlers live in villages with their concessions radiating out like spokes of a wheel, were not very successful. The Canadians insisted on having river frontage and living apart, lords of their own little domains, with access to the wider world beyond by way of the river.

By the mid-eighteenth century the farm houses in the first range and the churches, were nearly all of stone, thick-walled, substantial; steep Norman roofs were modified by a graceful curving wide eave, to afford shade in the hot Canadian summers. Peter Kalm, a Swedish professor of natural history who visited Canada in 1749, going by boat from Montreal to Quebec remarked:

> The country on both sides was very delightful to-day, and the fine state of its cultivation added to the beauty of the scene. It could really be called a village, beginning at Montreal and ending at Quebec, which is a distance of more than one hundred and eighty miles, for the farmhouses are never above five arpents and sometimes but three apart, a few places excepted. The prospect is exceedingly beautiful when the river flows on for several miles in a straight line, because it then shortens the distance between the houses, and makes them form one continued village . . . We sometimes saw *windmills* near the farms. They were generally built of stone, with a roof of boards, which together with its wings could be turned to the wind.[2]

The principal crop grown was wheat but the climate of the St. Lawrence Valley was not particularly suitable for this cereal. Heavy rains sometimes caused serious loss from smut; early frosts were a constant menace; and plagues of caterpillars occasionally destroyed everything growing. Yet crop failures appear to have been no more frequent than in France, where they were anticipated, on an average, once in five years.[3] In the early years the yield was high, the natural result of rich virgin soil. By the mid-eighteenth century it had declined considerably, despite the increase in the number of cattle and the consequent increased use of manure.

Peter Kalm was very critical of the inefficient agricultural methods he had observed in the English colonies. He was not less critical of those in New France; they both compared unfavorably with farming methods that he had studied in England, which he stated were the most advanced in Europe. One factor that militated against efficient agricultural production, in New France as in the English colonies, was the chronic shortage of labor. When able-bodied men could obtain land very cheaply, they were not inclined to work for others, except at excessively high wages. The wages paid skilled tradesmen were also high, resulting in a drift from the country to the three towns, which contained 25 percent of the colonial population. A much more important factor, however, was the large number of men, of necessity the young and physically fit, who were continually out of the colony on voyages to the west.

All the evidence indicates that the Canadian *habitants* and the laboring class in the towns enjoyed a higher standing of living and much more personal freedom than did their counterparts in Europe. This undoubtedly accounts, to some degree, for the difference in their attitudes and character that visitors from Europe all remarked on. But what seems to have had an even greater influence was their frequent contact, on terms of equality, with the Indian nations. Nor did they have to voyage far for this contact. Within the confines of the colony, or close by, were several resident Indian bands. Near Quebec, at Lorette, resided a band of Huron, survivors of the 1649 diaspora. A few miles south of Quebec was the Abenaki village of St. François, removed from Acadia to protect the colony's southern approaches from Anglo-American incursions up the Connecticut River. Near Montreal were two Indian settlements: the Mission Iroquois at Sault St. Louis and

87

the Sulpician mission that had first been established on the lower slopes of Mount Royal, then, as the town grew, had been moved first to the north side of the island, later to the western tip, and finally across the Lake of Two Mountains to Oka. The Mission Iroquois at Sault St. Louis (Caugnawaga to the Iroquois) were originally Mohawks who had been converted to Christianity by the Jesuits and had then removed to New France the better to preserve their new faith.[4] Members of other of the Iroquois nations, after conversion, subsequently moved to Caugnawaga to spare themselves the constant taunts of their fellow tribesmen who had remained pagan.

Another reason for this Iroquois defection to Canada was the desire to avoid the Albany rum traders. Not all the Indians were incapable of resisting the temporary delights that intoxication brought; the authorities of both New France and New York were frequently asked by the chiefs of Iroquois and Algonkin nations to keep liquor away from their villages. The governors of New France, for the most part, did their best to comply and managed to curb the abuse to a considerable degree. The same could not be said of the authorities at Albany. There, rum and whiskey of such appalling quality that it was little better than poison was the main item of trade, used to get the Indians drunk before they traded their furs and then defraud them. This practice was so common that the Dutch traders at Albany were little more than Canada's secret weapon, for although many of the western Indians would bypass the French posts to go to Albany where they were given all the liquor they could drink,[5] they were not so besotted that they did not later realize the consequences. This is not to say that there were no Canadian traders willing to use liquor in the same way in their commercial dealings with the Indians. The Jesuit missionaries at Sault St. Louis waged a constant struggle to keep such traders away from their charges, and the Oka mission had removed to this site largely to keep the converts away from the taverns and unscrupulous purveyors.

The members of this latter mission were a mixture of Iroquois and northern Algonkin; the common factor was their conversion to Christianity. During the colonial wars these warriors, particularly those of Sault St. Louis, performed valiant service; indeed, the authorities at Albany were greatly concerned lest most of the Five Nations should remove to Canada. Had this occurred Albany and all the northern settlements would have had to be abandoned. Although in expeditions against the villages of the Five Nations the Mission Iroquois could not be depended on — they frequently gave their kinsmen warning — the devastating raids on the settlements of New England were carried out by war parties composed largely of these domiciled tribesmen, combined with Canadian militia, and led by officers in the colonial regulars, the Troupes de la Marine. Thus the Canadians were closely associated with the Indians, waging war after their fashion, using their techniques and becoming as adept in the harsh, cruel methods as any Iroquois or Abenaki. There was therefore a demonstrable degree of truth in the opinion of the Canadians expressed by one French officer: "They make war only by swift attacks and almost always with success against the English who are not as vigorous nor as adroit in the use of fire arms as they, nor as practiced in forest warfare."[6]

In peacetime, too, the Canadians were in constant association with the Indians. The Indians were frequent visitors to Montreal, and to prevent constant blood baths, the intendant had to set aside certain taverns for the Indian trade, allocated by nation, and strictly regulated. It is, therefore, hardly surprising that the Canadians early adopted much of the Indian way of life and became imbued with some of their character traits. Native foods such as corn, squash, and pumpkins found ready acceptance. Indian means of travel — the snowshoe, toboggan, and canoe — were quickly mastered. Many of the Canadians, who were inveterate pipe smokers, preferred to mix their locally grown tobacco with the inner bark of the cherry or dogwood tree, a custom borrowed from the Indians. In their mode of dress the *habitants* copied the Indians, with an effect rather startling to European eyes. The women, except when dressed up fine for Sunday mass, wore a short jacket or blouse and a short skirt which, Peter Kalm several times observed "does not reach to the middle of their legs."

89

It was during their frequent trips to the west that the Canadians were most exposed to the Indian way of life. Immediately following the establishment of royal government in 1663 the population of the colony expanded rapidly, from approximately 2500 to an estimated 15,000 by the end of the century. Of the latter number as many as five hundred of the active males were always off in the west on trading expeditions. It was during these years that senior officials, newly arrived from France, began to comment on the striking difference between the Canadians and their peers in France. Inevitably, these officials were first struck by what seemed to them the deleterious social and economic effects of the metamorphosis.

The Marquis de Denonville, governor general from 1685 to 1689, was appalled by certain attitudes and habits of the Canadians. Instead of laboring on the land, they preferred to spend their lives in the bush, trading with the Indians, where their parents, the *curés*, and the officials could not govern them, and where they lived like savages. Even when they returned to the colony these youths showed a shocking proclivity for going about half naked in the hot weather, as did the Indians. "I cannot emphasize enough, my lord, the attraction that this Indian way of life has for all these youths," Denonville wrote to the minister. But he then went on to say, "The Canadians are all big, well built, and firmly planted on their legs, accustomed when necessary to live on little, robust and vigorous, very self willed and inclined to dissoluteness; but they are witty and vivacious."[7] The intendant Jean Bochart de Champigny in 1691 wrote in much the same vein, stating, "It is most unfortunate that Canadian youths, who are vigorous and tough, have no inclination for anything but these voyages where they live in the forest like Indians for two or three years at a time, without benefit of any of the sacraments."[8]

Peter Kalm in 1749 was also much impressed by the martial qualities of the Canadians, acquired through their frequent sojourns in the west. He noted that they were exceptional marksmen: "I have seldom seen any people shoot with such dexterity as these. . . . There was scarcely one of them who was not a clever marksman and who did not own a rifle." He then went on:

It is inconceivable what hardships the people of Canada must undergo on their hunting journeys. Sometimes they must carry their goods a great way by land. Frequently they are abused by the Indians, and sometimes they are killed by them. They often suffer hunger, thirst, heat, and cold, and are bitten by gnats, and exposed to the bites of snakes and other dangerous animals and insects. These (hunting expeditions) [sic] destroy a great part of the youth in Canada, and prevent the people from growing old. By this means, however, they become such brave soldiers, and so inured to fatigue that none of them fears danger or hardships. Many of them settle among the Indians far from Canada, marry Indian women, and never come back again.[9]

Some of the Jesuit missionaries in the west took a much more jaundiced view of the effects of the close relations between the Canadians and the Indians. Fathers St. Cosme and Carheil at Michilimackinac made that post appear, from their description, a veritable Sodom or Gomorrah, where the only occupations of the Canadians, apart from trading furs, were drinking, gambling, and lechery. Things had come to such a pass that the *coureurs de bois* took Indian women with them rather than men on their trading expeditions. The men claimed that these women worked for lower wages than men demanded, and were willing to perform such chores as cutting firewood and cooking. The missionaries refused to be persuaded that other fringe benefits were not involved.[10] The governor general Vaudreuil, although he did not support the Jesuit proposal to keep the Canadians and Indians as far apart as possible, was strongly opposed to mixed marriages. He claimed that the children of mixed blood incorporated the worst character traits of both races and were a constant source of trouble. He therefore issued orders forbidding such marriages at Detroit, the main French post in the west at that time (1709).[11]

These complaints on the part of the missionaries have to be taken with a pinch of salt. To them chastity, or failing this monogamy with the benefit of the marriage sacrament, was the ideal. They expected these *voyageurs* who, if married, had left their wives in the colony to live like monks while in the west. The Indians had different moral values and chastity was not among them. Father Charlevoix, who was not a missionary, took a more tolerant view of Canadian society in the 1740s. He commented:

Our Creoles are accused of great avidity in amassing, and indeed they do things with this in view, which could hardly be believed if they were not seen. The journeys they undertake; the fatigues they undergo; the dangers to which they expose themselves, and the efforts they make surpass all imagination. There are, however, few less interested, who dissipate with greater facility what has cost them so much pains to acquire, or who testify less regret at having lost it. Thus there is some room to imagine that they commonly undertake such painful and dangerous journeys out of a taste they have contracted for them. They love to breathe a free air, they are early accustomed to a wandering life; it has charms for them, which make them forget past dangers and fatigues, and they place their glory in encountering them often. . . . I know not whether I ought to reckon amongst the defects of our Canadians the good opinion they entertain of themselves. It is at least certain that it inspires them with confidence, which leads them to undertake and execute what would appear impossible to many others. . . . It is alleged they make bad servants, which is owing to their great haughtiness of spirit, and to their loving liberty too much to subject themselves willingly to servitude.[12]

These observations on the cupidity of the Canadians, coupled with their spendthrift attitude, are significant for these same traits were quite pronounced among the Indians. Like the Indian, the Canadian did not see any merit in storing up worldly goods; both looked down on those who did, and up to those who spent their money ostentiously on good living. The Canadians, too, became proud, independent, and improvident, glorying in their physical strength, their hardihood, and their contempt for danger, caring little for the morrow. One French officer commented, in 1757:

"They are not thrifty and take no care for the future, being too fond of their freedom and their independence. They want to be well thought of and they know how to make the most of themselves. They endure hunger and thirst patiently, many of them having been trained from infancy to imitate the Indians, whom, with reason, they hold in high regard. They strive to gain their esteem and to please them. Many of them speak their language, having passed part of their life amongst them at the trading posts."[13]

91

It would seem an obvious conclusion that the Canadians had acquired this attitude from the Indians, and were able to do so because the necessities of life were relatively easily come by in Canada. In other words, this character trait was a product of relative affluence and the frontier environment. It was to no small degree the fact that the Canadians did come to share this attitude with the Indians that their individual relations with them were usually better than were those of the Anglo-Americans. Ruette D'Auteuil, the attorney general at Quebec, spoke the truth for his day when he claimed that, the price of trade goods being equal, the Indians preferred to have dealings with the French rather than with the English.[14] This view was later corroborated by a British commentator who stated that, "the French have found some secret of conciliating the affections of the savages, which our traders seem stranger to, or at least take no care to put it in practice."[15]

Not only did the Canadians travel to the far west, they also voyaged northeastward, serving as crews on fishing boats in the Gulf and in the seal- and whale-hunting expeditions along the coast of Labrador. There, too, they came in frequent contact with Indians, and also with the Eskimo. In wartime they served on privateers, preying on shipping along the New England coast. French privateer captains frequently called at Quebec to take on crews, Canadians being very highly regarded for their toughness and bellicosity.

Canadians in all sections of the colony were accustomed to make trips to distant parts of the continent and to live among peoples of an entirely different culture. The whole continent from Labrador and Hudson Bay to the Rocky Mountains and the Gulf of Mexico was their world. Unlike their counterparts in Europe who rarely moved beyond the confines of their native parish, there was nothing parochial about them; they were men of broad horizons and a continental outlook able to accommodate themselves to almost any conditions anywhere. Were life to become too restrictive in the settlements along the St. Lawrence or were a wife to nag too constantly, some of them at least could hire out as *voyageurs* for the west or as crew on a voyage to Labrador, France, or the West Indies. Even those who never made such a trip could feel that the opportunity was there, and this must have given them a sense of freedom. They could not help but hear the tales of those who had voyaged far afield, of the strange peoples with stranger customs in these distant lands. They, too, shared the experience, vicariously.

Royal officials in the eighteenth century, upon first arriving in the colony, were quick to remark that the Canadians had become a distinct people with values and manners markedly at variance with those of the same class in the mother country. Usually they were quite taken aback by the attitudes and way of life of the Canadians. Only after they had been in the colony for a few years did they come to appreciate the positive side of what had at first seemed a society and people sadly in need of discipline and reform. It was the free and easy, seemingly dissolute, ways of the Canadians, their independent attitude, their insistence on being led not driven, that irked the officials, both civil and military. Other observers were struck by their profligacy, their feast or famine attitude, their recklessness. A Sulpician priest upon arrival in the colony in 1737 remarked that the bulk of the people — military officers, merchants, artisans, and *habitants* alike — were "as poor as artists and as vain as peacocks" and spent every sou they had on ostentatious living. He was shaken to see country girls who tended cows during the week, on Sundays bedecked in lace and hoop skirts, wearing their hair in the very elaborate, high-piled style known then as *à la Fontange*.[16]

Despite these shortcomings, all observers agreed that the Canadians were tough and hardy, gloried in feats of endurance that made Europeans blanch, could travel from one end of the continent to another while living off the land, and had no equal in forest warfare. It was also noted that these same men, when in their homes, were uncommonly courteous, with a natural air of gentility more usual among the nobility than the lower classes.[17] In this respect they compared very favorably with their counterparts, the peasants of France and the settlers in the English colonies. Peter Kalm was particularly struck by this and in his journal he noted that:

> The inhabitant of Canada, even the ordinary man, surpasses in politeness by far those people who live in these English provinces. . . . On entering one of the peasant's houses, no matter where, and on beginning to talk with the men or women, one is quite amazed at the good breeding and courteous answers which are received, no matter what the question is. . . . Frenchmen who were born in Paris said themselves that one never finds in France among country people the courtesy and good breeding which one observes everywhere in this land. I heard many native Frenchmen assert this.[18]

It would, of course, be very easy to ascribe these peculiarities to the frontier environment of New France. There can be no doubt that the frontier had a good deal to do with this, but the changes that took place in Canadian society were very complex. It is therefore necessary to examine conditions in the colony closely to discover the various elements that differed from those of France and then decide which ones were occasioned by the frontier.

Perhaps the basic factor was the abundance of free, fertile land, and the peculiar terms of land tenure under the seigneurial regime. This meant that the Canadian *habitants* were assured of as much land as they could cultivate, and they paid for it only very modest seigneurial dues, if they paid any at all, amounting to less than 10 percent of their annual income from the land.[19] Apart from this obligation, and the tithe for the church, fixed by royal decree at one twenty-sixth of the wheat grown, the *habitants* paid no other taxes. Labor service for the seigneurs, in the form of *corvées*, was very rarely imposed and was, in fact, a violation of the *Coutume de Paris*. In the few seigneuries where it was imposed it consisted of one day's labor in March or an exemption payment of two *livres*. Parish and royal *corvées* for work on the seigneurial common land, roads, bridges, or fortifications were a form of taxation but they usually amounted to not more than three or four days of labor a year, and the seigneur was supposed to do his share, under the supervision of the militia captain.

93

Unlike the peasant in France who spent his life sweating, scrimping, cheating, and saving to put aside enough money to buy a small piece of land or to purchase exemption from manorial obligations, and who had to keep his little hoard well hidden, wearing rags, living in a hovel, giving every appearance of near starvation to prevent the tax collectors from seizing his savings, the Canadian could spend what he had earned without a care. He could buy land for his sons so as to have them near him and spare them the necessity of clearing virgin forest on a new seigneury, or he could spend his earnings on consumer goods and entertainment. Whereas the economics of the situation would tend to make the French peasant mean and grasping, the Canadian could afford to be openhanded, with little care for the morrow.

In 1699 the intendant Jean Bochart de Champigny commented that for the most part the *habitants* lived well, enjoying the right to hunt and fish, privileges that were stringently denied their European counterparts. In that age wood and leather were vital commodities; the Canadians had ample supplies of both. Canadians who moved to France complained bitterly of the shortage and high cost of firewood, and declared that they suffered far more from the damp winter cold there than they ever had in Canada. In the eighteenth century the intendant Gilles Hocquart remarked that no one starved in Canada. Of few lands in Europe could this have been said. The normal consumption of meat was half a pound per person a day, and of white wheat bread, two French pounds a day. Moreover, the climate allowed the Canadians to keep plentiful supplies of meat, fish, and game frozen hard for use throughout the winter; but a mid-winter thaw that lasted too long could be calamitous. At the town markets fish were sold frozen and cut with a saw. Eels, taken at Quebec by the thousand, were a staple food; smoked or salted, they were described by Frontenac as the *"habitants'* manna." They were also a major export item to France, being considered far better than the European variety. Ice houses were common, making possible iced drinks and desserts all summer, not just for the wealthy as in France, but for the majority of the population. The colored ices served by the French in hot weather were a source of wonderment to visiting Indians when entertained by the governor, and their effect on the decayed teeth of certain elderly chiefs was electric.

The vitamin content of the Canadian diet, being much richer in protein, was considerably higher than that of the peasants and urban working class in France, who had to exist on coarse bread and vegetable stews with meat only on very rare occasions.[20] In Europe the bulk of the population went to bed hungry most nights. Such was rarely the case in Canada. Mme. Marie-Isabelle Bégon, widow of the governor of Trois-Rivières, who in 1749 moved from Montreal to the family estate near Rochefort querulously asked, "Where are those good partridges we left for the servants? I would gladly eat them now."[21] It is not surprising that the fine physical stature of the Canadians occasioned frequent comment from persons recently come from France. In fact, the Canadians were better fed then than a sizable percentage of North Americans are today.

94

If the Canadians had been willing to work hard, they could all have been very prosperous. Some of the royal officials, charged with improving the colonial economy, declared that the men showed a marked distaste for hard work and that the unbridled vanity of their womenfolk kept them poor. In 1699 Champigny noted: "The men are all strong and vigorous but have no liking for work of any duration; the women love display and are excessively lazy."[22] Denonville, thirteen years earlier, had also remarked that the indolence of the men and the desire of the women to live like gentle ladies kept the people poor and the colony's economy backward. Such comments have to be considered in context.

The Canadian *habitant* could provide for his basic needs without too much effort, and he preferred to devote his extra time, not to produce an agricultural surplus to please the intendant or to add to his own store of worldly goods, but to the relaxed enjoyment of his leisure hours. He would grow enough flax or hemp to supply his own needs, but frequently declined to raise a surplus for export. Rather than raise more cattle, he raised horses; by the early eighteenth century all but the poorer families had a carriage and sleigh for social occasions, and every youth had his own horse, used not for the plow but for racing, or to pay calls on the neighborhood girls. During the War of the Spanish Succession the governor and intendant became concerned over this, claiming that in winter the men no longer used snowshoes because they always traveled by horse and sleigh. It was difficult, they stated, to find enough men who could use snowshoes when they were needed for war parties against New England. The question might well be asked; how many peasants in Europe owned horses and carriages, let alone used them for mere social purposes. The average horse cost forty *livres* (roughly $80.00 in today's money) and a good one a hundred *livres* or more,[23] thus the Canadian *habitants* were relatively affluent, and this could not help but have influenced their social attitudes.

Given these conditions it is hardly surprising that the Canadians were by no means as submissive or even respectful, on occasion, toward their social superiors as was thought fitting. As early as 1675 the members of the Sovereign Council were incensed by derogatory graffiti on walls in Quebec, and several years later the intendant had to threaten stern action against those who composed, distributed, or sang songs that he regarded as libelous and defamatory of certain prominent persons in the colony. This last, however, might be regarded as merely the continuance of an old French tradition that had flourished in the days of the *Mazarinades*. Thus, rather than the frontier environment, economic affluence and the French temperament were the more significant factors here.

95

Much is made of the prevalence of lawlessness on the Anglo-American frontier. To a limited degree this was also true of New France, and it is significant that it was at Montreal, the fur trade and military base, the main point of contact between European and Indian cultures, more than at Quebec, that respect for law and order was sometimes lacking. In 1711 the governor and intendant had to establish a police force in Montreal, consisting of one lieutenant and three archers, to make the citizens keep the peace and to control drunken Indians. An educated soldier in the colonial troops, newly arrived in Canada, remarked that the citizens of Montreal called those of Quebec "sheep," and that the character of the latter was gentler and less proud. The Quebecers reciprocated by calling the men of Montreal "wolves," a label that the soldier thought apt since the Montrealers spent much of their time in the forest among the Indians. In 1754 an officer recommended that Quebec men be employed to transport supplies to the Ohio forts because they were much "gentler" and almost as vigorous as those from the Montreal area.

Despite the frequent tavern brawls and duels, the incidence of crimes of violence was not great. But what is much more significant is that, given the nature of the populace, accustomed to the relatively unrestrained, wild, free life that the fur trade afforded, very rarely was there any overt resistance to authority. On the few occasions when the people protested openly and vigorously something done, or not done, the authorities were able to subdue them quickly without recourse to punitive measures. Most of these manifestations — some five in all — were occasioned by high prices charged for certain commodities, leading the people to believe that the merchants were profiteering and that the authorities were delinquent in not taking steps to stop them. The heaviest penalty inflicted on the leaders of these "seditious gatherings" appears to have been less than two months in jail.[24] The conclusion to be drawn from all this is that the Canadian people had little to complain about, but when they did complain too vigorously, order was maintained without the overt use of force.

The attitude of the Canadians toward the religious authorities makes it plain that their opinions had to be taken into account. When it was decided, immediately after the inauguration of royal government in 1663, to impose tithes on the people for the support of a secular clergy, the bishop stipulated that it be at the rate of one thirteenth of the produce of the land, payable in wheat. The people protested vigorously, claiming this to be more than they could afford. The bishop reduced his demand to one twentieth, but the *habitants* and seigneurs would agree to pay only one twenty-sixth of their wheat, not of all their produce, with a five year exemption for newly settled concessions. With this the clergy had to be satisfied. That it was not enough is made plain by the fact that the crown had to provide the clergy with an annual subsidy to make up the difference between what the tithe produced and what the *curés* needed. By the 1730s however, as more land came into production, many of the parish priests were relatively well off.

96

Further evidence that the Canadians were anything but subservient to clerical authority is provided by the frequent *ordonnances* of the intendant ordering the *habitants* of this or that parish to behave with more respect toward the cloth; to cease their practice of walking out of church as soon as the *curé* began his sermon; of standing in the lobby arguing, even brawling, during the service; of slipping out to a nearby tavern; of bringing their dogs into church and expostulating with the beadle who tried to chase them out. Frequently the bishop thundered from the pulpit against the women who attended mass wearing elaborate coiffures and low-cut gowns. But all to no avail; décolletage remained that of the Paris salons. When Bishop St. Vallier somehow learned that the female members of his flock wore nothing but petticoats under their gowns he was horrified. In a curiously phrased pastoral letter he demanded that they immediately cease to imperil their immortal souls in this manner.[25] What the response was is not known. And a practice that might be advanced in support of the thesis that the frontier bred initiative was the Canadian custom of *mariage à la gaumine*, a form of "do it yourself" marriage ceremony which both the clergy and the civil authorities frowned on severely.[26]

At the upper end of the social scale, the most significant feature of this Canadian society was the aristocratic and military ethos that dominated it. This was not unique to Canada; it was part of the French old régime heritage. In the seventeenth century the aim of the rising, powerful bourgeois class was to gain entry into the ranks of the nobility, or at least to emulate the way of life of the aristocracy. Molière made this plain in *Le Bourgeois Gentilhomme*. Despite the fact that the Canadian economy was basically commercial and dependent largely on the fur trade, bourgeois commercial values did not dominate society; indeed, they were scorned. The ambitious Canadian merchant wished to be something more than prosperous. That was merely one rung on the ladder. The ultimate goal was entry into the ranks of the *noblesse* and receipt of the coveted Order of

St. Louis for distinguished service. More than wealth, men wished to bequeath to their sons a higher social status and a name distinguished for military valor, some great achievement, or the holding of high office. The proverb, *"Bon renom vaut mieux que ceinture dorée,"* summed up the Canadian philosophy at all levels of society.[27]

Wealth was, of course, desired, and ethics frequently went by the board in its pursuit. Men who might well have been ennobled for valiant service were denied if they lacked the means to live in a fitting manner. Wealth was sought, not for itself, but to enable men to live in the style of the class they sought to enter. Father Charlevoix, the Jesuit historian, writing in the 1740s commented on one aspect of this proclivity: "There is a great fondness for keeping up one's position, and nearly no one amuses himself by thrift. Good cheer is supplied, if its provision leaves means enough to be well clothed; if not, one cuts down on the table in order to be well dressed." He then went on to compare the Canadians with the English colonists to the south: "The English colonists amasses means and makes no superfluous expense; the French enjoys what he has and often parades what he has not. The former works for his heirs; the latter leaves his in the need in which he is himself to get along as best he can"[28]

In Canada it was in some ways much easier than in France for ambitious men to adopt the values and attitudes of the nobility and even to become ennobled. Despite the fact that society was very much status ordered, it was relatively easy for a talented, ambitious man or women to move up the social scale. Four factors help account for this: the availability of free land, the economic opportunities presented by the fur trade, the Royal edict of 1685 which permitted members of the nobility resident in Canada to engage directly in commerce and industry, something that, with a few notable exceptions such as the manufacture of glass and paper, was not permitted in France, and the presence of a large corps of regular troops in the colony in which Canadians could obtain commissions as officers.

It is rather ironic that when the king issued the edict of 1685 allowing nobles in Canada to engage in trade, he intended merely to stimulate the colonial economy.[29] It quickly came, however, to function in a way not anticipated by Louis XIV, for if those who were of noble status could engage in trade, there was nothing to prevent merchants and entrepreneurs who were not noble from aspiring to become so, provided they fulfilled the other requirements. Thus a Canadian of humble origin could make his fortune in the fur trade, acquire a seigneury, have his sons, if not himself, commissioned in the Troupes de la Marine, and hope that one day he, or his sons, would be ennobled for valiant service. Enough Canadians accomplished this feat to encourage a much larger number to govern their lives accordingly. It was the old story, few are chosen but many hear the call.

To be a seigneur, the first rung up the social ladder, was a distinct mark of social superiority, made manifest in a variety of ways; hence there was never any lack of applicants,[30] but it necessitated accepting rather onerous

97

responsibilities and in the seventeenth century most seigneurs had a hard time making ends meet. Yet so eager were the Canadians to attach the coveted particle *de* to their names that by 1760 there were nearly 250 seigneuries in the colony. Even more significant, it is estimated that there were some 200 *arrière fiefs*, or sub-seigneuries, that is, small seigneuries granted by a seigneur within his own seigneury to a friend or relative whom he wished to see get on in the world. Another significant point is that many seigneurs, the majority of whom lived in the towns and not on their lands, did not bother to collect the stipulated dues, *the cens et rentes*, from their *censitaires*. Clearly, many seigneurs were not interested in the economic aspect of land holding. The only other motive would appear to be the social prestige attached to the title. In other words, Joseph Blondeau was undoutedly a good name, but Joseph Blondeau de Grandarpents, or even de Petitarpents, was much better.

There were some who sought to gain entry into the *noblesse* through the back door, by simply assuming a title and claiming its privileges. In 1684 a royal edict was enacted levying a fine of 500 *livres* on any Canadian who falsely claimed noble status. A few years later the intendant Champigny stated that there were many such in the colony, but in time of war he thought it unwise to initiate an enquiry lest it cool their ardor for military campaigns. He also declared that several officers had requested to be ennobled, and although some of them merited it, he could not support their requests because they lacked the means to live as members of the *noblesse* should.[31] Although gaining entry into the ranks of the nobility was by no means easy, it was remarked in the mid-eighteenth century that there was a greater number of nobles in New France than in all the other French colonies combined. It was not the actual number of nobles that was important; rather it was the scale of values that they imparted to the whole of society, the tone that was set, and the influence it had on the way of life of the Canadian people.

Inextricably mingled with, and greatly strengthening, this aristocratic ethos was the military tradition of New France. In Europe wars were fought by professional armies, and civilians were not directly involved unless they happened to get in the way while a battle was being fought. This was more true of France and Britain than of other countries, since they both had sense enough to wage their wars on other nations' territory. In Canada when war came, all the settled areas were a battlefield and everyone was obliged to be a combatant. The administration of the colony was organized along military lines. The entire male population was formed into militia companies, given military training, and employed in campaigns. In 1665 the Carignan Salières regiments arrived in the colony to quell the Iroquois; it comprised over a thousand officers and men, and many of them stayed on as settlers. This greatly enhanced the influence of the military, for at that time the total population was less than 3000. Twenty years later the Troupes de la Marine were permanently stationed in the colony, some 1300 men and 400 officers by the end of the century among a total population of 15 000.

In the campaigns against the Iroquois and the English colonies it was quickly discovered that Canadians made better officers in forest warfare than did regulars from France. Consequently this career was opened to the seigneurs and their sons. They seized on it eagerly. Youths in their teens were enrolled as cadets and served on campaigns with their fathers or elder brothers to gain experience, then were sent out in command of scouting and small raiding parties to capture prisoners for intelligence purposes. The minister, however, thought they were being enrolled at far too early an age, while still mere children, and suspected the practice was merely a means for their families to draw military pay and allowances. Mme. de Vaudreuil, wife of the governor general, declared, "It would be advantageous for the well-being of the colony to accept youths of good families as cadets in the troops at fifteen or sixteen; that would form their characters early, render them capable of serving well and becoming good officers." The minister and Louis XIV were not convinced; they ordered that cadets had to be seventeen before they could be enrolled.[32] The dominant values of Canadian society were clearly those of the soldier and the noble, the military virtues those held in highest regard.

99

The social circles of Montreal and Quebec, comprising the senior officials, the army officers, and seigneurs, were undoubtedly very urbane, reflecting the polish and social graces of the French *noblesse*. Certainly Peter Kalm found this society much more civilized than that which he encountered in the English colonies where few people thought of anything but making money and not spending it.[33] Some of the senior officials who came from France in the eighteenth century, men like the intendant Claude Thomas Dupuy and the Comte de la Galissonière, took a keen interest in natural science, as had earlier the doctor and surgeon Michel Sarrazan who was a corresponding member of the Académie Royale des Sciences, but few Canadians showed much interest in intellectual pursuits.

The parish schools provided a basic education for those who wished it, and the Jesuit college at Quebec offered facilities as good as those in the larger French provincial cities. The letters and dispatches of Canadian-born officers and merchant traders in the mid-eighteenth century demonstrate that, with the rare exception of an officer such as Claude-Pierre Pécaudy de Contrecoeur who although a competent commandant had obviously had little schooling, they were all well-educated men. They expressed themselves succinctly and quite often felicitously: their syntax was good, the subjunctive employed where required; the literary style as well as the contents of their letters make them a pleasure to read. In fact, these men appear to have been as well educated as their counterparts in the French and British armies.

Yet the colony did not develop a literary tradition; the published journals depicting life in the colony were written by men from France and were intended for a metropolitan audience. But then, Canadians would see little merit in describing what was familiar to all their compatriots.

Several Canadians had large private libraries, but there was no public library. Nor was there a printing press in the colony, hence no newspaper, not because of any sinister repression of thought by the clergy, but because there was no great need therefore no demand for one. In these realms of activity Canada lagged far behind the English colonies. In short, New France was the Sparta, not the Athens of North America.

Notes

1. *Chronological List of Canadian Censuses*, Bureau of Statistics, Demography Branch, Ottawa.
2. Adolph B. Benson (ed.), *Peter Kalm's Travels in North America*, 2 vols. (New York, 1966), vol. II, pp. 416–417.
3. Le Roi à Vaudreuil et Raudot, Versailles, 6 juillet 1709, *Rapport de l'Archiviste de la Province de Québec*, 1942–1943 (hereafter cited as *RAPQ*), p. 408.
4. E. B. O'Callaghan and J. R. Brodhead, *Documents Relating to the Colonial History of New York*, 15 vols. (Albany, 1856–1883), vol. IV, p. 693.
5. Benson (ed.), *Peter Kalm's Travels in North America*, vol. II, p. 600.
6. Papiers La Pause. *RAPQ, 1931–1932*, pp. 66–67.
7. Denonville au Ministre, Que., 13 nov. 1685, Archives Nationales, Colonies, Series C11A, vol. 7, pp. 89–95.
8. Memoire instructif sur le Canada, 10 may 1691, *ibid.*, vol. 11, pp. 262–268.
9. Benson (ed.), *Peter Kalm's Travels in North America*, vol. II, pp. 522, 563.
10. Etienne de Carheil, S.J. à Champigny, Michilimackinac, 30 d'auest 1702, Public Archives of Canada, Series M, vol. 204, part 1, pp. 177–179; Fr. J.-F. St. Cosme, Michilimackinac, 13 sept. 1689, *RAPQ, 1965*, p. 37.
11. In a dispatch to the minister, Vaudreuil stated, "tous les françois qui ont épousé des sauvagesses sont devenus libertins feneans, et d'une independence insuportable, et que les enfans qu'ils ont esté d'une feneantise aussy grande que les sauvages mesmes, doit empescher qu'on ne permette ces sortes de mariages." Vaudreuil et Raudot au Ministre, Que., 14 nov. 1709, *RAPQ*, 1942–1943, p. 420.
12. Charlevoix, *Histoire de la Nouvelle France*, vol. II: *Journal d'un voyage fait par order du Roi dans l'Amérique septentrionale addressé à Madame la Duchesse de Lesdiguières* (Paris, 1744), pp. 247–249.
13. Papiers La Pause, *RAPQ, 1931–1932*, p. 67. See also Fernand Ouellet, "La mentalité et l'outillage économique de l'habitant canadien 1760. . . ." *Bulletin des Recherches Historiques* (1956), pp. 131–136.
14. Memoire sur les affaires au Canada, Avril 1689, *RAPQ, 1922–1923*, p. 7.
15. *The American Gazetteer*, 3 vols. (London, 1762), vol. II, entry under Montreal.
16. Relation d'un voyage de Paris à Montréal en Canadas en 1737. *RAPQ, 1947–1948*, pp. 16–17.
17. See Benson (ed.), *Peter Kalm's Travels in North America*, vol. II, pp. 446–447, 558; H. R. Casgrain (ed.), *Voyage au Canada dans le nord de l'Amérique septentrionale fait depuis l'an 1751 à 1761 par J.C.B.* (Quebec, 1887), p. 169.
18. Benson (ed.), *Peter Kalm's Travels in North America*, vol. II, pp. 558, 626.
19. Richard Colebrook Harris, *The Seigneurial System in Early Canada* (Madison, Wis., 1966), p. 81.
20. Robert Mandrou, *Introduction à la France moderne. Essai de psychologie historique 1500–1640* (Paris, 1961), pp. 17–39.
21. Mme Bégon à son gendre, Rochefort, 8 déc. 1750. *RAPQ 1934–1935*, p. 129.
22. Champigny au Ministre, Que., 20 oct. 1699. Archives Nationales, Colonies, Series C11A, vol. 17, pp. 106–110.
23. Benson (ed.), *Peter Kalm's Travels in North America*, vol. II, p. 536.
24. For a revealing account of one such protestation, which could have become dangerous, and the cool way it was subdued without the *habitants* concerned being treated at all harshly, see Vaudreuil au Conseil de la Marine, Que., 17 oct. 1717, Archives Nationales, Colonies, Series C11A, vol. 38, pp. 123–124. It is interesting to note that in this dispatch Vaudreuil is justifying his having had the ten ringleaders summarily arrested and kept in cells for nearly two months without trial. He considered that the circumstances had warranted the use of his exceptional powers, which permitted arrest and imprisonment without trial only in cases of sedition and treason. The Council of Marine subsequently approved his action in this instance. The common sense attitude of the government toward the governed is illustrated in another incident, which at first appeared to be a seditious assembly but was treated as being much less serious. See Raudot au Ministre, Que, 11 nov. 1707, *ibid.*, vol. 26, pp. 202–203.
25. Mandement de Jean évêque de Québec, 26 avril 1719 ("Trivia," Cameron Nish), *William and Mary Quarterly*, 3rd Series, vol. XXIII (July, 1966), pp. 477–478.
26. See Les Mariages à la Gaumine, *RAPQ, 1920–1921*, pp. 366–407.

27. Mme de Contrecoeur à son Mari, Montreal, 23 mai 1755. Fernand Grenier (ed.), *Papiers Contrecoeur et autres documents concernant le conflit Anglo-Français sur l'Ohio de 1745 à 1756* (Quebec, 1952), p. 349. The context in which the proverb is cited is quite revealing.
28. Pierre-François-Xavier de Charlevoix, S. J. *Histoire de la Nouvelle France*, vol. III: *Journal d'un voyage fait par ordre du Roi dans l'Amérique septentrionale addressé à Madame la Duchesse de Lesdiguières* (Paris, 1744), p. 79.
29. Arrest du Conseil d'Estat qui permet aux Gentilshommes de Canada de faire Commerce, du 10 mars 1685, Archives Nationales, Colonies, Series F3, vol. 7, p. 214; Le Roy au Sr. de Meulles, Versailles, 10 mars 1685, *ibid.*, *Series B*, vol. 11, p. 99.
30. Roland Mousnier, "L'évolution des institutions monarchiques en France et ses relations avec l'état social," *XVIIe Siècle*, 1963, nos. 58-59.
31. Extrait des Registres du Conseil d'Estat, 10 avril 1684, Bibliothèque Nationale, Collection Clairambault, vol. 448, p. 369; Champigny au Ministre, Que., 10 mai 1691. Archives Nationales, Colonies, Series CllA, vol. 11, p. 255; Memoire Instructif sur le Canada, *ibid.*, pp. 265-267.
32. Le Ministre à M. de Vaudreuil, Versailles, 30 juin 1707, *RAPQ, 1939-1940*, p. 375; Résumé d'une lettre de Mme de Vaudreuil au Ministre, Paris, 1709. *RAPQ, 1942-1943*, p. 416; Mémoire du Roy à MM de Vaudreuil et Raudot, à Marly, 10 May 1710, *RAPQ, 1946-1947*, p. 376; Archives du Seminaire de Quebec, Fonds Verreau, carton 5, no. 62.
33. Benson (ed.), *Peter Kalm's Travels in North America*, vol. I, 343-346, 375-376, 392-393, vol. II, pp. 446-447, 558, 626, 628.

101

The Family in New France*
JOHN F. BOSHER

One of the fundamental changes in Quebec since the 1940's is a marked decline in the birth rate which has lately become the lowest in Canada.[1] The large family is quickly disappearing, but until recently it was, as is well known, characteristic of French-Canadian society. Furthermore, if we go back to the history of that century and a half before 1763, when Quebec was a French colony, we find that the family, large or small, was a stronger and more prominent group than it is now. It was, indeed, one of the main institutions in New France. The study of it may help to explain how early Canadian civilization is so different from our own.

The typical family of New France may be described in figures drawn from statistical histories, making a sort of statistical portrait.[2] In the early eighteenth century, families had an average of five or six children, but this average includes families in which one of the parents had died and so stopped its growth. Those "arrested" families had, on the average, four or five children, whereas the complete family, in which neither parent had died, had eight or nine. These averages conceal the variety, of course: some 16% of all families had from ten to fourteen children and 2.8% had no less than fifteen children. Death among the children also kept numbers down, and to a degree staggering in comparison with our present-day infant mortality. We now lose twenty or twenty-one babies out of every thousand; but in New France 246 out of every thousand died during the first year of life, and that was normal

*From *In Search of the Visible Past: History Lectures at Wilfrid Laurier University, 1973-1974*, ed. Barry M. Gough. Copyright 1975 by Wilfrid Laurier Press. Reprinted by permission.

in the eighteenth century. What the figures suggest is that the small families at the bottom of the statistical scale were made so by the hazards of death, not by the habits or the wishes of the parents. If no parents or children had died, most families would have numbered a dozen or more children. These figures are for the early eighteenth century, it should be added, after the immigration from France had fallen off; and an analysis of the population in 1663 shows it at an earlier stage when four-fifths of all families had no more than from one to six children. But at every stage the family was enormous compared to the average Quebec family in 1951 which had only 2.2 children.

Taken by themselves, the statistical facts for New France may seem to confirm two common traditions about the family habits of all our ancestors: first, that women married very young; and secondly, that they tended to be eternally pregnant thereafter and to have a baby every year. Yet the facts for New France — as for Old France and England also — contradict both those traditions. The average age of women at their first marriage was nearly twenty-two in New France and about twenty-five in Old France. There are, of course, some well-known cases of girls being married at twelve, which was the youngest a girl might legally marry in New France. In 1637, the explorer, Jean Nicollet, set an extreme example by marrying an eleven-year-old girl, Marguerite Couillard, who was Champlain's god-daughter. Not many girls followed that example, it appears, because on 12 April 1670 the royal government ordered the Intendant to pay a premium — or a bounty, perhaps — to every girl under sixteen who found a husband, and to every man who married under twenty. The Crown thought it necessary to encourage people to marry younger. For the same purpose, the Crown also decided to help poor families with the dowries for their girls, and this brings to our notice one of the impediments to an early marriage: the dowry, often a struggle for a father to find for a numerous family of girls. For this and other reasons, too, no doubt, some 18% of women did not marry until they were thirty or more; 10% waited until they were thirty-five or over; and 6% until they were over forty. Women married later than tradition and a few famous examples have led us to believe that men, too, married older — on the average at nearly twenty-seven.

As for the frequency of births in a family, we learn that in New France women tended to have babies about every two years, not every year as legend has held. The demographic effects of such a difference were, of course, enormous; and one historian has concluded that the reason for this pause between babies, a pause of some twenty-three months from birth to birth or fourteen months plus nine months of pregnancy, was that women tended to remain temporarily sterile during the period of breast-feeding.[3]

To sum up, a typical "complete" family, which had not lost a parent, might consist of a father just over forty, a mother in her middle thirties and about eight children ranging from fourteen years of age down to a few weeks old. This may seem to be a very simple conclusion, disappointingly obvious, but it has the great merit of some basis in historical fact.

It leaves us wondering how to account for the phenomenal rate of the population's growth. In 1663, there were just over 3,000 people in New France, and a century later there were perhaps 70,000[4]. The population had multiplied by more than twenty-three. During that century, it appears that less than 10,000 immigrants came from the mother country. The remaining 57,000 people had all been born to the 3,000 Canadian families or to immigrant families as they came in, in less than five generations. If the French population had multiplied at that rate during the same century there might have been some 400 million Frenchmen by 1763, whereas there were, in fact, only twenty-two or twenty-three million. Lest we should be tempted to dismiss the figures for New France as improbable, we should glance at the increase during the two centuries after 1763 which amounts to an even more staggering rise of from 70,000 to 5½ million, or an eighty-fold increase. If the French had multiplied as quickly as the French Canadians since 1763 there would be nearly two billion Frenchmen by now, or more than half the population of the entire world. In this context, the figures for the twenty-three-fold increase in New France during the century before 1763 do not seem improbable. But they are nevertheless in need of explanation.

Leaving the mathematics of the problem to the demographers, we may sum up in general terms as follows: if women did not marry so young as we thought; if they had babies half as often as we thought; if nearly one-quarter of those babies died before they were a year old and nearly another fifth of them died before the age of ten; and if the annual crude death-rate for the country was somewhere between twenty and forty per thousand; then why did the population increase so quickly? Why was the crude birth-rate so much higher than the crude death-rate or from forty-eight to sixty-five per thousand? The answer (and the missing fact in the problem as I have posed it) is that the people of New France had a high propensity to marry. They were exceptionally fond of the married state.

People in Quebec today marry at an annual rate of about seven or eight per thousand, which is below our national average. The French during the eighteenth century used to marry at the rate of about 16.5 per thousand. But in the colony of New France, the marriage rate was between 17.5 and 23.5 per thousand. The result of this high marriage rate was that from 30% to 40% of the total population were married or widowed, and this proportion seemed to be increasing in the first half of the eighteenth century.[5]

In addition to this, we find a marked tendency to re-marry. Nearly one-fifth of married men married twice, and nearly one-fifth of families had fathers who had been married before. Widows were not snapped up quite so quickly as Peter Kalm and other travellers like to think, but the average widow re-married after three years of widowhood. One way or another very few women reached the age of forty without having married and even re-married. The re-marriage rate was 163 per thousand or nearly twice as high as in 1948.

Another figure that may reflect the strong propensity to marry is the low rate of illegitimacy: it seems to have been not more than ten or twelve per thousand whereas in 1969 the average in Quebec was seventy-six per thousand. We are, I think, obliged to conclude from all the evidence that Canadians were fond of the married state and that this is one reason for the high birth rate. For all that the frontier, like any frontier, had large numbers of single young men, and for all that many Canadians were attracted by the adventurous life of the *coureur de bois,* the society as a whole consisted mainly of married people with families. After all, the *coureurs de bois* were not very numerous and not many girls went into religious orders. There were forty-one women in religious orders in 1663 and in 1763 all seven of the orders of nuns numbered only 190 women altogether, a large number of them from France.

The marriage ceremony which these early Canadians went through in such large numbers left people in no doubt about what their main duty was as a couple. Immediately after the couple had been blessed by the officiating priest, the marriage bed was blessed with the sprinkling of holy water, prayers, and exorcisms. The exorcisms were intended to ward off the evil effects of an especially dangerous curse which some enemy of the couple might put on the marriage to make it barren. This curse was known as the *nouage de l'aiguillette,* and on occasion the Church would dissolve a marriage which produced no children on the grounds that this evil magic had made it barren, so important was the procreation of children in that society. And yet the bed in which children were to be conceived and born was not supposed to be a place for pleasure, as the official ceremony for Quebec, *Le Rituel du diocèse de Québec,* made very clear. The priest was to say to the newly-weds,

Remember that your wedding bed will some day be your death bed, from whence your souls will be taken to be sent before God's Tribunal. ...[6]

When we come to consider why the people of New France married so willingly and in such large numbers we may at first be tempted to think that the Church forced them into it. Marriage was, after all, a Christian institution, one of the seven sacraments of the Church. There was no civil marriage, nor any civil status at all, in New France. All marriages had to be Catholic marriages and priests were forbidden to marry anyone who was not a Catholic. Very few Canadians married Indians, baptized or not, and very few married Protestants. Priests had to make sure that people who wanted to marry were satisfied that God had called them to marriage; that they had been instructed of the duties and religious principles of marriage (for instance, that it was for having children and for no other purpose); that they had made a full and true confession and communion in their parishes; and that they intended to appear and to behave decently on their wedding day, not to give way to the Devil's temptation to dress vainly or to eat and drink too much. In 1682, Bishop Laval spoke out against women coming to church "in scandalous nakedness of the arms, of the shoulders and the throat or being satisfied to cover them with transparent cloth which often serves only to give more lustre to these shameful nudities."[7] We might be inclined to conclude that it was as good and faithful Catholics in a theocracy that the people of New France were drawn to marriage.

However, we do not have to look very far to see that marriage in that society was not only a religious sacrament, but much else besides. For one thing, weddings were one of the main social events, famous for celebrations lasting several days or even weeks together. That was why most marriages were held in November, January or February, the idle months of the year between the labours of autumn and the labours of spring. Marriage was also set about with pagan customs like the *charivari*, a ritual gathering of young people who made a disturbance outside the house of a widow who had just been married soon after being widowed, or of people of very unequal ages who had married. The crowd shouted until the newly-weds came out and either explained their actions or else paid a fine.[8] Another folk custom, brought from France, like nearly all Quebec customs, was for young people who wished to marry without their parents' consent, or without a proper wedding, to attend a regular church service and announce at the end of it that they regarded themselves as married. This was called *mariage à la gaumine* and was based on a strict and (said the clergy) illegitimate interpretation of the Papal ruling that marriage required the Church's blessing. Although it died out in the eighteenth century, this custom showed that some people viewed the Church's rules as hindrances to marriage. But all these things are only small clues to the irreligious side of marriage. Much more importantly marriage was an act of the family as a business and social enterprise. It was only rarely an act of two free individuals.

105

In New France, and in Europe at the time, the family was truly the fundamental unit of society and not the frail and limited group we know today. But in New France, the family was particularly important because some of the other French social groups had not taken root here. The typical French peasant lived in a close-knit village with common lands, common taxes, and a collective or communal life reflected in the word "commune" still used in France more or less as a synonym for "village."[9] However, the *habitants* of New France were not peasants, for the most part, and they lived dispersed across the countryside without common lands or duties in a pattern of rural settlement known as *le rang*.[10] Again, tradesmen in France were organized in guilds or *corporations* which governed most aspects of their working lives, but in New France they worked in a much freer and more independent way. The family was therefore a relatively more important social unit.

In both France and New France, however, as Guy Fregault writes, "The ties of family relationship had extraordinary strength at that time."[11] Four of its basic features will show what I mean. First, the family tended to be a business or agricultural unit with every member expecting to live on the family wealth and in turn expected to take part in the family enterprise. It was also a social enterprise in which every member tried to assist in the advancement of the whole. Families climbed socially like ivy up a wall. The mentality of social advancement at the time may be glimpsed in, for instance, some statements by an eighteenth-century governor whose attitudes may be taken as exemplary in the colony. This is Vaudreuil, who wrote to the minister at Versailles on 15 November 1703: "We have chosen the Honourable Chevalier de Courcy to carry these letters...to you because he is the nephew of Monsieur de Callieres. We have been pleased to give him this honour to let him know the respect we have for the memory of his late uncle." A year later, Vaudreuil wrote to the Minister on behalf of his own children: "I have eight boys and a girl who need the honour of your protection. Three of them are ready for service. I entered the musketeers when I was as young as my oldest. I hope you will have the goodness to grant me for him the company of the Sieur de Maricourt who has died." He then discusses his wife's relations and concludes, "On my side [of the family] I have only one relation, to whom the late Sieur Chevalier de Callières gave a small office as ensign. I beg you to grant him a lieutenancy...."[12]

Of course patronage extended beyond the family, but the strongest claims were on blood relations and for them. We cannot read very far in any official correspondence of the time without encountering such claims, for there was almost no other way of getting ahead in life. The system of patronage is revealed in a vocabulary all its own, peculiar to the *ancien regime* whether in France or in Canada: *protection* meant patronage; *grâce* referred to a post, a promotion, a pension or a title conferred by a patron or at his request; *estime* was the attitude of the patron towards his *créature* and it was the reason they both alleged for the *grâce*. And *crédit* was the power a friend or relation had to obtain a *grâce* from someone else; whereas *faveur* expressed the power he had to obtain something for himself.

A second feature of the family is that the act of marriage was in part a business event. In particular, the family had to find a dowry for a girl or else she would probably never find a husband. Trying to marry a girl off without a dowry would have been like fishing without bait on the hook. To use another image, the dowry was a sort of marriage "scholarship," and this metaphor seems all the more true when we remember that Talon gave the *filles du Roi* dowries of fifty *livres* in linen and other goods, and that in 1711 the government of New France set aside the sum of 3,000 *livres* to be distributed as dowries among sixty girls. In New France, dowries varied a good deal and they reflect roughly the social level of the family. Here is an example of a modest dowry which Magdeleine Boucher brought to her husband, Urbain Baudry Lamarche:

Two hundred *livres* in silver; four sheets; two table-cloths; six cloth and hemp napkins; a mattress and a blanket; two plates; six pewter spoons and six pewter plates; a pot and a cauldron; a table and two benches; a flour bin; a chest with a lock and key; one cow; two pigs, male and female. The parents gave the bride a suit of clothes and as much underwear as she wanted.[13]

This was an *habitant* family affair, of course. A rich shipping merchant's daughter, at the other end of the scale of commoners, might bring thousands of *livres* to her marriage: Denis Goguet, who retired to La Rochelle after making his fortune in Canada, put up dowries of 50,000 *livres* for his daughters.[14]

The main point about such dowries is that they were family property transferred by legal contract. At the time of the marriage a contract was drawn up before a notary stating this transfer of property and other business terms pertaining to the marriage. Marriage thus had a business side to it and the business negotiations were usually between the families rather than the betrothed couple. As a rule, the families signed these contracts in large numbers; we find the signatures of uncles, aunts, cousins and so on scrawled on the last page. One of the interesting effects of this system is that the wife, represented by her family and bringing considerable property to the marriage, tended to have a greater material equality with her husband than most wives in our time.

Needless to say, therefore, both families were very much interested in arranging the marriage in the first place, and this brings up my third point about the family as enterprise: marriage was a major theatre of the family struggle for social advancement or for security. To marry above the family station was a triumph, a step upward for the entire family. The new link with a grander or more noble family was a source of benefit through the influence if afforded. If the daughter of a successful merchant married a government official or his son, the assumption was likely to be that henceforth they were allies in a common struggle for advancement.

107

Why, we may wonder, would a family ever allow a marriage with a lesser family? The answer is that wealth attracted the poor but respectable; and respectability attracted the rich but low-born. Or else a powerful merchant or clerical family might be glad to marry into a large family of military officers with strong connections in the army. The benefit would still be mutual. Professor Cameron Nish has shown with many examples how the various social spheres intermarried in New France, there being only one ruling class and no such thing as purely military, purely seigneurial or purely administrative families.[15]

The fourth feature of the family was its hierarchy with the father in command, captain of the family enterprise. It is all too easy these days to imagine that paternal authority was merely a rank injustice or a quaint superstition. Far from it. Every enterprise in a competitive world must be under the command of someone or some group with authority to make decisions: a manager, a president, a ship's captain, a general in the army, a board in a company, and so on. The family enterprise in New France and Old France was nearly always under the father, though there were no impediments to a widow taking over her husband's family firm. In France, especially, there were many firms with "widow" in their titles: *La Veuve Charly* of La Rochelle, *La Veuve Augier et fils aîné* of Tonnay-Charente; *La Veuve Courrejolles et fils* of Bayonne, and so on.

It has been said that circumstances in Canada tended to put women and children much higher in the social scheme of things than French women and children and to make them more equal with the husband and father.[16] Yet such a difference was not sanctioned either by custom or by law, and normally the father's authority extended to most things, unless he died in which case his widow might assume some, though by no means all, of his authority. Parental authority over children may be seen very clearly in the field of marriage. No child could marry without his father's or widowed mother's consent until the age of twenty-five for girls and thirty for men. Until those ages, the children were considered minors. And in a world where life was shorter than it is now, we must add several years to those ages in order to appreciate the significance of that law. Marriage was primarily the family's business and by law as well as by custom the children were expected to make their marriages according to the best interests of the family.

French law provided that if a son, for example, wanted to marry a girl of whom his father did not approve, he might draw up three "respectful applications" *(sommations respectueuses)* at a notary's office, one after the other at a few weeks' intervals. Let me read to you the first respectful application that a certain Jean-Claude Louet made to his father in January 1733. He was then thirty years old and wanted to marry a shoemaker's daughter, but the father did not approve of the marriage.[17]

108

My Very Dear Father,
I am in the throes of misery at finding myself deprived of the kindness that I was used to receiving from you. I am extremely pained that your tender impulses which have moved me so often and so deeply are entirely extinct. However, dear father, if I withdraw the obedience and submission that I owe you it is out of an indispensable obligation to restore the reputation of the one whom I have lost, without which there is no salvation for me.
Finally, dear father, I entreat you in your paternal love, and by all that is dearest to you of your own blood, to let yourself be touched and persuaded by the pitiable fate of the poor girl and the lamentable state to which I have been reduced for so long. You have spoken; I have obeyed. You have sent me away to a place where I have nothing but tears and sighs to console me and keep me company.
I believe, however, that today you will be moved by my woes and will grant me the favour I am asking of you.

From he who is,
My Dear Father,
Your most humble and submissive son,
C. Louet

After the third such letter, the son was then legally entitled to marry because he was thirty years old. Under thirty, if his father still refused to consent the son would have had to wait.

We see in all this that the family was engaged in a collective struggle for survival or advancement, and children could not usually please themselves as individuals but had to act as members of the family team. This state of affairs was not merely a quaint custom, but enforced by the law of the kingdom. The law in New France, as in Old France, was prepared to punish children who disobeyed and defied their fathers; for the government, the Church and the society saw the family in that age as though it were itself a tiny kingdom in which the father, like a king, had almost total authority to rule, reward and punish. In other words, in that society the family appeared as the smallest political cell in the kingdom, modelled on the kingdom itself.

This metaphor is, however, reversible, and if we reverse it we find that the family in that eighteenth-century society served as a general pattern of organization and authority. The Church, for example, appeared to the people as a sort of family because God was presented as a father to be obeyed as one obeyed one's own father. The letter of Claude Louet above reads a little like a prayer. And not only was God a fatherlike figure, but beneath him there was a whole hierarchy of fathers in authority: the archbishops, the bishops and the priests. Catholic priests were addressed as "father" while the lay brothers were "brothers." The head of an order of nuns was, of course, a "mother superior," and the nuns were either "mother" or "sister." Girls first entering religious orders were expected to bring dowries as though they were being married, and a nun's dowry was not merely a symbol but a substantial sum of money, a piece of land or a parcel of goods. Records of dowries brought to Quebec orders are a useful guide to the wealth of the girls' families: some brought several thousand *livres* in cash, others came with a dowry of annuities or planks, barrels of wine, linen, furniture, wheat and so on.[18] When a Canadian girl chose to go into a monastery, she and her family prepared for the event in somewhat the same way as if she were going to be married, for they saw her as marrying into the Church. She joined the Church just as she might have joined a husband's family. Of course there were differences, but the similarities are striking.

Listen to the following ecstasies of love written by a women who spent most of her life in New France: "Oh, beloved of my soul! Where are you and when shall I possess you? When shall I have you for myself and entirely for myself? Ah, I want you, but I do not want only half of you. I want all of you, my Love and my Life....Come, then, come Oh my Love! The door of my heart is open to you..." and so on. Now who was this passionate woman? And who was the fortunate man to whom she was so passionately drawn? She was none other than Marie de l'Incarnation, a nun in the seventeenth century and now a saint in the Canadian Catholic calendar; and all these emotional outpourings were addressed to God. She was expressing her vocation, her call to a life in New France in God's service to which she devoted herself passionately. The point is that as these and other such passages show she saw herself as in some sense married to God or to Jesus and in her writings often referred to him as "my dear Husband."[19]

The image of the family was also present in the army. When a soldier wanted to marry, he needed the consent of his captain or other senior officer and of the Governor of New France. These two consents, which were not merely perfunctory, were duly registered by the officiating clergy. Military authority was thus in some measure paternal authority. But all authority which is not defined by clear regulations must inevitably appear as paternal in the sense that it has no limits and may extend, like a father's authority, into personal and family matters.

The political hierarchy, too, was organized on the family plan. What was the King in the Bourbon kingdom but a great father with paternal care for his subjects and paternal authority over them? Under him, the Governor and Intendant were also father figures expected to enforce not the law, but

109

the King's paternal will. They themselves had paternal rights and duties; and this explains why they used their authority in many matters great and small which astonish us. Paternal authority had very different limits from those of men in authority in our world. "You must maintain good order and peace in families," the minister at Versailles wrote to one Canadian Governor, "refrain from joining in private discussions except to bring them to an end and not join in them if you cannot settle them, never listen to women's talk, never allow anyone to speak ill of someone else in front of you and never do so yourself...." As the Intendant Raudot said, the colony was supposed to be managed "as a good father of a family would manage his estate."[20] When, for instance, the Minister happened to hear of an officer who was not supporting his impoverished mother, he arranged to have the officer punished and part of his pay withheld for the mother.[21]

There were, then, a number of hierarchies of authority in Canada all patterned on the family and all helping to reinforce one another in the Canadian mind. To introduce the rule of law into such a society, as the British tried to do after 1763, was a difficult task. How could it be introduced in a society where all authority was regarded as personal and paternal? Still, under British rule, the change began in New France a quarter of a century before it began in Old France during the French Revolution. Since then the French have reverted frequently to the paternal authority of a father figure such as the Bonaparte emperors and General de Gaulle, not to mention Marechal Petain whose regime used the motto, *Famille, Patrie, Travail*. Let us hope that in Quebec the rule of law has taken a firmer hold on the minds of the people during the past two hundred years, and that the ancient vision of the polity as a family has faded away.

Notes

1. *The Canada Yearbook for 1972*, pp. 241-242.
2. Jacques Henripin, *La Population canadienne au début du XVIIIᵉ siècle* (Paris, 1954); Henripin, "From Acceptance of Nature to Control: The Demography of the French Canadians since the Seventeenth Century," in M. Rioux and Y. Martin, *French-Canadian Society*, vol. 1 (Toronto, 1964), pp. 204-216; Marcel Trudel, *La Population du Canada en 1663* (Montreal, 1973); J.N. Biraben, "Le Peuplement du Canada français," *Annales de démographie historiques* (Paris, 1966), pp. 104-139.
3. Jacques Henripin, "La Fécondité des ménages canadiens au début du XVIIIᵉ siècle," *Population*, vol. 9 (Paris, 1954), pp. 74-84.
4. Marcel Trudel, *op. cit.*, p. 11. Professor Trudel lists 3,035 people, but admits that he is not sure of 221 of them. On immigrants, see Biraben, *op. cit.*, and Henripin, *La Population canadienne*, chap. II, quoting Georges Langlois, *Histoire de la population canadienne française de Montréal* (1934).
5. Trudel finds that in 1663, the proportion was nearly 50 per cent (*op. cit.*, p. 74).
6. Robert-Lionel Seguin, *La Vie libertine en Nouvelle-France au XVIIᵉ siècle*, vol. 2 (Ottawa, 1972), pp. 365-366.
7. Paul-André Leclerc, "Le Mariage sous le régime français," *Revue d'Histoire de l'Amérique française*, vol. XIII (1959), p. 525.
8. *Ibid.*, pp. 229ff. On "mariage à la gaumine," see *Le Rapport de l'Archiviste de la Province de Québec* (henceforth cited as R.A.P.Q.), 1920-21, pp. 366-407.
9. Marc Bloch, *Les Caracteres originaux de l'Histoire rurale française* (Paris, 1952) [first published in 1931], chap. V.
10. Pierre Deffontaines, "The *Rang* — Pattern of Rural Settlement in French Canada," in Rioux and Martin, *French-Canadian Society*, pp. 3-18.
11. Guy Frégault, *Le XVIIIᵉ siècle canadien* (Montreal, 1968), p. 179.

12. *R.A.P.Q.*, 1938-39, pp. 21-22 and 49-50.
13. Leclerc, *op. cit.*, p. 59.
14. Archives départementales de la Charente maritime (La Rochelle), minutes of the notary Delavergne, 10 December 1760 and 4 June 1770.
15. Cameron Nish, *Les Bourgeois-Gentilshommes de la Nouvelle-France, 1729-1748* (Montreal and Paris, 1968), chap. X, "La Bourgeoisie et le mariage."
16. Philippe Garigue, *La Vie familiale des canadiens français* (Montreal and Paris, 1962), pp. 16-17.
17. *R.A.P.Q.*, 1921-22, pp. 60-63.
18. Micheline d'Allaire, "L'Origine social des religieuses de l'Hôpital-général de Québec," *La Revue d'Histoire de l'Amérique française* 23 (March 1970): 559-583.
19. Dom Albert Jamet, ed., *Le Témoignage de Marie de l'Incarnation, Ursuline de Tours et de Québec* (Paris, 1932), pp. 70-72.
20. Guy Frégault, *Le XVIIIᵉ siècle canadien*, pp. 162-163.
21. *Ibid.*, pp. 163-164.

The Golden Age: Acadian Life, 1713-1748*
NAOMI GRIFFITHS

111

Until the 1950s Acadian history was most frequently written either as epic or as case study — as the drama of a people or as an example of the political and diplomatic struggles between great powers. The tragic nature of the deportation in 1755 seemed the obvious and fundamental starting point for all that the Acadians experienced since, and equally the culmination of everything that had occurred in their previous history. In the last thirty years, however, an ever-increasing number of scholarly works have been devoted to the examination of Acadian history from much more complex perspectives. These include attempts to analyze not merely 1755 as an event of major importance in the war between English and French for North America, but also works centred upon Acadian language,[1] folklore,[2] geography,[3] sociology,[4] as well as upon Acadian history as the history of a developing community.

Acadian studies have, in fact, come to an impressive maturity over the past thirty years. This maturity is magnificently documented in the work edited by Jean Daigle, *Les Acadiens des Maritimes*, where some twenty scholars present complex essays outlining the problems, the work done and the work to be done in every area of Acadian studies from history to folklore, from political science to material culture.[5] The result of all this publication is, of course, the temptation, if not the necessity, for present scholars to look at past syntheses of Acadian history, to discover where the new information demands new theories and to build, if not entirely new interpretations of the Acadian past, at least interpretations which are more richly decorated and more densely structured.

This challenge is as dangerous as it is irresistible, for the amount of material is considerable indeed. As a result, this paper is a cautious one. Its main aim is to paint Acadian life between 1713 and 1748 in such a way that the reader may sense the complex nature of the Acadian community during these

*From *Histoire sociale — Social History*, 17 (May 1984): 1-11.

years. This was the period to be remembered by the community in exile after 1755. All those over the age of ten or eleven in 1755 would have had some knowledge of these years. It was the time that would be recalled in exile and the time which would form the basis for the stories of past life as the Acadians once more established themselves in the Maritimes. It spanned the decades from the Treaty of Utrecht to that of Aix-la-Chapelle, during which years the lands on which the Acadians lived turned from being the border between two empires to the frontier between enemies.

The political geography of "Nova Scotia or Acadia", as the lands were called in the contemporary international treaties, had meant turmoil for its inhabitants from the outset of European colonization. As J.B. Brebner wrote, these lands were "the eastern outpost and flank for both French and English in North America". They made, in his words, a "continental cornice". Throughout the seventeenth century this cornice frequently changed hands between English and French. It became a true border, for whatever name it was given and whatever limits were claimed, it lay "inside the angle between the St. Lawrence route to French Canada and the northern route to New England which branched off from it south of Newfoundland."[6] Those who settled there in the seventeenth century would quickly find their situation akin to such people as the Basques caught between France and Spain, the Alsatians moulded by French and German designs, and those who lived on the borders between England and Scotland or England and Wales.

It was the French who began the first permanent settlement in the area in 1604. Whatever the international designation of the colony over the next century, it's non-Indian people would be called the Acadians. While predominantly French-speaking and Catholic, they were nevertheless a people who also absorbed English-speaking migrants such as the Melansons[7] and the Caisseys.[8] They also had a considerable knowledge of the Protestant religion, and it is very probable that some of the families who joined them from near Loudun in the 1630s were of the reform church.[9] By the end of the century the Acadians had known one lengthy and legitimate period of English rule, 1654-1668, as well as a number of much shorter periods of English control as a result of raids out of Massachusetts. By 1700 the Acadians were, as the detailed work of Professors Daigle and Reid has shown,[10] almost as accustomed to dealing with the officials of England as those of France. Thus the defeat of Subercase in 1710 and the subsequent transfer of the colony once more to English control by the treaty of Utrecht was for the Acadians yet one more step in a complicated ritual, an exchange of control over them from France to England, something which had happened before and would most probably be reversed in the not too distant future.

This fundamental belief in the mutability of power, this dominant sense of the probability of alternate French and English control of the colony, became the cornerstone of Acadian politics during the years 1713 to 1748. It was the basis for the Acadian action over requests made by the English officials that they swear an oath of allegiance to the King of England. From

112

the Acadian viewpoint, it would have been folly indeed to engage in any action which would bind them irrevocably to one Great Power when the other was still not only obviously in the neighbourhood, but even more obviously still interested in the future status of the colony and its inhabitants. Thus the Acadians built a policy compounded of delay and compromise. The oath to George I was first rejected outright; among other reasons they presented for the refusal, the Acadians of Minas remarked that "pendant que nos ancetres ont étés sous la domination angloise on ne leur a jamais exigé de pareille Sermente...."[11] Later on oaths were taken to George II, but in such circumstances as to enable the Acadians to believe that they had been granted the right to remain neutral. In fact, as Brebner pointed out, the practice of both English and French of referring to them from 1730 on as either "les français neutres" or "the Neutral French" indicates that this accommodation was generally tolerated, if not accepted, by those in power during these years.[12]

However it might have looked to outsiders, the question of neutrality was serious enough to the Acadians. It was in fact a consistent policy that was first enunciated in 1717 by the Acadians of Annapolis Royal and later adhered to by them, and others in time of war. On being asked for an oath of allegiance to George I, the response of Annapolis Royal Acadians was a refusal, the reasons given being that matters of religious freedom were not yet clarified and danger from Indians, who were bound to disapprove friendship between Acadian and English, led to fears for Acadian security. Nevertheless, the response continued, "we are ready to take an oath that we will take up arms neither against his Britannic Majesty, nor against France, nor against any of their subjects or allies."[13] In 1744 when hostilities broke out between English and French in North America, Mascerene, then the lieutenant-governor of the colony, wrote to his masters in London: "These latter [i.e., the French inhabitants] have given me assurances of their resolutions to keep in their fidelity to his Majesty".[14] Mascerene was convinced that had the Acadians not remained neutral during the hostilities, the colony would have fallen to the French.[15] Certainly there is more than enough evidence to show the Acadian dislike of the war, including a most strongly worded letter from those of Grand-Pré to the French, pointing out forcibly that the village preferred peace to war, tranquility and food to soldiers fighting across their farmlands.[16]

There is no doubt that between 1713 and 1748 the majority of the Acadians strove to live on their land truly as neutrals, giving loyalty to neither French nor English. This policy procured for their communities nearly thirty-five years of peace, but its final failure in 1755 has overshadowed its earlier success. It is worth emphasizing that it was a policy, not merely a series of inconsistent, unconnected reactions to the demands made by English and French. It was transmitted by delegates from the several Acadian communities to the English officials on a number of separate occasions and, as has been suggested, adhered to during a time of considerable pressure in the 1740s. It was a policy that produced peace and quiet for the Acadian communities, however catastrophic it finally proved to be. Its evolution and development gave the Acadians a knowledge of political action and a sense of their independent reality that would prove invaluable to them when they confronted the vicissitudes of the deportation.[17] Above all, it was the framework for the expansion and development of the Acadian communities between 1713 and 1748.

The demographic expansion of the Acadians during these years is a commonplace in one sense; in another it is something acknowledged rather than fully understood. As Gysa Hynes wrote in 1973, "the rapid natural increase of the population of the Acadians during the period from 1650 to 1750 . . . has long been recognised, but no historian has explored the demography of Acadia before the Dispersion."[18] As a result, while it is generally agreed that the Acadian population probably doubled every twenty years between 1713 and the early 1750s without the aid of any considerable immigration, there has been little real analysis of this development.[19] Gisa Hynes's excellent article was a pioneer study relating above all to Port Royal/Annapolis Royal and has not been followed by much else. Enough raw material does exist, however, to outline the tantalizing landscape waiting to be fully explored, a demographic territory which differs significantly from contemporary Europe and also, in some considerable measure, from that of other colonial settlements in North America.

114

It is a debatable point whether the longevity of the Acadians or their fertility should receive most comment. At a time when only 50 percent of the population reached the age of 21 in France, 75 percent reached adulthood in Port Royal.[20] Further, while mortality did take its toll during the middle years, death coming through accident and injury rather than epidemic, old age was a common enough phenomenon. In fact at the time of the Treaty of Utrecht, when the French were making every effort to withdraw the Acadians from land ceded to the English and to establish them on Isle Royal (Cape Breton), one of the priests noted that the Acadians refused to go because

It would be to expose us manifestly [they say] to die of hunger burthened as we are with large families, to quit the dwelling places and clearances from which we derive our usual subsistence, without any other resource, to take rough, new lands, from which the standing wood must be removed. One fourth of our population consists of aged persons, unfit for the labour of breaking up new lands, and who, with great exertion, are able to cultivate the cleared ground which supplied subsistence for them and their families.[21]

The presence of an older generation in the community meant a rich heritage of memories of past politics. Any Acadian over forty-two in 1713 would have been born when the colony was controlled by the English, for the terms of the Treaty of Breda were not honoured by Temple until 10 January 1671. Any Acadian over twenty-five would have personal memories of the stormy raids by New Englanders on their villages and of the French counter-measures. The reality of life on a border would be a commonplace for Acadian reminiscences in a community whose people lived long enough to remember.

If Acadians could see relatively long life as a possibility, they could also see life itself as abundant. From the travelling French surgeon-poet Dièreville to the almost equally travelling English official, Governor Philipps, the observations were the same. In 1699 the Frenchman wrote that "the swarming of Brats is a sight to behold."[22] The Englishman commented in 1730 on the Acadians' ability to increase and spread "themselves over the face of the province . . . like Noah's progeny."[23] Present day research has confirmed the accuracy of these impressions. Gisa Hynes discovered in her analysis of Port Royal that four out of five marriages were complete, that is "were not disrupted by the death of husband or wife before the onset of menopause."[24] In these marriages, if the women were under 20 on their wedding day, they had some ten or eleven children; those wedded between 20 and 24, nine children; and those married in their late 20s, seven or eight children.[25] For the population as a whole, it is probable that the average family in the colony had six or seven children.[26]

These bare statistical bones of Acadian family life can now be covered first *115* with the skin of individual family genealogy and then clothed with the fabric of community life. As an example of the first, there is the life of Claude Landry, born in 1663, the youngest of some ten children of René Landry of Port Royal, who himself had arrived in the colony sometime in the 1640s from Loudun.[27] When he was about eighteen, Claude married Catherine Thibodeau, whose father had been an associate of Emmanuel LeBorgne and come to the colony from around Poitiers in the 1650s.[28] She was the fifth child in a family of sixteen, eleven of whom reached adulthood.[29] Catherine was apparently fifteen when married and bore her first child within the year. She had some ten children in all, eight of whom lived to maturity.

The young couple moved very early in their marriage to Grand-Pré where they brought up their family and watched their children's children flourish. When Claude Landry died in 1747, aged eighty-six, his grandchildren through the male line numbered forty-six and his great-grandchildren, also through the male line, eleven. Claude's last child, a son, had been born in 1708; his first grandson was born in 1710. Between 1717 and 1747 there was only one year in which no birth is recorded for his sons, and it is not unlikely that one of Claude's two daughters might have had a child that year. 1735 saw the birth of the first great-grandchild within the male line.[30]

The growth of such extended families was supported by a healthy mixed economy, based upon farming, hunting and fishing with enough trade, both legal and illegal, to make life interesting. In Grand-Pré the Landry family was part of the flourishing development which Mascerene had described in 1730 as "a platt of Meadow, which stretches near four leagues, part of which is damn'd [*sic*] in from the tide, and produced very good wheat and pease."[31] Westward this great marsh is edged by the massive presence of Cape Blomidon, the tides of the Bay of Fundy curve across its northern shore, and wooded uplands circumscribe its other boundaries. Between 1710, when the first grandson was born, and 1747, when Claude died, the population of the area grew from well under a thousand to something more than four thousand.[32] The community lived in houses scattered across the landscape, not grouped close together in a village. Charles Morris, who was commissioned by Governor Shirley of Massachusetts to make a survey of the Bay of Fundy area in 1747, reported that the dwellings were "low Houses fram'd of timber and their Chimney framed with the Building of wood and lined with Clay except the fireplace below . . ."[33] Very often the houses sheltered a mixture of families, and the sheer work required to provide them necessities of life must have been considerable.[34]

The daily life of both men and women would be governed by the seasons, for the frame of the economy was what was grown and raised for food and clothing. Fishing, hunting and trade could and did provide important additions to this base, but the standard of living of the majority of the Acadians depended upon the produce of their land-holdings. At the very least a household would possess a garden, and from the seventeenth century on travellers had noticed the variety and abundance of vegetables grown. Dièreville, whose evidence is of the close of the seventeenth century, remarked upon the wealth of cabbages and turnips,[35] and another report of the same period lists the gardens as including "choux, betteraves, oignons, carottes, cives, eschalottes, navets, panets et touttes sortes de salades."[36] Most families would have also an amount of land varying in size between that of a smallholding and a farm, depending on where the community was in the colony and what level of resources the family in question could command. A.H. Clark considered that the households of Grand-Pré and the surrounding area usually had five to ten acres of dyked and tilled farmland within the marsh, supplemented with an orchard situated on the upland slopes. Morris reported the marshlands to be "Naturally of a Fertile Soil . . . and . . . of so strong and lasting a Nature that their Crops are not Diminished in ten or twenty years Constant Tillage".[37] The crops sown included most of the grain crops common to western Europe: wheat, oats, rye and barley, as well as peas, hemp and flax. Writing in 1757 another traveller remarked on the abundance of fruit trees, apples, pears, "cherry and plumb trees", and noted that "finer flavoured apples and greater variety, cannot in any other country be produced."[38]

Working with the land, whether garden or farm, did not only imply digging and ploughing, weeding and gathering. There was also the care of livestock. Poultry was everywhere about, as much for feathers as for the eggs and meat. Down-filled mattresses and coverlets were a noted Acadian possession, and the export of feathers to Louisbourg a common item of trade.[39] Pigs rooting around the houses were so common that few surveyors interested in estimating Acadian wealth even bothered to count them. A number of observers, however, remarked on the Acadian liking for fat-back *(le lard)*, which could be cooked with cabbage or fried and added to whatever vegetables were available.[40] Sheep were also numerous, raised for wool rather than for meat. Most households would also possess cows and a horse. The estimation of the total livestock in the colony varies widely since the Acadians, like most peasant populations, had no great wish to inform any of-

116

ficial of the true extent of their possessions. Life must have been sustained at considerably more than bare subsistence, however, since extant records show that in the 1740s the Acadians, particularly those of Grand-Pré and of the Minas basin in general, were able to export cattle, sheep, pigs and poultry to Louisbourg.[41] While the authorities at Annapolis Royal thundered against such trade, they also admitted that the Acadians were no worse than others, noting that "there is so great an illicit Trade carried on by the People of Massachusetts Bay and New Hampshire."[42] As has been suggested, the trade that existed was enough to make life for the Acadians interesting, and the goods imported included not only necessities such as "Spanish Iron, French Linnens, Sail Cloth Wollen cloths", but also "Rum, Molasses, Wine and Brandy."[43]

The sum of this evidence suggests an excellent standard of living among the Acadians, something which showed, of course, in the population increase of the first half of the eighteenth century. While there is little evidence of luxury, there is less of poverty. The staples of life, food, shelter and *117* clothing were abundant, even if the abundance was available only after hard work. Further, the absence of conspicuous consumption and the lack of development of towns and industry in no way meant an absence of specie. It is clear from the records of the deportation itself that Acadians took coinage with them into exile.[44] The Acadian community did not have the rate of economic growth that the New Englanders possessed, but it provided amply for the totality of individuals. Fishing and hunting added to the resources of the households. Charles Morris remarked that the population around Grand-Pré "had some shallops, in which they employed themselves in the catching of Fish just upon their Harbours, being out but a few days at a Time; This was rather for their Home Consumption than the foreign Market . . ."[45] Clark remarked that the Acadians were "particularly interested in salmon, shad, gaspereau, and the like during their spring runs up the rivers and creeks . . ."[46] As for hunting, it was less the meat that was immediately valued than the furs. Game was sought in order to sell it in Annapolis Royal,[47] but "avec les fourrures d'ours, de castor, de renard, de loutre, et de martre", they had material which gave them "non seulement le confort, mais bien souvent de jolis vêtements."[48] Dièreville had also commented on the way in which the Acadians made shoes from sealskin and the hides of moose.[49]

Given the considerable work necessary to turn the resources of their environment into food and clothing for the family, it is extraordinary that the Acadians should have been criticized for being idle.[50] The tools they worked with were scarcely labour-saving devices and were basically of their own manufacture. Clark has listed the main implements available to them as "pickaxes, axes, hoes, sickles, scythes, flails, and wooden forks and rakes," as well, of course, as spades, essential for dyke-building.[51] They were known as competent carpenters and joiners, and the census made by the French during the seventeenth century reported the existence of blacksmiths, locksmiths and nailmakers among them.[52] Working basically in wood, the

Acadians built their own houses, barns and the occasional church, made their own furniture, including enclosed beds which must have provided considerable privacy in the crowded households, tables, chairs, chests, kegs and barrels, as well as looms and spinning-wheels.[53] There was a remarkably fluid, though not entirely egalitarian social structure. Considerable importance was attached to the actual possession of land, and the recognition of proper boundaries.[54]

Specie did not serve as a major regulator of the internal economy. The available evidence shows that it was rare indeed for Acadian communities to pay one another, except in kind, for goods and services rendered. The gold gained through trade, or through wages from French and English officials, was kept for trade and most reluctantly handed over for any other purposes, especially rents and taxes.[55] Labour relations among the Acadians tended to be either barter-based (perhaps two days' digging or ploughing in exchange for some quantity of seed grain), co-operative (three or four people engaged in quilt-making or fishing, the resultant produce being divided equitably), or communal (several households joined together to build another dwelling and ready to be reconvened for such a purpose whenever the occasion warranted). The social ambiance produced by such labour relations encouraged the development of a community where family connections were as important as the particular attainments of an individual. Marriage would be seen as the connection between kin rather than the limited engagement of two individuals of particular social status. As Dièreville remarked, to his considerable surprise social barriers seemed to have no part to play in the regulation of marriage.[56]

In sum, Acadian life between 1713 and 1748 centred around the demands and rewards of family and land, although this did not mean isolation from a wider environment. During these decades the care and nurture of children must have been the dominating factor in the lives of most Acadians, male or female. A child born every two or three years on average in individual families meant the arrival of a child almost every year in multi-family households. Even with the importation of some yard goods, the provision of clothes and coverings for the children demanded continuous thought and activity. Records emphasize the extent to which the Acadians were self-sufficient in this area. Dièreville remarked on the way in which they made their own outfits, including caps and stockings.[57] Raynal, writing for Diderot's *Encyclopaedia* with information supplemented by the memorials of those Acadians exiled to France, asserted that they depended for their daily clothing on ''leur lin, leur chanvre, la toison de leurs brebis.''[58] From diapers to shawls, from shirts to shifts, with considerable liking for mixing black with red for ornament, and binding their skirts with ribbons,[59] the Acadians spun, wove, knitted and sewed their garments. Even with every economy between one generation and the next, even with children fully accustomed to hand-me-downs, the sheer number of bonnets and mittens, stockings and shoes, cloaks, coats, and trousers, shirts, blouses and jackets that would be needed is difficult to envisage.

118

Organizing the clothing was probably as much a year-round occupation for the women as the provision of meals was their daily chore. Grains were usually ground at grist-mills rather than within each household, although there is a tradition that most families possessed pestles and mortars capable of making coarse flour for porridge.[60] Bread would be baked in each household and was considered by Isaac Deschamps to have been the staple of Acadian diets.[61] Linguistic studies by Massignon show that doughnuts and pancakes were also common. She discovered references to documents dated 1744 referring to *croxsignoles,* a form of doughnut, as part of the Acadian diet.[62] It is also probable that those who came to the community from Normandy and Ile-et-Vilaine brought with them a taste for buckwheat pancakes, something that was certainly common among Acadians in northern New Brunswick at the close of the eighteenth century.[63] There is a strange debate about whether the Acadians grew potatoes before 1755, since a number of popular guides such as the *Guide Bleu de Bretagne* refer to them introducing the vegetable to France.[64] Again, it is certainly true that the potato was a staple of Acadian diets by the opening of the nineteenth century,[65] but more evidence is needed before one can accept that it was a common food for the Acadians fifty years earlier. Milk was abundant[66] and the Acadians found in exile that they had been particularly fortunate in this respect.[67] Its plenteousness must have been a great help in coping with what was known as the *pourginés d'enfants.*[68]

119

This charming word for a numerous family invites consideration of the emotional climate in which families grew and developed. The evidence here is, at present, somewhat sketchy. The extent to which the Acadians cared for one another during their exile, seeking news of brothers and sisters as well as advertising for husbands and wives, suggests the importance of family relations.[69] As to the actual treatment of children during these decades, one has very few concrete details. It is possible that the reputation the Acadians had for long and faithful marriages was not coupled with a bitterness against those whose lives followed other patterns. One of the few cases relating to children that reached the English officials at Annapolis Royal between 1720 and 1739 was one where grandparents fought for the privilege of raising an illegitimate child.[70] The folklore research of Jean-Claude Dupont reveals a considerable amount about children's toys and games current in the nineteenth century, and it is probable that some of these, at least, were also part of Acadian life during the eighteenth century. Certainly the early mobile-rattle, a dried pig's bladder filled with peas and hung so an infant could bat it about and watch it swing, listening to its noise, which Dupont has reported for the nineteenth century, would have been a useful toy to have in the house in the eighteenth century.[71]

There were, of course, the usual arguments and quarrels among the Acadians, the kinds of disputes common to any group of people. The court records of Annapolis show not only debates over landholdings and boundaries, but also slander actions, particularly between women, and at least one appeal for aid to control a nagging wife.[72] But the tenor of life was undoubtedly rendered easier by the ready supply of necessities, a supply which might depend on continuous hard work but one that was available. There was no major shortage of food for the Acadians between 1713 and 1748; shelter was readily available; clothing was adequate; and, above all, there were no major epidemics. Even when plague did reach the colony its ravages were confined, both in 1709 and 1751, almost exclusively to the garrisons.[73]

Quite how the Acadians escaped the general epidemics of the eighteenth century has yet to be fully determined. It is obvious from the mortality rates they suffered during the early years of exile that during the first half of the eighteenth century they had acquired no community levels of immunity to smallpox, yellow fever or typhoid. When those diseases struck as the exiles reached Boston, Philadelphia, South Carolina or the British seaports, a third or more of the Acadians died.[74] Yet the idea that this vulnerability developed because of the more or less complete isolation of the communities from outside contact is a theory which demands a great deal more examination. The Acadian tradition of trading-cum-smuggling which was established in the seventeenth century took at least some of the men regularly enough to Boston and probably to points south.[75] In the eighteenth century this activity was continued and Acadian connections with Louisbourg were also developed. The fact that between 1713 and 1748 no large body of immigrants came to the area has tended to overshadow both the trickle of newcomers to the settlements and the continuous nature of the relationships between this "continental cornice" and the wider world. The parish records of Grand-Pré examined by Clark show that of the 174 marriages for which detailed information is available almost exactly one-third involved partners either from elsewhere in the colony or from abroad, sixteen coming from France, eight from Quebec and three from Cape Breton.[76] As for travellers, most of the settlements encountered them in the form of soldiers and traders as well as government and church officials. Given the normal rate of the spread of infections during these decades, it is extraordinary that no epidemics seem to have come to the settlements via contact with Boston or Quebec, Annapolis Royal or Louisbourg.

If the life of the Acadian settlements was much more open to outside influences than has been generally thought, it was also much less controlled by religious devotion than has been generally supposed. There is no question that the Acadians cherished the Catholic faith. There is also no doubt that they were as much trouble to their priests as any other group of humanity might be. The immense political importance of the Catholic religion to the community has overshadowed questions about its social importance. Acadians' delight in litigation was not their only cross-grained trait. Quarrels that sprung up through their drinking were also matters that concerned their pastors. A report of the archdiocese of Quebec of 1742, which drew particular attention to this flaw, also inferred that bars *(cabarets)* were not only open on Sundays and feast-days, but also kept open during the celebration of Mass.[77] This same report also went on to condemn some of the Acadian communities that allowed men and women not only to dance together after sunset but even permitted the singing of "des chansons lascives". The lack of detail in the report is frustrating: was the alcohol spruce beer? Cider? Rum? Were the *cabarets* found in the front room of the local smuggler, or did Grand-Pré have something close to a village hostelry? Was the dancing anything more than square-dancing? Was the music played on flutes, whistles and triangles only? Or were there also violins? And the songs—which of the presently known folklore airs might they have been: "Le petit Capucin"? "Le chevalier de la Tour ronde"?

Considerably more work needs to be done in the relevant archives before the nature of Acadian beliefs before 1755 can be fully described. The document just cited suggests only that the Acadian interpretation of Catholicism before 1755 owed very little to Jansenism. This would be scarcely surprising. There is little indication, even with the present evidence, that the Acadians indulged in major projects of ostensible devotion, either public or private. There are no stone churches built by them before 1755 nor are there any records of vocations among them before that date, either to the priesthood or to the religious life. Religion among the Acadians seems to have been a matter of necessity but not a question of sainthood, an important and vital ingredient in life, but not the sole shaping force of the social and cultural life of their communities.[78]

121

For, in sum, the life of the Acadians between 1713 and 1755 was above all the life of a people in fortunate circumstances, the very real foundation for the later myth of a "Golden Age". The ravages of the Four Horsemen of the Apocalypse were remarkably absent, for famine, disease and war barely touched the Acadians during these years. There was sufficient food for the growing families and apparently enough land for the growing population. One's nearest and dearest might have been as aggravating as one's kin can often be, but circumstances not only did not add the burdens of scarcity to emotional life but in fact provided a fair abundance of the necessities. Certainly the daily round for both men and women must have been exhaustingly busy; but work did have its obvious rewards and, for both sexes, it would be varied enough and carried out with companionship and sociability. While the season would often have imposed harsh demands for immediate labour, for seeds must be sown, crops gathered, fish caught and fuel cut as and when the weather dictates, the year's turning would also have brought its own festivities and holidays. Massignon's work suggests that the Acadians kept the twelve days of Christmas, the customs of Candelmas as well as the celebrations common to Easter.[79] The long winter evenings knew card-playing, dancing and pipe-smoking, as well as storytelling and sing-songs. The spring and summer months would see the celebrations of weddings and the most frequent new-births. Quarrels, scandals, politics, the visits of priests, the presence of Indians, people whose children occasionally married with the Acadians and who instructed the settlers in the use of local foods,[80] the presence of the English, now and again also marrying with the Acadians,[81] — there is no doubt that Acadians life before 1755 was neither crisis-ridden nor lapped in the tranquility of a back-water. It was instead a life of considerable distinctiveness. It was a life rich enough to provide the sustenance for a continuing Acadian identity, based not only upon a complex social and cultural life, but also upon the development of a coherent political stance, maintained throughout the settlements over a considerable period of years. It is not surprising that, fragmented in exile, the Acadians remembered these years and that this remembrance would be built into their future lives.

Notes

1. For example, Geneviève Massignon, *Les Parlers français d'Acadie*, 2 vol. (Paris: C. Klincksieck, n.d.).
2. For example, Antonine Maillet, *Rabelais et les traditions populaires en Acadie* (Québec: Presses de l'université Laval, 1971); Anselme Chiasson, *Chéticamp, histoire et traditions acadiennes* (Moncton: Éditions des Aboiteaux, 1962); Catherine Jolicoeur, *Les plus belles légendes acadiennes* (Montréal: Stanké, 1981).
3. A.H. Clark, *Acadia: the Geography of Early Nova Scotia to 1760* (Madison: University of Wisconsin Press, 1968), and J.C. Vernex, *Les Acadiens* (Paris: Éditions Entente, 1979).
4. Jean-Paul Hautecoeur, *L'Acadie du Discours* (Québec: Presses de l'université Laval, 1976).
5. Jean Daigle, ed., *Les Acadiens des Maritimes: Études thématiques* (Moncton: Centre d'Études Acadiennes, 1980). See my review in *Histoire social—Social History*, XVI (May 1983): 192-94.
6. J.B. Brebner, *New England's Outpost* (New York: Columbia University Press, 1927), pp. 15-16.
7. While there has been considerable debate about whether this family had Anglophone roots (for example, see Clark, *Acadia*, p. 101), there now seems no doubt of their origins. For details of their ancestry as recorded in declarations made by their descendants in Belle-Île-en-Mer after the deportation, see M.P. and N.P. Rieder, *The Acadians in France*, 3 vol. (Metairie, La.: M.P. & N. Rieder, 1972), 2: *passim*.
8. Bona Arsenault, *Histoire et Généalogie des Acadiens*, 2 vol. (Québec: Le Conseil de la vie française en Amérique, 1965), 2: 550.
9. This is suggested, in particular, in the reports of discussions with the second Mme La Tour, in Candide de Nantes, *Pages glorieuses de l'épopée Canadienne: une mission capucine en Acadie* (Montréal: Le Devoir, 1927), pp. 150f.
10. Jean Daigle, "Nos amis les ennemis: relations commerciales de l'Acadie avec le Massachusetts, 1670-1711" (Ph.D. dissertation, University of Maine, 1975); and John Reid, *Acadia, Maine and New Scotland: Marginal Colonies in the Seventeenth Century* (Toronto: University of Toronto Press, 1981).
11. This document, headed "answer of several French inhabitants, 10 February 1717", is printed in the *Collection de documents inédits sur le Canada et l'Amérique publiés par le Canada français*, 3 vol. (Québec: Le Canada français, 1888-90), 2: 171. The collection was published anonymously, but its editor is known to be the abbé Casgrain. The original of the document is in the Public Records Office, London (hereafter PRO), CO/NS 2, as part of the Nova Scotia government documents.
12. Brebner, *New England's Outpost*, p. 97.
13. T.B. Akins, ed., *Selections from the Public Documents of the Province of Nova Scotia* (Halifax, 1869), pp. 15-16.
14. Mascerene to the Lords of Trade, 9 June 1744, printed in *Collection de Documents inédits*, 2: 80.
15. This was also the opinion of the French officer in charge of the attack on Grand-Pré, Duvivier. He defended himself at his court-martial on the charge of failure, by protesting that Acadian neutrality had rendered his task impossible. Robert Rumilly, *Histoire des Acadiens*, 2 vol. (Montréal: Fides, 1955), 1: 304.
16. Letter from the inhabitants of Minas, Rivière aux Canards and Piziquid to Duvivier and de Gannes, 13 October 1744, printed in ibid., 1: 304-5.
17. The full story of the Acadian years in exile remains to be told, but some indication of the strength of the community is given in Naomi Griffiths, "Acadians in Exile: the Experience of the Acadians in the British Seaports", *Acadiensis*, IV (Autumn 1974): 67-84.
18. Gisa I. Hynes, "Some Aspects of the Demography of Port Royal, 1650-1755", *Acadiensis*, III (Autumn 1973): 7-8.
19. For a good overview of what is available, see Muriel K. Roy, "Peuplement et croissance démographique en Acadie", in Daigle, *Acadiens des Maritimes*, pp. 135-208.
20. Hynes, "Demography of Port Royal", pp. 10-11. In recent years scholarship about demography has been prolific. One of the most readable accounts of the French reality during the late seventeenth century is that of Pierre Goubert: "In 1969 the average expectation of life is something over seventy

years. In 1661 it was probably under twenty-five . . . Out of every hundred children born, twenty-five died before they were one year old, another twenty-five never reached twenty and a further twenty-five perished between the ages of twenty and forty-five. Only about ten ever made her sixties." Pierre Goubert, *Louis XIV and Twenty Million Frenchmen* (New York Random House, 1972), p. 21. On the demography of New England, see esp. James H. Cassedy, *Demography in Early America: Beginnings of the Statistical Mind, 1600-1800* (Cambridge, Mass.: Harvard University Press, 1969). Cassedy points out that the demographic scale was at first weighted towards mortality, but at a different time for each colony, "this precarious balance righted itself". The incidence of disease, malnutrition and frontier warfare were demonstrably greater for New England than they were for Acadia. The conditions of life along the St. Lawrence were much closer to those along the Bay of Fundy. In the eighteenth century the population of Canada doubled every thirty years. In Acadia, however, the increase was even higher: it doubled every fifteen years between 1671 and 1714, and every twenty years between 1714 and 1755. Furthermore, migration was a minimal factor in Acadian demography after 1740. On Canada, see Jacques Henripin, *La population canadienne au début du XVIIIe siècle* (Paris: Institut national d'études démographiques, 1954); on Acadia, see Roy, "Peuplement", p. 152.

21. Father Felix Pain to the governor of Isle Royale, September 1713, printed in Clark, *Acadia*, p. 187.

22. Sieur de Dièreville, *Relation of the Voyage to Port Royal in Acadia or New France*, ed. J.C. Webster (Toronto: Champlain Society, 1933), p. 93.

23. Public Archives of Canada (hereafter PAC), MG 11, CO 217, vol. 5, Phillipps to the Board of Trade, 2 September 1730 (PAC reel C-9120).

24. Hynes, "Demography of Port Royal", p. 10.

25. Ibid., pp. 10-11.

26. Clark, *Acadia*, pp. 200f, arrived at somewhat different statistics, concluding that the average family size was closer to four or five.

27. Massignon, *Parlers français* 1:45; Arsenault, *Généalogie*, 1: 432, 433; 2: 666.

28. Ibid., 1: 518.

29. This calculation rests partly upon the assumption that the Acadians followed a common contemporary practice of using the name of a child that died for the next-born of the same sex.

30. Arsenault, *Généalogie*, 1: 518; 2: 666, 667f.

31. PAC, MG 11, CO 217, vol. 2 (PAC reel C-9119).

32. These figures are my own estimations, based upon the work of Clark, *Acadia*, p. 216, and the overview by Roy, "Peuplement", pp. 134-207.

33. "A Brief Survey of Nova Scotia" (MS in Library of the Royal Artillary Regiment, Woolwich, n.d.), 2: 25-26, cited in Clark, *Acadia*, p. 217.

34. There is considerable debate about the kin system of these households. Grandparents can only have lived in one home, and there is still debate on how siblings linked house-keeping arrangements.

35. Dièreville, *Relation*, p. 256.

36. PAC, MG 1, Series C 11 D, vol. 3, pp. 199-203, Villebon to the Minister, 27 October 1694.

37. Cited in Clark, *Acadia*, p. 237.

38. Captain John Knox, *An Historical Journal of the Campaigns in North America for the Years 1757, 1758, 1759 and 1760*, ed. A.B. Doughty, 3 vol. (Toronto, 1914-18), 1: 105.

39. PAC, AC 2B, p. 12, "Supplied from Acadia entering Louisbourg, 1740", printed in Clark, *Acadia*, p. 259.

40. L.U. Fontaine, *Voyage de Sieur de Dièreville en Acadia* (Québec, 1885), p. 56.

41. "Supplies from Acadia", in Clark, *Acadia*, p. 259; and "Report of custom collector Newton" (PAC, AC, NSA-26, 29-33), printed in A. Shortt, VK Johnston and F. Lanctot, eds. *Currency, Exchange and Finance in Nova Scotia, with Prefatory Documents, 1675-1758* (Ottawa, 1933), pp. 223-24.

42. PAC, AC, NSA-26, 52, cited in Clark, *Acadia*, p. 258. See also the chart of Louisbourg trade on pp. 324-25.

43. PAC, AC, NSA-26, 51, cited in Clark, *Acadia*, p. 258.

44. For example, the Acadians sent to Maryland and South Carolina were able to purchase ships. See PAC, NS A/60, "Circular to the governors on the continent, July 1st, 1756, Halifax".

45. Morris, "A Brief Survey", 2: 4, quoted in Clark, *Acadia*, p. 244.

46. Ibid., p. 246.

47. Fontaine, *Voyage*, p. 56.

48. Observations made by Moise de Les Derniers shortly after 1755 and printed in Casgrain, *Un pèlerinage au pays d'Évangéline* (Paris, 1889), App. III, p. 115.

49. Dièreville, *Relations*, p. 96.

50. It was Perrot who first commented upon this in 1686 (PAC, AC, C11D-2[1], 119, mémoires généraux); and many later observers, such as Dièreville and Phillipps, insinuated similar flaws.

51. Clark, *Acadia*, p. 232.

52. PAC, MG1, series C11D, vol. 2, pp. 96-106, report on Menneval, 10 September 1688.

53. R. Hale, "Journal of a Voyage to Nova Scotia Made in 1731 by Robert Hale of Beverley", *The*

Essex Institute Historical Collections, XLII (July 1906): 233.

54. Comments on the litigious nature of the Acadians span all regimes. See Clark, *Acadia,* p. 198, and Brebner, *New England Outpost,* p. 140.

55. In particular, note the trouble that Subercase faced collecting taxes, in Shortt et al., *Currency,* p. 16.

56. Dièreville, *Relation,* p. 93.

57. Ibid., p. 96.

58. Guillaume Thomas François Raynal, *Histoire philosophique et politique des établissements et du commerce des Européens dans les deux Indes* (Paris, 1778), 6: 309.

59. Moise de les Derniers, cited in Casgrain, *Un pèlerinage,* p. 155.

60. Massignon, *Parlers français,* 2: 548, 1316. The *bûche à pilon* is illustrated in Paul Doucet, *Vie de nos ancêtres en Acadie — l'alimentation* (Moncton: Éditions d'Acadie, 1980), p. 17.

61. Deschamps, cited in Clark, *Acadia,* p. 237.

62. Massignon, *Parlers français,* 2: 550, 1320.

63. Ibid., 2: 551, 1322; Ph.F. Bourgeois, *Vie de l'Abbé François-Xavier LaFrance* (Montréal, 1925), p. 83.

64. *Les Guides Bleus de Bretagne* (Paris, 1967), p. 662.

65. Bourgeois, *Vie de l'abbé LaFrance,* p. 83.

66. Dièreville, *Relation,* pp. 266, 110.

67. Records of the complaints of Acadians exiled to Brittany, described by Naomi Griffiths, "Petitions of Acadian Exiles, 1755-1785: A Neglected Source", *Histoire sociale — Social History,* XI (May 1978): 215-23.

68. Massignon, *Parlers français,* 2: 648, 1702.

69. Griffiths, "Petitions of Acadian Exile", pp. 218f.

70. A.M. MacMechan, ed., *Nova Scotia Archives, III: Original Minutes of H.M. Council at Annapolis Royal, 1720-1739* (Halifax, 1908), pp. 112, 122.

71. Jean-Claude Dupont, *Héritage d'Acadie* (Québec: Leméac, 1977), p. 172, and *Histoire populaire de l'Acadie* (Montréal: Leméac, 1979).

72. MacMechan, *Nova Scotia Archives, III,* pp. 3, 17.

73. W.P. Bell, *The "Foreign Protestants" and the Settlement of Nova Scotia: The History of a Piece of Arrested British Colonial Policy in the Eighteenth Century* (Toronto: University of Toronto Press, 1961), pp. 44-45, 64-85, 328-35.

74. Griffiths, "Petitions of Acadian Exiles", pp. 216f.

75. Jean Daigle, "Les Relations commerciales de l'Acadie avec le Massachusetts: le cas de Charles-Amador de Saint-Étienne de la Tour, 1695-1697", *Revue de l'Université de Moncton,* IX (1976): 353-61.

76. Clark, *Acadia,* pp. 203-4.

77. Têtu et Gagnon, *Mandements, lettres pastorales et circulaires des évêques de Québec, 1888,* pp. 15-16, reprinted in E. de Grace, G. Desjardins, R.-A. Mallet, *Histoire d'Acadie par les Textes,* 4 fascicules (Fredericton: Ministère de l'éducation du Nouveau-Brunswick, 1976), 1 (1604-1760): 19.

78. A most interesting question which needs further investigation and which reinforces the theory of Acadian respect for, but not subservience to, the Catholic church, is the matter of dispensations for marriage between second cousins accorded at Annapolis Royal between 1727 and 1755, the usual reason for such dispensations being pre-marital pregnancy. Cf. Clark, *Acadia,* pp. 203-4, *passim.*

79. Massignon, *Parlers français,* 2: 691-99.

80. Not only fiddle-heads but also *titines de souris (salicornia Europaia)* and *passe-pierre (saxifraga Virginiensis).* See ibid., 1: 183.

81. Knox, *Historical Journal,* 1:94-6, quoted in A.G. Doughty, *The Acadian Exiles* (Toronto: Glasgow, Brook & Company, 1916), p. 40.

Topic Four
The Conquest

The Seven Years' War in Europe, which set France, Austria, Sweden, and
a few small German states against Britain and Prussia, might well be termed
the First World War. Hostilities were waged from 1756 to 1763 over as large
a portion of the world as in 1914-1918. Britain engaged in naval campaigns
against France (and later Spain) in the Atlantic, the Caribbean, the Mediter-
ranean, and the Indian Ocean.

In North America the struggle between Britain and France had begun
in 1754 with a clash between French troops and Virginia militia in the Ohio
country, the result of an attempt by the American colonists to expel the
French from the area immediately west of the Alleghany Mountains. The
following year the British under General Braddock experienced a disastrous
defeat at Monongahela (present-day Pittsburg, Pennsylvania). In 1756 this
North American struggle merged into the Seven Years' War. Until 1757 New
France, although outnumbered in population twenty to one by the American
colonies, continued to hold the upper hand.

The whole character of the war changed in 1758 with the accession of
William Pitt as England's prime minister. Pitt regarded the North American
campaign as a primary, not as a secondary, theatre of the war. Instantly he
redirected the emphasis on Britain's war effort to a concentration on North
America. The British fleet, which had twice as many ships as its French
counterpart, blockaded the French navy, keeping it to its home ports thus
cutting off supplies and troop reinforcements to New France. Yet despite
the extent of the British commitment, New France held out for another
two years, until 1760. W.J. Eccles chronicles the final round of conflict for
the control of Northeastern North American in "The Preemptive Conquest,
1749-1763," a chapter from *France in America*.

It has been the impact, more than the events of the Conquest, that has
concerned historians. Guy Frégault in his short pamphlet, *Canadian Society
in the French Regime*, evaluates the impact of the Conquest by comparing
French-Canadian society before, and after, the event. Another French Canadian historian, Fernand Ouellet (a summary of his views appears in Topic
Six, "Post-Conquest Quebec") challenges Frégault's views.

For a thorough discussion of the various interpretations of the Conquest, see Ramsay Cook, "The Historian and Nationalism," in *Canada and the French-Canadian Question* (Toronto: Macmillan, 1966), pp. 119-142; and his essay, "Conquêtisme," in *The Maple Leaf Forever* (Toronto: Macmillan, 1971), pp. 99-113.

For a review of the nearly one-half century of armed conflict between the French and English in the New World, students should consult I.K. Steel's *Guerillas and Grenadiers* (Toronto: The Ryerson Press, 1969). For a more detailed examination of New France's final years, see George F.G. Stanley's *New France: The Last Phase, 1744-1760* (Toronto: McClelland and Stewart, 1968), and Guy Frégault's *La Guerre de la conquête* (1955), translated by Margaret Cameron as *Canada: The War of the Conquest* (Toronto: Oxford University Press, 1969). C.P. Stacey's *Quebec, 1759: The Siege and the Battle* (Toronto: Macmillan, 1959) examines that crucial year in the struggle. See as well his "Generals and Generalship before Quebec, 1759-1760," *Canadian Historical Association Report*, 1959, pp. 1-15. The articles by W.J. Eccles "The French Forces in North America during the Seven Years' War," and C.P. Stacey "The British Forces in North America during the Seven Years' War," in the *Dictionary of Canadian Biography*, Volume III (1741-1770), pp. xv-xxiii, and pp. xxiv-xxx, review the military strengths of the two opponents.

126

The Preemptive Conquest, 1749-1763*
W.J. ECCLES

In the Americas the War of the Austrian Succession had changed nothing and settled nothing. After 1748 France wanted an enduring peace to rebuild and restore, but the British commercial community wanted a renewal of the war at the earliest opportunity. The latter powerful group, with Newcastle and Pitt as its political agents, was convinced that peace was good for France, but bad for England. The struggle just ended had achieved sufficient success to demonstrate that were Britain to concentrate her resources on a commercial war, France as a competitor in world markets could be destroyed and British merchants could then pick up the pieces.[1] This aggressive policy found a counterpart in North America where the planters and land speculators of Virginia and Pennsylvania were now eyeing the rich lands of the Ohio Valley. Land companies were formed in both provinces to seize and parcel out these lands for settlement. Meanwhile, fur traders, who in some instances were also agents of the land companies, had established trading posts in the region and drawn the local tribes into a commercial alliance.[2]

The French in Canada were acutely aware of the danger posed by this encroachment on lands they claimed. Were it to go unchallenged the English

*From *France in America*, by W.J. Eccles. Copyright by Harper and Row. Reprinted by permission.

colonials would not only threaten their hold on the northwest fur trade but, by expanding down the Ohio to the Mississippi, would eventually sever communications between Canada and Louisiana. Looking even further ahead, were the English to seize and settle the lands between the Alleghenies and the Mississippi their rapidly expanding population would grow immeasurably in numbers and wealth, and with that, England's commerce. Since military power was determined to a considerable degree by the size of a country's population, by the number of trained men with muskets that could be put in the field, the much larger population of France compared to England's would eventually be offset by that of the English colonies. In America, therefore, English expansion had to be checked.

At Quebec the governor general, the comte de La Galissonière, took note of these dangers and recommended measures to circumvent them. He proposed that garrisoned forts be established in the Ohio Valley and the Indian tribes brought into the French alliance. In this way English expansion would be blocked. But more than that, from Canada and the proposed Ohio bases, the English colonies could be threatened by Canadian and Indian war parties. All that would be needed was a small force of French regulars to garrison the bases. In the previous wars the Canadians had more than held their own against the English colonials. In Britain's balance of trade those colonies were such an important item the English would have to respond to such a threat. They would have to send troops to aid the ineffectual colonial militia, and this would require the support of sizable elements of the Royal Navy which would then not be available for attacks on the French West Indies, or French maritime commerce, or to blockade the French ports as they had done so successfully in the past war. In other words, the role of the French in North America was to be that of a fortress, with a small garrison to tie down a much larger force of the enemy.[3]

With the approval of the Ministry of Marine, La Galissonière lost no time initiating this policy. In 1749 he dispatched an expedition, led by the veteran western commander Pierre-Joseph de Céloron de Blainville, to the Ohio to show the flag, claim the region for France, and drive out the Anglo-American traders. Céloron discovered that British infiltration of the region and influence over the Indian nations was far more serious than had been imagined. La Galissonière's successor, Pierre-Jacques de Taffanel, marquis de la Jonquière, strengthened the French forts in the Great Lakes area, but did little more. The governor of Louisiana, however, Canadian-born Pierre de Rigaud, marquis de Vaudreuil, showed a greater awareness of the need for action. He strengthened the garrisons at the posts in the Illinois country and began the construction of Fort Chartres, near Kaskaskia; but even after receiving reinforcements in 1751, he had only some two thousand indifferent regulars to hold the Mississippi Valley from New Orleans to the Illinois River. The French hold on this region had to depend on retaining the active allegiance of the Indian nations.[4]

On the Atlantic coast the French greatly strengthened the defenses of Louisbourg and sent out fifteen hundred garrison troops under officers who

127

this time maintained discipline. Some of the Acadians of Nova Scotia were enticed to remove to Île Royale (Cape Breton); merchants and fishermen, with their families, reestablished themselves there until by 1752 the population stood at 5,845.[5] Other Acadians were persuaded to settle on Île St. Jean (Prince Edward Island), and at Beaubassin where the French had a fort. The swift economic recovery of Louisbourg fully justified the sacrifices made to regain it at the peace table. The fishery expanded rapidly, and the old trade with Canada, the West Indies, and New England throve. Yet in this region too the French had to count on the Indian tribes, the Micmacs and Abenaquis, and, hopefully, on the Acadians still resident in Nova Scotia. The English, however, were fully conscious of this revival of French power that threatened their North Atlantic trade. In 1749 they began the construction of a naval base and fortress at Halifax, which not only countered the menace to English shipping but precluded the possibility of the Acadians liberating Nova Scotia.

128

In the west the French seized the initiative.[6] Unlike the Anglo-Americans, the governor general of New France was able to mobilize the colony's entire military resources with no regard for cost. In 1753 he dispatched two thousand men to Lake Erie to construct a road from southeast of that lake to the headwaters of the Ohio and build a chain of forts at strategic points. The Indian nations, impressed by this show of strength, began to sever their trade connections with the Anglo-Americans. All that the latter could do to counter this erosion of their position was to send a major of militia, George Washington, with an escort of seven men and a letter from Governor Robert Dinwiddie of Virginia, protesting the French invasion of lands claimed by Great Britain and demanding their immediate withdrawal. Jacques Legardeur de Saint-Pierre, commandant at Fort Le Boeuf, a tough veteran of the west, received Washington politely, but contemptuously rejected his blustering ultimatum.

The following year a small force of Virginia militia attempted to establish a fort at the junction of the Ohio and the Monongahela. Before they were well begun a French force, five hundred strong, swept down the upper Ohio and forced them to retire over the crest of the Alleghenies, which the French claimed to be the border between their territory and that of the English colonies. The French now built Fort Duquesne on the site and thereby dominated the whole region. The Anglo-American response was to send George Washington back, at the head of a motley collection of militia, to drive the French out. They ambushed a small French party sent to order them to retire. The officer in command, Ensign Joseph Coulon de Villiers de Jumonville, and nine of his men were killed, twenty-one taken prisoner. This was the first clash of arms in what was to become a global war. Significantly, it began while both powers were at peace. It also began under very dubious circumstances.[7]

The French reacted swiftly. Washington, with some 350 undisciplined colonial militia, made a stand at Great Meadows, where 500 French, after a short engagement, compelled them to surrender. Washington signed the capitulation terms without taking the trouble to inquire too closely into their meaning and subsequently dishonored them, then fled precipitately with his men back to Virginia. In his haste he abandoned his baggage containing his journal. The contents of that journal were to be used by the French government to brand the English as perfidious throughout Europe.[8] Washington's ignominious defeat brought the last of the wavering Indian nations to the French cause. From that point on, the English had not a single Indian ally in the west, while the strength of the French was enhanced immeasurably. At every turn of events the French had overreached the Anglo-Americans. They were securely in possession of the Ohio country, from its upper reaches to the Mississippi, and from their advanced forts war parties could fall on the rear of the English colonies at any time. For the time being, however, they kept their Indian allies securely on leash, determined on no account to give the enemy an excuse for attack.

The English colonies, with the exception of New York, which had no desire to have its profitable contraband trade with the French colonies disrupted, *129* clamored for war to drive the French out of North America once and for all. In the previous wars England had furnished scant aid to her American subjects. This time the war party, led by Cumberland, Henry Fox, and William Pitt, forced Newcastle to agree to full-scale hostilities against the French in America and on the seas without bothering with the formality of declaring war.[9]

In October, 1754, Major General Edward Braddock, commanding two battalions, eight hundred men, was ordered to North America with orders to capture Fort Duquesne, while the colonial forces attacked Fort Niagara, the French forts on Lake Champlain, and those on the Nova Scotia border. This force could not sail until the following April, and on the eve of its departure the French obtained a copy of Braddock's orders. Immediately, they raised six battalions, three thousand men from the better regiments of the *troupes de terre*.[10] In April they too were ready to sail. When the British cabinet learned of this they issued secret orders to Admiral Edward Boscawen with two squadrons composed of nineteen ships of the line and two frigates to intercept the French convoy, seize the ships, and if resistance were offered, give battle. A few days after he sailed, on April 27, the French ambassador to the Court of St. James's received word that Boscawen had orders to attack the French squadron. On May 10, however, two cabinet ministers dined at his house and cheerfully reassured him that such rumors were completely false, that no such orders had been issued.[11]

Off Newfoundland Boscawen succeeded in intercepting only three ships of the French convoy. When Captain Toussaint Hocquart hailed Captain Richard Howe, asking if they were at peace or war, the reply came, "At peace, at peace," followed by shattering broadsides.[12] Two of the French ships were captured; the third escaped to Louisbourg. The rest of the convoy, with all but eight companies of troops, and with the newly appointed governor general of New France, Pierre de Rigaud, marquis de Vaudreuil, on board, reached Louisbourg and Quebec safely.[13] Elsewhere the Royal

Navy had better luck. More than three hundred French ships and eight thousand sailors were seized in English ports or on the high seas.[14] This was a serious blow to French maritime strength. Needless to say, the French lost no time proclaiming the English to have been guilty of the blackest treachery.[15]

On land in North America, now that hostilities had begun in earnest, but still without a declaration of war, the British did not fare so well. Braddock, at the head of 2,200 men, British regulars and colonial troops, got his army over the mountains and within a few miles of Fort Duquesne — by itself no mean feat. In an almost forlorn hope Captain Daniel de Beaujeu led 108 Troupes de la Marine, 146 Canadian militia, and 600 Indians to oppose him. The ensuing clash was a disaster for the British. The Canadian and Indian forces took cover on the forested flank of the enemy, encumbered by siege artillery and a vast wagon train. The measured British volleys had little effect against the concealed foe. The Canadians and Indians advanced close. Noting that the British ranks reloaded to ordered drumbeats, they picked off the officers and drummers.[16] Confusion, then panic, spread through the British ranks. The battle became a slaughter. The troops broke and fled. More than two-thirds of the British force were killed or captured, along with the cannon and a vast store of supplies. This, at a cost to the French and their allies of twenty-three killed and twenty wounded.[17]

In the mortally wounded Braddock's captured baggage the plans for the attacks on the other fronts were found. Thus, by the time the ill-organized colonial forces had mustered for an attack on Niagara, the French had moved reinforcements to oppose them. The acting commander in chief of the Anglo-Americans, William Shirley, governor of Massachusetts, after his 2,400 colonial troops had been reduced to 1,400 by sickness and desertion, abandoned the campaign. On the Lake Champlain front the Anglo-Americans failed to reach the lake, being forestalled by the French, led by the commander of the regular troops Jean-Armand, baron de Dieskau, who had the misfortune to be wounded and captured in the brief and inconclusive engagement that both sides claimed as a victory.

Only on the Acadian frontier did the British enjoy any success. Fort Beauséjour, at the foot of the Bay of Fundy, was captured and the threat to the English in Nova Scotia effectively removed. Then followed one of the most controversial acts of the war, the expulsion of the Acadians.[18] Not only were the Acadians, both those captured in arms and those who had sworn the oath to His Britannic Majesty, expelled in brutal fashion, but the Indians were likewise driven off their land to make way for New England settlers. Many of the Acadians managed to elude the New England troops sent to seize them, and made their way to Quebec. They constituted a warning to the Canadians of what they could expect should they be conquered. Nothing could have been better calculated to make them fight with a ferocity born of despair. The French authorities at Quebec made the most of this.

Although war had not been declared, and would not be until May, 1756,

130

the British assaults on New France permitted Vaudreuil to take the offensive. Indian war parties led by Canadian officers ravaged the frontiers of Virginia and Pennsylvania; but Vaudreuil's strategy was defensive. His purpose was to use the advanced French bases in the west to hold the Indian nations in the French alliance, thereby offsetting the Anglo-American superiority in numbers. Thus small Canadian and Indian guerrilla detachments could force the British to maintain large defensive forces on their frontier. To take the offensive against these bases the British would require an army, have to build roads through the wilderness to move and supply it, and employ large bodies of men to maintain their supply lines. With their command of the rivers the French could move men and supplies much more easily than could the British. Moreover, the Anglo-American militia usually fled at the mere rumored approach of the enemy.[19]

On the New York frontier Vaudreuil's strategy was to block the Lake Champlain invasion route by maintaining a strong garrison at Fort St. Fréderic and by building an advanced fort at the head of the lake, Fort Carillon, later known as Ticonderoga. When the enemy attempted to attack Canada by this route, a relatively small force could delay them at Carillon and hold them at the narrows by Fort St. Fréderic while the Canadians and Indians harassed their supply lines. Carillon would also serve as an advance base to threaten Albany and the American frontier settlements, thereby containing sizable enemy forces. The main dangers to Canada were the threat of invasion from Lake Champlain, from Lake Ontario down the St. Lawrence, and a maritime assault up the river against Quebec. On the Lake Ontario front, the English fort at Oswego was the major threat, and Vaudreuil made plans in 1755 to destroy it. As for an assault on Quebec, the best that could be done there was to harass an invading fleet as it came up river, then rely on the natural defenses of the town to prevent its capture.

If necessary, the extended defense lines could be pulled back to Niagara, Fort Frontenac, and Fort St. Fréderic. The enemy's communications and supply lines would then be lengthened and more vulnerable to attack by the French irregulars. Thus the British would have to employ vastly superior forces, and their need to build roads through the forest to supply their armies on the periphery of New France, growing ever longer, would limit the number of troops they could bring into action.[20] The British could, of course, transport whole armies to America without much danger of attack from the smaller French fleet.[21] Moreover, Britain could use ports from Halifax to Charleston; Canada had only one. An English fleet in the St. Lawrence could isolate Canada completely. Without reinforcements and supplies from France, the colony could be starved into surrender. Yet, not until 1760 did the Royal Navy succeed in blocking the St. Lawrence. French supply ships reached Quebec every year until the city fell. Much, however, depended on the food the colony could itself provide, and this became crucial with all the additional mouths to feed, the army, the Acadians, and the allied Indians who had to be fed and provided with military supplies before they would take the field. When the crops failed in 1758 famine threatened, and inadequate food supplies, to some degree, dictated military tactics; yet food

131

was never the major factor that it has sometimes been claimed. The people went hungry at times, but they did not starve. It was not a food shortage that caused the eventual fall of New France.

In 1756 a replacement for Dieskau arrived in the person of Louis-Joseph, marquis de Montcalm-Gozon de Saint-Véran, a battle-tried regimental commander. He had the rank of *maréchal de camp*, equivalent to major-general, and command over the *troupes de terre* only. He was subordinate to the governor general, Vaudreuil, who had overall command of all the military forces, *troupes de terre*, Troupes de la Marine, the naval detachments, and the Canadian militia; all told, some 16,000 men. In addition there were the Indian allies. One reason for Vaudreuil's appointment as governor general was his intimate knowledge of, and ability to control, these proud, independent, and unpredictable warriors. Although he had served in the Troupes de la Marine from childhood and in 1738 had been recommended by Governor General Beauharnais for the post of commander of the companies stationed in Canada, he had served only briefly in one campaign in the west. Most of his experience had been administrative, lately as governor of Louisiana, where he had performed very creditably.[22]

Unfortunately, Montcalm and Vaudreuil quickly came to detest each other. Both were vain, each very jealous of his authority, each convinced of the other's incompetence and his own superior judgment. Vaudreuil did, however, know the country and what warfare in it entailed. He could, as much as anyone could, handle the Indians; and he was respected by both the Canadian militia and the Troupes de la Marine. He had contrived the strategy of extended defense lines and wanted to take full advantage of the differing capabilities of his motley forces. Montcalm rejected this strategic concept. He recommended that the French abandon the Ohio Valley and Lake Champlain, then concentrate the forces at the colony's inner defense line.[23] He wished the war to be conducted on European lines, sieges and set battles, in which superior discipline, training, and his leadership would bring victory. The sort of warfare that the Canadians excelled at he regarded with contempt, as accomplishing no worthwhile purpose. As for the Indian allies, he had no use for them at all.[24] But his greatest weakness was his confirmed defeatism. He quickly convinced himself that the French position was hopeless and devoted much of his time and energy to casting blame on Vaudreuil for the disasters he was sure would ensue. Nor did he make any attempt to hide his opinion of the governor general. He criticized Vaudreuil and all things Canadian before his officers, thereby fanning the latent hostility between the Canadian officers of the Troupes de la Marine and those newly come from France with the *troupes de terre* who looked down on the colonials. Naturally, the Canadian officers, with their much greater experience in forest warfare and their unblemished record of victory, resented the attitude of Montcalm and his staff. Montcalm's defeatism, and his attitude toward the Canadians, could not fail to sap the morale of both troops and militia.

Another factor that helped to lower morale, and to some degree to hinder

132

the French war effort — although not to the extent that has been claimed — was the malversation of the intendant François Bigot. By a series of clever devices he and his associates mulcted the Crown of millions of livres. Supplies sent to the colony, or produced in the colony, were bought at low prices by Bigot's agents, then sold at upwards of thirty times as much to the Crown. That Bigot was able to organize this very lucrative looting operation and get away with it for so long was a measure of his cleverness and ability.[25] He was an extremely efficient administrator, and although a scoundrel, he did keep the army and the colony supplied. To what degree military operations were hindered by his activities is extremely difficult to discern.

Despite these internal problems, the French forces won a succession of victories during the first two years of hostilities. Before Montcalm's arrival Vaudreuil had made plans to destroy Oswego and remove that threat to French communications with the west. In February, 1756, he sent a war party which, by destroying Fort Bull, cut Oswego's supply route to Schenectady. Other detachments hovered about Oswego, cutting down the supply columns, keeping it blockaded. In July Montcalm, with many misgivings, took command of a three-thousand-man assault force which captured Oswego after a four-day siege. Thirty Americans were killed, seventeen hundred taken prisoner, and a vast store of boats, cannon, and supplies captured, with only thirty casualties among the French. This was stunning blow to the Anglo-Americans, opening up the northwest frontier of New York to invasion. The entire western frontier of the English colonies was now ravaged by Canadian and Indian war parties. The early confidence that Canada would quickly be destroyed was replaced by fear that the French would soon invade the English colonies in force. Pleas for aid, recriminations, fears of conquest were voiced in the middle colonies. Far from winning the war, they were losing it.

133

The following year Vaudreuil continued this strategy of forcing the Anglo-Americans onto the defensive in the west with his raiding parties, supplied and sent out from Fort Duquesne.[26] On the central front Vaudreuil had to expect the British to mass their forces for an assault on Lake Champlain to drive the French back and open the invasion route into Canada. To forfend this he sent Montcalm with 3,600 men and 1,500 Indian allies to destroy the advanced British fort, William Henry, and then press south to threaten Albany. Arriving at the fort on August 3, Montcalm went through all the motions of a siege in the accepted European style and mounted his batteries. On the ninth the garrison commander, Colonel George Monro, asked for terms. He, with his 2,331-man garrison, was granted the honors of war and freedom to withdraw on condition they did not serve in operations against the French for eighteen months. After they had surrendered and were marching off, Montcalm's Indian allies, enraged at seeing their hated foe walk away unharmed, and inflamed by the liquor with which the Americans had foolishly tried to appease them, fell on the straggling columns. The French then did everything they could to stop the massacre, but twenty-nine were killed, over a hundred taken prisoner.

Regardless of this nasty episode, which afforded the British an opportunity to brand the French as war criminals, Montcalm had dealt the Anglo-Americans a severe blow. Their forward base was destroyed, they were deprived of a large body of troops and large stores of arms and cannon, and some three thousand barrels of pork and other valuable food supplies were added to the French stores. All this at a cost of thirteen killed and forty wounded. The Anglo-American troops defending the northern front were completely demoralized; Montcalm's were ready for anything. At New York the Provincial Council waited to hear that the French had taken the next strongpoint, Fort Edward, and fully expected Albany to fall. They wrote to Lord Loudoun, the commander in chief, who was at Halifax, "We may fear New York also."[27] Yet although Montcalm knew the dispirited and disorganized state of the enemy, that Fort Edward was only sixteen miles away, that its capture would have created panic in Albany and further reduced the offensive spirit of the Anglo-Americans, he refused to follow up his victory. He claimed the road was bad, his men worn out, and the militia needed back on their farms for the harvest. Since the harvest in Canada did not usually begin until September, even if the militia could not have been kept in the field beyond the first week of that month, it still allowed the French more than a fortnight to take Fort Edward, and that would have been enough time as things stood. Montcalm here betrayed his grave weakness as a commander. He was not aggressive; he could not seize the initiative when the opportunity presented itself. He preferred to react to the enemy's moves rather than make the enemy react to his.

134

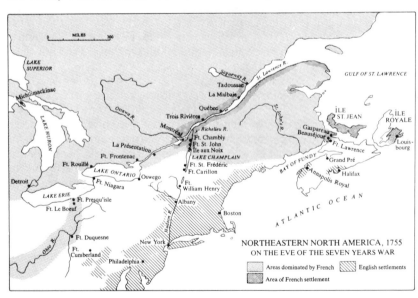

NORTHEASTERN NORTH AMERICA, 1755
ON THE EVE OF THE SEVEN YEARS WAR

Vaudreuil, of course, was infuriated by Montcalm's failure to execute his orders to march on Fort Edward. Their latent animosity now surfaced, and they quarreled openly. Their dispatches to the minister made their attitude all too plain. For his part, Vaudreuil infuriated Montcalm by taking credit for the victories; first at Oswego, then at Fort William Henry, as though he had commanded the troops during the actions, from his desk at Quebec.

Despite these victories, Canada had to have continued support from France to withstand the assaults that had been delayed but were sure to come.[28] Vaudreuil sent one of his Canadian officers to Versailles to explain the strategic and tactical situation and outline the additional forces needed to defend New France. He also allowed Montcalm to send two of his officers, Colonel Louis-Antoine de Bougainville and the commissary Doreil, to add their pleas. They were listened to much more attentively than was Vaudreuil's emissary. The dispute between the governor general and Montcalm was resolved in the latter's favor. Montcalm was promoted to lieutenant-general and given overall command of all the military forces in the colony. Vaudreuil *135* now had to defer to Montcalm's decisions in all military matters. In addition, the government ordered that Vaudreuil's extended lines defensive strategy be abandoned and Montcalm's instituted. The French forces were to fall back on the settlements in the St. Lawrence Valley as the enemy advanced and strive only to hold them on the doorstep of the colony proper. This meant that the enemy would be allowed to advance almost unopposed through the wilderness and consolidate their supply lines for a massed assault. Everything, therefore, would depend on the ability of the French forces to hold Quebec and defeat much larger enemy armies south and west of Montreal. The French were, in short, to conduct the war in Canada on European lines and strive to hold the rump of New France in the hope that some part of the territory could be retained until hostilities ceased. If France still had a foot-hold in North America it would be in a much stronger position when the bargaining began at the peace table. Montcalm, through his emissaries, had painted such a bleak picture of the military position that the King's council apparently decided it would be folly to commit large forces in a forlorn hope. Thus fewer than five hundred replacements for the army in Canada accompanied Bougainville on his return to Quebec, raising the effective strength of the regular troops to less than six thousand.

Ironically, the French government, although its armies in the field had won startling victories, reducing the authorities in some of the English colonies to plead for peace on any terms before further defeats rendered even those terms unobtainable, had adopted the defeatist attitude of Montcalm, whereas the British government, now dominated by Pitt, took determined measures to drive the French, not just out of the territory claimed by Britain, but out of North America. More British regiments were shipped to the colonies until more than 20,000 regulars of an army now totaling 140,000 soldiers and marines were in the theater, and one-quarter of the Royal Navy, in addition to 22,000 colonial troops and militia. The French army, on the other hand, had only twelve of its 395 battalions serving in Canada and

Louisbourg plus 2,000 Troupes de la Marine.[29] To that degree, fortress Canada was fulfilling its intended role in French imperial strategy; with a handful of troops it was tying down a much larger enemy force, preventing its being employed in some other theater.

In 1758 Pitt, who dictated military strategy, planned three concerted campaigns against Louisbourg, Quebec, and Fort Duquesne. Louisbourg, without a strong naval detachment, withstood a sixty-day siege by 8,000 troops under Jeffrey Amherst, but under fierce bombardment had finally to capitulate. It had, however, held out long enough to force the abandonment of the intended maritime assault on Quebec for that year. Brigadier James Wolfe acidly commented: "If this force had been properly manag'd, there was an end of the French colony in North America in one Campaign."[30] The fall of Louisbourg, by removing that potential threat to British shipping in the North Atlantic, allowed Pitt to transfer a large naval force to the West Indies. The object there was to capture Martinique to exchange at the peace table for Minorca, taken by the French in June, 1756, and so avoid the necessity to give back Louisbourg. The French defenses of Martinique proving too strong, the assault was transferred to Guadeloupe. Not, however, until May 1, 1759, were that island's defenders forced to capitulate, but Pitt now had the gage his strategy required. The war had taken a new direction. Previously it had been waged for commercial aims. Now territorial conquest was the chief end.[31]

On the central Canadian front Major General James Abercromby massed an army of 15,000, 6,000 of them British regulars, to drive down Lake Champlain to the Richelieu and the heart of Canada. He got no farther than Ticonderoga, where Montcalm and 3,500 regulars and militia had hastily entrenched themselves behind a wall of logs and felled trees. Cannon would have blasted this breast-work asunder. Abercromby, however, chose to send his regulars against it in a frontal column attack. They suffered heavy losses, but returned again and again until even these disciplined troops could take no more. The British withdrew to Fort William Henry, their losses nearly 2,000 men. The French had lost only 527 killed and wounded. The demoralized British had suffered another stunning defeat. Their retreat was almost a rout. They abandoned boats, arms, and supplies, as though the devil had been after them. Although a large contingent of Canadians reached Montcalm immediately after his victory, he made no attempt to follow it up by pursuing the beaten foe. Vaudreuil pleaded with him to send raiding parties to harass the enemy and their supply lines, and hammer it home to them that the route to Canada was impregnable. Montcalm, however, appeared satisfied with what he had already accomplished. And certainly, he had put a stop to the drive on the colony for that year. But that was not enough.

In the west the British had better success. In August Lieutenant Colonel Bradstreet with nearly 3,000 men caught the French at Fort Frontenac off guard.[32] Although the fort was very poorly sited, its walls no protection against cannon fire, the commandant, Pierre-Jacques Payen de Noyan, conducted the defense very ineptly. With his armed sloops he could have intercepted the attackers in their bateaux and shot them out of the water. Instead they were allowed to land and bring up their cannon. Three days later the fort surrendered. After destroying the store of provisions, the small French fleet, and the fort itself, Bradstreet swiftly retired across the lake. It was not the destruction of the fort but the loss of the stores, and the boats to transport them to Niagara and the Ohio, that hurt the French.

Farther west the British slowly mounted a campaign to drive the French out of the Ohio Valley. Montcalm convinced himself that this was merely a feint to draw troops away from Lake Champlain. Unfortunately for the French, they were now deprived of their Indian allies in the midwest. In October the authorities of Pennsylvania had met with delegates of the war-weary Ohio tribes at Easton and there negotiated a peace, a principal condition of which was a renunciation by Pennsylvania of all claims to lands beyond the crest of the mountains. The Indians guilelessly assumed that the Americans would honor the treaty; thus having achieved their main objective, they withdrew from the war. When Brigadier-General John Forbes, whose forces had been badly mauled by small Canadian war parties, learned from a French prisoner that the garrison at Fort Duquesne was far less than the reputed thousand, and with the Indian menace removed, he pressed on against the fort. The commandant, François Le Marchand de Ligneris, his supplies almost exhausted, his men in like condition, stripped the fort of its cannon, blew it up, and retreated to Fort Machault, there to await reinforcements and supplies from Montreal. He fully intended, when they were received, to counterattack and drive the Anglo-Americans back over the mountains.

In Canada, that winter of 1758-1759, food supplies were again short. The mass of the population was reduced to bare subsistence rations. Not so their leaders. Bigot and his entourage wanted for nothing. Gambling for desperately high stakes was the principal amusement. Vaudreuil remained aloof. He knew that Bigot was protected by senior officials in the Ministry of Marine, and this likely explains why he did not use his authority to curb the excesses. Montcalm, in his journal and his correspondence, was bitterly critical, but felt that his presence was required at the constant round of dinners and balls with which the senior officials and his officers beguiled themselves during the long winter nights.

Another scourge, inflation, hit the junior officers hard. They were no longer paid in specie, but in postdated letters of credit to be redeemed three years hence. The merchants in the colony accepted them at a mere quarter of their face value. Lieutenants were paid 1,330 to 1,500 livres a year, and it cost them more than 7,500 to live. Fortunately, the ordinary soldiers who were billeted on the *habitants* when not on campaign did not suffer. They received their rations and worked for inflated wages, earning up to a pistole a day sawing firewood. Many of them married Canadian girls and were determined to remain in Canada when hostilities ended.

137

With the regular troops dispersed among the civilian population in this fashion, discipline suffered and training proved impossible. The battalion commanders did not know how many men they had on strength, except at the beginning of the campaigns in the spring and again in the autumn when muster parades were held. The lack of regular training exercises was to prove fatal. The reinforcements sent from France in 1757 had been a particularly poor lot; as casualties thinned the ranks of the regulars, Montcalm pressed Canadian militia into the battalions to maintain them at full strength. For the type of set battle that he wished to fight, it required eighteen months of training on the drill ground to turn a civilian into a soldier, capable of maneuvering en masse, marching up to the enemy and firing in volleys on command, and standing fast in the face of the enemy's volley or bayonet charge. By 1759 Montcalm's troops were no longer capable of that style of warfare. Although he and his staff officers in their letters and dispatches expressed nothing but defeatism and the belief that the colony was doomed — indeed, Montcalm eventually proposed retiring to Louisiana with the army should the British break through his lines — yet his second in command, the Chevalier de Lévis, and some at least of the junior officers were more sanguine about the outcome.[33]

Fortunately for the French, twenty-two supply ships reached Quebec in May, 1759, bringing enough food to keep the army in the field until the harvest. Hard on their heels, however, came the Royal Navy, bringing an army of 8,000 seasoned troops commanded by Major General James Wolfe, for an assault on the bastion of New France. On the Lake Champlain front Jeffrey Amherst, the commander in chief of the British forces in America, had massed an army of 6,236 regulars and provincials to dislodge the French from their forts. It took him a month to get his army in motion. The French officers had orders to fight delaying actions only at Carillon and St. Fréderic, then retire on Fort Île aux Noix to make a stand. After Amherst had spent several days preparing trenches and gun emplacements at Carillon the French mined the fort, lighted the fuses, and slipped away. They did the same at Fort St. Fréderic, but Amherst made no move to pursue them. Instead he devoted the remainder of the summer to repairing the fort at Ticonderoga and building a massive new fort near where Fort St. Fréderic had stood. The only purpose these forts could serve was to block an army advancing south from Canada. Were Quebec to be taken there was no danger whatsoever of that. Obviously, Amherst did not expect Quebec to fall. This was a view shared by others in the British forces.

In the west, de Ligneris renewed his raids on the British supply lines to Fort Pitt, constructed near the ruins of Fort Duquesne. He was, however, forced to desist and rush to the aid of the small garrison at Niagara, under siege by an American provincial army 2,500 strong. De Ligneris never got there. His force was ambushed and cut to pieces by the Americans. On July 26 Fort Niagara capitulated. The Americans had finally achieved their original war aims. Their hold on the Ohio Valley and Lake Ontario was now secure. Moreover, the St. Lawrence was, at last, open for a descent on Montreal.

At Quebec, however, things were not going so well for the British. Although Montcalm had proposed siting batteries downriver at three spots which dominated the river channel and could have made the passage very costly for a fleet at the mercy of wind, current, and tide, nothing had been done. Admiral Charles Saunders was able to bring up the army and land it unopposed on Île d'Orléans on June 27. Only when the British fleet was in the river were measures taken to fortify the immediate approaches to Quebec. Entrenchments were dug on the Beauport flats, across the St. Charles River from Quebec. On the insistence of the Chevalier de Lévis they were extended to the Montmorency River, but, incredibly, Montcalm made no attempt to fortify the cliffs across the river from Quebec. To oppose the British, Montcalm had a total of nearly 16,000 men, regulars, militia, and Indians at his disposal, double the number that Wolfe commanded.

The French had prepared a flotilla of fire ships. On the night of June 28 they were sent down on the British fleet. The operation was a fiasco. Set alight too soon, British sailors in longboats were able to tow all seven clear before they reached their objective. The next day, on the insistence of Admiral Saunders, the British occupied Point Lévis and French attempts to drive them out failed miserably. The British were now able to mount heavy mortars to bombard the town across the mile-wide river. They were also able to get their ships upriver above Quebec and to threaten a landing on either side of the town. A landing above Quebec was particularly to be feared since Montcalm had established his main supply depot at Batiscan, some sixty miles upriver. Wolfe, however, stuck resolutely to his original plan to break the Beauport lines, but every assault was beaten back.[34]

139

Still convinced that if he could only force Montcalm to give battle on open ground he could defeat his foe, Wolfe, in his last letter to his mother, remarked, ''The Marquis de Montcalm is at the head of a great number of bad soldiers, and I am at the head of a small number of good ones, that wish for nothing so much as to fight him — but the wary old fellow avoids an action doubtful of the behavior of his army.'' There was more than a little truth in his judgment, as events were to prove. Although Wolfe was a poor strategist, he had always been an excellent regimental officer, a great admirer of Prussian military methods.[35] The training, discipline, and morale of his troops was now vastly superior to that of Montcalm's regulars. The Canadians, however, could be counted on to fight with savage desperation to protect their homeland and avoid the fate meted out earlier to the Acadians.

As July became August, Wolfe, frustrated at every turn and suffering from poor health, quarreled with his brigadiers. They regarded his tactics to date inept and resented his secretive, arrogant manner. Unable to force the enemy to come out of his lines, Wolfe gave orders for the systematic destruction of the colony. The Canadian settlements were to receive the same treatment as had the Scottish Highlands after Culloden, in which Wolfe had played an active part. Upon first landing on the Île d'Orléans he had issued a manifesto ordering the Canadian people not to assist the ''enemy,'' warning them that if they took up arms in defense of their homeland they would be punished with fire and sword, treated as Indians, who Wolfe had earlier declared merited extermination.[36] He took no account of the fact that every Canadian male between fifteen and sixty was a member of the militia, and thus had to obey the orders of his officers and fight the invader. To Wolfe war was the prerogative of regular uniformed troops; the civilian population had to stand aside and accept the outcome, regardless of its consequences for their lives and the lives of their descendants. At the end of July Wolfe repeated his proclamation, then turned loose the American Rangers, whom he had labeled "the worst soldiers in the universe," to burn the houses, buildings, and crops in all the parishes up and down the river. When any resistance was met, and prisoners taken, they were shot and scalped. At least fourteen hundred farms were destroyed, most of them fine stone buildings in the earlier-settled and more prosperous part of the colony. Bigot tersely commented: "M. Wolfe est cruel."

140 Wolfe claimed that this devastation was intended to force Montcalm to emerge and give battle. In this it failed. At the same time he increased the number of cannon bombarding Quebec from the Lévis side to forty pieces. Hardly a building in the city was left undamaged; 80 percent of Quebec was destroyed. It was the civilian population, not the army, that suffered. The bombardment served no useful military purpose. This whole policy of calculated destruction of Quebec and of the seigneuries about it made no military sense whatsoever, unless it had been concluded that Quebec could not be taken, and Canada not conquered. In his journal, under date of August 13, Major Patrick Mackellar noted that the bombardment of Quebec had been stepped up, and commented, "This was thought to be done either to favor a storm by water, or to do the town all possible damage if it could not be taken, which was now becoming doubtful, as there was little or no appearance of making good a landing upon that coast, it being so well fortified and defended by such Superior Numbers."[37] Wolfe himself, in his dispatch of September 2 to Pitt, in which he reviewed the course of the campaign, expressed profound pessimism as to the outcome, declaring: "In this situation, there is such a choice of difficulties, that I own myself at the loss how to determine." At that late date only a few weeks remained before the fleet would be forced to withdraw, taking the army with it. Of his original troop strength of 8,500 barely half were fit for duty. Casualties had been heavy. The men were now on short rations, reduced to eating horse flesh. More than a thousand men were in sick bay. Dysentery and scurvy were taking a heavy toll. At the end of August, in a letter to Admiral Saunders, Wolfe stated, "Beyond the month of September I conclude our operations cannot go." He then made the revealing comment that Barré had prepared a list of where the troops would be quartered, "supposing (as I have very little hope of) they do not quarter here."[38] But Wolfe could not give up without making one last attempt to conquer Quebec.

He wanted to launch another attack on the Beauport lines below Quebec, but when he proposed three variants of this plan to his brigadiers they rejected the concept of any attack there. Instead they proposed a landing above

Quebec between the city and the supply depot at Batiscan. Such a landing would, they pointed out, cut the road to Montreal. The brigadiers argued that there a landing in strength would force Montcalm to emerge from behind his defense works and give battle in the open. Ever since the fleet had forced a passage above Quebec, British raiding parties had landed above the town periodically. This had forced Montcalm to detach 3,000 of his better troops under Bougainville to march up and down abreast of the British ships to counter the threat.

Wolfe accepted the brigadiers' suggestion for a landing above Quebec; but whereas they had intended the landing to be made well above the city, he chose the Anse au Foulon, at the foot of the 175-foot cliff, less than two miles from Quebec. The operation required the troops to be transported above the city by the fleet, then, during the night, to embark in the landing craft, drift down with the tide, land, make their way up the steep path to the top of the cliff, overpower the French outpost stationed there, then assemble on the heights before the city walls and wait for the French reaction. It was a most desperate gamble, requiring the complete cooperation of the elements — and also of the French. Rear Admiral Charles Holmes, who was in charge of the operation, afterward described it: "The most hazardous and difficult task I was ever engaged in: For the distance of the landing place; the darkness of the night; and the chance of exactly hitting the very spot intended, without discovery or alarm; made the whole extremely difficult."[39]

141

Everything depended on surprise. Were the French to have had a battalion of troops on the heights above the Anse au Foulon, the landing could never have succeeded. Montcalm was convinced that Wolfe would not lift the siege without one last assault, and reading his adversary's mind, he anticipated an attack on the right of the Beauport lines.[40] The fleet movements above Quebec he regarded as a diversion. He had moved a battalion to the heights near the Anse au Foulon on September 5 but recalled it the following day to the Beauport lines.[41] As it was, the small French detachment on top of the cliff was taken completely by surprise, routed by the first British troops to scale the heights. The way was open for the army to follow. When Wolfe himself landed, the situation still looked desperate. His comment reveals that he regarded the enterprise as a forlorn hope: "I don't think we can by any possible means get up here; but, however, we must use our best endeavour."[42] This they did, and the surprise of the French was complete. By daybreak Wolfe had more than 4,400 men on the Plains of Abraham, a thousand yards from the city walls. But they were in an extremely vulnerable position. Before them was Quebec, poorly fortified, but still protected by a wall that would have to be breached by heavy guns, brought up the cliff, before an assault could be made. In Quebec and the Beauport lines Montcalm had some 6,000 troops, and a few miles above Quebec was Bougainville with 3,000 more. Wolfe's army was between the two. Moreover, he had to win a complete victory. Few generals have burned their bridges more successfully than did Wolfe. Retreat was virtually impossible. The army would have had to withdraw down the steep cliff path, then wait to be taken off the narrow beach by the ships' long boats. Such an operation would have invited slaughter. The alternatives for the British would have been: be shot, be drowned, or surrender. It is doubtful that many would have escaped. The army most likely would have been destroyed, and the fleet would have had to sail back to England with the shattered remnants. But none of this happened. Yet the possibility must have been in the minds of the soldiers as they climbed the cliff. It speaks volumes for their morale and discipline.

Upon finding the British army on the heights, Montcalm had several courses of action open to him, and ample time to carry them out. He could have sent word immediately to Bougainville, ten miles away, to bring his forces up to attack the British in the rear while he launched a frontal assault. He could have marched his army around the British and joined up with Bougainville for a consolidated attack. He could have withdrawn his main force into the city and forced Wolfe to launch an assault while Bougainville and the Canadian militia harassed the British rear. Montcalm could afford to wait; Wolfe could not. Bringing up supplies for his army from the fleet would have been difficult, to say the least. A siege was out of the question. The British had only two or three weeks left in which to take Quebec or be forced to withdraw. In short, Montcalm could have forced Wolfe to fight on his terms. Instead, he chose to throw away all these advantages and fight on the ground and at the time chosen by the British, employing only half his available forces.

By nine o'clock he had some 4,500 men mustered on the plain in front of the walled city, facing the British. The Canadian militia, fighting from cover on the flanks in their traditional manner, had engaged the enemy and were inflicting casualties. Then Montcalm gave the order for a frontal attack. The French regiments, bolstered by untrained Canadian militia, advanced at a run, fired volleys at long range, then dropped to the ground to reload. Their lines quickly became ragged. The disciplined British lines held their fire until the French were close, fired measured volleys, reloaded, advanced out of the gunsmoke, then fired again. When the lines were thirty yards apart, volleys all down the British line shattered the reeling French ranks. The French turned and fled toward the city, the British in pursuit. All that saved the remnants of the army was the withering fire of the Canadian militia on the flanks that forced the British to turn and regroup. By noon Wolfe's men were in command of the field. The actual battle had lasted only fifteen minutes. Half of North America was lost and won in that short engagement.

When it was over, Vaudreuil, who had never thought Montcalm would attack so precipitately, arrived on the field with reinforcements. Bougainville appeared later still, then quickly retired. The British still held only the Plains of Abraham.[43] The French had more than twice as many effectives and held the town. Casualties on both sides had been very heavy: 658 for the British,[44] almost as many for the French. Among the killed was Wolfe, and among the dying, Montcalm. For the generals on both sides to be killed

142

in a battle was indeed remarkable. True to form, Montcalm's last action before expiring was to address a letter to Brigadier General George Townshend, who had succeeded Wolfe in command, yielding up Quebec.

Vaudreuil, meanwhile, was struggling to rally the French forces to attack the British the following day, but the colonels of the *troupes de terre* had no stomach for it. Vaudreuil, therefore, gathered up all the troops and militia, then withdrew around the British to join Bougainville and regroup above the Jacques Cartier River, thirty-two miles from the city. In Quebec he had left the Chevalier de Ramesay with a token force and ill-conceived instructions to hold out as long as possible but not necessarily to wait for a British assault before surrendering. The Chevalier de Lévis, come posthaste from Montreal, now took command of the French army and prepared to counterattack. Before he could do so Ramesay surrendered Quebec and the British marched in. The French then fell back and established their forward outpost at Jacques Cartier, while the main forces retired to Montreal.

In Quebec, when the fleet finally sailed in October, Brigadier James Murray was left in command with the bulk of the army. He likely did not receive a letter until the following year written by Thomas Ainslie at Louisbourg and dated October 28: "I now congratulate you on your success at Quebec a thing little expected by any here, and posterity will hardly give credit to it, that such a handful of men should carry a point against such numbers, and with such advantages, thank God you have escaped, it is a miracle that you have."[45] After the British ships had sailed, the French got some of their ships past Quebec with dispatches for France pleading for a strong naval squadron to be sent early to block the St. Lawrence and prevent the British garrison at Quebec from being reinforced. Ten thousand troops, artillery, and supplies were also demanded to repel the British assaults that were sure to come the following year.

Murray's troops suffered cruelly during that winter in the city they had shattered. Sentries froze to death. Wood-cutting parties were savaged by the Canadians. Scurvy took a heavy toll.[46] In April Lévis gathered up his forces, 7,000 men, and marched back to try to retake Quebec. On the twenty-seventh he was at Ste. Foy, five miles from the city. Ironically, Murray committed the same tactical error as Montcalm had done. He marched his troops out, 3,866 strong, to give battle.[47] Lévis had 3,800 on the battlefield. Again the armies were evenly matched. But this time the British were routed. Abandoning their guns, they were pursued right to the city gates. Lévis then laid siege to the town while awaiting the relief ships from France. Those ships never came. Versailles had decided that Canada was irretrievably lost. The Duc de Choiseul sagely concluded that the British, by conquering New France, would merely strengthen their American colonies and their latent urge to strike out for independence. There was, therefore, no point in risking France's remaining naval strength, thousands of troops, and adding to the nation's hideous load of debt to achieve an end that the loss of Canada would achieve in due course at no cost to France. A token force was sent to Canada — five ships escorted by one frigate, bearing four hundred soldiers

143

and some supplies. They sailed late. When they arrived in the Gulf of St. Lawrence a powerful British fleet was already in the Gulf. After putting up a gallant fight the French ships were sunk in Restigouche Bay.

By mid-May the British ships of the line were at Quebec. Lévis had to raise the siege and retire on Montreal, where he intended to make a last stand — not to save the colony, for that was clearly impossible, but to save the honor of the French army and his own reputation. Three British armies now moved in to crush what remained of Canada. Murray moved upriver, by-passing the French defense points, and pressed on toward Montreal. To quell the resistance of the Canadians the homes at Sorel along a four-mile stretch were put to the torch. Even though their situation was hopeless, the consequences of further resistance cruel, many of the Canadians kept on fighting. Many, however, gave up.

On the Lake Champlain front the French had to fall back before Brigadier William Haviland's army, abandoning the chain of forts on the Richelieu after a heavy artillery bombardment. To the west Amherst at long last put in an appearance, moving down the St. Lawrence from Oswego. On September 6 he landed at Lachine. Seventeen thousand British troops now confronted Lévis. His forces had shrunk to two thousand. More than fifteen hundred of his regulars had deserted.[48] On the seventh Vaudreuil asked Amherst for terms. With a conspicuous lack of gallantry Amherst refused to grant the honors of war. Lévis protested violently. He demanded that the regulars be allowed to make a final stand rather than accept such shameful conditions. Vaudreuil, fearing savage reprisals on the Canadian people and recognizing the futility of further resistance, ordered that Amherst's terms be accepted. That night Lévis ordered his regiments to burn their colors to avoid the dishonor and anguish of spirit of handing them over to Amherst. On September 9 the British marched into Montreal. What remained of the French and Canadian regulars stacked their arms on the Champ de Mars. Before the month was out, they and the administrative officials were transported to France.[49] According to the terms of the capitulation the troops could not serve again during the continuance of the war.

Canada had finally been conquered. Yet that conquest had, by no means, been inevitable. Had no regular troops been involved on either side it is highly unlikely that the Anglo-Americans could have conquered New France. Fifteen years later, on the eve of the American Revolution, Chief Justice Hey at Quebec remarked: "I believe it to be as true as anything can be that has not been reduced to absolute proof that the Colonies without the assistance of England, would have been reduced from North to south by this province in the last war. They thought so themselves. . . ."[50] And against Louisiana, where no British troops were engaged, the Indian allies of the French punished the American frontier so severely that no attempts were made to invade that province. Had Montcalm not employed such disastrous tactics at Quebec on September 13, 1759, the fortress city would not have fallen; instead the British army might well have been destroyed. Then, the wavering, war-weary British government would have been more inclined to seek an end to the war. Ineptitude in the French military command and government at home, and the fortunes of war, gave Britain dominion over the vast French territory. But what might have been was now of no account. All that mattered to the conquered Canadians was to restore their destroyed homes before the onset of winter. Beyond that their main concern was what their ultimate fate would be. They were all disarmed and obliged to swear an oath of allegiance to the British monarch. Over them all hung the terrible fear of deportation, not to be dispelled for three generations. Yet the war still raged in Europe. They could still hope that France might win victories elsewhere with which to purchase their liberation. Meanwhile they had to make the best they could of life under the military rule of their conquerors.

Notes

145

1. See Paul Vaucher, *Robert Walpole et la Politique de Fleury (1731-1742)* (Paris, 1924), pp. 298-302; Sir Julian S. Corbett, *England in the Seven Years' War* (2 vols., London, 1918), I, 23-29; E.E. Rich (ed.), *The Cambridge Economic History of Europe* (Cambridge Univ. Press, 1967), IV, 536-537.
2. It is not without significance that the furs of the Ohio Valley were considered by the Canadians to be of very little value. See the informed comments by D'Aigremont; Paris, Archives Nationales, Colonies, C11A, vol. 29, p. 61. On Anglo-American aims and activities in the Ohio Valley see John Mitchell, *The Contest in America Between Great Britain and France with Its Consequences and Importance* (London, 1757), pp. iii-xlix, 17-38; Alfred P. James, *The Ohio Company: Its Inner History* (Univ. of Pittsburgh Press, 1959).
3. See W.J. Eccles, *The Canadian Frontier, 1534-1760* (New York, 1969), pp. 157-160.
4. Guy Frégault, *Le Grand Marquis: Pierre de Rigaud de Vaudreuil et la Louisiane* (Montréal, 1952), pp. 163-177.
5. George F.G. Stanley, *New France: The Last Phase, 1744-1760* (Toronto, 1968), p. 60.
6. On the events, strategy, and tactics of the war see Stanley, *New France: The Last Phase;* Eccles, *The Canadian Frontier,* pp. 157-185; Guy Frégault, *Canada: The War of the Conquest* (Toronto, 1969); Corbett, *England in the Seven Years' War;* Lawrence Henry Gipson, *The British Empire Before the American Revolution,* Vols. IV-VIII (New York, 1939-54); Gerald S. Graham, *Empire of the North Atlantic: The Maritime Struggle for North America* (Toronto, 1950).
7. This incident has long been a subject of controversy, American historians seeking to excuse Washington, while French and French-Canadian historians, for the most part, declare his act to have been that of a common assassin. See Stanley, *New France: The Last Phase,* pp. 54-55.
8. The journal was sent to Governor General Duquesne at Quebec, who predictably commented: "Rien de plus indigne et de plus bas Et meme de plus noir que les sentimens Et la facon de penser de ce Washington, Il y auroit eu plaisir de luy Lire Sous le nez Son outrageant journal." He had a translation made, a copy of which is in the Archives du Séminaire de Québec. See Fernand Grenier (ed.), *Papiers Contrecoeur et autres documents concernant le conflit anglo-français sur l'Ohio de 1745 a 1756* (Québec, 1952), pp. 133-181, 251.
9. Walter L. Dorn, *Competition for Empire, 1740-1763* (New York, 1963), pp. 287-289.
10. *Troupes de terre* were the regiments of the regular army, so designated because many of them took their nomenclature from the provinces where they were raised, e.g., Régiment de Languedoc, Régiment de Béarn.
11. See Corbett, *England in the Seven Years' War,* I, 45-46; Richard Waddington, *Louis XV et le renversement des alliances* (Paris, 1896), pp. 96-97.
12. Waddington, *Louis XV et le renversement des alliances,* pp. 104-110.
13. The strength of the four battalions sent to Quebec, on arrival, was 108 officers, 1,693 other ranks. See Paris, Archives Nationales, Colonies, D2C, XLVI, 254.
14. See A.T. Mahan, *The Influence of Seapower upon History* (New York, 1890; paperback ed., New York, 1957), 1957 ed., p. 251. The strength of the French navy was depleted further by an epidemic of typhus that swept through the fleet and naval ports in 1757. It was this, rather than the greater strength or efficiency of the Royal Navy, that allowed the latter eventually to blockade the French ports and dominate the Atlantic. Seamen and dockyard workers fled the ports; ships could not be manned for lack of crews and sometimes had to go into action with a handful of seamen amid

impressed landsmen. See Ruddock F. Mackay, *Admiral Hawke* (Oxford 1965), pp. 204, 213, 227, 234, 249.

15. For an example of the use made of these incidents by French diplomats abroad on instructions of the foreign minister see *Rapport de l'Archiviste de la Province de Québec, 1949-1951*, p. 5, M. Durand d'Aubigny, Résident du Roi à Liège, au Ministre, Liège, 27 juillet 1755; *ibid.*, p. 9, D'Aubigny au Ministre, à Liège le 11 oct. 1755.

16. See *Rapport de l'Archiviste de la Province de Québec, 1931-1932*, p. 19, Mémoire du Chevalier de la Pause.

17. The most detailed and frequently cited study of this action is Stanley M. Pargellis, "Braddock's Defeat," *American Historical Review*, XLI (1936), 253-269. It is, however, dated; the limitations of the musket were not taken sufficiently into account, and the effectiveness of guerrilla tactics against regular troops untrained for such warfare had not been as clearly demonstrated in 1936 as it was to be in subsequent years.

18. On this issue many historians have allowed national sentiment to weight their judgment. This is particularly true of Francis Parkman, *Montcalm and Wolfe* (London, 1964 ed.), pp. 175-208, and Gipson, *The British Empire Before the American Revolution*, VI, 212-344. Waddington, *Louis XV et le renversement des alliances*, pp. 372-417, gives a detailed account of events and roundly condemns the British. For a judicious view see Guy Frégault, *Canada: The War of the Conquest*, pp. 164-200; "La déportation des Acadiens," *Revue d'Histoire de l'Amérique Française*, VIII, 3 (1954-55), 309-358.

19. A contemporary American observer put the situation very succinctly: "Our colonies are all open and exposed, without any manner of security or defense. Theirs are protected and secured by numbers of forts and fortresses. Our men in America are scattered up and down the woods, upon their plantations, in remote and distant provinces. Theirs are collected together in forts and garrisons. Our people are nothing but a set of farmers and planters, used only to the axe or hoe. Theirs are not only well trained and disciplined but they are used to arms from their infancy among the Indians; and are reckoned equal, if not superior in that part of the world to veteran troops. Our people are not to be drawn together from so many different governments, views, and interests; are unable, unwilling, or remiss to march against an enemy, or dare not stir, for fear of being attacked at home. They are all under one government, subject to command like a military people. While we mind nothing but trade and planting. With these the French maintain numbers of Indians — We have none, — These are troops that fight without pay — maintain themselves in the woods without charges — march without baggage — and support themselves without stores and magazines — we are at immense charges for those purposes. By these means a few Indians do more execution, as we see, than four or five times their number of our men, and they have almost all the Indians of that continent to join them." Mitchell, *The Contest in America Between Great Britain and France*, pp. 137-138. See also *ibid.*, pp. 118-119, 125-126, and Charles Henry Lincoln (ed.), *The Correspondence of William Shirley* (2 vols., New York, 1912), II, 133-134, Shirley to James Delancey, Boston, Feb. 24, 1755.

20. See Henri-Raymond Casgrain (ed.), *Collection des manuscripts du maréchal de Lévis* (12 vols., Montréal and Québec, 1889-95). Vol. IV, *Lettres et pièces militaires, instructions, ordres, mémoires, plans de campagne et de défense, 1756-1760* (Québec, 1891), p. 153.

21. In 1756 France had 45 ships of the line ready for sea, 15 in dock being readied, several under construction (Waddington, *Louis XV et le renversement des alliances*, p. 246). England had 130 ships of the line, but they were inferior to the French; the reverse was true of the officers of the two navies. (Dorn, *Competition for Empire*, pp. 105-121), In 1756, with war declared, the French government decided on an invasion of England. The American theater tied down a sizable part of the Royal Navy; a diversionary assault on Minorca would tie down more. Diversionary assaults were to be made on Scotland and Ireland, then the main invasion launched against England. It was anticipated that all the ships and troops in the latter assault would be lost, but not before they had caused worse panic than the Jacobite march on London in 1745, the collapse of the country's financial structure, and a consequent willingness of the ruling class to accept reasonable peace terms to avert worse losses. See Corbett, *England in the Seven Years' War*, I, 83-95; Dorn, *Competition for Empire*, p. 355.

22. See Frégault, *Le grand marquis*.

23. See Frégault, *Canada: The War of the Conquest*, pp. 241-243.

24. His attitude is revealed by a comment in his journal: "A quoi donc sont bons les sauvages? A ne pas les avoir contre soi." Casgrain, *Collection des manuscrits*, VII, 591.

25. Bigot's activities were regarded as criminal, and he later paid for them; but to a degree, he appears to have been used as a scapegoat. It is interesting to note the difference in attitude toward his malversations and the bland acceptance in England of Henry Fox's amassing of a fortune, perhaps as large as that acquired by Bigot, while serving as paymaster-general. See Lucy S. Sutherland and J. Binney, "Henry Fox as Paymaster-General of the Forces," *English Historical Review*, LXX (Apr. 1955). For Bigot's checkered career see Guy Frégault, *François Bigot: Administrateur français* (2 vols., Montréal, 1948).

26. For a brief contemporary description of the nature of this guerrilla warfare see *Rapport de*

l'Archiviste de la Province de Québec, 1931-1932, Mémoire et observations sur mon voyage en Canada, Chevalier de la Pause, p. 43.

27. New York State Archives, Albany, Colonial Documents, LXXXIV, 149.

28. Historians who accept — usually as an unstated, and likely unconscious, premise — that what happened had to happen, and therefore regard the conquest of New France as inevitable, always advance as a main argument the dependence of Canada on France for support. They thereby ignore that the English colonies were more dependent on England for military aid than Canada was on France.

29. In 1758 the British army and marines numbered 140,000. Rex Whitworth, *Field Marshall Lord Ligonier: A Study of the British Army, 1702-1770* (Oxford, 1958), pp. 208, 246. The French army at maximum strength, 1757-1762, was slightly under 330,000 men in line units. Lee Kennet, *The French Armies in the Seven Years' War* (Duke Univ. Press, 1967), pp. 75-78.

30. McCord Museum, McGill University, Wolfe Papers, No. 1288.

31. On the West Indies campaign and Pitt's strategy see Corbett, *England in the Seven Years' War,* I, 371-395; Gipson, *The British Empire Before the American Revolution,* Vols. V and VIII.

32. Mr. James Turnbull, presently preparing a Ph.D. thesis on the role of Governor General Vaudreuil during the war, has advanced the proposition, on good evidence, that the French suffered a breakdown in the intelligence service provided them by the Five Nations. Previously the Iroquois had kept Vaudreuil well informed of English plans and preparations. On this occasion they conspicuously did not. It may be that they regarded it as in their interests to have the British destroy Fort Frontenac, located as it was on lands they claimed as theirs. When the French destroyed Oswego in 1756 the Iroquois pointedly thanked Vaudreuil for having thus "reestablished the Five Nations in possession of lands that belonged to them." See *Rapport de l'Archiviste de la Province de Québec, 1932-1933,* p. 327.

33. See Archives de la Guerre, Series A1, Vol. 3540, pt. 1, pp. 115, 138-139.

34. On August 11 he wryly remarked: "We had a lively skirmish this morning — we are as usual victorious and yet I am afraid we lost more than the enemy owing to our original disposition and partly to the irregularity and folly of our men. . . ." Public Archives of Canada, James Murray Papers, Wolfe to Brig.-Gen. Murray, Aboard Sterling Castle, 11 Aug. 1759.

35. See Wolfe to Captain Maitland, August 5, 1757: "I have ever entertained a profound admiration for the King of Prussia as the first soldier of this Age and our Master in the Art of War. . . . Some of H.M.'s manouvres are curious and the Deployments display uncommon ingenuity. They doubtless will be adopted by us if Occasion arises." McCord Museum, McGill University, Wolfe Papers, M1385. On Wolfe's generalship see E.R. Adair, "The Military Reputation of Major-General James Wolfe," *Canadian Historical, Association Report, 1936;* C.P. Stacey, *Quebec, 1759* (Toronto, 1959), pp. 170-178.

36. For Wolfe's views on the Indians, see McCord Museum, McGill University, Wolfe Papers, No. 1288. His manifesto is printed in Casgrain, *Collection des manuscrits,* IV, 273-276.

37. Public Archives of Canada, MG23, GII-1, Series 2-7, P. Mackellar's short account of the expedition against Quebec, p. 20.

38. Christopher Hibbert, *Wolfe at Quebec* (London, 1959), p. 165; Stacey, *Quebec, 1759,* p. 102.

39. Stacey, *Quebec, 1759,* pp. 132-133.

40. C.P. Stacey, *Quebec, 1759,* pp. 111-112, 168, opines that Montcalm lacked one essential quality of a good general, the ability to divine his antagonist's intentions, citing his failure to anticipate the landing above Quebec as an example. Montcalm gave abundant evidence of poor generalship, but in this particular case he cannot be faulted, for he had read Wolfe's mind very accurately. What he failed to divine was that Wolfe would defer to the tactics proposed by his brigadiers. He could not have been expected to know that this had transpired.

41. For the confusion that this incident occasioned in the minds of Canadian historians see the intriguing critique by C.P. Stacey, "The Anse au Foulon, 1759: Montcalm and Vaudreuil," *Canadian Historical Review,* XL, 4 (Mar., 1959), 27-37.

42. See C.P. Stacey, "Quebec, 1759: Some New Documents," *Canadian Historical Review,* XLVII, 4 (Dec., 1966), 344-355; Frégault *Canada: The War of the Conquest,* p. 253.

43. In 1711 Governor General Philippe de Rigaud de Vaudreuil, father of the governor general of 1759, had prepared to repel an English seaborne assault on Quebec. He had entrenchments made and cut all the roads everywhere the enemy could effect a landing on both sides of the city, from Beauport to Cape Rouge. He stated that even should the enemy break through these defenses, which they could not do without suffering heavy losses, "they would still hold nothing." *Rapport de l'Archiviste de la Province de Québec, 1946-1947,* pp. 433-434.

44. The total British casualties in the Quebec campaign were 21 officers killed, 93 wounded, 1,384 other ranks killed, wounded, and missing. McCord Museum, McGill University, No. 824, A Return of the Kill'd & Wounded etc. of H.M. Forces up the River St. Lawrence from the 27th June to the Reduction of Quebec 10 [*sic*] Sept. 1759.

45. Public Archives of Canada, James Murray Papers, Vol. (1), 3, pp. 8-9.

147

46. Vaudreuil proposed to detach 1,500 to 1,800 men to harass the British garrison continually and by preventing their obtaining firewood force Murray to surrender. The proposal was rejected owing to the shortage of food supplies for such a detachment and also because the French were sure that Murray would retaliate by burning the homes of all the Canadians within his reach. This might indicate that the British policy of *schrechlichkeit* had served a purpose. See *Rapport de l'Archiviste de la Province de Québec, 1938-1939*, p. 2.

47. The best brief account of this battle to date is G.F.G. Stanley, *New France: The Last Phase*, pp. 242-250.

48. Their officers reported that the majority of the regulars were resolved not to return to France. Many of them had married Canadian girls, with the consent of Montcalm, who had promised them that they could take their discharge and remain in the colony at the war's end. See Eccles, *The Canadian Frontier*, pp. 176, 184. For a graphic contemporary account of the collapse of French resistance see *Rapport de l'Archiviste de la Province de Québec, 1931-1932*, p. 120, Relation de M. Poularies.

49. A handful of officers in the Troupes de la Marine, six captains, three lieutenants, four *enseignes*, were granted permission in 1760 to remain in the colony either to recuperate from serious wounds or to attend to urgent family affairs. Only three Canadian merchants returned to France at the capitulation. Guillaume-Michel Perrault, d'Étienne Charest, Louis Charly de Saint Ange. See Claude Bonnault de Méry, "Les Canadiens en France et aux colonies après la cession (1760-1815)," *Revue de l'Histoire des Colonies Françaises*, XVII (1924), 495-550.

50. Shortt and Doughty, *Documents Relating to the Constitutional History of Canada, 1759-1791* II, 669.

148

Canadian Society in the French Regime*
GUY FRÉGAULT

The General Characteristics of Colonial Societies in America

During the French regime the structure of Canadian society differed in many respects from that of other North American colonies. At the same time Canadian society in the seventeenth and eighteenth centuries had certain basic qualities which can also be found at that date in all the rest of the new continent. These similarities and differences derived from their European origin and from the geographical conditions in which they had developed.

European Colonization

The four chief powers which colonized in North America, Spain, France, England and Holland, belong to a common civilization, that of the West. Shortly after the middle of the seventeenth century England eliminated Holland. There were left behind, however, 10,000 Dutch colonists, three times more than the population of Canada at that date; but, beset on all sides by British settlements, the Dutch colonists, were destined to be gradually absorbed into the Anglo-Saxon majority. In the last quarter of

*From *The Canadian Historical Association Booklet* No. 3 (1954). Copyright by the Canadian Historical Association. Reprinted by permission.

the seventeenth century, then, the situation was as follows: the south of the continent was Spanish; the Atlantic seaboard was in English hands; and France held the valley of the St. Lawrence and, after having explored the Mississippi, was making preparations to establish herself there also.

These three great nations had certain points of resemblance. In the first place they were Christian; but each in its own way. While Spain had kept a jealous eye on the preservation of its Catholic faith, France had passed through the crucible of the Wars of Religion, and England had nationalized its ecclesiastical structure before it developed a doctrine different from that of Rome. On the political level, religious problems were to preserve their importance for some time. The same is true to an even greater degree in the colonies. Various Protestant sects took root in the English settlements; and until 1627 Canada welcomed Catholics and Calvinists alike and the latter exercised an important economic influence. However, when he founded the Company of New France, Richelieu laid it down that the hundred shareholders "should populate the colony with a French and Catholic stock". *149* As this decision was reached when Canada had a very small population and French immigration did not develop until later, the population would inevitably become exclusively Catholic. The society of the country would be profoundly influenced by that fact.

The three metropolitan countries were monarchic as well as Christian, but each in its own way. The most noticeable differences were those between England and France. Both of them were shaken by political disturbances: after lasting for two centuries, absolute monarchy in England was broken down by the aristocracy, which substituted for the omnipotence of the King that of a Parliament under its control; whereas in France the monarchy of divine right triumphed, since in that country geographical considerations, and the risks which they implied, forbade political experiments of the kind that England could afford. These widely different developments reacted on the political institutions of the American colonies.

Here it is necessary to emphasize the fact that the mercantile system, the real source of imperialism, originated in England before the revolution of 1689. It was developed by the Navigation Act of 1660, the Staple Act of 1663, and the Plantation Duties Act of 1673. The fact is that society in France and in England assumed at approximately the same time a definitely capitalistic character, differing in this respect from Spain. This movement coincided with the rise of the upper middle class. In England, the leaders in commerce and finance ruled in close alliance with the territorial aristocracy, to which they were related by ties of family and of interest. In France, Colbert did all he could to favour the middle class, to which he belonged, by promoting industry and commerce and by making policy, as far as possible, further economic activity. Towards 1680 many signs suggested that the industrial revolution would occur in France rather than in England. Saint-Simon bewailed the fact that the long reign of Louis XIV was that of "vile bourgeoisie". As colonial societies have a tendency to model themselves on the mother country, the middle class was to play as important a role in Canada as in the British Colonies.

The social structures of Canada and of the British colonies differed in one important aspect: namely in their land law. In the eighteenth century, France still lived, theoretically, under a "feudal regime"; but if those vestiges of the middle ages, vassalage and fiefs, continued to exist, "it was only as legal forms which for some centuries had been practically void of substance". A "seigneurial regime", however, existed in fact as well as in law. The Canada of the seventeenth and eighteenth centuries was in no respect a feudal colony; but all land was held in seigneuries, a system of tenure by which various individuals shared, under different titles, a number of rights and dues connected with the same concession, the absolute antithesis of *dominium plenum* (freehold, in the modern sense). This principle brought about the existence in Canada of two classes of society which were practically unknown in the English colonies: the seigneurs and tenants.

150   On the cultural level, the evolution of Canada differs more clearly from that of the British colonies than the situation in France does from that of England. A little like Spanish societies, Canada stood outside those new ideas, stemming from the scientific revolution, which essentially modified the intellectual outlook of the modern world and which, from the end of the seventeenth century, shook the very foundations of religious life. Quite early, rationalism, belief in progress, and humanitarian ideas made an appearance in newspapers, pamphlets and books published in English America. One finds nothing of the sort in Canada, where there was no press, where higher education was in its infancy, and where all instruction was in the hands of the clergy who were, however, fully competent for their task.

Thus, as is usually the case, the colonial societies in the New World developed, as far as possible, on the model of the mother country to which they owed their existence. Since they formed part of a common civilization, metropolitan societies generally revealed a fundamental unity; but, since they varied along national lines in their interpretation of this great culture, they emphasized its rich diversity.

The American Milieu

To these national factors we must add the effect of geography. Climate and soil determined the form of agriculture which each colony developed. The South, both French and British, produced semi-tropical crops, rice, cotton, tobacco, and indigo, which lent themselves to large-scale cultivation; this necessitated huge plantations and a large supply of unskilled labour, a fact which favoured the introduction of slavery. Thus, as a result of his way of life, the Louisiana planter was more akin to the Carolinean than to the Canadian agriculturalist; while the latter had a closer affinity with the farmer of New England and, even more, with the farmer of New York.

Moreover, these same factors of climate and soil decided the status of agriculture in the economy of each colony. As the cereals of the North were marketed less easily in Europe than the exotic products of the South, the relative importance of agriculture was smaller there and the tendency towards industrialisation was more marked. The North tried to find in the fur trade and in the fisheries compensation for the economic deficiency of its agriculture. This was particularly true of Canada, which was compelled to send the bulk of its exports to France at a time when that country did not want Canadian wheat.

In the third place, the geographical situation of the colonies influenced the outlook of the societies which grew up there. Situated on the Atlantic seaboard, the English colonies looked towards the sea and were able to maintain uninterrupted communication with the mother country. Canada, on the other hand, spread up the valley of the St. Lawrence; it looked towards the interior of the continent and literally turned its back on the mother country, since its only seaport, Quebec, could not be used for half the year.   *151*

Canadian Society — Its Evolution, 1608-1750

The full bloom of Canadian society came in the middle of the eighteenth century. It would be impossible, however, to grasp its real nature without first of all following its development from the beginning of the previous century.

When he founded Quebec in 1608, Samuel de Champlain laid the permanent basis of the future of Canada. Why did this sailor, after having explored the Atlantic coast almost to the very place where later on New York was to rise, inspire his financial backer, de Monts, to choose the River St. Lawrence, far away inland, as the site of a new colony? Because he hoped to find a water passage to Asia; and because he reckoned on the fur trade to provide the means by which his promoter might recover the money which he had lost in Acadia. A little later he was still banking on the fur trade to interest merchants in financing the peopling of Canada. The business men did indeed take the furs; but they did not send colonists. Champlain, while he opened up possibilities for an extensive commerce, strove unsuccessfully to form an agricultural colony. In 1626, according to the *Jesuit Relations*, if there were in the whole country some 18 to 20 arpents of cultivated land "that was all there was". The same document, however, underlines the importance of the fur trade, which totalled some 200,000 *livres* per annum. In 1628 there were only 76 persons settled in Canada and they all lived in Quebec, which was a trading post. The individual who counted in this little society was not the peasant, but the trader with his interpreters. In 1641 the colony reckoned 300 souls living around two trading posts, Quebec and Three Rivers.

During the following 25 years, Canada grew at a quickening pace. Two factors hastened its growth. In the first place, France experienced a wave of religious feeling which unleashed a great missionary effort. In Canada, the Orders realized that their efforts would be all the more efficacious if they were supported by a strong colony. The intelligent propaganda of the Jesuits encouraged population. Montreal, for example, was launched as an enterprise that was primarily religious. Secondly, there was rapidly developing in the colony an upper class which devoted its time to the fur trade and occupied itself with public affairs. Profiting by the growing weakness of the Company of New France, it organized The Company of the Habitants in 1645 in order to seize the fur trade. The term *"habitant"* must not be confused with *"Paysan".* *"Habitant"* is a word borrowed from the West Indies meaning a factor in charge of a colonial enterprise. These colonists formed an oligarchy which possessed seigneuries and which controlled the Councils that were associated with the Governor from 1647 on.

152

The upper class was not wanting in ambition. In his *Histoire véritable et naturelle . . . de la Nouvelle-France* (Paris, 1664), the Governor of Three Rivers, Pierre Boucher, noted the work of the English in America. He wrote, "They are building many vessels of all kinds, they are opening up iron mines, they have fine cities, they have stage and mail connections from one colony to another, they have carriages as in France; those who invested in these places are now getting their money back. Yet that country is not different from ours; what can be done there can be done here". Boucher did not urge his contemporaries to confine themselves to agriculture; he suggested that they should adopt the British colonies as models.

The census of 1666 provides interesting details of Canadian society. The population had now grown to 3,418 inhabitants, of whom 1,600 lived in the towns of Quebec (555), Three Rivers (461) and Montreal (584). Thus almost half of the colonists were townsmen. The clergy (parish priests, regular clergy, and nuns) were numerous; almost a hundred individuals. The well-to-do middle class, higher civil servants and big business men, accounted for some sixty or seventy families, perhaps a little more than three hundred persons. Minor officials, employed by the state or by the Company of the West Indies (which had been founded in 1664), were to be found in about twenty families. At the bottom of the social scale were 400 indentured servants, most of them in the service of the clergy or of the well-to-do middle class. This leaves a populace of workers and peasants which totaled about 2,500.

At this time Jean Talon began his work. The Intendant was most vigorous and active in peopling the country; it had 7,833 inhabitants by 1675, three years after he had left. He distributed rewards and seigneuries to many officers of the Carignan regiment, which the King had used to pacify the Iroquois. He thus set up, beside the first group of colonists, another element to which the bourgeoisie was reluctant to open its ranks. Along with these officers, some hundreds of soldiers were settled on the land. Furthermore, a good number of immigrants came also. At the same time as he populated the country, Talon began a rapid development of its economy.

He directed the country dwellers towards the cultivation of non-food crops (like hemp), established manufacturers and in every way encouraged trade: in agricultural and forest products as well as in furs, the Company having lost its monopoly. He saw quite clearly that commerce was the only activity which would keep in the colony a middle class which had little interest in agriculture.

When Talon left, his work perished. Frontenac's political egotism provoked a long crisis. Not content with fighting against the clergy, who could not approve the brandy trade, the new governor also attacked the well-to-do and middle class. To compete with them for the fur trade, he built a fort higher up than Montreal, Fort Frontenac, today called Kingston. He protected and did business with unlicensed traders, and obtained for La Salle, a brilliant adventurer but a poor businessman, the monopoly of the Mississippi. La Salle went bankrupt; while such traders as La Chesnaye, Le Moyne, Le Ber and several others saw themselves ousted from the fur trade. It is not surprising, then, that the "Beaver" aristocracy, whose members dominated the Sovereign Council, quarrelled with the representative of the King. As soon as the first period of Frontenac's governorship ended in 1682, fourteen big traders launched the Company of the North to exploit Hudson Bay. A contemporary document describes the associates as "the chief *habitants* and merchants of the country". French shareholders were joined with this group and in 1693 they held the greater part of the capital of the Company. Thus it soon became a Canadian enterprise owned by the financiers of the mother country.

In 1689, a conflict which was evident since 1686 brought Canada into a war with the English colonies which, excluding a truce for several years after the Peace of Ryswick in 1697, lasted until 1713. The cause of this war cannot be understood unless it is realized what was included in New France. New France was not Canada alone. It was a great political and economic unity embracing, before the Treaty of Utrecht, the French portion of Newfoundland, Acadia, Hudson Bay, Canada, and Louisiana. If Canada should fall, New France would disintegrate: on the other hand, torn away from the framework of New France, Canada was not likely to live. Up to the end of the seventeenth century Canada had developed slowly, protected by the distances which separated the valley of the St. Lawrence from the English colonies. This isolation had come to an end when the Intendant Talon, realizing what was necessary for the further development of the fur trade, drew up the plan to connect the St. Lawrence valley with the rest of America, a plan which Pierre Le Moyne d'Iberville carved out, sword in hand, between 1686 and 1710 in Hudson Bay, in Acadia, in Newfoundland, and on the Mississippi. It was not from choice that Canada headed this movement for expansion. Two compelling factors forced it upon her. The first was economic: her prosperity depended on the export of furs. The second was social: her governing class, unable to live on the produce of the seigneuries, was supported by the network of trading posts and forts which commanded the trade routes of New France.

153

If it had been self-supporting, a small agricultural Canada, restricted to the middle St. Lawrence, could have existed beside the English colonies. But New France could not maintain itself without expansion and could not expand without coming into collision with British North America. Despite its ephemeral victory in 1697 (Ryswick), New France was dismembered in 1713 (Utrecht). Newfoundland, Acadia and Hudson Bay were lost. At the same time Great Britain secured the protectorate over the Iroquois, a status upon which she would call to prevent Canada expanding south of the Great Lakes and so effecting a junction with Louisiana. This move, implicit in Article XV of the Treaty of Utrecht, would permit the English to cut New France in two and would reduce it to two modest agricultural colonies: Louisiana at the mouth of the Mississippi and Canada on a section of the St. Lawrence. In 1713, one policy was imperative for the Canadians, to annul the effects of the Treaty of Utrecht. For fifty years they sought to anchor their country at Cape Breton, to extend it towards the west and to block the British advance into the continent. This meant that they must hold the line of the Ohio.

154

Why did Canada succeed in postponing for half a century the effects of the defeat of 1712? Because it benefited from two conditions which were to disappear between 1760 and 1763: it remained within the orbit of French colonization and it preserved its upper middle class.

It should not be assumed that France embarked on a policy of colonization on a grand scale immediately after the Treaty of Utrecht. She was passing through a serious economic crisis which also affected the colony. For example, the war had necessitated huge supplies which the Government had partly obtained locally by issuing paper money. The decline of the state's credit led to the depreciation of this money. In 1714 the Government of France agreed to redeem it, but only at three-eighths of its value. This state of bankruptcy followed closely the failure of the Company of the Colony, which the Canadians had established in 1710 to reorganize the fur trade. Certain administrative mistakes, and even more the war and the saturation of the French market, had hastened the collapse of this ambitious project. Far from coming to its aid, the Court compelled the Company's supporters to seek the aid of French bankers who took over the lion's share of the assets. The colony might well have received better treatment.

However, it was not abandoned. France always assumed the heaviest part of the cost of the administration of Canada, and a big part of these moneys came into the hands of the Canadians. The home government also built up the frontier defences of the colony. Niagara was rebuilt (1720-1727), St. Frederick was erected (1731) and, most important of all, Cape Breton was occupied. In 1718 the construction of Louisbourg was begun. A military base, Louisbourg became one of the busiest ports in America. Before long it was only surpassed by Boston, Philadelphia, and New York. The money which was spent in fortifying Île Royale (Cape Breton) had a good effect on the metropolitan economy, and also, indirectly, on the Canadian economy. One can say as much and even more of the capital spent in the building of forts like Niagara and St. Frederick, since that money went into the pockets of local contractors and purveyors and thus came to nourish the trade of the colony.

While French aid to Canada was often only indirect, the contribution of the upper middle class to the well-being of the country was also made for reasons of self interest. For the upper class pursued its own interests with single-minded devotion. Hard hit by the failure of the Company of the Colony and by the financial crisis of 1714, it yielded to the temptation to put the screws on the tenants; but Versailles quickly compelled the colonial administration to put a stop to such measures. The Court was less successful, however, when it attempted to suppress the contraband trade with the Albany merchants which the fur traders had organized. According to the Intendant Bégon, who wrote in 1715, 50,000 pounds' weight of beaver fur went every year to the English, to the great loss of the trade of Metropolitan France, but "to the great profit of the business men of Montreal" who thus evaded the 25% tax on beaver fur, and at the same time obtained prices higher than those on the French market. By this means the middle class was able to recoup its losses. It also revived the lumber industry and shipbuilding, which had been neglected since the time of Talon; but only with limited success. As for the tillers of the soil, they were experiencing hard times, particularly because of the inadequacy of the domestic market and because of the lack of an export trade. Moreover, as everyone was to some extent a trader, especially those in the Montreal district, everyone suffered from the instability of the fur trade.

155

By 1730, by dint of hard work, the crisis was overcome. For the next fifteen years, prosperity was general. The opening of the market of Louisbourg began a period of expansion in agriculture. The acreage of cultivated land doubled in ten years: it rose from 61,000 arpents in 1720 to more than 130,000 in 1730. The figures of population are proof of the fact that external trade caused this progress. The 24,951 inhabitants in Canada in 1721 had only increased to 33,682 by 1730. The Richelieu region took a new lease on life. Seven wealthy concessionaires, almost all high officials and big traders, undertook with success to open La Beauce to colonization. The country profited by these favourable circumstances to improve its network of roads.

Because of state aid, industry expanded more than agriculture. Yielding to the entreaties of the Intendant, Hocquart, the Court built warships at Quebec. These contracts made it possible to increase the equipment of the naval dockyards. Subsequently, some *protégés* of Bigot set the royal yards to work for their private profit, built a small merchant fleet, and made themselves masters of sea transport and of the longshore business, both of them essential industries in wartime and, in consequence, very profitable. Like the story of naval construction, that of the St. Maurice Forge is typical of industrial enterprises operating in the colonial economy. Some business men formed a company, obtained capital from the French government, laid the foundation of a big enterprise and lived a gay life while the company ran so much into debt that the state had to take it over in 1741. There were other industries started as well, but none of them were as important as ship-building and iron smelting.

Agriculture and industry can only advance along with trade. Tables of imports and exports furnish an index of prosperity. In 1730 imports balanced exports. In 1731 the former outweighed the latter. If in 1733 the colony consumed more than it sent out, from 1739 to 1742 the excess of its sales over its purchases amounted to more than a quarter of a million livres. In 1745 the favourable balance was more than 330,000 livres. Year after year, furs accounted for about two-thirds of Canadian exports. On the average, a million and a quarter livres' worth were sent out annually, apart from the illegal trade through Albany and through Louisbourg. The sale of agricultural products thus occupied only a modest place in the colonial economy by contrast with the situation in the centrally located British col-onies and even in New England, where nine-tenths of the population lived on the farms. But this modest place was more important now than in the previous period when Canada had subsistence farming only. That the com-mercial situation now exercised a profound influence on agriculture was proved in 1745, when wheat fell suddenly to half its price in the Quebec market upon receipt of news that the English had entered Louisbourg.

This brief review of the development of Canada from the founding of Quebec shows that in time of peace as in time of war, in prosperity as in depression, one factor dominated economic life as well as political, namely, big business. The trade curve coincides with that of the general well-being of the country. Its interests dictated local politics and promoted territorial expansion. Its leaders were at the head of Canadian society.

Canadian Society Around 1750

After having seen how it developed, it is now possible to describe the socie-ty of Canada around the middle of the eighteenth century.

One point strikes the observer: the Canadian population was not numerous. This numerical weakness stemmed from two causes. Economic and social conditions in France did not promote emigration to the colonies; and the Canadian climate and the economic activity with which it was iden-tified did not allow the absorption of a large population. The census of 1754 only credits the colony with a population of 55,009 inhabitants. This figure is certainly inaccurate; but even if one added five or six thousand, it would still be small. Moreover, as nothing suggests that the census was taken better in the towns than in the country, it will do to establish proportions.

Of the 55,000 inhabitants, about 42,000 lived in the country. Their liv-ing standards appear to have been high. La Hontan, early in the century, and Montcalm, fifty years later, compared them with "the minor gentry of France". Hocquart wrote that they "do not have the rude and rustic air of our French peasants", a fact upon which Charlevoix had already commented. Such would not have been the case if they had not enjoyed more than a subsistence level economy. Whence came the surplus? It is explained first of all by the fact that the seigneurial regime benefited the tenant more directly than the seigneur. In the eighteenth century, moreover, the system became more and more liberal. Besides receiving his land free and usually paying only small dues, the peasant paid no personal tax. The sale of his agricultural products allowed him to make a limited profit, small enough since the domestic market was restricted to a quarter of the population (that part which lived in the towns) and since the produce of the farms made up at most but a third of the colony's exports. What really helped the peasant to ease his lot was the fur trade which gave regular employment to almost 4,000 men.

This prosperity was not without consequences. It showed itself in the "insubordination" and "independence" of character which the French officials denounced with one accord. It was related also to the relatively high level of elementary education. Peter Kalm, who visited Canada in 1749, noted *157* that every church was flanked by a presbytery and "a school for boys and girls". These latter seemed better taught than the former, whence came, no doubt, the influence of women in the home. A French official, Louis Franquet, believed that the education of girls was carried too far and saw in it "a slow poison tending to depopulate the countryside".

As a matter of fact, the town exerted so strong a pull on the rural population that, in 1749, the Intendant took rigorous measures to prevent peasants from settling down in Quebec. In 1758 an official document deplored the fact that "the towns had been allowed to grow faster in population than the country". In 1759, Quebec had 7,995 inhabitants, Montreal 4,432, and Three Rivers about 800. One Canadian out of four was a townsman.

Quebec, the capital of Canada and of all New France, was a political centre and the seat of culture. It was the home of the public authorities. As in the mother country, the political regime in Canada was authoritarian. This was simply a matter of French practice and local necessity. Unit of command would permit the colony to offer a prolonged resistance to the superior, if uncoordinated, forces of the British colonies. That is why Canada was, in many respects, organized on military lines. The Governor-General, at the head of affairs, was above all things a soldier. The officers who formed his court, while still seeking to make their fortunes, were almost all from good families. They commanded the colony's regulars and, on expeditions, the militia also. The first were recruited in France and the second in the Canadian parishes. In the organization of the armed forces, the captain of the militia, a simple *habitant*, served as a modest helper to the regular officers. The officials who were subordinate to the Intendant, the civil administrator, formed two groups, one group exercising judicial power and the other controlling the finances. The latter usually came from France; the former, which included the members of the Superior Council, belonged generally to the commercial middle class of the colony.

As the centre of culture, Quebec had the Jesuit College, founded in 1645.

Like the houses which that Order controlled in France, the Quebec college met the needs of both upper and middle classes. It would be a mistake to think that it was especially devoted to the instruction of young men proceeding to theology. For that purpose there existed, from 1668, a small seminary whose boarders took courses at the college. It is a case of there being two distinct institutions: the chief one was for the use of laymen, the other served a particular need of the Church; and both were maintained by the clergy. With its great political figures, its ecclesiastical dignitaries, its magistrates, and its officials, Quebec society was the most brilliant in New France.

Montreal had a society that was less fashionable than that of the capital. When Bigot first announced that he was going to pay a visit, the townsmen and their wives hastened to take dancing lessons. But these townsmen were keen men of business. As early as 1718 the Chief Surveyor, Lanouiller, said that they "had possessed almost all the trade of the colony . . . and Quebec must only be regarded as a warehouse". Situated at the cross-roads of the routes of communication of the continent, the city built up its fortunes on trade. When the export of agricultural products was added to that of furs, Montreal took for itself a large part of the profits, for, as the Governor and Intendant wrote in 1737, "this area had always been the granary of the colony".

In the light of present information, it is harder to describe the living conditions of the workers than it is to describe those of the peasants. It is known that, owing to the shortage of skilled craftsmen, workers had high wages. A carpenter was better paid than a member of the Superior Council. Being well paid, they had to do as they were told. One day when the naval dockyard workers in Quebec decided to go on strike, Hocquart threw them all into prison, the proper way, in his opinion, to deal with a strike.

Quite different were the social conditions of the merchants. They constituted the only class which was organized during the French regime. In 1717, they obtained from the metropolitan government the right to meet daily at Montreal and Quebec to discuss business, and the right to choose two "syndics" to represent them before the authorities. Here is an interesting development. On occasions the syndics spoke in the name of the whole community. This was natural because the business men were the most important element.

It is not easy to draw precisely the line which separated the middle class from the upper middle class, or that which divided the latter from the aristocracy. As a matter of fact, the last two groups were really only one. In the seventeenth century, the King gave Charles Le Moyne patents of nobility; but after becoming a noble Le Moyne continued to engage in trade. In the colony, nobility lent prestige to a man who had either acquired or inherited it, but it gave him hardly any more privileges than a commoner. There were commoners who were seigneurs, and nobles who were not. Nobles lived in just the same way at the middle classes. It could not be otherwise since land or property provided little and the offices were insufficient to maintain those who received them. Titled or not, the lesser nobility or the upper middle class, the upper stratum of society, enriched by commerce, set the tone of Canadian society. It constituted an oligarchy which shared the trading posts, occupied most of the public offices, and distinguished itself in military expeditions. In fact it was that group which had built up Canada, the Canada which disappeared in 1760, by developing its economy, directing its territorial expansion and inspiring its politics.

The economic basis of Canadian society was thus a luxury trade, the fur trade. Even in years of prosperity (1730-1744) furs constituted two-thirds of the value of the exports. Hence the considerable difference which existed between the living standard of the farmers and that of the commercial and political aristocracy which controlled the fur trade. It followed that there was a similar difference between the social importance of the two groups. So, of these two classes, that which really counted, that which set the tone, was not the mass of peasants, but the great commercial middle class.

Such seemed to be, around 1750, the social structure of Canada. At the *159* bottom, the peasants on the seigneuries and the artisans in the towns; above, the commercial groups, including a middle class and an aristocracy in which were included the civil and military officers, who, having control of affairs, had the destiny of their country in their hands.

The Collapse of 1760-1763

In 1760 Canada was completely crushed. The colony which passed to Britain three years later was an economic ruin. It was also a political ruin. When the French government put Montcalm over the head of Vaudreuil at the end of 1758, a revolution could not have shaken more brutally what was called at that time "the constitution of the colony". A scion of the Canadian aristocracy, Vaudreuil typified the level of political life which the Canadians had achieved. Finally, in 1763 the country was ruined socially. It had lost the most influential and competent part of its ruling class, a part which could not survive outside of the political and economic framework of New France and the French empire. The latter now disappeared from America, and the former from the map.

During the years of 1760-3 Canada was not merely conquered and ceded to England; it was defeated. Defeat means disintegration. When an army is defeated there are still soldiers, but there is no longer an army. In 1763 there were still Canadians, but Canada was no more. Eliminated from politics, from commerce, and from industry, Canadians turned back to the soil. If they came to boast that they were "children of the soil", it was because defeat had affected not only their material civilization but also their ideas. They had had higher pretensions when their community was more complete.

The social development described in the preceding pages does not conform with the account given by most historians of Canada. The reason is that most of them attempted to reconstruct the society of the French regime on the lines of that broken society which they could examine in the period following 1760. They have read history backwards. It is only because of this dubious approach that they came to conclude that, under the French regime, the chief factors which conditioned Canadian society were neither the existence of the French motherland nor the fur trade but only the peaceful work of the countryside. The behaviour of the mother country was shown as being inadequate and, at times, uninspired; but that does not mean that it was superfluous. A simple examination of the facts brings into sharp relief the importance of big business and of the economic activity which implied the existence of a middle class.

In truth, the old-time Canadian society was something more than a rustic community. It had all the elements which made up the society of a normal colony. Like other American settlements, Canada possessed political and social institutions borrowed from the motherland and adapted to the conditions of the New World. Like other colonies it had its rustics and its townsmen, its clergy and its faithful, its workers and its merchants, it soldiers, its officials and its politicians, its middle classes and its aristocracy. Between Canada and the British colonies the chief difference was not one of kind but of size. It had very few people; they were populous. Hence, after an inevitable conflict, it was defeated.

160

Topic Five

The Impact of the Fur Trade on the Northwest

In 1670 Charles II granted a royal charter to the "Company of Adventurers of England trading into Hudsons Bay." The Hudson's Bay Company, as it became known, gained an exclusive monopoly over the fur trade in "Rupertsland" — all the territory whose rivers drained into Hudson Bay. Rupertsland, named after Prince Rupert, the Hudson's Bay Company's first governor, comprised almost half of present-day Canada.

Until the conquest in 1760 French traders operating out of Montreal opposed the Hudson's Bay Company's monopoly. Thereafter a new challenge arose when British traders working out of Montreal allied with the French to form the North West Company. Only after the forced union of the two companies in 1821 did the Hudson's Bay Company have a practical monopoly of the northern fur trade, and then it truly enjoyed the rights and privileges granted to it in 1670.

The Woodland Indians in the Northwest welcomed the English and French traders with their iron manufactured goods: axes, knives, spears, and kettles. These durable items made hunting, cooking, and warfare much easier and more efficient than with their former implements made of stone, wood, and bone. As a result of the trade, however, the Cree Indians living near the Hudson's Bay Company's posts on Hudson and James Bay came to rely on the white newcomers. Did the European fur traders, and in particular the Hudson's Bay Company, exploit the native peoples? Arthur Ray examines the Indians' role in the exchange in his essay, "Fur Trade History as an Aspect of Native History."

An important consequence of the fur traders' arrival was the rise of a mixed-blood, or Metis, population, the result of the white fur traders' intermarriage with Indian women. Until recently, historians of the fur trade ignored the role of these Indian wives. Sylvia Van Kirk analyzes their contribution in "'Women in Between': Indian Women in Fur Trade Society in Western Canada."

E.E. Rich has written the standard account of the Hudson's Bay Company *The History of the Hudson's Bay Company, 1670-1870*, 2 vols. (London: The Hudson's Bay Record Society, 1959). A shorter treatment by the same author which includes a discussion of the Hudson's Bay Company's rivals is *The Fur Trade and the Northwest to 1857* (Toronto: McClelland and Stewart, 1967). A recent review of "The Fur Trade and Eighteenth-Century Imperialism," by W.J. Eccles, appears in the *William and Mary Quarterly*, 3rd series, 40 (1983): 341-362. The first notable study of the fur trade is H.A. Innis, *The Fur Trade in Canada* (1930; reprint edition, New Haven: Yale University Press, 1962). A.J. Ray provides a more recent study in his *Indians in the Fur Trade* (Toronto: University of Toronto Press, 1974). Dan Francis has written a very readable account of the personalities of the fur trade in Western Canada, *Battle for the West: Fur Traders and the Birth of Western Canada* (Edmonton: Hurtig, 1982). A scholarly analysis of the fur trade in one specific region is the study by Dan Francis and Toby Morantz, *Partners in Furs: A History of the Fur Trade in Eastern James Bay 1600-1870* (Kingston: McGill-Queen's University Press, 1983). An excellent popular summary of the trade is the beautifully illustrated *Where Two Worlds Meet: The Great Lakes Fur Trade* (St. Paul: Minnesota Historical Society, 1982), by Carolyn Gilman.

162

Sylvia Van Kirk in *"Many Tender Ties:" Women in Fur-Trade Society, 1670-1870* (Winnipeg: Watson and Dwyer, 1980), and Jennifer S.H. Brown in her *Strangers in Blood: The Fur Trade Company Families in Indian Country* (Vancouver: University of British Columbia Press, 1980), have written two excellent accounts of women in the fur trade. Olive Patricia Dickason has taken a pan-Canadian view of the rise of a mixed-blood population in her "From 'One Nation' in the Northwest to 'New Nation' in the Northwest: A Look at the Emergence of the Metis," *American Indian Culture and Research Journal*, 6:2 (1982): 1-21. For a survey of the history of the Metis, see D. Bruce Sealey and Antoine S. Lussier, *The Metis, Canada's Forgotten People* (Winnipeg: Manitoba Metis Federation Press, 1975).

Fur Trade History as an Aspect of Native History*

ARTHUR J. RAY

Howard Adams, among others, has made the point that the dominant white Euro-Canadian culture has projected racist images of the Indians that, "are so distorted that they portray natives as little more than savages

*An article from *One Century Later: Western Canadian Reserve Indians since Treaty 7*, edited by Ian A. L. Getty and Donald B. Smith. Copyright 1978 by University of British Columbia. Reprinted by permission.

without intelligence or beauty."[1] He argued further that the Indians "must endure a history that shames them, destroys their confidence, and causes them to reject their heritage."[2] There is a great deal of truth in Adams's statements, and clearly a considerable amount of historical research needs to be done to correct these distorted images. One important aspect of any new meaningful Indian history necessarily will be concerned with the involvement of the Indian peoples in the fur trade and with the impact of that participation upon their traditional cultures as well as those of the European intruders. Work in this area will be important not only because it holds a potential for giving us new insights into Indian history, but also because it should serve to help establish Indian history in its rightful place in the mainstream of Canadian historiography. As some of Canada's most prominent historians have emphasized, the fur trade was a molding force in the economic, political, and social development of Canada,[3] and the Indian peoples played a central role in this enterprise. For these reasons Indian history should not simply be devoted to recounting the manner in which the aboriginal peoples of Canada were subjugated and exploited, but it must also consider the positive contribution that the Indian peoples made to the fur trade and, hence, to the development of Canada. If this positive contribution is recognized, it should help destroy some of the distorted images that many Canadians have of Indians and their history.

163

Given that fur trade history and Indian history are inextricably bound together, several questions immediately arise. How much attention have historians devoted to the roles that the Indians played in the fur trade in the considerable body of fur trade literature that already exists? What images of the Indian peoples emerge from this literature? What aspects of Indian involvement have yet to be explored fully?

Until relatively recently the Indian peoples have not figured prominently in works dealing with the fur trade.[4] Rather, they generally appear only as shadowy figures who are always present, but never central characters, in the unfolding events.[5] In part, this neglect appears related to the fact that historians have been primarily concerned with studying the fur trade as an aspect of European imperial history or of Canadian business and economic history.[6] And, reflecting these basic interests, the considerable biographical literature that fur trade research has generated deals almost exclusively with Euro-Canadian personalities.[7] Relatively few Indian leaders have been studied to date.[8]

Although the tendency to consider the fur trade primarily as an aspect of Euro-Canadian history has been partly responsible for the failure of scholars to focus on the Indians' role in the enterprise, other factors have been influential as well. One of the basic problems with most studies of Indian-white relations has been that ethno-historians and historians have taken a retrospective view. They see the subjugation of the Indian peoples and the destruction of their lifestyles as inevitable consequences of the technological gap that existed between European and Indian cultures at the time of contact.[9] From this technological-determinist perspective, the Indian has been rendered as an essentially powerless figure who was swept along by the tide of European expansion without any real hope of channeling its direction or of influencing the character of the contact situation. The dominance of this outlook has meant that in most fur trade studies the Indian has been cast in a reflexive role. Reflecting this perspective, until recently most ethno-historical research has been approached from an acculturation-assimilation point of view. The questions asked are generally concerned with determining how Indian groups incorporated European technology as well as social, political, economic, and religious customs into their traditional cultures.

While also interested in these issues, historians have devoted a considerable amount of attention toward outlining the manner and extent to which Euro-Canadian groups, particularly missionaries and government officials, helped the Indians to adjust to the new socio-economic conditions that resulted from the expansion of Western cultures into the new world.[10] Often historical research has taken a certain moralistic tone, assuming that members of the dominant white society had an obligation to help the Indians adopt agriculture and European socio-economic practices and moral codes, so that the Indian peoples could fit into the newly emerging social order.[11] Thus, historians who undertake these types of studies are frequently seeking to determine whether or not the traders, missionaries, and government officials had fulfilled their obligations to help "civilize" the Indian.

Granting that much good work has been done in the above areas, it is my opinion that many new insights into Indian history can be obtained if we abandon the retrospective, technological-determinist outlook and devote more attention to an examination of Indian involvement in the fur trade in the context of contemporary conditions. Such an approach would necessarily recognize that the nature of the trading partnerships that existed between Indian groups and various European interests changed substantially over time and place, making it difficult, frequently misleading, and certainly premature, given the amount of research that still needs to be done, to make any sweeping statements at this time about the nature of Indian-white relations in the context of the Canadian fur trade.

In order to pursue this work effectively, two courses of action need to be followed — one is not currently popular, and the other is extremely tedious. First, students of Indian history need to abandon the assumption that the Indians were ruthlessly exploited and cheated in all areas and periods by white traders. At present this is a very popular theme for both Indian and liberal white historians. All of us have heard the story many times of how the Indians sold Manhattan Island for a few pounds of beads, and we have been informed of the many instances when Indians parted with valuable furs for trinkets and a drink. But, why are we never informed of what the Indians' perceptions of trade were? It may well be that they too thought they were taking advantage of the Europeans. For example, in 1634, when commenting on Montagnais beaver trapping in eastern Canada, Father Le Jeune wrote:

> The Castor or Beaver is taken in several ways. The Savages say it is the animal well-beloved by the French, English and Basques, — in a word, by the Europeans. I heard my [Indian] host say one day, jokingly, *Missi picoutau amiscou*, "The Beaver does everything perfectly well, it makes kettles, hatchets, swords, knives, bread; and in short, it makes everything." He was making sport of us Europeans, who have such a fondness for the skin of this animal and who fight to see who will get it; they carry this to such an extent that my host said to me one day, showing me a beautiful knife, "The English have no sense; they give us twenty knives like this for one Beaver skin."[12]

While there is no denying that European abuses of Indians were all too common, there are several things wrong with continually stressing this aspect of the fur trade and Indian history. As the previous quote suggests, it gives us only half the story. Of greater importance, by continually focusing only on this dimension of the trade, we run the serious risk of simply perpetuating one of the images in Indian historiography that Adams, among others, most strongly objects to, namely, the view that the Indians were little more than "savages without intelligence." It also glosses over a fundamental point that must be recognized if the Indian is to be cast in an active and creative role. We must not forget that the Indians became involved in the fur trade by their own choice. Bearing that in mind, an objective and thorough examination of the archival records of the leading trading companies, admittedly a wearisome task, gives considerable evidence that the Indians were sophisticated traders, who had their own clearly defined sets of objectives and conventions for carrying on exchange with the Europeans.

165

This can be demonstrated by following several lines of inquiry. One of these involves attempting to determine the kind of consumers the Indians were at the time of initial contact and how their buying habits changed over time. Probably one of the most striking pictures that emerges from an examination of the early correspondence books of the Hudson's Bay Company is that, contrary to the popular image, the Indians had a sharp eye for quality merchandise and a well-defined shopping list. In short, they were astute consumers and not people who were easily hoodwinked.

If this is doubted, the early letters that the traders on Hudson Bay sent to the governor and committee of the Hudson's Bay Company in London should be read carefully. A substantial portion of almost every letter deals with the subject of the quality of the company's trade goods and with the Indians' reactions to it. Not only do these letters reveal that the Indians could readily recognize superior merchandise, but they also indicate that the Indians knew how to take advantage of the prevailing economic situation to improve the quality of the goods being offered to them. The following quote, typical of those that were written in the period before 1763, demonstrates the point and at the same time indicates one of the problems that is associated with carrying on research of this type. On 8 August 1728, Thomas McCliesh sent a letter from York Factory to the governor and committee in London informing them:

I have sent home two bath rings as samples, for of late most of the rings [which] are sent are too small, having now upon remains 216 that none of the Indians will Trade. I have likewise sent home 59 ivory combs that will not be traded, they having no great teeth, and 3900 large musket flints and small pistol flints, likewise one hatchet, finding at least 150 such in three casks that we opened this summer which causes great grumbling amongst the natives. We have likewise Sent home 18 barrels of powder that came over in 1727, for badness I never saw the like, for it will not kill fowl nor beast at thirty yards distance: and as for kettles in general they are not fit to put into a Indian's hand being all of them thin, and eared with tender old brass that will not bear their weight when full of liquid, and soldered in several places. Never was any man so upbraided with our powder, kettles and hatchets, than we have been this summer by all the natives, especially by those that borders near the French. Our cloth likewise is so stretched with the tenter-hooks, so as the selvedge is almost tore from one end of the pieces to the other. I hope that such care will be taken so as will prevent the like for the future, for the natives are grown so politic in their way of trade, so as they are not to be dealt by as formerly . . . and I affirm that man is not fit to be entrusted with the Company's interest here or in any of their factories that does not make more profit to the Company in dealing in a good commodity than in a bad. For now is the time to oblidge [sic] the natives before the French draws them to their settlement.[13]

166

From McCliesh's letter one gets the impression that few of the goods on hand were satisfactory as far as the Indians were concerned. Taken out of context, comments of this type, which are common in the correspondence from the posts, could be construed to indicate that the governor and committee of the Hudson's Bay Company hoped to enhance their profits by dealing in cheap, poor quality merchandise whenever possible. However, such a conclusion would distort the reality of the situation and overlook important developments that were underway in the eighteenth century. If one examines the letters that the governor and committee sent to the Bay during the same period, as well as the minutes of their meetings in London and correspondence with British manufacturers and purchasing agents, other important facts emerge.

These other documents reveal that from the outset the governor and committee were concerned with having an array of the types and quality of goods that would appeal to the Indians. From the minute books of the company we learn that in the earliest years of operations the London directors relied heavily upon the experience and judgement of Pierre-Esprit Radisson to provide them with guidance in developing an inventory of merchandise that would be suitable for their posts in Canada. Radisson helped choose the patterns for knives, hatchets, guns, and so forth that manufacturers were to use, and he was expected to evaluate the quality of items that were produced for the company.[14] The governor and committee also sought the expertise of others in their efforts to maintain some quality control. For instance, in 1674 they attempted to enlist the services of the gunsmith who inspected and approved the trade guns of the East India Company.[15] They wanted him to evaluate the firearms that the Hudson's Bay Company was purchasing.

In their annual letters to the posts on the Bay, the governor and committee generally asked the traders to comment on the goods that they received and to indicate which, if any, manufacturer's merchandise was substandard. When new items were introduced, the directors wanted to know what the Indians' reactions to them were.

The question that no doubt arises is, if the governor and committee were as concerned with the quality of the products they sold, as suggested above, then why was there a steady stream of complaints back to London about their goods? Before a completely satisfactory answer to this question can be given, a great deal more research needs to be done in these records. However, several working hypotheses may be put forth at this time for the sake of discussion and research orientation. In developing its inventory of trade goods, the Hudson's Bay Company, as well as other European groups, had to deal with several problems. One of these was environmental in character. Goods that may have been satisfactory for trade in Europe, Africa, or Asia, often proved to be unsuitable in the harsh, subarctic environment. This was especially true of any items that were manufactured of iron. For example, one of the problems with the early flintlocks was that the locks froze in the winter.[16]

167

The extremely cold temperatures of the winter also meant that metal became brittle. Hence, if there were any flaws or cracks in the metal used to make mainsprings for guns, gun barrels, knives, hatchets, or kettles, these goods would break during the winter. In this way the severe environment of the subarctic necessitated very rigid standards of quality if the goods that were offered to the Indians were going to be satisfactory. These standards surely tested the skills of the company's suppliers and forced the company to monitor closely how the various manufacturers' goods held up under use.

Besides having to respond to environmental conditions, the traders also had to contend with a group of consumers who were becoming increasingly sophisticated and demanding. As the Indians substituted more and more European manufactures for traditional items, their livelihood and well-being became more dependent upon the quality of the articles that they were acquiring at the trading posts. This growing reliance meant that the Indians could no longer afford to accept goods that experience taught them would fail under the stress of hard usage and the environment, since such failures could threaten their survival. It was partly for these reasons that the Indians developed a critical eye for quality and could readily perceive the most minute defects in trade merchandise.

Indian groups were also quick to take advantage of competitive conditions. They became good comparison shoppers and until 1821 used European trading rivalries to force the improvement of quality and range of goods that were made available to them. For example, during the first century of trade on Hudson Bay, the Indians frequently brought to Hudson's Bay Company posts French goods that they judged to be superior to those of English manufacture. The Indians then demanded that the Hudson's Bay Company traders match or exceed the quality of these items or risk the loss of their trade to the French. Similar tactics were used by the Indians in later years whenever competition was strong between

Euro-Canadian groups. Clearly such actions were not those of "dumb savages," but rather were those of astute traders and consumers, who knew how to respond to changing economic conditions to further their own best interests. The impact that these actions had on the overall profitability of the trade for Euro-Canadian traders has yet to be determined.

The issue of profits raises another whole area of concern that is poorly understood and should be studied in depth. To date we know little about how the economic motivations of the Europeans and the Indians influenced the rates of exchange that were used at the posts. In fact, there is still a great deal of confusion about the complicated system of pricing goods and furs that was used in Canada. We know that the Hudson's Bay Company traders used two sets of standards. There was an official rate of exchange that was set by the governor and committee in London which differed from the actual rate that was used at the posts. Of importance, the traders advanced the prices of their merchandise above the stated tariff by resorting to the use of short measures. Contemporary critics of the Hudson's Bay Company and modern native historians have attacked the company for using such business practices, charging that the Indians were thereby being systematically cheated, or to use the modern expression, "ripped off."[17] But was this the case? Could the company traders have duped the Indians over long periods of time without the latter having caught on? Again, common sense and the record suggests that this was not the case.

The traders have left accounts of what they claimed were typical speeches of Indian trading leaders. One central element of all of these addresses was the request by these leaders that the traders give the Indians "full measure and a little over."[18] Also, the Indians usually asked to see the old measures or standards. Significantly, the Indians do not appear to have ever challenged the official standards, while at the same time they knew that they never received "full measure." What can we conclude from these facts?

In reality, the official standards of trade of the Hudson's Bay Company, and perhaps those of other companies as well, served only as a language of trade, or point of reference, that enabled the Indians and the traders to come to terms relatively quickly. The traders would not sell goods at prices below those set in the official standard. The Indian goal, on the other hand, was to try to obtain terms that approximated the official rate of exchange. An analysis of the Hudson's Bay Company post account books for the period before 1770 reveals that the company traders always managed to advance prices above the standard, but the margin of the advance diminished as the intensity of French opposition increased.[19] And even under monopoly conditions such as existed in Western Canada before the 1730's, the Hudson's Bay Company traders were not able to achieve an across-the-board increase that exceeded 50 per cent for any length of time.[20] This suggests strongly that the Indians successfully used competitive situations to improve the terms of trade and that they had their limits. If prices were advanced beyond a certain level, the Indians must have perceived that their economic reward was no longer worth the effort

168

expended, and they broke off trade even if there was no alternative European group to turn to.

These remarks about the *overplus* system apply to the period before 1770. What we need to know is the extent to which the Indians were able to influence the rates of exchange during the time of bitter Hudson's Bay Company and North West Company rivalry. A preliminary sample of data from that period suggests their impact was much greater and that range of price variation was much more extreme than in the earlier years. Similarly, it would be helpful to have some idea what effect the re-establishment of the Hudson's Bay Company's monopoly after 1821 had on trade good prices and fur values in Western Canada. Being able to monitor prices under these contrasting conditions would enable us to obtain some idea of how the Indians were coping with the changing economic situation and how their responses influenced the material well-being of the different tribal groups.

Although this sample of the early accounting records shows that the *169* Indians were economic men in the sense that they sought to maximize the return they obtained for their efforts, the same documents also indicate that, unlike their European counterparts, the Indians did not trade to accumulate wealth for status purposes. Rather, the Indians seem to have engaged in trade primarily to satisfy their own immediate requirement for goods. On a short-term basis their consumer demand was inelastic. In the early years this type of response was important in two respects. It was disconcerting to the European traders in that when they were offered better prices for their furs, the Indians typically responded by offering fewer pelts on a per capita basis. This type of a supply response was reinforced by gift-giving practices. Following the Indian custom, prior to trade tribal groups and the Europeans exchanged gifts. As rivalries for the allegiance of the Indians intensified, the lavishness of the gifts that the traders offered increased.

The ramifications that Indian supply responses to rising fur prices and to European gift-giving practices had for the overall conduct of the fur trade have yet to be fully explored. Clearly the costs that the Europeans would have had to absorb would have risen substantially during the periods when competition was strong, but to date no one has attempted to obtain even a rough idea of the magnitude by which these costs rose during the time of English–French or Hudson's Bay Company–North West Company rivalry. Nor has serious consideration been given to the manner in which such economic pressures may have favoured the use and abuse of certain trade articles such as alcohol and tobacco.

Concerning the use of alcohol, the excessive consumption of this drug was an inevitable consequence of the manner in which the economies of the Indian and European were linked together in the fur trade and of the contrasting economic motives of the two groups. As rivalries intensified, the European traders sought some means of retaining their contacts with the Indians, while at the same time keeping the per capita supply of furs that were obtained at as high a level as was possible. However, in attempting to accomplish the latter objective, the Europeans faced a number of problems. The mobile life of the Indians meant that their ability to accumulate material wealth was limited, especially in the early years when the trading posts were distant from the Indians' homelands. And, there were social sanctions against the accumulation of wealth by individual Indians.[21] To combat these problems, the traders needed to find commodities that could be transported easily or, even better, consumed at the trading post.

Unfortunately, alcohol was ideal when viewed from this coldly economic perspective. It offered one of the best means of absorbing the excess purchasing power of the Indians during periods of intensive competition. Furthermore, alcohol could be obtained relatively cheaply and diluted with water prior to trade.[22] Hence, it was a high profit trade item, an article that helped the traders hold down their gift-giving expenses, and it could be consumed at the forts. Given these characteristics, the only way that the abusive use of alcohol in trade could have been prevented in the absence of a strong European or native system of government was through monopoly control.

The traditional Indian consumer habits and responses to rising fur prices were important in another way. They were basically conservationist in nature although not intentionally so. By trapping only enough furs to buy the goods they needed in the early years, the pressures that the Indians exerted on the environment by their trapping activities were far less than they would have been had the objective been one of accumulating wealth for status purposes. If the latter had been the primary goal, then the Indians would have been tempted to increase their per capita supply of peltry as fur prices rose, since their purchasing power was greater.

In light of the above, the period between 1763 and 1821 is particularly interesting and warrants close study. During that period Euro-Canadian trading rivalries reached a peak, and one of the consequences of the cut-throat competition that characterized the time was that large territories were over-hunted and trapped by the Indians to the point that the economies of the latter were threatened.[23] The question is, had the basic economic behaviour of the Indians changed to such an extent that it facilitated their over-killing fur and game animals? Or, was the heavy use of addictive consumables such as alcohol and tobacco a major factor in the destruction of the environment?

Yet another aspect of the fur trade that has received too little attention is the connection that existed between the European and eastern North American markets and the Western Canadian operations of the trading companies. It needs to be determined how prices for trade goods and furs in these markets, as well as transportation costs, influenced rates of exchange at the posts. For instance, it has become popular to cite cases where European traders advanced the prices of certain articles by as much as 1000 per cent over what it cost the companies to buy them in Europe.

Similarly, accounts of occasions when the Indians received a mere pittance for valuable furs[24] are common. But, it is rarely reported, and indeed it is generally not known, what percentage of the total gross revenues of a company were made by buying and selling such items. Nor is it known if losses were sustained on the sales of other commodities. Equally important, there is not even a rough idea of what the total overhead costs of the companies were at various times. Hence, their net profit margins remain a mystery, and what was considered to be a reasonable profit margin by European standards in the seventeenth, eighteenth, and early nineteenth centuries is not known. Answers to all of these questions must be found before any conclusions can be reached about whether or not the Indian or the European trader was being "ripped off."

And indeed, the Indian side must be considered when dealing with this question and when attempting to understand how the trading system responded to changing economic conditions. Even though Harold Innis pointed out that Indian trading specialists played a crucial role in the development and expansion of the fur trade, a common view of the Indians in the enterprise is still one that portrays them basically as simple trappers who hunted their own furs and accepted whatever prices for these commodities that the traders were willing to give them. The fact of the matter is that the records show that in the period before 1770, probably 80 per cent of all of the furs the Europeans received in central Canada came from Indian middlemen who acquired their peltry through their own trading networks.

171

Furthermore, these middlemen charged the Europeans substantially more for these furs than they had paid to obtain them from the trapping bands with whom they dealt. In turn, the middlemen advanced the prices for their trade goods well above the levels they had been charged by the Europeans, sometimes by margins of almost 1000 per cent.

These practices of the Indian middlemen raise a difficult question. If the Indians were not engaged in the trade to accumulate wealth, as suggested earlier, then why did the middlemen advance their prices to the extent that they did? Did their price levels simply enable them to maintain a material standard that they had become accustomed to? Before this question can be answered, a great deal more needs to be known about the problems that the Indian middlemen had to cope with in their efforts to acquire and transport goods and furs. A clearer understanding of their motives for engaging in the trade is also required. For example, why did some Indian groups quickly assume the middleman role while others were apparently content to continue as trappers? How did middlemen groups fare, economically, in comparison with trapping groups?

The Indians played a variety of other roles in the fur trade. They served as provision suppliers, canoe builders, canoe and boat men, and farm labourers around the posts, to name only a few. The Indians quickly assumed these roles as economic conditions changed, rendering old positions obsolete and opening up new opportunities.

This brings to mind another broad research area that should be explored more fully than it has been to date. It deals with determining how the various Indian groups perceived and responded to changing economic situations. Work in this area would serve to destroy another distorted image that many Euro-Canadians have of Indian societies, namely, the view that these societies are rigid and incapable of responding to change. Historically there is little evidence to support such a notion for the period before 1870. While the fur trade was a going concern and the Indians were not tied to the reserves and shackled with bureaucratic red tape, they made many successful adaptations to new circumstances. More needs to be written about this aspect of Indian history. If this work is done, perhaps a picture will emerge that shows the Indians to be innovative, dynamic, and responsive people, whose creativity and initiative have been thwarted in the post-treaty period.

172 In conclusion, this paper has focused upon the early phases of the Western Canadian fur trade, and the discussion has been restricted primarily to the economic dimension of trade. However, this restriction is justified because many of the problems of Indian-white relations are rooted in the past. Also, many of the distorted images that Euro-Canadians currently hold regarding Indians, thereby causing problems in the relationships between the two groups, have been generated and perpetuated by the manner in which the fur trade history has been written. Correcting these images requires starting at the beginning, and it is not simply a matter of rewriting what has already been done. New research has to be conducted in the various archival collections across the country and records that have received little attention to date, such as accounting records, need to be exhaustively explored. In conducting this research and presenting our results, the urge to overcompensate for past wrongs and inaccuracies by placing the Indian on a pedestal must be resisted. If the latter course of action is taken, a new mythology that will not stand the test of time will be created. Even more serious, it would probably serve only to perpetuate the warped images that such research set out to destroy, because it would fail to treat the Indians as equals with their own cultures and sets of values. Finally, if one of the objectives of studying the fur trade is to attempt to obtain a better understanding of Indian-white relations, it must be based on solid objective historical research.

Notes

I would like to thank Charles A. Bishop, SUNY–Oswego, James R. Gibson and Conrad Heidenrich, York University, and Carol Judd, Ottawa, for commenting on earlier drafts of this paper. The author, of course, is responsible for this paper.

1. Howard Adams, *Prison of Grass* (Toronto: New Press, 1975), p. 41.
2. *Ibid.*, p. 43.
3. The most notable example was probably Harold Innis. See H. A. Innis, *The Fur Trade in Canada* (1930; reprint ed., New Haven: Yale University Press, 1962), pp. 386–92.
4. See, for example, Innis, *The Fur Trade*; A. S. Morton, *The History of the Canadian West to 1870–71*,

2nd ed. (Toronto: University of Toronto Press, 1973); and E. E. Rich, *The Fur Trade and the Northwest to 1857* (Toronto: McClelland and Stewart, 1967).

5. C. Jaenen, *Friend and Foe* (Toronto: McClelland and Stewart, 1976), pp. 1–11.

6. Innis and Rich deal extensively with the fur trade as an aspect of imperial history. See Innis, *The Fur Trade*, p. 383; and Rich, *Fur Trade and Northwest*, pp. xi and 296. Several corporate histories have been written. See as examples, L. R. Masson, *Les Bourgeois de la Compagnie du Nord-Ouest*, 2 vols. (1889–90; reprint ed., New York: Antiquarian Press, 1960); E. E. Rich, *The History of Hudson's Bay Company 1670–1870*, 2 vols. (London: Hudson's Bay Record Society, 1958–59); and W. S. Wallace, *Documents Relating to the North West Company* (Toronto: Champlain Society, 1934).

7. One of the problems, of course, is that biographical details regarding Indian personalities are few. The historical record often does not provide information regarding births, deaths, and family relationships of Indian leaders.

8. There are some notable exceptions such as Dempsey's study of Crowfoot and Sluman's of Poundmaker. See H. Dempsey, *Crowfoot: Chief of the Blackfoot* (Edmonton: Hurtig, 1972); and N. Sluman, *Poundmaker* (Toronto: McGraw-Hill Ryerson, 1967).

9. This point of view was perhaps most strongly expressed by Diamond Jenness. See Diamond Jenness, "The Indian Background of Canadian History," Canada, Department of Mines and Resources, National Museum of Canada Bulletin No. 86 (Ottawa, 1937), pp. 1–2; and Diamond Jenness, *Indians of Canada*, 6th ed. (Ottawa: National Museum of Canada, 1963), p. 249. See also George F. Stanley, "The Indian Background of Canadian History," Canadian Historical Association, *Papers* (1952), p. 14.

10. A notable example of this interest as it pertains to Western Canada is the early work of Frits Pannekoek. See Frits Pannekoek, "Protestant Agricultural Missions in the Canadian West in 1870" (M. A. thesis, University of Alberta, 1970). More recently, Pannekoek has begun to consider the divisive role these groups played in terms of race relations in Western Canada. See Frits Pannekoek, "The Rev. Griffiths Owen Corbett and the Red River Civil War of 1869–70," *Canadian Historical Review* 57 (1976): 133–49.

11. A notable exception to this viewpoint is that expressed by Stanley in 1952. He pointed out that programmes oriented towards assimilating the Indians into the dominant white society lead to cultural extinction of the former group. This is offensive to any people having a strong sense of identity. See Stanley. p. 21.

12. R. G. Thwaites, ed., *The Jesuit Relations and Allied Documents*, vol. 6 (New York: Pagent Book Company, 1959), pp. 297–99.

13. K. G. Davies, ed., *Letters from Hudson Bay, 1703–40* (London: Hudson's Bay Record Society, 1965), p. 136.

14. E. E. Rich, ed., *Minutes of the Hudson's Bay Company, 1671–74* (Toronto: Champlain Society, 1942), pp. 26–27, 58–59.

15. Ibid., p. 91.

16. A. J. Ray, *Indians in the Fur Trade* (Toronto: University of Toronto Press, 1974), p. 75.

17. For example, in the eighteenth century Arthur Dobbs charged that the company advanced the prices of its goods above the Standards of Trade to such an extent that it discouraged the Indians from trading. Arthur Dobbs, *An Account of the Countries Adjoining to Hudson's Bay in the Northwest Part of America* (London, 1744), p. 43. More recently the company has been attacked for its pricing policy by Adams, *Prison of Grass*, p. 24.

18. C. E. Heidenreich and A. J. Ray, *The Early Fur Trades: A Study in Cultural Interaction* (Toronto: McClelland and Stewart, 1976), pp. 82–83.

19. A. J. Ray, "The Hudson's Bay Company Account Books As Sources for Comparative Economic Analyses of the Fur Trade: An Examination of Exchange Rate Data," *Western Canadian Journal of Anthropology* 6, no. 1 (1976): 44–50.

20. The principal exception was at Eastmain where the prevailing rates exceeded the 50 per cent markup level from the late 1690's until about 1720. However, it should be pointed out that French opposition was relatively weak in this area. See Ray, "Hudson's Bay Company Account Books," pp. 45–50.

21. For example, one of the virtues of Indian leaders was generosity. And, generalized reciprocity or sharing was practised amongst band members. These values and practices served to discourage any individual, regardless of his position, from accumulating wealth in excess of that of his kinsmen.

22. Generally, alcohol was diluted with water by a ratio of one-quarter to one-third at the Hudson's Bay Company posts in the eighteenth century. See Davies, *Letters from Hudson Bay*, p. 268.

23. Ray, *Indians in the Fur Trade*, pp. 117–24.

24. Adams, *Prison of Grass*, p. 51; and Susan Hurlich, "Up Against the Bay: Resource Imperialism and Native Resistance," *This Magazine* 9, no. 4 (1975): 4.

173

"Women in Between": Indian Women in Fur Trade Society in Western Canada*

SYLVIA VAN KIRK

In attempting to analyse the life of the Indian women in fur trade society in Western Canada, especially from her own point of view, one is immediately confronted by a challenging historiographical problem. Can the Indian women's perspective be constructed from historical sources that were almost exclusively written by European men? Coming from a non-literate society, no Indian women have left us, for example, their views on the fur trade or their reasons for becoming traders' wives.[1] Yet if one amasses the sources available for fur trade social history, such as contemporary narratives, journals, correspondence and wills, a surprisingly rich store of information on Indian women emerges. One must, of course, be wary of the traders' cultural and sexual bias, but then even modern anthropologists have difficulty maintaining complete objectivity. Furthermore, the fur traders had the advantage of knowing Indian women intimately — these women became their wives, the mothers of their children. Narratives such as that of Andrew Graham in the late eighteenth century and David Thompson in the nineteenth, both of whom had native wives, comment perceptively on the implications of Indian-white social contact.[2] The key to constructing the Indian woman's perspective must lie in the kinds of questions applied to data;[3] regrettably the picture will not be complete, but it is hoped that a careful reading of the traders' observations can result in a useful and illuminating account of the Indian women's life in fur trade society.

174

The fur trade was based on the complex interaction between two different racial groups. On the one hand are the various Indian tribes, most importantly the Ojibway, the Cree and the Chipewyan. These Indians may be designated the "host" group in that they remain within their traditional environment. On the other hand are the European traders, the "visiting" group, who enter the Northwest by both the Hudson's Bay and St. Lawrence-Great Lakes routes. They are significantly different from the Indians in that they constitute only a small, all-male fragment of their own society. For a variety of factors to be discussed, this created a unique situation for the Indian women. They became the "women in between" two groups of males. Because of their sex, Indian women were able to become an integral part of fur trade society in a sense that Indian men never could. As country wives[4] of the traders, Indian women lived substantially different lives when they moved within the forts. Even within the tribes, women who acted as allies of the whites can also be observed; certain circumstances per-

*From the *Canadian Historical Association* Historical Papers 1977, pp. 30-47. Copyright by the Canadian Historical Association. Reprinted by permission.

mitted individual women to gain positions of influence and act as "social brokers" between the two groups.

It is a major contention of this study that Indian women themselves were active agents in the development of Indian-white relations.[5] A major concern then must be to determine what motivated their actions. Some themes to be discussed are the extent to which the Indian woman was able to utilize her position as "woman in between" to increase her influence and status, and the extent to which the Indian woman valued the economic advantage brought by the traders. It must be emphasized, however, that Indian-white relations were by no means static during the fur trade period.[6] After assessing the positive and negative aspects of the Indian woman's life in fur trade society, the paper will conclude by discussing the reasons for the demise of her position.

I
175

Miscegenation was the basic social fact of the western Canadian fur trade. That this was so indicates active cooperation on both sides. From the male perspective, both white and Indian, the formation of marital alliances between Indian women and the traders had its advantages. The European traders had both social and economic reasons for taking Indian mates. Not only did they fill the sexual void created by the absence of white women,[7] but they performed such valuable economic tasks as making moccasins and netting snowshoes that they became an integral if unofficial part of the fur trade work force.[8] The traders also realized that these alliances were useful in cementing trade ties; officers in both the Hudson's Bay and North West companies often married daughters of trading captains or chiefs.[9] From the Indian point of view, the marital alliance created a reciprocal social bond which served to consolidate his economic relationship with the trader. The exchange of women was common in Indian society where it was viewed as "a reciprocal alliance and series of good offices . . . between the friends of both parties; each is ready to assist and protect the other."[10] It was not loose morality or even hospitality which prompted the Indians to be so generous with their offers of women. This was their way of drawing the traders into their kinship circle, and in return for giving the traders sexual and domestic rights to their women, the Indians expected equitable privileges such as free access to the posts and provisions.[11] It is evident that the traders often did not understand the Indian concept of these alliances and a flagrant violation of Indian sensibilities could lead to retaliation such as the Henley House massacre in 1755.[12]

But what of the women themselves? Were they just pawns in this exchange, passive, exploited victims? Fur trade sources do not support this view; there are numerous examples of Indian women actively seeking to become connected with the traders. According to an early Nor'Wester, Cree women considered it an honour to be selected as wives by the voyageurs, and any husband who refused to lend his wife would be subject to the general condemnation of the women.[13] Alexander Ross observed that Chinook women on the Pacific coast showed a preference for living with a white man. If deserted by one husband, they would return to their tribe in a state of widowhood to await the opportunity of marrying another fur trader.[14] Nor'Wester Daniel Harmon voiced the widely-held opinion that most of the Indian women were "better pleased to remain with the White People than with their own Relations", while his contemporary George Nelson affirmed "some too would even desert to live with the white".[15] Although Alexander Henry the Younger may have exaggerated his difficulties in fending off young Indian women, his personal experiences underline the fact that the women often took the initiative. On one occasion when travelling with his brigade in the summer of 1800, Henry was confronted in his tent by a handsome woman, dressed in her best finery, who told him boldly that she had come to live with him as she did not care for her husband or any other Indian. But Henry, anxious

176 to avoid this entanglement partly because it was not sanctioned by the husband whom he knew to be insatiably jealous, forced the woman to return to her Indian partner.[16] A year or so later in the lower Red River district, the daughter of an Ojibway chief had more luck. Henry returned from New Year's festivities to find that "Liard's daughter" had taken possession of his room and the devil could not have got her out".[17] This time, having become more acculturated to fur trade life, Henry acquiesced and "Liard's daughter" became his country wife. The trader, however, resisted his father-in-law's argument that he should also take his second daughter because all great men should have a plurality of wives.[18]

The fur traders also comment extensively on the assistance and loyalty of Indian women who remained within the tribes. An outstanding example is the young Chipewyan Thanadelthur, known to the traders as the "Slave Woman".[19] In the early eighteenth century after being captured by the Cree, Thanadelthur managed to escape to York Factory. Her knowledge of Chipewyan made her valuable to the traders, and in 1715-16, she led an H.B.C. expedition to establish peace between the Cree and the Chipewyan, a necessary prelude to the founding of Fort Churchill. Governor James Knight's journals give us a vivid picture of this woman, of whom he declared: "She was one of a Very high Spirit and of the Firmest Resolution that ever I see any Body in my Days."[20]

Post journals contain numerous references to Indian women warning the traders of impending treachery. In 1797, Charles Chaboillez, having been warned by an old woman that the Indians intended to pillage his post, was able to nip this intrigue in the bud.[21] George Nelson and one of his men only escaped an attack by some Indians in 1805 by being "clandestinely assisted by the women".[22] It appears that women were particularly instrumental in saving the lives of the whites among the turbulent tribes of the Lower Columbia.[23] One of the traders' most notable allies was the well-connected Chinook princess known as Lady Calpo, the wife of a Clatsop chief. In 1814, she helped restore peaceful relations after the Nor'Westers had suffered a raid on their canoes by giving them important information about Indian custom in settling disputes. Handsome rewards cemented her attachment to the traders with the result that Lady Calpo reputedly saved Fort George from several attacks by warning of the hostile plans of the Indians.[24]

The reasons for the Indian women's action are hinted at in the traders' observations. It was the generally held opinion of the traders that the status of women in Indian society was deplorably low. As Nor'Wester Gabriel Franchère summed it up:

Some Indian tribes think that women have no souls, but die altogether like the brutes; others assign them a different paradise from that of men, which indeed they might have reason to prefer . . . unless their relative condition were to be ameliorated in the next world.[25]

Whether as "social brokers" or as wives, Indian women attempted to manipulate their position as "women in between" to increase their influence and status. Certainly women such as Thanadelthur and Lady Calpo were able to work themselves into positions of real power. It is rather paradoxical that in Thanadelthur's case it was her escape from captivity that brought her into contact with the traders in the first place; if she had not been a woman, she would never have been carried off by the Cree as a prize of war. Once inside the H.B.C. fort, she was able to use her position as the only Chipewyan to advantage by acting as guide and consultant to the Governor. The protection and regard she was given by the whites enabled Thanadelthur to dictate to Indian men, both Cree and Chipewyan, in a manner they would not previously have tolerated. Anxious to promote the traders' interests, she assaulted an old Chipewyan on one occasion when he attempted to trade less than prime furs; she "ketcht him by the nose Push'd him backwards & call'd him fool and told him if they brought any but Such as they ware directed they would not be traded."[26] Thanadelthur did take a Chipewyan husband but was quite prepared to leave him if he would not accompany her on the arduous second journey she was planning to undertake for the Governor.[27] It is possible that the role played by Thanadelthur and subsequent "slave women" in establishing trade relations with the whites may have enhanced the status of Chipewyan women. Nearly a century later, Alexander Mackenzie noted that, in spite of their burdensome existence, Chipewyan women possessed "a very considerable influence in the traffic with Europeans."[28]

Lady Calpo retained a position of influence for a long time. When Governor Simpson visited Fort George in 1824, he found she had to be treated with respect because she was "the best News Monger in the Parish"; from her he learned "More of the Scandal, Secrets and politics both of the out & inside of the Fort than from Any other source."[29] Significantly, Lady Calpo endeavoured to further improve her rank by arranging a marriage alliance between the Governor and her carefully-raised daughter. Although

177

Simpson declared he wished "to keep clear of the Daughter", he succumbed in order "to continue on good terms with the Mother."[30] Many years later, a friend visiting the Columbia wrote to Simpson that Lady Calpo that "'fast friend' of the Whites" was still thriving.[31]

As wives of the traders, Indian women could also manoeuver themselves into positions of influence. In fact, a somewhat perturbed discussion emerges in fur trade literature over the excessive influence some Indian women exerted over their fur trader husbands. The young N.W.C. clerk George Nelson appears to have spent long hours contemplating the insoluable perplexities of womankind. Nelson claimed that initially Cree women when married to whites were incredibly attentive and submissive, but this did not last long. Once they had gained a little footing, they knew well "how to take advantage & what use they ought to make of it."[32] On one of his first trips into the interior, Nelson was considerably annoyed by the shenanigans of the Indian wife of Brunet, one of his voyageurs. A jealous, headstrong woman, she completely dominated her husband by a mixture of "caresses, promises & menaces". Not only did this woman render her husband a most unreliable servant, but Nelson also caught her helping herself to the Company's rum. Brunet's wife, Nelson fumed, was as great "a vixen & hussy" as the tinsmith's wife at the market place in Montreal: "I now began to think that women were women not only in civilized countries but elsewhere also."[33]

Another fur trader observed a paradoxical situation among the Chipewyan women. In their own society, they seemed condemned to a most servile existence, but upon becoming wives of the French-Canadian voyageurs, they assumed "an importance to themselves and instead of serving as formerly they exact submission from the descendants of the Gauls."[34] One of the most remarkable examples of a Chipewyan wife rising to prominence was the case of Madam Lamallice, the wife of the brigade guide at the H.B.C. post on Lake Athabasca. During the difficult winter of 1821-22, Madam Lamallice was accorded a favoured position because she was the post's only interpreter and possessed considerable influence with the Indians.[35] George Simpson, then experiencing his first winter in the Indian Country, felt obliged to give in to her demands for extra rations and preferred treatment in order to prevent her defection. He had observed that the Nor'Westers' strong position was partly due to the fact that ". . . their Women are faithful to their cause and good Interpreters whereas we have but one in the Fort that can talk Chipewyan."[36] Madam Lamallice exploited her position to such an extent that she even defied fort regulations by carrying on a private trade in provisions.[37] A few years later on a trip to the Columbia, Governor Simpson was annoyed to discover that Chinook women when married to the whites often gained such an ascendancy "that they give law to their Lords".[38] In fact, he expressed general concern about the influence of these "petticoat politicians" whose demands were "more injurious to the Companys interests that I am well able to describe."[39] The Governor deplored Chief Factor James Bird's management of Red River in the early 1820s because of his habit of discussing every matter "however trifling or important" with "his Copper

Cold. Mate'', who then spread the news freely around the colony.[40] Too many of his officers, Simpson declared, tended to sacrifice business for private interests. Particular expense and delay were occasioned in providing transport for families. Simpson never forgave Chief Factor John Clarke for abandoning some of the goods destined for Athabasca in 1820 to make a light canoe for his native wife and her servant.[41]

It is likely that Simpson's single-minded concern for business efficiency caused him to exaggerate the extent of the Indian women's influence. Nevertheless, they do seem to have attempted to take advantage of their unique position as women "in between" two groups of men. This fact is supported by the traders' observation that the choice of a husband, Indian or white, gave the Indian women leverage to improve her lot. Now she could threaten to desert to the whites or vice versa if she felt she were not being well-treated:

She has always enough of policy to insinuate how well off she was while living with the white people and in like manner when with the latter she drops some hints to the same purpose.[42]

179

Although Chipewyan women who have lived with the voyageurs had to resume their former domestic tasks when they returned to their own people, they reputedly evinced a greater spirit of independence.[43] Considerable prestige accrued to Chinook women who had lived with the traders; upon rejoining the tribes, they remained "very friendly" to the whites and "never fail to influence their connections to the same effect."[44]

From the Indian woman's point of view, material advantage was closely tied to the question of improved influence or status. The women within the tribes had a vested interest in promoting cordial relations with the whites. While George Nelson mused that it was a universal maternal instinct which prompted the women to try to prevent clashes between Indian and white,[45] they were more likely motivated by practical, economic considerations. If the traders were driven from the country, the Indian woman would lose the source of European goods, which had revolutionized her life just as much if not more than that of the Indian man. It was much easier to boil water in a metal kettle than to have to laboriously heat it by means of dropping hot stones into a bark container. Cotton and woolen goods, saved long hours of tanning hides. "Show them an awl or a strong needle," declared David Thompson, "and they will gladly give the finest Beaver or Wolf skin they have to purchase it."[46]

Furthermore, it can be argued that the tendency of the Indians to regard the fur trade post as a kind of welfare centre was of more relevance to the women than to the men. In times of scarcity, which were not infrequent in Indian society, the women were usually the first to suffer.[47] Whereas before they would often have perished, many now sought relief at the companies' posts. To cite but one of many examples: at Albany during the winter of 1706, Governor Beale gave shelter to three starving Cree women whose husband had sent them away as he could only provide for his two children.[48]

The post was also a source of medical aid and succour. The story is told of a young Carrier woman in New Caledonia, who having been severely beaten by her husband managed to struggle to the nearest N.W.C. post. Being nearly starved, she was slowly nursed back to health and allowed to remain at the post when it became apparent that her relatives had abandoned her.[49] The desire for European goods, coupled with the assistance to be found at the fur trade posts, helps to explain why Indian women often became devoted allies of the traders.

In becoming the actual wife of a fur trader, the Indian woman was offered even greater relief from the burdens of her traditional existence. In fact, marriage to a trader offered an alternative lifestyle. The fur traders themselves had no doubt that an Indian woman was much better off with a white man. The literature presents a dreary recital of their abhorrence of the degraded, slave-like position of the Indian women. The life of a Cree woman, declared Alexander Mackenzie, was "an uninterrupted success of toil and pain."[50] Nor'Wester Duncan McGillivray decided that the rather singular lack of affection evinced by Plains Indian women for their mates arose from the barbarous treatment the women received.[51] Although David Thompson found the Chipewyan a good people in many ways, he considered their attitudes toward women a disgrace; he had known Chipewyan women to kill female infants as "an act of kindness" to spare them the hardships they would have to face.[52]

180

The extent to which the fur traders' observations represent an accurate reflection of the actual status of Indian women in their own societies presents a complex dilemma which requires deeper investigation. The cultural and class biases of the traders are obvious. Their horror at the toilsome burdens imposed upon Indian women stems from their narrow, chivalrous view of women as the "frail, weaker sex". This is scarcely an appropriate description of Indian women, particularly the Chipewyan who were acknowledged to be twice as strong as their male counterparts.[53] Furthermore, while the sharp sexual division of labour inflicted a burdensome role upon the women, their duties were essential and the women possessed considerable autonomy within their own sphere.[54] Some traders did think it curious that the women seemed to possess a degree of influence in spite of their degraded situation; indeed, some of the bolder ones occasionally succeeded in making themselves quite independent and "wore the breeches".[55]

A possible way of explaining the discrepancy between the women's perceived and actual status is suggested in a recent anthropological study of the Mundurucú of Amazonian Brazil. In this society, the authors discovered that while the official (male) ideology relegates women to an inferior, subservient position, in the reality of daily life, the women are able to assume considerable autonomy and influence.[56] Most significantly, however, Mundurucú women, in order to alleviate their onerous domestic duties, have actively championed the erosion of traditional village life and the concomitant blurring of economic sex roles which have come with the introduction of the rubber trade. According to the authors, the Mundurucú woman "has seen another way of life, and she has opted for it."[57]

This statement could well be applied to the Indian woman who was attracted to the easier life of the fur trade post. In the first place, she now became involved in a much more sedentary routine. With a stationary home, the Indian woman was no longer required to act as a beast of burden, hauling or carrying the accoutrements of camp from place to place. The traders often expressed astonishment and pity at the heavy loads which Indian women were obliged to transport.[58] In fur trade society, the unenviable role of carrier was assumed by the voyageur. The male servants at the fort were now responsible for providing firewood and water, although the women might help. In contrast to Indian practice, the women of the fort were not sent to fetch home the produce of the hunt.[59] The wife of an officer, benefitting from her husband's rank, enjoyed a privileged status. She herself was carried in and out of the canoe[60] and could expect to have all her baggage portaged by a voyageur. At Fond du Lac in 1804 when the wife of N.W.C. *bourgeois* John Sayer decided to go on a sugar-making expedition, four men went with her to carry her baggage and provisions and later returned to fetch home her things.[61]

While the Indian woman performed a variety of valuable economic tasks around the post, her domestic duties were relatively lighter than they had traditionally been. Now her energies were concentrated on making moccasins and snowshoes. As one Nor'Wester declared, with the whites, Indian women could lead "a comparatively easy and free life" in contrast to the "servile slavish mode" of their own.[62] The prospect of superior comforts reputedly motivated some Spokan women to marry voyageurs.[63] The ready supply of both finery and trinkets which *bourgeois* and voyageurs were seen to lavish on their women may also have had an appeal.[64] Rival traders noted that luxury items such as lace, ribbons, rings and vermilion, which "greatly gain the Love of the Women", were important in attracting the Indians to trade.[65] The private orders placed by H.B.C. officers and servants in the 1790s and later include a wide range of cloth goods, shawls, gartering, earrings and brooches for the women.[66] When taken by a trader *à la façon du pays*, it became common for an Indian woman to go through a ritual performed by the other women of the fort; she was scoured of grease and paint and exchanged her native garments for those of a more civilized fashion. At the N.W.C. posts, wives were clothed in "Canadian fashion" which consisted of a shirt, short gown, petticoat and leggings.[67]

The traders further thought that Indian women benefitted by being freed from certain taboos and customs which they had to bear in Indian society. Among the Ojibway and other tribes, for example, the choicest part of an animal was always reserved for the men; death it was believed would come to any woman who dared to eat such sacred portions. The Nor'Westers paid little heed to such observances. As Duncan Cameron sarcastically wrote: "I have often seen several women living with the white men eat of those forbidden morsels without the least inconvenience."[68] The traders were also convinced that Indian women welcomed a monogamous as opposed to a

181

polygamous state. Polygamy, several H.B.C. officers observed, often gave rise to jealous and sometimes murderous quarrels.[69] It is possible, however, that the traders' own cultural abhorrence of polygamy[70] made them exaggerate the women's antipathy toward it. As a practical scheme for the sharing of heavy domestic tasks, polygamy may in fact have been welcomed by the women.

II

Thus far the advantages which the fur trade brought to Indian women have been emphasized in order to help explain Indian women's reactions to it. It would be erroneous, however, to paint the life of an Indian wife as idyllic. In spite of the traders' belief in the superior benfits they offered, there is evidence that fur trade life had an adverse effect on Indian women. Certainly, a deterioration in her position over time can be detected.

182

First there is the paradox that the supposedly superior material culture of the fur trade had a deleterious effect on Indian women. It was as if, mused Reverend John West, the first Anglican missionary, "the habits of civilized life" exerted an injurious influence over their general constitutions.[71] Apart from being more exposed to European diseases, the Indian wives of traders suffered more in childbirth than they had in the primitive state.[72] Dr. John Richardson, who accompanied the Franklin Expedition of the 1820s noted, that not only did Indian women now have children more frequently and for longer periods, but that they were more susceptible to the disorders and diseases connected with pregnancy and childbirth.[73] It was not uncommon for fur traders' wives to give birth to from eight to twelve children, whereas four children were the average in Cree society.[74]

The reasons for this dramatic rise in the birth rate deserves further investigation, but several reasons can be advanced. As recent medical research had suggested, the less fatiguing lifestyle and more regular diet offered the Indian wife could have resulted in great fecundity.[75] The daily ration for the women of the forts was four pounds of meat or fish (one half that for the men);[76] when Governor Simpson jokingly remarked that the whitefish diet at Fort Chipewyan seemed conducive to procreation he may have hit upon a medical truth.[77] Furthermore sexual activity in Indian society was circumscribed by a variety of taboos, and evidence suggests that Indian men regarded their European counterparts as very licentious.[78] Not only did Indian women now have sex more often, but the attitudes of European husbands also may have interfered with traditional modes of restricting family size. The practice of infanticide was, of course, condemned by the whites, but the Europeans may also have discouraged the traditional long nursing periods of from two to four years for each child.[79] In their view this custom resulted in the premature aging of the mothers,[80] but the fact that Indian children were born at intervals of approximately three years tends to support the recent theory that lactation depresses fertility.[81]

The cultural conflict resulting over the upbringing of the children must have caused the Indian women considerable anguish. An extreme example of the tragedy which could result related to the Chinook practice of head-flattening. In Chinook society, a flat forehead, achieved by strapping a board against the baby's head when in its cradle, was a mark of class; only slaves were not so distinguished. Thus it was only natural that a Chinook woman, though married to a fur trader, would desire to bind her baby's head, but white fathers found this custom abhorrent. The insistence of some fathers that their infants' heads not be flattened resulted in the mothers murdering their babies rather than have them suffer the ignominy of looking like slaves. Gradually European preference prevailed. When Governor Simpson visited the Columbia in the early 1820s, he reported that Chinook wives were abiding by their husbands' wishes and no cases of infanticide had been reported for some years.[82]

In Indian society, children were the virtual "property" of the women who were responsible for their upbringing;[83] in fur trade society, Indian women could find themselves divested of these rights. While the traders acknowledged that Indian women were devoted and affectionate mothers, this did not prevent them from exercising patriarchal authority, particularly in sending young children to Britain or Canada so that they might receive a "civilized" education.[84] It must have been nearly impossible to explain the rationale for such a decision to the Indian mothers; their grief at being separated from their children was compounded by the fact that the children, who were especially vulnerable to respiratory diseases, often died.[85]

183

It is difficult to know if the general treatment accorded Indian women by European traders met with the women's acceptance. How much significance should be attached to the views of outside observers in the early 1800s who did not think the Indian woman's status had been much improved? Some of the officers of the Franklin Expedition felt the fur traders had been corrupted by Indian attitudes toward women; Indian wives were not treated with "the tenderness and attention due to every female" because the Indians would despise the traders for such unmanly action.[86] The first missionaries were even stronger in denouncing fur trade marital relations. John West considered the traders' treatment of their women disgraceful: "They do not admit them as their companions, nor do they allow them to eat at their tables, but degrade them *merely* as slaves to their arbitrary inclinations."[87] Such statements invite skepticism because of the writers' limited contact with fur trade society, and in the case of the missionaries because of their avowedly hostile view of fur trade customs. Furthermore, the above statements project a European ideal about the way women should be treated, which apart from being widely violated in their own society, would have had little relevance for Indian women. It is doubtful, for example, that the Indian women themselves would have viewed the fact that they did not come to table, a custom partly dictated by the quasi-military organization of the posts, as proof of their debased position.[88] The segregation of the sexes at meals was common in Indian society, but now, at least, the women did not have to suffice with the leftovers of the men.[89]

Nevertheless, there is evidence to suggest that Indian women were misused by the traders. In Indian society, women were accustomed to greater freedom of action with regard to marital relationships than the traders were prepared to accord them. It was quite within a woman's rights, for example, to institute a divorce if her marriage proved unsatisfactory.[90] In fur trade society, Indian women were more subject to arbitrary arrangements devised by the men. Upon retiring from the Indian Country, it became customary for a trader to place his country wife and family with another, a practice known as "turning off". Although there was often little they could do about it, a few cases were cited of women who tried to resist. At a post in the Peace River district in 1798, the Indian wife of an *engagé*, who was growing tired of wintering *en derouine*, absolutely rejected her husband's attempt to pass her to the man who agreed to take his place.[91] At Fort Chipewyan in 1800, the estranged wife of the voyageur Morin foiled the attempt of his *bourgeois* to find her a temporary "protector"; she stoutly refused three different prospects.[92] Indian women also did not take kindly to the long separations which fur trade life imposed on them and their European mates. Although the Indian wife of Chief Factor Joseph Colen was to receive every attention during his absence in England in the late 1790s, Colen's successor could not dissuade her from taking an Indian lover and leaving York Factory.[93]

184

Indian wives seem to have been particularly victimized during the violent days of the trade war when rivals went so far as to debauch and intimidate each other's women. In 1819 at Pelican Lake, for example, H.B.C. servant Deshau took furs from a N.W.C. servant and raped his wife in retaliation for having had his own wife debauched by a Nor'Wester earlier in the season.[94] A notorious instance involved the Indian wife of H.B.C. servant Andrew Kirkness at Isle à la Crosse in 1810-11. In the late summer, this woman in a fit of pique had deserted her husband and sought refuge at the Nor'Westers' post. She soon regretted her action, however, for she was kept a virtual prisoner by the Canadians, and all efforts of the H.B.C. men to get her back failed. The upshot was that Kirkness himself deserted to the rival post, leaving the English in dire straits since he was their only fisherman. Kirkness was intimidated into remaining with the Nor'Westers until the spring with the threat that should he try to leave "every Canadian in the House would ravish his woman before his eyes." Eventually Kirkness was released, but only after his wife had been coerced into saying that she did not want to accompany him. As the H.B.C. party were evacuating their post, the woman tried to escape but was forcibly dragged back by the Nor'Westers and ultimately became the "property" of an *engagé*.[95]

Such abusive tactics were also applied to the Indians. By the turn of the century, relations between the Indians and the Nor'Westers in particular showed a marked deterioration. In what seems to have been a classic case of "familiarity breeding contempt", the Nor'Westers now retained their mastery through coercion and brute force and frequently transgressed the bounds of Indian morality. An especially flagrant case was the Nor'Westers' exploitation of Chipewyan women at its posts in the Athabasca district. By the end of the eighteenth century, they had apparently built up a nefarious traffic in these women; the *bourgeois* did not scruple at seizing Chipewyan women by force, ostensibly in lieu of trade debts, and then selling them to the men for large sums.[96] The situation became so bad that the Chipewyan began leaving their women behind when they came to trade, and when Hudson's Bay traders appeared on Lake Athabasca in 1792, the Indians hoped to secure their support and drive out their rivals. The English, however, were too weak to offer any effective check to the Nor'Westers who continued to assault both fathers and husbands if they tried to resist the seizure of their women. Since they were not powerful enough to mount an attack, the Chipewyan connived at the escape of their women during the summer months when most of the traders were away. Resentful of their treatment, many of the women welcomed the chance to slip back to their own people so that the summer master at Fort Chipewyan was almost solely preoccupied with keeping watch over the *engagés* women.[97] By 1800 at least one voyageur had been killed by irate Chipewyan, and the *bourgeois* contemplated offering a reward for the hunting down of "any d--nd rascal" who caused a Frenchman's woman to desert.[98]

185

The Indians appear to have become openly contemptuous of the white man and his so-called morality. A northern tribe called the Beaver Indians took a particularly strong stand. At first they had welcomed the Canadians but, having rapidly lost respect for them, now forbade any intercourse between their women and the traders.[99] Elsewhere individual hunters boycotted the traders owing to the maltreatment of their women.[100] Sporadic reprisals became more frequent. Whereas Indian women had previously played a positive role as a liaison between Indian and white, they were now becoming an increasing source of friction between the two groups. Governor Simpson summed up the deteriorating situation:

It is a lamentable fact that almost every difficulty we have had with Indians throughout the country may be traced to our interference with the Women of the Forts in short 9 murders out of 10 Committed on Whites by Indians have arisen through Women.[101]

Although there is little direct evidence available, it is possible that the Indian women themselves were becoming increasingly dissatisfied with their treatment from the whites. In spite of the initiative which the women have been seen to exercise in forming and terminating relationships with the traders, there were undoubtedly times when they were the unwilling objects of a transaction between Indians and white men. Certainly not all Indian women looked upon the whites as desirable husbands, a view that was probably reinforced with experience. George Nelson did observe in 1811 that there were some Indian women who showed "an extraordinary predilection" for their own people and could not be prevailed upon to live with the traders.[102]

The increasing hostility of the Indians, coupled with the fact that in well-established areas marriage alliances were no longer a significant factor in trade relations, led to a decline in the practice of taking an Indian wife. In fact in 1806, the North West Company passed a ruling prohibiting any of its employees from taking a country wife from among the tribes.[103] One of the significant factors which changed the traders' attitudes toward Indian women, however, was that they were now no longer "women in between". By the turn of the century a sizeable group of mixed-blood women had emerged and for social and economic reasons, fur traders preferred mixed-blood women as wives. In this way the Indian women lost their important place in fur trade society.

The introduction of the Indian woman's perspective on Indian-white relations serves to underscore the tremendous complexity of inter-cultural contact. It is argued that Indian women saw definite advantages to be gained from the fur trade, and in their unique position as "women in between", they endeavoured to manipulate the situation to improve their existence. That the limits of their influence were certainly circumscribed, and that the ultimate benefits brought by the traders were questionable does not negate the fact that the Indian women played a much more active and important role in the fur trade than has previously been acknowledged.

186

Notes

1. The lack of written Indian history is, of course, a general problem for the ethnohistorian. Indeed, all social scientists must rely heavily on the historical observations of the agents of white contact such as fur traders, explorers and missionaries. Little seems to have been done to determine if the oral tradition of the Indians is a viable source of information on Indian-white relations in the fur trade period.

2. Glyndwr Williams, ed. *Andrew Graham's Observations on Hudson's Bay 1769-91* (London, Hudson's Bay Record Society, v. XXVII, 1969); Richard Glover, ed. *David Thompson's Narrative 1784-1812* (Toronto, Champlain Society, v. XL, 1962).

3. A fascinating study which indicates how the application of a different perspective to the same data can produce new insights is *Women of the Forest* by Yolanda and Robert Murphy (New York, 1974). Based on field work conducted twenty years earlier in Amazonian Brazil, the authors found that by looking at the life of the Mundurucú tribe from the woman's point of view, their understanding of the actual as opposed to the official functioning of that society was much enlarged.

4. Marriages between European traders and Indian women were contracted according to indigenous rites derived from the Indian custom. For a detailed explanation, see Sylvia Van Kirk, "'The Custom of the Country': An Examination of Fur Trade Marriage Practices" in L.H. Thomas, ed., *Essays in Western History* (Edmonton, 1976), pp. 49-70.

5. See Murphy, *Women of the Forest*, Ch. 6 for a useful comparison. Mundurucú women actively welcomed the social change brought about by the introduction of the rubber trade into their traditional economy.

6. An instructive study of the Indians' economic role in the fur trade is provided by Arthur Ray in *Indians in the Fur Trade* (Toronto, 1974). He shows that the Indian played a much more active, although changing role in the dynamics of the fur trade than had previously been acknowledged.

7. H.B.C. men were prohibited from bringing women to Hudson Bay. It was not until the early nineteenth century that the first white women came to the Northwest.

8. In 1802 H.B.C. men defended their practice of keeping Indian women in the posts by informing the London Committee that they were "Virtually your Honors Servants", H.B.C. Arch., B.239/b/79, fos. 40d-41. For a discussion of the important economic role played by native women in the fur trade, see Sylvia Van Kirk, "The Role of Women in the Fur Trade Society of the Canadian West, 1700-1850", unpublished Ph.D. thesis, University of London, 1975.

9. H.B.C. Arch., Albany Journal, 24 Jan. 1771, B.3/a/63, f. 18d; "Connolly vs. Woolrich, Superior Court, 9 July 1867, *Lower Canada Jurist*, vol. XI, p. 234.

10. Charles Bishop, "The Henley House Massacres", *The Beaver* (Autumn), 1976, p. 40.
11. *Ibid.*, p. 39. For a more technical look at the socio-economic relationship between the Indians and the traders, see the discussion of "balanced reciprocity" in Marshall Sahlins, *Stone Age Economics* (Chicago, 1972), Ch. 5.
12. In this instance the Indian captain Woudby attacked Henley House because the master was keeping two of his female relatives but denying him access to the post and its provisions.
13. Alexander Henry, *Travels and Adventures in Canada and the Indian Territories 1760-1776*, ed. by Jas. Bain. (Boston, 1901), p. 248.
14. Alexander Ross, *The Fur Hunters of the Far West*, Vol. 1, (London, 1855), pp. 296-97.
15. W. Kaye Lamb, ed., *Sixteen Years in the Indian Country: The Journal of Daniel Williams Harmon 1800-1816* (Toronto, 1957), p. 29; Toronto Public Library, George Nelson Papers, Journal 1810-11, 24 April 1811, p. 42.
16. Elliot Coues, ed., *New Light on the Early History of the Greater North West: The Manuscript Journals of Alexander Henry and David Thompson 1799-1814*, (Minneapolis, 1965), pp. 71-73.
17. *Ibid.*, p. 163.
18. *Ibid.*, p. 211.
19. For a detailed account of the story of this woman, see Sylvia Van Kirk, "Thanadelthur", *The Beaver*, (Spring), 1974, pp. 40-45.
20. *Ibid.*, p. 45.
21. Public Archives of Canada (P.A.C.), Masson Collection, Journal of Charles Chaboillez, 13 Dec. 1797, p. 24.
22. Nelson Papers, Journal and Reminiscences 1825-26, p. 66.
23. Ross, *Fur Hunters*, Vol. 1, p. 296.
24. Coues, *New Light*, p. 793; Frederick Merk, ed. *Fur Trade and Empire: George Simpson's Journal, 1824-25* (Cambridge, Mass., 1931), p. 104.
25. Gabriel Franchère, *Narrative of a Voyage to the Northwest Coast of America 1811-14*. ed. R.G. Thwaites, (Cleveland, Ohio, 1904), p. 327.
26. Van Kirk, "Thanadelthur", p. 44.
27. *Ibid.*, p. 45.
28. W. Kaye Lamb, ed. *The Journals and Letters of Sir Alexander Mackenzie* (Cambridge, Eng., 1970), p. 152.
29. Merk, *Fur Trade & Empire*, p. 104.
30. *Ibid.*, pp. 104-105.
31. H.B.C. Arch., R. Crooks to G. Simpson, 15 March 1843, D. 5/8, f. 147.
32. Nelson Papers, Journal 1810-11, pp. 41-42.
33. Nelson Papers, Journal 1803-04, pp. 10-28 *passim*.
34. Masson Collection, "An Account of the Chipwean Indians", p. 23.
35. E.E. Rich, ed. *Simpson's Athabasca Journal and Report 1820-21* (London, H.B.R.S., v. I, 1938), p. 74.
36. *Ibid.*, 231.
37. H.B.C. Arch., For Chipewyan Journal 1820-21, B.39/a/16, fos. 6-21d. *passim*.
38. Merk, *Fur Trade & Empire*, p. 99.
39. *Ibid.*, pp. 11-12, 58.
40. H.B.C. Arch., George Simpson's Journal 1821-22. D. 3/3, f. 52.
41. Rich, *Athabasca Journal*, pp. 23-24; see also Merk, *Fur Trade & Empire*, p. 131.
42. "Account of Chipwean Indians", pp. 23-24.
43. *Ibid.*, p. 23.
44. Ross, *Fur Hunters*, vol. 1, p. 297.
45. Nelson Papers, Journal and Reminiscences 1825-26, p. 66. Nelson claimed that around 1780 some Indian women had warned the Canadian pedlars of impending attack because in their "tender & affectionate breast (for women are lovely all the world over) still lurked compassion for the mothers of those destined to be sacrificed."
46. Glover, *Thompson's Narrative*, p. 45. Cf. with the Mundurucú women's desire for European goods, Murphy, *Women of the Forest*, p. 182.
47. Samuel Hearne, *A Journey to the Northern Ocean*, edited by Richard Glover, (Toronto, 1958), p. 190.
48. H.B.C. Arch., Albany Journal, 23 Feb. 1706, B.3/a/1, f. 28.
49. Ross Cox, *The Columbia River*, edited by Jane and Edgar Stewart, (Norman, Okla., 1957), p. 377.
50. Lamb, *Journals of Mackenzie*, p. 135.
51. A.S. Morton, *The Journal of Duncan McGillivray . . . at Fort George on the Saskatchewan 1794-95* (Toronto, 1929), p. 60.
52. Glover, *Thompson's Narrative*, p. 106.
53. Hearne, *Journey to Northern Ocean*, p. 35: "Women," declared the Chipewyan chief Matonabee, "were made for labour; one of them can carry, or haul, as much as two men can do."

54. There has been a trend in recent literature to exalt the Indian woman's status by pointing out that in spite of her labour she had more independence that the pioneer farm wife, see Nancy O. Lurie, "Indian Women: A Legacy of Freedom", *The American Way*, vol. 5 (April), 1972, pp. 28-35.

55. Morton, *McGillivray's Journal*, p. 34; L.R.F. Masson, *Les Bourgeois de la Compagnie du Nord-Ouest*, Vol I, p. 256.

56. Murphy, *Women of the Forest*, pp. 87, 112.

57. *Ibid.*, p. 202.

58. Lamb, *Journals of Mackenzie*, p. 254; Glover, *Thompson's Narrative*, p. 125.

59. Masson Collection, Journal of John Thomson, 15 Oct. 1798, p. 10.

60. J.B. Tyrrell, *Journals of Samuel Hearne and Philip Turnor 1774-92* (Toronto, Champlain Society, vol. XXI, 1934), p. 252.

61. Michel Curot, "A Wisconsin Fur Trader's Journal 1803-04, *Wisconsin Historical Collections*, vol. 20, pp. 449, 453.

62. Nelson Papers, Journal 1810-11, p. 41: Reminiscences, Part 5, p. 225.

63. Cox, *Columbia River*, p. 148.

64. Coues, *New Light*, p. 914; Ross, *Fur Hunters*, vol. 11, p. 236.

65. Tyrrell, *Journals of Hearne and Turnor*, p. 273.

66. H.B.C. Arch. Book of Servants Commissions, A.16/111 and 112 *passim*.

67. Lamb, *Sixteen Years*, pp. 28-9.

68. Masson, *Les Bourgeois*, Vol. II, p. 263.

69. Hearne, Journey to Northern Ocean, p. 80; Williams, *Graham's Observations*, p. 158.

70. Alexander Ross, *Adventures of the First Settlers on the Oregon or Columbia River* (London, 1849) pp. 280-81; Glover, *Thompson's Narrative*, p. 251.

71. John West, *The Substance of a Journal during a residence at the Red River Colony 1820-23* (London, 1827), p. 54.

72. The traders were astonished at the little concern shown for pregnancy and childbirth in Indian society, see for example Lamb, *Journals of Mackenzie*, p. 250 and Williams, *Graham's Observations*, p. 177.

73. John Franklin, *Narrative of a Journey to the Shores of the Polar Sea 1819-22* (London, 1824), p. 86.

74. *Ibid.*, 60. The Indian wives of Alexander Ross and Peter Filder, for example, had thirteen and fourteen children respectively.

75. Jennifer Brown, "A Demographic Transition in the Fur Trade Country", *Western Canadian Journal of Anthropology*, Vol. VI, No. 1, p. 68.

76. Cox, *Columbia River*, p. 354.

77. J.S. Galbraith, *The Little Emperor* (Toronto, 1976), p. 68.

78. Nelson Papers, Reminiscences, Pt. 5, p. 155.

79. Brown, "A Demographic Transition", p. 67.

80. Margaret MacLeod, ed. *The Letters of Letitia Hargrave* (Toronto, Champlain Society, v. XXVIII, 1947), pp. 94-95; Alexander Ross, *The Red River Settlement* (Minneapolis, 1957), pp. 95, 192.

81. Brown, "A Demographic Transition", p. 65.

82. Merk, *Fur Trade & Empire*, p. 101.

83. Williams, *Graham's Observations*, pp. 176, 178.

84. Ross, *Adventures on the Columbia*, p. 280; W.J. Healy, *Women of Red River* (Winnipeg, 1923), pp. 163-66.

85. Lamb, *Sixteen Years*, pp. 138, 186.

86. Franklin, *Narrative of a Journey*, pp. 101, 106.

87. West, *Red River Journal*, p. 16.

88. Cox, *Columbia River*, p. 360.

89. Hearne, *Journey to the Northern Ocean*, p. 57.

90. Williams, *Graham's Observations*, p. 176.

91. Thomson's Journal, 19 Nov. 1798, p. 20.

92. Masson, *Les Bourgeois*, Vol. II, pp. 384-85. We are not told whether she also escaped being sold when the brigades arrived in the spring as the *bourgeois* intended.

93. H.B.C. Arch., York Journal, 2 Dec. 1798, B. 239/a/103, f. 14d.

94. H.B.C. Arch. Pelican Lake Journal, 18 Jan. 1819, D. 158/a/1, f. 7d.

95. This account is derived from the Isle à la Crosse Journal, H.B.C. Arc., B. 89/a/2, fos. 5-36d *passim*.

96. Tyrrell, *Journals of Hearne and Turnor*, pp. 446n, 449.

97. *Ibid.*, 449-50.

98. Masson, *Les Bourgeois*, Vol. II, pp. 387-88.

99. Lamb, *Journals of Mackenzie*, p. 255; Rich, *Athabasca Journal*, p. 388.

100. Masson Collection, Journal of Ferdinand Wentzel, 13 Jan. 1805, p. 41.

101. Merk, *Fur Trade & Empire*, p. 127.

102. Nelson Papers, Journal 1810-11, pp. 41-42.

103. W.S. Wallace, *Documents relating to the North West Company* (Toronto, Champlain Society, v.

XXII, 1934), p. 211. This ruling was not enforced in outlying districts such as the Columbia. Even after the union in 1821, Governor Simpson continued to favour the formation of marital alliances in remote regions as the best way to secure friendly relations with the Indians, see Rich, *Athabasca Journal*, p. 392.
104. For a discussion of the role played by mixed-blood women in fur trade society, see Van Kirk, "Role of Women in Fur Trade Society."

189

Topic Six
The Economy and Society of Post-Conquest Quebec

In the Treaty of Paris of 1763 France ceded New France to England. The British now faced the difficult task of formulating a policy to govern a colony whose population was different in language, culture, and religion from their own. That policy, as outlined in the Proclamation of 1763, limited New France, now renamed the Province of Quebec, to the St. Lawrence Valley. It was designed to transform the former French colony into a British one through the establishment of British institutions and laws; in short, it was designed to assimilate the French Canadian population.

The policy failed, however. Very few English-speaking immigrants came to Quebec, preferring to settle in the more fertile Ohio Valley rather than in the colder region to the north (amidst an alien French-speaking population). Furthermore, the first two governors of Quebec, James Murray and Guy Carleton, sided with the French-speaking seigneurs against the aggressive, English-speaking merchants in the colony. Realizing that there was little likelihood of the colony becoming anglicized, Governor Carleton recommended the reinstatement of French civil law, the seigneurial system of holding land, and the right of the Roman Catholic Church to collect the tithe. London accepted his proposals and thus completely reversed its earlier policy of 1763, in the Quebec Act of 1774.

Although the old French civil law — the seigneurial system and the tithe — had been restored, the basic economic structure of the colony had changed. The few English-speaking colonists who had settled in Quebec had taken a prominent role in the economic life of the colony. While limited in numbers, this Anglo-American commercial class had obtained enormous influence — enough to lead to the recall of James Murray, the first governor, in 1766. In terms of economic power they even commanded (by 1777) a majority of the investments in the fur trade. How had this tiny English-speaking groups prospered so? Was it due to the return to France of the commercial class of New France, the superior abilities of the English-speaking merchants, or the favouritism of the British administrators? Fernand Ouellet offers one explanation in the following excerpt from *Canada:*

Unity in Diversity. In his pamphlet, *French Canada and the Early Decades of British Rule, 1760-1791*, Michel Brunet presents an alternative viewpoint. José Igartua's "A Change in Climate: The Conquest and the Marchands of Montreal," examines the rise of the English-speaking merchants in the fur trade.

For an overview of the period, see A.L. Burt's *The Old Province of Quebec* (2 vols.; Toronto: McClelland and Stewart, 1968, first published in 1933), and Hilda Neatby's more recent *Quebec: The Revolutionary Age, 1760-1791* (Toronto: McClelland and Stewart, 1966). Fernand Ouellet has fully developed his argument in *Histoire économique et sociale du Québec, 1760-1850* (Montreal: Fides, 1966), translated in English as *Economic and Social History of Quebec, 1760-1850* (Toronto: Macmillan, 1980), while Michel Brunet presents his case in *Les Canadiens après la Conquête, 1759-1775* (Montreal: Fides, 1969). Dale Miquelon's *Society and Conquest* (Toronto: Copp Clark, 1977) contains a very useful collection of texts on the effect of conquest on French-Canadian society.

191

The Legacy of New France Restored to Favour*
FERNAND OUELLET

By the Royal Proclamation of 1763, England had brought about a sort of social revolution in Quebec. The promoters of this radical transformation had believed that, through the superior business techniques of the British and a massive wave of immigration from New England, it would be possible in a few years to institute a "Mercantile State" in Quebec, populated by an Anglo-Saxon majority. The measures they had adopted in 1763 would then be justified. However, this was merely a utopian dream: the situation prevailing some years later led to the opposite result. The British authorities were forced to confirm the social and institutional heritage left by New France. The history of the Royal Proclamation of 1763 is simply the history of its disintegration. In 1774, England sanctioned this reversal by adopting the Quebec Act.

Between 1765 and 1774 there was no revolutionary change in the economy. Any reconstruction was faced with a tangle of problems that affected all levels of society. Although very real progress was made in all sectors of the economy — the fur trade, agriculture, fisheries and the Saint Maurice foundries — and new enterprises were begun, the economic situation remained essentially that of the French era. In this respect, the

*Chapter 14 from *Canada: Unity in Diversity*, edited by P. G. Cornell et al. Copyright 1967 by Holt, Rinehart and Winston of Canada, Limited. Reprinted by permission.

consequences of the change of political control were scarcely important. The slight quantitative gains that were achieved were based firmly on the traditional economic structure. The revival of the fur trade immediately raised again the traditional rivalry between Montreal and Albany; both wished to control the western trade. The British who had settled in the country allied themselves spontaneously with the French Canadians in the bitter competition. The struggle became so intense that the government instituted a policy which was, in fact, favourable to Albany and detrimental to the interests of the French-Canadian and British fur traders. The restraints placed on the ambitions of the inhabitants of the Saint Lawrence Valley were essentially those used by the administration of New France.

The reinstatement of these controls had several causes. The government administrators were convinced that the irresistible attraction that the fur trade held for the inhabitants had in the past hindered harmonious economic development. Also, the administration had been placed under considerable pressure, both in Canada and in London, by the fur trade merchants of New England and by the shareholders of the Hudson's Bay Company, who were trying to secure supremacy in the lucrative fur trade. The boundaries laid out in 1763 were the result of these factors. Finally, the governors, in their desire to maintain the stability of the trade in the West, had adopted a series of restrictive measures all of which were unfavourable to the local fur trade. Trading permits were brought back into force, and security equal to twice the value of the merchandise to be carried on a given expedition had to be posted to obtain such a permit. In addition, the traders were forbidden to go into an Indian village and extend credit to Indians. These decisions, which effectively confined the traders to the environs of the posts, clearly favoured Albany, since the businessmen of New England were in a better position, having the advantages both of lower transportation costs and a greater supply of trading goods.

Albany's favourable position in the fur trade not only enabled most of the furs to be channelled toward the port of New York, but also gave this port a considerable advantage in the provisioning of the western posts with trade goods. In effect, Quebec ran the risk of becoming a dependency of New England, but Canadian businessmen of both origins wanted to establish themselves independently in the English and West Indian markets. To become well rooted in the West Indian market, the Canadian merchants needed the support of established fisheries, a thriving timber trade and a stable agricultural production. With these assets, they could have controlled their import trade themselves.

In spite of these handicaps, the fur trade continued to expand after 1763, and the records of the French Regime were rapidly exceeded. Nevertheless, after 1770, the resources of beaver began to be exhausted in the areas exploited since the Conquest. The Quebec Act, which returned the far West and the Ohio Valley to Canada as fur reserves, made possible an extension of the area that could be exploited and a further increase in the fur trade. Montreal's dominance was henceforth assured.

Although agriculture was also beset with problems, it made considerable progress as well. After 1763, production rose. The cycle reached its ceiling by 1770 — in 1774 the surplus of wheat was estimated at more than one-half million *minots*. All levels of society benefited from this increase, which, however, was not consistent. In 1765–1766, and again three years later, bad crops and epidemics brought hard times.

Aside from the attempts to diversify production through the introduction of new crops, such as potatoes, hemp and flax, the most interesting feature of this agricultural evolution was the development of an external market. The colony made considerable efforts to dispose of its surpluses by provisioning the fisheries, and by entering the West Indian market and even, on occasion, the markets of the mother country. These sales did not, however, entirely alleviate the persistent over-production, and as a result agriculture was not as prosperous as it might have been.

Low prices and the lack of currency indicated a stagnation in the economy, but it was in other areas that difficulties were more prolonged. The merchants had to fight long and hard to secure the abolition of the restrictions imposed upon the sedentary fishery by the Proclamation of 1763, for this industry lay on the fringes of the great Atlantic cod fishery which was minutely regulated to conform with the British mercantile system. By attaching these fishing posts either to Newfoundland or to Nova Scotia, England theoretically excluded the inhabitants of the Saint Lawrence Valley from this area of business, and limited the prospect of a well organized and diversified trade with the Antilles and Great Britain.

193

Although the Saint Maurice iron industry was in a fairly advantageous position, such was not the case with lumbering. Strong competition from the countries of Northern Europe and from New England considerably reduced the possibilities of expansion in an industry that was later to become one of the most important resources of Canada. In the meantime, it had to be content with modest development.

In short, the Canadian economy expanded slowly in spite of the efforts of the businessmen. The gains made could not mask the durability of the older centres of competition; the great economic changes still lay in the future.

The Enduring Social Structure

After the Conquest, the French Canadians remained the chief source of population expansion. After the Seven Years' War, the population increase returned to normal because of a heavy wave of marriages and a rapid lowering of the death rate. Between 1767 and 1775 the birth rate fluctuated around fifty-four per thousand, the marriage rate about 8.3, and the death rate about 26.7. The population doubled in less than twenty-eight years. This exceptional growth contrasted strongly with the light immigration.

Clearly, local economic conditions and the situation in the mother country scarcely favoured the initiation of mass immigration. Immigration was in progress, but at a desperately slow pace in the opinion of those who wanted to make the colony British. On the other hand, the colonists who settled in the Saint Lawrence Valley were ambitious and full of initiative, and wished to play a role in the colony far out of proportion to their numbers.

The repercussions of the Conquest, the policy of the Proclamation of 1763, the economic situation and the attempts to implant a large English population had all been unable to upset the social structure of the French Regime. Socially, the replacement of the French bureaucracy by a group of administrators who were predominantly English hardly constituted a shaking of the basic structure. The elite remained the same, and the masses conserved their traditional characteristics.

The clergy and the seigneurs were still the dominant groups. The clergy continued to occupy a prominent social position in the colony. It controlled 26 per cent of the seigneurial lands; was firmly established in the parishes; and held exclusive jurisdiction over education, hospitalization, and aid to the poor. Its moral influence and privileged status within the State contributed powerfully to its assurance of a continued position as a dominant class. The lay seigneurs were in essentially the same category.

The aura of attraction around aristocratic values and the monarchic nature of the political regime were the reasons for the lasting prominence of the landed aristocracy. It saw its social utility in relation to the defence of the country, and felt that such social functions should form the basis of its political importance and justify its privileged status in the economy and the administration. However, the new regime's proclamation of freedom of trade deprived the seigneurs of State protection in the fur trade and thus generally restricted them to the development of their fiefs. Economically speaking, the seigneurs soon realized that their future, because of their customs and because of lack of business acumen, was not bright.

This society had been created to incorporate the social usefulness of the various groups and was based on the seigneurial system. The demarcation between "seigneur" and "censitaires" was indicative of the relative importance of each group. The first group charged the rent and the second paid it. Clearly, the acquisition of a seigneurie by a merchant or a rich habitant contributed to his rise in the social scale. The prestige already enjoyed by the nobility and the social significance of real property drove the bourgeoisie to acquire seigneuries. Although these periodic recruitments renewed the seigneur class, they did not help the cause of the bourgeoisie. Once he had achieved his ends and had become a seigneur, a businessman often lost the dynamism that he showed in his business enterprises, and adopted the attitudes and style of life appropriate at the time to the nobility. This lack of dynamic motivation had, during the French Regime, prevented the local bourgeoisie from becoming truly great and developing lasting traditions. This characteristic remained under the English regime, and continued to influence the majority of French Canadians and even claimed victims among a minority of British.

However, under the English regime the development of the bourgeoisie did take a different turn. The British immigrants brought different business traditions and different ideals. They believed in free enterprise and distrusted State intervention. In addition, they were convinced that only parliamentary institutions would enable the bourgeoisie to fulfill its socio-economic role, and a great many French-Canadian businessmen were willing to accept their viewpoint, in whole or in part.

The bourgeoisie was small in numbers to begin with but was continually gathering strength all through the period. It was no more English than French-Canadian. The fur trade attracted investments quite readily and was, until 1775, dominated by the French Canadians by virtue of their experience, numbers and invested capital. Nevertheless, the British showed a more marked inclination to coordinate their interests, seeking means to develop partnerships and to invest to money gained in the fur trade into other channels like the timber trade, fisheries, grain trade, the Saint Maurice foundaries and import trade in general. The French Canadians seemed to remain too absorbed in fur. *195*

Although both French Canadians and British were well entrenched, and fought together against the State and foreign competition in the fur trade and the fisheries, such was not the case in most other areas. The British seem to have been the prime movers of new enterprises. Their efforts to commercialize agriculture and to stimulate and diversify production are well known, and they did the same thing for lumbering. In the long run this superiority of initiative had decisive results.

As a group, the bourgeoisie grew in force and influence. If it did not obtain the reforms it demanded or promote objectives in its own interest, it was because it did not have a sufficient weight of numbers. The bourgeoisie remained, in spite of its demands, a group that was active enough, but in the last analysis marginal and not representative of the interests of the majority. Its sense of frustration is understandable.

Between 1760 and 1775 the evolution in economic and social affairs contributed as much as the military situation to the continuing predominance of the elite groups from the *Ancien Régime*; both ensured the decline of the policy of 1763.

The Decline in the Policy of 1763 and the Quebec Act

The economic conditions and the slow immigration made the governors, already predisposed to absolutism, realize that the British regime would have to rely on the French Canadians. There could be no doubt that their overwhelming numerical superiority, though not permanent, would continue. The unleashing of radical agitation in New England raised urgent questions about the current policies. In these circumstances, it was not only the numerical superiority of the French Canadians that was valued, but all the social and political structures inherited from the French Regime. The seigneurial system, the *Coutume de Paris*, the status of the

Church, and even the French criminal law were seen as the bases of an hierarchical society wherein the people moved at the will of the upper strata and were filled with the strongest military traditions. Thus, the administrators were inclined to see the functions of the clergy and the lay seigneurs as of more than ordinary importance, and endeavoured to impose their views in England.

That England recognized the tithe in law, abolished the Test Oath, and accepted in practice the union of the Catholic Church to the State is all understandable in the light of the thinking of the era. By officially restoring the *Coutume de Paris*, maintaining the seigneurial system and refusing to establish parliamentary institutions, she showed her willingness to ensure the survival of the traditional organization of the colony. The solution reached in the question of boundaries in the West and in the fishing zones reflected similar preoccupations. These decisions had been dictated by the circumstances and by consideration of the unusual situation in the Saint Lawrence Valley, but made reforms necessitated by later developments very difficult indeed.

196

THE QUEBEC ACT
Anno Decimo Quarto
GEORG II III. REGIS
Cap. LXXXIII.

An Act for making more effectual Provision for the Government of the Province of *Quebec* in *North America*.

Whereas His Majesty, by His Royal Proclamation, bearing Date the Seventh Day of October, in the Third Year of His Reign, thought fit to declare the Provisions which had been made in respect to certain Countries, Territories, and Islands in America, ceded to His Majesty by the definitive Treaty of Peace, concluded at Paris on the Tenth Day of February, One thousand seven hundred and sixty-three: And whereas, by the Arrangements made by the said Royal Proclamation, a very large Extent of Country, within which there were several Colonies and Settlements of the Subjects of France, who claimed to remain therein under the Faith of the said Treaty, was left, without any Provision being made for the Administration of Civil Government therein; and certain Parts of the Territory of Canada, where sedentary Fisheries had been established and carried on by the Subjects of France, Inhabitants of the said Province of Canada, under Grants and Concessions from the Government thereof, were annexed to the Government of Newfoundland, and thereby subjected to Regulations inconsistent with the Nature of such Fisheries: May it therefore please Your Most Excellent Majesty that it may be enacted; and be it enacted by the King's most Excellent Majesty, by and with the Advice and Consent of the Lords Spiritual and Temporal, and Commons, in this present Parliament assembled, and by the Authority of the same, . . .

And whereas the Provisions, made by the said Proclamation, in respect to the Civil Government of the said Province of Quebec, and the Powers and Authorities given to the Governor and other Civil Officers of the said Province, by the Grants and Commissions issued in consequence thereof, have been found, upon Experience to be inapplicable to the State and Circumstances of the said Province, the Inhabitants whereof amounted, at the Conquest, to above Sixty-five thousand Persons professing the Religion of the Church of Rome, and enjoying an established Form of Constitution and System of Laws, by which their Persons and Property have been protected, governed, and ordered, for a long Series of Years, from the first Establishment of the said Province of Canada; be it therefore further enacted by the Authority aforesaid, That the said Proclamation, so far as the same relates to the said Province of Quebec, and the Commission under the Authority whereof the Government of the said Province is at present administered, and all and every the Ordinance and Ordinances made by the Governor and Council of Quebec for the Time being, relative to the Civil Government and Administration of Justice in the said Province, and all Commissions to Judges and other Officers thereof, be, and the same are hereby revoked, annulled, and made void, from and after the First day of May, One thousand seven hundred and seventy-five.

And, for the more perfect Security and Ease of the Minds of the Inhabitants of the said Province, it is hereby declared, That His Majesty's Subjects, professing the Religion of the Church of Rome, of and in the said Province of Quebec, may have, hold, and enjoy, the free Exercise of the Religion of the Church of Rome, subject to the King's Supremacy, declared and established by an Act, made in the First Year of the Reign of Queen Elizabeth, over all the Dominions and Countries which then did, or thereafter should, belong to the Imperial Crown of this Realm; and that the Clergy of the said Church may hold, receive, and enjoy, their accustomed Dues and Rights, with respect to such Persons only as shall profess the said Religion . . .

Provided nevertheless, That it shall be lawful for His Majesty, His Heirs or Successors, to make such Provision out of the rest of the said accustomed Dues and Rights, for the Encouragement of the Protestant Religion, and for the Maintenance and Support of a Protestant Clergy within the said Province, as he or they shall, from Time to Time, think necessary and expedient.

Provided always, and be it enacted, That no Person, professing the Religion of the Church of Rome, and residing in the said Province, shall be obliged to take the Oath required by the said Statue . . .

And be it further enacted by the Authority aforesaid, That all His Majesty's Canadian Subjects, within the Province of Quebec, the religious Orders and Communities only excepted, may also hold and enjoy their Property and Possessions, together with all Customs and Usages relative thereto, and all other their Civil Rights, in as large, ample, and beneficial Manner, as if the said Proclamation, Commissions, Ordinances, and other Acts and Instruments had not been made, and as may consist with their Allegiance to His Majesty, and Subjection to the Crown and Parliament of Great Britain; and that in all Matters of Controversy, relative to Property and Civil Rights, Resort shall be had to the Laws of Canada, as the Rule for the Decision of the same; . . .

And whereas the Certainty and Lenity of the Criminal Law of England, and the Benefits and Advantages resulting from the use of it, have been sensibly felt by the Inhabitants, from the Experience of more than Nine Years, during which it has been uniformly administered; be it therefore further enacted by the Authority aforesaid, That the same shall continue to be administered, and shall be observed as Law in the Province of Quebec as well in the Description and Quality of the Offence as in the Method of Prosecution and Trial; . . .

And whereas it may be necessary to ordain many Regulations for the future Welfare and good Government of the Province of Quebec, the Occasions of which cannot now be foreseen, nor, without much Delay and Inconvenience, be provided for, without intrusting that Authority, for a certain Time, and under proper Restrictions, to Persons resident there: And whereas it is at present inexpedient to call an Assembly; be it therefore enacted by the Authority aforesaid, That it shall and may be lawful for His Majesty, His Heirs and Successors, by Warrant under His or Their Signet or Sign Manual, and with the Advice of the Privy Council to constitute and appoint a Council for the Affairs of the Province of Quebec, to consist of such Persons resident there, not exceeding Twenty-three, nor less than Seventeen, as His Majesty, His Heirs and Successors, shall be pleased to appoint; and, upon the Death, Removal, or Absence of any of the Members of the said Council, in like Manner to constitute and appoint such and so many other Person or Persons as shall be necessary to supply the Vacancy or Vacancies; which Council, so appointed and nominated, or the major Part thereof, shall have Power and Authority to make Ordinances for the Peace, Welfare, and good Government, of the said Province, with the Consent of His Majesty's Governor, or, in his Absence, of the Lieutenant-governor, or Commander in Chief for the Time being.

. . . . .

Canada during the American Revolution

The American Revolution was an event of singular historic importance. It not only broke the unity of the British Empire, but heralded an era of revolution, on a world stage, aimed at the liberation of dominated peoples and the internal transformation of established institutions. In North America, it secured the political independence of a people, but mainly of an elite already possessing a national consciousness. The values propounded by this group, socially, economically, and politically, were quite distinct from those of the Empire and its representatives. The democratic ideal this group pursued was a fundamental element of its national consciousness. Canada, on the other hand, was not ready for independence. The American Revolution might have drawn the inhabitants of the Saint Lawrence Valley into its wake; but the motives that led New England to favour independence did not apply in the Province of Quebec. On the contrary, it might be said that the American Revolution, by clarifying obscurities surrounding loyalty to the Empire, reinforced the ties between Canada and England.

The American Invasion

Nonetheless, the Americans wished to associate Canadians with their movement, for the defection of the colonists in the Saint Lawrence Valley to their side would have added weight to their cause. Also, it is obvious that the existence of a colony entirely controlled by the British just beyond their borders constituted a permanent danger.

In 1774 and 1775, the rebelling forces confined themselves to inciting Canadians of all origins to join them. This propaganda did not produce the expected results, and it was decided to invade Canada. Accordingly, on June 27, 1775, Congress adopted a plan to this effect. Preparations began at once but it was the beginning of September, after numerous delays, before Shuyler, the senior in command of the future expedition, and Arnold could contemplate marching on Montreal and Quebec. The first army, commanded by Shuyler, set out by way of the Richelieu on September 6. Sick and uncertain, he was forced to turn his command over to Montgomery about ten days later. Montgomery was held up more than a month at Fort Saint-Jean which did not surrender until November 2, a few days after Fort Chambly. The general then marched on Montreal, which yielded on November 12.

Meanwhile, Arnold's forces had followed the route of the Kennebec River and had begun the siege of Quebec. He had no more than two thirds of his troops, and awaited Montgomery's arrival to begin the assault on the town. The latter did not arrive until December 2, when he could finally assess the difficulties involved. The cold, the lack of money, the hostility of a large part of the population, and finally the desertions among his volunteers forced him to attempt the assault on December 31. It was a failure; he himself was killed and Arnold was wounded. The siege continued, however, until May when the arrival of General Burgoyne at the head of more than nine thousand men forced the Americans to withdraw. Their retreat increased in pace thereafter, until by June 18 all the Canadian territory had been returned to British control. This defeat did not end all thought of invading Canada. Each year until the end of the Revolution the Americans planned a revenge.

The Economic Situation during the Revolution

In one sense the American revolution stimulated economic activity. It was responsible for the great demand for consumer goods that lasted throughout the conflict, since it was necessary to supply the combatants as well as the civilians engaged in paramilitary activities. Production and imports were highly stimulated by these demands; and importers, army suppliers and all businessmen in general had periods of varying degrees of real prosperity. The situation encouraged the habitant to clear more land and to increase and diversify his production. Furthermore, the financing of the war seems to have raised no serious problems, since the mother country sent out the funds necessary to defray the expenses of military undertakings.

Aside from the short period when the invasion forcibly restrained all activity, Canada seems to have enjoyed considerable prosperity. In spite of the scarcity of certain trading commodities and a considerable rise in the cost of transporting goods, the fur trade expanded into new areas and *199* increased considerably. The disappearance of competition from Albany allowed this trend to become firmly established.

Agriculture also benefited extensively from this set of circumstances. The internal market remained largely untouched and this, plus the rise in prices which the war occasioned and the above-mentioned factors, promised considerable profits to the farmer and the dealer in farm supplies. It is important to note that, during the entire war, production far outran local needs. Almost every year, at least until 1779, the export of grain was maintained; although its volume was not very great, this surplus is an excellent indication of the favourable circumstances that prevailed in agriculture. Beginning in 1779, however, famine settled on the land for an interlude of several years.

Prospects were no less encouraging for the fisheries. The American Revolution seemed to promise a weakening of that country's hold on the West Indian market. In reality it was not so simple, for the insecurity that prevailed during the hostilities considerably limited fishing enterprises. Replenishing of supplies became difficult, and the fishermen found that they were frequently at the mercy of privateers. Though it is true that independence theoretically meant a withdrawal of the Americans from the West Indies, it did not necessarily mean a revolution in the sedentary fishing industry. Newfoundland and Nova Scotia were the first colonies to benefit, as they had been well established for some time in international fisheries and foreign markets.

The lumbering industry was passing through a difficult period at this time, but on the other hand the Saint Maurice iron industry found the war advantageous. In general, the American Revolution caused an expansion in the economy and permitted the development of trade between Canada and the West Indies; but contributed in no way to changing the conditions of the development, for Canada remained subjected to her former handicaps.

The Society

It might be said that the Quebec Act and the American Revolution confirmed the entrenchment of the *Ancien Régime*'s social structure. The clergy benefited most from this affirmation. As landowners and as members of a dominant and privileged social class, the clergy could face the future with confidence.

The lay seigneurs understood that the military situation, because it emphasized their military role, gave them unparallelled relief from pressure. From this time on, their pretensions knew no bounds. They were firmly convinced that the Quebec Act was the first step in a restoration and reinforcement of their privileges. They made no effort to disguise their contempt for the bourgeoisie; nor did they have the slightest fear of inducing discontent among the peasants by raising seigneurial rents. This exaggerated attachment to their social status was not a healthy sign. They were vulnerable on the economic level, and were equally so in other respects: the American invasion had tested the precise measure of their influence on the people. The habitants' resistance to the seigneur's propaganda threw serious doubt on the latter's popularity.

The most important social changes occurred among the merchant class. The bourgeoisie grew in numbers, power and wealth. New merchants came, of course, from the local inhabitants, but they were also drawn from among the immigrants. Some, such as Dobie, Forsyth and Gregory came from England and Scotland and others came from New England. E. Ellice, Simon McTavish and Peter Pond were the most representative of this second group.

The importers and the grain dealers, as well as those engaged in the transport business, were the first to benefit from the expanded economy produced by the American Revolution. Quite prominent were a group of individuals having interests in all areas, including the fur trade and the fisheries. In the fur trade, moreover, blocks of capital took shape. The once vague concentration of efforts and means became quite clearly outlined.

The expansion of the area of exploitation, the rise in transportation costs and salaries, the general inflation, and the disastrous consequences of the competition among traders made a regrouping of interests into more extensive organizations imperative. It was in the Northwest, where the factor of distance was even more crucial, that this tendency was most strongly asserted. In 1775, talk arose about forming an organization to be known as the Northwest Company. In the southwest, although less pressing, the same evolution was occurring. Four years later, eight societies with interests in the Northwest trade did join forces. Then in 1783, a reorganization took place that gave the McTavish-Frobisher group the dominant position. This group had fully grasped the possibilities in the Northwest, and accelerated the tendency toward concentration.

As these movements towards a vast monopoly progressed, the French-Canadian enterprise was gradually outdistanced by the British in the exploitation of the West. The prolonged hesitance of the French-Canadians to accept the necessity to organize seemed to be responsible for this change. For the most part, they continued to develop alone or in small groups, and thus made themselves increasingly vulnerable to the competition of the more complex enterprises. In addition, their comparative weakness in the import field at a time when trading commodities were rather scarce served them particularly badly. Whatever the reasons, the American Revolution marked the end of their primacy in the fur trade. From this time on, French-Canadian enterprise was widely outdistanced by the English-Canadian.

Public Opinion in Lower Canada

When the American Revolution broke out, not all groups in Canadian society were in a position to make a decisive choice. The difficulties of the economic reconstruction and certain social tensions, many referred to in the Quebec Act, explain the uncertainty that permeated society. For the habitant, the businessman, the seigneur, the cleric and the official this revolution carried varied implications and produced very diverse attitudes.

201

The state of mind prevalent among the bourgeoisie at the outbreak of the Revolution is quite understandable. In 1774, the merchants had suffered an immense disappointment, for the Quebec Act had thwarted their ambitions and ideals. In spite of the revision of the boundaries in the West, they remained scarred by the hard competition they had sustained with New England. The fur trade did link them to London but they were wondering about the future. It is understandable, then, that under these conditions certain merchants would be attracted to the American dream. This reaction, however, was only temporary and the bourgeoisie in general quickly realized that its interests would link it to imperial unity for a long time to come.

The clergy was not subject to such hesitation. Their way was quite clear. English policy as reaffirmed in the Quebec Act satisfied all their expectations, since the administration depended on the survival of the *Ancien Régime* in its political and social aspects. This does not explain entirely the uncompromising loyalty of the clerics who, by reason of their politico-religious beliefs, considered themselves completely bound up with the established regime. The values propounded by the Americans deeply offended the French-Canadian clergy. The bishop's letter from Mgr. Briand reminded Catholics of the nature of their duty and clearly stated the penalties risked by those who disobeyed or shirked their obligations; it was typical of the ideology commonly accepted among the French Canadians of the period. A belief in monarchy founded on divine rights was an integral part of their creed.

This ideology was also prevalent among the lay seigneurs whose military role was somewhat amplified by the war. Hostilities, they believed, would give them the opportunity to become the true supporters of the monarchy, and they tried to become integrated into the regular troops as well as at the head of the militia. This unmistakable recognition of their military functions led to a no less absolute realization of their social importance, and their zeal was therefore unflagging.

The reaction of the peasants was far more complex than the reaction of the upper classes. The seigneurs, clerics, and civil and military chiefs tried in vain to induce the habitant to take up arms. In general the latter chose a passive role. Why? Was a strong tendency towards disloyalty discernible behind this attitude? It is difficult to believe that the peasant could have been sensitive to the ideological message of the American revolutionaries. In choosing neutrality, the habitant did not believe himself disloyal. In this regard, the Conquest had produced important consequences, since under the French Regime loyalty and territorial defence were intimately connected. Under the British regime things changed. The British had disarmed the population; and at the time of Pontiac's rebellion, had inaugurated the system of voluntary enlistment. No more was necessary to convince the habitant that henceforth the defence of the country would be undertaken almost entirely by the troops of the mother country while their own participation remained voluntary and paid. The habitant, then, could remain neutral should a conflict arise, and still be loyal to the English crown. In short, his zeal depended entirely on the circumstances. The civil and military directors, forgetful of the past or blinded by the exigencies of the present, found the attitude of the rural population incomprehensible.

On the eve of the invasion, insecurity was prevalent in the countryside. The weakness of the government forces was very well known by the populace, and the Americans carried on intensive propaganda whose echoes rang throughout the rural parishes. The habitants were soon convinced that the British wanted to enlist them only to deport them more easily to the Spanish colonies. This fear of deportation, firmly instilled in the mind of the peasant after the Acadian expulsions, expressed itself intensely in 1775.

The habitant's actions were also based on self-interest. It must be remembered that for several past years harvests had been exceptionally good. By remaining on his land, the farmer was convinced he could bring in a great deal of money with his wheat. He seems to have acted with a desire to seize the opportunity since he had been forced to stand by (especially during the Seven Years' War) and pay the expenses of the military operations while helplessly watching speculators accumulate fortunes. The image of Bigot and *La Grande Société* was still clear in the minds of all.

The Loyalist Immigration

The American Revolution, as all wars do, forestalled the natural increase in population. This tapering affected the French Canadians most of all, but was on the whole temporary and slight. The most important demographic phenomenon during these times was the altering nature of immigration to the colony. For a few years this immigration was heavy and still came primarily from the British Isles, but the most important influx was now coming from New England. These "Loyalists," who for many reasons refused to support the aims of the American Revolution, flowed into the other English colonies remaining loyal to the mother country.

The majority of these 35,000 immigrants settled in the Maritimes. The total of those who chose the Saint Lawrence Valley did not, it seems, exceed four or five thousand. Although the volume soon decreased, the immigration of this period nevertheless changed the demographic balance. The British minority increased from 4 or 5 per cent of the total population to 10 or 15 per cent in a few short years. No more was needed to provoke a review of the policies that had prevailed until now.

Beyond the pioneer spirit characteristic of these people and the business traditions of a small group of them, it is their ideological tendencies that must be emphasized. Through these immigrants, pro-British and anti-American feeling gathered momentum in the English colonies, and had a considerable influence on the immediate and long-term development of Canada.

203

French Canada and the Early Decades of British Rule, 1760–1791 *

MICHEL BRUNET

The Capitulation of Montreal (September 8, 1760), which as Professor A. L. Burt remarks should be called the Capitulation of Canada, fulfilled the hopes of the most ambitious leaders of the New England colonies and of the British empire. After a ruthless struggle lasting more than seventy years, the Anglo-Americans had triumphed. France and the Canadians could not obstruct any further the expansion of British colonization in North America.

Both in London and in the American colonies, great rejoicing welcomed Amherst's victory. From that moment, the leading political figures, both in the colonies and at home, worked to convince their compatriots and the imperial government that it was vital to retain Canada. Certain British statesmen and business men would have preferred the acquisition of Guadeloupe. There were two opposing conceptions of the British empire: that of a narrow mercantilism, according to which colonies only existed for commerce, and that which envisaged the growth of new Englands abroad, firmly linked to their metropolis. Those who dreamed of an Anglo-Saxon North America defeated the mercantilists.

Canadian Historical Association Booklet No. 13. Copyright 1971 by Canadian Historical Association. Reprinted by permission.

Military Occupation or the Return of Peace

Although the war had ended on the American continent, it still continued for some months both in Europe and in India. The conclusion of the Family Compact between the different branches of the Bourbons — French, Spanish and Neapolitan (1761) — encouraged some Canadians to think that Spanish help would reverse the situation. These hopes were quickly cut short. As early as the summer of 1762, although a few might still imagine that France would recover the St. Lawrence Valley, the majority seemed to have become accustomed to the idea that the British would remain, at least for several years. However, the Canadians of the first generation after the Conquest, while submitting to British rule, always held the dream that France had not said her last word in North America. When the hour of revenge came, their former mother country would be able to rely upon them. Meanwhile, they bore their lot with resignation.

204   The judicious conduct of the British authorities greatly helped to reconcile the Canadians to the new regime. Amherst, Murray, Gage, Burton and Haldimand were prudent administrators, careful to reassure a population which had expected the worst. Official French propaganda had repeatedly stated that defeat would mean terror. But the measures taken by the military commanders aided a rapid return to normal daily life. The militia captains continued to exercise their former functions, the tribunals established by the victors rendered justice according to the established laws of the colony, the clergy had freedom to attend to the spiritual needs of the faithful, trade regained its former vigour. The inhabitants of the colony had only one thought: to profit from the return of peace to repair the damages of war.

The long conflict had left behind it much destruction and a general apathy. The death of Bishop Pontbriand, four months before the Capitulation of Montreal, placed the clergy in a particularly delicate situation. Bigot's administration as Intendant had made the French regime very unpopular during its last years. The bankruptcy of Louis XV's government, which had only redeemed a portion of the paper money and bonds drawn on the public treasury, had increased the chaos and augmented the discontent of the population. The victors had before them an exhausted populace, ready to be governed. All circumstances and factors helped to render the establishment of British rule easy.

The King is Dead — Long Live the King!

French Canadians showed in general no astonishment when they learned of the ratification of the Treaty of Paris. The clergy and the middle class hurried to acclaim the new king given them by the fortunes of war. At that period the prestige of monarchical institutions was of a kind that those living in the second half of the twentieth century find difficult to understand. For the Canadian leaders of the eighteenth century, the king was the source and symbol of all power. Society, they thought, could not exist without monarchy, which they believed sincerely to be the will of God. This idea formed part of the mental equipment of the principal societies of the North Atlantic world. Under such circumstances, the support of monarchy formed a rallying point and a bond between the leaders of all western countries. The historian must take this factor into account when he observes the behaviour and reactions of the clergy and the leading spokesmen of the Canadians on the morrow of the Conquest.

The *élite* of Canadian society showed a spirit of open collaboration with the victors. Immediately after the surrender of Quebec and Montreal, several young girls married officers of the victorious army. A few people were shocked but they represented the opinion of a minority. Canon Briand, grand vicar of the district of Quebec, ordered prayers to be said for George III at mass, even though the peace negotiations had not been concluded. To those who expressed astonishment at his decision he replied that the British "are our masters; and we owe to them what we owed to the French when they ruled." The Treaty of Paris could only confirm the leaders of Canadian society in their desire to collaborate with the British authorities. In any case, as long as they continued to live in the colony, they had no opportunity to do otherwise.

205

Emigration and the Decapitation of Society

Canadians of the upper class, who refused to submit to the victors, emigrated. They foresaw that their personal future was compromised in a colony where the principal channels of social promotion would, in future, be occupied by the British. The former administrators did not have to rack their brains overlong to discover who would succeed them. The most powerful business men understood that their enterprises would not prosper within the British commercial system.

It is true that some of these emigrants were forced to return to France in order to account for their administration and their scandalous fortunes. Nevertheless, only a few of those who left Canada were functionaries and traders guilty of embezzlement. The majority was drawn from honourable families who did not wish to suffer the humiliation of foreign occupation and who wanted to keep all the advantages which the French empire provided: royal pensions, access to public office, business relations with the capitalists of the metropolis, official protection, contracts with the government and so on. It has been calculated that at least two thousand Canadians left their native land during the ten years which followed the surrender of Montreal.

Can one speak about the loss of social leadership? Some historians, building upon the fact that the emigration of the ruling class was not overwhelming, maintain that Canadian society retained its form. Have they asked themselves what became of the former leaders who remained in Canada? Their fall, which was inevitable in a vanquished colony where a new body of administrators and executives of British origin was being assembled, is the most striking social phenomenon of the first generation after the Conquest. Canadian society no longer offered its most ambitious and dynamic members either the opportunity or the means to win prestige in public life. During the French colonial era, no career was closed to the Canadians. The French empire counted upon their help to continue and prosper. The situation was completely different under British rule. The administration, the army, the navy and external trade were all preserves of the British. The Canadians could not meet the competition of newcomers who came as conquerors. It could not be otherwise.

The Canadians had to learn to limit their ambitions and their horizons, which shrank to fit their diminished chances of social success. Deprived of the indispensable backing of its mother country, left to its own resources, submitting to the rule of a foreign upper class, French Canada lived in a state of subordination.

Hopes and Dreams of the Canadians

For the majority of the population there was no question of emigration. Faithful to the monarchic ideal, they recognized George III without protest as their new sovereign. However, in giving their allegiance to the king of Great Britain, the Canadians had no intention of renouncing the right to define and protect their own interests. The clergy, conforming to the traditional teaching of the Church, were ready to have *Te Deum's* sung to celebrate the peace and to do homage to "the legitimate authority". At the same time, they counted on the latter for the nomination of a bishop and the freedom to exercise their ministry. The seigneurs and the Canadian officers, to whom the defeat meant loss of prestige in the eyes of the habitants and the militia, deluded themselves into thinking that the British government, following the example of Louis XV, would have recourse to them for the administration and defence of the colony.

The Canadian business men, delighted by the departure of Bigot, his associates and favourites, hoped to improve their lot quickly. Had they not been told that the colony, thanks to its entry into the British market and to the freedom of trade which the English practised, would experience soaring prosperity? They had, for a few short years, the *naïveté* to imagine that they would be the principal beneficiaries of this upsurge of economic activity. They were soon to realize that their British competitors were basically the only ones equipped to benefit from it. Also, the middle-class Canadian traders who remained in the colony, influenced by the British business men who were coming in, had convinced themselves they would supplant the seigneurs in the social hierarchy.

As to the lowest strata, that is to say the immense majority of the population, what did they think? First of all, there was a strong impression of having been betrayed by those in authority. The latter suddenly appeared as being unworthy of their honours, their privileges and their responsibilities. In all societies, the immediate consequence of an unsuccessful war is a loss of authority and prestige by the former governing class. This particular group, however, as well as having been defeated on the battlefield, had to suffer occupation by the victorious army and had to collaborate with it, and thus lost even the possibility of regaining popular support. But the Canadians had no other leaders to whom they could give their loyalty. Obedient to both their seigneurs and clergy, they echoed "Long live the king!" At the same time, they took refuge in a state of passive resistance. Both the British authorities and the Canadian leaders realized this when an attempt was made to raise a volunteer battalion to help suppress Pontiac's rising (1764). The militia, in spite of alluring promises, showed no haste to enroll. The people, although submitting themselves to George III, felt no obligation to serve the interests of their enemies and conquerors. Sooner or later, they thought, the "Londoners", the English, would be forced to quit the country.

207

The Failure of the Royal Proclamation

A royal proclamation of October 7, 1763, announced that Canada, along with other new British colonies, was to have an elected assembly and that its inhabitants could expect "the enjoyment of the benefits of the laws of . . . England". General James Murray, who had been military governor since October 1759, was appointed civil governor of the colony, now called the Province of Quebec. His instructions (December 7, 1763) provided for a council including, besides officials, eight of the "most considerable" residents of the colony appointed on his recommendation. Murray was instructed to honour the treaty guarantee of religious toleration, but not to allow any papal or "any other foreign ecclesiastical jurisdiction whatever". He was also to have vacant lands surveyed in townships and to publish regulations for granting land in English tenure, the grantees to pay quit-rents. Quebec, in fact, was to be remade into an English colony. This programme, intended to attract immigrants from the comparatively crowded English colonies to the south, simply did not face the fact that the Canadians formed more than ninety-nine per cent of the white population in the St. Lawrence Valley.

Murray, sympathetic to the Canadians but obedient and unimaginative, attempted to obey his instructions impartially. The result was the total disorganization of justice. The Canadians were delivered into the hands of judges and officials who were ignorant or contemptuous of their language and traditions, and some of whom exploited them shamelessly. The governor tried to set limits to the havoc by recognizing the right of Canadians to jury service and by creating lower courts. In them the judges were to take notice of French laws and customs and Canadian lawyers (who, being Catholic, could not practice in the Court of King's Bench) were allowed to represent their clients. This concession to the "natives", however, was stated to be only temporary.

Those who could legitimately regard themselves as the leaders of the Canadian community discovered, not without astonishment, that they had no public rights in their own country. The Test Act barred them, as Catholics, from careers in the administration, whether as councillors or as mere justices of the peace. They were totally ignorant of the English law which now replaced their own. Surely, they thought, their willingness to collaborate and their protestations of loyalty to the Crown merited greater consideration than this?

Murray, realizing that the number of British colonists was too small, decided to postpone the election of an assembly. This brought him the enmity of the group one can call the English party. The British merchants and adventurers who had come to Canada immediately after the Conquest expected, for the most part, to become its ruling class. They had been patient during the military regime, but they regarded the establishment of civil government (which came into force on August 10, 1764) as the beginning of their triumph. They had expected to dominate the assembly which Murray now postponed and to control both the Canadians and the officials sent out from Great Britain. They expressed their disappointment in a manifesto of the Grand Jury of Quebec (October 16, 1764) and in petitions sent direct to Westminster. Murray, in response, moved closer to the Canadian leaders and defended them before the imperial government. At the same time, he was plagued by the hostility of the military commanders, who were themselves also at odds with the spokesmen of the British mercantile community.

Some members of the British minority were well-disposed towards the Canadians, and formed a political group called the "French party". The most influential of these advocates of paternalism was Adam Mabane, a Scottish surgeon who in 1764 was appointed a judge and a member of the governor's council. With this support and with Murray's, the Canadians demanded from the imperial government the redress of their grievances.

The British ministers had begun to doubt the wisdom of their policy towards His Majesty's new subjects in the Province of Quebec. Since they had no intention of persecution, deportation or liquidation, they were forced, while guarding the fundamental interests of the British empire, to take into account the presence of the Canadians. They were willing, for example, to accept a bishop recognized by Rome and consecrated in France. Canon Briand, who had been one of the vicars-general chosen to govern the diocese after Bishop Pontbriand's death, was allowed after several months' waiting in London to seek consecration discreetly. In June 1766 he returned as the head of the Canadian clergy. In the same month Murray, who had been recalled, left Quebec.

Under the Benevolent Rule of Carleton

The Canadians had thus scarcely found a protector when he was removed. Sir Guy Carleton replaced him. Carleton was ambitious, able and intent upon demonstrating his administrative capacity. From the beginning he sought, by both force and flattery, to impose his authority on all parties. Authoritarian by nature but pliable when necessary, he was soon in control of the situation. He succeeded in convincing all parties that he was their ally and all agitation ceased. The lieutenant-governor — he did not become governor until the beginning of 1768 — decided almost immediately that the royal proclamation and the instructions written for his predecessor were inapplicable. He was shocked by the chaos in the administration of justice. He found the pretentions of the English party unacceptable. He thought it impossible to govern the colony without recourse to the services of the Canadian leaders. Thus he proposed to re-establish at least French civil law, to maintain the seigneurial system, to give legal recognition to the tithe and to include Canadians in the conduct of public affairs. He took care, however, to state that they should play only a secondary role. There should be no elected assembly; all legislative power should lie with the governor and his council, whose members would be appointed by the Crown. Some Canadians would be named to it. This policy was finally implemented in the Quebec Act of 1774.

209

Carleton's paternal despotism fulfilled the dreams of the principal Canadian leaders. In particular, Carleton received the enthusiastic support of the higher clergy, who in the circumstances of the moment were the most influential representatives of the Canadian community. A personal friendship grew up between Bishop Briand and the governor.

Some Canadians, it is true, recognized and mistrusted the way in which Carleton's programme led to enhanced personal power for the governor. These critics were accused of envy for their compatriots whom the governor had honoured with his confidence. They were reproached, too, with falling under the influence of the English party. The British merchants were still demanding an assembly, but they were now willing to accept one elected by the whole population, and containing some Canadian members. For the Canadian community, the choice was thus between the paternalism of the governor and that of the English minority. The Quebec Act definitely instituted the former.

The Era of Mutual Disappointment

In Carleton's view, the vital problem was to build confidence between the Canadian population and the British authorities. It was necessary to end the misgivings and disorder arising from the royal proclamation, the sudden introduction of English law, the exclusion of Canadians from the administration and the agitation of the English party. Carleton knew that this could only be done with the support of the clergy and the seigneurial class. How else could a foreign power establish itself in a country except by ensuring the cooperation, or at least the neutrality, of its former leaders? By the Quebec Act, Carleton won the confidence and obtained the cooperation of the Canadian *élite*.

It appeared at first as if he had hoped to get even more than this. While he was formulating his programme for Quebec, the thirteen American colonies had been moving towards rebellion. As a soldier, Carleton wanted to make his province a secure base for a British army if it should have to re-establish order in the American colonies. Further, he imagined that the Canadian militia would contribute to the defence of imperial authority, or at least protect the St. Lawrence Valley from rebel attack. The seigneurs and the higher clergy encouraged his hopes. They did not realize, or would not admit, that the bulk of the population offered a kind of passive resistance to the British occupation.

When the American invasion came, Carleton and the Canadian leaders suffered a bitter disappointment. In general, the people refused to take up arms, despite the authoritative appeals of bishop, clergy and seigneurs. The Canadians took the occasion to show their hatred of or indifference to the English and their mistrust of those who cooperated with them. On the other hand, the Americans had nothing to offer; while the rudimentary equipment and poor organization of their forces did not escape notice. Most of the population adopted a prudent neutrality.

The entry of France into the war on the side of the Americans (February 6, 1778) created a particularly delicate situation. The majority of the people expected, hopefully, that their former mother country would re-conquer the colony. The Canadian leaders lived through several months of anguish. While they hoped spontaneously for the defeat of British arms, prudence recommended that they show themselves submissive to the government of George III. Haldimand, who succeeded a disappointed and frustrated Carleton in 1778, had good reason to be nervous and suspicious. Neither the Canadians nor the British administrators knew, at this point, that the French government had no intention of demanding the return of Canada. In 1783, many Canadians considered the Treaty of Versailles a further betrayal by France. It was difficult for them to understand why she had not used her victory to return and continue her work of colonization in the St. Lawrence Valley. Their reaction sprang both from a completely natural attachment to the country which would always remain in their eyes the mother country and from anxiety concerning their continued existence as an ethnic entity. It did not take into account the demands of international politics which France had to heed.

The Quebec Act on Trial

Once they had accepted the fact that Quebec was to remain a British colony, the Canadians questioned their collective lot more sharply and concluded that it ought to be bettered. The Quebec Act had not fulfilled the hopes of its Canadian supporters.

In the administration and in the council the Canadians formed a feeble minority whose influence was strictly limited. The few who were in a position to benefit from official protection had little prestige in the eyes of their compatriots. English wealth dominated the economy of the province. The English business men had prospered during the war years and the arrival of the Loyalist immigrants had increased their opportunities. Several Canadian merchants had failed or retired, or had merged with their British competitors.

The Church lacked priests and was forbidden to recruit them in France. The clergy knew themselves to be under constant surveillance. This weighed upon them more and more heavily and several began to complain openly. The diocese of Quebec no longer drew from France the revenues which it had enjoyed before the Conquest. The bishop, whom the government considered as one of its officials and to whom it paid a small annual salary, lived very poorly. His clergy, too, lived in straitened circumstances. If he was able to retain a certain financial independence it was due to a small pension, voted by the assembly of the French clergy, which the king of France sent on to him without the official knowledge of the British government. This pension continued until 1792.

211

The institutions of learning, which the French government had always generously supported, stagnated. The closure of the College of Quebec and the confiscation of the Jesuits' property appeared to the Canadian leaders as most unjust measures, leaving no fund for education. The most far-seeing leaders of the Canadian community were alarmed by the extent to which the education system had deteriorated in a single generation. Immediately after the Conquest attempts had begun to bring over teachers from France and to obtain the re-opening of the College of Quebec. They were unsuccessful. English reproaches of Canadian ignorance thus added insult to injury. In a memorandum to Judge William Smith (1789), Bishop Hubert remarked that parents might be more enthusiastic about the education of their offspring if more Canadians were employed in public administration. The government, he complained, too often gave preference to "old subjects and even foreigners". When a number of English people in the colony took an interest in the progress of education amongst the Canadians, for the most part it was with some motive of anglicization.

The Quebec Act had not even succeeded in making the administration of justice efficient. The re-establishment of French civil law and the support of the seigneurial regime had given rather more security to Canadians. Most of their leaders agreed on this point. But several pointed out that the colony was developing a hybrid judicial system that bordered on anarchy. The judges, several of whom lacked competence, had established a jurisprudence where the principles of French and English law intermingled. Permanent strife existed between the Court of Appeal and the lower courts. The ordinances of the council, where the members of the "French party" and the English faction fought openly, left confusion worse confounded. Every kind of influence and of conflicting interest tended to corrupt the administration of justice. The inquiry conducted by Judge Smith in 1787 brought this into the open.

Another matter greatly perturbed the Canadian leaders: the influx of Loyalists. A census of 1785 gives the figure of 6800 for those already established in the St. Lawrence Valley. These newcomers to the colony, who had left their native lands in order to remain loyal to the British Crown, were astounded to realize that they had to obey foreign laws. In particular, the seigneurial system was repugnant to them. They protested, and accused the government of depriving them of their rights as British subjects. Invited to legislate in their favour, the council showed itself in no hurry to accede to their requests. The majority of Canadian councillors and of the "French party" had no sympathy for the Loyalists. The newcomers meant a series of new problems and the reinforcement of the English minority.

Towards Constitutional Reform

212   Both Canadians and colonists of British stock were in favour of a revision, either minor or major, of the Quebec Act. Even its most ardent Canadian supporters — whose support was not always disinterested — admitted the necessity for some kind of alteration and reform.

The aims of the Canadian leaders did not alter: to consolidate and to increase the influence of their community, which formed the largest part of the population. Naturally, this meant more prestige and power for those who had either the right or the ambition to become the spokesmen for the community. However there was a considerable lack of agreement as to the best means to achieve this end. Conservatives, who feared to set out on a new path, wanted to keep the Quebec Act as a charter of Canadian liberties. They contented themselves with a demand for greater Canadian participation in the government of the colony, in order to protect the established order against the introduction of English laws and institutions. The return of Carleton, who became governor for a second term in 1786, raised great hopes among the members of the "French party", whose influence had been declining during the past few years, and among the Canadian leaders who counted on his paternalism to uphold and extend their privileges. A few had even imagined that a Canadian would be named lieutenant-governor. This group dreamt of a colonial government created and maintained by the British Crown, but operated by Canadians.

Another group, whose origins can be traced to the period 1770–1774, did not put all their hopes in the benevolence of a governor backed by a council favourable to Canadian interests. Its members tried to understand what the benefits of a system of representative government would be for their compatriots. They were not afraid of the idea. On the contrary, since they realized that numbers would inevitably favour them, they concluded that an elected assembly should be adopted. The members of this reform movement represented a new wave of Canadian leaders, who dissociated themselves from the seigneurial and military class of the first generation after the Conquest. The majority belonged to what we would call today the middle class: small shop-keepers — very few among them had the stature or influence of big business men — notaries, lawyers, surveyors, book-keepers. A few seigneurs supported them. Several of the higher clergy sympathized with them and helped circulate their petitions among the populace. These reformers had no sympathy for the Canadian favourites of Carleton, Haldimand and Hope (lieutenant-governor, 1785–86). They rejected, too, the tutelage of the remnants of the "French party". In fact, the Canadian community had discovered new spokesmen.

The Complaints and Plans of the British Merchants

The Quebec Act had never been accepted by the principal leaders of the colony's British minority. The royal proclamation of 1763 had promised them their rights as British subjects. The Act, they thought, abandoned and betrayed them. It placed them under French civil law and under a colonial government not supported by an elected assembly. Every other British colony in North America enjoyed representative institutions.

213

They considered the powers of the governor and council under the Act to be arbitrary. Conscious of the central role they played in the economic development of the St. Lawrence Valley, they were nevertheless confronted by a colonial government over which they had little influence. Their indignation reached new heights when they found that Carleton had concealed instructions to introduce some English commercial law, trial by jury in certain civil cases and the privilege of *habeas corpus*.

During the War of Independence, the British minority had to hold back its complaints. Several of its members had shown sympathy for the rebellious colonies before and in particular during the American invasion of Quebec. This, fully exploited by its opponents, had brought the English party into disrepute. With the end of the war, the need for cautious silence was over. The British minority had grown in numbers and could count on powerful friends and protectors in London. Post-war financial difficulties made the merchant community more aggressive. The Treaty of Versailles, moreover, limited the expansion of their trade in the interior. The coming of the Loyalists, whom they naturally sought to take under their protection, strengthened their position. In sum, the British merchants, like the Canadians, decided to indulge in an examination of the Quebec Act. In a petition of September 30, 1783, they asked for the immediate repeal of the Act and for a constitution that would make Quebec, at last, a true British colony.

Both in Quebec and in Montreal, Citizens' Committees were formed to bring together all those in favour of constitutional reform. This involved an alliance between the English party and some of the more influential of the new middle-class Canadian spokesmen. The two parties to this alliance did not have the same motives. The Canadians intended to use British representative institutions to further their own collective interests. The

British business men seem never to have been bothered by the risk they were inviting, that a Canadian majority in the assembly would swamp them. Under-estimating the resources of their new allies, they confidently expected to substitute their own brand of paternalism for that of the governor and the former "French party". The Citizens' Committees drew up a petition to the king in November 1784, substantially repeating the demands in the merchants' petition of the preceding September. Both they and their opponents held public assemblies to demonstrate their popular support. Actual political parties now faced each other and attempted to rally the apathetic majority. Their rivalry made the administration of the colony extremely awkward during the months immediately following Haldimand's departure (November 1784). In permitting all parties to express themselves, Lieutenant-Governor Hamilton definitely brought to an end the atmosphere of constraint that had prevailed during the war years.

214

Dorchester and Smith against Carleton

The hopes raised by the return of Carleton have already been described. Now elevated to the peerage as first Baron Dorchester, he arrived at Quebec at the end of October 1786. He might have united under his paternal yoke all the spokesmen of the Canadian community; but Dorchester no longer had the same ideas as Carleton.

In 1774 he had worked for the adoption of the Quebec Act because he thought it would serve the best interests of the British empire in North America. He had not believed that a British colony could be founded in the St. Lawrence Valley and had therefore not hesitated to ignore the claims of the British minority settled there. Its members, in his view, were simply adventurers come to seek their fortune in a newly conquered territory; he had even supposed that they would not stay long.

Twelve crowded years later, Dorchester brought a new perspective to his old post. There was now a British population in the St. Lawrence Valley, re-inforced by Loyalists, for whose welfare he had shown himself concerned while commanding the British troops in New York. It was now his mission to consolidate British colonial efforts in North America. There were some, their faith in the British empire unshaken by the War of Independence, who were determined to create a prosperous and dynamic British North America — one that might even make the Americans regret their break with the Crown. William Smith, lately Chief Justice of New York, was one of the most eloquent of such imperialists; he had won Dorchester's confidence and was appointed Chief Justice for the Province of Quebec. It was not long before his influence was felt in all parts of the administration. Dorchester wanted to correct, according to the advice of Smith, the work he himself had done as Carleton.

His freedom of action was however somewhat limited and he never rose to command circumstances as he had done during his first administration. The change in his conduct was the result of his personal dilemma. He was reluctant to break with his old allies and supporters, who counted on him to defeat the reformers and the English party. At the same time, he recognized the necessity of reform. Realizing that the American continent favoured democracy, he nevertheless retained many aristocratic ideas on the proper distribution of power. Alive to the demands of the present, Dorchester thus remained to a certain extent a prisoner of the past. This, far more than the poor state of his health, explains why he lacked energy and decisiveness during the critical period 1787 to 1790.

In those years the struggle between the different parties — the "French party", the seigneurs allied to it, those Canadians who wanted a slight improvement in the Quebec Act, those Canadians who wanted an elected assembly and the English party — became more intense. Acrimonious debates were raised by Smith's interpretation of the Quebec Act in one of *215* his first decisions as president of the Court of Appeal, by his criticism of the judges of the Court of Common Pleas, by the inquiries he started into the administration and by his proposed reforms, particularly in the field of education. Even within the Canadian community, public opinion was deeply divided. The advocates of constitutional reform, profiting from the confusion, acquired greater influence and new confidence. The Citizens' Committees, which had spokesmen in London, redoubled their activity.

The Constitution of 1791 or the Confirmation of the Quebec Act

The imperial government, which had wavered for a long time, at last decided to amend the Quebec Act. Buffeted from all sides by contradictory demands and not very well informed on the real state of the colony, the ministry drafted the Constitutional Act. This piece of legislation did not reverse the Quebec Act. It provided a bicameral legislature: an appointed Legislative Council and an elected assembly. At the same time an order-in-council, signed on August 24, 1791, created the two separate colonies of Upper and Lower Canada.

The British merchants of Quebec, Three Rivers and Montreal, who for over twenty-five years had demanded their rights as British subjects, learned with stupefaction that the imperial government had upheld the major part of the Quebec Act and that it had separated them from the Anglo-Protestant population established in Upper Canada. They had not foreseen the division and had every reason to suppose that their interests, both as merchants and as an ethnic minority, would suffer from it. They tried, but failed, to prevent it. They persisted, nevertheless, in their usual expectation that the Canadians would accept their paternalism without much resistance. The more optimistic of them managed to believe that the assembly in Lower Canada, with a majority of Canadian members entirely ignorant of parliamentary institutions, would be easy to dominate. Although the "French party" had been defeated, the victory of the English party was incomplete.

As for the Canadian leaders, if one omits the seigneurs linked with the "French party", the few beneficiaries of government patronage under the Quebec Act and those who did not grasp the opportunities of the new constitution, they were largely satisfied. A few were even enthusiastic. French civil law remained in force, the clergy retained the rights acknowledged by the Quebec Act, some Canadians at least would continue to be appointed to public office. The franchise for the new assembly was wide, and those Canadians who had been involved in the Citizens' Committees were particularly well aware of what numbers would mean in a democratic regime. The division of the province was welcome, both for its guarantee of a continued Canadian majority and for the chagrin it caused the English party. The Canadians, particularly the new middle-class spokesmen, foresaw that the new constitution would confirm the rights already recognized by the Quebec Act; for it provided new and more powerful methods of collective action. It remained to learn their use. By undertaking a political apprenticeship, the Canadian spokesmen were able gradually to develop an effective opposition to the English minority and to British officials. A new era had begun in the history of French Canada and of British colonization in the St. Lawrence Valley.

216

A Change in Climate: The Conquest and the *Marchands* of Montreal*

JOSÉ IGARTUA

When the British government issued the Royal Proclamation of 1763, it assumed that the promised establishment of "British institutions" in the "Province of Quebec" would be sufficient to entice American settlers to move north and overwhelm the indigenous French-speaking and Papist population. These were naive hopes. Until the outbreak of the American Revolution, British newcomers merely trickled into Quebec, leading Governor Carleton to prophesy in 1767 that "barring a catastrophe shocking to think of, this Country must, to the end of Time, be peopled by the Canadian Race . . ."[1] But the British newcomers, few though they were, had to be reckoned with. By 1765 they were powerful enough to have Governor Murray recalled and by 1777 they would be strong enough to command the majority of investments in the fur trade.[2] Did their success stem from superior abilities? Did the British take advantage of the situa-

*From *Canadian Historical Association Historical Papers*, 1974, 115–134. Copyright by the Canadian Historical Association. Reprinted by permission.

tion of submission and dependence into which the Canadians had been driven by the Conquest? Did the newcomers gain their predominance from previous experience with the sort of political and economic conditions created in post-Conquest Quebec?

Historians of Quebec have chosen various ways to answer these questions. Francis Parkman was fond of exhibiting the superiority of the Anglo-Saxon race over the "French Celt."[3] More recently the studies of W. S. Wallace, E. E. Rich, and D. G. Creighton took similar, if less overt, positions.[4] One of the best students of the North West fur trade, Wayne E. Stevens, concluded: "The British merchants . . . were men of great enterprise and ability and they began gradually to crowd out the French traders who had been their predecessors in the field."[5]

The French-Canadian historian, Fernand Ouellet, attributed the rise of the British merchants to the weaknesses of the Canadian trading bourgeoisie: "Son attachement à la petite entreprise individuelle, sa réponse à la concentration, son goût du luxe de même que son attrait irrésistible pour les placements assurés étaient des principaux handicaps." No evidence is given for this characterization and the author hastens to concede that before 1775 "le problème de la concentration ne se pose pas avec acuité," but for him it is clear that the economic displacement of the Canadians resulted from their conservative, "ancien Régime" frame of mind, bred into them by the clergy and the nobility.[6] Ouellet painted British merchants in a more flattering light as the agents of economic progress.[7]

217

Michel Brunet has depicted the commercial competition between the British newcomers and the Canadian merchants as an uneven contest between two national groups, one of which had been deprived of the nourishing blood of its metropolis while the other was being assiduously nurtured. For Brunet the normal and natural outcome of that inequality was the domination of the conqueror, a situation which he sees as prevailing to the present day.[8]

Dale B. Miquelon's study of one merchant family, the Babys, shed new light on the question of British penetration of Canadian trade. It outlined the growth of British investments in the fur trade and the increasing concentration of British capital. The author concluded:

The French Canadians dominated the Canadian fur trade until the upheaval of the American Revolution. At that time they were overwhelmed by an influx of capital and trading personnel. English investment in the top ranks of investors jumped by 679% and was never significantly to decline. Even without explanations involving the difference between the French and English commercial mentalities, it is difficult to believe that any body of merchants could recover from an inundation of such size and swiftness.[9]

This conclusion had the obvious merit of staying out of the murky waters of psychological interpretations. But Miquelon's own evidence suggests that the "flood theory" is not sufficient to account for the Canadians' effacement; even before the inundation of 1775–1783, British investment in the fur trade was growing more rapidly than Canadian. By 1772, to quote Miquelon, the "English [had] made more impressive increases in the size of their investments than [had] the French, and for the first time [had] larger average investments in all categories."[10]

It is difficult not to note the ascendancy of the British in the fur trade of Canada even before the American Revolution. The success of the British merchants, therefore, was rooted in something more than mere numbers. It was not simply the outcome of an ethnic struggle between two nationalities of a similar nature; it was not only the natural consequence of the Canadians' conservative frame of mind. It arose out of a more complex series of causes, some of them a product of the animosities between Canadians and British, others inherent to the differences in the socio-economic structures of the French and British Empires; together, they amounted to a radical transformation of the societal climate of the colony.

The aim of this paper is to gauge the impact of the Conquest upon a well-defined segment of that elusive group called the "bourgeoisie" of New France. It focuses on Montreal and its Canadian merchants. Montreal was the centre of the fur trade and its merchants managed it. Historians of New France have traditionally seen the fur trade as the most dynamic sector of the colony's economy; by implication it is generally believed that the fur trade provided the likeliest opportunities for getting rich quickly and maintaining a "bourgeois" standard of living.[11] It is not yet possible to evaluate the validity of this notion with any precision, for too little is known about other sectors of the economy which, in the eighteenth century at least, may have generated as much or more profit. Research on the merchants of Quebec should provide new information on the wealth to be made from the fisheries, from wholesale merchandising, and from trade with Louisbourg and the West Indies. But if one is concerned with the fate of Canadian merchants after the Conquest, one should examine the fate of men involved in the sector of the economy of Quebec which was the most dynamic *after* the Conquest, the fur trade. The paper examines the impact of the arrival of (relatively) large numbers of merchants on the Montreal mercantile community, the attitude of British officials towards the Canadians, and the changing political climate of the colony. It is suggested that it was the simultaneous conjunction of these changes to the "world" of the Montreal merchants, rather than the effect of any one of them, which doomed the Canadian merchants of Montreal.[12]

The Montreal Merchants at the End of the French Regime

In 1752 a French Royal engineer passing through Montreal remarked that "la plupart des habitants y sont adonnés au commerce principalement à celui connu sous le nom des pays d'en haut."[13] It was only a slight exaggeration. By the last year of the French regime one could count over one hundred *négociants*, merchants, outfitters, traders, and shopkeepers in Montreal. The overwhelming majority of them had been in business for some years and would remain in business after the Conquest. Over half were outfitters for the fur trade at some time or other between 1750 and 1775; these men comprised the body of the merchant community of Montreal. Above them in wealth and stature stood a handful of import merchants who did a comfortable business of importing merchandise from France and selling it in Montreal to other merchants or directly to customers in their retail stores. Below the outfitters a motley group of independent fur traders, shopkeepers, and artisans managed to subsist without leaving more than a trace of their existence for posterity.[14]

The fur trade, as it was conducted by the merchants of Montreal before 1760, had little to do with the glamorous picture it sometimes calls to mind. For the outfitter who remained in Montreal, it was not physically a risky occupation; its management was fairly simple and the profits which it produced quite meager. For the last years of the French regime the fur trade followed a three-tier system. Fort Frontenac (present-day Kingston) and Fort Niagara were King's posts; they were not lucrative and had to be subsidized to meet English competition. The trade of Detroit and Michilimackinac, as well as that of the posts to the South West, was open to licencees whose numbers were limited. Some *coureurs de bois* (traders without a licence) also roamed in the area. The richest posts, Green Bay and the posts to the northwest past Sault Sainte-Marie, were monopolies leased by the Crown to merchants or military officers.[15] The export of beaver was undertaken by the French *Compagnie des Indes,* which had the monopoly of beaver sales on the home market. Other furs were on the open market.

219

The system worked tolerably well in peace time: there was a stable supply of furs, prices paid to the Indians had been set by custom, the prices paid by the *Compagnie des Indes* were regulated by the Crown, and the prices of trade goods imported from France were fairly steady. There was competition from the Americans at Albany and from the English on the Hudson Bay, to be sure, but it appeared to be a competition heavily influenced by military considerations and compliance with Indian customs.[16]

The system faltered in war time. Beaver shipments to France and the importation of trade goods became risky because of British naval power. Shipping and insurance costs raised the Canadian traders' overhead, but the Indians refused to have the increase passed on to them. This was the most obvious effect of war, but it also produced general economic and administrative dislocations which led H. A. Innis to conclude that it ". . . seriously weakened the position of the French in the fur trade and contributed to the downfall of the French *régime* in Canada."[17]

Nevertheless, outside of war-time crises, the fur trade of New France was conducted with a fair dose of traditionalism. This traditionalism resulted from two concurrent impulses: Indian attitudes towards trade, which were untouched by the mechanism of supply and demand and by distinctions between commercial, military, political or religious activities; and the mercantilist policies of France, which tried to control the supply of furs by limiting the number of traders and regulating beaver prices on the French market. While the fur trade structure of New France had an inherent tendency towards geographic expansion, as Innis argued, it also had to be oligopolistic in nature, if investments in Indian alliances, explorations, and military support were to be maximized. Open competition could not be allowed because it would lead to the collapse of the structure.[18]

It is not surprising, therefore, that most outfitters dabbled in the fur trade only occasionally. On the average, between 1750 and 1775, the Canadian merchants of Montreal invested in the trade only four times and signed up about eleven *engagés* each time, not quite enough to man two canoes. Few merchants outfitted fur trade ventures with any regularity and only six men hired an average of twelve or more *engagés*, more than twice before 1761 (See Table 1). Three of these were unquestionably wealthy: Louis Saint-Ange Charly, an import merchant who, unlike his colleagues, had a large stake in the fur trade, realized 100 000 livres on his land holdings alone when he left the colony for France in 1764; Thomas-Ignace Trotier Desauniers "Dufy," who in a will drawn up in 1760, bequeathed 28 000 livres to the Sulpicians; the illiterate Dominique Godet, who in a similar document of 1768, mentioned 5000 livres in cash in hand, land in three parishes in the vicinity of Montreal, "Batiment & Bateaux qui en dependent," around 5000 livres in active debts, and two black slaves.[19] Two other large outfitters left relatively few belongings at the time of their death: Alexis Lemoine Monière left less than 1000 livres, all

Table I–Largest Canadian Fur Trade Outfitters in Montreal, 1750–1760

Name	Total No. of Years	Total No. of Hirings	Yearly Average
CHARLY, Louis Saint-Ange	6	85	14.1
GODET, Dominique	5	85	17.0
LECHELLE, Jean	4	130	32.5
LEMOINE MONIERE, Alexis	7	300	42.8
L'HUILLIER CHEVALIER, François	7	90	12.6
TROTIER DESAUNIERS, Thomas-Ignace "Dufy"	5	129	25.8

Source: "Répertoire des engagements pour l'ouest conservés dans les Archives judiciaires de Montréal," *Rapport de l'Archiviste de la province de Québec*, 1930-31, pp. 353-453; 1931-32, pp. 242-365; 1932-33, pp. 245-304.

of it in household goods, and François L'Huillier Chevalier just slightly more.[20] Little is known about the sixth man, Jean Léchelle.

If the fur trade made few wealthy men among those who invested heavily in it, it would be hard to argue that less considerable investors were more successful. It is not unreasonable to conclude that the fur trade was not very profitable for the overwhelming majority of outfitters and that it only sustained a very limited number of them each year. Yet the French had reduced costly competition to a minimum and had few worries about price fluctuations. How would Canadian outfitters fare under a different system?

The Advent of the British Merchants

With the arrival in Montreal of British traders, the workings of the fur trade were disrupted. At first, the licensing system was maintained and some areas were left to the exclusive trade of particular traders.[21] But from the very beginning the trade was said to be open to all who wanted to secure a licence, and the result could only be price competition. With individual traders going into the fur trade, the organization of the trade regressed. The previous division of labour between the *Compagnie des Indes,* the import merchants and outfitters, the traders, the voyageurs, and the *engagés* was abandoned and during the first years of British rule the individual trader filled all of the functions previously spread among many "specialists."

The story of Alexander Henry, one of the first British merchants to venture into the upper country, illustrates the new pattern of trade. A young man from New Jersey, Alexander Henry came to Canada in 1760 with General Amherst's troops.[22] With the fall of Montreal Henry saw the opening of a "new market" and became acquainted with the prospects of the fur trade. The following year, he set out for Michilimackinac with a Montreal outfitter, Etienne Campion, whom he called his "assistant," and who took charge of the routine aspects of the trip.[23] Henry wintered at Michilimackinac. There he was urged by the local inhabitants to go back to Detroit as soon as possible for they claimed to fear for his safety. Their fears were not without foundation, but Henry stayed on. His partner Campion reassured him: ". . . the Canadian inhabitants of the fort were more hostile than the Indians, as being jealous of British traders, who . . . were penetrating into the country."[24] At least some of the Canadians resented the British traders from the outset and a few tried to use the Indians to frighten them away.[25]

Henry proceeded to Sault Sainte-Marie the following year. In the spring of 1763, he returned to Michilimackinac and witnessed the massacre of the British garrison during Pontiac's revolt.[26] He was eventually captured by the Indians and adopted into an Indian family with whom he lived, in the Indian style, until late June 1764. Undaunted, Henry set out for the fur trade again, exploring the Lake Superior area. He was on the Saskatchewan River in 1776, tapping fur resources which the French had seldom reached.[27] Finally he settled down in Montreal in 1781 and while he did join the North West Company after its formation, he seldom returned to the upper country himself.[28]

Henry was not the first British merchant to reach the upper country. Henry Bostwick had obtained a licence from General Gage before him in 1761,[29] and the traders Goddard and Solomons had followed Henry into Michilimackinac in 1761. By early 1763 there were at least two more British merchants in the area.[30] In Montreal alone there were close to fifty new merchants by 1765. Governor Murray's list of the Protestants in the district of Montreal gives the names, the origins, and the "former callings"

221

of forty-five.[31] Over half of them came from England and Scotland and 20 per cent were from Ireland. Only 13 per cent came from the American colonies and an equal number came from various countries (Switzerland, Germany, France, Guernsey). In the proportion of more than three to one, the newcomers had been merchants in their "former calling." The others had been soldiers and clerks. Many of the newcomers were men of experience and enterprise. Among them were Isaac Todd, Thomas Walker, Lawrence Ermatinger, Richard Dobie, Edward Chinn, John Porteous, William Grant, Benjamin Frobisher, James Finlay, Alexander Paterson, Forrest Oakes, and the Jewish merchants Ezekiel and Levy Solomons, all of whom became substantial traders.[32]

The arrival of so many merchants could only mean one thing: strenuous competition in the fur trade. Competition ruthlessly drove out those with less secure financial resources or with no taste for sharp practices. Among the British as among the French, few resisted the pressures. The story of the trader Hamback is not untypical. Out on the Miami River in 1766 and 1767, he found that competition left him with few returns to make to his creditor William Edgar of Detroit. "I live the life of a downright exile," he complained, "no company but a Barrel of drunken infamous fugitives, and no other Comfort of Life."[33]

The Canadian merchants of Montreal had competition not only from British merchants in their town, but also from American merchants moving into Detroit and Michilimackinac. William Edgar, a New York merchant, was at Niagara in late 1761.[34] In 1763 he was established at Detroit, where he conducted a brisk trade supplying individual traders at Michilimackinac and in the South West District.[35] From Schenectady, the partnership of Phyn and Ellice also carried on a profitable supply trade for the fur traders of the interior.[36]

Competition also came from the French on the Mississippi, who were trading in the Illinois country and the Lake Superior region. These French traders could all too easily link up with French-speaking traders from Canada, whose help, it was feared, they could enlist in subverting the Indians against British rule.[37] This always troubled Sir William Johnson, the Superintendent for Indian Affairs, who refused to abandon his suspicions of the French-speaking traders from Canada.

This many-sided competition produced a climate to which the Canadian merchants were not accustomed. The increased numbers of fur traders led to frictions with the Indians, smaller returns for some of the traders, and unsavory trade practices.[38] Even the retail trade was affected. Merchants from England flooded the market at Quebec "with their manufactures, so much so that they are daily sold here at Vendue Twenty per Cent. below prime Cost."[39] In 1760 alone, the first year of British occupation, £60 000 worth of trade goods had been brought into Canada.[40] From 1765 to 1768 the pages of the *Quebec Gazette* were filled with notices of auctions by merchants returning to England and disposing of their wares after unsuccessful attempts to establish themselves in the trade of the colony.[41]

By 1768 some thought the Canadians still had the advantage in the fur trade, even though there was "Competition" and a "strong Jealousy" between Canadian and English. The Canadians' "long Connections with those Indians," wrote General Gage, "and their better Knowledge of their Language and Customs, must naturaly for a long time give the Canadians an Advantage over the English . . ."[42] Sir William Johnson had expressed a similar opinion the previous year and had deplored the British merchants' tactics: "The English were compelled to make use of Low, Selfish Agents, French, or English as Factors, who at the Expence of honesty and sound policy, took care of themselves whatever became of their employers."[43]

Another observer, the Hudson's Bay Company trader at Moose Factory, complained of "Interlopers who will be more Destructive to our trade than the French was." The French had conducted a less aggressive trade: they "were in a manner Settled, their Trade fixed, their Standards moderate and Themselves under particular regulations and restrictions, which I doubt is not the Case now."[44] Competition was forcing the British merchants in Montreal into ruthless tactics, a development which upset the Hudson's Bay Company man and which would unsettle the Canadians.

The pattern of British domination of the fur trade began to emerge as early as 1767. Trading ventures out of Michilimackinac into the North West were conducted by Canadians, but British merchants supplied the financial backing. The North West expeditions demanded the lengthiest periods of capital outlay, lasting two or three years. British merchants, it seems, had better resources. Of the fifteen outfitters at Michilimackinac who sent canoes to the North West in 1767, nine were British and six were Canadian; the total value of canoes outfitted by the British came to £10 812.17 while the Canadian's canoes were worth only £3 061.10. The British outfitters — most notably Alexander Henry, Isaac Todd, James McGill, Benjamin Frobisher, Forrest Oakes — invested on the average £1 351.12. and the Canadians only £510.5. The average value of goods invested in each canoe stood at £415.17. for the British and £278.6. for the Canadians.[45] The Canadians' investment per canoe was only two-thirds that of the British and the Canadians were already outnumbered as outfitters in what would become the most important region of the fur trade.[46]

Open competition was not conducive to the expansion of the fur trade and an oligopolistic structure reminiscent of the French system soon reappeared as the only solution.[47] This led to the formation of the North West Company in the 1780's but already in 1775, those Montreal merchants who had extended their operations as far as the Saskatchewan felt the need for collaboration rather than competition. Again developments in the more remote frontiers of the fur trade foretold of events to occur later in the whole of the trade: the traders on the Saskatchewan were almost all of British origin.[48] The fur trade was returning to the structures developed by the French, but during the period of competition which followed the Conquest the Canadians were gradually crowded out. They was some irony in that. Why had the Canadians fared so badly?

The Attitude of Government Officials

Much has been made of the natural sympathies of Murray and Carleton towards the Canadians and their antipathies towards the traders of their own nation. Yet for all their ideological inclinations there is no evidence that the governors turned their sentiments into policies of benevolence for Canadians in trade matters. Rather, it is easier to discover, among the lesser officials and some of the more important ones as well, an understandable patronizing of British rather than Canadian merchants. Colonial administrators may not have set a deliberate pattern of preference in favour of British merchants. But the Canadian merchants of Montreal, who put great store by official patronage, cared not whether the policy was deliberate or accidental; the result was the same.

Official preferences played against the Canadian traders in many ways. First, the lucrative trade of supplying the military posts was given to British and American merchants as a matter of course, and this occasion for profit was lost to the Canadians. Under the French regime some of the Montreal merchants, notably the Monières and the Gamelins, had profited from that trade.[49] Now it fell out of Canadian hands. This advantage did not shift to the sole favor of the British merchants of Quebec. New York and Pennsylvania traders were also awarded their share of the trade. The firms of Phyn, Ellice of Schenectady and Baynton, Wharton, and Morgan of Philadelphia received the lion's share of that business while the upper country was under the jurisdiction of Sir William Johnson.[50] But this was of little comfort to the Canadians.

Less tangible by-products of the British occupation of the former fur trading areas of New France are more difficult to assess than the loss of the supply trade; they were, however, quite real. One was the British military's attitude towards Canadians. The military were wary of French-speaking traders in Illinois and on the Mississippi. Although the French from Canada had been vanquished, French traders in the interior could still deal with France through New Orleans. No regulations, no boundaries could restrain French traders operating out of Louisiana from dealing with the Indians, and the Canadians who were confined to the posts protested against the advantage held by the French traders.[51] But who were these French traders? Did they not include Canadian *coureurs de bois* and wintering merchants? How could one really tell a French-speaking trader from Canada from a French-speaking trader out of New Orleans? Were not all of them suspect of exciting the Indians against the British, promising and perhaps hoping for France's return to America?[52] As late as 1768, when Indian discontent in the West threatened another uprising, General Gage failed to see any difference between French-speaking Canadians and the French from New Orleans:

There is the greatest reason to suspect that the French are Endeavoring to engross the Trade, and that the Indians have acted thro' their Instigation, in the Murders they have committed, and the Resolutions we are told they have taken, to suffer no Englishman to

224

trade with them. And in this they have rather been Assisted by the English Traders, who having no Consideration but that of a present gain, have thro' fear of exposing their own Persons, or hopes of obtaining greater influence with the Indians, continually employed French Commissarys or Agents, whom they have trusted with Goods for them to Sell at an Advanced price in the Indian Villages.[53]

Gage's suspicions of the French traders were nurtured by Sir William Johnson, who had to keep the Indians on peaceful terms with one another and with the British. It was part of Johnson's function, of course, to worry about possible uprisings and about subversive individuals. His job would be made easier if he could confine all traders to military posts where they could be kept under surveillance. But the traders had little concern for Sir William's preoccupations. If British traders were irresponsible in their desires of "present gain," the Canadian traders' vices were compounded by the uncertainty of their allegiance to the British Crown:

Since the Reduction of that Country [Canada], we have seen so many Instances of their [the Canadian traders'] Perfidy false Stories & Cª. Interested Views in Trade that prudence forbids us to suffer them or any others to range at Will without being under the Inspection of the proper Officers agreeable to His Majesty's Appointment . . .[54]

225

Johnson's attitude spread to the officers under him, even though Carleton had found nothing reprehensible in the Canadians' behavior.[55] Johnson's deputy, George Croghan, believed there was collusion between the French from Canada and the French from Louisiana.[56] In 1763 the commandant at Michilimackinac, Major Etherington, had displayed a similar mistrust of the Canadians.[57] Major Robert Rogers, a later commandant at Michilimackinac, checked the Canadians by trading on his own account.[58]

The British military's mistrust of the French traders from Canada was understandable. Before 1760, one of the major reasons for the American colonials' antagonism towards New France had been the French ability to press the Indians into their service to terrorize the western fringes of American settlement. Thus there was a historical as well as a tactical basis for the military's attitude towards the Canadians. But British officers failed to recognize that not all Canadian traders were potential trouble-makers and that there was indeed very little tangible evidence, as Carleton had reminded Johnson, of any mischief on their part. The military's attitude was directed as much by ethnic prejudice as by military necessity.

The Canadian traders could not fail to perceive this prejudice, and it dampened their spirits. Perhaps the military's attitude, as much as competition, forced the Canadians into partnerships with British merchants. (The express purpose of the bonds required for the fur trade was to ensure loyal conduct; what better token of loyalty could there be for a Canadian trader than a bond taken out in his name by a British partner?) The military's mistrust of the Canadian traders did not lessen with time. The advantage which this prejudice gave British traders would continue for some twenty years after the Conquest, as the American Revolution rekindled the military's fears of treasonable conduct by the Canadians.

Other patronage relationships between British military officials and British traders also deprived the Canadians of an equal chance in the competition for furs. It is hard to evaluate precisely the effect of such patronage; only glimpses of it may be caught. Late in 1763 a Philadelphia merchant who had lost heavily because of Pontiac's uprising wrote to William Edgar in Detroit that Croghan was in England where he was to "represent the Case of the Traders to his Majesty" and that General Amherst had "given us his faithful promise that he will do everything in his power in our behalf."[59] In 1765 Alexander Henry was granted the exclusive trade of Lake Superior by Major Howard, the military commandant at Michilimackinac. Nine years later Henry received the support of such patrons as the Duke of Gloucester, the consul of the Empress of Russia in England, and of Sir William Johnson in an ill-fated attempt to mine the iron ore of the Lake Superior area.[60]

These were obvious examples of patronage; other forms of cooperation were less visible. Another correspondent of William Edgar, Thomas Shipboy, asked Edgar to represent him in settling the affairs of a correspondent at Detroit and at Michilimackinac where, he added, "if you find any Difficulty in procuring his effects I dare say the Commanding officer will be of Service to you if you inform him in whose [sic] behalf you are acting . . ."[61] Benjamin Frobisher also asked Edgar to "use your Interest with Capt. Robinson" to put a shipment of corn aboard the government vessel which sailed from Detroit to Michilimackinac.[62] Such shipping space was scarce and was only available through the courtesy of military officers or the ships' captains. Here again British traders put their social connections to good use. A last resort was sheer military force. Out on the Miami River, the trader Hamback saw "little hope of getting any thing from [Fort] St. Joseph at all, if I don't get protected, by the Commanding Officer, who might easily get those [Canadian] rascals fetch'd down to Detroit if He would . . ."[63]

None of this patronage appears to have been available to Canadians. It is impossible to ascertain the degree to which military suspicions and patronage lessened the Canadians' chances in the fur trade. But more important, perhaps, than the actual loss of opportunities was the psychological handicap imposed upon the Canadians. What heart could they put in the game when the dice were so obviously loaded?

The Merchants' Political Activities

The enmity between British merchants and the military, the merchants' growing agitation in favour of "British liberties" and their sentiments of political self-importance have been ably told by others and need not be retold here.[64] What needs to be underlined is that political agitation was unfamiliar to the Canadians. They had had no experience in these matters under French rule. Only on rare occasions during the pre-Conquest years

226

had the Canadian merchants engaged in collective political representations; such representations were elicited by the governor or the intendant to obtain the merchants' advice on specific issues.[65] As French subjects, the Canadian merchants of Montreal had lacked the power to foster their economic interests through collective political action.

After 1760, the Canadian merchants would gradually lose their political innocence under the influence of the British merchants. During the thirty years which followed the Conquest they would make "l'apprentissage des libertés anglaises" and in 1792 they would take their place in the newly-created legislative assembly more cognizant of the workings of the British constitution than the British had expected.[66] But that is beyond the concern here. In the years preceding the American Revolution the Montreal merchants were still looking for bearings. They showed their growing political awareness by following in the *Quebec Gazette* the political and constitutional debates which were rocking the British Empire. The merchants also began to voice their concerns in petitions and memorials to the authorities in the colony and in London.

227

The *Quebec Gazette* was the province's official gazette and its only newspaper before 1778. The paper published public notices for the Montreal district and occasional advertisements sent in by Montrealers as well as matters of concern to Quebec residents. It also made an effort to publish Canadian news of a general character. It closely followed the debates raging across the Atlantic over the Stamp Act and the general issues of colonial taxation. It reported on changes in the Imperial government and on contemporary political issues in England, notably the Wilkes affair.[67]

The pages of the *Gazette* also served on occasion as a forum for political discussion. In September 1765 a "Civis Canadiensis" declared his puzzlement at all the talk of "British liberties" and asked for enlightenment. The following year, a Quebec resident wrote a series of letters arguing that the colony should not be taxed.[68] In 1767, a debate arose on the British laws relating to bankruptcy and their applicability in Quebec.[69] Because of the pressures of Governor Carleton the *Gazette* stifled its reporting of controversial issues after 1770 and thereafter had little to print about American affairs.[70] In 1775 the *Gazette*'s political outpourings were directed against the American rebels and towards securing the loyalty of those Canadians who read the *Gazette* and had been made familiar with the concepts of personal liberty, of "no taxation without representation," of the limited powers of the sovereign, and of the rights of the people. The *Gazette*'s readers most probably included the leading merchants of Montreal.

The *Gazette* was not the only instrument for the learning of British liberties. Anxious to give the appearance of a unanimous disposition among all merchants in Montreal, the British merchants often called on their Canadian confreres to add their names to various memorials and petitions dealing with the political and the economic state of the colony. The Canadian merchants who signed these petitions and memorials represented the top layer of the Canadian mercantile group in Montreal. Those who signed most often were the import merchants and the busy outfitters.

These Canadian merchants followed the political leadership of the British merchants. From 1763 to 1772 their petitions were either literal translations or paraphrased equivalents of petitions drafted by British merchants. It was only in December 1773 that they asserted views different from those of their British counterparts.[72] They petitioned the King that their "ancient laws, privileges, and customs" be restored, that the province be extended to its "former boundaries," that some Canadians be taken into the King's service, and that "the rights and privileges of citizens of England" be granted to all.[73]

The Canadians were becoming aware of their own position and were seeking to consolidate it against the attacks of the British element. The demand for the maintenance of the "ancient laws" was designed to counter British demands for British laws and representative institutions. The Canadians opposed the latter since, in their view, the colony was "not as yet in a condition to defray the expences of its own civil government, and consequently not in a condition to admit of a general assembly."[74] The demand for "a share of the civil and military employments under his majesty's government" came naturally to those who had lived under the French system of patronage. The Canadians had been accustomed to seek official patronage as the main avenue of upward mobility. The prospect of being denied such patronage was "frightful" to them, since they had little familiarity with alternate patterns of social promotion.[75]

In style as well as in content the Canadian merchants' petitions and memorials revealed differences in attitudes between Canadians and British. British memorials and petitions were rarely prefaced by more than the customary "Humbly showeth" and went directly to the point. In their own memorials and petitions, the Canadians first took "the liberty to prostrate themselves at the foot" of the royal throne and surrendered themselves to the "paternal care" of their sovereign. They often appealed to the wisdom, justice, and magnanimity of the King.[76] Their formal posture of meekness contrasted sharply with the self-assertion of the British. The Canadians' "Habits of Respect and Submission," as one British official put it,[77] may well have endeared them to Murray and Carleton, but those habits constituted a psychological obstacle against their making full use of their new-found "British liberties" to foster their own economic interest.

Conclusion

With the fall of Montreal to British arms in September 1760 something was irrevocably lost to the Canadian merchants of that city. More than the evil effects of the war or the post-war commercial readjustments, the most unsettling consequence of the Conquest was the disappearance of a familiar business climate. As New France passed into the British Empire, the Montreal outfitters were thrown into a new system of business competition, brought about by the very numbers of newly-arrived merchants, unloading goods in the conquered French colony and going after its enticing fur trade. In opening up the trade of the colony to competition, the British presence transformed Canadian commercial practices. The change negated the Canadian merchant's initial advantage of experience in the fur trade and created a novel business climate around them.

Competition in trade, the new political regime, the Canadian merchants' inability to obtain the favors of the military, all these created a mood of uncertainty and pessimism among the Montreal merchants. The merchants could only conclude from what was happening around them that the new business climate of the post-Conquest period favoured British traders at their expense. They can be understood if they were not eager to adapt their ways to the new situation.

It may be argued, of course, that the changes which produced the new situation are subsumed under the notion of "Conquest" and that the previous pages only make more explicit the "decapitation" interpretation advanced by the historians of the "Montreal school."[78] It is true enough that the new business climate described here may not have been created after the Seven Years' War had Canada remained a French possession. But there is no guarantee that other changes would not have affected the Montreal merchants. During the last years of the French regime they had reaped few profits from the fur trade. After the Conquest they continued in the fur trade much on the same scale as before. The Montreal merchants were not "decapitated" by the Conquest; rather, they were faced in very short succession with a series of transformations in the socio-economic structure of the colony to which they might have been able to adapt had these transformations been spread over a longer period of time.

This paper has attempted to show that the fate of the Canadian merchants of Montreal after the Conquest followed from the nature of trade before the Conquest and from the rate at which new circumstances required the merchants to alter their business behavior. But it should be remembered that the decapitation hypothesis still remains to be tested in the area of the colony's economy which was most heavily dependent upon the control of the metropolis, the import-export trade of the Quebec merchants. Only a detailed examination of the role and the activities of the Quebec merchants, both before and after the Conquest, will fully put the decapitation hypothesis to the test.

229

Notes

1. Public Archives of Canada [hereafter PAC], C.O.42, vol. 27, f. 66, Carleton to Shelburne Quebec, 25 November 1767; quoted in A.L. Burt, *The Old Province of Quebec* (2 vols. Toronto, 1968), I, p. 142.
2. See Burt, *Old Province*, I, Chapter VI; Dale B. Miquelon, "The Baby Family in the Trade of Canada, 1750–1820" (Unpublished Master's thesis, Carleton University, 1966), pp. 145–146.
3. Francis Parkman, *The Old Regime in Canada* (27th ed. Boston, 1892), Chapter XXI, especially pp. 397–398.

4. W. Stewart Wallace, ed., *Documents Relating to the North West Company* (Toronto, 1934); *Wallace, The Pedlars From Quebec and Other Papers on the Nor'Westers* (Toronto, 1954); E. E. Rich, *The Fur Trade and the Northwest to 1857* (Toronto, 1967); Rich, *The History of the Hudson's Bay Company*, II (London, 1959); D. G. Creighton, *The Empire of the St. Lawrence* (Toronto, 1956).

5. Wayne E. Stevens, *The Northwest Fur Trade 1763–1800* (Urbana, Ill., 1928), p. 25.

6. Fernand Ouellet, *Histoire économique et sociale du Québec 1760–1850* (Montreal, 1966), p. 77.

7. *Ibid.*, pp. 104–106.

8. Michel Brunet, *Les Canadiens après la Conquête, 1759–1775* (Montreal, 1969), pp. 173–174, pp. 177–180.

9. Miquelon, "The Baby Family," p. 158.

10. *Ibid.*, p. 142.

11. The implication is unwarranted. A given economic sector can be dynamic and even produce the largest share of marketable commodities and still provide individual entrepreneurs with meager profits. The macro-economic level of analysis should not be confused with the micro-economic level. Jean Hamelin showed that only around 28 percent of the profits from the beaver trade remained in Canada. Since the Canadians had an assured market for beaver, one can wonder how much more profitable it was for them to deal in other peltries. See Hamelin, *Economie et Société en Nouvelle-France* (Quebec, 1960), pp. 54–56.

12. The obvious economic explanation for the downfall of the Canadian merchants after the Conquest has to be dismissed. The liquidation of Canadian paper money by France hurt most of all those British merchants who bought it from Canadians for speculation. Canadian merchants had already compensated in part for the anticipated liquidation by raising prices during the last years of the Seven Years' War. Those Montreal merchants who had the greatest quantity of French paper were not driven out of business; on the contrary the most prominent merchants were able to open accounts with British suppliers soon after the Conquest without too much difficulty. See José E. Igartua, "The Merchants and *Négociants* of Montreal, 1750–1775: A Study in Socio-Economic History" (Unpublished Ph.D. thesis, Michigan State University, 1974), Chapter VI.

13. Franquet, *Voyages et mémoires sur le Canada en 1752–1753* (Toronto, 1968), p. 56.

14. For a more elaborate description of the size and the socio-economic cnaracteristics of the Montreal merchant community at this time, see Igartua, "The Merchants and *Négociants* of Montreal," Chapter II.

15. See H. A. Innis, *The Fur Trade in Canada* (Rev. ed. Toronto, 1956), pp. 107–113.

16. See Abraham Rotstein, "Fur Trade and Empire: An Institutional Analysis" (Unpublished Ph.D. thesis, University of Toronto, 1967), p. 72.

17. Innis, *Fur Trade*, p. 117. For his discussion of the impact of war on the fur trade and on New France, see pp. 114–118.

18. In theory, the French licensing system set up to restrict the trade remained in operation from its re-establishment in 1728 to the end of the French regime; only twenty-five *congés* were to be sold each year. In practice, military officers in the upper country could also acquire for a modest fee exclusive trade privileges for their particular area. With some care, concluded one author, they could make an easy fortune. See Emile Salone, *La Colonisation de la Nouvelle-France* (Trois-Rivières, 1970), p. 390, pp. 392–393. No clear official description of the licensing system was found for the period from 1750 to 1760, but the precise way in which the fur trade was restricted matters less than the fact of restriction.

19. On Charly see PAC, RG 4 B58, vol 15, 19 September 1764, pass by Governor Murray to "Monsr. Louis Saint-Ange Charly [and his family] to London, in their way to France agreeable to the Treaty of Peace . . ."; Archives Nationales du Québec à Montreal [formerly Archives judiciaires de Montréal; hereafter ANQ-M], Greffe de Pierre Panet, 16 août 1764, no. 2190. Trotier Desauniers "Dufy"'s will is in *ibid.*, 29 juillet 1760, no. 1168, and Godet's will is in *ibid.*, 28 décembre 1768, no. 3140.

20. The inventory of Monière's estate is in *ibid.*, 28 décembre 1768, no. 3141; that of L'Huillier Chevalier's in *ibid.*, 15 [?] juin 1772, no. 3867.

21. See Alexander Henry, *Travels and Adventures in Canada* (Ann Arbor. University Microfilms, 1966), pp. 191–192.

22. W. S. Wallace, *Documents Relating to the North West Company*, Appendix A ("A Biographical Dictionary of the Nor 'Westers"), p. 456.

23. See Henry, *Travels*, pp. 1–11, p. 34.

24. *Ibid.*, p. 39.

25. *Ibid.*, p. 50. Cf. the rosier picture by Creighton, *The Empire of the St. Lawrence*, p. 33.

26. Henry, *Travels*, pp. 77–84. The Indians killed the British soldiers but ransomed the British traders, giving to each according to his profession.

27. Henry, *Travels*, pp. 264–292.

28. See Wallace, *Documents*, p. 456; Milo M. Quaife, ed, *Alexander Henry's Travels and Adventures in the Years 1760–1776* (Chicago, 1921), pp. xvi–xvii.

29. Henry, *Travels*, p. 11; Quaife, *Henry's Travels*, p. 12 n. 6.

30. Rich, *History of the Hudson's Bay Company*, II, p. 9.

31. See PAC, C.O. 42, vol. 5, ff. 30–31, Murray's "List of Protestants in the District of Montreal," dated Quebec, 7 November 1765.

32. See Miquelon, "The Baby Family," pp. 181–187.

33. PAC, MG 19 A1, 1, William Edgar Papers, vol. 1, p. 97, F. Hamback to W. Edgar, 2 November 1766. See also *ibid.*, p. 95, Hamback to D. Edgar, 29 October 1766, and pp. 104–106, same to Edgar, 23 March 1767.

34. *Ibid.*, vol. 1, p. 12.

35. See *Ibid.*, vols. 1 and 2.

36. R. H. Fleming, "Phyn, Ellice and Company of Schenectady," *Contributions to Canadian Economics*, IV (1932), pp. 7–41.

37. See Marjorie G. Jackson, "The Beginnings of British Trade at Michilimackinac," *Minnesota History* XI (September, 1930), 252; C. W. Alvord and C. E. Carter, eds., *The New Regime 1765–1767* (Collections of the Illinois State Historical Library, XI), pp. 300–301; Alvord and Carter, eds., *Trade and Politics 1767–1769* (Collections of the Illinois State Historical Library, XVI), pp. 382–453.

38. See "Extract of a Letter from Michilimackinac, to a Gentleman in this City, dated 30th June," in *Quebec Gazette*, 18 August 1768; see also Rich, *History of the Hudson's Bay Company*, II, p. 26: "The suspicions between the Pedlars [from Quebec], and their encouragements of the Indians to trick and defraud their trade rivals, especially by defaulting on payments of debt, were widespread and continuous."

39. *Quebec Gazette*, 7 January 1768.

40. Burt, *Old Province*, I, p. 92.

41. The flooding of the Quebec market by British merchants was part of a larger invasion of the colonial trade in North America. See Mark Egnal and Joseph A. Ernst, "An Economic Interpretation of the American Revolution," *William and Mary Quarterly*, Third Series, XXIX (1972), pp. 3–32.

42. Quoted in Alvord and Carter, eds., *Trade and Politics*, p. 288.

43. *Ibid.*, p. 38.

44. Quoted in E. E. Rich, *Montreal and the Fur Trade* (Montreal, 1966), p. 44.

45. These figures are somewhat distorted by the inclusion of a single large British investor, Alexander Henry, who outfitted seven canoes worth £3400 in all. See Charles E. Lart, ed., "Fur-Trade Returns, 1767," *Canadian Historical Review*, III (December, 1922), pp. 351–358. The definition of the North West as including Lake Huron, Lake Superior, and "the northwest by way of Lake Superior" given in Rich, *Montreal and the Fur Trade*, pp. 36–37, was used in making these compilations. The French traders were "Deriviere," "Chenville," St. Clair, Laselle, "Guillaid [Guillet]," and "Outlass [Houtelas]."

46. See Rich, *Montreal and the Fur Trade*, pp. 36–37.

47. Jackson, *Minnesota History*, XI, pp. 268–269.

48. Rich, *History of the Hudson's Bay Company*, II, p. 68.

49. On the Monières, see Igartua, "The Merchants and *Négociants* of Montreal," Chapter II. On the Gamelins, see Antoine Champagne, *Les La Vérendrye et les postes de l'ouest* (Quebec, 1968), *passim*.

50. See R. H. Fleming, *Contributions to Canadians Economics*, IV, 13; on Baynton, Wharton and Morgan, see *The Papers of Sir William Johnson* [hereafter *Johnson Papers*], 14 vols., (Albany, 1921–1965), V, VI, XII, *passim*.

51. PAC, C.O. 42, vol 2, ff. 277–280, petition of the "Merchants and Traders of Montreal" to Murray and the Council, Montreal, 20 February 1765; *Johnson Papers*, V, pp. 807–815, memorial and petition of Detroit traders to Johnson, 22 November 1767; XII, pp. 409–414, 1768 trade regulations with the merchants' objections.

52. See Alvord and Carter, eds., *The New Regime*, pp. 118–119, and *Trade and Politics*, p. 39, p. 287; see also Stevens, *The Northwest Fur Trade*, p. 44.

53. *Johnson Papers*, XII, p. 517, Thomas Gage to Guy Johnson, New York, 29 May 1768.

54. *Ibid.*, V, p. 481. See also Alvord and Carter, eds., *The New Regime*, pp. 118–119; *Johnson Papers*, V, p. 362; Alvord and Carter, eds., *Trade and Politics*, p. 39; *Johnson Papers*, V, pp. 762–764; XII, pp. 486–487; Stevens, *The Northwest Fur Trade*, p. 28.

55. PAC, C.O. 42, vol. 27, ff. 81–85, Carleton to Johnson, Quebec, 27 March 1767.

56. *Johnson Papers*, XII, pp. 372–375, Croghan to Johnson, 18 October 1767.

57. Henry, *Travels*, pp. 71–72.

58. See PAC, C.O. 42, vol. 26, f. 13, Court of St. James, Conway [Secretary of State] to the Commandants of Detroit and Michilimackinac, 27 March 1766. See also Alvord and Carter, eds., *Trade and Politics*, pp. 207–208, Gage to Shelburne, 12 March 1768; p. 239, Johnson to Gage, 8 April 1768; p. 375, Gage to Johnson, 14 August 1768; p. 378, Gage to Hillsborough, 17 August 1768; p. 384, Johnson to Gage, 24 August 1768; p. 599, Gage to Hillsborough, 9 September 1769. More than trading on his own account, Rogers was suspected of setting up an independent Illinois territory. He was eventually

cleared. See "Robert Rogers," *Dictionary of American Biography,* XVI (New York, 1935), pp. 108–109, and *Johnson Papers,* V, VI, XII, XIII, *passim.*
59. PAC, William Edgar Papers, vol. 1, pp. 43–44, Callender to Edgar n.p., 31 December 1763.
60. Henry, *Travels,* pp. 191–192, p. 235.
61. PAC, William Edgar Papers, vol. 1, p. 90, Thos. Shipboy to Rankin and Edgar, Albany, 21 August 1766.
62. *Ibid.,* p. 201, Benjamin Frobisher to Rankin and Edgar, Michilimackinac, 23 June 1769.
63. *Ibid.,* pp. 104–106, F. Hamback to Edgar, 23 March 1767.
64. The most detailed account is given in Burt, *Old Province,* I, Chapters VI and VII. See also Creighton, *Empire of the St. Lawrence,* pp. 40–48.
65. See for instance E.-Z. Massicotte, "La Bourse de Montréal sous le régime français," *The Canadian Antiquarian and Numismatic Journal,* Third Series, XII (1915), pp. 26–32.
66. See Pierre Tousignant, "La Genèse et l'avènement de la Constitution de 1791" (Unpublished Ph.D. thesis, Université de Montréal, 1971).
67. See the *Quebec Gazette* of 15 September 1766 and the issues from June to September 1768.
68. See *Quebec Gazette,* 26 September 1765. Tousignant, "La Genèse," pp. 21–39, points out the political significance of this letter.
69. See texts, by "A MERCHANT" in the 10 and 17 December 1767 issues, and rebuttals in the 24 and 31 December 1767 and 7 and 21 January 1768 issues.
70. Tousignant, "La Genèse," p. 39.
71. See issues of 13 and 27 July, and 5 October 1775.
72. Canadian notables of Quebec broke with the "Old Subjects" earlier: a petition, thought to date from 1770 and signed by leading Canadians of that city, asked for the restoration of Canadian institutions. See Adam Shortt and Arthur G. Doughty, *Documents Relating to the Constitutional History of Canada* (2nd. ed. Ottawa, 1918) [hereafter *Docs. Const. Hist. Can.*], I, pp. 419–421.
73. The petition and the memorial are reproduced in *Docs, Const. Hist Can.,* I, pp. 504–506, pp. 508–510.
74. *Ibid.,* I, p. 511. The British merchants of Montreal signed a counter-petition in January 1774, requesting the introduction of an assembly and of the laws of England. See *ibid.,* I, pp. 501–502.
75. Recent historians have highlighted the influence of the military and civil administrations as sources of economic and social betterment in New France. See Guy Frégault, *Le XVIIIe siècle canadien* (Montreal, 1968), pp. 382–384; W. J. Eccles, "The Social, Economic, and Political Significance of the military Establishment in New France," *Canadian Historical Review,* LII (March, 1971), pp. 17–19; and Cameron Nish, *Les Bourgeois-Gentilhommes de la Nouvelle-France* (Montreal, 1968), *passim.*
76. See PAC, C.O. 42, vol. 24. ff. 72–73v.; *ibid.,* ff. 95–95v; *ibid.,* vol. 3, f. 262; *Docs. Const. Hist. Can.,* I, pp. 504–508.
77. See *Docs. Const. Hist. Can.,* I, p. 504.
78. Maurice Séguin, of the History Department of the Université de Montréal, was the first to present a systematic interpretation of the Conquest as societal decapitation. His book, *L'Idée d'indépendance au Québec: genèse et historique* (Trois-Rivières, 1968), which contains a summary of his thought, was published twenty years after its author first sketched out his thesis. Guy Frégault's *Histoire de la Nouvelle-France,* IX. *La guerre de la Conquête, 1754–1760* (Montreal, 1955) is a masterful rendition of that conflict, cast as the *affrontement* of two civilizations. Michel Brunet, the most voluble of the "Montreal school" historians, has assumed the task of popularizing Séguin's thought. See Brunet, "La Conquête anglaise et la déchéance de la bourgeoisie canadienne (1760–1793)," in his *La Présence anglaise et les Canadiens* (Montreal, 1964), pp. 48–112. Brunet developed the point further in *Les Canadiens après la Conquête, I: 1759–1775* (Montreal, 1969). An abridged version of Brunet's position is provided in his *French Canada and the Early Decades of British Rule, 1760–1791* (Ottawa, 1963). For a review of French-Canadian historiography on the Conquest up to 1966, see Ramsay Cook, "Some French-Canadian Interpretations of the British Conquest: une quatrième dominante de la pensée canadienne-française," Canadian Historical Association *Historical Papers,* 1966, pp. 70–83.

Topic Seven

The Impact of the American Revolution on the Maritime Colonies

Ironically, Britain's success in expelling France from North America con-tributed to its own expulsion from the Thirteen Colonies only fifteen years later. The removal of the French threat from Quebec and Louisbourg had, in the minds of many American colonists, ended the need for Britain. This realization, in addition to a growing sense of nationalism among the Thirteen Colonies, led to the demand for greater self-government. Britain's attempt to tax the colonies finally led to open rebellion. The first armed clash at Lexington, Massachusetts, in mid-April 1775, officially began the American Revolution.

The Nova Scotians had to make a difficult decision: to support Britain, to join the American cause, or to remain neutral. Though three-quarters of Nova Scotia's roughly 20,000 settlers in 1775 were New Englanders with strong economic and family ties with the New England colonies, in the end they chose to stay loyal to the Crown. George Rawlyk offers an explanation of their loyalty in "The American Revolution and Nova Scotia Reconsidered."

During the Revolutionary War thousands of farmers, craftsmen, and small merchants, as well as large landowners and governments officials, had sided with the Crown. After Britain's defeat about 80,000 of these United Empire Loyalists chose, or were forced, to depart with the British garrisons, over half of them settling in two of the remaining British colonies to the north: Nova Scotia and Quebec. Approximately 30,000 went to Nova Scotia, almost doubling the size of the existing population; about 5,000 came to the St. Lawrence Valley, doubling, perhaps even tripling the English-speaking population there from four or five percent, to ten or fifteen percent of the total population; and nearly 10,000 settled in the western portion of the Province of Quebec, which became Upper Canada in 1791. The Loyalist migration led to the founding of two new colonies, New Brunswick and Upper Canada. In "The United Empire Loyalists: A Reconsideration" W.G. Shelton outlines the importance of the Loyalists in Canadian history.

The classic account of Nova Scotia's response to the revolutionary struggle in the Thirteen Colonies is John Bartlet Brebner's *Neutral Yankees of Nova Scotia* (Toronto: McClelland and Stewart, 1969; first published in 1937). For a recent history of Nova Scotia-New England relations see George Rawlyk, *Nova Scotia's Massachusetts: A Study of Massachusetts-Nova Scotia Relations, 1630 to 1784*, (Montreal: McGill-Queen's University Press, 1973). *Revolution Rejected, 1775-1776*, edited by George Rawlyk (Scarborough, Ontario: Prentice-Hall, 1968) and W.S. MacNutt's chapter, "Revolution and Reorganization, 1775-1785," in *The Atlantic Provinces, 1712-1857* (Toronto: McClelland and Stewart, 1965), are also useful. J.M. Bumsted's *Henry Alline* (Toronto: University of Toronto Press, 1971), reviews the career of the leader of an important religious revival in Nova Scotia during the years of the American Revolution.

The anthology *The United Empire Loyalists* (Toronto: Copp Clark, 1967), edited by L.F.S. Upton, provides a general overview. In *The Atlantic Provinces, 1712-1857* (Toronto: McClelland and Stewart, 1965), W.S. MacNutt reviews the impact of the Loyalists. His essay "The Loyalists: A Sympathetic View" appeared in *Acadiensis*, 6 (Autumn 1976): 3-20. On the background of the American Loyalists see: W.H. Nelson, *The American Tory* (Toronto: Oxford, 1961). A very helpful study remains J.J. Talman, ed., *Loyalist Narratives from Upper Canada* (Toronto: Champlain Society, 1946).

Two new studies of the Loyalists are: Wallace Brown and Hereward Senior, *Victorious in Defeat: The Loyalists in Canada* (Toronto: Methuen, 1984), and Christopher Moore, *The Loyalists, Revolution, Exile, Settlement* (Toronto: Macmillan, 1984).

Robert S. Allen has compiled a useful bibliography, *Loyalist Literature: An Annotated Bibliographical Guide to the Writings on the Loyalists of the American Revolution* (Toronto: Dundurn Press Ltd., 1982). For books and articles produced after 1981, consult Bruce Bowden, "The Bicentennial Legacy — A Second Loyalist Revival," *Ontario History*, 77 (1985): 65-74.

The American Revolution and Nova Scotia Reconsidered*

GEORGE A. RAWLYK

On the eve of the American Revolution, Nova Scotia was little more than a political expression for a number of widely scattered and isolated communities. These stretched from Halifax to Maugerville on the St. John River and to the tiny outpost of Passamaquoddy on the St. Croix. At the end of the Seven Years' War many land-hungry settlers from Rhode Island, New Hampshire, Massachusetts, and Connecticut pushed up into the fertile

*From *Dalhousie Review*, 43 (1963/64): 379-394. Reprinted by permission.

regions bordering the Bay of Fundy which had been abandoned by the Acadians when they were expelled from the peninsula in 1755. In 1775 Nova Scotia had a population of only approximately 20,000 inhabitants,[1] three-quarters of whom were New Englanders with strong economic, cultural, and family ties with their former homeland.[2]

In spite of the fact that Nova Scotia was virtually New England's northeastern frontier and was peopled by a majority of recently arrived New Englanders,[3] the colony refused in 1775 and 1776 to join in attempting to shatter the framework of the British colonial system. Instead, most of the inhabitants, especially the New Englanders, endeavoured to pursue a policy of neutrality, even though their moral support was firmly behind the "rebels". It is interesting to note that this policy of neutrality was exactly the same policy that the New Englanders severely condemned when it had been adopted by the Acadians two decades earlier. However, toward the end of the Revolution, the sympathies of the neutral New Englanders, largely as the result of serious depredations committed by American privateers throughout Nova Scotia from 1777 to 1782, shifted towards Great Britain.[4]

Why did Nova Scotia not join the Thirteen Colonies in attempting to break away from Britain in 1775 and 1776? Three distinct schools of thought have emerged in the effort to answer this question. First, the proponents of the "Halifax-merchant" school have stressed that the influential Halifax merchants were directly responsible for keeping Nova Scotia loyal to the Crown.[5] The merchants, believing that the Revolution was a Heaven-sent opportunity to supplant the New England colonies in the West Indian trade, and also that in the long run their colony would gain more than it would lose in retaining political and economic ties with Britain, were able to impose their will upon the other inhabitants. This is indeed an interesting interpretation, but one without any real foundation, since in 1775 the population of Halifax was only 1800 and the influence of the Halifax merchants was largely confined chiefly to the area of the Bedford Basin.[6] It is clear that their economic ties with Britain were strong, but it is just as clear that they were in no effective position to impose their will upon the other Nova Scotians, who in actual fact reacted violently to the merchant clique that was attempting to manipulate the economic and political life of the colony.

Second, W.B. Kerr, who has written far more about Nova Scotia during the Revolutionary period than any other historian, has strongly argued that as early as 1765 it was inevitable that Nova Scotia would remain loyal to George III. Kerr maintains that there was an almost total absence of "national sentiment"[7] among the New Englanders of Nova Scotia and that, because of this lack of "nationalism",[8] there was very little popular support for the Revolutionary cause in Nova Scotia.[9] It appears that Kerr has clearly underestimated the general significance of the widespread sympathy for Revolutionary principles. This feeling was prevalent throughout Nova Scotia, with the notable exception of Halifax, in 1775 and 1776. Moreover, he has failed to draw sufficient attention to the profound impact that the isolation of most of the Nova Scotian settlements and the British control of the North

235

Atlantic had upon seriously weakening the indigenous Revolutionary movement.

Third, J.B. Brebner, in his excellent work, *The Neutral Yankees of Nova Scotia*, has asserted that the Revolutionary movement failed in Nova Scotia because "the sympathizers with rebellion among the outlying populace could make no headway because their friends in the rebellious Colonies had no navy and because they themselves could not assemble from the scattered settlements an effective force for unassisted revolt."[10] Brebner's is certainly the most satisfactory answer to the original question regarding Nova Scotia and the Revolution. A careful and critical examination of events in the Chignecto region of Nova Scotia in the years 1775 and 1776 will not only serve to prove the validity of Brebner's thesis, but will also cast a considerable amount of light upon the relations between Nova Scotia and the colonies to the south during a most critical period.

The Isthmus of Chignecto provided the stage upon which a somewhat inconsequential scene from the American Revolutionary drama was played. The Eddy Rebellion of 1776 had most of the characteristics of a tragic comedy; a glorious failure, it was nevertheless accompanied by death and destruction.

The Chignecto Isthmus is a narrow neck of land joining the peninsula of Nova Scotia to the North American mainland. Roughly ten miles in width and twenty in length, the Isthmus is bordered on the north-east by Baie Verte, on the south-west by the Cumberland Basin, and on the north-west and south-east by the Sackville and Amherst Ridges respectively. J.C. Webster, one of New Brunswick's outstanding historians, has asserted that "no area of its [Chignecto's] size anywhere in America has a greater or more varied wealth of historical memories and traditions."[11] There is much evidence to support Webster's sweeping generalization.

The vacuum created by the expulsion of the majority of the Acadians from the fertile Isthmus in 1755 was quickly filled at the end of the Seven Years' War by settlers from New England.[12] Unlike the Acadians, these men energetically began to clear and to cultivate the ridge lands which had a heavy forest cover.[13] Only after many frustrating failures were the New Englanders able to master marsh agriculture.[14] From 1772 to 1775 they sullenly observed the arrival of over 500 Yorkshire immigrants seeking "a better livelihood"[15] in the New World. These newcomers had been recruited by the aggressive Lieutenant-Governor of Nova Scotia, Michael Francklin.[16]

Thus in 1775 the general Chignecto Isthmus region contained three important elements within its population. The New Englanders were the most numerous, but the Yorkshiremen were not too far behind. Together these two groups numbered 220 families.[17] The third element was the Acadian; there were thirty Acadian families, most of the members of which worked on the land belonging to the English-speaking farmers.[18]

There was considerable friction and ill-feeling between the New Englanders and the newcomers from the north of England on the one hand, and between the former and the Halifax government on the other. Most of the

236

New Englanders detested their new neighbours, not only because the Yorkshiremen had settled on land that the New Englanders had long coveted and considered to be rightfully theirs, but also because the outlook of the Englishmen was almost diametrically opposite to that of the Americans. The Yorkshiremen were Methodists closely tied to the Mother Country and all she represented, while the New Englanders were Congregationalists who had been greatly influenced by the North American environment and whose ties with the Mother Country were extremely tenuous. The Old World was in conflict with the New on this narrow neck of land.

The New Englanders, moreover, were greatly dissatisfied with the Halifax government. Had not Francklin encouraged the Yorkshiremen to settle in the Isthmus? Furthermore, the New Englanders reacted violently to the fact that a small clique of Halifax merchants controlled the legislative and executive functions of government,[19] stubbornly refusing to grant to the New Englanders the right of "township form of government" which Governor Lawrence had promised them in 1758 and 1759.[20]

237

A spark was needed to set the kindling discontent ablaze. The American Revolution provided the spark, but the fire was quickly and easily extinguished before it could spread and result in any serious damage.

The centre of organized activity against Nova Scotia during the first years of the Revolution was the tiny lumbering outpost of Machias, a few miles west of the St. Croix River.[21] Most of the inhabitants wanted to grow rich by sacking the prosperous Nova Scotian settlements, particularly Halifax. These freebooters, these eighteen-century filibusters, unsuccessfully endeavoured to hide their real selfish motive beneath a veneer of concern for Revolutionary principles.

In the summer of 1775 they proposed to General Washington to invade Nova Scotia if supported by a force of 1000 soldiers and four armed vessels.[22] When Washington was asked to act upon this bold plan in August, he tactfully refused; all available men and supplies were needed for the proposed Quebec invasion. His reasoned arguments justifying his refusal are of considerable consequence since they explain why Washington refused to mount any kind of offensive against Nova Scotia in 1775 and 1776:

As to the Expedition proposed against Nova Scotia by the Inhabitants of Machias, I cannot but applaud their Spirit and Zeal; but, after considering the Reasons offered for it, there are Several objections . . . which seem to me unanswerable. I apprehend such an Enterprise inconsistent with the General Principal upon which the Colonies have proceeded. That Province has not acceded, it is true, to the Measures of Congress; and therefore, they have been excluded from all Commercial Intercourse with the other Colonies; But they have not Commenced Hostilities against them, nor are any to be apprehended. To attack *them*, therefore, is a Measure of Conquest, rather than Defence, and may be attended with very dangerous consequences. It might, perhaps, be easy, with the force proposed, to make an Incursion into the Province and overawe those of the Inhabitants who are Inimical to our cause; and, for a short time prevent the Supplying the Enemy with Provisions; but the same Force must continue to produce any lasting Effects. As to the furnishing Vessels of Force, you, Gentlemen, will anticipate me, in pointing out our weakness and the Enemy's Strength at Sea. There would be great Danger that, with the best preparation we could make, they would fall an easy prey either to the Men of War of that Station [Halifax] or some who would be detach'd from Boston.[23]

Washington was no doubt right in the long run, but the inhabitants of Machias almost intuitively realized that in the summer of 1775 Nova Scotia was ripe for plucking from the British colonial tree. American economic pressure had resulted in a serious recession,[24] Governor Legge was alienating leading elements of the population, and the exploits of the Revolution had captured the imagination of the New Englanders.[25] In addition, there were only thirty-six British regulars guarding Halifax,[26] and Legge, who seriously believed that the New Englanders "were rebels to the man", sadly observed that "the fortifications [of Halifax] were in a dilapidated state, the batteries . . . dismantled, the gun-carriages decayed, the guns on the ground."[27] If the men from Machias had had their way, the invading force would have been enthusiastically welcomed and openly supported by the vast majority of "Yankees" and would have easily gained control of the colony. However, the lack of suitable land communications between the various settlements in Nova Scotia, as well as between Nova Scotia and the other colonies, together with the British control of the Atlantic, would have probably forced the American troops to abandon Nova Scotia after a brief occupation. Washington's refusal to attack Nova Scotia when it was ripe for conquest and the arrival of military reinforcements in Halifax in October[28] virtually made certain that the Colony would remain within the framework of the British colonial system during the war years.

In the summer months an indigenous revolutionary movement came into being in the Chignecto region.[29] It was led by John Allan, a Scot who had been won over to the American revolutionary cause, and Jonathan Eddy, who had left Massachusetts to settle in the Isthmus after the Seven Years' War. Sam Rogers, Zebulon Rowe, Obadiah Ayer, and William Howe, among others, all respected and prosperous New Englanders, supported Allan and Eddy. These men were greatly encouraged by the successful sacking in August of Fort Frederick, a tiny British military outpost at the mouth of the Saint John River, by a small Machias force,[30] and also by the bold pronouncement of the inhabitants of Maugerville in favour of the Revolution. The Maugerville settlers declared that they were willing "to submit ourselves to the government of the Massachusetts Bay and that we are ready with our lives and fortunes to share with them the event of the present struggle for liberty, however, God in his providence may order it."[31]

Towards the end of November, Allan, Eddy, and their not insignificant following were given an excellent opportunity to precipitate a crisis that could have conceivably led to a successful rebellion. The long-simmering discontent with the government authorities finally boiled over when the assembly, controlled by the small Halifax merchant clique with strong commercial ties with Britain, passed two acts, one to call out a fifth of the militia, the other to impose a tax for its support.[32] Almost immediately the two bills were loudly denounced throughout the colony, but especially in the Chignecto region. Allan and Eddy, instead of quickly harnessing the deep dissatisfaction within the framework of armed rebellion, decided to widen first the popular basis of their support by sending a rather mildly-worded yet firm protest against the two bills to Governor Legge. In the protest, which was eventually signed by almost 250 inhabitants including many Yorkshiremen, the Chignecto settlers objected to the new tax and to the possibility of being forced to "march into different parts in arms against their friends and relations."[33] Allan and Eddy had succeeded in gaining much popular support for their attack upon the Halifax government, but at the moment when they attempted to use this support to emulate the example of the colonies in revolt, Legge suddenly pulled the rug from under their unsuspecting feet. Realizing the seriousness of the discontent as reflected in the Chignecto petition, the governor promptly suspended the two contentious acts. In so doing, Legge had removed the catalyst from the potential revolutionary situation not only in the Isthmus but throughout Nova Scotia.

Failing to grasp the significance of Legge's clever manoeuvre, Allan and Eddy decided during the first weeks of January, 1776, that the time was propitious for fomenting an insurrection. Nothing could have been further from the truth. Having won the support of the Acadians, but the equally enthusiastic disapprobation of the Yorkshiremen, Allan and Eddy decided that before taking any further steps on the road to rebellion it was first imperative to sound out carefully the general feeling of the mass of New Englanders towards the proposed vague plan. The two leaders were genuinely shocked to discover that the vast majority of New Englanders, even though they "would have welcomed an army of invasion",[34] stubbornly refused to support the planned insurrection. Ground between the millstones of contending forces, most of the Chignecto New Englanders, as well as those throughout the colony, had decided to walk the tightrope of neutrality until it was clear that a strong rebel invading force would be able to gain effective control of Nova Scotia. Allan and Eddy were forced to alter drastically their proposed policy; they decided to petition General Washington and the Continental Congress to send an "army of liberation" to Nova Scotia. The Machias plan of August 1775 had been resurrected.

239

Jonathan Eddy, with a band of fourteen men, had set out in February from Chignecto to persuade Washington and the Continental Congress to invade Nova Scotia. On March 27, Eddy met with the American general at Cambridge.[35] Washington carefully considered Eddy's often illogical arguments, but believing that the British forces that had abandoned Boston[36] ten days earlier were now in Halifax, the General informed the ambassador that "in the present uncertain state of things . . . a much more considerable force [than Eddy had even requested] would be of no avail."[37] Washington reaffirmed the policy he had first enunciated on hearing of the Machias plan in August of the preceding year.[38] The disillusioned Eddy next went to the Continental Congress in Philadelphia, but as he expected, here too his urgent appeal fell on unresponsive ears.[39] After his return to the Isthmus in May it was decided that, as a last resort, the government of Massachusetts should be approached for military aid. The persistent Eddy, accompanied by Howe, Rogers, and Rowe, immediately set sail for Boston.

During the months of January and February the Halifax government had been strangely indifferent to developments in the Chignecto Isthmus. The loyalist leaders, Charles Dixon and the Rev. John Eagleson, had bombarded the Governor and his Executive Council with frantic letters.[40] A delegation had been sent to General Washington by the New Englanders;[41] and on hearing a rumour that the American army had captured Bunker Hill, the supporters of Allan and Eddy had procured "a chaise and six horses, postillion and a flag of liberty, and drove about the isthmus, proclaiming the news and blessings of liberty."[42] Dixon and Eagleson demanded immediate government action. In March the Executive Council resolved "that the lieutenant-governor [Francklin] be desired to proceed, as soon as possible to [Chignecto] . . . and there make a strict inquiry into the behavior and conduct of the inhabitants, and to make report thereof to the governor; also, that he will apprehend all persons, who, on due proof, shall be found guilty of any rebellious and treasonable transactions."[43] Francklin, however, was able to accomplish absolutely nothing. It was not until June that the government exerted some semblance of authority on the troubled Isthmus. This delay was at least partly the result of the recall of Legge in May and his replacement by Lieutenant-Colonel Arbuthnot.[44] In June, 200 Royal Fencibles[45] under the command of Lieutenant-Colonel Joseph Gorham were sent to occupy Fort Cumberland, which had been abandoned by the British eight years earlier.[46] Fort Cumberland, the reconstructed French Fort Beauséjour, was strategically located at the extreme southern tip of the Fort Cumberland Ridge which, together with the Fort Lawrence Ridge, cuts through the Chignecto marshlands until it almost touches the waters of the Bay of Fundy. Gorham found the fort in a state of serious disrepair. He reported that "the face of the Bastions, Curtains, etc., by being so long exposed to the heavy rains and frost were bent down to such a slope that one might with ease ascend any part of the fort."[47] Gorham set about repairing the fort, and he went out of his way to overlook what he considered to be the harmless activities of the energetic American sympathizers. He hoped that a simple show of strength would completely undermine the position held by the Eddy-Allan faction.

It was not until July that the Halifax authorities, at last convinced of the seriousness of the revolutionary movement in the Isthmus, considered it necessary to strike against the leaders of the "American Party". A proclamation was issued offering a reward of £200 for the capture of Eddy and £100 for Allan, Howe, and Rogers.[48] On hearing that he was a man with a price on his head, Allan decided to join his friends in Massachusetts and left a committee in charge of "the revolutionary interests".[49]

Eddy was unsuccessful in his attempt to persuade the General Court of Massachusetts to send a military expedition "supplied with some necessaries, as provisions and ammunition . . . [to] destroy those [Nova Scotian] forts and relieve our brethren and friends."[50] Nevertheless, he had not entirely failed. He was promised sufficient ammunition and supplies to equip properly whatever force he himself could muster. Eddy immediately rushed off to Machias, where he knew there was a group of men still vitally interested in attacking Nova Scotia. By carefully playing upon their cupidity Eddy was able to recruit twenty-eight men from Machias.[51] On August 11, just as the invading army was embarking, Allan arrived. Fully aware of the weakness of the revolutionary movement on the Isthmus, Allan endeavoured in vain to dissuade Eddy from carrying out his rash and hopeless plan. Eddy refused to come to grips with the hard facts of reality; he hoped that his force would build up like a giant snowball at Passamaquoddy and Maugerville and that the Chignecto New Englanders would eagerly rally to his banner. He seemed to believe that it would be only a matter of time before his liberating army would force the British to abandon "New England's Outpost".

At Passamaquoddy, a few miles to the east of Machias, Eddy added seven new recruits and then sailed to Maugerville in three whale boats.[53] At the settlement on the upper Saint John River he found the inhabitants "almost universally to be hearty in the cause",[54] but was able to enlist only twenty-seven settlers and sixteen Indians.[55] Eddy's liberating army, now numbering some eighty men, returned to the mouth of the Saint John River to await the arrival of the promised ammunition and supplies from Boston.[56] There was an unexpected prolonged delay, and the force was unable to move eastwards until the last week of October. On October 29, Eddy's men easily captured fourteen of Gorham's troops who were stationed at the military outpost of Shepody, to the south of present-day Moncton.[57] The invaders[58] then swung sharply to the north and made their way up the Petitcodiac and Memramcook Rivers to the Acadian settlement of Memramcook, where Eddy had no trouble whatsoever in persuading a number of Acadians to support him.[59] From Memramcook, on November 5, Eddy and his men marched eastwards towards their immediate objective — Fort Cumberland.[60]

241

The supporters of Allan and Eddy on the Isthmus loudly "expressed their Uneasiness at seeing so few [invaders] . . . and those unprovided with Artillery."[61] They vehemently argued that, taking everything into consideration, there was no possible chance of success. Even if Fort Cumberland were captured, and this was highly unlikely, British reinforcements would readily rout Eddy's motley collection of undisciplined freebooters, Indians, and Acadians. Eddy was forced to resort to outright intimidation and to false promises in order to win the unenthusiastic support of his friends. His policy was objectively described by his associate Allan:

That they [Chignecto New Englanders] had supply'd the Enemys of America which had much displeased the States. That the Congress doubted their integrity, that if they would not rouse themselves and oppose the British power in that province [Nova Scotia] they would be looked upon as enemies and should the country be reduced by the States they would be treated as conquered people and that if they did not Incline to do something he [Eddy] would return and report them to the States. But if they would now assert their rights publickly against the King's Govt, he was then Come to help them and in Fifteen days Expected a reinforcement of a large body of men.[62]

These reinforcements existed only in Eddy's active imagination.

Only fifty New Englanders, against their better judgment, rallied to Eddy's banner, and they were joined a short time later by twenty-seven men from the Cobequid region of Nova Scotia.[63] The invading army now numbered roughly 180 men.[64] Eddy must be given a considerable amount of credit for using his relatively small force to gain virtual control of the entire Chignecto Isthmus, except, of course, for Fort Cumberland. Most of the Yorkshiremen, fearing the destruction of their property if they supported Gorham, quickly surrendered their guns and ammunition to the invaders.[65] It should be noted that well over half of the New Englanders supported neither Eddy nor Gorham, but instead carefully pursued a policy of neutrality.

Eddy was not a demagogue, nor was he a megalomaniac. He was convinced that all ties with Britain should be severed, and his fanatical enthusiasm for the Revolutionary cause seriously dulled his already undeveloped sense of military strategy. In spite of fantastic rumours regarding the size of Eddy's invading force which spread like wildfire throughout Nova Scotia during the months of October and November, the inhabitants could not be aroused from their lethargic neutrality.

242

As early as August, Gorham had heard of Eddy's invasion plans, but it was not until the beginning of November that he learned that Eddy was in the Chignecto region.[66] With fewer than 200 troops at his command[67] and believing that Eddy had at least 500 men,[68] Gorham was of the opinion that he was in no position to attack the invaders.[69] Therefore he felt that the only alternative was to adopt a defensive policy and to wait for reinforcements from Halifax. This was the right policy at the right time.[70]

During the early morning hours of November 7, Eddy's forces experienced their only real victory in the futile Chignecto campaign. Taking advantage of a thick fog which had settled over the coastal region, Zebulon Rowe and a handful of men thirsting for excitement and possible loot set out to capture a sloop filled with supplies for the Fort Cumberland troops.[71] Because of the low tide the sloop lay on the broad mud flats to the south-west of the fort. Eddy's description of this most humorous incident of the rebellion makes fascinating reading:

After a Difficult March, they arrived opposite the Sloop; on board of which was a Guard of 1 Sergt and 12 men, who had they fir'd at our People, must have alarmed the Garrison in such a Manner as to have brought them on their Backs. However, our men rushed Resolutely towards the sloop up to their Knees in Mud, which made such a Noise as to alarm the Centry, who hailed them and immediately called the Sergt of the Guard. The Sergt on coming up, Ordered his Men to fire, but was immediately told by Mr. Row[e] that if they fired one Gun, Every Man of Them should be put to Death; which so frightened the poor Devils that they surrendered without firing a Shot, although our People Could not board her without the Assistance of the Conquered, who let down Ropes to our Men to get up by.[72]

As the working parties from the fort arrived to unload the sloop, they too were easily captured.[73] Altogether thirty-four of Gorham's troops, including Captain Barron, Engineer of the Garrison, and the Chaplain, the bibulous Rev. Eagleson, were seized by Rowe's detachment.[74] The captured sloop was sailed away at high tide in the direction of the Missiquash River, but not before the Royal Fencibles "fired several cannon shots"[75] at the brazen enemy.

Only two attempts were made to capture Fort Cumberland, one on November 13[76] and the other nine days later.[77] Both were miserable failures. Before Eddy could organize a third attempt, British reinforcements arrived.

On November 27 and November 28, the British relieving force, consisting of two companies of Marines and one company of the Royal Highlanders, finally landed at Fort Cumberland.[78] The relieving force had sailed from Halifax and Windsor.[79] On the 28th Gorham ordered Major Batt, an officer who had accompanied the reinforcements, to lead an attack on Eddy's camp, one mile north of the fort.[80] At five-thirty in the morning of the 29th, Batt marched out of Fort Cumberland with 170 troops, hoping to surprise the "rebels."[81] If it had not been for an alert young Negro drummer who furiously beat the alarm when he sighted the enemy,[82] Eddy's men would have been slaughtered in their sleep. Wiping sleep from their eyes, Eddy's confused followers ran into the neighbouring woods in search of cover.[83] In the skirmish that followed only seven "rebels" and four British soldiers were killed.[84] Seeing the hopelessness of the situation, Eddy ordered his men to retreat westwards "to the St. John River . . . and there make a stand."[85] Batt refused to pursue the "rebels"; instead he had his men put to the torch every home and barn belonging to those inhabitants of the Isthmus who had openly supported Eddy.[86] The billowing dark clouds of smoke could be seen by the defeated invaders as they fled in panic towards Memramcook.[87]

243

Eddy's rash attempt to capture Fort Cumberland failed not only because he lacked artillery, but also because his men were poorly trained, undisciplined, and badly led. With British control of the North Atlantic firmly established, with Washington's refusal to support the invasion, and with the great majority of Nova Scotians desperately trying to be neutral, Eddy's task was hopeless. Even though the Eddy Rebellion, by any broad strategic standards, was quite insignificant in the larger Revolutionary context, it is of some importance as an illustration of the fact that in 1775 and 1776, under their superficial neutrality, the New Englanders tacitly supported the Revolutionary movement. Moreover, the Eddy Rebellion helps to indicate how effectively British naval power and the isolated nature of the settlements of Nova Scotia had "neutralized the New England migrants."[88]

From 1777 to 1782 almost every Nova Scotian coastal settlement (with the notable exception of Halifax) from Tatamagouche on Northumberland Strait to the Saint John River was ravaged by American privateers.[89] As a result of these freebooting forays many New Englanders in Nova Scotia, who had originally been rather sympathetic to the Revolution, became increasingly hostile to their brethren to the south. In 1775 and 1776 most of the Nova Scotians "divided betwixt natural affection to our nearest relations, and good Faith and Friendship to our King and Country",[90] had decided to walk the tightrope of neutrality even though they appeared to lean precariously in the direction of their "nearest relations". By the closing years of the conflict, however, as the "Neutral Yankees" reached the end of their hazardous journey, they had begun to lean towards the opposite extreme, towards the King.

What real impact did the Revolution have upon the inhabitants of Nova Scotia? Of course most of them resolved to adopt a policy of neutrality; many suffered because of the depredations of the American privateers; while a few, especially the Halifax merchants, grew rich from the usual profits of war. But was there nothing else? M.W. Armstrong has convincingly argued that probably the most important impact of the Revolution upon Nova Scotia was in precipitating the "Great Awakening of Nova Scotia."[91] In addition, Armstrong has emphasized that the "Great Awakening" encouraged the development of neutrality:

> Indeed, the Great Awakening itself may be considered to have been a retreat from the grim realities of the world to the safety and pleasantly exciting warmth of the revival meeting, and to profits and rewards of another character . . . an escape from fear and divided loyalties . . . an assertion of democratic ideals and a determination to maintain them, the Great Awakening gave self respect and satisfaction to people whose economic and political position was both humiliating and distressing.[92]

244

The prophet and evangelist of the spiritual awakening was Henry Alline who, when he was twelve, had moved from Rhode Island to Falmouth, Nova Scotia.[93] An uneducated farmer, Alline had experienced an unusual "Conversion",[94] and in 1776 he began to preach an emotional Christian message that has been described as being a combination of "Calvinism, Antinomianism, and Enthusiasm."[95] The flames of religious revival[96] swept up the Minas Basin in 1777, across the Bay of Fundy in 1779, and to the South Shore in 1781.[97] All Protestant Churches in Nova Scotia were in one way or another affected by the "Great Awakening", and largely as a direct result the evangelical wing of the various Protestant Churches was able to dominate Maritime religious life throughout the nineteenth century.

British sea power, the isolated nature of the settlements, the refusal of Washington to mount an offensive against Nova Scotia, and perhaps the religious revival, all combined to keep the "Yankees" neutral during the Revolution.

Notes

1. W.B. Kerr, "Nova Scotia in the Critical Years, 1775-6", *The Dalhousie Review* (April, 1932), 97.
2. S.D. Clarke, *"Movements of Political Protest in Canada, 1640-1840* (Toronto, 1959), 63.
3. It should be borne in mind that there was a significant German-speaking population in the Lunenburg region and that there were pockets of Highland Scots, Yorkshiremen, Acadians, and Scots-Irish scattered throughout the peninsula of Nova Scotia. Most of these settlers (a few Acadians and Scots-Irish are the exception to the rule) also remained neutral during the Revolution even though their sympathies lay with the Crown.
4. J.B. Brebner, *The Neutral Yankees of Nova Scotia* (New York, 1937), 329-337.
5. V. Barnes, "Francis Legge, Governor of Loyalist Nova Scotia, 1773-1776", *New England Quarterly* (July, 1931), 420-447. See also a convincing criticism of this view in W.B. Kerr, "The Merchants of Nova Scotia and The American Revolution", *Canadian Historical Review* (March, 1932) 21-34.
6. A.L. Burt, *The United States, Great Britain, and British North America* (Toronto, 1940), 13.
7. W.B. Kerr, *The Maritime Provinces of British North America and the American Revolution* (Sackville, n.d.), 59.
8. *Ibid.*, 60.

9. *Ibid.*, 53-60.
10. Brebner, *Neutral Yankees of Nova Scotia*, 352.
11. J.C. Webster, *The Forts of Chignecto* (Sackville, 1930), 5.
12. W.C. Milner, *History of Sackville, New Brunswick* (Sackville, 1955), 14-21.
13. B.J. Bird, "Settlement Patterns in Maritime Canada, 1687-1876", *The Geographic Review* (July, 1955), 398-9.
14. *Ibid.*
15. W.C. Milner, "Records of Chignecto", *Collections of the Nova Scotia Historical Society*, Vol. XV (Halifax, 1911), 41-45.
16. *Ibid.*, 40.
17. W.B. Kerr, *The Maritime Provinces . . . and the American Revolution*, 68.
18. *Ibid.*
19. J.M. Beck, *The Government of Nova Scotia* (Toronto, 1957), 22-25.
20. D.C. Harvey, "The Struggle for the New England Form of Township Government in Nova Scotia", *Canadian Historical Association Report* (1933), 18.
21. D.C. Harvey, "Machias and the Invasion of Nova Scotia", *C.H.A.R.* (1932), 17.
22. J.C. Fitzpatrick (ed.), *The Writings of George Washington* (Washington, 1931), III, 415.
23. *Ibid.*, III, 415-416.
24. The Petition of the Chignecto Inhabitants, December 23, 1775, *Nova Scotia Archives*, A 94, 330-8.
25. Kerr, "Nova Scotia in the Critical Years 1775-6", 98.
26. Governor Legge to the Secretary of State, July 31, 1775, *Canadian Archives Report for 1894* (Ottawa, 1895), 334.
27. E.P. Weaver, "Nova Scotia and New England during the Revolution", *American Historical Review* (October, 1904), 63.
28. B. Murdoch, *A History of Nova Scotia* (Halifax, 1860), II, 554.
29. Kerr, *The Maritime Provinces*, 69.
30. *Ibid.*, 63.
31. Quoted in F. Kidder, *Military Operations in Eastern Maine and Nova Scotia During the Revolution* (Albany, 1867), 64.
32. Kerr, *The Maritime Provinces*, 70.
33. The Petition of Chignecto Inhabitants, *Nova Scotia Archives*, A 94, 330-8.
34. Quoted in Kerr, *The Maritime Provinces*, 73.
35. Fitzpatrick, IV, 437.
36. H. Peckham, *The War For Independence* (Chicago, 1959), 32.
37. Fitzpatrick, IV, 438.
38. *Ibid.*
39. Kerr, *The Maritime Provinces*, 73.
40. See *Canadian Archives Report for 1894*, 345.
41. *Ibid.*
42. Kerr, *The Maritime Provinces*, 74.
43. Quoted in Murdoch, II, 568.
44. In the administrative shuffle Francklin was demoted to Indian Agent.
45. The Royal Fencibles were mostly recruited from the Loyalists in the Thirteen Colonies.
46. W.B. Kerr, "The American Invasion of Nova Scotia, 1776-7", *Canadian Defense Quarterly* (July, 1936), 434
47. Gorham's Journal, *C.A.R.*, *1894*, 360.
48. Kerr, *The Maritime Provinces*, 78.
49. Kidder, *Military Operations in Eastern Maine and Nova Scotia During the Revolution*, 12.
50. Petition of Jonathan Eddy, Aug. 28, 1776, in P. Force (ed.), *American Archives, Fifth Series* (Washington, 1851), II, 734.
51. *Ibid.*
52. Kidder, *Military Operations in Eastern Maine and Nova Scotia During the Revolution*, 12.
53. Gorham's Journal, 355.
54. Quoted in Harvey, "Machias and the Invasion of Nova Scotia", 21.
55. Kerr, "The American Invasion of Nova Scotia, 1776-7", 434.
56. *Ibid.*, 435.
57. *Ibid.*
58. The description of the Rebellion is to be found in Gorham's Journal, *C.A.R.*, 355-7 359-365 and in Eddy's Journal, Harvey, "Malchias and the Invasion of Nova Scotia", 22-24.
59. Eddy's Journal, 22.
60. *Ibid.*
61. *Ibid.*
62. Allan's Journal, Harvey, "Machias and the Invasion of Nova Scotia", 24.
63. Kerr, "The American Invasion of Nova Scotia, 1776-7", 435.

64. Eddy's Journal, 23.
65. Kerr, "The American Invasion of Nova Scotia, 1776-7", 436.
66. Gorham's Journal, 355.
67. *Ibid.*, 360.
68. *Ibid.*, 356.
69. *Ibid.*, 360.
70. For the opposite point of view see Kerr, "The American Invasion of Nova Scotia", 441: "A well-directed sortie could at any time have broken up Eddy's camp."
71. Eddy's Journal, 22.
72. *Ibid.*
73. *Ibid.*, 22-3.
74. *Ibid.*
75. *Ibid.*, 23; Gorham's Journal, 356.
76. Gorham's Journal, 361-362.
77. *Ibid.*
78. *Ibid.*, 362.
79. *Ibid.* This point must be emphasized especially, after examining Stanley's inaccurate reference to an overland march. See G.F.G. Stanley, *Canada's Soldiers, 1605-1954* (Toronto, 1954), 118.
80. Gorham's Journal, 362.
81. *Ibid.*
82. C.E. Kemp, "Folk-Lore About Old Fort Beauséjour", *Acadiensis* (October, 1908), 301-302. Also see Kerr, "The American Invasion of Nova Scotia", 440.
83. Gorham's Journal, 362.
84. Kerr, "The American Invasion of Nova Scotia, 1776-7", 441.
85. Eddy's Journal, 23.
86. Gorham's Journal, 362.
87. The contest for present-day western New Brunswick continued until the end of the Revolutionary War. In the summer of 1777 Allan's invading force of some 100 men from Machias was compelled to retreat overland from the St. John Valley towards the St. Croix when confronted by a strong British military expedition led by Major Gilford Studholme and Francklin. For the remainder of the war Allan unsuccessfully attempted to persuade the St. John River Indians to join the Revolutionary cause.
88. Brebner, *The Neutral Yankees of Nova Scotia*, 353.
89. *Ibid.*, 324-335.
90. Petition of the Inhabitants of Yarmouth, Dec. 8, 1775. Quoted in Brebner, 291.
91. M.W. Armstrong, "Neutrality and Religion in Revolutionary Nova Scotia", *The New England Quarterly* (Mar., 1946), 50-61.
92. *Ibid.*, 57, 58, 60.
93. *Ibid.*, 55.
94. See W. James, *The Varieties of Religious Experience* (New York, 1958), 134-135: "My sins seemed to be laid open; so that I thought that every one I saw knew them, and sometimes I was almost ready to acknowledge many things, which I thought they knew; yea sometimes it seemed to me as if every one was pointing me out as the most guilty wretch upon earth."
95. Quoted in Armstrong, "Neutrality and Religion in Revolutionary Nova Scotia," 58.
96. The following is Alline's description of the Liverpool revival of 1776: "We had blessed days, the Lord was reviving his work of grace. Many under a load of sin cried out, what shall we do to be saved? and the saints seemed much revived, came out and witnessed for God. In a short time some more souls were born to Christ, they came out and declared what God had done for their souls and what a blessed change had taken place in that town." Quoted in Armstrong, 55-56.
97. *Ibid.*, 55.

The United Empire Loyalists: A Reconsideration*

W. G. SHELTON

The United Empire Loyalists occupy a strangely equivocal place in Canadian history. Although regarded with honour by some Canadians for

*From *Dalhousie Review*, 45 (1965):5–16. Reprinted by permission.

having saved part of North America for the British connection, they are suspected by others of being not quite respectable political ancestors in this democratic age. As a result, especially since this country has become more independent of Great Britain, the Loyalists have received little attention from serious historians, and their role in the founding of Canada has been de-emphasized to the point where they appear as just another group of immigrants making their contribution to our cultural mosaic.[1]

A search through standard histories of Canada fails to reveal much agreement on the significance of the Loyalists. Edgar McInnis implies that they were a conservative group accustomed to a privileged position in society, many of whom were expelled from the United States for their opinions.[2] The motives of the Loyalists are not discussed by Donald Creighton, although he does mention that many of those who settled in Ontario were poor and illiterate.[3] D. C. C. Masters agrees that they came from all walks of life, but adds that they brought to Canada "a liking for an aristocratic society of privilege with themselves as the privileged group."[4] J. B. Brebner feels that the emigration of American settlers to Ontario was part of a general westward movement unrelated to principle. He, too, emphasizes the conservatism of the Loyalists which, interacting with British Toryism, consolidated an "anti-republican, anti-democratic, politico-economic system in Britain and America."[5] For J. M. S. Careless, also, they were conservative in outlook, but he recognizes that they "represented a declaration of independence against the United States", and that "they helped to create not only a new province, but a new nation."[6] W. L. Morton says that they were "for the most part" conservative, although the largest number was "like the revolutionaries, Whiggish by persuasion."[7] G. M. Craig, in his recent study of Upper Canada, sees the Loyalists as "a large and varied group" which "opposed the resort to force against British authority."[8]

247

Almost alone among Canadian historians, A. R. M. Lower thinks that the Loyalists are worth more than a passing mention. Like Careless, he sees Canada as a "by-product" of the American Revolution, which was "the great tragedy of history, the breaking of the unity of race, the drawing of those of like blood apart." Canadians have since regarded it as a "foul and treasonable occurrence", and there has been "little understanding of the essential nature of the Revolution — still less sympathy with the fine generosity of the ideals that had inspired it and which it in turn inspired." Canada was the offshoot of the losing and conservative side of a great radical upheaval — a struggle between classes and masses in a "frankly anti-democratic" society, with the classes retreating to Canada after their defeat. Others who joined the trek north had merely put their money on the wrong horse and were repudiated by the victors. He does find it difficult to understand why so many Loyalists were non-British in origin but explains it on the basis that "those with whom tradition is an acquired one are often apt to be more tenacious of it than those with whom it originated, to whom it is familiar and perhaps threadbare."[9]

From these opinions, three conclusions seen to emerge. The first is that, considering their importance, surprisingly little attention is paid to the Loyalists in Canadian histories. Secondly, what is said about them is often contradictory, or at least confusing. For example, they did not want to break the unity of the race, but many were of different racial backgrounds; or they hoped to establish an aristocratic society on the frontier, but many could not read or write. Thirdly, to the extent that a consistent picture emerges, it is unfavourable: words such as "privilege", "anti-democratic", and "conservative" in a pejorative sense occur most often.

Why are the Loyalists handled in this way? Two possible reasons come to mind. One is their association, for many people, with the Family Compact and other self-perpetuating ruling cliques in British North America. It is assumed that the Loyalists would naturally dominate the social and political life in the colonies where they settled. This may have been true in New Brunswick but, since practically the entire population was composed of refugees from the American colonies, the inhabitants who were outside the charmed circle of authority and patronage were just as much Loyalists as those on the inside.

In Upper Canada, where the influx of immigrants soon made the genuine Loyalists a minority, we find that studies of the personnel of the legislative and executive councils show that between 1791 and 1841 there were only 22 Loyalists out of 105 appointees, and that many of these owed their position to Bishop Strachan rather than to their Loyalism. That Loyalists were not unduly prominent in the Family Compact is further indicated by the absence of such well-known Loyalists names as Johnson, Grass, Butler, and Van Alstine.[10]

A second factor probably responsible for the treatment meted out to the Loyalists is that they were on the wrong side in the American Revolution. The singularly unattractive portrait of the American Tories painted by earlier American historians has been to some extent corrected by more recent research. On the whole, American historians have been extremely generous in their reappraisal, but the fact remains that the Loyalists were on the losing side, and the victors went on to make a huge success of the American republic. This outcome cannot help being reflected in the writings of Americans on this subject.

The Loyalists have had their supporters in Canada, but the nature of this support has often done them more harm than good. They have been used by some of their descendants to reinforce claims of social superiority which do not sit well in a democratic society, and the emphasis on the purity of their Britishness has been an embarrassment in a country where other races now form a majority.

The main reason, however, why more attention has not been devoted to the Loyalists in Canadian history is that the formative period of their lives was spent in the American colonies and is therefore officially part of American history. Although true in a strict geographic sense, this fact has had the unfortunate effect of depriving the Loyalists of their past and much of their meaningfulness. The result is a strange impression of one group called American Tories vanishing into well-deserved oblivion, and another group known as United Empire Loyalists suddenly appearing in the Canadian wilderness clutching their Union Jacks.

Only a study of the American Revolution from a Loyalist rather than an American or British point of view can give an insight into their motivation and a fair evaluation of their role. It is too easy to assume, because the revolutionaries were fighting for self-government, equality, democracy, and liberty, that the Loyalists who opposed them also opposed these honourable ideals. This conclusion is not always drawn, but it certainly lurks in the background.

If we are permitted then to trespass on American territory for a moment, the first thing we should note is that, whether American grievances against Britain were completely justified or not, most Loyalists objected just as strongly as did the Whigs to British attempts to impose new taxes on the colonies. Furthermore, even the most extreme Tory admitted that some change was necessary in the constitutional relations between the colonies and the mother country. In other words, most Loyalists were not blind supporters of the British government — they were just as American in outlook as their opponents. Some of the Loyalists were recent arrivals, it is true, but so were Tom Paine and many of the recruits in Washington's army.

The major difference between the two sides was in their opinion of the seriousness of the British threat to American liberties and what action should be taken. The Loyalists believed that the Patriots were exaggerating their grievances out of all relation to fact — that in reality the American colonists were fortunate in living under laws that were about as mild and just as one could expect in an imperfect world. As T. B. Chandler, a Connecticut Congregationalist turned Anglican minister, put it, "A small degree of reflection would convince us, that the grievances in question, supposing them to be real, are, at most, no more than just grounds for decent remonstrance, but not a sufficient reason for forcible resistance."[11]

Many Tory pamphleteers were led to question the sincerity of the revolutionary leaders, who, they felt, were really seeking independence from the beginning. The fate of Joseph Galloway's Plan of Union seemed convincing evidence. Galloway, a leading Pennsylvania politician, provided in his scheme for a Grand Council representing all the colonies and possessing a large measure of autonomy. Although the moderate leaders of the first Continental Congress praised it warmly, and it was "tabled" by a vote of only 6 to 5, all reference to it was later expunged from the record, and the radical Whigs moved on quickly to uncompromising measures which led to eight years of war. Despite public denials, many of them admitted privately that they were seeking complete independence, and in any case, the demands they were making on Great Britain amounted in fact to independence. Their reluctance to bring their real intentions out into the open seems to indicate that they were afraid public opinion did

249

not support independence at that time and that it was necessary to build up anti-British feeling by provoking violence and avoiding conciliation. For example, although Congress began secret negotiations to obtain help from France as early as the fall of 1775, Tories still ran the risk of being tarred and feathered in the spring of 1776 for accusing Whigs of advocating independence.

In response to protests in the past, Britain had given way in practically everything except a token tax on tea. The Loyalists felt that it was reasonable to expect that peaceful negotiations would result in a redress of the latest grievances without recourse to violence. If the colonists were truly united, passive resistance alone could accomplish a great deal, as it had in the past. Americans already possessed a large degree of self-rule — it was just a matter of solving a number of questions relating to the constitutional link with Britain. The cautious New York lawyer Peter Van Schaack knew his Locke as well as any of his fellow Whigs, but he questioned whether there was enough tyranny on the part of the British to warrant a repetition of 1688.

250

From all the proofs I had, I could not, on a fair estimate, think them sufficient to establish the fact of an intention to destroy the liberties of the colonies. I saw irregularities, but I thought time would work out our deliverance, and it appeared to me, that, balancing conveniences and inconveniences, we were, upon the whole, a happy people. The idea of a civil war appeared to me to involve the greatest of human calamities, — I thought policy should make that in us the *last* resort.[12]

If, then, British tyranny was not the real reason for the revolution, what was? Hector St. John Crevecoeur, a Huguenot farmer and author of well-known sketches of colonial life, answered this question for many Loyalists:

Ambition, we well know, an exorbitant love of power and thirst of riches, a certain impatience of government, by some people called liberty, — all these motives, clad under the garb of patriotism and even of constitutional reason, have been the secret but true foundations of this, as well as many other revolutions. But what art, what insidious measures, what deep-laid policy, what masses of intricate, captious delusions were not necessary to persuade a people happy beyond any on earth, in the zenith of political felicity, receiving from Nature every benefit she could confer, that they were miserable, oppressed, and aggrieved, that slavery and tyranny would rush upon them from the very sources which before had conveyed them so many blessings.[13]

With the revolutionary Whigs occupying the high ground of liberty, equality, and self-government, those who opposed them were outmanoeuvred. Many could not accept their arguments but, finding it dangerous to antagonize the Whig mobs, hoped to remain quiet. However, this became increasingly difficult as the situation deteriorated into outright war, and the Patriots began taking the attitude that those who were not with them were against them. At this point many Americans who did not support independence gave in to the threats and intimidation of the revolutionaries and switched their allegiance. How many times did something similar to the following take place? In the spring of 1776, a Pennsylvanian, Thomas Smith, is reported to have said, that the Measures of Congress had already enslaved America and done more damage than all the Acts of Parliament ever intended to lay upon us, that the whole was nothing but a scheme of a parcel of hot-headed Presbyterians and that he believed the Devil was at the bottom of the whole; that the taking up Arms was the most scandalous thing a man could be guilty of and more heinous than an hundred of the grossest offences against moral law, etc., etc., etc., etc.[14]

The Bucks County Committee of Safety decided that he be "considered an Enemy of the Rights of British America and that all persons break off every kind of dealing with him until he shall make proper satisfaction to this Committee for his conduct." By the time this appeared in the press, Smith had already decided to recant and make his peace. Some put up a stouter resistance than he did, but in most areas life became extremely difficult, even unbearable, for those who refused to conform, and they were eventually forced to make a choice between acquiescing or fleeing behind the British lines.

Those who chose the latter course were as varied in background as the Revolutionaries themselves. Occupational lists show that the Loyalists formed a cross-section of the population of the Thirteen Colonies in every respect. Some were rich and socially prominent, but so were the Washingtons, the Livingstons, and the Hancocks of the Patriot party. Many were so poor that they made no claim for compensation from the British government because they had owned no property which could be confiscated by the victors. There is no doubt that some of the Loyalists were anti-democratic, but for every statement which could be interpreted in this way by a Tory, one can probably find a dozen from the mouths of the Whigs. It is a waste of time to attempt to differentiate the Loyalists from the Patriots on the basis of conservatism, regardless of how one defines it, since the American Revolution is widely recognized as an essentially conservative movement.

251

One thing, however, many of the Loyalists did have in common, as W. H. Nelson points out in his recent book, *The American Tory*.[15] A study of their ethnic, religious, and economic composition indicates that most of them came from groups which were minorities in the localities where they lived, such as Anglicans in the north, Presbyterians in the south, Quakers and Mennonites from Pennsylvania, Highlanders from North Carolina, Lowlanders from New York, seaboard merchants in some colonies and frontiersmen in others, Indians, and of course Negroes. These people felt that they had more to fear from the unrestricted power of those around them than they did from the distant British government, which had often protected them by disallowing discriminatory colonial legislation.

This is a very useful approach but it is not completely adequate, since only a portion of each minority became active Loyalists. Families often split over the issues at stake, so that generalisations about types and categories do not really do justice to the individual human being. It must be remembered that each person had to make a decision, often an agonizing one, involving the loss of friends as well as property, and long periods of separation from wife and children as well as physical hardship and perhaps even death. For many this decision was made on the basis of conscience, self-respect, integrity, call it what you will. Social upheavals like the American Revolution force many people to make a choice between what seems safe, sensible, and expedient and what they feel to be right. Even for those not politically minded many painful dilemmas were created.

Here are several examples. The Anglican clergyman who was ordered to abjure the king would have to violate an oath taken at his ordination. The merchant who had undertaken to ship goods to a firm in England which had advanced him credit might very well drive old business friends into bankruptcy if he agreed to the export embargo called for by Congress. Officeholders are often looked upon as men who were Loyalists out of self-interest, but in most cases their personal welfare would have been better served by forgetting their oaths of office and throwing in their lot with the revolutionaries. This was especially true in New England, where the patriots formed an overwhelming majority. Typical of New England Loyalists was Colonel William Browne of Salem, who had extensive properties in Massachusetts and Connecticut. Fourteen valuable farms in the latter colony alone were later confiscated. He was so highly respected by the inhabitants that he was offered the governorship by the Committee of Safety, and a delegation which included Elbridge Gerry (whose idea of democracy is preserved in the term "gerrymander") pleaded with him to join them. He refused, saying that neither persuasion nor threats could make him do anything derogatory to the character of his office, and he ultimately went into exile.[16]

It was the very pressures by which the Whigs attempted to coerce the rest of the population into conformity with their wishes, however, which aroused the opposition of countless ordinary people and turned them into active Loyalists. Lorenzo Sabine, an early American student of the Loyalists, pointed out over a century ago that persecution made half the "king's friends."[17]

This contradiction between Whig theory and Whig practice was a source of never-ending amazement to their opponents. At the time of an earlier non-importation agreement, a Boston storekeeper published the following statement in a local paper:

> Upon the whole, I cannot help saying — although I never have entered far into the mysteries of government, having applied myself to my shop and my business — that it always seemed strange to me that people who contend so much for civil and religious liberty should be so ready to deprive others of their natural liberty; that men who are guarding against being subject to laws [to] which they never gave their consent in person or by their representative should at the same time make laws, and in the most effectual manner execute them upon me and others, to which laws I am sure I never gave my consent either in person or by my representative.[18]

This perplexity was echoed many times in Loyalist pamphlets during the Revolution. It seemed perfectly evident to them that the tyranny of Congress was much more severe and all-embracing than anything known under British rule.

252

Although originally in favour of avoiding bloodshed and arriving at a negotiated settlement with the home government, the active Loyalists eventually realised, especially after the Declaration of Independence, that the issue would be decided by force. As a result they volunteered for service with the British in such large numbers that it has been estimated that about half as many Americans enlisted on the British side as did in the Continental Army. Their aim was not to reimpose harsh foreign rule, as the Whigs would have it, but to liberate their homeland from the usurped authority of a ruthless faction claiming without justification to be acting for all Americans, and to restore the civil liberties guaranteed by the British constitution. They were fighting, in other words, for their own conception of freedom.

There was more, however, to the Loyalist position than mere response to the actions of the Whigs. For those Loyalists, at least, who published their ideas in contemporary pamphlets and newspapers and in memoirs and histories, there was fundamental disagreement with the political theory of the revolutionaries. They had, of course, to assume that the Whigs were sincere in their use of the vocabulary of freedom, since self-determination, in the words of Alfred Cobban, is "the usual demand of those who want to oppose others." However, whether these ideas were believed in or not by those who advocated them, they were obviously expected to influence public opinion by their self-evident rightness. The basis for revolt was found originally in the British constitution; but as that would hardly serve for independence, natural law became the final authority. Although other writers may have been cited more often by the revolutionaries than John Locke, it was his name which lent respectability to their cause. As interpreted by them, Locke sanctioned a rebellion such as the Glorious Revolution of 1688, if the sovereign violated certain natural rights, especially that of property. All that the revolutionaries had to do, according to this formula, was to demonstrate the tyranny of King George III, declare him deposed, and provide a substitute administration. This they did by the Declaration of Independence.

However, the Loyalists did not accept the analogy of 1688. In that case the country changed rulers but remained united, whereas in the 1770s the issue was nullification and secession. What the patriots did was to nullify certain laws which they did not like and then to secede when they were not allowed what amounted to *de facto* independence. Today, in Canada, it would be called separatism. The Loyalists objected that any argument which could be used against British tyranny would be just as effective against the tyranny of Congress: if pushed too far, the contract theory could lead to anarchy. Daniel Leonard, a lawyer who carried on a pamphlet debate with John Adams, put it this way:

253

Admitting that the collective body of the people, that are subject to the British Empire, have an inherent right to change their form of government, or race of kings, it does not follow that the inhabitants of a single province, or of a number of provinces, or any given part under a majority of the whole empire, have such a right. By admitting that the less may rule or sequester themselves from the greater, we unhinge all government.[19]

The argument for separation against which Leonard wrote came home to roost 85 years later, with the side which adopted the Loyalist position, the North, emerging the victor at that time. In fact, Abraham Lincoln's arguments against secession in his First Inaugural address are strikingly similar to those of Leonard. Another Loyalist, Galloway, forecast a civil war should independence come, in which the North would fight the South over control of the West, with the "ruthless and cunning Yankees" emerging triumphant.[20]

Today, of course, the right of a people to govern themselves is taken for granted; it is even made explicit in the United Nations Charter. But, as the Loyalists were aware, there are difficulties. The only way the Patriots could justify the break with Great Britain was on the grounds of their favourite Latin adage, *vox populi, vox dei*. It is indeed difficult to find a more obvious authority for legitimizing power, but the question immediately arises: Who are the people? "Popular demagogues", wrote Leonard, "always call themselves the people, and when their own measures are censured, cry out, the people, the people are abused and insulted."[21] However, the Loyalists objected not only to discontented politicians claiming to speak for everyone but also to the idea that the raw will of the "people" as exemplified in mobs, or the arbitrary actions of self-constituted committees and irregularly elected congresses, could ever be a substitute for the justice and order provided by a government which, though responsive to the people, must be to some extent above their momentary passions. They feared that public opinion was being deified at the expense of all other standards of morality, as in a Loyalist's portrait of *The Factious Demagogue:*

254

As for his Religion, he could mix,
And blend it well with politics,
For 'twas his favourite opinion
In mobs was seated all dominion:
All pow'r and might he understood
Rose from the sov'reign multitude:
That right and wrong, that good and ill,
Were nothing but the rabble's will:
Tho' they renounce the truth for fiction,
In nonsense trust, and contradiction;
And tho' they change ten times a day
As fear or interest leads the way;
And what this hour is law and reason,
Declare, the next, revolt and treason;
Yet we each doctrine must receive,
And with a pious grin believe,
In ev'rything the people's choice
As true as God Almighty's voice.[22]

The Loyalists thus anticipate some of the judgments of Alexis de Tocqueville and others who have been critics of the tyranny of the majority, or what is sometimes called "totalitarian democracy."

In sum, then, the case presented here is that the Loyalist was no more reactionary than the Whig, that he believed the dispute with Britain could be settled peacefully, that he felt he had more to lose than to gain by giving up the protection of British laws for the unlimited sovereignty of public opinion, that the actions of the revolutionaries very often put him in a position where there was no alternative to taking the British side if he wanted to preserve his self-respect, that he fought not to defend tyranny but to free his country from what he regarded as tyranny, and that he was aware of some flaws in the overoptimistic and sometimes hypocritical slogans of the Whigs.

It is not necessary to pretend either that independence was wrong or that it would not have come very soon in order to justify the stand taken by the Loyalists. Such a justification is particularly desirable from the standpoint of Canadian history because that preference for evolution rather than revolution, for patient negotiation rather than impatient violence, which is supposed to be a characteristic of the Canadian temper, can be traced directly back to the United Empire Loyalists. As the chief point of differentiation between the Canadian and American forms of democracy, it is surely worth emphasizing.   *255*

Notes

1. For example, not one of the papers presented at the annual meetings of the Canadian Historical Association since it was founded in 1922 has had the Loyalists as its subject, except in connection with land allotment.
2. Edgar McInnis, *Canada* (New York, 1960), 160–165.
3. D. G. Creighton, *Dimension of the North* (Boston, 1944), 177, 172.
4. D. C. C. Masters, *A Short History of Canada* (Princeton, 1958), 22–23.
5. J. B. Brebner, *Canada, A Modern History* (Ann Arbor, 1960), 106–107.
6. J. M. S. Careless, *Canada, A Story of Challenge* (Cambridge, 1953), 113.
7. W. L. Morton, *The Kingdom of Canada* (Toronto, 1963), 174–5.
8. G. M. Craig, *Upper Canada — The Formative Years* (Toronto, 1963), 2–3.
9. R. M. Lower, *Colony to Nation* (Toronto, 1959), 77, 84, 113–120.
10. James J. Talman, ed., *Loyalist Narratives from Upper Canada* (Toronto, 1946), lxiii. The figures are from Alison Ewart and Julia Jarvis, "The Personnel of the Family Compact, 1791–1841", *Canadian Historical Review*, VII, 209–221.
11. [Thomas Bradbury Chandler], *A Friendly Warning to All Reasonable Americans* (New York, 1774).
12. H. C. Van Schaack, *Life of Peter Van Schaack* (New York, 1842), 261.
13. Hector St. John Crevecoeur, *Sketches of Eighteenth Century America* (New Haven, 1925), 251.
14. Quoted in W. H. Siebert, *The Loyalists of Pennsylvania* (Columbus, Ohio, 1920), 26.
15. W. H. Nelson, *The American Tory* (Oxford, 1961), 91.
16. James H. Stark, *The Loyalists of Massachusetts and the Other Side of the American Revolution* (Boston, 1910), 450.
17. Lorenzo Sabine, *Biographical Sketches of the Loyalists of the American Revolution*, 2 vols. (Boston, 1864), I, 78.
18. *Ibid.*, 311.
19. John Adams and Daniel Leonard, *Novanglus and Massachusettensis* (Boston, 1819), 225.
20. [Joseph Galloway], *A Candid Examination of the Mutual Claims of Great Britain and the Colonies* (New York, 1775), 59.
21. Adams and Leonard, 225.
22. Winthrop Sargent, ed., *The Loyalist Poetry of the Revolution* (Philadelphia 1857), 129. *The Factious Demagogue* was dated at Halifax, May 13, 1780, and was probably written by the Rev. Jacob Bailey, the frontier missionary.

The Society of Upper Canada

256   On the eve of its creation in the Constitutional Act of 1791, Upper Canada had a population of roughly 20,000 (one half white settlers and one half Indians). By 1850 Canada West (as the colony became known after the Act of Union of 1841) had become the largest British North American colony with a population of over one million white colonists (and only approximately 10,000 Indians). Two groups predominated: Americans who came either as the United Empire Loyalists in the 1780s — settling mainly in the Niagara Peninsula and along the St. Lawrence River, or as later settlers (many without any Loyalist background) arriving between 1791 and 1812; and the British migrants who came in great numbers in the 1830s, 1840s and 1850s. Naturally such rapid population growth created a society in transition. The following readings examine the nature of that society in the early nineteenth century.

    Jean Burnet explains the gradual evolution of social classes in the backwoods settler society of Upper Canada in "Occupational Differences and the Class Structure," a chapter from her *Ethnic Groups in Upper Canada*. The conditions of wealth in the rural areas are examined by Peter Russell in "Upper Canada: A Poor Man's Country? Some Statistical Evidence."

The best surveys of Upper Canada are the two volumes in the Canadian Centenary Series, Gerald M. Craig's *Upper Canada: The Formative Years, 1784-1841* (Toronto: McClelland and Stewart, 1963), and J.M.S. Careless, *The Union of the Canadas: The Growth of Canadian Institutions 1841-1857* (Toronto: McClelland and Stewart, 1967). Fred Landon's study, first published in 1941, is still useful, *Western Ontario and the American Frontier* (Toronto: McClelland and Stewart, 1967). Cole Harris, a historical geographer, provides a survey of "Ontario," in *Canada Before Confederation: A Study in Historical Geography* (Toronto: Oxford University Press, 1974), pp. 110-168. J.K. Johnson's *Historical Essays on Upper Canada* (Toronto: McClelland and Stewart, 1975) is a valuable collection of articles. The condition of urban poor is treated by Patricia E. Malcolmson in "The Poor in Kingston,

1815-1850," in *To Preserve and Defend, Essays on Kingston in the Nineteenth Century,* ed., Gerald Tulchinsky (Montreal: McGill-Queen's University Press, 1976), pp. 281-297.

Gerald Craig's edited work, *Early Travellers in the Canadas: Extracts from the Writings of Thirty Visitors to British North America 1791-1867* (Toronto: Macmillan, 1955) is very useful. Three of the most cited contemporary witnesses of early Upper Canada are women: Catharine Parr Traill, Susanna Moodie and Anna Jameson. Two of Catharine Parr Traill's books, *The Backwoods of Canada* (1836) and *The Canadian Settler's Guide* (1854), and Susanna Moodie's *Roughing it in the Bush* (1852), and Anna Jameson's *Winter Studies and Summer Rambles in Canada* (1838) are available, in abridged editions, in McClelland and Stewart's New Canadian Library Series. Marian Fowler's *The Embroidered Tent: Five Gentlewomen in Early Canada* (Toronto: House of Anansi, 1982), contains sketches of these women's lives.

For a full review of the Iroquois residents of Upper Canada and their society in the early nineteenth century consult Charles M. Johnston, ed. *The Valley of the Six Nations: A Collection of Documents on the Indian Lands of the Grand River* (Toronto: The Champlain Society, 1964). A general review of the changes in Indian society is provided by Elizabeth Graham in *Medicine Man to Missionary: Missionaries as Agents of Change Among the Indians of Southern Ontario, 1784-1867* (Toronto: Peter Martin Associates Limited, 1975). Several chapters in Robin W. Winks, *The Blacks in Canada* (Montreal: McGill-Queen's University Press, 1971) deal with the arrival, and the lives, of Blacks in Upper Canada.

257

Occupational Differences and the Class Structure*
JEAN BURNET

In early Upper Canada there was, in the main, one occupation and one social class. No one could hold aloof from his neighbours because there was no landless proletariat to perform for wages the chores that were beyond the capacity of the family unit. Medical care and other functions that required special knowledge or skills were provided by people who spent more of their time as working farmers.[1] Differences in wealth existed: the sects were frequently as groups richer than the rest of the community, and included individuals of considerable wealth.[2] But the rich were not marked off from the rest of the community by social status.

This was the condition of Upper Canada especially in the years before the War of 1812-1814, when the agrarian class was largely made up of

*From *Ethnic Groups in Upper Canada*, by Jean Burnet. Copyright 1972, by Ontario Historical Society. Reprinted by permission.

Loyalists, sectarians and Yankee pioneer farmers whose home previous to migration had been in the United States. Robert Gourlay wrote of the Americans in Upper Canada:

> They are here distinguished rather by their occupations than by their political connexions, or the places of their birth. A due proportion of them are in the professional, mercantile, and mechanic employments; but the most numerous classes are engaged in agriculture, and have the appropriate views, manners, and sentiments of agriculturists.[3]

They had been used to a democratic way of life admirably suited to a rural community. Their log or frame houses did not even provide private sleeping quarters; their "help", sons and daughters of neighbouring farmers, ate their meals with the family; and the "bee", as a means of building houses, barns or mills, was a peerless social equalizer. Free social intercourse, accompanied by similarity in occupation, led to community of interest and lack of class consciousness.

258   However, before the end of the eighteenth century the towns of the lakeshore had a social elite, sharply distinguished from the farmers. It was composed of military men, government officials, ecclesiastical dignitaries, and well-to-do merchants. The first three groups consisted of a sprinkling of overseas people, who frequently did not intend to remain in the province, and a larger number of "the well-educated, the ambitious, and the well-versed in politics"[4] from among the U. E. Loyalists. The British Government and Lt. Gov. John Graves Simcoe had tried to create of these people an aristocracy that would "offset the rising tide of colonial democracy,"[5] by bestowing upon them grants of land and offices under the Crown. The merchants were largely Scots. The Scots were already established as the builders of empire, and the prestige, the wealth and the organization that they acquired as traders in the outpost colonies gained them a place in the Upper Canadian aristocracy alongside the Loyalists. The Scottish merchants who had established themselves in Lower Canada in the fur trade[6] had been able to extend their lines of influence into the upper province, and their position there was most advantageous. They constituted the sole link between the farmer and the outside world, carrying on trade in a "species of indirect barter."[7] That they seized the opportunity thus afforded them is suggested by La Rochefoucault-Liancourt's remark concerning the Newark merchants. "The shops are few," he wrote, "and the storekeepers combining against the public fix what price they choose upon their goods".[8] Another traveller noted the factors involved in the success of the Scottish merchants:

> The persons of greatest weight, in the Canadas, are the merchants, or store-keepers. Among these, the gentlemen from Scotland take a decided lead. I have been informed that they have the same ascendancy in the West Indies. They are sent out at an early period of life from Scotland, and, by the time they arrive at manhood, are perfectly conversant in a knowledge of the country. If superior industry and activity are grounds to pretension of affluence, I know no men whose claims are equal to those of the Scotch.[9]

The Scots were readily assimilated into the ruling clique, for they formed a prominent part of the Family Compact. Indeed, they are said to have been the original members of that group.

If it were necessary to put one's finger on the point at which, more than any other, the Family Compact may be said to have come into existence, that point might reasonably be the end of General Hunter's administration in 1805, when an element among the public officials secured the selection of Alexander Grant as president and administrator of the province over the head of Peter Russell, who had been president from 1796 to 1799. It was this element which those in opposition to the government denominated 'the Scotch faction' or 'the clan'. The lieutenant-governor, wrote Robert Thorpe in 1806, is "surrounded with the same Scotch pedlars, that had insinuated themselves into favour with General Hunter, and that have so long irritated and oppressed the people. There is a chain of them linked from Halifax to Quebec, Montreal, Kingston, York, Niagara and so on to Detroit."[10]

To the Loyalists and Scots, the overseas immigration after 1815 added a number of officers on half-pay and younger sons, chiefly from England and Scotland. The three elements merged into a self-conscious, almost endogamous upper class, preoccupied with land speculation and preferments, and trying to retain intact the old stratified social structure of Great Britain. They defended privilege in every form; in particular, they supported the endowed Anglican Church's endeavour to maintain its rights in land and education. They emphasized the social distance between themselves and the lower classes in every way possible. They visited almost exclusively among themselves,[11] and married among themselves. Travellers could not gain admission to their circle, whatever their quality, unless they had letters of introduction to the Governor, or Bishop or other social leader.[12] They were punctilious in observing conventions in paying calls, in conducting themselves at social gatherings, and indeed in all matters associated with gentility. Fashion in dress, usually of great importance in aristocracies,[13] was much stressed, as Mrs. Moodie noted:

259

They dress well and expensively, and are very particular to have their clothes cut in the newest fashion. Men and women adopt the reigning mode so universally that they look all dressed alike. The moment a fashion becomes at all obsolete, the articles of dress made to suit it are discarded. In England, a lady may please herself in the choice of colours, and in adopting as much of a fashion as suits her style of person and taste, but in Canada they carry this imitation of the fashions of the day to extremes. If green was the prevailing colour, every lady would adopt it, whether it suited her complexion or not; and, if she was ever so stout, that circumstance would not prevent her from wearing half-a-dozen more skirts than was necessary, because that absurd and unhealthy practice has for a long period prevailed.[14]

On the whole, the manners of the people were "thoroughly English"[15] but with the difference that folkways of English society became mores in Upper Canada. Great significance was attached to the various social rituals, so that no one dared deviate, however inconvenient it was to comply. This suggests that the first class of provincial society was insecure, straining to maintain itself in the face of some kind of threat. What that was has already been suggested. Because of the great difference in orientation between the élite and the agrarian class in the frontier community, the former could not fulfill any real function; therefore its very survival was jeopardized. Cultural and political leadership requires not only freedom from the necessity of earning a living by manual labour, but also membership in the community,[16] and the aristocrats in Upper Canada possessed the first requisite but lacked the second. Hence they tried to perpetuate their class and its privileges by overstressing good form. Mrs. Jameson observed:

I did not expect to find here in this new capital of a new country, with the boundless forest within half a mile of us on almost every side — concentrated as it were the worst evils of our old and most artificial social system at home, with none of its *agremens*, and none of its advantages. Toronto is like a fourth or fifth rate provincial town, with the pretensions of a capital city. We have here a petty colonial oligarchy, a self-constituted aristocracy, based upon nothing real, nor even upon anything imaginary; we have all the mutual jealousy and fear, and petty gossip, and mutual meddling and mean rivalship, which are common in a small society of which the members are well known to each other, a society composed, like all societies, of many heterogeneous particles; but as these circulate within very confined limits, there is no getting out of the way of what one most dislikes: we must necessarily hear, see, and passively endure much that annoys and disgusts anyone accustomed to the independence of a large and liberal society, or the ease of continental life. It is curious enough to see how quickly a new fashion, or a new folly, is imported from the old country, and with what difficulty and delay a new idea finds its way to the heads of the people, or a new book into their hands.[17]

Mrs. Jameson wrote in 1837, when the formality and the tension in Upper Canadian society was probably at its height. The problem of the assimilation of plutocracy to aristocracy, always acute in Western European culture,[18] was sharpened by the ethnic differences between the elite, with its European way of life, and the wealthy, who were largely American, although the Scotch still ranked high among the storekeepers and merchants. The restriction placed upon land holding in the 1812-14 period had brought about a radical change in the position of the Americans in the Upper Canadian occupational structure. Now it could be said of the Yankees that:

These people had come over in large numbers. They did not usually take up land. They preferred some occupation in which their hands were nearer the pockets of the public. To keep a store or a tavern suited them best.[19]

They constituted most of the active business people in the province, and took a lead in its industries.[20] Among the prominent men of capital and technical experience were Joseph Van Norman, Hiram Capron, George Tillson and Elijah Leonard, all associated with iron works and other enterprises; Simeon Morrill and Ellis Walton Hyman, connected with the tanning industry; James M. Williams, active in oil refining and the manufacture of railway cars, tinware and glass; Edward and Charles Gurney, the Hamilton stove manufacturers; the tinsmith Edward Jackson; the railway and financial magnate Samuel Zimmerman.[21] There were also outstanding professional men, notably in medicine,[22] and the fact that many of the early printers and hotel-keepers were American[23] made for the wide extension of American points of view. It was to these people that the community often looked for leadership, rather than the office-holding clique.

If the upper class overseas immigrants who lived in the towns of Upper Canada found it hard to maintain their social position, those who settled in the backwoods found it impossible. Except in a few isolated cases, such as the Peterborough and the Woodstock settlements,[24] the English and Irish half-pay officers and gentlemen in reduced circumstances were unable to segregate themselves from their fellow farmers. They had to adopt the same occupation, for labour was both scarce and expensive, and sometimes unobtainable to those who would not admit the claims of the lower orders to equality.

....the farmer who is willing to place his servant upon terms of equality with himself, is never at a loss for help, and his work is well and cheerfully performed; while on the other hand, those coming from the old country, and who feel disposed to stand upon their dignity, more or less experience great difficulty in meeting with suitable servants, and still greater difficulty in retaining their services. The annoyance to such persons from this cause is sometimes very great. Thus, a female help newly arrived one day, frequently disappears the next, simply because she was asked to sleep in an attic, or had not pickles, pies and preserves served for her tea, or perhaps was not invited to spend the evening in the drawing room. Another because she was not allowed to sit with the family, or a third because she was expected to milk cows, draw water from the well, or carry an armful of wood to the cooking stove. In like manner a help of the masculine gender, has before now bid us good morning, because he was asked to clean out a pig stye, or dig a post hole, or a ditch.[25]

261

In default of hired labour, the aristocrats had to work in the bush and the potato field, take their own grist to the mill, and join with the rest of the community at bees.[26] Class distinctions in occupation thus broke down, and although this had its advantages, in that storekeeping and other profitable work could be undertaken without degradation,[27] it meant that one basis of class had disappeared.

While following the same occupation as his humbler neighbours the gentleman found it imperative to change many other cultural traits. Distinctive styles of clothing were discarded for what was almost a uniform in the backwoods: homespun trousers, shirt open at the neck, and broad-brimmed straw hat. Even among the young university men of Sturgeon Falls, proprieties of dress were soon surrendered, despite a firm determination to preserve them, as two extracts from John Langton's letters to his father show:

York, Feb. 3rd, 1834

....Your fears lest we should grow bearish in our manners are, I think, needless — at our end of the lake at least; our dress, of course, is not in the style of a town dandy, but we have agreed to keep up a degree of form which sometimes amuses me when I look round on the accompaniments of the scene.

Blythe, Oct. 10th, 1835

....I have run on at such a rate about climate, crops etc., that I have no room left to answer your letters; I must however acknowledge receipt of the two packages, all the contents of which were very welcome; but the stock and waistcoat might have been dispensed with as they are articles of attire which I never wear. I couldn't help smiling when I unpacked them, so strongly did they contrast with my usual dress, viz., white trousers or such as were white on Sunday morning, a red shirt open at the breast and tucked up above the elbows — et voila tout — a coat never comes over my back, except at Peterborough, or when I call on Mrs. Frazer.[28]

Because of the pressure of farm chores and the imperfect communication between the farmer and the outside world provincial politics did not become a live issue in the backwoods, and the upper class colonist could not count on maintaining his prestige by giving political leadership. Mrs. Moodie, commenting upon the Rebellion of 1837, stated that "The political struggles that convulsed the country were scarcely echoed in the depths of those old primeval forests", and that the "people in the backwoods . . . . were profoundly ignorant of how the colony was governed, and many did not even know which party was in power".[29] The talents required for municipal affairs, were not knowledge of the outer world and refinement of manner; the aristocrat had no better claim than, and perhaps not so good a claim as, the illiterate farmer with only common sense to recommend him, and indeed he frequently scorned to fill the highly useful function of "pig regulators or cattle impounders."[30]

262

Literary and artistic abilities were of no advantage in coping with a backwoods farm. "The sin of authorship," complained Mrs. Moodie, "meets with little toleration in a new country . . . . A new country, where all are rushing eagerly forward in order to secure the common necessaries of life, is not a favourable soil in which to nourish the bright fancies and delusive dreams of the poet".[31] Moreover, the facilities, energy and time required to maintain cultivated tastes in adults and to inculcate them in children were not available. Paper and books were few in the backwoods, musical instruments other than the violin and flute almost lacking,[32] and life crowded with all manner of fatiguing and time-consuming tasks. Mrs. Stewart of Douro was keenly sensible of the pleasures of literary and artistic endeavour, but repeatedly spoke of having no opportunity to indulge in them, or teach them to her children. "Various and endless are the obstacles to any employment which requires quietness", she wrote, "and sometimes I am almost in despair about being able to do anything but nurse or fuss a little over housekeeping."[33] Perhaps the fact that so many of the diaries, letters and books from the backwoods were written by women settlers indicates that men were too busy even for those literary endeavours.

The gentlemen settlers in the backwoods could not base their claims to prestige entirely on wealth, since among the backwoods farmers the correlation between wealth and social status at the time of immigration was not always maintained. The poor industrious immigrant, with a large family of healthy children, frequently surpassed the settler who had possessed inherited wealth within a short time.[34]

In short, there was a levelling downwards of social classes in the backwoods proceeding primarily from lack of occupational differentation.

In the backwoods education or refined tastes brought very little immediate profit. It was as physically difficult for the rich man as for the poor man to build his log cabin, clear his land, extract the first unwilling crop, and raise the children through the perils of childhood. There were few luxuries that money could buy in the form of either goods or service, and less leisure to enjoy these, even if within the reach of the settler. For all there was the prospect chiefly of grinding labour. The backwoods recognized no differences in station or rank because almost all were engaged in a similar type of work.

There the son of a gentleman became a hewer of wood and a drawer of water. He studied the art of chopping trees, piling brush heaps, splitting rails for fences, attending fires during the burning season. Dressed in a coarse overgarment of hempen cloth, called a logging suit, with trousers to correspond, a Yankee hat flopped over his eyes. To tend and drive oxen, plough, sow, plant Indian corn and pumpkins, and raise potatoes were among some of the emigrant's needful accomplishments. At the bees magistrates, counsellors and colonels might work side by side without any feeling of degradation. The fact that all men laboured at the same occupation tended to give rise to a sense of equality.[35]

The descent of the upper class overseas immigrant did not take place without resistance. Mrs. Moodie spoke of struggles against old prejudices that had to be won and proud swellings of the heart that had to be subdued by her and her family before they became reconciled to social intercourse with uneducated people,[36] and probably most people of her class tried to maintain a degree of segregation as long as it was at all possible. Eating at the same table was a widespread symbol of equality and even intimacy, and the upper class settlers stoutly resisted eating with servants. A young traveller set down his feelings after a visit to Clifton House at Niagara Falls:

263

I felt my English blood almost boil in my veins when I found myself sitting in company with two servant women at the table d'hote, at the same time that their mistress occupied a place at the other end of the table. I could have very well accommodated myself to such neighbours in the States, but never expected to have found the levelling system introduced into the British provinces to such an extent.[37]

Sleeping in the same room or the same bed with servants was of course relished just as little, and sometimes a sleepless night was preferred to the alternative.[38] Marriages involving disparagement also were not uniformly successful.[39]

For the overseas immigrants of the lower classes, the social system of the backwoods frequently meant a levelling upward rather than downward. They were no longer limited to menial occupations, and they became independent proprietors, with pride in their status. Samuel Strickland painted a picture of the effects of this:

It is astonishing how a few years' residence in Canada or the United States brightens the intellects of the labouring classes. The reason is quite obvious. The agricultural population of England are born and die in their own parishes, seldom or never looking out into a world of which they know nothing. Thus, they become too local in their ideas, are awake to naught but the one business they have been brought up to follow; they have indeed no motive to improve their general knowledge.

But place the honest and industrious peasant in Canada, and, no matter how ignorant he may be, when he sees that by his perseverance and industry he will in a short time better his situation in life, and most likely become the possessor of a freehold, this motive for exertion will call forth the best energies of his mind, which had hitherto, for want of a proper stimulus, lain dormant. Having to act and think for himself, and being better acquainted with the world, he soon becomes a theoretical as well as a practical man, and consequently a cleverer and more enlightened person, than he was before in his hopeless servitude in the mother country.[40]

However, though this was the long-run effect of the disintegration of class lines, the temporary effects were often less gratifying. The poor man from the British Isles had been accustomed to consider land ownership a mark of membership in a privileged class, and now he himself was a farm owner. Moreover, he had previously never doubted that he had been called to a certain station in life, and now he came in contact with American ideas of freedom and equality of opportunity. The constraints of a comparatively rigid class system were gone, and the new liberty was unsettling.

> Possessing farms which render them independent of the better classes of society they can, within certain limits, be as bold, unconstrained, and obtrusive, as they please, in their behaviour towards their superiors; for they neither look to them for subsistence nor for anything else. They now consider themselves on an equality with those to whom, in former times, the hope of gain would have made them crouch like slaves; and tacitly avow their contempt of the better part of society, by avoiding the slightest approximation towards them, so far as regards habits, appearance, or mode of life.[41]

It was generally conceded that their incivility surpassed that of the Americans, though the manners of the latter were distasteful enough to the upper class settlers and travellers particularly at inns.[42] The overseas settler, long accustomed to the codes and traditions of a stratified society, could not take his new situation for granted. Just as the town aristocrat's insecurity led him to excessive ritualism, the lower class settler's insecurity led him to excessive flouting of the prescriptions of a culture from which he was not as yet able to dissociate himself completely. He could not forego ostentatious demonstration, because he had not yet fully convinced himself or others of his rights. While the American could take equality for granted, the overseas immigrant could not. Thus it was that Thomas Need[43] and Mrs. Traill[44] found the manners of the British a caricature of those of the real American, and E.A. Talbot wrote with his usual malignance:

264

> These emigrants, having generally been of the lowest class of society in their respective countries — and consequently mere cyphers except in their own immediate spheres, — as soon as they arrive in Canada, begin to assume an appearance of importance, and to be quite ashamed of their former unassuming manners and native customs. The most absurd notions of equality and independence take instant possession of their vertiginous and unreflecting minds. As they travel through the Province and mingle with its inhabitants, they hear the dialect and peculiarities of their respective nations decried and ridiculed, while those of America, both Republican and Monarchical, are invariably defended and extolled. The first, and as they conceive it the most essential study in which they can engage in this new state of existence, is therefore to imitate everything American; and so successful are they in their endeavour to copy the example of those by whom they are surrounded, that, before they have spent a single season in the Province, they exhibit the most ludicrous specimens of ignorance and affectation that this or any other country can produce. Not a single trace of native simplicity or of native manners remains. Everything must give place to the influence of example; and American vanity must be grafted onto the stock of foreign diffidence. No magpie was ever more assiduous in mimicking his music master, than these imported mocking birds are in copying the fashionable slang of their immaculate neighbours. They are indefatigable in acquiring a knowledge of THE RIGHTS OF MAN, THE JUST PRINCIPLES OF EQUALITY, AND THE TRUE NATURE OF INDEPENDENCE, and, in a word, of everything which characterises an American; and then they quickly become divested of common manners, and common civility, and not unfrequently of common honesty too — indeed, this latter virtuous quality is rather uncommon on this side of the Western Ocean.[45]

There was no servant class to which the aggressive attitudes of independence did not communicate themselves. Labourers and domestics, being scarce and in demand, could insist on high wages and good treatment. They also expected to become farm owners within a few years, no matter how poor they were on arrival, and therefore shared the attitudes and values of the agrarian class rather than having distinct proletarian attitudes and values. Captain Basil Hall showed insight into this fact:

....it happens that the power of getting servants even at Cobourg, York, and other considerable towns in Canada, varies very much from year to year. When a fresh batch of settlers arrives, there is no difficulty, nor for some time afterwards; but exactly in proportion as the emigrants succeed in establishing themselves, and thus acquire independence, so the difficulty of obtaining servants increases. The inconvenience to which even the wealthiest residents are put.... from their attendants being called home, and from there being absolutely no distinct order of persons bred in that line of life, is greater than can well be conceived in England. With us, at home, fortunately, a class does exist, whose sole object and pleasure it is to employ themselves in this particular line of useful industry.... In Canada, however, and throughout America generally, there is a deep-rooted, but surely very idle prejudice against this description of labour; caused probably, by some associations connected with the existence of negro slavery over so great a portion of the United States. Be this as it may, the fact is one which goes farther to make a residence on the western side of the Atlantic inconvenient, than people can easily comprehend who have never been subjected to the absolute want of servants; or, what is often worse, to the necessity of submitting in patience to the ungracious, capricious, sluggish, disrespectful, and, at the very best, ill-qualified nature of American attendance, which prevails from end to end of that country.[46]

Women who brought out servants with them were often seriously inconvenienced by their rapid adoption of independent, and even insolent, manners, and by their readiness to leave. The hard work and the social deprivations to which the domestic and farm labourers had been accustomed in the old land they now would not accept. It was often the upper class employers who were the suppliants in transactions with servants. Mrs. Moodie was one of many backwoods women who were forced to pay considerable attention to the servant problem:

Servants that understand the work of the country are not easily procured, and such always can command the highest wages. The possession of a good servant is such an addition to comfort, that they are persons of no small consequence, for the dread of starving no longer frightens them into servile obedience. They can live without you, and they well know that you cannot do without them. If you attempt to practise upon them the common vice of English mistresses, to scold them for any slight omission or offence, you rouse into active operation all their new-found spirit of freedom and opposition. They turn upon you with a torrent of abuse; they demand their wages, and declare their intention of quitting you instantly. The more inconvenient the time for you, the more bitter become their insulting remarks. They tell you, with a high hand, that "they are as good as you, that they can get twenty better places by the morrow, and that they don't care a snap for your anger." And away they bounce, leaving you to finish a large wash, or a heavy job of ironing, in the best way you can.[47]

Gradually, however, the opportunities for immigrants without capital to rise to a position of independence disappeared, while the number of wage occupations increased. A group of people emerged who had only a limited

265

prospect of improving their social status by becoming their own masters. The first members of this group were almost all Irish Roman Catholics.[48] They constituted the vast majority of the labourers on the public works, their riotous behaviour earning them as evil reputation in all regions in which canal-building was in progress.[49] Many writers mentioned that their drivers in their travels were Irish, and very often praised their eloquence,[50] and Mrs. Moodie implied that the poor cabmen of Toronto belonged to the same ethnic group:

> The steamboat had scarcely been secured to her wharf before we were surrounded by a host of cabmen who rushed on board, fighting and squabbling with each other, in order to secure the first chance of passengers and their luggage. The hubbub in front of the ladies' cabin grew to a perfect uproar; and, as most of the gentlemen were still in the arms of Morpheus, these noisy Mercuries had it all their own way — swearing and shouting at the top of their voices, in a manner that rivalled civilized Europe. I was perfectly astounded at their volubility, and the pertinacity of their attentions, which were poured forth in the true Milesian fashion — an odd mixture of blarney, self-interest, and audacity.... One of these Paddies, in his hurry to secure the person and baggage of several ladies, who had been my fellow-passengers in the cabin, nearly backed his crazy old vehicle over the unguarded wharf into the lake.[51]

Frequently no distinction is made between Roman Catholics and Protestants, but the hypothesis that the former constituted the kind of proletariat which was emerging, is borne out by John A. Godley:

> The Protestants became farm-labourers, or domestic servants in good families, for a time, but always aim at settling, as soon as possible, on land of their own, while the Roman Catholics, who are invariably of the poorest class, constitute, for the most part, as in the States, the Pariah class, or "proletaires": they are the porters, carters, waiters at inns, etc., and above all, they monopolise almost entirely the public works, which absorb a great portion of the labouring population in this country....[52]

Thus ethnic, religious and occupational lines coincided in marking off the lowest social class in Upper Canada.

The Roman Catholic Irish became the object of prejudice, presumably on account of their low social status, but they suffered much less than another section of the emerging proletariat, the small body of Negroes who had come into the province as fugitives from slavery in the United States. The Negroes, except for a few farmers, and a number of pastors, merchants and lawyers serving fellow blacks, were concentrated in such occupations as serving in hotels, whitewashing, plastering, carting, barbering and entertaining,[53] all tasks frequently performed by pariah groups. At first the Negroes probably entered these occupations because of their low qualifications for other work, but soon they were prevented from entering others by racial prejudices operating either directly or indirectly. John C. Geikie's comments upon the menial nature of the employments in which blacks were found suggest the development of myths justifying occupational segregation:

> In all the hotels, most of the workers, and a large proportion of the cooks, seemed to be colored. They take to these employments naturally, and never appear to feel themselves in

greater glory than when fussing about the table at meals, or wielding the basting-ladle in the kitchen. They very seldom turn to trades, and even their children, as they grow up, are not much more inclined to them. I used to think it was, perhaps, because, as slaves, they might not have learned trades, but this would not apply to those born in Canada, who might learn them if they liked. They become, instead, whitewashers, barbers, or waiters, and cooks, like their fathers before them.[54]

Far from enjoying menial occupations, James B. Brown considered that the Negroes were made by discrimination "too bitterly to feel themselves to be merely the hewers of wood and drawers of water" among the white population, who were also enforcing a measure of spatial segregation upon them in many places.[55]

By this time a distinct working class developed, the tensions in the upper class of Upper Canadian society were decreasing. The office-holding cliques were beginning to absorb the rich merchants into its circles, and the combination to exercise a measure of dominance not previously possible.[56] This development, like the growth of the working class with no orientation toward proprietorship of the land, signalized the passing of the agrarian economy of Upper Canada from the frontier expansionist phase of its economy to stability and maturity. In the 'forties and 'fifties, the multiplication of social classes was related not to the agricultural frontier but to the rise of the towns, and not to the occupation of farming but to new occupational developments.

267

Notes

1. Cf. C.O. Ermatinger, *The Talbot Regime or the First Half Century of the Talbot Settlement*, (St. Thomas, 1904), p. 104.
2. Logan, *Notes on a Journey Through Canada, the United States of America, and the West Indies*, p. 47.
3. Gourlay, *Statistical Account of Upper Canada*, Vol. I, p. 142.
4. Rev. Egerton Ryerson, *The Loyalists of America and Their Times*, Vol. II, p. 143.
5. Macdonald, *Canada 1763-1841*, pp. 52-3.
6. Cf. Lambert, *Travels through Canada and the United States of North America, in the years 1806, 1807 & 1808*, Vol. I, pp. 232-6, 523-4; also John M. Duncan, *Travels through a part of the United States and Canada in 1818 and 1819*, (Glasgow, 1823), Vol. II, p. 156; Frances Hall, *Travels in Canada and the United States in 1816 and 1817*, (London, 1818), pp. 143-4.
7. Gourlay, *Statistical Account of Upper Canada*, p. 226.
8. La Rochefoucault-Liancourt, *Travels in Canada 1795...*. edited by W.R. Riddell, in Alexander Fraser, *Thirteen Report of the Bureau of Archives for the Province of Ontario* (Toronto, 1917), p. 43; cf. J.J. Bigsby, *The Shoe and Canoe, or Pictures of Travel in the Canadas*, (London, 1850), Vol. I, pp. 261-2, and others.
9. "Canadian Letters. Description of a tour thro' the provinces of Lower and Upper Canada, in the course of the years 1792 and '93," Reprinted from *The Canadian Antiquarian and Numismatic Journal*; Vol. IX, Third Series, No. 3 and 4, July-October, 1912, by Thomas O'Leary, p. 80.
10. William Stewart Wallace, *The Family Compact: a chronicle of the rebellion in Upper Canada*, Chronicles of Canada Series, edited by G.M. Wrong and H.H. Langton, Vol. 24, (Toronto, 1915), pp. 4-5. Cf. Alison Ewart and Julia Jarvis, "The Personnel of the Family Compact, 1791-1841," *Canadian Historical Review*, Vol. VII, No. 4 (Toronto, 1926). Note, however, D. M'Leod, *A Brief Review of the Settlement of Upper Canada, by the U.E. Loyalists and Scotch Highlanders, in 1783*, (Cleveland, 1841), p. 2.
11. Moodie, *Life in the Clearings Versus the Bush*, p. xiii.
12. Cf. Rev. Isaac Fidler, *Observations on Professions, Literature, Manners, and Emigration in the United States and Canada, made during a Residence there in 1832*, (London, 1833), p. 338; Godley, *Letters from America*, Vol. I, p. 167; Rose, *The Emigrant Churchman in Canada*, Vol. I, p. 87.
13. Arthur Livingston, "Theory of the Gentleman," *Encyclopaedia of the Social Sciences*, (New York, 1935), Vol. VI, pp. 616-620.

14. Moodie, *Life in the Clearings Versus the Bush*, pp. 87-8.
15. Kingston, *Western Wanderings*, Vol. II, p. 38; cf. *The Canadas as they now are, by a late resident*, (London, 1833), p. 67; Geikie (ed.), *Life in the Woods*, p. 396; Eliot Warburton (ed.), *Hochelaga, or England in the New World*, (n.p., 1846), Vol. I, p. 225.
16. Daniel Katz and Richard L. Schank, *Social Psychology*, (New York, 1938), pp. 187-8.
17. Jameson, *Winter Studies and Summer Rambles in Canada*, pp. 50-1.
18. Dixon Wecter, *The Saga of American Society, A Record of Social Aspiration 1607-1937*, (New York, 1937).
19. W.A. Langton, (ed.), *Early Days in Upper Canada: Letters of John Langton from the Backwoods of Upper Canada and the Audit Office of the Province of Canada*, (Toronto, 1926), pp. XXV-VI.
20. Shirreff, *A Tour through North America*, pp. 38-9.
21. Fred Landon, *Western Ontario and the American Frontier* (Toronto, 1941), pp. 50-55.
22. *Ibid.*, pp. 56-9.
23. *Ibid.*, pp. 55-6.
24. Cf. Shirreff, *A Tour through North America*, p. 123; Godley, *Letters from America*, Vol. I, pp. 167-9, 176-7, 208; Langton (ed.), *Early Days in Upper Canada*; Need, *Six Years in the Bush*; Rose, *The Emigrant Churchman in Canada*, Vol. II, pp. 278-80.
25. James Croil, *Dundas, or a Sketch of Canadian History and more particularly the County of Dundas, one of the earliest settled counties in Upper Canada*, (Montreal, 1861), pp. 216-7.
26. Cf. T.W. Magrath, *Authentic Letters from Upper Canada*, edited by Rev. T. Radcliff (Dublin, 1833), pp. 117-9; Moodie, *Roughing It in the Bush*, p. 519; Rose, *The Emigrant Churchman in Canada, being letters from the wife of an emigrant officer* (London, 1846), p. 122; Pickering, *Inquiries of an Emigrant*, pp. 42-3.
27. Need, *Six Years in the Bush*, pp. 102-3; Langton, (ed.), *Early Days in Upper Canada*, p. 99; Moodie, *Life in the Clearings Versus the Bush*, pp. xii-xiii; Traill, *The Backwoods of Canada*, pp. 81-2.
28. Langton (ed.), *Early Days in Upper Canada*, pp. 75, 155; cf. Need. *Six Years in the Bush*, p. 70.
29. Moodie, *Roughing It in the Bush*, p. 466, and *Life in the Clearings Versus the Bush*, p. 50.
30. Rose, *The Emigrant Churchman in Canada*, Vol. I, p. 116.
31. Moodie, *Life in the Clearings Versus the Bush*, pp. 61-2.
32. Traill, *The Backwoods of Canada*, p. 29; E.C. Guillet, *The Victoria College Manuscript Discoveries, The New Outlook*, (Toronto, April 8, 1931), p. 322.
33. Dunlop (ed.), *Our Forest Home*, pp. 114-5.
34. William Dunlop, *Statistical Sketches of Upper Canada, for the use of emigrants, by a backwoodsman* (London, 1833), pp. 6-7.
35. M.A. Garland, "Some Frontier and American Influences in Upper Canada prior to 1837", London and Middlesex Historical Society, *Transactions*, Part XIII, (London, 1929), pp. 12-3.
36. Moodie, *Roughing It in the Bush*, p. 238.
37. Coke, *A Subaltern's Furlough*, Vol. II, pp. 36-7; cf. William Lyon Mackenzie, *Sketches of Canada and the United States*, p. 70.
38. John C. Geikie, (ed.), *Life in the Woods*, pp. 161-2.
39. *Ibid.*, p. 178-9.
40. Strickland, *Twenty-seven Years in Canada West*, Vol. I, p. 265-6.
41. Howison, *Sketches of Upper Canada*, pp. 136-7.
42. Howison, *Sketches of Upper Canada*, pp. 118-9; William Bell, *Hints to Emigrants in a series of letters from Upper Canada* (Edinburgh, 1824), pp. 65-6; Jameson, *Winter Studies and Summer Rambles in Canada*, p. 127; Need, *Six Years in the Bush*, pp. 15-6; Traill, *The Backwoods of Canada*, p. 50.
43. Need, *Six Years in the Bush*, p. 22.
44. Traill, *The Backwoods of Canada*, p. 83.
45. Talbot, *Five Years' Residence in the Canadas*, Vol. II, pp. 10-11; cf. Howison, *Sketches of Upper Canada*, pp. 174-5; Moodie, *Life in the Clearings Versus the Bush*, p. 54.
46. Captain Basil Hall, *Travels in America in 1827 and 1828*, Vol. I, pp. 299-300.
47. Moodie, *Roughing It in the Bush*, pp. 242-3.
48. Rev. James Beavin, *Recreations of a Long Vacation; or, A visit to the Indian missions in Upper Canada* (London, 1846), pp. 86-7; Bonnycastle, *Canada and the Canadians in 1846*, Vol. II, pp. 63-4; Godley, *Letters from America*, Vol. I, p. 156.
49. Jameson, *Winter Studies and Summer Rambles in Canada*, pp. 66-7; Bonnycastle, *Canada and the Canadians in 1846*, Vol. I, p. 43.
50. Kingston, *Western Wanderings*, Vol. I, p. 301, Vol. II, pp. 1-2; Traill, *The Backwoods of Canada*, pp. 77-8.
51. Moodie, *Life in the Clearings Versus the Bush*, pp. 282-3.
52. Godley, *Letters from America*, Vol. I, p. 251.
53. Fred Landon, "Fugitive Slaves in London Before 1860", London and Middlesex Historical Society, *Transactions*, Part X, (London, 1919), pp. 28-9; Sir James E. Alexander, *L'Acadie*, Vol. I, p. 139.
54. Geikie, (ed.), *Life in the Woods*, p. 378.

55. Brown, *Views of Canada and the Colonists*, p. 289.
56. Moodie, *Life in the Clearings Versus the Bush*, p. ix.

Upper Canada: A Poor Man's Country?
Some Statistical Evidence*

PETER A. RUSSELL

I

The price of the land, too, is still so Low, and may yet be had on terms so easy that the poorest individual can here procure for himself and family a valuable tract; which, with a little labour, he can soon convert into a comfortable home, such as he could probably never attain in any other country — *all his own!*[1]

The Settlers in Gwillimburry, Vaughan, and Markham, in the Home District, who entered the province at an early period, and who chiefly came from the States, occupy a tract of country highly cultivated, and are now affluent farmers. The Settlers of Peter-boro'; and those of Cavan and Monaghan; chiefly composed of Irish, have also succeeded. The Military Settlers established in the Bathurst District, though placed on bad land are now independent.[2]

269

How long did it take "the poorest individual" to turn his "valuable tract" into a "comfortable home"? What stages of economic prosperity are indicated by the terms "affluent farmers" and "independent"? How many settlers came to Upper Canada with capital? Previous studies have offered only anecdotal answers.[3] In an attempt to deal with such quantitative questions I have used a selection of township tax assessment records to indicate the pattern of land holdings and clearing. By studying fifteen townships in three districts between 1812 and 1842, we can get some ideas as to the distribution of cultivated land (including "average farm size"), the rate of clearing, the approximate proportion of new farmers who possessed some capital, and the ownership pattern of "wild land."[4] These empirical observations will give a solid base from which to draw inferences about the economic and social structure of at least part of the Upper Canada farm community.

II

Since the objective of this study is to examine the distribution of cultivated land, the focus of attention is the farmer — not pioneer, whose primary interest was clearing the land, nor the land speculator. The pioneer's principal return from his work came in the appreciated capital value of his farm, not from any cash crop he might have raised incidental to his main purpose.[5] The speculator's gain came from the enhanced value of his lands as the neighbouring farms were cleared. The farmer's economic position

*From *Canadian Papers in Rural History*, ed. Donald H. Akenson, 3 (1982): 129-147. Reprinted by permission.

depended on the amount of cleared land he had to cultivate.

The available statistics are used selectively to focus on the data most useful for learning about farmers. There exist assessment rolls for about seventy townships in Upper Canada between 1812 and 1842.[6] (Some rolls cover more than one township.) As many of these townships were sparsely populated — and included many pioneers — it is desirable to narrow the study to such townships as would be likely to have a higher concentration of farmers. After an examination of the 1836 census for population and cultivated land, it appears that a division can be made between "unsettled" and "settled" townships. The latter are defined as having about or over 2,000 in population, with 5,000 or more acres in cultivation. By this measure there were seventy-five settled townships.[7] Assessment rolls are available for parallel years from 1812 for ten of these, and from 1822 to 1842 for fifteen of those townships, or 20 percent of the total. Thus, we have data on one in five settled townships. Further, the six counties in which the townships are located constitute a wide section of the province. Only the Niagara region and the Lake Erie shore are not represented.

Some line needs to be drawn to distinguish between the pioneer clearing and the land speculator's mandatory clearing to establish title, on the one hand, and the settled farm on the other. The settlement requirements in land grants usually required a three-acre clearing after a period of years. There is ample evidence from the period that speculators commonly made a small clearing simply to secure their patent.[8] While an argument could be made for drawing a line at three acres or less, to obtain the most comprehensive estimate of the number of farms, this study sets one acre or less as the boundary between pioneer (and speculator) and the farmer.

III

The valuation part of Upper Canada's assessment law set up an honour system, which operated under certain constraints. Each ratepayer was to give the assessor (appointed by Quarter Sessions) a statement of his or her own rateable property. The assessor was responsible for compiling these statements into an accurate list, which he deposited with the Clerk of the Peace, for public inspection prior to the spring Quarter Sessions. The assessor had to swear under oath as to the accuracy of his list, and was subject to a fine if it were proved false. The ratepayer took no oath as to the accuracy of the statement and was subject to no penalty if it were found to be false.[9]

The ratepayer's own statement of rateable property was taken as valid, subject to three checks. Although nowhere specifically required to do so in the legislation, the assessor had an interest in keeping his list reasonably accurate, especially in keeping ratepayers from drastically underestimating their property. First, the responsibility for the accuracy of the total list fell on the assessor: it was he, not the ratepayer, who would be penalized if it were found gravely wanting. Second, the assessor's remuneration was based on the property tax. He was paid £4 for every £100 collected in assess-

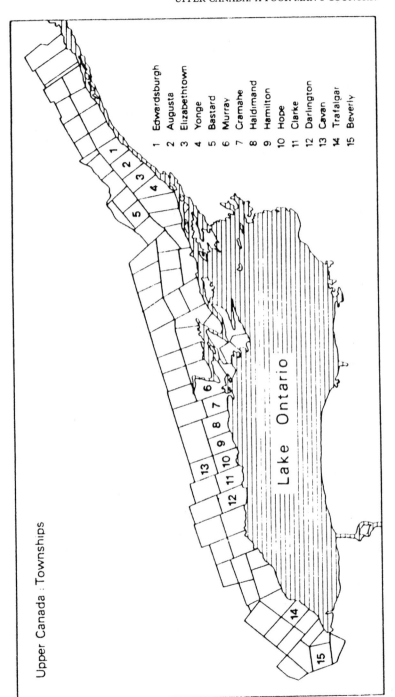

Upper Canada : Townships

Lake Ontario

1 Edwardsburgh
2 Augusta
3 Elizabethtown
4 Yonge
5 Bastard
6 Murray
7 Cramahe
8 Haldimand
9 Hamilton
10 Hope
11 Clarke
12 Darlington
13 Cavan
14 Trafalgar
15 Beverly

271

ment. Thus, the assessor's personal interest in avoiding trouble with the law and in obtaining a fair return for his work would incline him to use moral suasion with any ratepayers inclined radically to undervalue their own holdings. The second monitor upon the honour system came in the public posting of the assessor's list for the township. A person's neighbours would be likely to object to someone with the same size farm attempting to pay less tax than themselves.

The last constraint upon the ratepayer (after 1819) was a provision in the Assessment Act which required the Surveyor General to provide the treasurer in each district with a list of all lands granted or leased by the Crown, broken down by township and concession. This was done to enable the collection of rates from absentee land owners. But it also provided a partial check on any resident ratepayer who might be inclined to "forget" a second (or third) farm holding located in another district. This check only operated on the total amount of land one held. It told nothing about how much was cultivated or uncultivated.

The Assessment Act of 1819 defined cultivated land as "every acre of arable, pasture, or meadow land," which it rated at twenty shillings each. Uncultivated land was rated at four shillings per acre.[10] Since the rate for uncultivated land was one-fifth that for cultivated, it made a great difference

TABLE I — **Number of Farms and Average Number of Cleared Acres Per Farm For 10-15 Townships, 1812-42**

Townships	1812		1822		1832		1842	
	no. of farms	aver. farm size	no. of farms	aver. farm size	no. of farms	aver. farm size	no. of farms	aver. farm size
Augusta	159	43.8	187	48.0	342	30.3	466	31.78
Edwardsburgh	77	30.0	130	26.5	228	21.4	363	20.43
Elizabethtown	189	46.6	281	46.8	448	31.2	559	32.7
Yonge	158	27.1	230	24.8	325	26.4	395	36.6
Bastard	78	25.4[1]	125	30.8	204	35.4	340	28.3
Cramahé	59	30.7	124	35.2	209	33.1	362	36.3
Haldimand	101	33.3	150	44.2	241	54.4	353	47.4
Hamilton	76	36.6	135	44.8	265	41.9	381	46.2
Murray	25	25.5	124	22.9	209	24.9	411	28.2
Hope	69	35.9	114	37.3[2]	136	45.9[4]	387	40.2
Clarke			16	41.6	107	35.2	428	36.2
Darlington			47	35.2	117	30.1[4]	411	29.7 [5]
Cavan			98	13.3	334	19.4	401	31.5
Beverly			63	31.4	128	34.6	438	33.8
Trafalgar			182	22.4[3]	393	33.0[4]	869	40.9
Total	991	36.2	2,006	33.6	3,686	33.1	6,540	34.7

(For some townships the years vary: [1]1810, [2]1821, [3]1823, [4]1833, [5]1841)

to each ratepayer how much land was considered in each category. Since the act placed the power of deciding on this division in the hands of the ratepayers, we may assume the estimates of cultivated acreage were consistently conservative, subject to the constraints of the assessor's and the neighbours' scrutiny. A number of practical problems in assessment were thus left to the ratepayers individually.[11] Given the absence of any clear mandate to review the ratepayers' statements, we may take it for granted that assessors would be inclined to accept the most generous interpretation of these gray areas in the law.[12] Consequently, the assessment figures for cultivated land may be seen as severely conservative estimates.

IV

The impact of immigration into Upper Canada is readily visible in the farm settlement pattern shown in Table I. As large numbers of new settlers began their clearing, there was a sharp rise in the proportion of small farms, and the attendant decline in the average number of acres cleared per farm. Between 1812 and 1822, average farm size declined from 36.2 cleared acres to 33.6 acres, then to 33.1 acres in 1832. With the easing off of immigration after the mid-1830s, the new small farms grew, as did the older farms, without any comparable influx of new farmers. Consequently, the average farm size rose again to 34.7 cleared acres by 1842.[13] Closer examination of the figures makes the pattern of increasing farm size clearer (see Table II). From 1812 to 1822, the principal growth was in the number of cleared farms of up to nineteen acres. From 1822 to 1832, the numbers in this category still increased, though the proportion dropped. The largest growth was in the next category, of twenty- to twenty-nine-acre farms. Between 1832 and 1842 the proportion of small farms (nineteen acres and under) had dropped

273

TABLE II — **Change in the Percentage of Farms in Each Farm Size Category For Townships, 1812-42**

Number of Acres	1812-22*	1822-32**	1832-42**
1-9	+2.87	-4.1	-4.5
10-19	+1.17	+0.3	-3.3
20-29	-1.17	+4.1	+0.1
30-39	-4.74	+0.9	+2.4
40-49	+0.8	-0.5	+0.16
50-59	+0.9	-0.4	+1.7
60-69	-1.74	-0.1	+1.4
70-79	+1.18	-0.1	+0.4
80-89	-0.5	0	+0.5
90-99	+0.13	-0.1	+0.3
100+	+1.12	-0.5	+0.8

* Comparing 10 townships in 1812 and 1822
** Comparing 15 townships in 1822, 1832, and 1842

further, and the growth appeared in the higher categories — especially those from thirty to thirty-nine acres and from fifty to sixty-nine acres. Thus, we are able to plot with some precision the growth of the farm community, both in total numbers and in the proportions of various sized farms.

While the averages are useful for seeing the overall impact of immigration, they do not tell us much about the patterns of farm land distribution. The pattern which emerges from the graph (see Table III) shows that, far from being homogeneous, farmers varied greatly in the amounts of cultivated land they held (and, by inference, in their income). The large peak on the left of the graph represents about one-half of the farms which had thirty acres or less. The gradual "tail" to the right shows a substantial minority of just under one-fifth with holdings of between fifty and one hundred cleared acres. Last, the small peak (really a false peak) on the right indicates a minority of 2 to 5 percent — present in every settled township — that held over one hundred acres of cultivated land.[14] That pattern is of some significance for an understanding of the social structure of the Upper Canadian farm community.

274

TABLE III — Farm size distribution in 10-15 townships, 1812-1842.

| 10 Townships | 1812 | 15 Townships | 1822 | 1832 | 1842 | 20 | 15 | 10 | 6 | 0 |

| 1-9 | 20-29 | 40-49 | 60-69 | 80-89 | 100+ | 100 + | Number of acres cleared on each farm |

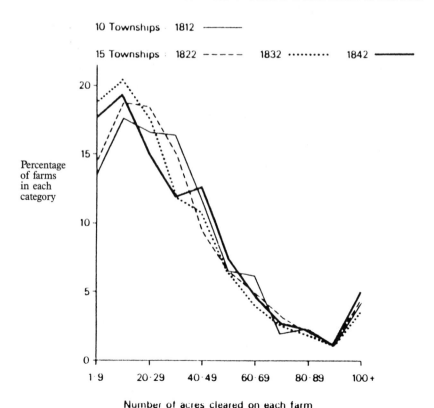

10 Townships   1812   ———
15 Townships   1822   – – – –   1832 ··········   1842 ———

Number of acres cleared on each farm

To establish the wealth of the largest farms it is necessary to make certain, quite reasonable, assumptions. Most farmers in the settled townships would probably have been part of the commercial rather than the subsistence economy. Given a farm of one hundred cleared acres devoted to wheat, with a modest yield of twenty bushels per acre, and a good (but not high) price of $0.75 per bushel, then a large-scale farmer's potential income would have been $1,500.[15] That compares favourably with the salary of $1,200 paid such high officials as the Attorney General, the Surveyor General or the President of King's College in York.[16] The contrast between this group of farmers and their proper neighbours was in the amount of land cleared rather than in the total owned. The promise of social mobility was there for every smallholder; if he could just get his lot cleared, he would be amongst the richest people in the province.

The critical importance of clearing land leads us to the average rate of clearing. There were various methods of clearing the forest from the land. The quickest way was to cut away the underbrush, and leave the most substantial trees to die while still standing, by slashing (called "girdling"), or by fire. In time, these dead trees would rot and fall down by themselves. The more laborious, but safer, method demanded that the trees be chopped down after clearing the brush and the timber piled in heaps to be burnt.[17] These different methods — and the varieties of forest cleared — meant that a certain amount of variation in clearing rates is to be expected.

Writers then and since have offered a wide range of estimates on the rate of clearing. Edwin Guillet refers to several accounts that claim one could variously chop ten to twelve acres in four months; or chop, cut, and pile an acre in eight days; or clear, seed, and fence ten acres a year. The latter

275

TABLE IV — **Townships Ranked By Acres Cleared Per Farm Per Year**

1812-22		1822-32		1832-42	
Edwardsburgh	2.64	Augusta	3.03	Augusta	3.18
Hamilton	2.41	Clarke	2.89	Trafalgar	2.88
Augusta	2.32	Haldimand	2.68	Clarke	2.82
Haldimand	2.18	Edwardsburgh	2.14	Hope	2.67
Cramahé	2.06	Trafalgar	2.06	Darlington	2.64
Murray	1.78	Hamilton	1.91	Beverly	2.36
Hope	1.75	Beverly	1.91	Edwardsburgh	2.04
Elizabethtown	1.54	Bastard	1.65	Cramahé	1.72
Bastard	1.24	Cavan	1.55	Hamilton	1.71
Yonge	0.63	Darlington	1.45	Murray	1.55
		Cramahé	1.22	Cavan	1.53
		Hope	1.22	Yonge	1.49
		Murray	1.13	Haldimand	1.03
		Yonge	0.88	Elizabethtown	0.77
		Elizabethtown	0.18	Bastard	0.71

estimate he considered highly optimistic. An average settler would not accomplish half that. His more sober estimates appear to range from four to seven acres a year per farm.[18] Robert L. Jones, after reviewing several sources, estimated that an able-bodied man could clear four to five acres in a year. He cited Anna Jameson's encounter with a backwoodsman, who said he cleared an acre a year. Her reply indicated that she considered the common clearing rate four times that. This provoked from the man an admirably concise statement of one of the variables in land clearing.

He replied, almost with fierceness, "Then they had money, or friends, or hands to help them; I have neither. I have in this wide world only myself! and set a man with only a pair of hands at one of them big trees there! — see what he'll make of it."[19]

Besides extra help (from family, neighbours, or hired hands), one's own skill, the method of clearing, and the nature of the forest to be cleared determined the rate of clearing. Except for Jameson's backwoodsman, the conservative overall rate commonly mentioned is about four acres per farm per year.

The actual average rate of clearing shown by the assessment rolls, however, is much lower — from 1.23 acres per farm per year (1822) to 1.47 (1832), and 1.55 (1842). Even the highest recorded rates of clearing (Augusta, 1832 and 1842) are only 3.03 and 3.18 acres per farm per year (see Table IV). Variations above the overall average can be attributed to the availability of more labour for clearing, owing to either large families or to settlers having more capital to hire "choppers." Only three townships (Yonge, Elizabethtown, and Bastard) have clearing rates consistently below the average of one and a half acres per farm per year. These form a geographical unit coinciding with the southern tip of the Precambrian Shield. There may be a relation between the low clearing rates in these townships with large areas of poor land and the high rates of their two eastern neighbours, Edwardsburgh and Augusta. Farmers, finding that to clear their own property was unprofitable, may have readily hired out to those nearby with better land.

The figures for average land clearing seriously challenge the conventional view that the backwoods of Upper Canada could rapidly transform a pauper immigrant into a yeoman farmer.[20] Both contemporary Upper Canadian assumptions and subsequent scholarly thought have held that the transition from immigrant to yeoman would be readily accomplished. R.L. Jones estimated that a farm could be cleared in five to six years.[21] In fact, at one and a half acres a year, it would take a healthy, hard working immigrant working by himself just over thirty years to create a fifty-acre farm.

In considering the rate of clearing, however, the use of the aggregate rate for all farms in a township might conceal marked variations between the clearing rates on large farms and those on small ones. To check whether any significant differential did exist, the percentage of larger farms (fifty arable acres and over) for each township was correlated to the clearing rate of that township, for each of 1822, 1832 and 1842. For the first period, the correspondence was quite low: 0.17. However, in each succeeding period

276

it rose, most markedly in 1832 (0.62), and further (0.67) in 1842. As those increased rates in clearing parallel the rapid increase in immigration, the rising correlation might reasonably be linked to an inflow of well-to-do immigrants. Yet, even in 1842, the correspondence of a high proportion of large farms and high clearing rates is not so close as to establish a firm relationship between the two. Thus, such differential as existed between the clearing rates on large as compared to small farms could not have been very great.

That conclusion appears to be confirmed by the data on Cavan township. On the government's initiative, it was principally settled by a group of Irish poor. There was practically no previous settlement in Cavan before 1815. The Irish took up their lots of 100 acres and cleared them themselves. The factors of previous settlement or wealthy immigrants thus were not significant.[22] Cavan, "the poor man's township," had a consistent clearing rate of just over one and a half acres per farm, per year.

Yet many immigrants were not destitute of funds. Not all new farmers began with only the £100 or so that was considered just sufficient to clear a farm.[23] There is ample evidence that some came out with capital — intending to be "gentlemen farmers," purchasing a cleared farm or hiring the necessary labour to make a farm.[24] Other immigrants, though coming to Upper Canada with little, worked for a time — as was commonly advised — to raise the needed capital to begin their own farms in the bush.[25] Some of these latter could have raised more than the minimum. Thus, like the immigrant capitalists, they would have been able to hire labour to assist them in clearing. But how many new farmers with capital to hire labour or extra human resources were there?

277

The data is comprehensive enough only to allow us an estimate of the numbers of new farmers with either money or human capital. We know the number of small farms and large farms (however we may choose to define these) for a series of years. We can assume either, first, that all small farmers expanded their clearings to become large farmers or, second, that none of them did. This establishes the possible range of new farmers with capital. If the number of small farms, in the second year of a pair of years being compared, is greater than the total increase in the number of farms, then (taking the first possibility — that all small farms are new farms) the number of new farmers with capital will be equal to the total increase in the number of farms minus the number of small farms in the second year. In summary, the difference between the number of new farms and the number of small farms (assuming all small farms are new) gives the minimum number of new farmers who have large farms. Taking the second assumption — that none of the small farmers in the first of the two years being compared were able to increase their clearing to large ones — then the largest possible number of new farmers with capital would be equal to the increased number of large farms.

There is a possible third assumption. Large farms may be broken into smaller ones, as land passes from one generation to another. This "diffusion by inheritance" would not likely have been a significant factor in Upper Canada. As Attorney General J.B. Robinson noted during a debate on M.S. Bidwell's Intestate Bill in 1826, the common procedure evidenced by the records of the provincial Surrogate offices was to settle the cleared farmland on one of the children, not to divide it up amongst them all.[26] Sons and daughters were more likely to be given wild land of their own to develop, rather than have the cleared land which a family possessed divided.[27] To the extent to which such diffusion did take place, the maximum number of new farmers with capital would be higher.[28]

R.L. Jones groups immigrants into three classes, according to their means. There were those with enough capital to purchase a farm ready-made. Then there were immigrants who could afford only a backwoods lot, but who were able to support themselves while clearing it. Lastly, there were those who would need to labour several years on someone else's farm to obtain enough capital even to begin clearing a farm in the bush.[29] The second class and most of the third class, who earned a good deal more than the £100 basic stake — along with settlers who had the human capital of a large family — would appear as new farmers with capital. If we take a "small farm" as comprising nine acres or less, then the estimated range of new farmers with capital is from one-quarter to one-third of the total (see Table V). Given the clearing rate established earlier, it would be unlikely that all small farms would become large farms in a single decade. Therefore, the more conservative estimate of new farmers with capital is probably the closer approximation.

278

TABLE V — **Estimated Range of New Farmers with Capital (Where "a Small Farm" is 9 Acres or Less) For 10-15 Townships, 1812-42**

	Numbers	Percentages
10 townships:		
1812-22	422-441	26.5-27.7
15 townships:		
1822-32	1,113-1,375	30.4-37.5
1832-42	2,148-2,549	33.04-39.9

V

The study of township assessment rolls also yields information about the pattern of holding uncultivated land. It does not tend to confirm Lillian Gate's picture of a "lavish land granting policy" which "had established speculator control over the most fertile parts of Upper Canada."[30] Most townships in 1812 or 1822 had about 20 to 30 percent of the privately owned wild lands in the hands of non-residents or resident large holders (i.e., those with more than 400 acres not cleared). The latter almost always account for more of the land so held than the former (see Table VI). Moreover, almost all of the non-residents held less than 1,000 acres. These conclusions tend to agree with Leo Johnsons' finding about certain townships in the Home

District. "By far the majority of absentee-held lands were in the hands of the general population who hoped to realize something worthwhile on their patrimony."[31] Of the fifteen townships in three districts covered by this study, it may be said that the great majority of the privately owned wild lands were held by farmers as the uncleared remainder of their own properties.

The striking exception to this generalization appears in the townships of Augusta, Edwardsburgh, and Elizabethtown between 1812 and 1822. In these three, for 1812, between two-thirds and three-quarters of the wild lands were held in large blocks by resident and non-resident holders. But within ten years' time that share dropped drastically, falling into line with most other townships. The key to this puzzle is that the total amount of privately held wild lands also dropped sharply in these townships — from 171,114 acres to 97,978 acres. The large private holdings — 115,826 to 24,311 acres — account for that drop. (The holdings of resident farmers with less than 400 acres rose by 18,379 acres.) Within ten years the Crown resumed title to 91,515 acres, almost all of that certainly formerly held by large land owners.

279

The most likely explanation for this massive shift appears to be the forfeiture of lands granted to Loyalists, as a result of the tightening of settlement duty regulations in 1818.

On October 14, 1818, public notice was given that grantees of land would be required to erect a habitable house and to clear and fence 5 acres in every 100 . . . Another regulation attempted to undo the errors of the past by providing that all locations subject to settlement duties made before August 1, 1819, would be rescinded unless a certificate showing the duties to have been performed was presented within twelve months' time and the patent sued out within one month thereafter.[32]

Governor Maitland, by this action, provoked a protest from several of the members of the assembly who represented the areas affected. The wonder is that, involving as much land as it apparently did, the protest against the new regulation was not more forceful. Gates concluded that "Maitland was but little more successful . . . [in enforcing his regulation] than his predecessors."[33] On the basis of the assessment rolls, it appears that Maitland's regulation worked very well, at least in some of the old Loyalist townships.

Other factors could be cited for a return of lands to the Crown in that period. The losses of the war and the commercial crisis of 1819-20 may have forced some to give up lands to the Crown in lieu of taxes due. Such considerations, however, would apply to most townships. They would not account for the massive resumption of title to wild lands in Augusta, Edwardsburgh, and Elizabethtown.

VI

What is the relationship of these economic realities of the Upper Canadian farm community to the social structure of the colony? Does the preponderance of very small farms and the low rate of clearing (low, relative to previous assumptions) mean that what Robert Wolfe called "the myth

TABLE VI — Ownership Pattern of Wild Lands in 10-50 Townships, 1812-42

Township	1812					1822				
	Acres of wild land	Held by non-res.	More than 100 acres held by res.	Held by both	Percentage held by both	Acres of wild land	Held by non-res.	More than 100 acres held by res.	Held by both	Percentage held by both
Augusta	59,367	6,000	32,335	38,335	64.4	27,262	1,665	5,785	7,450	27.3
Edwardsburgh	35,341	1,350	25,141	26,491	75.0	31,460	1,039	5,159	6,198	19.7
Elizabethtown	76,406	4,800	46,120	51,000	66.7	39,256	1,440	9,223	10,663	27.2
Yonge	26,137	1,895	6,448	8,343	31.9	26,485	1,392	3,753	5,145	19.4
Bastard	11,670	1,850	750	2,600	22.3(a)	14,038	660	1,080	1,740	12.4
Cramahé	9,813	577	1,902	2,479	25.3	16,567	2,821	1,067	3,888	23.5
Haldimand	16,913	1,470	4,770	6,240	36.9	17,332	2,204	2,345	4,549	26.2
Hamilton	18,556	1,175	6,403	7,578	40.8	18,222	1,970	2,308	4,278	23.5
Hope	18,210	350	9,152	9,502	52.2	22,556	1,394	10,483	11,877	52.7(b)
Murray	8,642	1,357	4,164	5,521	63.9	16,453	1,355	2,039	3,394	20.6
Clarke						5,522	1,206	2,412	3,618	65.5
Darlington						7,704	190	2,116	2,306	29.9
Cavan						15,069	400	492	892	5.9
Beverly						8,184	1,224	490	1,714	20.9
Trafalgar						23,813	1,920	1,554	3,474	14.6(c)

TABLE VI — (continued)

Township	1832					1842				
	Acres of wild land	Held by non-res.	More than 100 acres held by res.	Held by both	Percentage held by both	Acres of wild land	Held by non-res.	More than 100 acres held by res.	Held by both	Percentage held by both
Augusta	35,285	2,615	2,470	5,087	11.4	38,279	1,564	792	2,356	6.2
Edwardsburgh	25,814	2,077	2,673	4,750	18.4	30,729	1,425	600	2,025	6.6
Elizabethtown	46,363	2,490	3,743	6,233	13.4	47,784	919	2,763	3,682	7.7
Yonge	32,265	1,227	3,285	4,512	14.0	37,105	695	2,081	2,776	7.5
Bastard	17,230	947	—	947	5.5	25,443	1,885	—	1,885	7.4
Cramahé	20,643	1,749	2,755	3,389	16.4	29,803	2,069	1,925	3,994	13.4
Haldimand	23,322	1,640	4,768	6,408	27.5	23,680	970	2,033	3,003	12.7
Hamilton	25,646	2,544	3,810	6,354	24.8	26,198	1,432	4,908	6,331	24.2
Hope	17,187	510	7,547	8,057	46.8(d)	25,542	1,205	3,574	4,779	18.7
Murray	25,064	4,841	885	5,726	22.8	40,366	1,610	685	2,295	5.7
Clarke	15,424	3,709	3,326	7,035	45.6	25,387	1,507	1,704	3,211	12.6
Darlington	18,916	4,276	2,364	6,640	35.1(d)	31,961	4,310	1,985	6,295	19.7(e)
Cavan	34,431	2,004	1,165	3,169	9.2	61,310	790	615	1,405	2.3
Beverly	17,869	3,652	1,693	5,345	29.9	42,932	3,073	6,048	9,121	21.3
Trafalgar	40,117	2,375	2,330	4,705	11.7(d)	58,622	1,880	1,630	3,510	5.9

Note: For some townships the years vary: (a) — 1810, (b) — 1821, (c) — 1823, (d) — 1833, (e) — 1841.

281

of the poor man's country" was indeed a myth — in the common, pejorative sense? Did the poor of Britain come to Upper Canada and stay poor? If we look at the experience of the Primitive Methodist Church in Upper Canada during the 1830s, we can gain some insight into the interaction of economic and social factors in the lives of the poor immigrants.

The Primitive Methodists were a predominantly working class offshoot of English Methodism. They began organizing in Upper Canada in 1829 under the impetus of William Lawson, a lay preacher of independent means. In the early 1830s, under Lawson's direction, the group attempted to take over the leadership of the "respectable" Methodists (rudderless since the withdrawal of the Wesleyans in 1820) in opposition to the "republican" Methodists associated with the Ryersons. In doing so, it over-extended itself, establishing congregations and building chapels it could not support. That failure to meet optimistic goals led to a certain quarrelsomeness between the local organization and its parent group in Hull, England.[34]

In a letter "to the Brethren at Hull" on 2 March 1836, the members of the York Circuit set out their view of the situation. Among other points, they stressed the inadequacy of the preachers' salaries. "We would suggest that in our opinion one great cause of so many failures among the Preachers in America is the smallness of the Preachers' salary's (sic) . . . the commonest labourer can earn more than their allowance."[35] The Hull Conference replied rather testily that there could be nothing wrong with a preacher earning the wages of a common labourer. The York Circuit replied to this rebuke in a letter of 1 March 1837, by making the acute observation that "We suppose you have drawn the comparison between our Preachers & your common Labourers in England — not being aware that the Industrious Labourer here if he is steady, in a few years rises to be a landed Proprietor."[36] The Primitive Methodists of Upper Canada were trying to impress upon their English brethren a crucial social and economic reality about the colony. In Upper Canada a common labourer would soon have enough saved out of his wages to purchase a lot and begin clearing his own farm. In England there was no such handy ladder of social mobility to draw men away from preaching. A preacher had more status in England than in Upper Canada (in the eyes of God and men). As a labourer there he would hardly have earned more and would have had no prospect of social and material advancement. In Upper Canada, a steady labourer in good health had every chance of improving his condition. Consequently, the salary for a preacher in the colony needed to be higher than the labourer's to keep men from that attractive bottom rung of the social ladder.

While the optimistic predictions that an immigrant could make a substantial farm in six years have been shown as exaggerated, the attraction of farming remained. It took a lifetime for anyone lacking either a large family, or sufficient capital to clear a farm of fifty acres and so provide a comfortable living. But immigrants were aware of more than just the economic realities when they headed for the backwoods with an axe. They also perceived the social possibility that a landless labourer could become a landed proprietor. As the Primitive Methodist experience suggests, to be on the road to a comfortable material existence had concomitant social benefits in Upper Canada not available to similarly placed persons in England.

The study of selected township assessment rolls for 1812-42 enables us to make certain empirical observations about at least that part of the Upper Canadian farm community. Far from being homogeneous, "farmers" varied greatly in the amount of cultivated land that they held. About one-half had cleared farms of under thirty acres. Just under one-fifth had farms of between fifty and one hundred acres. A small minority of from 2 to 5 percent had farms of over one hundred acres in cultivation. The average rate of clearing is much lower than previous estimates — one and a half acres per farm per year. Consequently, as noted above, to make a farm out of the bush would have entailed a lifetime's work for someone without a large family or the necessary capital to hire labour. However, at least one-quarter of the new farmers did have capital in human resources or money to employ "choppers" for clearing. In contrast to the common impression of speculators with vast holdings, the settled townships of this study show most wild lands held by farmers with less than 400 acres as the uncleared remainder of their property. The difficulties experienced by the Primitive Methodists in retaining their preachers point the impact of Upper Canada's comparative opportunities for land ownership on working-class attitudes. While the rate of clearing has been over-estimated, and consequently the time needed to clear a farm much under-estimated, Upper Canada was, in the minds of many who settled it, a "poor man's country."

283

Notes

1. *The Canadian Emigrant*, 13 July 1833.
2. Public Archives of Canada (PAC), CO 42, "Q" series, vol. 354, p. 306, Sir John Colborne to Sir George Murray, 4 October 1830.
3. Robert L. Jones, *History of Agriculture in Ontario, 1613-1880* (Toronto: Univ. of Toronto Press, 1946). Edwin C. Guillet, *The Pioneer Farmer and Backwoodsman*, vol. I (Toronto: Univ. of Toronto Press, 1963). Kenneth Kelly, "The Agricultural Geography of Simcoe County, Ontario, 1820-1880," Ph.D. thesis, University of Toronto, 1968.
4. The townships whose assessment rolls were utilized in this study are: Johnstown District — Augusta, Bastard, Edwardsburgh, Elizabethtown, and Yonge; Newcastle District — Cavan, Clarke, Cramahé, Darlington, Haldimand, Hamilton, Hope, and Murray; Gore District — Beverly and Trafalgar.
5. For a discussion of pioneers, see Jones, *History of Agriculture*, p. 54; Guillet, *Pioneer Farmer*, pp. 303-306. See also Samuel Strickland, *Twenty-Seven Years in Canada West*, vol. I, (Edmonton: M.G. Hurtig Ltd. 1970), p. 136.
6. The available assessment rolls are listed in the Public Archives of Ontrio (PAO), in the *Preliminary Inventory of Municipal Records*, Record Group 21.
7. *Appendix to the Legislative Assembly Journals of Upper Canada*, Thirteenth Parliament, 1836-37, no. 8, "Return of the Population of the Province of Upper Canada," and no. 9, "Assessment Returns."
8. Lillian Gates, *Land Policies of Upper Canada* (Toronto: Univ. of Toronto Press, 1968), pp. 20, 129-30. Strickland, *Twenty-Seven Years*, vol. I, pp. 88-89.
9. *Statutes of Upper Canada*, 1819, chapter VII.
10. Ibid., section ii.
11. Jones, *History of Agriculture*, p. 4.
12. Ibid., pp. 70-72. Strickland, *Twenty-Seven Years*, vol. I, pp. 165-66.

13. Compare this to Jones's estimate of 45-48 acres as the average farm size: excluding all with less than 3 acres cleared, Jones's estimate is a very close approximation.

14. The "false peak" really represents the total of all farms over 100 acres, which would actually be a tiny "tail" off to the right.

15. Jones, *History of Agriculture*, pp. 90-97, 123. John Howison, *Sketches of Upper Canada* (Edinburgh: Oliver and Boyd, 1821; Johnson Reprint Corporation, 1965), pp. 236, 251. Robert F. Gourlay, *Statistical Account of Upper Canada*, ed. S.R. Mealing (Toronto: McClelland and Stewart Ltd., 1974), pp. 130, 133, 136, 139, 150, 188, 199, 202, 242, 260, 263, 278.

16. PAO, John Strachan Papers, Lord Bathurst to Sir Peregrine Maitland, 31 March 1827. PAC, CO 42, "Q" series, vol. 352, pp. 4-10, Sir John Colborne to the Home Secretary, 10 July 1829.

17. Jones, *History of Agriculture*, pp. 69-71. Edwin C. Guillet, *Early Life in Upper Canada* (Toronto: Univ. of Toronto Press, 1967), pp. 274-76. Howison, *Sketches*, pp. 247-50. William Caniff, *History of the Settlement of Upper Canada with Special Reference to the Bay of Quinté* (Toronto: Dudley and Burns, 1869), pp. 186-88.

18. Guillet, *Pioneer Farmer*, p. 312.

19. Jones, *History of Agriculture*, pp. 71-73, citing Anna Jameson, *Winter Studies and Summer Rambles in Canada* (London: Saunders and Otley, 1838), vol. II, p. 227.

20. Gerald M. Craig, *Upper Canada: the Formative Years* (Toronto: McClelland and Stewart Ltd., 1963), pp. 124-25, 229. Strickland, *Twenty-Seven Years*, vol. I, pp. 134-39; vol. II, pp. 315-18. Susanna Moodie, *Roughing It in the Bush* (London: Richard Bentley and Co., 1852), vol. I, pp. viii-xiii; and her *Life in the Clearings* (ed. R.L. McDougall) (Toronto: The Macmillan Co. of Canada, 1959), p. xxxii. Robert D. Wolfe, "The Myth of the Poor Man's Country: Upper Canadian Attitudes to Immigration, 1830-1837," M.A. thesis, Carleton University, 1976, pp. 15-47. For a contrary view, see John MacTaggart, *Three Years in Canada* (London: Henry Colburn Ltd., 1829), vol. II, pp. 215, 241-42, 250.

21. Jones, *History of Agriculture*, p. 54.

22. Helen I. Cowan, *British Emigration to British North America* (Toronto: Univ. of Toronto Press, 1961), pp. 67-79.

23. Jones, *History of Agriculture*, p. 67.

24. Ibid., p. 60. Robert C. Good, "Letter Book of John Strachan, 1827-1834," M.A. thesis, University of Toronto, 1940, pp. 211-12. Like Strachan, Strickland and Moodie also warned gentlemen away, unless they took up cleared farms. Strickland, *Twenty-Seven Years*, vol. I, pp. 135-36. Moodie, *Life in the Clearings*, pp. xxx-xxxi.

25. Jones, *History of Agriculture*, pp. 60-61. Wolfe, "Poor Man's Country," pp. 9-10, 20. But MacTaggart rejected this view: ". . . They think the labourer will be able in a few years to obtain as much money by the sweat of his brow, as may enable him to purchase a farm of this land — a thing which does not happen in one case out of fifty." MacTaggart, *Three Years in Canada*, vol. II, p. 250.

26. *Kingston Chronicle*, 19 January 1827.

27. Canniff Height, *Country Life in Canada* (Belleville: Mika Silk Screening Ltd., 1971), pp. 2-4.

28. The estimates of new farmers with capital were established by the following formula.

$s(1)$	$s(2)$	$s(1)$ = small farms in the first year
		$L(1)$ = large farms in the first year
		$s(2)$ = small farms in the second year
		$L(2)$ = large farms in the second year
$L(1)$	$L(2)$	$T(1)$ = total farms in the first year
		$T(2)$ = total farms in the second year
$T(1)$	$T(2)$	$\triangle t$ = increase in the total number of farms
		NFC = new farmers with capital

Assumption 1: $s(1) \rightarrow L(2)$

All small farms were expanded into large ones. Then new farmers with capital will be the number of new farms minus the number of small farms in the first year, or

In A(1), $\triangle t - s(1)$ = NFC (the minimum number of NFC)

Assumption 2: $s(1) \rightarrow s(2)$

No small farms were able to expand, and thus they are all still small. Then new farmers with capital will be the increased number of large farms, or

In A(2), $L(2) - L(1)$ = NFC (the maximum number of NFC)

Assumption 3: $L(1) \rightarrow s(2)$

Large farms may be broken down into small farms, say by inheritance. The effect of this would be to underestimate the number of new farmers with capital, since there would then be more new large farms than the figures show. (Similarly, the effect of several small farms consolidating into one large holding would be to make the minimum estimate of Assumption 1 too low.) The greater the extent of diffusion, the higher the maximum number of new farmers with capital would be.

29. Jones, *History of Agriculture*, pp. 60-61.

30. Gates, *Land Policies*, p. 149, Norman Macdonald, *Canada 1763-1841, Immigration and Settlement* (Toronto: Longmans, Green & Co., 1939), pp. 511-12.

31. Leo A. Johnson, "Land Policy, Population Growth and Social Structure in the Home District," in J.K. Johnson ed., *Historical Essays on Upper Canada*, (Toronto: McClelland and Stewart Ltd., 1974), p. 44.

32. Gates, *Land Policies*, p. 129.

33. Ibid., p. 130.

34. John D. Hoover, "The Primitive Methodist Church in Canada, 1829-1884," M.A. thesis, University of Western Ontario, 1970, pp. v-22.

35. United Church of Canada Archives, Victoria University, Primitive Methodist Church in Canada, York Circuit, *Minutes of Preachers and Leaders Meetings, 1830-1838*, 2 March 1836.

36. Ibid., 1 March 1837. See also Albert Burnside, "The Bible Christians in Canada, 1832-1884," Toronto Graduate School of Theological Studies, 1969, p. 102, for a similar group's troubles with "the dangers of becoming materialistic in the new land of opportunity."

285

The Rebellions of 1837/1838 in Lower Canada, and Their Aftermath

The rebellions in Lower Canada followed a long period of constitutional strife. The appointed Executive and Legislative Councils were almost exclusively English-speaking, while the Assembly was almost entirely French-speaking. Louis-Joseph Papineau, an articulate bilingual lawyer, in 1837 led a number of the Lower Canadian Reformers into open rebellion against the entrenched Conservative elite, who retained control of the provincial revenue.

After the failure of the rebellion of 1837 the British government sent Lord Durham to Canada to investigate the causes of the uprising. He issued his *Report* in late 1838 just after the suppression of the smaller uprising of that same year. To the joy of the Reformers, Durham recommended that responsible government be granted; henceforth the Executive Council and the upper house (the Legislative Council) were to be responsible to the elected Assembly. But he made a second recommendation that, for the Reformers of Lower Canada, initially negated the first. He proposed a union of the Canadas, for the purpose of assimilating the French Canadians.

Britain, while rejecting Durham's recommendation of responsible government, favoured that of union and the assimilation of the French Canadians. In the proposed union the Colonial Office ruled that English would be the only official language and that Upper Canada (which still had a smaller population despite its faster growth rate) would obtain the same number of seats as Lower Canada. It was hoped that the Upper Canadian members would ally with the English-speaking members from Lower Canada (by 1840 the English-speaking minority constituted about twenty-five percent of Lower Canada's population) against the French Canadians.

The results of the union have been vigorously debated. In his essay "The 1840s," Jacques Monet argues that French-speaking reformers worked with the English-speaking allies in the Assembly of the United Canadas to overcome the assimilationist intentions of the union. Maurice Seguin presents an opposing opinion in "A Disaster." In his short contribution, "Insurrections," from *Canada: Unity in Diversity*, Fernand Ouellet extends the discussion by introducing the economic as well as the political factors that contributed to the Rebellions of 1837/38.

Fernand Ouellet's *Lower Canada, 1791-1840* (Toronto: McClelland and Stewart, 1980) is essential for any understanding of the Lower Canadian rebellion. Helen Taft Manning's *The Revolt of French Canada, 1800-1835* (Toronto: Macmillan, 1962), an older study, covers the constitutional struggle. A popular account is Joseph Schull's *Rebellion* (Toronto: Macmillan, 1971). Ramsay Cook has edited a valuable collection of essays on the background to the rebellion, *Constitutionalism and Nationalism in Lower Canada* (Toronto: University of Toronto Press, 1969). In *Les Rebellions de 1837-1838* (Montréal: Editions du Boréal Express, 1983), historian Jean-Paul Bernard includes a summary of the various interpretations of the Lower Canadian uprisings.

Jacques Monet has developed his argument on the Union at greater length in *The Last Cannon Shot: A Study of French-Canadian Nationalism, 1837-1850* (Toronto: University of Toronto Press, 1969), as has Maurice Seguin in *L'idée d'Indépendance au Québec: Génèse et historique* (Trois-Rivières: Le Boréal Express Limitée, 1968). *Lord Durham's Report* has been edited by Gerald M. Craig (Toronto: McClelland and Stewart, 1963). Chester New's *Lord Durham's Mission to Canada* (Toronto: McClelland and Stewart, 1963), first published in 1929, still is useful. For an overview of the 1840s and 1850s, see J.M.S. Careless's *The Union of the Canadas: The Growth of Canadian Institutions, 1841-1857* (Toronto: McClelland and Stewart, 1967).

287

The 1840s *

JACQUES MONET, S.J.

October 19, 1839, was a windy, cool, and dark day; but thousands of Quebecois lined the streets of their ancient city to watch the colourful parade as Sir John Colborne, erect on his black charger and in the full gold and scarlet of a major-general, led the officers of his staff out of the Chateau Saint-Louis towards the harbour. There, in the frigate *Pique*, awaited the Rt. Hon. Charles Poulett Thomson, later Lord Sydenham, the highly competent, forty-year-old English businessman who had been commissioned to come to the Canadas and by "frank and unreserved personal intercourse," reconcile them to Lord Durham's plan for their union. In mid-afternoon, after the whole garrison had assembled, the new governor general, short, slender, supremely self-confident, stepped briskly

*Chapter 9 from *Colonists and Canadiens, 1760–1867*, edited by J. M. S. Careless. Copyright 1971 by Macmillan of Canada. Reprinted by permission of Gage Publishing Limited.

off the gangplank, took the salute, and drove to the Chateau to issue a proclamation announcing his assumption of power. The decade of the rebellions in British North America had effectively ended. That of the union of the Canadas and responsible government had begun.

The Durham *Report* had reached Quebec and Halifax eight months before, and colonists and *Canadiens* had lost no time in expressing their frank and unreserved opinions about its chief recommendations for union and responsible government. They were not uninfluenced, of course, by the reaction of imperial statesmen in the mother country. While these had rather spontaneously agreed to union and assimilation in the Canadas, they had remained sceptical, to say the least, about responsible government. To the latter, the prime minister, Lord Melbourne, declared himself "entirely opposed," the leading spokesman of the opposition dismissed the idea as of "a perfectly subordinate nature," and the colonial secretary opined that responsible government "meant separate independent powers existing in Great Britain and in every separate colony. . . . It would be better to say at once 'Let the two countries separate'." Clearly, Canadian union was one thing, colonial responsible government another. And in the colonies as well, there were not a few ready to draw the same distinction. Some opposed both, others agreed with both, others yet welcomed or resisted either one.

Tory leaders in British North America felt instinctively that both of Durham's proposals would be fatal to their rule. In Nova Scotia Judge Haliburton, who had earned an international reputation with his literary creation Sam Slick, had not even awaited publication of the *Report* to ridicule it. After burying himself in eight hand-carts of assorted documents, he had emerged with his acid *The Bubbles of Canada*, in which, among many other remarks, he commented: "When a nobleman advocates democratic institutions, we give him full credit for the benevolence of his intentions, but we doubt his sanity." In Upper Canada, the chief justice, John Beverley Robinson, reacted in very much the same manner. He also shut himself up for days before publishing a retort which, naturally, censured the union and responsible government, both of which, he foresaw, would involve the upper province in all the troubles of Lower Canada. Later, his sentiments would be echoed by the Committee reports of each house of the tory-dominated legislature in Toronto: while the union might be acceptable for economic reasons, responsible government would "lead to the overthrow of the great Colonial Empire of England."

In Lower Canada, powerful voices had also arisen against Durham's plans. John Neilson, the veteran constitutional reformer and editor, since 1797, of the colony's leading newspaper, the bilingual *Quebec Gazette*, declared himself strongly. He attacked the union project. By its provisions for the rearrangement of the *Canadiens'* ancestral legal system, by its strictures upon French-Canadian culture, by its recommended reorganization of Lower Canadian education, it violated the special national rights repeatedly confirmed to the French by Great Britain, rights enshrined by prescription and defended in two wars at the price of *Canadien* and British blood; by joining two cultural groups into one legislative system, it threatened the whole social order in which property and freedom were secured. This strong opinion was seconded by the powerful French-Canadian clerical elite. The courtly, white-haired Archbishop of Quebec, Joseph Signay declared "notre opposition à un semblable plan," while Bishop Jacques Lartigue, his suffragan in Montreal, called it "très dangereux pour les Catholiques." They both left no doubt they would resist the policy designed, as Bishop Lartigue put it, "pour nous *anglifier*, c'est-à-dire nous décatholiser par une union législative et un système d'écoles neutres."

Some, however, approved. In Nova Scotia Durham's *Report* threw light and hope on Joseph Howe's long struggle for political reform. True, the editor of the *Novascotian* disagreed with any hint of a union with the Canadas: "A Confederation, instead of leaving the Province with its present evils in connection with the Colonial Office, would establish an Office in the backwoods of Canada, more difficult of access than that in London." But with responsible government he was in total accord. Indeed, he wished that "a copy of this *Report* was in the hands of every head of family in Nova Scotia." In Lower Canada, most of the anglophones — Quebec officials and Montreal business leaders — rejoiced expectantly over continued English-speaking rule under the proposed union. The mistake made in 1791 would be righted, interprovincial barriers would be removed from the rich trade which they could now fully control up the great Laurentian waterway, and, since they need no longer fear a hostile French majority in the Assembly, they could finish the St. Lawrence canal system and conquer the natural barriers to their hinterland. Their journals generally gave the *Report* a warm welcome. So, of course, did those of the reformers in Upper Canada. "No document has ever been promulgated in British North America that has given such general satisfaction as this report," wrote Francis Hincks in his Toronto *Examiner* before setting off to organize hundreds of "Durham meetings" and "Durham Constitutional Clubs" with "Durham flags" and "Durham songs," to the benefit of the reform cause. Indeed, in Hamilton, a gathering which mustered some two thousand people — half the population of that town — passed enthusiastic resolutions approving of "responsible government as recommended by Lord Durham." Within six months many such large meetings were held; by the end of the year 1839, the "Durhamites" seemed to constitute a large proportion of the population of Upper Canada. By then Durham's recommendations also seemed to have secured the support of an important number of French Canadians.

In Quebec the highly respected journalist Etienne Parent, editor since 1831 of the nationalist *Le Canadien*, had translated the *Report* as soon as it arrived, and published it by instalments. Then, in a remarkable series of articles published between May and November 1839, he carefully unfolded his thought upon it. Since Great Britain had now determined on the union, his compatriots had no choice but to resign themselves. They must,

289

however, insist on the union's twin: responsible government. "En nous résignant au plan de Lord Durham," he wrote on May 13, "nous entendons qu'on le suive dans toutes ses parties favorables." With and by these two, union and responsible government, he considered the margin of gain was worth the loss. The *Canadiens* would achieve at last their goal of thirty years, victory over the local oligarchy of officials and merchants. By the union they would be joined to the reformers of Upper Canada whose strength they needed and who also needed them. Together, as he foretold on August 2, they would force from English politicians "un gouvernement satisfaisant, responsable, condition indispensable de bonheur et de prospérité." In fact they would even gain the help of reformers throughout the whole of British North America.

290

Parent urged what appeared to French-Canadian *nationalistes* to be the supreme sacrifice. Yet, at the same time, he seemed to be aware that such cultural self-denial might not be necessary. For throughout his penetrating analysis of the *Report*, he underlined that *la survivance* of the *Canadiens* as a distinct national group went hand in hand with the British constitution. It was by using the constitution that had been granted to them that the *Canadiens* had, so far, preserved and developed their own distinctive cultural patterns, the survival of which still depended upon its flexibility and organic vitality. Without it, would they not long ago have fallen under the overwhelming numbers and influence of their immediate neighbours? Would they not have inevitably lost their identity? So, to save themselves, they had twice defended Britain's empire at the price of their blood, and — a subtle thought — had they not kept the other colonists British by setting up a rival culture to that of the merchants and American Loyalists? "Du moment qu'elle n'aura plus à craindre ou à jalouser une nationalité française dans le Bas-Canada," he argued, the English-speaking British American population would sound the tocsin of revolt exactly as it had in 1775.

The British constitution, therefore, and French Canada's distinct nationality were co-relatives: the stronger the nationality the greater the permanence of the Empire, and vice versa. And once the *Canadiens* had achieved responsible government, they could utilize it to nullify assimilation, and open up a broadening future for their language, their institutions, and their nationality. Or, as Francis Hincks wrote to Parent's close associate, the young politician Louis-Hippolyte LaFontaine: "On the Union question you should not mind Lord Durham's motives but the effect of the scheme. . . . I have already told you that I have always supported the Union *without reference to details* because by it alone I felt convinced we would have a majority *that would make our tyrants succumb*."

All this might well be, but as the new decade opened, the times for French Canada seemed dark and dangerous indeed. Disillusion and disappointment had set in. In November 1839, Governor Poulett Thomson had summoned Colborne's old Special Council to Montreal and submitted the union project in a closed session, calling for a vote before any of those likely to oppose it could discuss amendments. The terms, besides, were clearly unfair to Lower Canada. Its population of 650 000 was to have in the united legislature the same representation as the upper province's 450 000, and the Upper Canadian debt of £1 200 000 (huge compared to Lower Canada's £95 000) was to be charged to both. And obviously the terms contained nothing about responsible government. The governor next moved on to Toronto, where Durhamite ardour for union seemed to cool in proportion to the decline in guarantees of responsible government. He won acceptance for the union in the Upper Canadian legislature, but at the price of more discrimination against Lower Canada. Now, the *Canadiens* learned, the capital of the province would have to be moved to Upper Canada (to, of all places, what they came to call, "cet enfer de Kingston"); and English would become the only official language of the united Parliament. Clearly this was not the union Hincks had dreamed of, nor that Parent had been ready to accept. In any case the Union Act went through the British Parliament later in 1840. Yet when, on February 10, 1841, the union was officially proclaimed, almost every French Canadian greeted it with horror. "Nous entrons cette nuit dans une route obscure," sighed John Neilson, "à l'entrée de laquelle sont le mensonge et la corruption."

291

II

Despite *Canadien* misgivings, the decade would be for all the colonists as well as for themselves one of progress and resolvings. There would be growth and change of pace. There would be signs and symbols of prosperity. As Nova Scotia's seaborne commerce mounted further, Halifax — incorporated as a city in 1841 — virtually became the capital of the North Atlantic. The British North American Mail Steam Packet Company, founded by the native Haligonian Samuel Cunard, was sending "steamships on schedule" across the ocean, and gained a practical monopoly of transatlantic steam navigation. When the city was connected to Boston by telegraph in 1849, it was there that American newspapermen came to pick up the latest news from Europe which, arriving in the morning, could be published in New York evening journals. In New Brunswick, despite a short-lived decline in the second third of the century, the timber trade continued on its exciting upward curve. As for Prince Edward Island, where the four thousand inhabitants of Charlottetown proudly watched the rise of their fine new provincial building (in somewhat dated Georgian style), the province had now achieved a notable degree of farm-based self-sufficiency: oats forging ahead as its principal earner of credit. And Newfoundland, too, enjoyed increased prosperity, as sealing developed markedly. Vats for the manufacture of seal oil grew ever larger at Fogo, Twillingate, Greenspond, and Trinity. Some years as many as 650 000 seals were shot or clubbed to death (to be exact, 685 530 in the peak year, 1844). Gold bullion also was acquired as Spanish vessels, encouraged by the preferential duties of their government, came to buy fish at island ports.

Although during the widespread depression late in the decade there were business failures — Joseph Howe claimed that in New Brunswick there was "scarcely a solvent house from Saint John to Grand Falls," though skilled workmen abandoned the shores of Fundy for Australia and New Zealand, while Nova Scotia suffered from the shrinking of overseas trade after 1847, the Maritimes, generally, would end the 1840s in a sounder financial state than they had begun it. Howe, exhuberant and energetic as usual, might well exhort his fellow colonists: "Boys, brag of your country. When I'm abroad I brag of everything that Nova Scotia is, has, or can produce; and when they beat me at everything else, I turn around on them and say: 'How high does your tide rise?'"

In the new united Province of Canada, the tide continued to flow with British immigrants. They arrived, some 25 000 to 40 000 a year, to boost the total population up to near the two million mark — a net increase during the decade of some 692 000. Most travelled to the chief settlement frontier in the upper section, now denominated Canada West, doubling its population in ten years to some 952 000 (compared with some 890 000 in Canada East). There they established themselves on the large fertile land area stretching inland from Lake Huron, or southward towards Lake Erie, or again north of Toronto or along the Ottawa. Some went to the urban communities: London in the heart of the western peninsula with its population of some 2000 in 1841; Hamilton, 3400, at the head of Lake Ontario. Others went to Kingston, the stone-built garrison town of fewer than six hundred houses which had suddenly become the capital of an enormous province, where hundreds of labourers were busy remodelling the municipal hospital into a Parliament. More still travelled to Toronto, a city most definitely on the move: it would mushroom from 14 000 in 1841 to over 30 000 in 1851. There, according to one traveller in 1842,

all is in a whirl and fizz, and one must be in the fashion; everything and everybody seem to go by steam; and if you meet an acquaintance in the street he is sure to have arrived from some other place three or four hundred miles off, and to be starting upon a similar expedition in some other direction. After a short experience of this mode of life one quite forgets that there is such a thing as repose or absence of noise, and begins to think that the blowing of steam is a necessary accompaniement and consequence of the ordinary operation of the elements.

The fact was that in Toronto as throughout the West, the 1840s were breeding a considerable class of businessmen closely involved with the extensive growth of the western agrarian community, supplying its wants and marketing its crops. By the end of the decade, these would shape a new upper and middle class of merchants and enterpreneurs — men such as the Scots importer Isaac Buchanan, the Irish wholesale merchant William McMaster, or the American stove manufacturers Charles and Edward Gurney. They would ally with professional men and "gentry" in the towns or countryside to prompt and guide the results of the population explosion. They would prosper, of course, from the increased sales of wheat and the steady expansion of the Ottawa lumber empire. They would build numerous churches (in percentage the western population in 1841 was roughly 22 per cent Anglican, 20 per cent Presbyterian, 17 per cent Methodist, and some 14 per cent Roman Catholic). And they would support the constant proliferation of newspapers across Canada West, and even the foreshadowing of a periodical press, evidenced by the *Victoria Magazine*, "a cheap periodical for the Canadian people," founded at Belleville in 1846. This, indeed, was edited by Susanna Moodie and her husband; but though she also wrote for the similar (and longer-lived) Montreal *Literary Garland*, her classic account of pioneer life in Upper Canada, *Roughing it in the Bush*, was published in England, as were a number of other literary works on Canadian immigrant and pioneering experience, which then found a ready British market.

At the same time a more populous, settled Canada West was developing an effective, publicly maintained school system. In 1844 the powerful and controversial Methodist leader, Egerton Ryerson, was appointed Chief Superintendent of Education for Upper Canada. Under Governor Sydenham, the Union Parliament had passed the first of the decade's important series of school acts in 1841, essentially enabling the two sections of the union to develop their own patterns of state-supported education. That for the Upper Canadian half became basically one of non-discriminational schools, though with provisions for separate schools for the religious minority. That for the Lower Canadian section provided for religious-based, or confessional schools — Catholic for the majority, Protestant for the minority. But in Upper Canada it was the work of Ryerson, above all, that established a system of elementary public education across the West, dependent on central grants and standards but with a good deal of local authority (and some taxes) in the keeping of locally elected school boards. In short, the basis of the Ontario school system was laid during the 1840s. But more than that, the decade also witnessed notable beginnings in Ontario higher education. The Methodists' Victoria College emerged at Cobourg; Ryerson was its first president before he became educational superintendent, the post he was to hold for over thirty years. Queen's was founded as a Presbyterian college at Kingston in 1841, while the long-delayed Anglican King's College finally began teaching in Toronto in 1842.

As for the eastern, largely French-Canadian section of the united province, despite Neilson's dark forebodings — and perhaps even more so Durham's disparaging assessment of French Canada — the union soon generated a new ferment and vitality among the *Canadiens*. They grew out of the "grand découragement" that had hung over the beginnings of the decade. Gradually they caught the infectious nineteenth-century spirit of progress. They became more aware of their national identity and, as the 1840s moved on, they became restless to express it. In cultural affairs, in newspapers, literature, and thought; in their Church; in reviving industry; they looked at things with new pleasure. At the beginning of 1843 there were in French Canada five large bi-weeklies, *Le Canadien* and *Le Journal de Québec* in the old capital; *L'Aurore*, *Les Mélanges Religieux*, and *La Minerve* in Montreal. By 1850 these had multiplied to over a dozen, and the older

293

ones now appeared three times a week to compete with the new radical *L'Avenir* and with a host of other, keen little papers. There were also the anthologies such as Michel Bibaud's *Encyclopédie Canadienne*, in which the French could read chapters from François Xavier Garneau's new national *Histoire du Canada*, and a steady stream of productions from native authors: wild, romantic novels, like Joseph Doutre's *Les Fiancés de 1812*, theatrical plays like *Le Rebelle*, endless epic poems — uneven, ugly tangles of captive heroines, brigands, handsome officers, passionate lovers, but for all that, the first drafts of what would one day be the *Canadiens'* own national literature.

They also flocked to lectures, filling parish halls and hotel lobbies to hear new, exciting ideas percolating over from the salons of Europe on the most modern topics of the day: education, hygiene, exports, independence of character, and "la position de la femme." Especially they listened to Etienne Parent. In five great lectures delivered in Montreal between 1846 and 1849, the former editor of *Le Canadien* now turned civil servant, outlined a new social and economic philosophy which, had they heeded it, might well have given the *Canadiens* the key to the new economic order then being founded. He proposed sweeping reforms in all social, educational, and religious institutions; more importantly, in the habits of thought of the habitants. He was not followed, of course, as fully as he would have wished. "Il a exprimé," noted *La Minerve* on December 18, 1848, "beaucoup d'idées qui paraissaient toutes neuves à une grande partie de son auditoire." Still, in a way, he testified to the new mood.

So, in another way, did the new Bishop of Montreal, Monseigneur Ignace Bourget. Shortly after succeeding Bishop Lartigue in 1840, this energetic and authoritarian young churchman began to renew the face of Catholicism in French Canada. Within his first year, he had organized a great mission throughout his diocese, preached by Bishop de Forbin-Janson, one of France's foremost orators. Between September 1840 and December 1841 the latter travelled across French Canada, visiting some sixty villages and preaching rousing sermons to crowds numbering sometimes as many as ten thousand. Meanwhile the Bishop of Montreal had left for Europe to arrange for the immigration from France of the Oblate Order (December 1841) and the Jesuits (May 1842), of the Ladies of the Sacred Heart (December 1842), and of the Sisters of the Good Shepherd (June 1844). Before the end of the decade, he had also founded two Canadian religious congregations of his own, and established the Saint Vincent-de-Paul Society. Of course, this enthusiasm, this multiplication of religious houses and charitable foundations spread beyond Canada East to new fields in Toronto, the northwest and the Oregon country on the Pacific: "Cette vaste chaîne de sièges épiscopaux," commented the *Mélanges Religieux* in 1843 on the occasion of the consecration of a French-Canadian bishop in Oregon, "qui doit s'étendre un jour, nous l'espérons de la mer jusqu'à la mer: *a mari usque ad mare*." Essentially, however, it was a Lower Canadian phenomenon. So was the excess of enthusiasm over temperance.

In Canada West a temperance movement developed in response to the frontier brawling and family suffering caused by the "liquor evil." Toronto's Temperance Society had over a thousand members in 1841. In New Brunswick an unfortunate government would experiment with prohibition in the 1850s. But in French Canada East the movement was part of the Catholic revival and turned upon the personality of "le petit père Chiniquy," a sensitive, frail, passionate young abbé who was obsessed with the problem of alcohol. He began his crusade in March 1840 by administering the pledge to thirteen hundred of his parishioners at Beauport, near Quebec. Thence he progressed, brimful with temperance, across the Quebec diocese. In the Montreal district he sometimes enrolled as many as seventeen thousand people in one month. In fact, he moved Montrealers to such a pitch of sobriety that they planned to erect a marble statue of him on Place d'Armes: in his left hand he would carry a tablet with a bilingual history of the temperance cause and his own name in gold letters, and from his right hand there would fall through the fingers a fountain of water — the beverage he recommended so highly. In 1849, he gave some fifteen hundred sermons in one hundred and twenty parishes to over 200 000 people. In all of this, of course, the Apostle of Temperance was doing more than fostering sobriety: he was witnessing that the Catholic Church in French Canada had become one of the more powerful advocates of change.

295

Indeed, Bishop Bourget was concerned with more than spiritual things. He followed Parent's lectures with great interest, and detected among the *Canadiens* a growing regard for business matters. True, the French Canadians as a whole remained less overtly concerned with these than their new compatriots in the western section or in Montreal; but their leaders were. Bourget gave his patronage to a new *Banque d'Epargne*; the Sulpicians in Montreal became proprietors of large blocks of shares in the proposed Saint Lawrence and Atlantic Railway; other leaders started a new steamship company — La Compagnie du Richelieu — and invested in the *Banque du Peuple*. When Joseph Masson, owner of extensive seigneuries and a most influential importer, died in 1847, he was reputed to be the wealthiest merchant in the two Canadas.

As for the other classes, they could no longer consider economic activity to be subordinate: their newspapers were filled with stories of new railway projects and steamship services. Besides, the union had evidently brought them a return of prosperity. The first Canadian agricultural protective tariff in 1843; the acts of 1844 and 1845 that raised grants to farmers to £150 for each county in Lower Canada; the employment provided by the beginning of the new Beauharnois Canal, and by the gradual increase of shipping in Quebec city from about 12 000 tons in 1841–42 to 40 000 tons in 1846; the fleet of paddle-wheelers sailing the St. Lawrence between Montreal and Quebec, and the construction of the greatest of them all, the *John Munn*, the most luxurious and fastest ship in Canada, called "le roi du Saint Laurent," launched at Quebec on May 22, 1847 — all of this brought encouragement.

It may be that in bare numbers of population, the *Canadiens* had become a minority in the united province, but due especially to their high birth and declining death rates, they were growing proportionately in the eastern section. Montreal, where the proportion of the population of roughly 40 000 in 1841 was some 60 per cent anglophone, increased to 45 per cent (of 57 000) French-Canadian in 1851; Quebec would rise to 58 per cent French; the Eastern Townships from some 27 per cent French in 1841 to almost 41 per cent in 1851, as British immigration there tailed off. As for the chief cities, Quebec, of course, was the busy centre of the "immigrant trade," Canada's chief lumber port and shipbuilding centre, British North America's military headquarters, and French Canada's religious capital. But thanks to the union, Montreal was becoming the economic heart of the commercial metropolis of the province and in 1845 became the political capital as well. There the aggressive mercantile and financial community established along Notre-Dame and Saint James streets directed the economy, if not the lives, of the Irish and *Canadien* labourers, of the new immigrants from Scotland, and of the buoyant habitant farmers from the countryside come to the daily market.

As the climate of opinion in cultural, religious and economic affairs grew more enthusiastic, the *Canadiens* found anew their joyous and hospitable sense of fellowship. They began to join new social and patriotic clubs. Napoléon Aubin, a Swiss emigré and *littérateur*, founded the Société Saint Jean Baptiste in Quebec in June 1842, and seems to have set the example. In 1843, Ludger Duvernay, editor of Montreal's *La Minerve*, decided to resurrect the Saint Jean Baptiste Society there. Within the year several others were set up. And on December 17, 1844, some two hundred young Montrealers met in the chambers of another recent foundation, the *Société d'Histoire naturelle*, to start the more famous *Institut Canadien* that would have a noted influence as a centre for advanced liberal political and social thinking.

From commerce to literature, in church and in the salon, the *Canadiens* were out of discouragement, out of the misery of the thirties. They placed no limit now on their enterprise.

III

Before the end of the decade the *Canadiens* had become veritable political masters of the union. This was no easy task — after all, the project had been designed to crush their national aspirations. But it was Louis-Hippolyte LaFontaine's achievement, above all. He was not the scholar Parent was; he had none of Papineau's passion, none of John Neilson's urbanity. He had no charm, no sense of humour. But as circumstances would make him French Canada's main spokesman, he revealed that he could think clearly and practically about his nationality and about its connection with the British constitution. Like Etienne Parent, he understood how responsible government could bring the *Canadiens* to overcome the past. It was not retreat into a French Lower Canada they needed as much as to deal with the British on their own terms, to argue on grounds which no British subject or statesman could deny. Soon he came to identify his country's cause with his own ambitions, and then he found that his personality could be turned into an invaluable political asset. His strange mixture of ambition and stubborn idealism coincided well with the constant pressure needed to force the concession of responsible government. Before the end of the decade he would head a responsible cabinet, and be the first among his own people to actually express and direct the national aspirations of French Canada.

When union was proclaimed in 1841, most French Canadians agreed with John Neilson, the powerful Denis-Benjamin Viger, (Papineau's cousin and coadjutor), and the various other politicians of the Papineau family who favoured a separatist solution. Militant idealists, these found the key to *la survivance* in the isolation of French Canada upon a territory where the *Canadiens*, living as a compact national group, would be undisputed masters, secure against alien Anglo-Saxon contamination. The union having been adopted in spite of them, they decided to cooperate as little and as superficially in politics as possible. They decided to join on a mere temporary basis whichever one of the Upper Canadian parties offered them the most interesting concessions. Later, in 1845, in another form of abstention, they invented the theory of "double majority," a device according to which a law of the union would not be valid until it was sanctioned by a distinct majority of the two groups, English and French. Still later, after Neilson's death in 1847 and the return from his Paris exile of the great, uncompromising hero, Louis-Joseph Papineau, these ardent nationalists improved upon isolation by promoting the idea of a French-Canadian national republic, which, joining the American republic as a 34th state, could become a little Louisiana of the north.

297

LaFontaine thought otherwise. Ten days after the Act of Union was announced, he accordingly published his celebrated *Adresse aux Electeurs de Terrebonne*. In this, he admitted that the union was unjust — "elle est un acte d'injustice et de despotisme." But it did not follow, he argued, that the French should abdicate their rights as British subjects, and adopt a course which must inevitably lead to national suicide. No, they must play their rightful part, fight the next election, then unite with sympathizers from Upper Canada to form a political majority that could force through responsible government. With this, "le principal moteur de la constitution anglaise," they could win back all that they had lost. But without it, there could be no political liberty, no cultural future. The call was clear: accept the union, join with the reformers of Canada West, force the Colonial Office to grant responsible government. Fortunately he found western reform associates, like sharp-witted Francis Hincks, eager to urge the cause of "Reform alliance," and the austere, clear-sighted Robert Baldwin, who commanded wide respect for his unswerving devotion to the principle of responsible rule.

Nevertheless, LaFontaine spent nearly ten years accomplishing his purpose. It was not until the elections of 1844 that he succeeded in rallying a majority of his fellow *Canadien* politicians. And it was not until 1846 that he managed to win the support and influence of the clergy, which until then feared his projects of school reform. He had to suffer the effects of the political reversals of his friends, the reformers of Upper Canada, who were temporarily beaten by western tory-conservative forces between 1844 and 1847, led by able William Draper and the demagogic but forceful Sir Allan MacNab. LaFontaine even had to face the beginnings of a revolt among his own followers in 1846–47. Not until the end of the decade could he be certain of victory. Still, after a decade of fistfights on electoral platforms, scandals, riots and racial fury; after a luminous, dynamic, and flexible partnership with Robert Baldwin; and strengthened at last by the almost unanimous support of his compatriots, LaFontaine achieved his goal.

298

He needed Robert Baldwin as leader of the Upper Canadian reformers, who could prove to *Canadien* electors that Upper Canadians were aware of their sensitivities. This Baldwin did, for example, in refusing to enter the Executive Council in 1841 because he considered the Oath of Supremacy he was asked to take would be insulting to the Pope, and thus to French-Canadian feelings and traditions. Another time, in a warm gesture towards the *Canadien* leader, Baldwin persuaded his own constituents in the Fourth Riding of York in Canada West to elect LaFontaine in his place. At that time Etienne Parent underlined the significance of the gesture in his *Canadien*: "Que je vous dise un mot des braves gens que j'ai rencontrés à Newmarket. Si tous les habitants du Haut-Canada leur ressemblent, je peux prédire les plus brillants résultats de l'Union des Canadas." LaFontaine also needed the help of that gentle gentleman, the governor general, Sir Charles Bagot (Sydenham's successor) a man of the world, fluent in French, who moved through Lower Canada in 1842 conversing with *jeux d'esprit* and wit. It was his task to prove that the union did not necessarily mean assimilation, indeed that some good might come out of it. And this he did by conceding to the *Canadiens'* most urgent wishes in education, in the judiciary, in the area of municipal reform, indeed in a long list of popular appointments, not least of which were LaFontaine's and Baldwin's to the attorney-generalships of the province. Then, too, LaFontaine needed the help of Francis Hincks, the best election-winner in the two Canadas, who moved to Montreal in early 1844, and more than anyone else created the powerful reform alliance which allowed LaFontaine and Baldwin eventually to dominate the Assembly — and the Canadas.

Once he had become political master in his own house, LaFontaine set to work to transform the administration and implement reforms in the municipal and judicial systems, and much else besides. He also made certain, excellent politician that he was, that by a judicious allotment of favours all the *Canadiens* became permanently involved in self-rule. For two generations, the *Canadien* professional class had been struggling to secure an outlet for its ambitions: so now, with a kind of bacterial thoroughness it began to invade every vital organ of government, and divide up among its members hundreds of posts as judges, Queen's Counsels, justices of the peace, medical examiners, school inspectors, militia captains, postal clerks, mail conductors, census commissioners. And as the flatteries and salaries of office percolated to other classes of society — from merchants who wanted seats on the Legislative Council down to the impoverished habitants on the crowded seigneuries — the French Canadians came to realize how parliamentary democracy could be more than an admirable ideal. It was also a profitable fact. And henceforth, because of LaFontaine's crucial role in achieving responsible government, there could be guaranteed for all of them the possibility of room at the top.

In addition, LaFontaine turned his energies to development and expansion. In the Eastern Townships and the Saguenay region, he pushed forward a new policy of colonization, of improvement of agricultural methods, and of reform in depth of the seigneurial system. In education, he encountered the new primary schools being founded by the new Superintendent of Education for Lower Canada, Jean-Baptiste Meilleur, and the multiplication of new *collèges classiques* climaxed, after the end of the decade, by the grant of a royal charter to Laval University in Quebec. Indeed, by 1848, he had become identified with the mission to defend French culture and language. Hence when he finally came to power, he wished to inaugurate his regime by formally reinstating the official use of his mother tongue.

At the beginning of 1848, the reformers swept the elections in both Canadas. Lord Elgin, the statesmanlike governor general who had come to Canada the year before, called upon the leaders of the Assembly majority to form a government, as indeed it was now British policy to do. He turned to LaFontaine to head the ministry, since he had the larger following, with Baldwin as his leading colleague. LaFontaine now had his moment for the reinstatement of the French language, the supreme moment of the colony's political and ceremonial life: the opening of Parliament in his own city of Montreal. Accordingly, on January 18, 1849, amid traditional panoply, and through rows of troops that had taken their places like monuments along the route, bright scarlet against the snowbanks, Governor General Elgin slid smartly in a large sleigh down Notre-Dame Street to the Parliament at the Marché Sainte-Anne. There, white-plumed and splendid in his dark-blue and silver tunic he proceeded to the red chamber, crowded for the occasion by dark, formal-coated councillors and their wives in bright dresses. Seated under the huge red and gold canopy, he read his Speech from the Throne. He paused and, his courtly diction filling the chamber, he himself repeated it once over in elegant French. Thus, in one fine, royal, unprecedented gesture, he wiped out forever the last national iniquity of the union. And as he stepped out a few minutes later into the fresh and open air, the fanfare must have seemed to ring out with greater sound. In all events, as the vice-regal procession receded, LaFontaine's old opponent Denis-Benjamin Viger exclaimed in tears:

"Que je me sens soulagé d'entendre dans ma langue les paroles du trône!" Indeed, asked *La Minerve*, "Quand notre nationalité a-t-elle été plus respectée, plus honorée?"

IV

In Upper Canada, too, the LaFontaine-Baldwin combination that had taken office in March 1838, as the first completely reform party cabinet, brought notable changes to laws and institutions. For one thing the vexed "university question" of the decade — as to the nature of the publicly endowed Upper Canadian provincial university, King's College — was given a lasting settlement. In the mid-forties various bills had been put forward to make that institution a completely secular state university, to share its endowment among several religiously based colleges, or to work out some form of association for them all. None had succeeded, as advanced reformers sought full secularization, confirmed tories defended an Anglican King's College, and moderate conservatives sought some compromise, often backed by the various religious college interests. But in 1849, the reform government secularized King's College, though denominational institutions could have a loose affiliation with the new nonsectarian University of Toronto that replaced it. From this, ultimately, would stem a federation of private denominational colleges with the public university, a significant model for Canadian higher education.

Equally significant was the Municipal Corporations Act of 1849, that set up a pattern of municipal self-government throughout Canada West. This aptly christened "Baldwin Act" really extended its initiator's belief in responsible rule into the vital area of the local community. It created a complete system of elected, locally responsible authorities, both rural and urban, that would remain at the core of Ontario's political and administrative life for well over a century, and have influence as well on the development of other municipal institutions in the far broader Canada of a later day. Also important, at least for its own day, was the Guarantee Act of 1849, put through by Francis Hincks as the finance minister of the new regime. The guarantee it offered for the bonds of projected railways that everyone was talking about by the close of the forties did much to encourage their rapid construction in the next decade.

Whatever the consequences of the coming of responsible government in Canada, it no less made its impact in the Atlantic provinces. Indeed, Nova Scotia was actually first to achieve it in British North America, for in January 1848, two months before Canada, a responsible party cabinet of reformers took office in Halifax, headed by James Boyle Uniacke and Joseph Howe. Howe himself had shaped a powerful campaign for the cause, skilfully directing Durham's ideas against the Halifax oligarchy and, in particular, writing a widely read set of public letters to Lord John Russell, then colonial secretary, refuting the latter's objections to colonial self-government with telling wit and realism. After bringing down one government by duly parliamentary methods, Howe perhaps was ill-advised to join a supposedly "non-party" coalition Executive Council in 1840 under a new governor, Lord Falkland. But when he found he could make no further headway with his tory colleagues there, he went into opposition in 1843, and worked vigorously at building a strong party front in the Assembly. Success came under still another governor, Sir John Harvey, who now — like Elgin in Canada — was authorized by changed imperial policy to accept a government from whatever party could control the elected house. And the reformers carried the elections of 1847, so that when the Assembly met in 1848, they took office. Nova Scotia had achieved democratic self-government "without the shedding of a drop of blood . . . the breaking of a pane of glass," as Howe liked to proclaim.

New Brunswick did less to attain self-government for itself. Indeed, politics in that province were relatively uneventful during most of the decade. The external irritant of the disputed Maine-New Brunswick boundary was finally settled by the Ashburton Treaty of 1842, although New Brunswickers might complain that the settlement took away valued tracts of timberland as well as blocking off their shortest land routes to Quebec. In internal affairs, the Assembly by the late thirties had already gained such full control of crown revenues and lands (and thus timber resources) that reform leaders like Lemuel Wilmot saw little need to press further. There was a shifting succession of coalition administrations under Sir William Colebrooke, governor from 1841 to 1848, but personal contests for office and patronage did not really alter the general political tranquility — "the Reign of Smoothery," the Saint John *Loyalist* termed it. In 1848 an earnest new governor, Sir Edmund Head (who would later succeed Elgin in Canada) did seek to apply the principles of responsible government that had now been recognized by the imperial authorities; yet New Brunswick was only gradually adapting to that system at the end of the decade. More meaningful perhaps, was the underlying fact that by 1850 the business power of Saint John had wrestled ascendancy away from the old conservative gentry of Fredericton, and so would dominate in politics thereafter.

In Prince Edward Island through much of the forties, Governor Sir Henry Huntley carried on a bitter feud with the Speaker of the Assembly, Joseph Pope, whom he regarded as one of the dangerous "party of the Escheators" who sought "unlimited control." Thus he opposed Pope's resolution in the house in 1846 for responsible government, and poured scorn on "this abstruse subject." But then the change in imperial policy revised his ideas. Still, there were further angry struggles in the little island political cockpit before a responsible ministry took office in 1851. As for the larger, still angrier cockpit of Newfoundland, political clashes there were so acute that the movement to popular self-government even went into reverse for part of the decade. Wild election violence at Carbonear in 1840 brought the suspension of representative government, and when it was resumed in 1843 it was within a single mixed chamber of appointed and elected members. Under more conciliatory leaders, chastened Newfoundland politicians made the system work. By 1848, in fact, as they saw

301

responsible government being applied to neighbouring colonies, they began to seek it for themselves, notably through a "Catholic Liberal" party that emerged under Philip Francis Little. The divided, scantily organized island was scarcely ready for it yet, however. And when responsible rule did come, in the next decade, it was chiefly because British policy was now generally granting it to all white colonies of settlement.

There was no question of granting responsible government to the rest of British North America. Apart from trading posts and missions, in the immense wilderness area west of the bounds of Canada there was still only the little colony at Red River in the keeping of the Hudson's Bay Company; and it was too remote and immature for such a grant, though it was developing a regular administrative and court system. In 1849, it is true, a new colony was founded on Vancouver Island, after the Oregon Treaty of 1846, extending the boundary along the 49th parallel from the Rockies to the Pacific, had brought British interests to withdraw from south of that line. But the island colony was still under Bay Company auspices, and it would not rise to representative institutions for several years. In all the lands between, from New Caledonia (that is now mainland British Columbia) to the posts along the Peace, Saskatchewan and Athabaska, the Bay Company fur trader held sway; and generally gave just treatment to the Indians of the region, who were, after all, the essential suppliers and customers of the great fur monopoly.

302

V

The Canadian union had turned out to be a positive achievement of the forties; responsible government assuredly was another. But the decade also had its disasters, its dangers and depression. Indeed, before its end it would see new violence and destruction. One such disaster was fire, given crowded, flimsy houses in the towns and inadequate water supplies. In Quebec in 1845 two spectacular conflagrations almost totally destroyed the city. In the fire of May 28 about one hundred Quebecois perished and nearly 16 000 were rendered homeless, while on June 28, 12 000 homes were burned, leaving another 18 000 without shelter. Colonists throughout British North America came to the relief of the ancient capital, and over £100 000 came from private donations in Britain, Queen Victoria herself contributing liberally from the privy purse. The Quebec disaster had another unexpected, but not uncharacteristic, effect: some ten dozen dispossessed and unemployed prostitutes had to move to Montreal.

A year later, on June 9, 1846, St. John's was almost wiped out, at a cost of over 12 000 homeless and a million pounds in estimated damages. Colonists and *Canadiens* were brought together in catastrophe, and liberal donations were subscribed to ease the grim tragedies.

Nor was this all. In 1847 a host of destitute and starving immigrants began arriving in British North America, fleeing from famine and dispossession in Ireland. With these "famine Irish" came dreaded disease, to be a constant threat to the end of the decade. "L'année 1847," wrote Ludger Duvernay in *La Minerve*, "sera nommée dans notre histoire l'année de l'émigration. Près de cent mille malheureux ont quitté l'Irlande pour venir chercher du pain sur le rivage du Saint Laurent; pour comble de malheur la fièvre les a décimés." "La fièvre" was the dreaded typhus. Within the year, some 16 000 Irish immigrants would die of it, and miserable thousands of *Canadiens* and colonists be infected. Government, the churches, and private charity struggled desperately but could not cope. Doctors and clergy died, newspapers listing new obituaries in each new issue. "I visited the [immigrant] sheds one Sunday afternoon," an old Montrealer reminisced some fifty years later. "They formed a large square with a court in the centre, where the coffins were piled; some empty awaiting the dead, and some full awaiting burial. I tried the weight of one coffin standing above, another which appeared to be empty, but on lifting the lid found a skeleton within. On one occasion I saw the mayor, [John Mills] and Lord Elgin visiting the ships on horseback, and after- *303* wards riding towards the sheds." Mayor Mills of Montreal, Bishop Michael Power of Toronto, Monseigneur Hyacinthe Hudon, the Vicar-General of Montreal, and eighteen nuns from Quebec all succumbed to the fever, along with so many other inhabitants and immigrants alike in port cities and inland towns across the country.

After these squalid miseries, 1848 seemed healthy by comparison. Yet, by the beginning of June, the abbé Félix Cazeau, who led the relief for the sick in Quebec, already had more orphans to place than he normally had in a whole year. Then in 1849 cholera replaced typhus; and between July and September, some 1200 died in Quebec and 974 in Montreal. 1850 would bring some relief. But throughout the colonies there lingered a feeling of disturbance and insecurity.

It might well. For throughout the last half of the decade, forces from outside the province, from the republic to the south and from the mother country, seriously threatened the colony's economic stability. In 1845 and 1846 the American Congress passed the Drawback Laws remitting duties on goods destined for Canada which were imported through the United States, and on Canadian exports sent overseas the same way. Upper Canadians would now be able to use the Erie Canal route to the sea. And in fact Montreal merchants grew increasingly desperate, as more and more western wheat went by the Erie and imports passing through Montreal for the inland country declined sharply. The whole St. Lawrence commercial system was now fully exposed to American competition. Meanwhile, in Britain, a vigorous railway boom was coming to an end, with consequent disastrous results for Canadian timber merchants. Moreover, in 1846 the powerful agitation of the British Anti-Corn Law League culminated in the repeal of the duties on grain, the climax of the advancing British movement to free trade. Britain's adoption of free trade might have removed earlier objections there to the recognition of responsible government, since free trade doctrines saw little need for closely controlled and subordinated colonies. But at the same time it loosened the bonds and removed preferential duties between 1846 and 1849 that had given Canada much of its economic prosperity. The results, wrote Lord Elgin, were to ruin "at once mill-owners, forwarders, and merchants. The consequence is that private property is unsaleable in Canada, and not a shilling can be raised on the credit of the Province."

The fact was that British North America, and especially the Canadian merchants in the staple trades, were feeling the impact of world trade depression, which spread from 1847 onward from Halifax to Sarnia, as well as through Europe and America. But the most obvious factor was the change in imperial trade policy, and the removal of the old protections given colonial commerce. To solve all this, somehow, the new prime minister, LaFontaine, turned to his new inspector-general, Francis Hincks, who set himself to the unenviable task with his customary efficiency. He began commercial negotiations which would eventually lead to a reciprocal trade treaty with the United States. And after persuading his fellow reformers Lemuel Wilmot of New Brunswick and William Young of Nova Scotia to initiate a trade conference in Halifax, he travelled down to the Maritime capital to exchange views — and talk railways. By the end of the 1840s the world depression was lifting. It grew apparent that the prosperity of the first two-thirds of the decade would return. But not quite yet.

There was still the question of rebellion losses — a complicated piece of legislation debated on and off throughout the decade and designed to compensate those whose property had been destroyed during the Rebellions of 1837–38. Upper Canadians had received £40 000 in 1845; and in February 1849 LaFontaine introduced a bill to cover damages suffered in Lower Canada. For the new prime minister and his council the measure was designed as a broad unstinting gesture that would finally put to rest the bitterness of 1837. But for many in Montreal's commercial class, already suffering the pangs of deep financial depression, and for many of the tory politicians who had just lost political control of Lower Canada for the first time since 1791, the issue became a symbol. They reacted with all the primitive, panic-stricken, almost standard fury of the recently dispossessed. On the evening after Lord Elgin had given his royal assent to the Rebellion Losses Bill (April 25, 1849), a tory mob gathered in Montreal, some fifteen hundred strong, and broke into the Parliament, rioting, tearing, smashing. Some threw rocks at the great clock, others hacked at the throne; one, mounting the steps of the speaker's chair pronounced: "I dissolve this French House"; another, seizing the splendid silver-gilt mace ornamented with Canadian beavers and the imperial crown, hurled it out a window to the excited crowd below. Someone set a fire. Soon the flames, feeding on the escaping gas and whipped by the wind blowing through the broken windows, were burning out of control, licking the walls about the roof. At midnight the rioters were still there running about the building, signing, cavorting, yelling, celebrating the ruin (they thought!) of French domination. They had turned away the firemen, cut the hose, and the huge bonfire raged uncontrolled high into the black night.

In the spring and summer of 1849, Montreal's tory commercial community could concentrate on nothing but French and reform domination. And after a contagion of violence — a senseless attack on the person of the governor general, the destruction of LaFontaine's home and Hinck's furniture, several weeks of breathless disorders which, if not in lives lost at least in property damage and national bitterness, formed a revealing counterpart to the rebellions that closed the previous decade — Montreal businessmen turned to what they considered more practical means of regaining control of the colony. By abolishing the Corn Laws, they reasoned, the British had ceased to protect their own; by acknowledging responsible government they had abandoned them to what they termed "the tender mercies of a voluble French faction." Why not, therefore, join the United States, and even at the cost of being American, regain control of the colony for Anglo-Saxon Protestants? On October 11, 1849, they issued the Annexation Manifesto.

305

To Louis-Joseph Papineau and the radical separatists dubbed *rouges* who had been campaigning for repeal of the union and for annexation, this "démarche imprévue," as Papineau put it, "semble être un secours providentiel qui nous advienne." They signed the Manifesto and with their new-found allies set off on what turned out to be a short-lived press and speech campaign in favour of "la colossale République du nouveau-monde." Short-lived because *Canadiens* remained unattracted by this small *nationaliste* republican head somehow attached to a larger anglophone tory body. Short-lived also because conservatives outside the metropolis and in Canada West seemed equally unimpressed, and reformers ardently hostile. At a grand meeting of the British North American League in Kingston in July, they had overwhelmingly declared their British allegiance. By the end of the year, annexationism in its tory and *nationaliste* varieties had been reduced to an ineffectual nuisance in Canada.

Indeed as the decade ended, prosperity was returning all across British North America. Responsible government and the British constitution were secure; LaFontaine, Baldwin and their united reform party solidly entrenched in Canada. Judge Haliburton and John Beverley Robinson had been proved wrong: the union and responsible government did not mean the end of the British connection. The end of Family Compact, oligarchic rule perhaps, but not of the connection. The Montreal merchants, the Roman Catholic bishops, and John Neilson had been proved wrong: the union had not crushed French Canada's nationality and religion. On the contrary, it had fortified them. It was Joseph Howe who had been right: responsible government had strengthened the British constitution. It was Francis Hincks, Robert Baldwin, Etienne Parent and Louis-Hippolyte LaFontaine who had been right: the union and responsible government had reinforced reform, nationality, and allegiance. And for the *Canadiens*, the union, responsible government and reform had saved "notre langue, nos institutions, et nos droits"; they had consecrated the Union Jacks flying over imperial citadels at Quebec, Kingston and Halifax.

A Disaster*

MAURICE SÉGUIN

Translated by E. Nish

Faced with interpreting the national history of French Canada, two attitudes are adopted. The most common, which since 1840 has dominated the traditional interpretation of the history of Canada, clings to the federalist ideology. Aware that nationality, spontaneous communal order, is not necessarily the same as the state, this school concludes that a collective minority can accept a sharing of powers in a federal union, consent to a certain degree of centralization, without losing, by doing so, mastery over the essentials of its national life, and that it may preserve its potential to expand in the political, economic and cultural fields. This is the thesis of the autonomists who believe they may be content with a fraction of independence.

The other attitude, very little held after 1840 among a people who had debated nationality and nationalism at length, pushes to its logical conclusion the idea of autonomy and ends in a concept of the rigorous principle of nationalities. To be a minority population in a federation is to be an annexed population. The state is not the nation, but the state is the principal instrument of national expansion. There is no political equality in any federation between the people who are a majority and the people who are a minority. The majority population has at its disposal internal and external autonomy. The minority population can place at its service only an internal autonomy.

Political annexation in a modern and dynamic economy brings with it, inevitably, economic subordination. When economic is joined to political inferiority, the situation becomes more serious. Culture itself, in the larger sense of the word, intimately linked to political and economic realities, is so greatly disordered that one cannot even speak, with reference to the minority population, of a real cultural autonomy. To the independentist school, political independence is absolutely necessary. It is to be sought as desirable in itself, and it is considered as an irreplaceable means of assuring mastery over economic and cultural life.

From the point of view of the independentist, the situation of Canada in the French empire should not be idealized but re-evaluated. That was the only epoch in its history when separatism was rooted in reality. For more than a hundred years the Canadians of French origin lived alone in a separate state. . . .

*From "Gènese et historique de l'idée separatiste au Canada français," from a series of three talks on the radio program *Conférences*, 18 March, 25 March, 1 April 1962. Published in *Racism or Responsible Government: The French Canadian Dilemma of the 1840s*, edited by E. Nish. Copyright 1967 by Copp Clark Limited. Reprinted by permission.

The two nations, through the instrumentality of their most advanced elements in Lower Canada, were reaching the point of exasperation. A general paralysis resulted. No more government, no more administration of justice, no more schools; capital fled, immigration languished, public works were suspended and Upper Canada was bankrupt. This was the result of the conflict of two incompatible nationalities.

The revolt of 1837 was, in reality, a double uprising; the uprising of the British of Lower Canada against the menace of a French Canadian republic, and the uprising of the most advanced section of the French Canadian nationalists against English domination. The clash of 1837 finally brought the suspension of the impolitic constitution of 1791. Durham, in 1839, agreed with the French Canadian reformers. He even admitted in theory the legitimacy of their racial struggle for supremacy. But he knew that French Canada was a futureless remnant of an old colonization, and that the precarious independence of French Canada would jeopardize the future of British North America. Even though he despised the pretensions of racial superiority, he was forced by circumstances to pronounce against the separatism of the French Canadians in order to save the only viable separatism of the epoch, English Canadian separatism.

Finally the union of the English forces of the two Canadas over the French Canadians was effected, a solution envisioned as early as 1810, which failed in 1822, and which could no longer be postponed in face of the general disorganization. It was the veto by all British Montreal, and behind this veto, by all of British North America, of the separatism of Quebec.

The union, the only logical solution, was imposed by force of circumstances. It was ordained by the higher interests of English colonization. It was not a caprice, a chastisement for a temporary fault of disloyalty. It was not the effect of a policy of momentary persecution. Masters since 1760 of all levels of command, the British, by the union, consolidated their hold not only on the valley of the St. Lawrence, but on Quebec itself. The union of 1840 confirmed, first through political inferiority, and afterwards through economic inferiority, the minority status of a French colonization that had failed. Faced with the inevitable democratic, political, economic and social inferiority of the small French Canadian population, some British seriously asked themselves whether it would not be better, even in the interests of the French Canadians, to work towards the total assimilation of the minority to assure social peace in the valley of the St. Lawrence. But as the solution to the French Canadian problem, assimilation is as unrealizable as the solution of independence.

If in 1840, English Canada, which was fifty-five per cent of the population of Canada, exercised its majority hold on the government and, thanks to the help of the metropolis, alone disposed of the necessary capital for industrialization; in brief, if English Canada out-classed all the sectors of French Canada, it was still impossible for it to assimilate the latter. The relations between the two nationalities congealed. As early as 1841 the

307

legislative union, which contained some concessions to the minority of a federal character, functioned spontaneously as a federation, and since that day, the French Canadians survived, annexed, provincialized, in a greater *British North American* Empire.

This solution which could not be rejected, Lafontaine and his successors accepted very easily. They even accepted it with a certain enthusiasm, for they found in it the application of the principle of federalism which contained no major inconveniences for them. The capitulation of Vaudreuil had led infallibly to the unconscious capitulation of Lafontaine, a necessary capitulation, even explicable, but one that remains nonetheless a capitulation. A population is forced to live, and must accept life, as a minority under a foreign majority, without being able to measure the gravity of the situation.

The political history of French Canada cannot be well understood unless one takes into account the inevitable disaster of these two times, forecast in 1760 by English colonization, and consolidated in 1840 by the union of the English forces. . . .

308

. . . English Canadians took eighty years to equal in number the French Canadians. They achieved it in 1840 by the union of the two Canadas. The four hundred thousand British of Upper Canada united with the hundred and fifty thousand British of Lower Canada to form a majority of five hundred and fifty thousand over the French Canadian minority of four hundred and fifty thousand. English Canada could now make the parliamentary regime function to its advantage. A majority of the population, and having a majority in the legislative assembly, a majority in the executive council, and supported by metropolitan capital, English Canada had completely declassed French Canada without being able to assimilate it. French Canada was literally annexed, provincialized in politics and in economics, transformed into a French appendix attached to a British nation. And English Canada could not avoid this without compromising her own chances of development, without placing her own separatism *vis-à-vis* the United States in danger.

It is important to pause here to outline the political and economic thought of progressive French Canadians following this annexation. On the political level, thanks to a federalist ideology, the French Canadian leaders, politicians like Lafontaine or journalists like Etienne Parent, quickly arrived at the belief that the union only juxtaposed two colonies which, by their common achievement of self-government, remained free each to administer his own area. They saw in the union a kind of juxtaposing of two colonial autonomies with regard to that which is essential to the national life of French Canada and of English Canada, even though some sectors, considered neutral, such as public finance, tariff policy, commerce, transportation, defense, and external policies were administered in common.

By 1842, and under the legislative union (one cannot emphasize it too much) the French Canadians proclaimed themselves free as a people. At the cost of long and difficult travails they claimed to have entered into the Promised Land. The French Canadian leaders boasted of having marched in the front rank in the conquest of colonial liberties, and even to have shown the road to the English Canadians. The French Canadians, who at the end of their struggle were annexed, and who gained only a limited provincial autonomy, affirmed their political equality with the English Canadian majority from the beginning of the legislative union. Did not the French Canadians have mastery over the internal policies of Lower Canada? A handy formula, this federalist ideology which permits bypassing the essential and not seeing the annexation.

On the economic level, a more concrete domain, a reality becomes apparent which does not furnish the same assurance. Here there can be no question of proclaiming oneself the equal of the English. But the French Canadians finally find the means to conserve the nice optimism which characterizes them in politics. The French Canadians are inferior in the economic domain. The progressives of 1846 admit it voluntarily. Where are, they say, our industrial leaders, our workrooms, our workshops? Have we the proportion in high finance we should have? In all branches we are only the exploited. Everywhere we let the riches of our country pass into the hands of others. Our merchants, in general, are but secondary agents of British merchants.

309

And who is responsible for this inferiority? It is, above all, the French Canadians, even if we admit that the English are naturally better equipped, belonging to the more industrious, the most commercial race that exists in the world. At the time of the new phase which began after the cession of the country — wrote Etienne Parent, the father of the nationalist thought which was said to be progressive, in 1846 — the people naturally had to turn to the remnants of the old families to find their leaders, guides to the new roads which were opening up, roads of social and industrial progress. Merchants, captains of industry, agriculturists, all were needed. How many have fulfilled this national mission? Some fled before the new flag, others took refuge in the idleness of the seigneurial customs. And Parent explained the economic inferiority of the French Canadians in big business entirely by the criminal negligence of the elite immediately following the conquest, and, for succeeding generations, by the laziness of the French Canadians and their ignorance of political economy.

The young people of 1847 took up this theme of an economic disaster attributable to the French Canadians themselves. They reproached the politicians for not having prepared the French Canadians on the economic level in order that they might enjoy their political triumph. The young people said they were neglected, abandoned, forgotten, by men of their origin who, while fighting for the cause of their nationality and for freedom, never thought to establish industries where the young *Canadiens* could have prepared themselves to struggle in commerce, in industry, fruitful sources of riches and influence, against the enemies of French

Canada. The politicians have overthrown, said the young people, an irresponsible system and have conquered constitutional government. The struggle was long and difficult, the victory is nice, complete, glorious. But has the French Canadian population advanced? No, for it is deprived of the influence that it should exercise on the new system. This influence is gained only with the wealth that is obtained from commerce and industry, and this influence they would possess today if they had had the wisdom and the patriotism to found institutions where the youth could have received a practical education.

Apart from the agricultural school, whose motto was: "Agriculture for the French Canadians and industry for the English," this supposedly progressive thought which proclaimed the importance of industry and commerce should be borne in mind. Let us be strong economically and we will be strong politically. Who makes social power in America? Industry, undoubtedly. We are in a world where everything is related. The future of civilization rests on the development of industry. Because of its geographic location and its natural resources, Quebec, it was said around 1850, has an industrial vocation. If the French Canadians tolerate economic servitude under another race much longer, their days are numbered. To neglect industry would be to commit suicide as a people. If we despise industry, it was said, it will bypass us completely and the mass of our population will pass body and soul under the domination and exploitation of another race. The French element would be absorbed or strangled by the economic ascendancy of the new race because the French Canadian people, in spite of its political abilities, would be subject to the denationalizing actions of the captains of industry of the rival race. The English prophecy that the French Canadians would be destined to be the bearers of water and hewers of wood, served the elite as a means to whip up nationalism.

No matter how sombre the present, the progressives of 1846 in no way doubted the future. As they said, the French Canadians knew how to triumph in the political arena; application would be sufficient in order to win in the economic domain. After all, inferiority is due only to negligence, to laziness, to ignorance; it will suffice only to desire large schools to have them. What is necessary, it was affirmed, was to create in time an industry that could be measured up to the industry of the other race in all ways and which would attract the esteem and the respect of the latter. The fathers had been tribunes, the sons would be economists. The children, the nephews of the men who had always made Lower Canada march at the head of the colonial ranks in the long struggle for political liberty, would know how to maintain their race in the front ranks during the discussions to be pursued in the field of material interests. And the young people respond in chorus: "How happy we will be, we too, to be able to prepare ourselves to place French Canada at the head of Canadian commerce, as it is already at the head of the colonial phalanges who demand, as British subjects, constitutional liberty!"

310

It can be contended, then, that about 1846, the thinking for this progressive illusion was completely formulated. For this school, the problem of political emancipation was solved. Thanks to federalism, there was political equality with English Canada. A serious economic problem existed, dangerous to the point of assimilation. However, all could be repaired if the French Canadians would only use their talents. This progressive thought of 1846 became the national credo, the traditional doctrine (today more than a century old) of the immense majority of those who, believing themselves to be the *avant garde*, claim that French Canada obtained a political autonomy sufficient to perfect, if it wished, its economic, social and cultural autonomy. It would take nearly ninety years for the counter-thought, separatist thought, to shake this old national credo.

Inspired by Papineau, who, returned from exile, demanded the repeal of the union, that is to say separation, the young democrats of the newspaper *L'Avenir* of Montreal attacked the position of Lafontaine in 1848. England, they wrote, conceded responsible government. To the people of Canada taken as a mass they accorded justice, but did they accord justice to the French Canadians? No, it was necessary to repeal the union. The French Canadians found themselves in a minority, and would always be so. Otherwise the purpose of the union would have failed. Never since the union have we considered nationality as a political link, said these young people. The link which it had formed until then was not strong enough for us to obtain this majority which we needed to counteract the worst consequences of the union. Our liberalism could form this majority. To obtain our political rights we must cease to consider ourselves as French Canadians. Thus, our nationality would be absorbed by liberalism. It is up to the French Canadians to understand the evils of the union and to ask for its repeal. If we are unanimous, this will not be refused. Events in Europe guarantee our success. The French revolution (that of 1848) will overthrow the world, and England, crushed, will not be able to refuse. If the union were repealed, responsible government would still be accorded to us for, as all avow, Great Britain has decided to intervene no longer in colonial affairs. Thus reasoned the young separatists of 1848. Papineau, on the other hand, denounced the union as a stupidly vicious principle, a shabby conception, without vitality, a sickly abortion, a conjurer's trick, an ephemeral measure, a destructive act planned solely in a spirit of vengeance, imposed, at a time of anger and hatred, by men animated by violence. The sooner separation was achieved, the better it would be for the two peoples.

The supporters of Lafontaine, defenders of the union, reply, "At what epoch in our history has the French Canadian nationality been more brilliant, more honoured, and occupied a higher position than that which it occupies today? It has gained more in a few years than it had before in half a century of combat. The union was made to ruin us, but the union has saved us, and after having obtained political rights for which we fought for fifty years, *L'Avenir* inveighs today against the union, but one could not choose a worse moment to revolutionize Canada. The people suffer from indigestion caused by [too much] theory."

L'Avenir's young democrats and Papineau were unable to bring to light the weaknesses of the federalist position of Lafontaine, because they too suffered from the same illness. As early as 1839, Papineau, in response to the Durham *Report*, pronounced himself in favour of the independence of Lower Canada, but equally in favour of the entry of Lower Canada in the great federation of the United States, where the individuality of each sovereign state is under the protection of a Congress which could not be a tyrant, and possessed no powers except in matters of peace or war and of external commerce. And these young admirers, in 1849, repeated: "We do not believe that immediate annexation to the United States would be of a character to do us great harm, that is to us French Canadians. Annexation to the United States would be less harmful than the present state in which we find ourselves. We would then have the elective system in all its plenitude, we would elect our governor who would probably be a French Canadian, we would elect a number of representatives in proportion to our numerical strength, we would elect senators to our taste, finally, we would also have a local House structured as we would want it. We would have government in our hands. The French language would be the legal language; finally we would be masters of our own house. The constitution of the United States leaves to each state of the Union the best means of safeguarding its nationality."

Answering Papineau and the young democrats, who were annexationists more than separatists, it was easy for Lafontaine to defend his federation with English Canada as superior to that dreamed of by Papineau and the young men. The conduct of the reformers of Upper Canada, Lafontaine said, established in fact and in right that the act of Union had not made a single province of the two Canadas, but had united two provinces under the operation of a single legislature which were distinct and separate until that time and would continue to be so to all intents and purposes. In a word, following the example of our neighbours, there was a confederation of two provinces, of two states. And it was by taking a stand on this principle of seeing in the Act of Union a confederation of two provinces that Lafontaine proclaimed that, by using the union, it would be possible for the French Canadians, even though placed in a minority, to make the constitution produce a result quite different than that expected by its authors.

If it was possible and very easy to avoid assimilation, the French Canadians did not avoid annexation, political subordination, provincialization, no matter what Lafontaine thought . . .

Faced with the spectacular role played in the House by the bloc of French Canadians, some Britishers cried "French domination." The Governor, Bagot, while appealing to the French Canadians as a people, all the same informed London that the French Canadians were and would remain in a minority. In 1849, Elgin, in turn, advised London not to worry. The

French Canadians did not form more than one-third of the population, had only one-tenth of the budget, and there was no reason to cry that the colony was "French ridden." Why then, do the British complain of the French Canadians? *L'Avenir* wrote in 1849. Are they under "French domination?" Those of British origin are in a majority in the ministry, in the assembly, in the legislative council, in the judiciary, and among the administrators. Everywhere the French Canadians are only exceptions. John Macdonald, in an election tour in Upper Canada, derided his audience, debunking the myth of "French domination." "In the council we are twelve, of whom three are French Canadians. Can we believe that nine British are menaced by three French Canadians? Where is this 'French domination?' Of one hundred and thirty deputies, there are eighty-eight British and forty-two French Canadians. Two to one. British blood dominates everywhere."

313

The Insurrections *

FERNAND OUELLET

The Origins of the Rebellions

To understand fully the nature and real repercussions of the rebellions of 1837–1838, it is not sufficient simply to cite the reactions to Russell's Resolutions, any more than it is to emphasize the preceding political conflicts. It is just as important to take into consideration the economic, social, demographic, and psychological aspects of this revolutionary attempt, since it is impossible to believe that the rural population with its low level of education and its traditions could have been aware of the constitutional principles involved in the debate. They were not trying to promote a democratic society by their action. The reaction of the habitant sprang from sources more intimately connected with his everyday existence and his mental outlook.

*Chapter 19 from *Canada: Unity in Diversity*, edited by P. G. Cornell et al. Copyright 1967 by Holt, Rinehart and Winston of Canada, Limited. Reprinted by permission.

Nor is it correct to assume that the insurrection was in the hands of isolated individuals, drawn at random from all social strata. Rather, it was the activating of certain social groups and the reacting of others against them. This indicates that a certain amount of cooperation was taking place among individuals working to transform society to conform to their common ideals. A knowledge of this social background is indispensable to the understanding of the events that ushered in the establishment of a new order.

The Economic Instability

The economic trends taking form at the turn of the century were thrown into sharper relief after 1815. As the decline of the fur trade gathered momentum, the agricultural situation of Lower Canada was becoming more critical. The lower prices which had prevailed for so long accentuated the problems facing the inhabitants of Lower Canada. This economic crisis was not, however, universal. The development of the lumbering industry and the expansion of agriculture in Upper Canada, in spite of violent fluctuations, did a great deal to alleviate the existing problems. Nevertheless, the economic situation remained, on the whole, unfavourable.

The decline in wheat production, in spite of occasional increases, continued without interruption after the War of 1812. Surpluses for export became progressively smaller, until after 1832 the deficits became chronic. At this stage the consumer in Lower Canada was obliged to import a large part of the grain necessary for subsistence either from Upper Canada or from the United States. The decline could not be attributed to a lesser demand from foreign markets, for as time went on these demands increased. Nor was its main cause the epidemic of wheat rust, since this did not occur in full force until 1835. It was owing, rather, to the continuance of outmoded techniques which inevitably caused an exhaustion of the land; however, it has a much greater significance for it was an expression of the deep agricultural crisis existent in Lower Canada during these times.

This decisive turn of events resulted in the restriction of agricultural production until it was aimed at mere subsistence. The habitant, in order to feed himself, was obliged to increase the number of his cattle and swine and resort to replacement crops, such as the potato, that had no foreign outlets. Furthermore, the impoverished farmer found it more difficult to obtain textiles and wools imported from Great Britain, and therefore was forced to devote more attention to the raising of sheep and the production of linen. In concentrating his efforts in this direction the habitant, instead of participating in the internal markets, was rather obeying a defence mechanism which led him to assert his agricultural independence. This reaction explains why Lower Canada remained a heavy importer of dairy products and butchered meats during this period. Technical progress did not keep pace with the increase in the quantities produced. Thus, after 1832, when the crisis forced the agricultural producer to substitute commodities, he was inevitably forced to watch a reduction in animal husbandry.

The extent of the crisis became more apparent as 1837 approached; it plunged the peasantry into debt, imperilled patrimonies and engendered rancour and discontent. Instead of looking for a remedy to his problems through technical improvements, the French-Canadian farmer was led to look outward for the responsibility for his misfortunes. The political elite, although occasionally rather patronizing toward the agricultural groups, did help the farmers to find scapegoats in the capitalist, the immigrant, the local government, and, before long, in the British Government as well — in a word, the *English*.

The Decline in Prices

After 1815, the habitant was faced with further difficulties — a universal fall in prices. This fall was consistent in spite of several vacillations and had a profound effect on the regional economics. It accented the seriousness of a problem already critical. The peasants' revenue tended to fluctuate in direct proportion to the general price vacillations, as did the salaries of city workers and agricultural labourers. The pressure affected even the seigneurs who reacted to it by demanding more from their tenants. Neither the business classes, nor the liberal professions escaped it. Profits were directly threatened by the economic situation, and this forced the merchants to look for solutions to the problems.

315

The New Image of the Seigneurial System

During these years the seigneurial system acquired an image that was considerably less benevolent than before. The idea of profit had by this time penetrated deep into this stratum of society and became more and more a motivating force. The seigneurs, whether they were businessmen, descendants of the older families, lawyers or ecclesiastics, were sensitive to the implications of the new definition of property. Property was becoming more mobile and took on a more personalized and intrinsic character. The new outlook and behaviour of the seigneurs is partly explained by the economic situation.

The new practices were most pronounced in the seigneuries owned by merchants where disposable land was more abundant. With a view to increasing the value of landed property and seigneurial rights, the holders of seigneuries restrained the rate of land concession. Not having the right to sell unsettled or uncleared land, the seigneurs did it indirectly. They demanded a gratuity (*pot-de-vin*) from those inhabitants desirous of obtaining a concession; or even transferred parcels of land to friends, retrieved them for non-clearance and then sold them afterward. If, in the older seigneuries, whose rates had been fixed at a time of rising prices, the proprietors confined themselves to exercising their rights, other seigneurs did not hesitate to raise the rates of *cens et rentes*. They also redoubled their own privileged rights in contracts and restored privileges that had fallen out of use, even going so far as to establish new rights. In addition, the surge in the lumbering business led all seigneurs, whatever their initial origin, to reserve the wood on their lands for themselves.

The seigneurial regime, which the merchants, even those who owned seigneuries, wished to abolish, became an increasingly heavy burden for the habitants. But the political upper castes were watchful. Fearing that the peasants would turn their aggressiveness upon this institution, which they considered as being of ultimate national value, the French-Canadian political leaders tried to divert the rural discontent against the English merchants, the habitant's main creditors. In this manner they hoped to preserve French Civil Law.

Lumbering

316   The preferential tariffs promoted considerable expansion in the exploitation of the forests during this period by supporting two sectors of the economy: naval construction, with its centre in Quebec, and the export of lumber which spread most of its benefits in the same area. At such a difficult time, lumbering had a profound significance. Not only did it sustain an important section of the middle classes, but it provided a wage to a large portion of the population, both urban and rural. This business tended, therefore, to temper the shock produced by the agricultural crisis and the drop in prices and to lessen the effect of the seigneurs' reaction to these events. It is of note that the political and social conflicts did not degenerate into a general crisis until the time when lumbering began to follow the other industries down the road of decline. These recessions, especially in the lumbering industry, never lasted more than a year or two. It might also be said that, in the circumstances, the British regime had been saved by the lumbering industry.

Demographic Pressure

Astonishing as it may seem, the rate of increase of the French-Canadian population remained the same during this entire period. It is evident (taking into account the economy at this period) that the population as a whole tended to become poorer year by year. The land not only produced less, but it became scarcer throughout the entire seigneurial region. By about 1820 the majority of the seigneuries were overpopulated or nearly so. The habitant was no longer able to settle his sons around him and felt that he was witnessing the dissolution of the family.

It was at this stage that the migrations began. Some of the emigrants were content to leave the seigneurie and move to the townships where they might settle near their former parishes. Others left their original localities and went further afield in search of land. A final group began to emigrate to the United States, a trend that continued and expanded during the nineteenth century.

The habitant had become, naturally enough, extremely sensitive to the problem of land. He felt limited in his natural expansion by the borders of the townships; and since he was frequently in debt, he feared he would lose the small portion of soil that was his basis of security. He held the government responsible for the scarcity of seigneurial land and reproached it for not converting the townships into seigneuries, and so giving him access to all the land in Lower Canada. He reproached the capitalists for their desire to possess land which he regarded as his right.

This hostility toward the capitalists and the State expressed itself most forcibly in the attitude toward the English immigrant. Immigration after 1815, instead of being a modest flow as before, became an actual tidal wave; and in the eyes of the rural French Canadian the immigrant was a competitor for land and employment; therefore, he represented a vital danger both to the rural population and to the inhabitants of the towns. The pressure of overpopulation, then, as it was experienced by the rural groups, promoted the racial conflicts to the same degree as the agricultural crisis.

317

Social Ills

The social misunderstandings were not solely the product of economic conditions, but were caused as well by purely social factors that in themselves implied conflicts of ideals and interest. The economic situation merely threw into bold relief the ambitions of the different groups composing the society.

Obviously the economic problem pre-occupied the merchant classes most. The decline in the cultivation of wheat in Lower Canada affected the business groups, who tried to revive its traffic by encouraging the clearance of new lands. The merchants, therefore, attached considerable importance to the development of Upper Canada. Having lost all hope of a renewal of agriculture in the lower province, these merchants looked to the immigrants as the only future hope for economic improvement. But the drop in prices and the distances between the centres of production necessitated a lowering in transportation costs; especially at a time when the Erie Canal, finished in 1825, had strengthened American competition to the point where it was seriously threatening the leadership of Montreal.

The building of a road network the length of Lower Canada and the system of canals on the Saint Lawrence constituted the two essential measures needed to revive the economy of the two Canadas. These improvements were impossible to attain without government support and the cooperation of the French-Canadian members in the legislative assembly; for they implied a new concept in public finance and a reassessment of tax responsibility. In addition, the support of Upper Canada was of the essence in this mutually beneficial project.

It was not enough to agree to these reforms and organize credit. Since foreign competition was so strong, it was essential to firmly unite the efforts of the two provinces against the English free-trade movement that was battling with increasing success against the tariffs protecting Canadian wood and lumber on the English market. Finally, for economic and social reasons, the mercantile middle class demanded the dissolution of the institutions that were the basis of the old social regime, namely the *Coutume de Paris* and the seigneurial system. They were, however, content with an extensive revision of these structures. The proposed program encountered the determined resistance of the liberal professions and a large part of the French-Canadian rural population. In their discouragement, the merchant interests became more and more aggressive, and finally demanded, both in Canada and in London, the union of the two Canadas.

The Liberal Professions

318
The influence of the liberal professions, especially the French-Canadian elements, deteriorated during this period, partly as a result of economic difficulties. However, the excessive multiplication of professional practitioners as a result of the growth of the classical colleges was another aspect of the problem. The professional men were living for the most part in hardship, and therefore, tended to place a high value on the security of former times and to share the fears of the rural population.

The professional men came, more and more, to identify their own future with that of the French Canadians. Their mistrust of the merchant classes and the objectives they advocated became more extreme. They felt that the French-Canadian nation was disappearing as a result of the prevailing circumstances and the aims of the Anglo-Saxon group. The lumbering industry and the fur trade seemed opposed to their interests for they supported their political and social adversary. Their reaction was the same toward the banks and the preferential tariffs which the professional men saw as a gross attack upon individual liberty. The efforts of the merchants to modify the *Coutume de Paris* and to abolish the seigneurial system were regarded as aimed at depriving the French-Canadian nation of the institutions essential to the support of the social structure and its upper classes. The proposals to revamp the transportation system were regarded as the logical concomitants of this general program to undermine French-Canadian institutions. They believed that its only possible objective was to flood Lower Canada with English immigrants in order to achieve union of the two Canadas, and thereby to drown the French Canadians in an Anglo-Saxon sea. The aggressive attitude of the more militant-minded British simply seemed to confirm them in their convictions. Above all, they feared the domination of large capitalists, Anglo-Saxon for the most part, upon whom a mass of salaried workers would be forced to depend.

Goaded by these fears and by their class ambitions, the professional men intensified their efforts to attain a greater control of the political structure, since it was at this level they believed that they might succeed in solving their own problems and those of the nation. Of course there were many who refused to look at the situation in such a tragic light, and believed in policies founded on moderation and a spirit of compromise.

But the most influential factions moved deliberately toward intransigence and radicalism. An unstable rural population exerted an additional pressure on the decisions of the professionals.

The Clergy

The clergy did not remain unaffected by the trends that became evident after the turn of the nineteenth century. They were temporarily disconcerted by the rapidity of the changes, and did not hesitate in their reaction. The actions of the Anglican bishop, the State intervention in education, and the attraction of the new liberal ideas upon the upper-class laity contributed to the rise of new problems. Under Mgr. Plessis, the reaction of the clergy *319* went no further than an opposition to new innovations. In addition, the clergy was deeply divided over the proposed establishing of a new episcopate at Montreal. But the founding of new classical colleges and the efforts schools, supervised by the curates, demonstrates that the episcopate had become aware of the need for positive action.

It was under Mgr. Lartigue that counteroffensive of the clergy really began. Mgr. Lartigue, the first bishop of Montreal, a cousin of Papineau and a former lawyer, did not have the same prejudices as his predecessors toward nationalism. What he deplored most about this new ideology was its association with liberalism, that flower of the French Revolution. But once the idea of brotherhood had been excised, nationalism might well serve to build up a society respectful of tradition and, perhaps, even theocratic in nature. Mgr. Lartigue had been educated under the influence of the French theocratic school of De Maistre, De Bonald and Lammenais, a school directly opposed to the Gallican school of which Msgr. Plessis was an advocate. Thus his hostility toward the French Revolution and to liberal and democratic ideas was even more pronounced.

Mgr. Lartigue was not content to confine his efforts to waging a fierce and desperate war against revolutionary ideas and their advocates, but worked diligently to restore the moral and temporal influence of the Church and to make the clergy the accepted dominant class. In struggling against the Royal Institution and the legislative assembly's scheme for public schools he hoped to restore the exclusive jurisdiction of the Church over education. He felt that education on all levels (primary, secondary and university) was solely the responsibility of the Church. Mgr. Lartigue, in addition to planning a religious revival in the population, worked to extend the social radius of the Church. The counter-offensive begun in these years carried on during the course of the nineteenth century.

Thus, relations between the liberal professions, especially those elements of it engaged in the political struggle, and the clergy had become increasingly strained. The attitude of Mgr. Lartigue during the rebellions of 1837–1838 stemmed from these social and ideological controversies. Moreover the clerical influence had not been strong enough to prevent the *patriote* movement from exerting a large measure of influence over the rural population.

The Principal Actors

The critical economic situation, the pressures of overpopulation, and a society in which racial delineations tended to coincide with class boundaries, together formed the stage upon which the political drama was to unfold. The aims and policies of the emergent political parties remained consistent with the circumstances of the particular sectors of society from which they arose. It would be wrong, however, to underestimate the influence of the individual personalities in the foreground; for instance, the personalities and attitudes of the governors influenced public affairs according to their support of one group or another. Historians have frequently been misled by contemporary caricatures of the governors engaged in the conflicts of that time. "Francophile" or "Anglophile" were the most common descriptions, and these often obscured the real issues and occasionally led to errors in diagnosing causes.

320

Among the outstanding personalities, none stands out more clearly than Louis-Joseph Papineau, who was born in 1786 and was educated at the Quebec Seminary. His father was a notary who had been politically active since the establishment of parliamentary institutions. After leaving the Seminary the young Papineau decided to become a notary; dissatisfied by his studies there, he shortly thereafter chose law, which he also disliked. In 1818, he bought the seigneurie of Petite-Nation from his father. He would have liked very much to live there but his wife objected, and although he was attracted by the charm and solitude of country life, he was too much in need of an audience to enjoy himself fully in the country. In 1809, he entered politics which seemed to bring him the outlet he needed.

In reality, Papineau did not especially like politics. He constantly complained that he was engaged in a combat he was not suited for; and moreover, attributed his continuing this way of life to a sense of patriotic duty and an ardent desire to rescue his countrymen from the ills that threatened them. However he rationalized it, it is true that Papineau was not cut out for political life; he was a visionary and intransigent, and was disposed to take upon himself the perils threatening the French-Canadian group and to assume the ambitions and interests of the liberal professions.

At the outset of his career, he did not belong to the extremist wing of the *Parti Canadien*, but among the moderates; and when the question of a successor for Pierre Bédard and Antoine Panet arose, Papineau was the only deputy to finally poll the majority of his party's votes. It was only after 1818 that he adopted his extreme attitudes. He gradually became the natural leader of the French Canadians whose hopes he claimed to represent. A reformer until 1830, he subsequently came to desire independence and to wish for the establishment of a French-Canadian republic, with himself as president. His ineptitude in practical action, which drove him to specialize in verbal action, was the source of his setbacks. Despite his deficiencies, Papineau was nonetheless the most outstanding personality of the period upon which he left his mark.

The Political Conflicts

All these factors were transposed to the political level, where the fluctuations followed those of the economy and the society. Two political parties, representing different social and ethnic groups were locked in combat. The *Parti Canadien* drew its support mainly from the rural sector of the population and was led by an elite drawn from the liberal professions; the merchants' party was supported by the capitalists and landed interests, and rallied the British and the affluent. Until 1830, the clergy and the *321* old seigneurial families supported or disapproved, more or less openly, the one or the other of the two parties, depending on the circumstances.

On the political scene there were as many irreconcilable views and opposing political ideas as there were in the social sphere. Each group wished to control the political structure in order to promote its own exclusive views on economic and social matters. Under these conditions, the constitutional issues were not, in themselves, very significant. If the legislature demanded "ministerial responsibility" and the control of finances, it was simply because they saw in these innovations a way to allow the liberal professions to assume not only political leadership, but also the social leadership, which would permit them to promote their concept of the future of the French-Canadian people. Until 1830, the French-Canadian political leaders were convinced that the mother country was not ill-disposed toward them; but the moment they believed that the latter did not favour the abolition of what they called the "reign of the oligarchy," they took the road toward political independence and the inauguration of a republican regime modelled upon the American political design. The *Parti Canadien* which had become the *Patriote* party in 1826, was not truly democratic; but was dominated by a nationalistic ideology, and thought it could attain its reactionary objectives by means of democratic institutions. On the other hand the Bureaucratic party, formerly the merchants' party, in spite of its urge for innovation in economic and social affairs, took the opposite course, putting its faith in a reactionary defensive policy executed with a measure of realism.

After 1830, the political atmosphere deteriorated more and more until the conflict between the legislative assembly and the councils, and between the lower house and the governors became so sharp that any compromise became extremely difficult, if not impossible. Elections were not only stormy, but they frequently gave rise to organized violence. During this period, associations were formed which merely aggravated the feeling of anarchy that reigned everywhere. The cholera epidemics and the acuteness of the economic crisis complicated the situation, and with the Ninety-Two Resolutions passed in 1834, the turbulence reached a peak. The extremists of both camps spoke of taking up arms, with the result that the slightest incident threatened to unleash an insurrection. The stage for revolution was set in the spring of 1837, when Lord John Russell presented to the Parliament in London a series of resolutions which constituted a total rejection of the demands of the *Patriotes*.

Russell's Resolutions rejected the *Patriotes'* demands for an elective legislative council and granted power to dispose of government funds without permission from the legislative assembly. The adoption of these Resolutions took place at the most inopportune moment. The agricultural crisis reached a new low; for the general crop failure, after several years of deficits that were more or less universal in the colony, had accentuated the discontent among the farmers. The recession in the lumbering industry and in naval construction, and the effects of a contemporary English financial crisis reached country and town at the same time. This critical situation added to the social instability and to the privations already suffered by the most underprivileged groups in society. On the political level, the atmosphere was even more strained as a result. The explosive nature of the Resolutions is understandable in this light.

A challenge had been presented to the *Patriotes*, which left them no alternative but to surrender or to take up arms. The first alternative was impossible in such troubled times; they could only turn to insurrection. It could not, however, be a spontaneous uprising, for practical preparations had to be made and some supplementary agitation undertaken to rouse the populace. Although the extremists in the *Patriote* party had wanted an armed confrontation ever since 1830, they had taken no practical steps in this direction.

The Pre-revolutionary Period: April 1837 to November 1837

It is difficult to ascertain with any degree of certainty the *Patriotes'* decisions following the divulgence of the contents of Russell's Resolutions, since they took care to destroy any documents likely to appear compromising. It is, however, obvious that they followed a precise program, whose general outlines can be traced both in their actions and through various sources of information.

The *Patriotes* were not unanimous in their aims. Some believed that the English Government would never stop at the stand taken by Russell, and that the only realistic solution was to organize the revolutionary forces as soon as possible and throw them into action. Others, nursing their illusions, continued to believe that systematic agitation would be sufficient to force England to revise her policy, and that recourse to armed rebellion would be unnecessary. Finally the two groups, the former one led by Dr. W. Nelson and the latter by Papineau, seemed to have agreed on a single plan.

The plan included two distinct phases. The first was constitutional agitation which was either to lead to the backing down of England, or to pave the way for revolutionary action should the English authorities refuse to yield to pressure. The armed uprising was projected for the beginning of December. The so-called constitutional agitation occurred on three levels. Firstly, a series of large public meetings were held to stir up the populace in both the urban and rural areas. A boycott of regular imports and the use of smuggling was also prescribed with a view to combating the merchant classes. Thirdly, a show of force was to be prepared either by enlisting volunteers or some other means.

During the summer of 1837, the campaign waged by the *Patriotes* throughout the province produced the desired results. From one assembly to the next the fever mounted, especially in the rural areas. Although the leaders tried, by and large, to remain within the legal limits, they did not always succeed, and were occasionally carried away by the atmosphere they created. After July, others, particularly the extremists, did not hesi- 323 tate to incite the populace to revolt, and numerous incidents occurred throughout the countryside. The founding of the revolutionary *association des Fils de la liberté* ("Association of the Sons of Liberty") increased the unrest in the city of Montreal. It had its counterpart in the *Doric Club*, a society equally counter-revolutionary.

Tension reached the breaking point when the *Patriotes* organized the "Assembly of the Six Counties." The speeches were extremely violent, and the nature of the meetings indicated that the climax was fast approaching. A declaration of human rights was issued at the meeting, and measures that were plainly revolutionary were adopted. It was decided that officers of the militia and justices of the peace, previously named by the government, were to be replaced by officials elected by the populace. The new organization set itself up to a certain extent as independent. From this point on the actual revolutionary phase had begun.

The Revolt

The increasing tension, which spread in the rural areas and the city of Montreal, was expressed with new vigour after the formation of the Assembly of the Six Counties. The British minority became alarmed and demanded that the government intervene, but the latter continued to interpret the movement as a blackmailing operation until the beginning of November 1837. Monseigneur Lartigue, Bishop of Montreal, was the first to feel it necessary to intervene; and on October 24, at the time the *Patriotes* published the manifesto of the Assembly at St. Charles, he sent out a letter unequivocally condemning the actions of the French-Canadian leaders. He condemned their revolutionary intentions and the liberal ideas that bore them, and implicitly formulated the penalties the Church attached to actions intended to overthrow the established order. In spite of this clerical influence the revolutionary movement swept on.

It was November before the government finally decided to act and ordered the arrest of the principal *Patriote* leaders. Some of them hid in the parishes, one small group headed toward St. Eustache and St. Benoit, and others went to St. Charles or St. Denis. Camps were established in these places as rallying points for the peasant forces. After the incident at Longueuil between the police and the *Patriotes*, the government sent an expedition against St. Denis which was repulsed on November 23, 1837; but two days later the government forces, captured St. Charles, at which point the resistance of the *Patriotes* collapsed. Colborne afterward succeeded in pacifying the parishes to the north of Montreal, and St. Eustache fell to him in spite of strong resistance from a small group of *Patriotes* commanded by Jean-Olivier Chénier.

324   The rapid collapse of the *Patriote* movement was not the result of a lack of planning of the revolt, but of weakness in the leadership. The *Patriote* chiefs, as far as the practical side of their venture was concerned, showed themselves to be very poor organizers; in combat, they were lamentable. Only Dr. Nelson, Charles-Ovide Perrault and Chénier were equal to the task. Papineau, the commander-in-chief, left St. Denis just before the battle; moreover, his conduct during the entire revolutionary period was most inconsistent. His continual hesitation, his fear of responsibility and his physical cowardice explain his flight in disguise, and account for a large part of the climate of anarchy that existed. It is true that the government forces mobilized much more swiftly than the *Patriotes* expected, but this is hardly a sufficient explanation. The French-Canadian leaders undoubtedly put too much faith in the ability of the farmer to act alone. Without well-established leadership, the habitants were a disorganized and ineffective fighting force.

The Mission of Lord Durham in Lower Canada

The revolt in Lower Canada and the troubles in Upper Canada profoundly shocked public opinion in England. The problems could not be regarded lightly. English political leaders now became preoccupied with finding the source of the problems and the nature of the conflicts, and with formulating satisfactory solutions. Lord Durham's mission was the result of this desire to rectify these ills.

Durham arrived in Quebec in May 1838 with two types of responsibilities. He was to decide the future of the political prisoners and set up committees of inquiry to study the causes of the uprising. All this was not easy. The atmosphere was extremely strained and each group seemed bent on securing official validation and forwarding its own version of events. Therefore, the commissioner had to avoid compromising himself in the eyes of all the different elements of the population. In such circumstances, impartiality would not be easy.

The most pressing task was to decide the fate of the political prisoners. Many different solutions were possible, of course, but Durham was quick to realize that trial by jury was unthinkable. With emotions running high, justice could not have been dispensed fairly whatever the jury chosen. On the other hand, a trial without a jury would have resulted in a long series of particularly severe comdemnations. The great volume of proof accumulated against the *Patriote* leaders guaranteed this. Wishing to avoid another popular uprising, Durham preferred another solution. He freed those prisoners who had played only a subordinate role in the insurrection, but showed more severity toward the principal instigators of the movement, exiling them to Bermuda. Those who had escaped to the United States he forbade to return under threat of punishment.

During this time, the committees formed by Durham were accumulating a large body of material dealing with all aspects of life in Lower Canada and in the other colonies. With the help of this material and his own personal observations, Durham was soon in a position to diagnose the problems of Lower Canada. Influenced by the European climate of ideas *Radical Jack* had thought he would find a genuine liberal conflict in Canada. He did discover traces of it, especially in Upper Canada, but to him it seemed that the conflict in Lower Canada had an entirely different character. The intensity of the racial conflict, which the liberal element masked but did not hide, seemed to him the most striking feature in the colony. "I found two nations warring in the bosom of a single State . . ."

325

According to Durham, these two nations not only possessed different characteristics of language, race and religion, but they differed in their degree of evolution as well. The French-Canadian society, he assumed, was essentially static and destined, as a result of its outlook, to remain so. The British, on the other hand, were sensitive to currents of progress in all their forms. Influenced by the atmosphere that existed in the society at the time of his stay, Durham finally concluded that the French sector was forever entrenched in inferiority and obstruction. He even saw in this element some organic and immutable tendency to be so. Hence the extreme nature of some of his recommendations.

Therefore, because he had observed the struggle at its greatest intensity, Durham saw no other solution to the ethnic problem except the assimilation of French Canadians into the English culture. For this reason he recommended the union of the Canadas and the undertaking of a policy aimed at absorbing the French group into the Anglo-Saxon. His *raciste* attitude was based on a distorted view of relations between the ethnic groups. Apart from the establishment of the union, necessary for other reasons, his solution was illusory. The future progress of Canada did not depend on the destruction of French culture, but on a change in attitude on the part of the French-Canadian population toward progress. In this sense, the French Canadians themselves held the key. By reversing their stand, they might prove Durham's conclusion unfounded. Instead of promoting assimilation, the union of the Canadas would prove to be no more than a means of achieving a number of economic and institutional reforms.

In his *Report*, which was published in the spring of 1839, Durham perceived another reform as indispensable as the union — the establishment of responsible government. His recommendation is not, of itself, startling. The commissioner had long been one of the main proponents of the English liberal movement, and even bore the reputation of being a radical. His background, together with a desire to find a solution to certain Canadian problems, explains Durham's proposal for ministerial responsibility. His recommendation seemed to him to be in tune with the natural evolution of the British Empire toward a thorough remoulding of its colonial structures. Ministerial responsibility, for Durham, was to be the political expression of this development, implying an increased autonomy of the colonies. It is from this point of view that the Durham Report marked a step toward the complete reform realized in 1848.

Fortunately, the enormous amount of work accomplished by his committees allowed Durham time to accumulate the information necessary to draw up his report, because his mission ended abruptly in 1838. He learned that the government in London had just overruled the decision he had made regarding the political prisoners. There was no other alternative under the circumstances but to tender his resignation.

326

The Second Outbreak: November 1838

A few days after Durham's departure another insurrection broke out in Lower Canada which was not, however, linked to the events surrounding his mission. It was, rather, a movement organized at long range by the Canadian refugees in the United States. After the setback of 1837, the *Patriotes* had never ceased to dream of avenging themselves; but deeply divided, they needed more than six months to recover and to agree on a new plan.

However, after July 1838, the *Patriote* leaders, having more or less rejected Papineau, succeeded in achieving a certain unanimity among themselves, and in establishing the *Société des Frères-Chasseurs*, a secret revolutionary organization drawing its adherents from the parishes of Lower Canada. The leaders counted on American aid in their insurrection planned for November 3. They hoped to capture St.-Jean, Chambly and Laprairie quickly, before marching on Montreal. Once Montreal was in their hands, they proposed to move on Quebec.

Events, however, did not occur as planned. On November 3, the *Frères-Chasseurs* agitated in all the parishes south of Montreal, and several thousand of them gathered at Napierville where independence for the country was once again proclaimed by two of their leaders, Robert Nelson and Côté. Anarchy prevailed everywhere. Once again the leaders were found incapable of commanding the movement and guiding it toward the desired objectives. A large mass of people gathered at Napierville but the majority dispersed before seeing any action, and government forces encountered no serious opposition.

This resounding failure, followed by severe repressive measures, was to have a profound influence upon the future course of the French Canadians. In 1840, the *Patriote* experiment had completely collapsed, and men with different objectives assumed the leadership of the French-Canadian group.

Topic Ten

The Conservative and Reform Traditions in Upper Canada/Canada West

After the Union of the Canadas in 1841 new political factions emerged in both Canada East and West. The Canada West members of the Assembly of the United Canada divided into various groups of Tories and Reformers. Under the leadership of John A. Macdonald the Canada West Tories — or Conservatives — allied with the *Bleus* in Canada East (the French-Canadian reformers who became increasingly conservative after 1848) led by George-Etienne Cartier. This alliance, the precursor of the Conservative Party of Canada, dominated the politics of the Canadas for most of the period from 1854 to 1867. S.F. Wise examines the contribution of the Upper Canadian Tories to the conservative tradition of Canada West in "Upper Canada and the Conservative Tradition."

In the late 1840s a new radical movement arose in Canada West, a revival of the group that had once supported William Lyon Mackenzie before the Rebellion of 1837. Known as Clear Grits (because they wanted in their ranks only pure-hearted men, those who were 'clear grit' through and through) they demanded an elective, democratic system of government, modelled on that of the United States. When George Brown, editor of the Toronto *Globe* and an ardent admirer of the British constitutional system, became leader of the Clear Grits in 1859, he modified their program and transformed them into a respectable British-type Liberal party. J.M.S. Careless outlines the policies of the Clear Grits' new leader in "The Political Ideas of George Brown."

In the Assembly the Clear Grits allied uneasily with the *Rouges* of Lower Canada/Canada East (a partial revival of the radicalism of Louis-Joseph Papineau), who also believed in an American-style democracy. Their anti-clericalism, however, weakened their position among French Canadians, undermining their electoral strength.

Paul Cornell's "The Genesis of Ontario Politics in the Province of Canada" (1838-1871) explains the complicated, but important, political developments that went into the formation of Canada West's politics on the eve of Confederation. His study explains why the conservatives, under Macdonald, formed the Canadian cabinets, and George Brown and the Clear Grits (often the majority group in Canada West) did not.

For an introduction to the political history of Upper Canada before the Act of Union see: Gerald M. Craig's *Upper Canada: The Formative Years, 1784-1841* (Toronto: McClelland and Stewart, 1963). David W.L. Earl's collection, *The Family Compact: Aristocracy or Oligarchy?* (Toronto: Copp Clark, 1967), contains a number of important essays on the conservative establishment, including excerpts from Robert E. Saunder's, "What was the Family Compact?" *Ontario History*, 49 (1957). For a review of the debate between the Tories and the Reformers before the Rebellion of 1837, consult Aileen Dunham, *Political Unrest in Upper Canada, 1815-1836* (Ottawa: McClelland and Stewart, 1963; first published in 1927). A new biography of a prominent member of the Family Compact is Patrick Brode's *Sir John Beverley Robinson: Bone and Sinew of the Compact* (Toronto: The Osgoode Society, 1984). A lively account of the radical reformer who led the Rebellion of 1837 in Upper Canada, is William Kilbourn's biography of William Lyon Mackenzie, *The Firebrand* (Toronto: Clarke, Irwin and Co. 1956). Frederick H. Armstrong reviews the various interpretations of Mackenzie in his, "William Lyon Mackenzie: Persistent Hero," *Journal of Canadian Studies* 6,3 (August 1971): 21-35. Two recent accounts of the Upper Canadian rebellion are Colin Read and Ronald J. Stagg, eds., *The Rebellion of 1837 in Canada: A Documentary History of the Rebellion of 1837* (Ottawa: Carleton University Press, 1985), and Colin Read's *The Rising in Western Upper Canada 1837-38: The Duncombe Revolt and After* (Toronto: University of Toronto Press, 1982).

329

Two of the best biographies of Canadian politicians concern the two leading antagonists of the 1850s: D.G. Creighton's *John A. Macdonald*, volume 1, *The Young Politician* (Toronto: Macmillan, 1952); and J.M.S. Careless, *Brown of the Globe*, volume 1, *The Voice of Upper Canada, 1818-1859* (Toronto: Macmillan, 1959). *Upper Canadian Politics in the 1850's* (Toronto: University of Toronto Press, 1967), ed. R.C. Brown, is a useful collection of essays as is J.M.S. Careless, ed., *The Pre-Confederation Premiers, Ontario Government Leaders, 1841-1867*, (Toronto: University of Toronto Press, 1980). J.M.S. Careless has also written the survey, *The Union of the Canadas. The Growth of Canadian Institutions, 1841-1857* (Toronto: McClelland and Stewart, 1967).

Upper Canada and the Conservative Tradition *

S. F. WISE

Two streams of conservatism met and blended in the two generations of Upper Canadian history before the Union. One was that brought by the Loyalist founders of the colony: an emotional compound of loyalty to King and Empire, antagonism to the United States, and an acute, if partisan sense of recent history. To the conservatism of the émigré was joined another, more sophisticated viewpoint, first brought by Simcoe and his entourage, and crystallized in the Constitutional Act of 1791: the Toryism of late eighteenth century England. What Upper Canada received from this source was not merely the somewhat creaking intellectual edifice of Blackstone and Warburton, but a conservatism freshly minted into a fighting creed through Edmund Burke's philippics against the French Revolution. The joining of two intensely counter-revolutionary outlooks in a colony as peculiarly situated as was Upper Canada had powerful consequences for the Canadian conservative tradition.

330

It is not, of course, usual to think of Upper Canadian Toryism in relation to the Canadian conservative tradition. Its contribution has not been freely acknowledged by later Conservatives, and probably not even dimly apprehended by them. There are good reasons for this state of affairs. For one thing, John A. Macdonald dominates the history of Canadian conservatism. His long career, his creative association with great acts of nation-building, his extraordinary attractiveness and complexity as an individual, and the very brilliance and persuasiveness of his biographer, have made it difficult for us to see beyond him to the society that produced him, and that shaped his approach to politics. Secondly, the evil repute in which Compact Toryism is held has made it difficult for Conservatives, from the day of Macdonald onwards, to own that anything in their tradition could conceivably derive from a period prior to his coming. Thus the Conservative party dates its origin from the coalition of 1854, which is normally depicted as a grand rejection of the past by essentially forward-looking men, who turned to building modern conservatism from the foundations up. This is a harmless myth, and like other ancient monuments should doubtless be treated with reverent care. Since it is highly improbable, however, that anything said here will have the slightest destructive effect upon it, we propose to examine briefly some of the contributions made by Upper Canadian Toryism to the conservative tradition in Canada.

In doing so, it is necessary to acknowledge at once that much of that

* From *Profiles of a Province: Studies in the History of Ontario*, edited by the Ontario Historical Society.
Copyright 1967 by the Ontario Historical Society. Reprinted by permission.

contribution was negative; that is, that the example set by the Family Compact in its exclusiveness, inefficiency, arbitrariness and occasional corruption had a salutary effect upon generations to come. High Toryism fell, once for all, with the system of government that had nurtured it; but its sins were recapitulated ad nauseam by succeeding generations of reform politicians. Thanks to their labours, and to those chroniclers and historians of Whiggish bent, it seems unlikely that the failings of the Compact will ever be forgotten; on this side of the ledger, at least, the historical record is complete. Nor is there any good reason why the record should be forgotten. Upper Canada's fifty years of oligarchic rule remain standing testimony to the weaknesses and dangers of government by an authoritarian and paternalistic élite.

But historians have a peculiar duty towards losers, not out of mere perversity, but because much is to be learned from them. This is the case with the conservatives of Upper Canada. Our reform tradition has telescoped the complexities of early conservatism into High Toryism, and has turned the phrase "Family Compact" into a term of political science, when it was nothing but a political epithet. The habit of viewing the first fifty years of Ontario's history as a political false start has obscured the essential continuity of Upper Canadian with subsequent provincial history, and has fostered the tendency to attach fundamental importance to the Rebellion and the Union as rejections of the colonial past, when they ought more accurately to be described as events which eliminated certain alternative lines of development, reform as well as conservative, implicit in the early circumstances of the colony. Beneath the polemics and violence which accompanied these events, beneath the clash of such personalities as Gourlay, Strachan, Mackenzie and Bond Head, beneath the struggles over constitutional change or clergy reserves, a provincial community was being born, and by 1841 it had taken on characteristics both distinctive and permanent.

331

In the building of the new Ontario society, conservative forces had been powerfully at work, and nowhere more so than in the sphere of politics. During Upper Canada's existence as a separate province, thirteen general elections were held, as well as a large number of by-elections. Although these elections have yet to be carefully analyzed, it is clear that their prime effect was to organize the population into its basic conservative and reform patterns. Since party, in the modern institutional sense, did not exist, political affiliations were quite fluid, and a sizeable body of electors shifted allegiance from election to election. Yet long before the Union, conservative and reform strongholds had emerged; areas from which the later Conservative and Liberal parties were to draw strength to the present day. The core of Tory support was in the eastern counties, the area of major Loyalist settlement, and in the towns, especially Kingston, Brockville, York-Toronto, Niagara and London. There was no significant variation from this pattern in the later Union period; indeed, there is a continuity between the electoral behaviour of colonial Upper Canada and the political geography of twentieth-century Ontario.

Conservative members were returned to the Assembly from ridings other than the eastern counties and the towns, but not quite so consistently. In the 1830's, the Tory cause was further strengthened by the addition of members from "frontier" constituencies, peopled by the recent flood of immigration from Britain. All this is to say that the political situation in Upper Canada was not invariably, or even normally, one in which a reform majority in the Assembly found its legislative programme blocked by the solidly Tory upper house. In the first few assemblies, political dissent was of little significance. A number of oppositionists were elected to the Fifth Assembly in 1808, and the habitual end-of-session absenteeism of the eastern county members seems occasionally to have given the opposition a temporary majority. There was no real unity of purpose among such men as Joseph Wilcocks, Samuel Sherwood and David McGregor Rogers, however, and these early stirrings disappeared with the wartime election of 1812. From 1812 to 1824, the provincial house was once more dominated by conservative-minded members. By no means did this guarantee to the executive government an acquiescent and docile Assembly. Both the American Loyalist and English Blackstonian traditions emphasized the separate and distinctive functions of the popular assembly in the constitution. Conservative Assemblies, especially when led by men as able and articulate as Robert Nichol, were quite capable of kicking over the traces, as the 1816 Assembly did, for example, on the issue of land and immigration policy.

332

It might be argued that the conservatism of the early Assemblies reflected an electorate not yet awakened to its grievances, and content to elect men who could benefit the locality through their connections with government. The real beginnings of reform strength in the Assembly date from the election of 1820, and unquestionably some of the Reformers then elected owed their success to the agitation of Robert Gourlay. Yet it would be incorrect to say that as reform sentiment became province-wide, conservatism as a force in the Assembly melted away. In the five elections from 1824 to 1836, there were two reform and two conservative victories, while another resulted in a virtual stalemate. The house elected in 1824 was very evenly divided, although on some issues the government could still find a majority. The mishandling of the alien question by the provincial executive had much to do with the reform sweep of 1828, yet in 1830 the conservatives were back in the saddle again, though by a relatively narrow margin. The 1834 Assembly was reform, but there was a substantial conservative opposition. The Thirteenth Assembly elected in 1836 was decisively conservative in composition. In sum, these elections demonstrate that conservatism met the democratic test of the hustings in Upper Canada, and that even after the rise of reform, men of conservative outlook had at least one chance in two of forming a majority in the Assembly. Long before the day of Macdonald, thousands of provincial voters had become habituated to voting on the Tory side, and a substantial voting base for the future Conservative party had been firmly established by 1841.

It must not be imagined that the Tories elected to the later Assemblies were a solid phalanx at one with themselves and with the ruling élite. They were no more united than were the reformers. Relatively few conservative assemblymen were prepared to go down the line with the "pure" Tories of the Councils on every issue. This is not to say that High Tories were not elected. John Beverley Robinson and Christopher Hagerman were repeatedly returned, despite their close association with official policy, and virtually every Assembly contained a few Tories who followed their lead. Most conservatives, however, were unwilling to follow Hagerman when he championed the views of Dr. Strachan on such matters as the clergy reserves the right to conduct the marriage ceremony, or the maintenance of the principle of primogeniture in cases of intestacy. Not even Hagerman would submit to official policies that conflicted sharply with the local interests he represented. Conservatives were frequently divided on banking legislation, the scale of appropriations for local services, proposals to tax unimproved lands in private hands, and hardy perennials such as the claims for war losses during the war of 1812; on these and other occasions, Tory assemblymen were at odds with the position taken by the official class. Members like Charles and Jonas Jones of Leeds and Brockville, William Morris of Perth, and Allan MacNab of Wentworth, all of whom have been identified with the Compact, took independent stands in the Assembly. On the whole, the brand of Toryism represented in the lower house was more moderate than that found in the councils; undoubtedly the need to get elected, and then to keep one's seat, helped to dilute High Tory principles. The lack of a constitutional connection between the Assembly and the other branches of government also encouraged independent behaviour in assemblymen, much as in the American congressional system, and allowed Tory candidates to distinguish themselves somewhat from government, although their reform opponents did what they could to obliterate this distinction in the minds of the electorate.

Undoubtedly the system of government under the Constitutional Act had something to do with swelling the ranks of conservatives in the assembly. Some moderate conservatives would have been quite as comfortable with the Baldwin reformers, had their business interests not induced them to retain official favour by maintaining some degree of orthodoxy on divisions. The permanence of officialdom, and the squeezing out of the moderate reform option in the 1830's, kept several men on the government side in politics. Perhaps the most prominent of these "business conservatives" was William Hamilton Merritt. Without the support of the provincial government, and of such figures in it as J. B. Robinson and John Strachan, Merritt's great undertaking, the Welland Canal, would have been impossible, and he trimmed his sails accordingly. Or was it his conversion to liberalism at the Union that is open to suspicion? In an intriguing correspondence with Robert Baldwin in 1840–41, Merritt admitted that he had never understood the principle of Responsible Government until he read Durham's Report, "but now that I see and feel the

333

necessity of that measure being fully carried out in this province, no person can be more firmly devoted to aid in its accomplishment." He was aware of his reputation for "inconsistency in advocating Lord Durham's Report & not having supported the Reform Party heretofore"; interestingly enough, he denied this charge on the grounds of his past independent performance in the legislature on such issues as the dismissal of Hagerman and Boulton, in which he had joined his fellow Tories in denouncing the interference of the imperial authorities! While it is quite possible that Merritt was a genuine convert, it is remarkable how nicely his conversion coincided with new directions in politics. To him, Responsible Government signified "the improvement of the St. Lawrence, a better and more abundant circulating medium, and unrestricted Emigration or at least on as liberal a footing as before the War of 1812": business objectives all, and much in keeping with the new Sydenham approach.

The thousands of recent immigrants from the British Isles who cast their first votes in the elections of the 1830's must have included many men of moderately liberal politics who, like Merritt, were forced by colonial realities to support Tory candidates. At an earlier time, the elector often could choose among five, six or even more competitors, but such smorgasbord politics diminished sharply after 1828. In many constituencies, the recent immigrant of Whiggish background found he had to choose between a Tory and a Mackenzie radical. "I feel myself fast growing a Tory", said John Langton, and many another must have made a similar choice.

If Upper Canada conservatism lacked uniformity and homogeneity, this is only another way of saying that it was an alliance of various groups, with different interests and outlooks. It is possible to express the nature of the alliance in several ways. A Tory of the time would certainly have said that conservative leadership came from the "respectable classes" in the community. In this sense, Toryism was the political expression of the province's small upper class, the people who considered themselves the natural leaders of society. For members of the professions, attachment to government conferred status and more tangible benefits. It is true that many reform leaders came from the legal and medical professions: John Rolph and William Warren Baldwin were members of both, while Dr. T. D. Morrison and the lawyers Robert Baldwin and Marshall Spring Bidwell testify to the lack of a Tory monopoly in this sphere. Yet most members of both professions seem to have been conservative. As for the military profession, its bias was instinctively conservative, among the hundreds of army and navy officers resident in Upper Canada on half-pay, a reform politician like Captain Matthews was very much a rare bird. Similarly, most landowners who thought of themselves as gentry, not farmers, were conservatives in politics. Yet, though the Tories were indisputably the representatives of the classes, to the dismay and mystification of reformers they were also able to win the support of many artisans and farmers, a phenomenon by no means confined to this period.

Merchants and other men of business were a special case. By and large, it was advantageous for them to be on the right side of government; as creditors, both their interests and their inclinations pushed them in that direction. Moreover, although the upper echelons of Toryism were almost exclusively bureaucratic in character, the official class proved reasonably responsive to the interests of the provincial mercantile community, and to the larger needs of St. Lawrence commercialism. Although there were exceptions, most substantial merchants, ship-owners and lumbering operators were Tory adherents, while many smaller tradesmen and shopkeepers tended the other way.

Early Toryism is usually associated with Anglicanism, and with the exclusive pretensions of the Church of England to the clergy reserves and to control over public education. This is not altogether an inaccurate impression, but it is a misleading one; obviously the Tories could not have achieved any measure of electoral success had they depended upon the votes of Anglicans alone. The situation has perhaps not been recognized in all its complexities. On the one hand, it is certainly true that for many years John Strachan spoke both for his church and for the executive government of the province upon religious policy, and that from first to last he never yielded an inch in his claims for the exclusive rights of the Anglican Church. Yet Strachan did not speak for all conservatives, probably not for a majority of Anglican laymen, and certainly not for the Tory politicians whose first concerns were to win elections and to keep their local supporters satisfied. Whatever the merits of Strachan's cause, from the political point of view his pronouncements were inept, and disastrously weakened the conservative alliance at some crucial stages in its history.

335

For an alliance, however precarious, did exist among Anglicans, members of the Church of Scotland and Catholics. There was not a great deal of difference, except in national origin, between well-to-do Anglicans and Presbyterians, and they met and mingled easily in society and business. All three denominations were united in their distrust of Protestant dissent, particularly that emanating from the United States. The clergy of all three churches were instinctively social and political conservatives; all believed that churches had a public role to play; and all accepted the principle that churches should support order and government through the promotion of public and private morality and the inculcation of ideas of subordination and of veneration for authority. Neither Presbyterians nor Catholics (with a few notable exceptions) objected to the principle of public endowment of churches, or to church control over public education. What they found objectionable was Strachan's insistence upon the exclusive jurisdiction of the Church of England in those spheres, and the style he chose to adopt in urging his case.

Nevertheless, an alliance, however fragile, was maintained politically among the members of three churches, and was manifested in a variety of ways. Through the provincial government, the clergy of the Catholic Church and of the Church of Scotland were accorded a status not extended to the clergy of the sects. Grants of Crown land for churches, and small grants of public money for the support of clergy and schoolmasters, were made to both churches from an early date. Bishop Alexander Macdonell was made a legislative councillor; so were a number of Catholic and Presbyterian laymen. In the Assembly, spokesmen of the three denominations combined to defend their common viewpoint on such matters as the right to perform marriages, or to denounce the radical proposal to secularize the reserves and devote the proceeds to a system of secular education. It was only at the critical election of 1836 that the Tories opened their ranks to admit Ogle Gowan and his Orangemen to a full political partnership; prior to that time the Orangemen had been regarded with deep distrust, not only by the Catholics, but by non-Catholic Tories as well, precisely because of the danger they posed to the religious foundations of the conservative coalition. Bishop Macdonell's address to the Catholic and Protestant free-holders of Stormont and Glengarry in 1836, advising them to vote the conservative ticket, was remarkable testimony of the religious base of Toryism.[1]

336

Upper Canadian Toryism was an alliance, or rather a system of alliances, between the bureaucratic élite attached to the government of the province, and local élites and their followings. Although the alliance was held together in part by natural affinities arising from common social, economic and institutional outlooks, its chief bond was political. Only in the central arena of politics did the interests of all the groups that made it up intersect, and only through the political process could tangible satisfaction for these interests be forthcoming. In other words, in order to meet the needs of the conservative coalition, something very like the modern political party was required, and something very like it was created. Under the shelter of the 1791 constitution, the Tories constructed the first province-wide political organization in Upper Canada. While it might be technically incorrect to employ the term "party" to describe a system that lacked the modern party's distinctive trappings, yet in the crucial test of function there was a provincial Tory party long before the reformers had begun to organize themselves. The constitution of Upper Canada was doubled — outwardly, it was the usual formal structure of the British colonial establishment; inwardly, the apparatus of government was virtually identical with the apparatus of party. There was no need for the Tories to band together in any permanent fashion, as reformers began to do under the leadership of W. W. Baldwin, William Lyon Mackenzie and Jesse Ketchum in the late 1820's. Little wonder that reformers writhed at Tory hypocrisy when their party organizations were denounced as "factions". So long as the constitution remained unreformed, conservatives had no need for political associations outside it.

The building of the Tory party into the constitution can best be traced briefly in the history of the distribution of Crown patronage in Upper Canada, since the handling of patronage illustrates clearly the dynamics of the system. During Simcoe's tenure, the dispensing of patronage remained in the hands of the lieutenant governor, though even Simcoe distributed jobs and other favours partly on the advice he got from his principal officers of government. He used patronage for the explicit purpose of cementing to government the loyalties of the most "respectable" members of society, whose principles through emulation would then be broadcast throughout their localities. Though Simcoe's political objective was never departed from, inevitably it became intermingled with motives of private advantage as population grew and as the process of selection became more complicated. Continuity in government patronage policy came to rest with the officials, whose tenure was permanent in fact if not in law, even though successive lieutenant governors exerted ultimate control, and sometimes intervened directly in the process. Those officials of government who enjoyed the particular confidence of the lieutenant governor used their favourable position to benefit their friends in various parts of the province. As a result, a simple clientage or "interest" system took shape, and by the time of the war of 1812 it was so well-established that it was impossible for a young man to make his way up the ladder of preferment without the necessary connections.

337

The inner political history of Upper Canada is largely the history of warring interests, and of their rise and fall. Peter Russell's interest was paramount for the first decade of provincial history, and through him the fortunes of families like the Baldwins and the Willcockses were advanced. Russell's influence waned after the turn of the century, and at his death in 1808, since the politics of patronage were personal, the Russell interest collapsed, and with it the hopes and prospects of his clientage. The ascendancy of Judge William Dummer Powell dates from shortly after the arrival of Lt. Gov. Francis Gore. Through Powell's help, usually obtained through such local intermediaries as Richard Cartwright of Kingston or Dr. Solomon Jones of Augusta, a large number of people received places or other benefits from government. Dr. John Strachan and his protégé, John Beverley Robinson, were both in Powell's debt at early stages in their careers — something of an irony, since they combined to ease the Chief Justice out of his place at the centre of power and of the web of patronage shortly after Sir Peregrine Maitland took over.

As the clientage system ramified, as indeed it was bound to do, since every prominent official at York had at least some jobs or perquisites in his gift, it hardened into a complex network joining officials at the capital to interest groups in every locality, in a bewildering maze of inter-relationships. As early as the 1820's, and probably well before then, each community had a local oligarchy — in effect, a party machine — through which the provincial government dispensed its favours. In Kingston, for example, a group headed by John Kirby, John Macaulay and Thomas and George Markland advised the York officials on questions of patronage, and submitted nominations for justices of the peace, local court officials, commissions and promotions in the local militia, the issuance of licences, or the allocation of government contracts of one kind or another. In Leeds and Grenville, the Joneses and Sherwoods performed the same functions; everywhere, in fact, across the province a voluminous political correspondence was maintained between the central bureaucracy and local Tory personages, from district chieftains like Allan MacNab of Wentworth and Mahlon Burwell of the London district down to party wheelhorses like Thomas Mears of Peterborough and George Hamilton of Hawkesbury.

The Tory "party", then, was a quasi-official coalition of the central and local élites united for the purpose of distributing honours and rewards to the politically deserving. The system was certainly effective in building, maintaining and disciplining a conservative coalition for electoral purposes, although that was by no means its only function. On the whole, it worked fairly smoothly, despite the inevitable faction fights among local groupings over division of the spoils, and tussles among higher officials over jurisdiction and influence. Its operations strengthened the social, economic, religious and ideological bases of the conservative alliance in the most tangible way. Thus, in the Perth area, the Presbyterian William Morris was given a leading voice in the allotment of jobs; in the eastern counties Bishop Macdonell had for many years a free hand in dispensing patronage among the Catholic population; while in Kingston, Christopher Hagerman took care to see that his Presbyterian and Catholic constituents got their share of plums. Some of the most intricate balancing of competing group claims was done whenever new writs for the commissions of the peace were issued. Nominations for justices of the peace went up to York from the localities, and then were sifted by the law officers of the Crown before the new commissions went out. It is worth noting that John Beverley Robinson, among others, was quite prepared occasionally to accept the appointment of known reformers as J. P.s, usually when there was a shortage of competent Tory candidates.

But because the patronage system hinged upon personal relationships, and had little to do ordinarily with forms of merit other than the political, its operations led inevitably to abuses that in the long run hurt the Tory cause. Too frequently men of real ability were passed over, and became permanently embittered. Robert Nichol, William Warren Baldwin, and an assortment of Ridouts, Jarvises and Smalls were given jobs of a demeaning kind, either in terms of their competence, or in terms of their personal measurements of their merit; such incidents had something to do with the making of a few reformers. In the 1830's, hundreds of able new Upper Canadians found that the official avenues of preferment were closed to them; the system had hardened too much, had become too exclusive and too inflexible to make room for enough of them. Pluralism, the cosy practice of passing offices down from father to son, and the maintenance in office of incompetent or unreliable men were abuses of the second generation of Upper Canadian Toryism that provided weapons for reformers, and sharpened their desire to turn the rascals out, and to get rid of a form of government that could foster such a system.

338

Political patronage was hardly the invention of the Upper Canadian conservatives. Yet their use of it to build up a coalition was the central fact of provincial politics, and established a political climate that profoundly affected reformers as well. It is true that the reforms of the 1840's and 1850's did much to regularize public administration, and to rid the structure of local government of many of its more spectacular abuses. But it was no accident that the reform-inspired conciliar crises of 1836 and 1843–4 centred upon control of Crown patronage, even though, on each occasion, the issue was masked in the lofty principles of Responsible Government. Nor is it an accident, as students of the Baldwin papers know, that well over half the surviving Baldwin correspondence is devoted to questions of patronage. The Tories pioneered in the use of patronage to build party; the reformers, despite their rhetoric, learned the lesson well, and played the same game as intensely, and perhaps more skilfully, than had their conservative teachers.

339

The Upper Canadian Tories contributed to subsequent politics on quite other planes than patronage. In the field of public policy, their major legacy was the Welland Canal, and to a lesser degree the St. Lawrence canal system. The Welland was a collaboration between the energy and enthusiasm of private projectors like William Hamilton Merritt, and the readiness of conservatives, official and otherwise, to pledge the cooperation of government in an enterprise of great provincial importance. Both elements were indispensable to the completion of this remarkable project, which in the end became a government-owned facility.

The Tories, in entering into collaboration with private initiative in the development of the Welland and other canals, were responding to a general desire for public improvements, and in particular to the threat posed by the building of the Erie Canal, which, if not countered, would drain off the commerce of the province to the south and New York. It is important to emphasize, however, that conservative canal policy was not just a response to public pressure. In the lengths to which they were prepared to go in mortgaging the public credit, the Tories far outran the views of a large section of provincial opinion. At first, the reformers had been quite as enthusiastic as conservative assemblymen in their support for the Welland, but as the real difficulties of its construction and financing unfolded, they became more and more hostile towards it, and more and more suspicious of the ties between it and government.

Some Tory Assembly members did oppose the Welland Canal, usually as a result of the same regional considerations that influenced reformers from the eastern part of the province. Many easterners could not accept the argument that the Welland, as an integral part of the whole St. Lawrence system, would benefit the whole province and not just the merchants and farmers of the west. On the whole, however, most opposition came from reformers, from whatever region. Some of them, like William Lyon Mackenzie, were convinced that the canal was a great engine of Tory corruption and patronage, although an Assembly investigation under Mackenzie's chairmanship disclosed nothing but inefficiency. Most reformers thought that Upper Canada was too small for such an immense undertaking. "This great overgrown concern", said Marshall Spring Bidwell in the Assembly debates of January, 1834, was "consuming the life's blood of this young province." "Is all to be subservient to this great Moloch?", Peter Perry asked; it should be left to rot, in his opinion, as "a monument of the folly of the Legislature of Upper Canada." By and large, reformers took a democratic view of their relationship to their constituents, and as mouthpieces for local electorates tended to be more parochial in outlook than most conservatives. Consequently, public improvements for them meant chiefly roads and bridges for their own constituencies. Conservative members were more responsive to the commercial interests that formed so important a part of their political support, and while quite ready to play the politics of roads and bridges, were more open to the appeal of enterprises that were provincial in scope.

340

Here they were following the lead given them by the official Tory élite. The list of substantial provincial subscribers to Welland stock under the charter of 1825 was dominated by the names of men in the inner circle of power: J. B. Robinson, William Allan, J. H. Dunn, H. J. Boulton, D'Arcy Boulton, and Col. Joseph Wells. Repeatedly, during the ensuing years, it was the influence of these men, and others like Strachan, Hagerman, MacNab and John Macaulay, that rescued the Canal from final disaster. Vested as they were with responsibility for the whole province, largely unconnected with popular politics and thus relieved of the inconvenient necessity of assuaging the doubts of a local electorate, acutely conscious of the military, economic and political menace of the United States, the Tory élite backed the Welland Canal to the hilt as a measure vital to the security as well as the prosperity of all. Robinson termed the prospect of private gain from the Welland "quite a secondary consideration"; it was well he did, for none was made. "The grand object", he said, "was to overcome a great natural impediment to the prosperity of the better half of our country." There was nothing doctrinaire in the readiness of conservatives to use public credit to supplement, and eventually to replace private capital; in a country so short of fluid capital as Upper Canada, in the face of so urgent a public necessity, government had to step in. When the legislative commissioners, John Macaulay, W. B. Robinson and Absolom Shade, found that the Welland Canal Company was no longer equal to maintaining the canal, they recommended public ownership without a tremor, so that "the Canal should be thus rendered in name, as it always has been in fact, and must be in effect, a *national concern.*" Despite their inefficiencies and miscalculations, there was an undeniable statesmanship in the pragmatic conservative acceptance of the positive role that government must play in order to counteract the vulnerabilities of the Canadian economy and polity. The example they set was to be followed by the next generation of canal builders, and by the Conservative party in the years to come, whether the object involved was one of national importance, as with the Intercolonial and Canadian Pacific railways, or of provincial concern, as with Ontario Hydro. In this realm of public policy, both Macdonald and Whitney were legatees of the Upper Canadian conservatives.

When the Tories used the term "national" to describe projects like the Welland and St. Lawrence canals, they meant only that they were natural monopolies, affecting so vitally the common weal that they were, or should be, removed from the sphere of private relationships. In all other senses, "national" still meant "British" or "imperial", since the conservative still regarded himself as a member of the British nation. Yet the seeds of a separate nationalism were implicit in the Upper Canadian Tory's approach to the economic problems involved in public improvements, trade, and banking, for though he might justify a particular policy on grounds of imperial interests, it was the provincial stake he had chiefly in view. Joined to the concern for local interests was a deeply defensive cast of mind. To most Tories, though perhaps not to the aggressive and optimistic merchants, a canal like the Welland was a protective device, to be visualised in political, social and cultural contexts as well as in the economic.

341

It is at this point that the conservative economic policy intersected with the total structure of conservative values; values which have had an influence far beyond the bounds of party, and which indeed lie at the roots of Canadian national feeling. Conservatism is concerned with the preservation of arrangements deemed good. The more highly such arrangements are prized, the more strongly the conservative will react under challenge to them. Upper Canada, in conservative eyes, was not merely challenged, but was under a state of permanent siege; hence the conservative mind in Upper Canada was a mind beleaguered. While conservatism flourished in all the provinces of British North America, only in Upper Canada was it professed with such passionate conviction, because Upper Canada was vulnerable in ways which the other provinces were not. The apprehended threat from the large American-born element in the population, and the quite genuine danger, military, political and cultural, from the United States, made "loyalty" the crux of conservative attitudes. Loyalty did not simply mean adherence to the Crown and the Empire, although it started there. It meant as well adherence to those beliefs and institutions the conservative considered essential in the preservation of a form of life different from, and superior to, the manners, politics and social arrangements of the United States. To the Tory, American democratic republicanism was the worst possible form of government, since it tempted politicians to play upon the worst appetites of men. The Tory was ignorant of such subtleties in the American constitution as the system of checks and balances, or if he was not, considered that their effect was rather to weaken executive government than to check the turbulence inherent in democracy. The deistic founding fathers, in their rejection of the connection between religion and the state, had sacrificed the most effective brake upon public disorder, and paved the way for anarchy. While it was true that men created the institutions under which they chose to live, the conservative believed quite as strongly that institutions made men and made nationality. The American, shaped by his secularized and revolutionary democracy, was a being altogether different from the British American; and his society was moving along another road. The shape of things to come was to be seen in the cities of the United States: swollen by non-British immigration, torn by crime and violence, and governed by corrupt machines kept in power by demagogic appeals to mass envy and greed. How preferable it was to live under the stable, orderly and peaceful government of Upper Canada, with institutions that encouraged both private and public morality, and that cherished true liberty, personal independence and a decent respectability.

Loyalty, then, meant much more than political allegiance. It signified acceptance of the special character of life in Upper Canada. Any attack upon the beliefs and institutions that guaranteed that life was an attack upon the order of things that made the Canadian different from the American, and hence the Upper Canadian conservative reacted with peculiar vehemence against reformers, particularly those who were "soft" on the American question. The relation of these attitudes to the fostering of an intense local patriotism, or, as S. R. Mealing has put it (having in mind the Union period), a spirit of Ontario sectionalism which "survived the Compact's disintegration", is fairly clear. What has not been apprehended so clearly is the extent to which early conservatism was assimilated into the dominant attitudes of nineteenth century Canadian society, and how significant a part of present day patterns of thought derives from colonial Toryism. For this transformation to come about, the focus of loyalty had to be shifted from Britain to British North America. As has been suggested, that process was well under way before 1841. (It is remarkable, incidentally, how conscious such Upper Canadian High Tories as J. B. Robinson, William Macaulay, H. J. Boulton, George Markland and Christopher Hagerman became of their separate identities as Canadians when, at various times, they visited the centre of Empire, and discovered with a sudden shock how greatly Britain differed from their picture of it.) It was necessary, too, for the concept of loyalty to be broadened to embrace the party system and the idea of responsible opposition. That was to be the work of the next generation.

In certain ways, Upper Canadian conservatism was a major formative influence upon the nature of the reform tradition in the province. This was so not only in the sense that the failings of Toryism provided reformers with a platform and with a catalogue of grievances, but also, and quite as significantly, because the long conservative dominance, and the effect this had upon Upper Canadian habits of mind and political behaviour, eliminated radicalism as a major political alternative. The mainstream of reform is represented by Robert Baldwin and George Brown, not by Robert Gourlay, William Lyon Mackenzie and "Coon" Cameron; by a mingling

342

of moderate political reformism and social and economic orthodoxy, not by across-the-board democratic radicalism; and by the observance of the proprieties in political discourse, rather than by the unfettered approach of the radical school. In all this, the reformers were adapting themselves to an environment largely created by early conservatism.

When, in the 1850s, a common political culture emerged in the Canadas, and the major parties, despite their surface antagonisms, came to be in agreement upon the fundamental assumptions without which a viable polity could not have existed, the foundations for a Canadian national feeling were laid. In the new synthesis, though both liberal and conservative, traditions were considerably modified, it was the values of conservatism that gave coherence to the whole. In this context, it was Macdonald's function to extend the values he had inherited from the Toryism of old Ontario to the rest of the country, in company with those thousands of Upper Canadians who took part in the peopling of the West.

343

Note

1. This analysis of the religious base of Toryism deals with its leading elements. There was, of course, scattered support from members of other denominations, and a notable, although temporary accession of strength from Methodism following Egerton Ryerson's dramatic break with reform in 1833.

The Political Ideas of George Brown*
J.M.S. CARELESS

Canadian political figures have generally skirted the discussion of ideas and doctrine by wide platitudes. Not George Brown, however, the journalist-politician and Clear Grit Liberal leader of the Confederation era — he was born to argue principle. In his powerful Toronto *Globe*, the most widely circulated newspaper in British North America, he had the ideal instrument for expressing his mind, and for over three decades, from the first *Globe* issue in 1844 to his death in 1880, it presented a massive documentation of the thinking of George Brown. Others, of course, shared in writing its columns, especially after Brown entered parliament in 1852. Yet he kept such strong control that the journal regularly exhibited the consistent pattern of his thought, consistent too with his lengthy, closely argued speeches in the House and about the Ontario countryside. This pattern may be best described in terms of three main threads that ran through it: his creed of anti-state-church Protestantism, his belief in free-trade, economic liberal doctrines, and his rooted preference for British parliamentary institutions over American republican models.

*From *The Canadian Forum*, February 1957, pp. 247-250. Reprinted by permission.

But to trace these threads to their beginnings, one must start in the classic way with the early life and family background of George Brown.

Born in Edinburgh in 1819, he grew up in the fervent atmosphere of reform movements that were striving to pry loose the dead hand of the eighteenth century from the Scottish church and state. On the one side was the struggle against the old narrow oligarchies in the boroughs that triumphed in the Reform Act of 1832. On the other was the mounting protest against the power of lay authority in the Church of Scotland, a protest which led ultimately to the disruption of 1843, when the "non-intrusionist" faction withdrew from the established Presbyterian church to set up the Free Kirk. Brown's own Edinburgh middle-class family were Whig-Reform in politics, evangelical and non-intrusionist in their Presbyterianism. And both stands were ardently expounded to him by his father, who undoubtedly did more than anyone else to mould the mind of his son.

344

Peter Brown, a prominent wholesale merchant active in civic affairs, was well acquainted with the capital's literary and Whig social circles, and well acquainted besides with constitutional history, the writings of the masters of Scots Presbyterianism, and contemporary liberal political and economic doctrine. From him a receptive George Brown learned the significance of the separation of the church and state for progress, liberty, and truth: that a church-connected state suffered from sectarian strife in politics and the danger of clerical domination, while a state-connected church was degraded by sordid struggles for worldly power and squabbles over benefits from the public purse. He learned as well of the natural laws of economic freedom so indisputably determined by Adam Smith and his successors. And he came to know the merits of a balanced liberal constitution, wherein the forces of the selfish aristocracy and the unenlightened masses could both be held in check by the weight of the responsible, respectable (and middle) classes of society.

Though he was not quite eighteen when he left Scotland, Brown continued under this sort of tutelage; for in 1837 he accompanied his father to New York to help prepare the way for the rest of the family. There he began his career in journalism by assisting Peter Brown to publish the *British Chronicle*, a little weekly for the emigrant Scots community, very Whig-Liberal in its full reports of British politics. At the same time both Browns began to react sharply to the American political scene. As they saw it, republicanism boasted of liberty but practised slavery, scorned the hidebound ways of Europe but kept up the old fallacy of tariff protection. Then too, its devotion to the false ideal of universal-suffrage democracy had merely led to the corrupt power of machine politicians and rule by the passions of the mob. And finally it seemed evident that Britain's parliamentary monarchy, cabinet system, and unwritten constitution were far superior to the unwieldy mechanism of American government, with its inflexible written prescriptions and jarring division of authority. George Brown did acquire a lasting respect for the vigor and free spirit of the individual American; but holding views such as these he could hardly live contentedly in the United

States. Consequently, when in 1843 the Browns received an invitation to found a Free Kirk journal in Canada (thanks to the *British Chronicle's* glowing support of the non-intrusionists on the disruption of the Scottish Church), the son was quick to urge his father to make the change.

Moving to Toronto, they began the *Banner* as a Presbyterian sectarian paper. But within a few months their strong political convictions had all but inevitably committed them to the Reform side in the contemporary Canadian struggle over responsible government, and George Brown launched out with his own secular Liberal political journal, the Toronto *Globe*. From the start in March of 1844, it expressed the basic ideas that he had acquired in his British background and American experience. Thus the principle of the separation of church and state resounded through the *Globe's* attacks on Anglican-controlled King's College, and determined its support of a wholly secular provincial university, the University of Toronto as erected by the Act of 1849. Thus Brown's free trade ideal made his paper welcome the ending of the old imperial preferences in the late 'forties, and look forward to the attainment of reciprocity with the United States as a step towards the rational removal of all tariff barriers. And hence as well, his enthusiasm for parliamentary institutions brought the *Globe* to view the pursuit of responsible government essentially as an effort to gain the crowning excellence of the British cabinet system for the colonial constitution.

345

The fifties brought the rise of sectional strife in the province of Canada, the collapse of the old Reform party, and the emergence of George Brown as leader of a reconstituted Upper Canadian Liberalism. His ideas were modified by existing conditions, but still the underlying pattern remained. Devotion to the British parliamentary model was expressed in his hostility to the new Clear Grit radical movement of the early 'fifties, whose demands for fully elective institutions he ardently condemned as republican and democratic, and destructive of the parliamentary principle. Furthermore, he kept up a rear-guard resistance to the widely supported proposal to make the upper house elective, on the grounds that two elected chambers would upset the workings of British cabinet government, which could hardly be responsible to two possibly opposed sets of representatives of the people. On the economic side, he fought protective tariff measures, not only as the evil consequences of government extravagance and the lobbying of special-interest groups, but because they flew in the face of the great truth of free trade. As for church-state relations, above all he identified himself, first, with the agitation that finally brought the abolition of the clergy reserves in 1854 — on the principle that there should be no state endowment for religion — and, second, with the opposition to mounting Roman Catholic demands for separate school provisions — in the contention that state supported education must be secular and not denominational in character.

In this last strenuous campaign, Brown has often been accused of simply giving vent to anti-Catholic bigotry. The harsh language of the *Globe* adds color to the charge, though vehemence was by no means all on one side in an age that violently expressed its religious and political antipathies. It is worth recalling that his stand against "Catholic aggression" in the matter of separate schools was based on a general political principle, which actually sought to take religious strife out of politics by denying any form of state connection to churches in a land of many different denominations. Yet Brown's fierce opposition to Catholic demands undoubtedly indicated more than the defence of a principle: rather, the influence of particular Canadian circumstances on the general pattern of his thinking. Canada then was an uneasy union of two discordant sections, the largely Protestant, English-speaking Upper Canada of the West and the strongly Catholic and French Lower Canada of the East. In terms of population Lower Canada was over-represented in the union parliament, and the compact power of French Canadian votes there could work to impose separate school legislation on the West against the will of its Protestant majority. And so, fired with Upper Canada's indignation at "French Catholic domination" and filled with his own Free Kirk evangelical Protestant fervor, Brown could readily translate his concept of the separation of church and state into militant anti-Catholicism.

Canadian circumstances brought another adjustment in his attitude, when in the mid-fifties he came to terms with the Clear Grits who had been among his most bitter foes. The change came out of the final break-up of the old Reform party in 1854, that put the Liberal-Conservative coalition, and soon John A. Macdonald, in control of government. The Brownite and Clear Grit Reform fragments left in opposition gradually joined to build a new Liberal party, a potent combination appealing to western sectional discontents that brought together Brown's talents for leadership, the strong voice of the *Globe*, and the growing weight of Grit numbers in the agrarian West. Brown, however, achieved the reconstruction largely by turning the erstwhile Grit radicals from ultimate projects for democratizing the constitution to the immediate question of Upper Canada's wrongs. His past differences with the Clear Grits were laid aside, but he by no means became a democrat himself or gave up his objections to elective institutions on the American plan (though he did accept the American party convention). In fact, he virtually grafted British middle-class urban Liberalism on to Grit agrarian democracy, so that the end-product was the staid and moderate Victorian Liberal party in Ontario which passed on to Oliver Mowat's keeping — a far cry from the root-and-branch democracy of the early Clear Grit radicals.

Nevertheless Brown did identify the forces he directed with the demand for representation by population to end Lower Canada's preponderance of power; and this was a demand that had an ominously democratic ring, and was so attacked by his Conservative opponents. But Brown and his journal frequently asserted that applying this just principle to the allotment of parliamentary seats in no way involved the wholesale introduction of democracy. The *Globe* explained, moreover, that while it was possible to have a good deal wider franchise in Canada than in England, this was because there was a far higher proportion of respectable, property-holding "yeomanry" in the population — which still sounded more like the British middle-class Liberal approach to the question of the suffrage than the

American democratic belief in the inalienable right of one man to one vote.

Yet the North American problem of sectionalism led to a further adjustment of Brown's thinking: to the acceptance of federalism, not closer legislative union, as the solution for Canada's problems. The result was the plan he advocated at the Reform Convention of 1859, a federal union of the two Canadas without the "organic changes" in political institutions which some Grit back-benchers still sought. British parliamentary patterns would be preserved, but combined with the federal principle: it was significant that the *Globe* termed this a "British-American" scheme of government. Within a few years Brown's Canadian federal plan was merged in the wider project for general British North American federation; but at the Quebec Conference of 1864 that drafted the design for Confederation he made clear that he had not forgotten his basic concern for the British parliamentary model. He again opposed an elective upper house in the new constitution, this time successfully. It was not that he expected great things from an appointed federal Senate. He stood rather on the ground that the American type of Senate, part of a system that divided power between President and two houses of Congress, could not be imported into a constitution that gave unity of power to a cabinet organically linked to a single elected chamber. Sectional feeling in the provinces might require a second federal chamber; the principles of British cabinet government no less required that it should not be a competing elected body.

347

In short, in Confederation as in other political issues, Brown sought to maintain British institutions while adapting them to Canadian needs. He could be sharply critical of things British on occasion, but always within the limits set by his acceptance of a British heritage as fundamentally valuable to Canada. In a sense, this attitude dictated his whole approach to questions in Canadian-imperial relations. Treating imperial affairs as family affairs, his paper was ready to make scathing criticisms of British politicians and policies, in a manner that allowed conveniently shocked Conservative opponents to denounce it as subversive and republican, ignoring the repeated proofs to the contrary, and the *Globe's* inherent belief in the value of imperial connection. Brown and his journal, in fact, saw Canada as a new nation in North America ("We too are Americans," he declared), but a nation still within the framework of the British Empire and subordinate in its immaturity. Such a view could be assailed both by the more conservative, as trenching on disloyalty, and by the more radical as timid and old-fogey. Both attacks were made before Confederation. Afterwards, in the new national enthusiasm roused in the early years of the Dominion the noise of battle rose chiefly on the left, from idealistic nationalists contending with the *Globe*. As that paper lashed back at the Canada First group of the 'seventies and their ally of the moment, Goldwin Smith, it might have seemed that Brown had grown colonially-minded with advancing age. Actually, however, even in his most angry moments of denouncing imperial bumbling in times gone by, he had never really felt the impatient yearning for national recognition which now infused some of the "four millions of Britons who are not free.'' No doubt the simple truth was that times were moving on, and what had seemed a progressive viewpoint in Brown's own generation was becoming old-guard to its successor — which only further indicates that the basic pattern of his thought remained unaltered.

In similar fashion his views on economic policy remained in much the form that he had brought them to Canada, though once more there might be some adaptation to fit them to the Canadian situation. He conceded, for example, that full free trade on the British plan was inapplicable to Canada, since in an undeveloped country the main source of government revenue had still to be the tariff. Yet this should be kept as low as possible, without "artificial" protective rates, and government expenditure accordingly be held to the minimum. His belief in reciprocity with the United States persisted; though when in 1865 the Americans made clear that they would abrogate the Reciprocity Treaty of 1854 he was not willing to seek its renewal at all costs, and even left the coalition government formed to carry Confederation on this specific issue. Nevertheless it was notable that in 1874, after he had been out of active politics for seven years, Alexander Mackenzie's Liberal government sent him to Washington to negotiate a new treaty; and while his efforts failed, they signified his abiding interest in the project.

348

Just as abiding was his faith in the doctrines of economic liberalism, which the *Globe* preached with ceaseless zeal. Its editorials — and his speeches — frequently expounded the revealed natural laws of economics: not only with regard to tariff matters, but in respect of the abolition of usury legislation, the falsity of legal-tender schemes for paper currency, and the wrongheadedness of trade unionism. In this last connection Brown spoke with particular feeling as a newspaper proprietor who had to meet some of the first manifestations of organized labor in Canada. When the *Globe* faced printers' strikes its readers were favored with specially full critiques of collective bargaining. In this Brown's reaction was merely that of most large employers of his day — and as an employer it seems that on the whole he was a fair-minded one. His trouble was that he was sufficiently well read in the prevailing canons to add intellectual horror to business annoyance over trade unions, and had the *Globe* in which to make it plain.

This comes close to a general conclusion on Brown's thinking. Many of his ideas were shared by large numbers of Canadians in his day: his distinction was that, as a leading journalist, he had the *Globe* in which to propound them so thoroughly. Yet this is not the full story. Brown's opinions were far more coherently organized on the basis of set principles, his ideas much more explicitly rendered, than were those of many of his contemporaries — including, specifically, most of his political colleagues and opponents. He may not have had the flexible practicality and intuitive understanding of a Macdonald. He may have lacked the depth of learning and intellectual grasp of a Goldwin Smith. But Macdonald had good reason to regard him as his ablest adversary, Smith to bewail his paper's "literary despotism". No one could dispute the force of Brown's mind, reasoning in supreme confidence from what were to him logical and tested propositions.

And when one finds his views echoed by the multitude of the *Globe's* faithful, reshaping Clear Grit Liberalism, and working to precipitate the decisive sectional crisis that issued in Confederation — who can deny that that mind was a vital influence on the emerging character of a young Canadian nation?

The Genesis of Ontario Politics in the Province of Canada (1838-1871)*

PAUL G. CORNELL

In 1838 Lord Durham reported on "the peculiar geographical character of the province [Upper Canada] . . . its inhabitants scattered along an extensive frontier, with imperfect means of communication, and a limited and partial commerce, have, apparently no unity of interest or opinion. The Province has no great centre with which all the parts are connected, . . . Instead of this, there are many petty local centres, the sentiments and interests (or at least what are fancied to be so) of which, are distinct, and perhaps opposed". If we accept his analysis without question we are driven to wonder whether the history of this Upper Canada region can be studied as a single social and political entity. In seeking reasons for political disaffection and retarded economic progress Durham gives no credit to his despised Family Compact for the co-ordination and leadership that they had in fact given in the province's first forty-five years of very primitive pioneer development.

349

Thirty years later Upper Canada had become a self-conscious and viable province of Ontario: with a sense of identity, a metropolitan centre in Toronto, its land fully settled, its commerce prosperous, new industries multiplying, and the whole welded together by a network of railways. All this had happened in the years 1840-1867 while it had been attached to Lower Canada in the united province of Canada. Statesmen of that era were baffled by the extraordinary complex of divergent pressures and tendencies of those years, and later historians continue to share their puzzlement. The facts of geography and economics dictated that Upper Canada establish and maintain intimate connections with Lower Canada, while most pressures in the maturing society urged on the consolidation of regional institutions fulfilling local needs. This study seeks to identify, particularly in the political field, the main foundations of the province of Ontario in the years 1837-1871.

I

Between the dying days of 1837 and September 1841 a perplexed British government had resolved upon a course of action to start the Canadian col-

*From *Profiles of a Province*, pp. 59-72. Copyright 1967, by Ontario Historical Society. Reprinted by permission.

onies on a new course of progress, and the policy had been set in motion by twenty-three months of unremitting activity by Lord Sydenham.

The new policy had various ingredients. The economic unity of the St. Lawrence River–Great Lakes region was to be recognized and the French-Canadian "problem" solved by joining Upper Canada and Lower Canada into one province. The stalled economy was to be sparked into new life by a large infusion of new capital for public works and a reform in public administrative procedures. Tensions between groups of Reformers and Tories were considered to be exaggerations of real social and administrative problems, grown out of proportion in an isolated backwoods society. They could be overcome by good effective administration. The rigid confrontation that had brought active rebellion could be thawed by isolating and ignoring the leaders of extreme groups while sponsoring practical men of moderate views. Theoretical ideas, current in the colonies and in Britain about applying the techniques of responsible cabinet government, were inadmissable and wrongheaded. Theoretically they would place the Governor at the mercy of two quite different masters: the British government and colonial public opinion. In practical terms, both Upper and Lower Canada were rent by the contentions of extreme, irresponsible political groups; the present colonial population would not be able to operate with moderation the highly sophisticated conventions of cabinet government.

For Canada West (the new official name of Upper Canada) Lord Sydenham's initiatives left several important legacies. He used his personal experience of British business and political methods with machiavellian shrewdness to get the wheels of government rolling again. A Colonial Office dispatch of October 16, 1839 authorized him to remove and replace members of the colony's Executive Council when public policy dictated. One main citadel of Compact Tory power was thereby immediately undermined. Sydenham used the threat of this power to secure the acquiescence of Upper Canadian Tories in his policies, and then he removed them from office. The governor masterminded the campaign strategy for the 1841 general election, and personally arranged the details. Compact Tories were excluded from a slate of officially favoured candidates, while middle-of-the-road independents and moderate Reformers were sought out and encouraged. These candidates were given every available aid and assistance and the personal attention of the governor. Their opponents were excluded from government patronage and pointedly snubbed. Of the forty-two members returned by Canada West only 6 Compact Tories and 7 ultra-Reformers consistently opposed the governor's policies in the Legislature. Sydenham's methods had reduced Tory representation to only 14%, while his manoeuvering among Reformers had disorganized their sense of party solidarity. For the moment he held the initiative in the political life of Canada West.

The *élan*, and even supercilious contempt, with which Sydenham manipulated his colonial demesne, did not disguise his use of every trick of contemporary British political life to achieve his immediate aims. Perhaps

Canadians did not need lessons in the use of influence, patronage and physical violence in political manoeuvre. There remained for a generation, however, the memory that the highest representative of the British government gloried in political expediency.

Finally, it had been a part of British strategy for solving the problems of 1837, that the English-speaking majority in the United Province should in time, effectively assimilate the French Canadian minority. Given the different well-established institutions in the provinces of Upper and Lower Canada, and the solidarity of the French Canadian community, the policy had no hope of success. Yet the formative months of 1840 and 1841 were the time to set the pattern for such changes, if they were to come about. There is no evidence that Sydenham tried to bring the institutions and people of Canada West into active co-operation with the English community of Canada East. On the contrary, he set the pattern of legislating separately for the institutions of the two sections of the province; and in organizing the 1841 general election he recognized two different campaigns, one in each of the late provinces, to be organized separately and dealt with by a different strategy. Tacitly, he recognized the continuation of the old provincial boundary.

351

II

With Sydenham's removal from the scene the various forces operating upon public life were freed to find their own equilibrium. Most significant in the long run was a new massive wave of immigration from the British Isles, gathering momentum from 1842 onward. The population had doubled before the end of the decade. New capital investment brought the rapid completion of the canals on the St. Lawrence with accompanying employment and increased circulation of money. Meanwhile the consolidation of fiscal and budgetary policy in one provincial government cleared the way for the expansion and articulation of private mercantile organizations throughout the whole area.

From well before 1837 energetic merchants in Niagara, Kingston, York, Hamilton, St. Catharines and London had opened up the commerce and markets of Upper Canada. They were and for years inevitably would remain the up-country agents and tributaries of Montreal wholesalers. Yet residence in Canada West gave insights and impressions about business prospects that differed subtly from the view in Montreal. Upstate New York on Lake Ontario, and Pennsylvania, Ohio and Michigan across Lake Erie all gave prospects of growing markets for Upper Canadian produce, while the Erie Canal opened at Buffalo an alternative route to the Atlantic and markets overseas. People travelling to Britain came and went quite regularly through the United States rather than by way of Montreal. Here was a basis for the gradual evolution of an Upper Canadian economy in the future. Meanwhile the merchant class of Canada West grew in numbers and in influence, and sparked the rapid growth of numerous towns.

These social and economic developments had their influence on political life, while the constitutional arrangements of 1841 presented new problems of their own. From the political battles of the 1830s there were legacies of party loyalties and alignments: particularly the idea of "Tories" opposed by "Reformers". Both these political camps were now transformed — the Tories dethroned from the inner councils of government, the Reformers systematically disorganized by Sydenham, and their radical wing in exile or hiding. Forty-two Lower Canadians had now to be included in all calculations of parliamentary manoeuvering — a new factor that would require new tactics. If a succession of governors general had been prepared to devote themselves to acting as their own chief minister and political agent they might have delayed the reappearance of party politics. Sir Charles Bagot was certain that this was not possible.

From the session of the Legislature in 1842 political party activity was again untrammelled by executive restraints. While the Compact Tories were no longer an official party, their staunchest followers were still at hand. The growing merchant community would want stability in society and a favourable, paternalistic government policy: they might be wooed to support the Tories. Farming populations tend to be conservative unless roused to deal with a collective wrong: they too might be organized by the Tories. There was still a strong "War of 1812 patriotism" in Upper Canada that had been exploited more than once by the Tories, an emotion not very different from the British patriotism alive in many of the new immigrants. All these tendencies seemed to be available if a reinvigorated Tory party could grasp and use them.

For the Reformers too there were hopeful tendencies. Compact Toryism had a repellent exclusive quality, and its Church of England connections grated on the sensibilities of the majority of the people. The popular interpretation of the Mackenzie Rebellion could be turned to portraying a Reform party as the defender of the people, frustrated by aristocratic and corrupt interests entrenched in power. Most important for the Reformers, however, was the absence of their radical wing, and the presence of Robert Baldwin and his fixed idea about Responsible Government. Without the radicals the Reformers could appeal to moderate merchants, traders and farmers as the advocates of good middle class government. Baldwin's idea of Responsible Government was a touchstone that encompassed all others, for if government responded exactly to the will of the people, it would, ideally, legislate for every man his heart's desire.

As the party battle developed, Baldwin and his Reformers held the winning hand, while the Tories could not seem to get organized under William Draper. In 1842 and 1843 Baldwin's Reformers developed a working alliance with LaFontaine's French Canadians to control a majority of the Legislative Assembly, while both leaders entered the Executive Council, and for some months ensured the co-ordination of executive actions with the general will of the Assembly. During this happy interval most of Sydenham's "official" moderate members from Canada West moved into support of Baldwin, so that his following numbered at least 25 members in the House. It is interesting that Baldwin was not overly punctilious about insisting on an Upper Canadian majority for all major executive acts at this time. On November 3, 1843, his supporters were in a minority of 14 to 27 (of members from Canada West) on the decision to move the seat of government from Kingston to Montreal. Thirteen days later they were in a minority of one (12 to 13) on the second reading of the Assessment Bill for Upper Canada.

What seemed to be a quite inevitable drift toward the functioning of cabinet government was halted abruptly in late November 1843, when Sir Charles Metcalfe, on orders from Britain, refused the proffered advice of his Executive Council on a matter of government patronage in Canada East. The issue was tried before the electorate in a general election in the summer of 1844 with a verdict in favour of the governor's contention. Baldwin's Reformers shrank in numbers to 12 (with 1 independent) and were faced in the new second parliament by 29 Tories and moderates. In referring the theory of Responsible Government from the confidential discussions of the council table to election propaganda for popular consumption, something of its clear theoretical purity was lost (to be restored later by historians and party politicians bent on establishing some neat pattern of development). For purposes of the election the principal aim of the moment was to secure the return of Baldwin, W.H. Blake, J.H. Price, J.P. Roblin, M. Cameron and other Reformers, rather than W.E.T. Corbett, G. Duggan, W.R. Graham, D.B. Stevenson, Alex. Fraser and other Tories and moderates who supported the governor. Personalities, the control of patronage, and immemorial political feuds in the ridings entered into the public contest.

In the following years from 1844 to 1847 the way was open for the reorganization of a new Tory party, an alternative to the Reformers, that would lead public life calmly and moderately into developing the new Canada West. The possibilities of the moment were understood by W.H. Draper, one of the province's leading barristers, and he rightly identified John A. Macdonald, J.H. Cameron and William Cayley as the nucleus of a new generation of Tories about whom the party might grow. Too many of the old guard, George and Henry Sherwood, W.B. Robinson, Sir Allan MacNab, J. Johnston and their ilk, were present with their long memories of older, better Tory days. They resented Draper and quarrelled among themselves. The crowning problem was one of political strategy: the need for a working alliance with a significant group of Lower Canadian members to control a dependable majority in the Assembly. Three major efforts by Draper to frame an alliance with the French Canadians failed. A new general election at the end of 1847 weighed the accomplishments of the recent Tory administration and found them wanting: 23 Reformers faced 18 Tories and one independent at the beginning of the third parliament.

The British government had come into the hands of the Whig party some months previously and had changed its stand on the question of cabinet government for mature colonies. The new governor general, Lord Elgin, was instructed to preserve absolute neutrality in the political warfare leading

353

up to the general election. Thus Baldwin and his Reformers had a free rein to present the principles of Responsible Government in the election campaign and implement them after their victory. It was the Reformers who had worked out the election-winning formula that appealed to the moderate electors. They now entered upon six years in office.

III

In 1848 and 1849 the Baldwin formula seemed to meet the needs of Canada West exactly. The Reformers had insisted upon the cabinet government principle and were now operating it with the full backing of the British government. A dynamic legislative programme brought moderate, common sense solutions to the need for more representative municipal institutions, the secularizing of university endowments, the revamping of municipal assessment procedure and the streamlining of judicial procedure. A resolution, popular with business people, urged the British government to secure the free importing and exporting of natural products with the United States. While it made no wide popular appeal in Canada West, the Baldwin Reformers maintained an intimate working agreement with LaFontaine and his French Canadian party of Canada East and were thereby assured of a dependable majority in the Assembly.

Almost in the hour of victory, however, the Baldwin Reformers' political position began to be outmoded. For one thing, the achievement of Responsible Government had removed that idea from the field of reforms to be fought for, and opened the question: what new goals lay open for reforming spirits? A spate of new political ideas and controversial religious positions gained currency in Canada West: some stemming from the climate of 1848 liberal revolutions in Europe and political radicalism in England, the Free Kirk disruption of the Scottish Church, and the Protestant resentment of the new Roman Catholic territorial dioceses in England. The large Irish immigration continued to import Orange-Roman Catholic tensions. All these new currents replenished the ammunition for continuing older controversies. The proclamation of amnesty for the revolutionaries of 1837 brought W.L. Mackenzie, Peter Perry and Caleb Hopkins back into public life, to join with a rising generation of radicals who were involved with the new ideas.

Baldwin's Reformers had never captured the confidence of the upper echelons of the Canadian business world, although he had a loyal following among the ranks of Upper Canadian merchants. It was still not certain in 1849-50 that Francis Hincks, the Reformers' chief financial expert, would be able to build lasting confidence between the Reformers and the business community in general, for its requirements from the government in capital aid, company legislation and tariff adjustments would become ever more importunate. It was perhaps a sign of the times when on July 24, 1850, Holmes (a liberal spokesman for Montreal business interests) seconded by W.B. Richards (a well connected Midland District Reformer) moved the third reading of a general Companies Incorporation Act for manufacturing, mining, mechanical and chemical industries, that it was Baldwin himself, seconded by J.H. Price, who moved a six month's hoist. In the ensuing division, not on party lines, Baldwin and Price were in a minority of 8 to 22 among members from Canada West.

In 1851 it became clear that Baldwin's political organization in Canada West was rent by disunity, caused by the pressing of the new radicals on the left of the party, for more constitutional and legal innovation. The process came to a head on June 26, 1851, when W.L. Mackenzie, seconded by Caleb Hopkins, moved for a special committee to report a bill for the abolition of the Court of Chancery in Upper Canada. The members from Canada West voted 25 to 9 in support of this proposition, which was intended to demolish Baldwin's own work of the previous year in reorganizing this Court. Baldwin resigned immediately, claiming that he had lost the confidence of his constituents.

The Reform ministry was reorganized in the next months with Francis Hincks undertaking the leadership in Canada West. Two principal problems had to be met: a new accommodation with the radical Reformers to silence their disruptive tendencies, and a new approach to the business community of Canada to meet its growing needs for government aid. In their whole approach to public life the two classes were mutually antagonistic. At the moment Hincks came to power the railway building mania was about to seize the imagination of the province, and Hincks led his government toward aiding and encouraging railway building. Very soon most radicals in the party drew back with distaste from involvement in the large scale capital borrowing that was the price of railways. As the provincial and municipal governments became more and more involved in railway financing the radicals proclaimed conspiracy by financial "interests." Hincks and his government became "corruptionist." In the constituencies and in parliament the Reformers had ceased to be an alliance, and presented a spectrum of political shadings from radical rebels of 1837 to moderate individualists like Sandfield Macdonald.

In the summer of 1854 these divisions among Reformers brought down the Hincks ministry. The proportions of the schism were exactly defined in the general election in August. To fill its 65 seats Canada West had returned 25 Hincksite Reformers, moderates of the centre. In opposition, 25 Conservatives on the right and 14 Reformers on the left together constituted a majority from their section of the province (one riding was vacant). Since the government still held the support of the majority from Canada East, the ministerial crisis was exclusively an Upper Canadian affair, and the 14 ultra-Reformers in opposition were the telling factor.

IV

A new generation of public men was coming into view with the general election of 1854 while the old was making its final appearance. It was, for in-

355

stance, the last general election for as different people as William Lyon Mackenzie and Sir Allan MacNab. John A. Macdonald was now recognized as heir apparent in the Conservative ranks, and with him were the stalwarts of the next decade: J.H. Cameron (Toronto), W.F. Powell (Carleton), E. Murney (Hastings North), D.B. Stevenson (Prince Edward), G. MacBerth (Elgin West), J. Langton (Peterborough) and others. The ultra-Reformers did not march in step as a homogeneous party. Joseph Hartman (North York), Billa Flint (Hastings South), J. Scatcherd (Middlesex West) and D. McKerlie (Brant East) had urgent reforming instincts; George Brown, in his second parliament, was beginning to find them kindred spirits; while Sandfield Macdonald, for instance, followed his own courses. In the ranks of Reformers that supported Hincks in September 1854, were many good Reform party men who in the following years would find it impossible to preserve a distinct middle way between the emerging political poles of Grittism and Conservatism. Some, like J. Gould (Ontario North), H. Munro (Durham North), R. Bell (Lanark North), H. Bigger (Brant West) drifted within a few months into the Clear Grit ranks, others like Angus and J.C. Morrison (Simcoe North, Niagara), D. Roblin (Lennox and Addington), R. Spence (Wentworth North) and Sydney Smith (Northumberland West) continued to claim to be Reformers, but voted the Conservative party line on most occasions.

356

Expediency, rather than far-seeing design brought a workable solution to the ministerial crisis of September 1854. It became clear in negotiation that there was much practical common ground between Hincks' moderate Reformers and the Conservatives. A rebuilding of the Upper Canadian wing of the ministry, excluding the ultra-Reformers Malcolm Cameron and John Rolph but including three Conservatives and two Hincksite Reformers, secured the necessary working majority. On the morrow of the cabinet changes on September 11, 1854, only 20 left-wing Reformers were in opposition while 44 Conservatives and moderate Hincksite Reformers supported the government.

Succeeding months and years brought a gradual readjustment in the alignment of individual members, and an evolution in the policies of the various political groups. In parliamentary terms, the ultra-Reformers began to use the name Clear Grit, and finding more and more common ground among themselves, developed a party *esprit de corps* and attracted many moderate Reformers into their ranks. Merchants and business men of stature joining the party further diluted its agrarian radicalism. The Tory party, too, was undergoing a transformation that would see it emerge as a Conservative party. There were visible tensions still between the Tory wing and the new moderate men. Expediency and shared goals brought moderate Reformers into alliance, or into the party's ranks. The exclusion of Sir Allan MacNab from the cabinet and from party leadership in 1856, and the succession of John A. Macdonald to leadership marked the completion of this process.

The division of the Upper Canadian political scene into two camps was evident in the general election of 1857. In most ridings the voters now had a simple choice between two candidates, one a "Ministerialist", usually a Conservative, but occasionally a Hincksite Reformer, and the other a Clear Grit. In retrospect, the arrangements of September 1854 stand out as a great watershed in Upper Canadian politics. Previously the followers of Baldwin and Hincks had really been a party of the centre. Soon after 1854, and for many generations, every little Ontarian born alive was either a Liberal or a Conservative.

V

Although since 1841 Canada West had been joined to Canada East like a Siamese twin, for over a decade its political life had stemmed from issues arising within its own borders. It is conceivable that political developments up to this point would not have been very different if Upper Canada had gone its own way, and not entered into the union. In its different circumstances Nova Scotia's experiences had "won" Responsible Government and evolved a two party system, with Tories transformed into Conservatives and Reformers become Liberals. From 1857 onward, however, many of the motives in the public life of Canada West became inextricably involved in the fact of union with Canada East. With the astonishing growth of population and its accompanying economic developments, the business and financial community of Canada West gained a sense of identity and began to make its own demands on the provincial government. The more effective electioneering propaganda for Canada West involved rivalry with the English-speaking financial interests of Montreal and Lower Canada's French Canadian community. The strategy for building a viable ministry began to depend very much on the political affairs of Canada East.

357

This change was in large part due to the emergence of the Clear Grit party as the champion of the special attitudes of Canada West. Particularist tendencies had of course been evident in both parts of the province from 1841, but the actual building of a party on these lines in Upper Canada began in 1855. Late in the session of that year a Separate School Bill for Upper Canada was introduced by a French Canadian and pushed through parliament against the votes of a majority of members from Canada West. Here was ammunition for a cry that Canada West was "dominated" by French Canadian Lower Canada. The party machinery of the Clear Grits was lying fallow awaiting the energy of a new cause, and in central and western Upper Canada the Toronto *Globe* was gaining prestige as the most widely circulated liberal paper. The necessary spark to galvanize all into action was provided in 1856 by George Brown, the *Globe's* proprietor, when he introduced the theme: Canada West would only find justice and its optimum development if it was represented in parliament in numbers corresponding to the population, without regard to any dividing line with Canada East. The proposition was soon contracted to the phrase "Rep. by Pop."

The Clear Grit party found unity in this cry, and won the 1857 general election: their 34 members were opposed by only 24 Conservatives and 5

Hincksite Reformers. (Two ridings were vacant.) With a majority of five in their section of the Province they hammered away at the Macdonald-Cartier government from February to late July of the new session, demonstrating beyond doubt that the ministry was kept in power by Lower Canadian votes. The earnest will of the Upper Canadian majority was frustrated by the arrangement of the constitution. However, quick victory was suddenly in sight when the Macdonald-Cartier government was defeated in a division concerning Ottawa as the permanent seat of government, and resigned. George Brown and Upper Canadian liberals, concluded an *ad hoc* arrangement with *Rouge* and liberal members from Canada East and were sworn in as a new ministry. The confidence of parliament was immediately tested on August 2, 1858, and the Brown-Dorion government was defeated. The old government under Georges Etienne Cartier and John A. Macdonald returned to power.

These events of August 1858 clearly demonstrated the essential difficulties of the constitutional situation: the liberal majority of Canada West was powerless to effect legislation for Canada West, and there was apparently no substitute for a ministry formed on the strength of the French Canadian party. The ranks of the Upper Canadian Clear Grit liberals began to fray again, when "Rep. by Pop." was seen to be ineffectual. There was a strong movement in favour of a solution that had been repeatedly urged in earlier years by W.L. Mackenzie: simply dissolve the Union of 1841. To arrest further disintegration, a full scale convention of Clear Grits and liberals was assembled in Toronto in late 1859 to hammer out a new policy. A movement in favour of simple dissolution of the Union was averted. Many of the delegates recognized that the Union had worked out well from an economic point of view and had removed the obstacles to Upper Canadian development that had been so evident in the 1830s. Further, there was fear that outside a union, Upper Canada would be inexorably drawn into annexation to the United States. Again it was George Brown who led the convention's thinking toward resolutions in favour of converting the union with Lower Canada into a federal arrangement. A federal union would preserve the economic unity of the St. Lawrence–Great Lakes area, and provide a strong enough base for the economic penetration of the prairie West. Meanwhile local parliaments for Upper and Lower Canada would allow "Rep. by Pop." full play in dealing with all the cultural and social matters that had brought Upper and Lower Canadians close to blows.

There is an inference in Liberal history writing that John A. Macdonald and his Conservatives were from 1858 onward somehow usurping power, with something less than honour in the process. In retrospect, it is not clear that a Clear Grit government could have taken power in February 1858 and from that date provided Upper Canada with complete self government but for the tie of union with Lower Canada. The gathering of various radical Reformers into a viable party in the period 1855-57, and their election victory in the latter year, depended upon their anti-Lower Canada emotion: a sectional emotion. With this motive removed, it is at least conceivable that moderate opinion would have supported either Hincks or Macdonald, or a coalition of both, to provide long years of government catering to the energetic expansion of the Upper Canadian economy. Given the circumstances of the Union in the late 1850s, the Conservatives and their Hincksite Reformer allies were providing just this sort of practical government.

The record of Upper Canadian politics in the following seventy months, though filled with manoeuvre and experiment, added little to the situation known in August 1858. The general election of 1861 returned Liberals and Conservatives in equal numbers from Canada West, while there was less party solidarity in Canada East. The Cartier-Macdonald government survived for some months but was eventually upset by the defection of many of its Lower Canadian supporters in May, 1862, over a question of defence policy. Curiously, on this vital division the government actually had a majority of six in Upper Canada.

Sandfield Macdonald undertook the formation of a Liberal ministry and again opened experiments seeking an alternative to the Cartier-Macdonald alliance. In theory, his prospects for success should have been very good for though he could depend on the general support of the Clear Grits he had never been one of them, nor had he ever voted in support of "Rep. by Pop." His moderate position might attract many Upper Canadians while of all the Upper Canadian Liberals, he should have had the best prospects for gaining broad support among Lower Canadians. As events worked out he stayed in power till March 1864, but it was an uneasy experience. Down to May 1862 he enjoyed a slim majority of about three in Canada West. When he was defeated in the House by Lower Canadian votes he called a general election for the summer of 1862 and won a resounding victory in Canada West — a majority of 25. From the viewpoint of the United Province, however, the election was a grave disappointment, for his Lower Canadian allies had been reduced to about 18. There was no scope for vigorous government with a majority of only two or three, dependent on the votes of a few independent members. The situation of 1858 had returned with slight variations: now it was a government with a large Upper Canadian contingent and a small Lower Canadian tail, faced with an opposition with a large Lower Canadian representation and a minute Upper Canadian tail. Deadlock was reached in June 1864 when both the Sandfield Macdonald-Dorion alliance and their Liberal-Conservative opponents had attempted to form a lasting ministry, without success.

359

VI

The final chapter in the political history of the United Province of Canada in the years 1864 to 1867 was prelude to Canadian federation. The political parties led by Cartier (Canada East — *Bleu*), Brown (Canada West — Grit) and John A. Macdonald (Canada West — Conservative), on the initiative of George Brown agreed in June 1864 to join in a drive to solve the political deadlock by introducing the federal principle to the Canadian constitution.

This was the Great Coalition that masterminded the Canadian federation of 1867.

As seen from Upper Canada the Great Coalition was a truce between Clear Grit Liberals and Conservatives to achieve a new degree of autonomy for their region. The two parties brought different approaches to the constitutional problem. Brown and his Liberals would have preferred to concentrate on remodelling the Union of Upper and Lower Canada, restoring to each its own Legislature, and providing a joint authority to administer interests common to the two regions. Hopefully Upper Canada would gain both a new initiative for its self-realization and expansion westward, and still retain the advantages of the economic unity of the Great Lakes–St. Lawrence River region. The operation of the "Rep. by Pop." principle in both the new provincial legislature and the federal joint authority would, it was thought, achieve Upper Canadian goals.

360

The Conservative approach to the Great Coalition was to concentrate first on seeking a federal union of all the British North American provinces, reverting to the smaller federation only in case of failure with the larger scheme. This insistence on the larger British North American union was at first not necessarily the expression of a new national sentiment, nor was it merely a partisan tactical move to assure the future of the party. It was the only practicable scheme. From 1854 onward the Conservatives had recognized mutual economic advantage in co-operating closely with the *Bleu* party in Lower Canada. The insistence by their Liberal opponents on particularist Upper Canadian attitudes had obviously led into the *cul-de-sac* of political deadlock: the creation of particularist attitudes in Lower Canada that exactly matched their own. The way out of the deadlock must be on the very practical lines of extending to all British North America the habit of co-operation among provinces for mutual economic benefit. It was a recipe that had worked well in Liberal-Conservative hands for 95 of the 117 months since the fall of Hincks' government in 1854.

The division in the Canadian Legislature which passed the Confederation Resolutions on March 11, 1865, recorded 54 members from Canada West in favour and only 8 opposed (7 Clear Grits and 1 Conservative). Soon thereafter activity in party ranks began to prepare for the realities of a federal political system. For the Liberal-Conservative leaders their best tactic was to perpetuate the semblance of a coalition ministry that had conceived the plans for federation and must now, logically, be the best equipped party to implement them. For the Liberals in Upper Canada the practical problem was more difficult, for they must either strike out independently on a new tack of their own, or have their identity lost, absorbed in the coalition ministry.

George Brown withdrew from the cabinet in December 1865; joining the seven anti-federalist Clear Grits, he began to recreate the Liberal party. Many of the party's faithful followers from the battles of the previous decade both in parliament and in the ridings responded to his lead. On the eve of the general elections of 1867 a Liberal party convention in Toronto attracted an enthusiastic attendance, and disowned the few Liberals of former years who continued to work in coalition with John A. Macdonald. Apparently they were prepared to give battle with the Conservatives on the old party lines.

VII

The general elections of 1867 were anticipated as a definitive testing of party alignment under the new constitutional arrangements. The British North America Act respected the principle of "Representation by Population" and assigned 82 seats in the House of Commons to the new province of Ontario, in place of the 65 seats Canada West held in 1866. Where a major part was faced previously with fielding candidates in 65 ridings, it had in 1867 to deal with 82 federal and 82 provincial ridings. Both parties were hard pressed to find sufficient candidates of good calibre, but in the end 157 federal and 164 provincial candidates stood for election. For the only time in history, the federal and provincial elections were held concurrently in each riding. There was no prohibition against a candidate offering himself for both the House of Commons and the Ontario Legislature. On July 1, when the Dominion of Canada was proclaimed, Sir John A. Macdonald and leaders of the Confederation movement were sworn to office in the federal government; Sandfield Macdonald became Premier of Ontario in a six man cabinet, half Conservative and half "Coalition Liberal." It was in these unique circumstances, with administrations already appointed to office at Ottawa and Toronto, that the general elections of 1867 hold unusual interest.

It was apparent that most of the veteran politicians of Canada West viewed the federal House of Commons as the important new political arena; 49 members of the Canadian Legislature in 1866 offered themselves for the Ontario seats in the 1867 federal election, and 36 were returned. By contrast, only seven sitting members ran in the Ontario provincial election and the four who succeeded (E.B. Wood, T.R. Ferguson, Sandfield Macdonald and John Carling) all held federal seats as well. In addition, 22 former members of the Canadian Legislative Assembly stood for election to the House of Commons, nine being successful. Nineteen other political veterans contested Ontario provincial seats, 12 with success. Thus the Ontario contingent to Ottawa in 1867 was much the same sort of group that would have been returned to a ninth parliament of the United Province of Canada, while the Ontario Legislature was largely a new group of men with only a few veterans.

Approximately 48 federal members from Ontario supported the Macdonald government in 1867, including five who had been Liberals or Reformers in the past. The hopes of the Liberal party were frustrated, for there was really no alternative to the appeal of Macdonald's federal policies in that year. Where Liberal members were returned it was from areas of the province which had demonstrated years of loyalty to the Clear Grit party.

Party alignment in the House of Commons was obvious, for it continued the lines of cleavage established in the Canadian Legislative Assembly before

361

1867. This was not the case, however, in the new Legislature of Ontario. Sandfield Macdonald's provincial government (dubbed the "Patent Combination" by its opponents) was carefully conceived both in membership and policy to appeal to all moderate men and avoid old partisan feuds. Most members were new to public life and had left no clue to their previous political loyalty. The absence of divisions in the House clearly testing confidence in the government increases the difficulty of assigning each member to one party or another. It is clear, however, that about 28 members, led by Edward Blake and Archibald McKellar, constituted themselves a coherent Liberal party in opposition. By actively advocating many of the old Clear Grit principles — an extended franchise, cheaper and simpler legal procedures, amelioration of the condition of debtors, and strict legislative control of appropriations — they developed a sense of party solidarity, in contrast to the uninspired ranks of Conservatives and moderates supporting Sandfield Macdonald. The Liberals defeated Sandfield in the second provincial general election in March and April 1871 and toppled his government soon after.

362

It is a curious fact, then, that the federal and provincial general elections of 1867, though held concurrently in each riding, produced quite different results. In many ridings there is a close correspondence between the proportions of the votes cast for each party in the federal and the provincial elections. For instance on September 24, Bothwell's returns show in the federal election: David Mills (Liberal) 1333, David Glass (Conservative) 1224; and in the provincial election: Archibald McKellar (Liberal) 1309, Kirby (Conservative) 1238. By contrast, Middlesex East sent a Conservative to Ottawa and a staunch Liberal to Toronto (federal: Crowell Wilson (Conservative) 1896, D. McFie 1756; provincial: James Evans (Liberall) 1821, Taylor 1791.) Three-sided contests, uncontested elections, the ambiguous stand of some moderate independents, all serve to make general conclusions about the political battle meaningless.

When Ontario was inaugurated as a province in 1867 it did not speak with either a decisively Liberal or a Conservative voice. For the moment the Clear Grit or Liberal party had lost both the federal and provincial contests to the Conservatives and their allies, though neither party could feel assured about its future. In the following years both the federal and Ontario governments came under the control of long-lived ministries that followed moderate policies in tune with the needs of economic expansion. It was the Liberal nucleus, first assembled by Blake and McKellar and soon to be led by Oliver Mowat, that controlled the province of Ontario's destinies down to the end of the century. Although not so consistent in their success, the federal Conservatives continued to dispute Ontario ridings with Liberals in support of Sir John A. Macdonald's governments.

Note

The original sources for this field are the *Journals* of the Legislative Assembly of the Province of Canada (1841-1867) and of the Legislative Assembly of the Province of Ontario (1867-1872), together with the newspapers of the day, especially the Toronto *Globe* and the Toronto *Leader*.

Much of the basic material before 1867 is compiled and interpreted from a general Canadian point of view in P.G. Cornell, *The Alignment of Political Groups in Canada, 1841-1867* (Toronto, 1962).

The excellent biographies of John A. Macdonald by D.G. Creighton and of George Brown by J.M.S. Careless are essential to unravelling the public life of the period after 1854.

Topic Eleven
Urban and Commercial Development in the Canadas in the Mid-Nineteenth Century

The colony of the United Canada in the mid-nineteenth century was still predominantly rural and agricultural. Out of a population of roughly 2 million, only 135,000 — approximately eight percent — lived in the three major urban centres of Montreal (60,000), Quebec (45,000) and Toronto (roughly 30,000). Yet already these urban centres were emerging as focal points for the commercial and social life of the Canadas. John McCallum reviews developments to mid-century in his "Urban and Commercial Development until 1850," a chapter from his *Unequal Beginnings: Agriculture and Economic Development in Quebec and Ontario until 1870.*

The British decision to abolish the old imperial preferences for Canadian flour and grain in the late 1840s forced British North Americans to look within North America for their trade and livelihood. This shift in emphasis necessitated in turn an extensive railway system that could link the urban centres of British North America with each other and with the prosperous American cities. The railways had decided advantages over the existing canal system for trade and communications: they were faster, more flexible in location, and operational year round. Together, the railways and the St. Lawrence canals held the potential to make the colony of the United Canadas one of the major centres of North American trade.

The 1850s was the great age of railway building in British North America. At the beginning of the decade, only 106 km of primitive track existed, but by the end, there were over 3,000. The construction of the Grand Trunk, which extended from Sarnia to Quebec City, developed into the most ambitious of all the projects. With 1800 km of track, it was, at the time, the longest railway system in the world. One of the best accounts of the excitement and unlimited optimism of the railways is Thomas Keefer's essay, *Philosophy of Railroads,* published in 1849 on the eve of the railway age.

One of the immediate effects of the railway industry was the rapid rise of towns and cities along the rail lines. Toronto in particular became an important trading centre, with rail lines extending into the northern part of the colony (the Georgian Bay area), into the American midwest, down to

New York via Buffalo, and east along the St. Lawrence to Montreal and Quebec City. Railways also brought the industrial revolution to the Canadas: iron foundries, locomotive shops and rolling mills were established in Toronto, Montreal, and other important Canadian towns. In "Transportation" John McCallum discusses the impact of the railways in the 1850s and 1860s.

Historian H.V. Nelles offers a good introduction to T.C. Keefer's *Philosophy of Railroads* in the *Social History Series* edition (University of Toronto Press, 1972). An earlier article on Keefer is D.C. Master's "T.C. Keefer and the Development of Canadian Transportation," *Canadian Historical Association Report*, 1940, pp. 36-44.

For a general history of railway development, the first volume of G.P. de T. Glazebrook's, *A History of Transportation in Canada* (Toronto: McClelland and Stewart, 1964) merits examination. Peter Baskerville offers a useful summary of developments in present-day Ontario in "Americans in Britain's Back Yard: The Railway Era in Upper Canada, 1850-1880," *Business History Review*, 55 (1981): 314-336. For a short review of the effect that the railway had on small towns, see J.J. Talman, "The Impact of the Railway on a Pioneer Community," *Canadian Historical Association Report*, 1955, pp. 1-12. Jacob Spelt's *Urban Development in South-Central Ontario* (Toronto: McClelland and Stewart, 1972) reviews urbanization of the north shore of Lake Ontario.

The best short review of the growth of cities in the Canadas is J.M.S. Careless, *The Rise of Cities in Canada Before 1914*, Canadian Historical Association Booklet, no. 32 (1978). *The Canadian City: Essays in Urban and Social History* (Don Mills, Ontario: Oxford, 1984), edited by G.A. Stelter and A.F.J. Artibise contains articles on the early urban history in the Canadas. Three major urban centres of the Canadas have been the subject of important studies: John Irwin Cooper, *Montreal: A Brief History* (Montreal: McGill-Queen's University Press, 1969), J.M.S. Careless, *Toronto to 1918: An Illustrated History* (Toronto: Lorimer, 1984), and John C. Weaver, *Hamilton: An Illustrated History* (Toronto: James Lorimer, 1982).

365

Urban and Commercial Development until 1850*

JOHN McCALLUM

Urban development in Quebec and Ontario is a study in contrasts. Between 1850 and 1870 the two largest cities of Quebec made up about three-quarters of the urban population of that province, while the equivalent figure for

*Chapter 5 from *Unequal Beginnings: Agriculture and Economic Development in Quebec and Ontario until 1870*. Copyright 1980, by University of Toronto Press. Reprinted by permission.

Ontario was between one-quarter and one-third. To arrive at the share of Quebec's urban population held by Montreal and Quebec City, one would have to include the fifteen largest towns of Ontario in 1850 and the thirty largest towns in 1870. Looking at the matter in a different way, dozens of urban centres filled the Ontario countryside, but outside Montreal and Quebec City the population of Quebec was overwhelmingly rural.

It is clear from Table 1 that these differences in urban structure had been firmly established by 1850 and that the differences merely intensified in the following two decades. Between 1850 and 1870 the number of towns increased increased faster in Ontario than in Quebec, and, while the share of Ontario's two largest cities in the urban population actually fell from one-third in 1850 to one-quarter in 1870, Montreal and Quebec City accounted for close to three-quarters of Quebec's urban population throughout the period. The causes of the basic differences in urban structure are therefore to be found in the years before 1850, and this chapter focuses on those years. Urban growth after 1850 cannot be separated from industrial and transportation developments.

Ontario

Regional patterns of wheat production and urban and industrial development may be seen at a glance in figures 1 to 4. In mid-nineteenth century Ontario there was a striking concentration of activity in the triangle bounded roughly by York County, the Niagara River, and London. The region varies somewhat, sometimes extending further east along Lake Ontario and

TABLE I — **Population in Quebec and Ontario, 1850-70**

1 Number of towns:

Town size:	Quebec 1850	1860	1870	Ontario 1850	1860	1870
25,000+	2	2	2	1	1	2
5000-25,000	0	1	3	4	8	10
1000-5000	14	18	22	33	50	69
Total	16	21	27	38	59	81

2 Urban and rural population (thousands):

Town size:	Quebec 1850	1860	1870	Ontario 1850	1860	1870
25,000+	100	141	167	31	45	83
5000-25,000	0	6	20	41	83	95
1000-5000	31	39	42	67	108	149
Total urban	131	187	229	139	236	328
Total rural	759	925	962	813	1160	1293
Total population	890	1112	1192	952	1396	1621
Urban as percentage of total	14.7	16.8	19.2	14.6	16.9	20.2

Source: Census of Canada

Figure 1

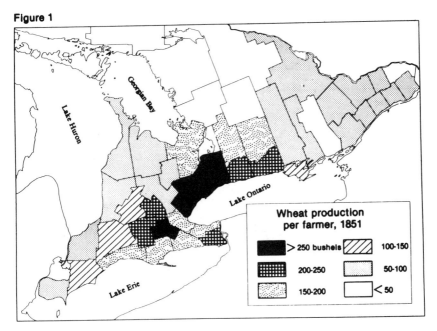

Wheat production
per farmer, 1851

■ > 250 bushels	▨ 100-150
▦ 200-250	▦ 50-100
▨ 150-200	□ < 50

Figure 2

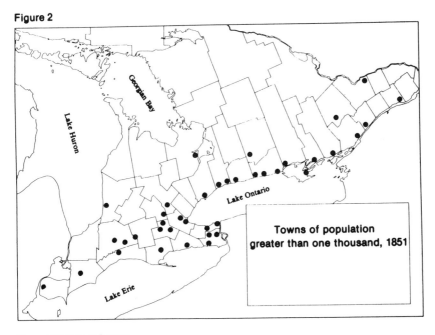

Towns of population
greater than one thousand, 1851

Source: Census of Canada

Figure 3

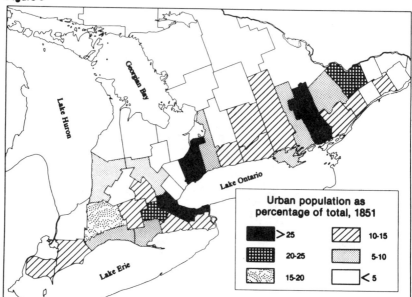

Urban population as percentage of total, 1851

Figure 4

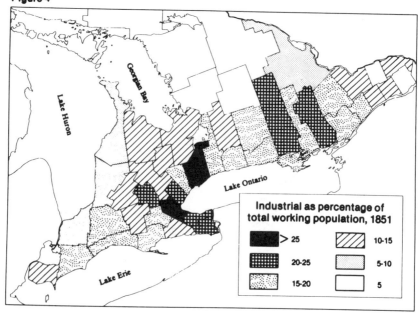

Industrial as percentage of total working population, 1851

Source: Census of Canada

sometimes stopping short of London on the west; but as a snapshot of a rapidly changing scene the general outline is remarkably clear: the areas of highest wheat production tended also to be the areas of greatest urban and industrial development. This was so despite the very recent settlement of the western regions, which, at mid-century, were in the midst of their period of most rapid growth. This pattern suggests that wheat was at the root of urban development, a supposition that will be confirmed by an analysis of the growth of Ontario towns.

Toronto

It was only by virtue of its position as provincial capital that the town of York, with its 'very trifling'[1] trade and its undeveloped hinterland, had reached the grand total of 1700 inhabitants by 1824. Starting in the mid-1820s, settlers poured into the Home district, and the district population of 17,000 in 1824 increased at an annual rate of 8.6 per cent to reach 168,000 in 1851. York (or Toronto, as it became in 1834) grew with its agricultural hinterland, attaining a population of 9252 in 1834 and 30,800 in 1851.[2]

369

The driving force behind the growth of Toronto was the demand for goods and services from the immigrant and farm population. Financed initially by the savings of British immigrants, this demand was maintained by the farmers' cash income from wheat. In the earlier years of settlement, the demand from new arrivals was the major element. In the second half of the 1820s, according to T.W. Acheson, 'the provision of housing, food, clothing, and tools for several hundred new family units each year created a demand which provided the economy with a dynamism otherwise inconceivable.'[3] At the time of the peak immigration of 1831-32, immigrants deposited not less than £300,000 in the Bank of Upper Canada.[4] As exports of wheat and flour accelerated during the 1840s, the demand for goods and services from established farmers was felt with ever-increasing intensity. Throughout the period wheat and flour dominated the export trade of Toronto, accounting for more than three-quarters of exports at mid-century.[5]

As population and trade increased, the importance of the city's position as provincial capital declined correspondingly. Thus, in 1845 W.H. Smith, author of the *Canadian Gazetteer,* wrote: '...the seat of government was moved to Kingston in 1841...Had this event taken place ten years sooner, it might have had a serious effect upon the prosperity of the town, but in 1841 Toronto had become a place of too great a commercial importance to feel much ill effect from the removal of the government offices, and the loss of the expenditure of a few thousand pounds per annum.'[6]

Under these circumstances the primary functions of Toronto were to export flour and to import goods for sale to established and prospective farmers. Acheson described the operations of the retailers around 1830. About 90 per cent of the market of Toronto's retailers was in rural areas, and consequently the pattern of sales was determined by the farming seasons. Peak sales occurred in October following the harvest, and business remained fairly strong throughout most of the winter when the farmers transported their wheat and flour to the town. Demand fell off during the spring thaw, and it picked up again in July when there was a steady demand for tools and implements. The 'struggling' patrons purchased cotton cloth and thread, glass, nails, scythes, and hardware supplies, while the more prosperous customers bought luxury articles such as Madeira, snuff, and silk. These prosperous customers, presumably mainly attached to government activities, were small in number, and it was the agricultural population which determined both the seasonal fluctuations and the principal commodity composition of retail sales.

Behind the retailers were the wholesalers. These were larger commercial enterprises which not only sold goods to the retailers but also purchased and exported flour. Manufacturing made modest progress in the years to 1850, and the goods supplied by the wholesalers were mainly imported. In the early years most imports were British goods purchased through Montreal, but after the opening of the Erie Canal in 1825 the wholesalers began to import more American goods. In the prosperous years of the late 1820s and early 1830s, larger and more specialized wholesalers established themselves, and to stay in business it became necessary to import goods directly from Britain.[7] In 1832 York had eight wholesalers; by 1850 this number had increased to twenty, fifteen of which had jettisoned retail activities altogether.[8]

Indeed, by mid-century a rising commercial group led by the wholesalers was challenging the position held by the old Toronto families. This group had arrived in the 1830s, and included such men as William McMaster (wholesaler and later banker) and F.C. Capreol (commercial salesroom operator and later railway promoter). Many of the old members of the Family Compact were still important in the economic life of the city, but by 1850 they were losing power to the newer group led by the wholesalers.[9]

While this commercial development based on settlement and wheat exports applied on a smaller scale to most other Ontario towns, a number of special factors favoured Toronto over other places. Between 1824 and 1829 York had the only bank in the province, but in the latter year the Bank of Montreal established a branch in York, and banks were established in Hamilton and Kingston in the first half of the 1830s. While the Bank of Upper Canada was sometimes credited with York's growing prosperity, it was remarked in 1831 that 'the fine back Country does infinitely more for the advancement of York than the Bank can do.'[10] To the advantages of an early lead in banking and an exceptionally large and fertile back country were added a good harbour, an early road, and the town's position as provincial capital, which made it a focal point for new arrivals to the province. It was only natural, then, that Toronto should be the main beneficiary of any trends in the direction of increased geographical concentration of economic activity.

370

In the years to 1850, such forces of concentration were limited. Toronto's export trade was not markedly higher than that of other lake ports, and according to Jacob Spelt its presence did not have any influence on the size or number of manufacturing establishments in York County. The one important sector of the economy in which forces of concentration had begun to assert themselves by mid-century was wholesale trade. In 1851 the value of direct imports to Toronto was $2.6 million, as compared with $2.2 million for Hamilton and $1 million for Kingston. The next largest importer was Chippewa at $318,000. By 1850 Toronto had established itself as the major distributing point for such ports as Oakville, Port Credit, and Whitby. There were economies to be gained in limiting the number of contacts with British and American suppliers, and 'it was only natural that this trade should concentrate on the capital, the largest city and market with the biggest banks and one of the best ports.'[11]

Furthermore, Toronto had started to invade the territory formerly held by Montreal. The city's direct imports (as opposed to goods imported through Montreal wholesalers) rose dramatically in the 1840s and imports from the United States more than doubled in the two years between 1849 and 1851. It has been seen that Toronto wholesalers began to import goods directly from the early 1830s, and in the same period they started to replace Montrealers as suppliers to merchants in smaller Ontario towns. Also, from the late 1840s a rising proportion of wheat and flour was shipped through the United States instead of through Montreal.

371

Toronto's development is therefore explained not only by the growth of its own hinterland but also by a start to its commercial penetration of other regions. In the process it began its escape from the control of Montreal. On the whole, however, the city's growth up to 1850 depended mainly on growth within its own territory, for, with the partial exception of wholesale trade, dispersion rather than concentration remained the hallmark of economic activity.

Finally, associated with all this was the accumulation of capital. Funds were derived first from the savings of immigrants and from the disposal of land held by the government and its associates, and then increasingly from the activities of the rising merchant class and its agricultural hinterland. Local governments, deriving their revenue directly from the wealth of the towns and countryside, were also important contributors. The point to be emphasized at present is that all these sources may be traced to the twin processes of settlement and wheat exports.

Hamilton

Hamilton owed its early growth to its position at the head of Lake Ontario. According to W.H. Smith, 'Hamilton is admirably suited for carrying on a large wholesale trade with the West, — being at the head of navigation of Lake Ontario, and in the heart of the best settled portion of the Province, it possesses peculiar advantages for receiving goods, and distributing them through the interior, while its central position makes it the depôt of a large extent of grain and other produce.'[12] The town's population reflected the course of settlement and the wheat trade. The Burlington Bay Canal, which connected Hamilton with Lake Ontario, was completed in 1825, and in 1831 it was said that 'since the Burlington Canal started, Hamilton has increased from 3 to 18 stores. Its former trifling trade and its houses have doubled.' Population rose from 1400 in 1833 to 3600 in 1837, 4300 in 1842, and 14,000 in 1851.[13]

As in the case of Toronto, this growth resulted from the rapid settlement of the city's back country and the acceleration of wheat exports during the 1840s. The population of the Gore district was 150,000 in 1851, or more than six times as high as in 1831. Exports of wheat and flour more than tripled between 1838 and 1844, and they had tripled again by 1850. By mid-century, Hamilton exported more wheat and flour than any Ontario town except Port Dalhousie, located at the mouth of the Welland Canal.

As Smith indicated, Hamilton was the major wholesale centre for points west of Lake Ontario. Douglas McCalla has produced a map that reveals, for the year 1857, the deep penetration into western Ontario by Hamilton's largest wholesaler, Buchanan, Harris and Company. Eighty centres from Niagara to Amherstburg and from Lake Erie to points north of Goderich contained one or more customers of this firm, and the most concentrated group of customers was located between London and Hamilton.[14]

Hamilton, then, was a commercial town. In his exhaustive study of the town in 1851 Michael B. Katz wrote that '...men in commerce, about a quarter of the workforce, controlled nearly 59% of the wealth, a figure which underscores the clear commercial basis of the city.' As in Toronto, the industrial sector, operating overwhelmingly in local markets, played a passive role in the years up to 1850. The settlement and development of Hamilton's rich and rapidly growing agricultural hinterland was the basis not only of the town's growth but also of the wealth and capital accumulation of the commercial class. The export of wheat and flour, the importation and distribution of manufactured goods, land speculation, and personal profit derived from municipal funds[15] were all based directly or indirectly on the settler's supply of wheat and demand for land and other goods and services. This capital accumulation and general prosperity may be seen in a number of developments: the replacement of wooden structures with brick buildings and the 'vast improvement' in the character of the city's buildings in the last few years of the 1840s, the location of two bank headquarters and four branches in Hamilton, improvements such as the introduction of gas lighting in 1851, and the ambitious but misguided decision of the city to subscribe £100,000 for the construction of the Great Western Railway.[16]

This is not to paint a picture of general affluence and social harmony. As Katz demonstrated minutely, inequalities were enormous and individual business failures were commonplace. The large-scale Irish immigration brought problems of disease, riots and violence. Nevertheless, during the last decade of the pre-railway age, Hamilton underwent a total transforma-

372

tion in its population, trade, social infrastructure, and wealth. It is impossible to attribute this transformation to anything other than agricultural settlement and the growth of wheat and flour exports.

Other Ontario towns

The maps in Figures 1 to 4 indicate that the three westernmost counties of Ontario were not large-scale wheat producers and that they were relatively underdeveloped in terms of both urban and industrial growth. The only two towns of a thousand or more were Amherstburg (1880) and Chatham (2070). The former was a frontier post and naval depot during the War of 1812, and it continued to be a garrison town until after 1850. In 1850 and 1851 almost all enumerated exports consisted of wheat, but the quantities involved were not large. By Ontario standards Amherstburg was stagnant. Joseph Bouchette in 1831 gave the population as over 1200 and mentioned 'the wealth and respectability of its inhabitants.'[17] In the twenty years to 1851 population rose by only 50 per cent. The difficulties of wheat growing in the region and the correspondingly low production levels would seem to have limited the growth of the town. Chatham, on the other hand, was a product of the wheat boom. Its population rose from 812 in 1841 to 2070 in 1851, and, according to Smith, 'Being situated in the midst of a fine agricultural country, it is a place of considerable business.' Or in the words of F.C. Hamil, 'The principal source of prosperity for the town was the prolific country about it, settled by industrious, intelligent, and thrifty farmers.'[18] During the 1840s property values rose rapidly, bank branches were established, and brick houses began to replace less solid structures. In 1850 the town had two steam grist mills, two steam sawmills, two foundries and machine shops, a brewery, two tanneries, a woollen factory, and four distilleries.[19] Nevertheless, taken as a whole, the three counties of the Western District grew relatively little wheat, and difficulties in this area had led to an effort to expand tobacco production and in general to adopt a more diversified agriculture. Tobacco and other products were not good substitutes for large quantities of wheat, and the overall development of the district was meagre.

373

Moving eastwards, London, St Thomas, and Ingersoll were within about thirty miles of each other in Middlesex, Oxford, and Elgin counties. The maps indicate that in 1850 this area was more developed than the counties to the west and somewhat less developed than the counties along the shores of Lake Ontario. This was a newer region which at mid-century was in the middle of its period of most rapid growth: the population of the London District tripled during the 1840s, while the town of London grew from 1100 in 1834 to 2600 in 1842 and 7000 in 1851.[20] London became the district town in 1826, and in 1838 an imperial garrison was stationed in the town. These factors were the major non-agricultural influences on London's development, and, while they may explain the town's ascendancy over St Thomas, they were relatively unimportant in the urban development of the region as a whole. Some town in the region had to be the district centre, and, while the coming of the garrison in 1837 was a shot in the arm for the town's economy, its departure in 1853 was 'almost unnoticed.'[21]

After London was given the right to hold a public market in 1835, it quickly became the trade focus of a rich but very partially settled agricultural area. It was during the 1840s that London's economy became firmly based on wheat. In the words of Orlo Miller: 'By the late 1840's, London's economy had become tied to a more stable commodity than either litigation or logistics [that is, district centre or garrison town]. That commodity was wheat... By the middle of the nineteenth century Western Ontario had become one vast granary and London one of its principal market towns and shipping centres.'[22]

374

As London grew, it attracted men with capital to invest and enriched those who were already there. Some of the town's leading citizens arrived with the settlers in the 1820s and early 1830s. This group included George Goodhue, merchant and land speculator, and Ellis Hyman and Simeon Morrill, both tanners. Men such as Elijah Leonard, iron founder and steam engine maker; John Birrell, dry goods wholesaler; and Thomas Carling, brewer, arrived soon after the Rebellion of 1837. John K. Labatt, brewer; Charles Hunt, miller; and the McClary brothers, warehousing, arrived in the late 1840s and early 1850s. These manufacturers and wholesalers served an area that 'stretched west to Chatham, Windsor, and Sarnia, north to Goderich, St Mary's, and Stratford, east to Ingersoll and Woodstock, and south to St Thomas and Port Stanley.' Strong commercial ties with Hamilton were developed from an early date. By 1850 London had four bank branches, two building societies, several insurance companies, three 'extensive' foundries, one grist and sawmill, three breweries, two distilleries, two tanneries, and three newspapers. While provincial funds were spent generously on London roads because the position of public works commissioner was held by a London citizen, it was the local capital of such families as the Labatts and Carlings which paid for the road to the Huron Tract in 1849 and for the London–Port Stanley railroad in the 1840s.[23]

Ingersoll, Woodstock, and St Thomas were rivals of London in the 1820s and 1830s, but by 1850 they were clearly of secondary importance. To some extent they suffered from London's success, as in the case of Elijah Leonard's departure from St Thomas to London in 1838 on the conviction that London was 'sooner or later to become the hub of Western Canada.'[24] Nevertheless, the populations of Ingersoll and Woodstock grew extremely rapidly in the late 1840s, and it was not until the railway age that these towns suffered severely from the forces of concentration. At mid-century they were market centres surrounded by a booming agriculture, and each had its five to ten mills and manufactories. The same was true on a lesser scale for the fifteen to twenty smaller villages which dotted the countryside within a twenty-mile radius of London.

Goderich served as district town headquarters of the Canada Company and port for the surrounding country. Population rose from 300 in 1831[25]

to about 1300 in 1851, and in the latter year the town had the usual assortment of mills, newspapers, and bank and insurance company agents. Exports were still very low, and the most important function in 1850 was to
supply settlers bound for the northern sections of the Huron Tract.

In Norfolk County only the district town of Simcoe had as many as one
thousand people. Lumber was more important in this county than elsewhere,
and in 1850 Ports Dover, Ryerse, and Rowan exported mainly wood, although
in the first of these, which was much the largest, wheat and flour made
up close to half the total value of exports. None of these ports contained
as many as a thousand residents. Simcoe, which had the usual quota of mills
and other establishments, derived its existence from a combination of wood,
wheat, and administrative functions.

We come now to the largest cluster of towns, those within about forty
miles of Hamilton in Brant and Wentworth counties and in the Niagara
Peninsula. A glance at Figure 1 shows that this region was second only to
the neighbourhood of Toronto in its wheat production. In Brant County
wheat production per farmer was the highest in the province in 1851 (370
bushels), and this county contained Paris and Brantford, with a combined
population of 5800 or 23 per cent of total county population. Brantford,
the largest of these towns, increased its population rapidly in the few years
before 1850. It had the advantage of being located on the Grand River and
on the Hamilton-London road. In 1850, 350,000 bushels of wheat and flour
(just under three-quarters of the total value of shipments) were shipped from
Brantford along the Grand River, and in addition 'large quantities of flour,
whisky and ashes are teamed down to Hamilton and shipped there.' The
manufacturing establishments seem to have been larger than average, for
Smith lists 'four grist mills, one of which is a large brick building; two foundries, doing a large business; a stone-ware manufactory, the only one yet in
operation in the west of Canada . . . two tanneries, two breweries, four
distilleries, a planning machine and a sash factory, &c. &c.'[26]

The other towns on the Grand River had similar, if somewhat lesser
manufacturing activities, and they too profited from their position on the
river in the midst of highly productive wheat farming. Galt and Guelph had
originated as supply centres for the Canada Company, but by mid-century
most of the lands in the region had been settled. Dunnville was located at
the mouth of the Grand River and was a point of trans-shipment of imports
as well as an export point. In 1850 wheat and flour made up about three-
quarters of the town's exports.

In Niagara District the largest town, St Catharines, benefited from its
position on the Welland Canal and had six grist mills. Thorold was also
on the Welland Canal, and it had grown rapidly in the few years prior to
1850, taking advantage of the hydraulic powers of the canal to establish a
number of large grist mills and other enterprises. Niagara and Chippewa
had declined somewhat with the opening of the Welland Canal: in 1851 they
had a combined population of about 4500.

The Lake Ontario wheat ports east of Hamilton and west of Belleville

375

were so similar that they may be described as a group. According to figures contained in Smith, for six of the eight ports in this region wheat and flour accounted for at least 80 per cent of total exports. The two exceptions were Port Hope and Cobourg, but these were also the only two towns (except Toronto) for which figures on exports to places other than the United States were not available. Most of the towns had wheat and flour exports between 175,000 and 300,000 bushels and total exports of $160,000 to $320,000, while the value of imports varied more widely. The ports competed for their respective back countries, and leading citizens were active in promoting and financing roads, and later railroads, to tap their agricultural hinterlands. Financial services and small-scale manufacturing of the type already described had developed in all of these towns by 1850.

This survey of towns in the wheat-producing areas of Ontario ends with Barrie and Peterborough, which were inland towns north of Lake Ontario. Barrie, with a population of 1007 in 1851, was the main supply centre for the settlers and farmers of Simcoe County, as well as the county town. Its growth had been moderate, and it contained a tannery, brewery, newspaper, and bank agency in 1850. Peterborough was more substantial, with a population of 2191 in 1851. Immigration and the settlement of the surrounding districts remained the town's most important function until about 1840, after which the export of wheat, flour, and lumber increased in importance. In 1850 wheat and flour exports were of about the same importance as exports of lumber and square timber.[27]

We come now to the towns in the part of the province which did not produce wheat as a staple product. From Hastings County eastwards there were in 1851 nine towns with population exceeding one thousand, of which the largest were Kingston (11,600), Bytown (7800), Belleville (4600), and Brockville (2200). For the region as a whole, the urban population made up 15.1 per cent of the total. This was a lower proportion then in the former districts of Niagara (19.1 per cent), Home (21 per cent), and Gore (18 per cent), but it was higher than in most counties west of Brant. Considering that this eastern section had been settled earliest, its urban development up to 1850 was not impressive.

In 1830 Kingston had a larger population than York and about four times as many people as Hamilton; by 1851 it had been surpassed by Hamilton and had less than 40 per cent of the population of Toronto. The economy of Kingston had traditionally been based on its position as entrepôt, together with civilian and military government establishments, the lumber trade through the Rideau Canal, and shipbuilding. The town's unproductive back country was said to have restrained its growth, and it suffered setbacks with the movement of the capital to Montreal in 1844 and the decline of its role as entrepôt. Smith wrote that 'the Government establishments, naval and military, with the shipping interest, are the principal support of the city.'[28]

Bytown (later Ottawa) was clearly a lumber town, and Belleville exported mainly wood in 1850, although wheat and flour were significant (28 per cent of exports). To a large extent, Prescott and Brockville were dependent on St Lawrence shipping, while Perth was originally the supply centre for local settlers and in later years had been connected to the Rideau Canal by private company. Cornwall lost population between 1845 and 1850, and the small towns of Napanee and Picton were market centres. Of the nine towns, only Belleville, Kingston, and Bytown had significant exports in 1850. Taken as a whole, the region from Belleville eastwards experienced slightly more than a doubling of its urban population between 1835 and 1850. West of Belleville, urban population rose by a factor of five over the same period.[29]

This analysis has covered the years up to 1850. In the next twenty years the number of towns increased from 38 to 81. Three-quarters of the newly established towns were located west of Trenton, and most of these were in the more recently settled inland counties which accounted for a rising proportion of wheat production as the older lands became exhausted. Dispersion remained the keynote of urban structure, as the share of the five largest cities in the urban population actually fell from 51 per cent in 1850 to 40 per cent in 1870.

377

Three sets of conclusions flow from this analysis. First, wheat was the driving force behind at least twenty-six of the twenty-nine towns west of Belleville (Amherstburg, Simcoe, and Peterborough were partial exceptions). All of these towns were either export ports or inland transportation terminals for Ontario wheat, all were market centres for the agricultural population, most had been supply centres for settlers, and many were import ports or wholesale centres. Wood and garrisons had been of secondary or passing importance. In addition to the centres of over a thousand people, there were literally hundreds of lesser centres, concentrated in the most productive wheat-producing areas, which performed similar functions on a smaller scale. By producing the region's only major export and by providing the market for its imports, agriculture was the foundation of commercial activity. Also, it was this wheat-generated activity that attracted men of capital to the region's commercial and nascent industrial sectors, that provided the basis for further capital accumulation, and that provided the tax base and savings that financed the roads and other projects of the time.

Furthermore, by the standards of the day the wheat economy of 1850 was an economic success story. In the words of I.D. Andrews, the compiler of the most comprehensive statistics on the trade of the province, 'The population of Toronto has doubled in the last 10 years, and is now 30,000. Hamilton, now containing 14,000, has been equally progressive. The imports show their commercial program to have been equally rapid; and there can be little doubt that in Upper Canada the export of produce, and the import and consumption of all the substantial and necessary products of civilization, are as high, per head, as in the best agricultural districts of the United States.'[30]

The second conclusion is that wood had much weaker effects on urban growth than wheat. The eastern part of the province had been settled earlier, and the Ottawa Valley was the major contributor to Canada's very large exports of forest products. Yet urban growth in this region had been meagre. The reasons for this are discussed in a later chapter.

The final conclusion concerns the pattern of urban growth. Why was this growth so dispersed instead of highly concentrated in a single city, as in the case of Winnipeg in the prairie wheat economy? Why, indeed, was the commercial activity located in Ontario at all, when, for example, most of the commercial activity associated with southern cotton and much of that flowing from prairie wheat took place outside the staple-producing region? To these questions, so vital to the prospects of any staple-producing region, there are two basic answers. The technology of the mid-nineteenth century favoured dispersion. We have already mentioned the case of the tiny port of Oakville which transported the wheat to its warehouses, constructed the steam engines and flour mill machinery that converted the wheat to flour, and built and manned the ships that carried the finished commodity to Montreal.[31] In 1847 a small Peterborough foundry manufactured most of the threshing mills used in the district, as well as a wide variety of the agricultural implements.[32] Such examples could be multiplied, but, in general, technology in the areas of transportation and manufacturing favoured the very local retention of a very high proportion of the linkages flowing from the wheat staple.

378

This technological bias in favour of the local level naturally promoted the retention of commercial activity within the province. However, even in 1850 technology favoured a higher degree of concentration of imports and wholesalers, and in subsequent years technological changes promoted centralization of other activities. The question was whether these centralized activities would take place in Ontario or Quebec, and it was the availability of direct American imports and the American trade route that tipped the balance in favour of Ontario. By contrast, fifty years later the prairie wheat economy had no such escape from eastern control, for the high Canadian tariffs and the monopolistic American freight rates made it difficult to import goods or export wheat through the United States.[33] In the case of Ontario, the effective challenge to Montreal's monopoly position had permitted a growing independence on the part of Toronto wholesalers from the 1830s, and the story was to be repeated in banking, transportation, and industry. Nevertheless, this was a gradual and partial process, for it will be seen in the next section that Montreal derived much benefit from the Ontario wheat economy.

Quebec

Montreal

Much, if not most, of the literature on this period has concerned itself with the commercial empire of the St Lawrence, and there is no need to repeat the story of the Montreal merchants here.[34] Suffice it to say that a series of shocks in the 1840s destroyed both the old colonial system and Montreal's aspirations for the trade of the American west. Abandoned by Britain and excluded from American produce and markets, the Montreal merchants were driven to the Annexation Manifesto of 1849, in which they declared that the only solution to their problems lay in 'going to prosperity, since prosperity will not come to us.'[35]

Excluding for the moment its role as supplier of cheap labour, Quebec agriculture had little to do with the development of Montreal. The local farmers had made no significant contribution to exports since the early years of the century, their demand for imports was limited by their low and fluctuating incomes, and their role in capital formation was minimal. They supplied a portion of the city's livestock requirements, little of its wheat, and most of its limited requirements for other vegetable products.

On the other hand, Ontario agriculture was a major factor in the economy of Montreal. While Montreal never became the great emporium of the American mid-west, such shipments as it did receive came increasingly from Ontario rather than from the United States. Thus, wheat and flour shipments via the St Lawrence rose from 2.9 million bushels in 1840 to a peak of 5.8 million bushels in 1847, and by 1851 shipments were 4.3 million bushels. Ontario produce was less than half the total in 1840 and virtually all of it in 1850. In the latter year, wheat and flour made up 78 per cent of the total tonnage passing down the St Lawrence canals. This excludes lumber products which accounted for 10 per cent of the tolls collected.[36] Thus, by 1850 Ontario wheat and flour were of dominant importance in the shipments received at Montreal via the St Lawrence canals. The total tonnage, while not as great as had been anticipated, would have been almost negligible without the wheat and flour of the upper province.[37]

379

Montreal's imports were closely tied to conditions in Ontario. According to Fernand Ouellet, even by 1820 the incomes of Montreal importers were 'directement fonction de l'agriculture haut-canadienne.'[38] As indicated by the following figures, the volume of merchandise passing up the Lachine Canal to Ontario rose dramatically:[39]

1826	1,500 tons
1830	8,300 tons
1835	15,800 tons
1844	27,500 tons
1850	70,000 tons

In 1851 *direct* imports to Ontario towns via Montreal amounted to $3.0 million, as compared with $9.2 million entered as imports at Montreal.[40] A significant but unknown percentage of the latter figure would have been re-exported to Ontario.

Thus Ontario provided the great majority of Montreal's exports and absorbed perhaps one-half of the imports which reached the city. For Montreal, the upper province was the one bright spot in an otherwise gloomy decade. This is all the more remarkable in the light of Ontario's shift to the American route for both its imports and exports: the province's growth was so rapid that Montreal's declining share of the trade did not prevent the city's absolute level from growing at impressive rates.

There was little progress in manufacturing during the 1840s, and this, together with the commercial disappointments of the decade, led to the emigration of large numbers of workers. Referring to 'Montreal and Quebec workmen' as the first class of emigrants, a Select Committee of the Legislative Assembly in 1849[41] described the causes of this emigration in the following terms:

— unsettled trade and industry for several years past
— want of manufactories for those previously in lumbering
— increase in U.S. wages and fall here
— lack of public works

380

It was not until the industrial growth of the 1850s and 1860s that Montreal began to call on the surplus labour of rural Quebec.

Other Quebec towns

The timber trade and shipbuilding dominated the economic life of Quebec City. Local agriculture was of minor importance. Neither did Ontario agriculture exert much influence on Quebec, for while the city was a major exporter of wheat this trade was much less important than the trade in timber and ships.

In the rest of the province the major activity was agriculture, and Quebec agriculture was a miserable base for urban growth. Worse than this, the crisis in Quebec agriculture destroyed the economic base of established merchants and artisans, and rural artisans who were 'réduits à la misère par l'effondrement du revenu de leurs clients' were forced to emigrate. The Select Committee of 1849 ascribed the emigration of 'workmen who had settled in the villages and county parts' to the fact that the farmers 'do themselves almost everything they might require from a tradesman,' with the result that 'the workmen...have little employment and lose courage.' Also, the inability of the inhabitants to repay debt to 'the fearful number of those who carry on trade in our country parts on a small scale' brought financial ruin to debtor and creditor alike.[42]

Outside Montreal and Quebec City the urban population made up 4 per cent of the total population in 1850 and 6 per cent in 1870. Even these figures understate the differential impact of agriculture in the two provinces. While the great majority of Ontario towns owed their existence to the wheat economy, most Quebec towns depended in large measure on activities other than agriculture. This has already been demonstrated for Montreal and Quebec City, and it was also the case for most of the remaining fourteen towns of mid-nineteenth-century Quebec.

The growth of Lachine was obviously not dependent on agricultural conditions, while Aylmer was an Ottawa Valley lumbering town. The economy of St Jean was based on its role as entrepôt for trade between Canada and the United States. Trois-Rivières was in the midst of a region of very poor soil and an agricultural back country which had little to buy or sell. Growth was based on the town's position as a half-way point between Quebec and Montreal, a minor administrative centre, and, from 1840, the exporter of wood from the country along the St Maurice. Laprairie was a commercial centre at the head of communication from Montreal to St Jean and the Richelieu, while Ste Thérèse was a lumbering centre.[43]

In Quebec the railway age began slightly before 1850. The Longueuil-St Hyacinthe section of the St Lawrence and Atlantic Railway was completed in 1847, and these towns had become distribution points based on the railway.[44] Sherbrooke, which had 350 people in 1830, had 2998 in 1851, thanks in large part to the local railroad construction going on at the time of the census. Without the railroad, Sherbrooke 'n'aurait jamais dépassé la taille d'un Lennoxville ou d'un Richmond.'[45] Joliette, or Industrie as it was called before 1864, originated as a sawmill site in 1823. Under the energetic direction of its founder, the site acquired a flour mill in 1824, a wool factory and nail factory in 1825, a distillery in 1840, and an foundry in 1844. In 1850 a railway was constructed at a cost of $55,000, and at that time population doubled to about 2500. The towns of L'Assomption and Berthier were the two terminal points of this railway.[46]

Sorel and Berthier had been important centres of the wheat trade in earlier years, and the timber trade and shipbuilding were also important in the former. Population of both towns slightly more than doubled in the twenty years to 1850.[47] Finally, Montmagny, which with the exception of Quebec was the only town east of Trois-Rivières with as many as a thousand people, was dependent on local agriculture. Small manufacturing enterprises were encouraged by water power, local raw materials, river transport, and 'l'emploi de l'abondante main-d'oeuvre d'origine agricole.'[48] Thus, Quebec towns were only partly based on agriculture. The wood industry and entrepôt and administrative functions were also important, and in some cases railways provided stimuli unrelated to local agriculture.

Consequently, the agricultural sector of mid-nineteenth-century Quebec sustained less than 20,000 town-dwellers. By contrast, the great majority of Ontario's 130,000 urban residents owed their livelihood to economic activity spawned by the wheat staple, and even Montreal, after its grander designs had been shattered during the 1840s, saw its fortunes tied increasingly to the Ontario wheat economy. On the other hand, for forestry sector, supporting a few small towns in both provinces as well as Bytown and Quebec City, had proven to be a much less potent generator of urban growth.

Notes

1. This was the phrase of John Howison, *Sketches of Upper Canada* (1821; Toronto 1965), 55.
2. Population figures for Toronto are from Edith G. Firth, ed., *The Town of York, 1815-1834* (Toronto 1966), xxvi; and Census of Canada, 1870, iv, 83, 131, 178. Unless otherwise stated, figures on town population are from the census.

3. Acheson, 'The Nature and Structure of York Commerce in the 1820's' (1969), in J.K. Johnson, ed., *Historical Essays on Upper Canada* (Carleton Library no 82, 1975), 171.
4. Jacob Spelt, *Urban Development in South-Central Ontario* (Carleton Library no 57, 1972), 79.
5. Unless otherwise stated, information on export and import values is from I.D. Andrews, *Report on the Trade, Commerce, and Resources of the British North American Colonies...*31st Congress, 2nd Session, ex. doc. no 23 (Washington 1851), and Andrews, *Report on the Trade and Commerce of the British North American Colonies and upon the Trade of the Great Lakes and Rivers*, 32nd Congress, 1st Session, ex. doc. no 136 (Washington 1853).
6. Smith cited in Spelt, *Urban Development*, 94.
7. Firth, *Town of York*, xxvi-viii.
8. Barry D. Dyster, 'Toronto, 1840-1860: Making It in a British Protestant Town,' unpublished PHD thesis, University of Toronto, 1970; and Firth, *ibid.*, 75-6.
9. Donald C. Masters, *The Rise of Toronto, 1850-1890* (Toronto 1947), 21-6; and Dyster, *ibid.*, 293.
10. John Macauly, agent of the bank at Kingston, cited in Firth, *Town of York*, xxxi.
11. Spelt, *Urban Development*, 75-6, 79.
12. Smith, *Canada: Past, Present and Future*, 2 vols. (Toronto 1851), I, 223.
13. *Western Mercury*, cited in Marjorie Freeman Campbell, *A Mountain and a City: The Story of Hamilton* (Toronto 1966), 65; population statistics, *ibid.*, 62.
14. McCalla, 'The Decline of Hamilton as a Wholesale Center,' *Ontario History*, LXV (1973), 253.
15. Katz, 'The People of a Canadian City: 1851-2,' *Canadian Historical Review*, LIII, (1972), 411. Katz, in *The People of Hamilton, Canada West* (Cambridge, Mass. 1975), provides evidence that these were the primary sources of income of the 'entrepreneurial' class.
16. Smith, *Canada*, I, 220-8; Campbell, *A Mountain and a City*, 76.
17. Bouchette, *The British Dominions in North America...and a Topographical Dictionary of Lower Canada*, 2 vols. (1831; New York 1968), I, 105-6.
18. Smith, *Canada*, I, 16; Fred Coyne Hamil, *The Valley of the Lower Thames, 1640 to 1850* (Toronto 1951), 263.
19. Unless otherwise stated, information on the industrial and commercial establishments of each town in 1850 is from Smith, *Canada*.
20. The population figure for 1834 if from Frederick H. Armstrong and Daniel J. Brock, 'The Rise of London: A Study of Urban Evolution in Nineteenth-Century Southwestern Ontario,' in Armstrong et al., eds., *Aspects of Nineteenth-Century Ontario* (Toronto 1974), 89.
21. Orlo Miller, 'The Fat Years, and the Lean: London (Canada) in Boom and Depression,' *Ontario History*, LIII (1961), 76.
22. *Ibid.*, 74.
23. Armstrong and Brock, 'Rise of London,' 83-4, 91; Miller, *Ibid.*, 76.
24. Cited in Armstrong and Brock, 'Rise of London,' 91.
25. Bouchette, *British Dominions*, I, 118.
26. Smith, *Canada*, I, 237-9.
27. Thomas W. Poole, *A Sketch of the Early Settlement and Subsequent Progress of the Town of Peterborough* (Peterborough 1867), 93-9. Estimate of price of square timber is from Smith, *Canada*, II, 229.
28. Smith, *Canada*, II, 278. Direct imports by Kingston were 74 per cent of direct imports of all Ontario ports in 1842. This ratio declined to an average of 30 per cent in 1844-46 and 10 per cent in 1848-51. Andrews, *Report on the Trade, Commerce, and Resources*, 198-9; *Report on the Trade and Commerce*, 457-8.
29. Estimates of urban population in 1835 are from Albert Faucher, *Québec en Amérique au XIXe siècle* (Montreal 1973), 301.
30. Andrews, *Report on the Trade and Commerce*, 430.
31. Hazel C. Mathews, *Oakville and the Sixteen: The History of an Ontario Port* (Toronto 1953), 204, 212.
32. Poole, *Sketch of the Early Settlement*, 62.
33. In comparison with mid-century Ontario, the prairies also faced more highly developed manufacturing and financial centres to the east, as well as a transportation network which denied to its nascent industry the 'natural protection' enjoyed by Ontario in its early years of industrial growth. The comparison with the prairies is analysed further in Chapter 8.
34. Works in this area include D.G. Creighton, *The Commercial Empire of the St. Lawrence, 1760-1850* (Toronto 1937); Gilbert N. Tucker, *The Canadian Commercial Revolution, 1845-1851* (New Haven 1936); and R.T. Naylor, 'The Rise and Fall of the Third Commercial Empire of the St Lawrence' in Gary Teeple, ed., *Capitalism and the National Question in Canada* (Toronto 1972).
35. Cited in Tucker, *Canadian Commercial Revolution*, 186.
36. Andrews, *Report on the Trade, Commerce, and Resources*, 276-7.
37. As noted above, the exclusion of shipments to Lower Canada and the Maritimes gives a false impression of the relative importance of the American route. This misleading impression is compounded by considering only wheat, in which case, according to Easterbrook and Aitken, as cited in Jean

Hamelin and Yves Roby, *Histoire économique du Québec, 1851-1896* (Montreal 1971), 47-8, the volume of Upper Canadian wheat exported by the American route was more than fifteen times that exported via the St Lawrence in 1850. The more meaningful figure, as given in Table S.2, includes flour shipments as well as shipments destined to Lower Canada and the Maritimes, and on this basis St Lawrence shipments were one-third greater than those via the United States in 1850 and 88 per cent greater in 1851.

38. Ouellet, *Histoire économique et sociale du Québec, 1760-1850* (Montreal 1971), 265.

39. 1826: *Journals of the Legislative Assembly of Lower Canada* (JLALC), 1830, app. D
1830: JLALC, 1831, app. G
1835: JLALC, 1835-36, app. Q
1844: *Journals of the Legislative Assembly of Canada* (JLAC), 1844-45, app. AA
1850: Andrews, *Report on the Trade, Commerce, and Resources*, 282-3
All figures refer to the Lachine Canal except in the year 1850, which refers to the St Lawrence canals. However, these would seem to be almost identical, since in 1844 shipments were 26,600 tons via the St Lawrence canals and 27,500 tons via the Lachine Canal.

40. Andrews, *Report on the Trade and Commerce*, 454-5, 458.

41. JLAC, 1849, app. AAAAA, 3.

42. Ouellet, *Histoire économique et sociale*, 475; JLAC, ibid., 3, 11.

43. Raoul Blanchard, *Le centre du Canada français* (Montreal 1947), 153-6, 159-62, 166-8; *L'ouest du Canada français* (Montreal 1953), 139, 145.

44. Hamelin and Roby, *Histoire économique*, 122-3, 125.

45. Blanchard, *Le centre du Canada français*, 320.

46. Blanchard, *L'ouest du Canada français*, 144.

47. Bouchette, *British Dominions*, I, 210, 305-6.

48. Raoul Blanchard, *L'est du Canada français*, 2 vols. (Montréal 1935), I, 177.

383

Philosophy of Railroads *

T. C. KEEFER

published at the request of the
directors of the Montreal and Lachine Railroad
by Thomas C. Keefer, civil engineer

Old winter is once more upon us, and our inland seas are 'dreary and inhospitable wastes' to the merchant and to the traveller; — our rivers are sealed fountains — and an embargo which no human power can remove is laid on all our ports. Around our deserted wharves and warehouses are huddled the naked spars — the blasted forest of trade — from which the sails have fallen like the leaves of the autumn. The splashing wheels are silenced — the roar of steam is hushed — the gay saloon, so lately thronged with busy life, is now but an abandoned hall — and the cold snow revels in solitary possession of the untrodden deck. The animation of business is suspended, the life blood of commerce is curdled and stagnant in the St. Lawrence — the great aorta of the North. On land, the heavy stage labours through mingled frost and mud in the West — or struggles through drifted snow, and slides with uncertain track over the icy hills of Eastern Canada.

* Abridged from *Philosophy of Railroads*, edited by H. V. Nelles. Published in 1972 by University of Toronto Press from the third edition published in 1850 by Armour & Ramsay printers of Montreal and Andrew H. Armour and Company of Toronto.

Far away to the South is heard the daily scream of the steam-whistle — but from Canada there is no escape: blockaded and imprisoned by Ice and Apathy, we have at least ample time for reflection — and if there be comfort in Philosophy may we not profitably consider the PHILOSOPHY OF RAILROADS.

New commercial enterprises, however well supported by dry and accurate statistics, are not often undertaken upon imperfect information — through the representations of theorists or politico-economical writers — or even when supported by bright analogies, and the most authentic records of the success of similar undertakings amongst similar communities. It is true, that well-established systems become the subjects of stock-jobbing and speculation by parties ignorant of their uses or real value; but their origin and maturity are the work of the well-informed few, whose foresight has been rewarded frequently before it has been acknowledged. In older countries the feasibility of public projects and their value as speculations are more speedily ascertained than in our young and thinly populated Province, and any attempt to transplant a system, or found arguments for the latter from the experience of the former, is at once met with disparaging and 'odious' comparisons. The intrinsic merit of the question — the absolute instead of the comparative value of our own projects — are not often investigated, because the nature of such investigations are not familiar to us, while they have long since become unnecessary and are therefore not canvassed in those countries where an established system exists.

384

Thus it is with the Railway System in Canada. We see, and to our cost, feel its effects around us; — we acknowledge its importance, the great results it has achieved, and the substantial expression of public opinion in its favour in the hundreds of millions which have been freely devoted to its extension in other civilized countries. We have talked about it for years — we have projected a great deal, and done very little, because the public — the real estate owners large and small — have not taken up the subject. Our Representatives have lately acquitted themselves nobly in this matter, but they have rather led than followed public opinion, and have themselves been acted upon by a 'glorious' minority, to whom the actual and efficient execution has hitherto been confined, and who have contended with the chilling influences of popular apathy, ignorance, and incredulity.

An attempt to investigate the Railway System in its applicability to new countries — to define its limitations by shewing where and why its application becomes justifiable — to disseminate popular information upon a too unpopular subject, and turn a portion of that earnest and eager covetousness of foreign prosperity back upon our own neglected resources — will it is hoped be received with public favour — or at least with public charity.

At the outset it may be objected that there is an insufficiency of disposable circulating capital in Canada, to construct a tithe of the length of projected Railways, and that *therefore* the discussion is premature. The premises will be admitted to any reasonable extent, but the conclusion, instead of the discussion is, we hope to show, premature.

The population, soil, and wealth of Canada are not inferior to Vermont, New Hampshire, Michigan, Georgia, and other States which have Railways; and the local resources of some portions of our Province, where Railroads are wanting, are at least equal to those in Ohio and many other States where these advantages have been enjoyed for years. Whatever is or was the condition of the circulating capital in the States mentioned, they have *found a way* to build their roads. This we believe has been done through the energy and perseverance of the local proprietors of real estate, who have convinced capitalists that they could have no better security for their investments, than that contingent upon the certain increase of population, wealth, and traffic, in rising countries like our own; — and thus have they secured improvements from which the land is the first to benefit, and without which its value in Canada is stationary; and this too, under circumstances when to stand still is to recede. The projectors of the Welland Canal were not Rothschilds; yet the untiring perseverance of one gentleman secured the construction of a work which for importance has no parallel in America.

385

There is a greater amount of unemployed capital amongst our agricultural and trading population than is generally supposed; and of fixed capital and absolute wealth there is more than sufficient both to need and to warrant the construction of all the roads proposed. A very considerable class of the stockholders in New England roads are farmers, with investments from £50 to £500.

Railway stocks, unlike most others, are a species of real estate immoveably attached to the soil, and have therefore become of late years favourite channels for investment with all classes of capitalists. Banks may fail — commerce may languish or be partially diverted — manufactures be rendered unprofitable — even the earth may for a time refuse to many a return for the capital invested in it; but as long as there are men to profit or to lose by speculations, there will be people to sustain a Railway; and if universal ruin be inevitable, *they* will be the last public works to succumb to the general prostration. The cart road is succeeded by the turnpike, this again by the macadam or plank roads, and these last by the Railway. The latter is the perfected system and admits of no competition — and this characteristic pre-eminently marks it out as the most desirable object for investment in the midst of an enterprising and increasing population.

With an *assessed* value of about thirty-five millions of dollars — with cultivated lands worth thirty-six millions of dollars, and an annual crop, valued at ten millions of dollars, in Upper Canada alone — with population, production and wealth, doubling in about ten years, we offer a security upon the industrial character and the increasing wants of a progressive people, for all judicious commercial investments. We therefore believe — although we could not borrow a dollar for any other purpose — that as the unavoidable customers of a well placed Railway, we have only to secure its receipts to those from whom we ask assistance and take those necessary preliminary steps which none but ourselves can take, in order to obtain the capital required to construct our works. This can scarcely be contested from the experience of the past, because the value of Railway investment is of comparatively recent discovery — and is even now but partially appreciated. Did we not find it so difficult to foresee the inevitable future instead of looking backward, we must acknowledge that with the same future as past progress, there will have taken place in the natural order of things, *before* such works as we propose to consider *could be* brought into perfect operation, such an improved change as is now only demanded by the most incredulous in order to secure their sanction to a Railway System for Canada.

What we need most is that faith in the works themselves which will produce sufficient fruit to bring them within the munificent provisions of our late Railroad Act. It is to present something of the 'substance hoped for,' and the unseen evidence required to produce these works, that these remarks have been offered to the public.

The initiative must be taken by us: we cannot expect the accumulated capital of commerce or of older countries to seek out *our* investments. We must do as others do — lay our projects before the money holders, and shew our earnestness and confidence by taking stock to the extent of our means; — but, above all, we must inform ourselves and them fully of the grounds upon which we found our expectations. Zeal and enterprize, directed by a knowledge of our subject, are more rare and efficient commodities than the mere possession of capital; because they will carry capital and all other things with them.

Let us take a case of which Canada (we are proud and sad to say) presents more than one instance. A well cultivated district, in which all the lands are occupied (perhaps by the second generation) with or without water power, but situated twenty to fifty miles from the chief towns upon our great highway, the St. Lawrence, and without navigable water communication with it. The occupants are all thriving and independent farmers, the water power is employed only to an extent to meet their local wants, and the village is limited to the few mechanics, and the one store required for this rural district. The barter of the shopkeeper is restricted by the consumption of his customers, and he becomes the sole forwarder of the surplus product of the district. There is no stimulus for increased production — there are less facilities for it: the redundant population have all been accustomed to agriculture, and as the field for this is unrestricted, they move Westward to prevent a subdivision of the homesteads, and to become greater landowners than their fathers. There exists the well known scarcity of labourers for the harvest, because there is no employment for them during the remainder of the year; and they have not yet been led by necessity to that subdivision of labour and that variety of employment which are the results of an increasing and more confined population. Each farmer has his comfortable house, his well stored barn, variety of stock, his meadows and his woodland; he cultivates only as much as he finds convenient, and his slight surplus is exchanged for his modest wants. Distance, the expense of transportation, and the absence of that energy which debt or contact with busier men should produce, have prevented any efforts to supply the commercial towns on the part of the contented denizens of our 'Sleepy Hollow.' To themselves, to the superficial observer, their district has attained the limit of improvement. If they have no water power, or one limited to the supply of the needful grist or saw mill, it is clear to their minds that they were never destined for manufacturing people; and if they have abundant water power, their local market would not support one manufactory, while land carriage, want of people, money, and more than all *information*, precludes the idea of their manufacturing for a distant market. It is still more evident, from their position, they are not to become a commercial people and build up large cities; they, therefore, jog along with evident self-satisfaction — the venerable churchyard is slowly filling up with tombstones — and the quiet residents arrive at the conclusion that they are a peculiarly favoured people in having escaped the rage for improvement. They are grateful that their farms have not been disfigured by canals or railroads, or the spirits of their sires troubled by the hideous screech of the steam-whistle.

387

We will now suppose, (we would we could more than suppose), that two of our cities should be moved to unite by the iron bond of a Railway, which in its course will traverse the district just described. Excitement prevails in the 'Hollow'; — sleep has deserted her peculiar people — the livelong night is passed in mutual contemplation of farms 'cut up' or covered over — visions of bloody skirmishes between 'Far downs' and Corkonians — of rifled gardens and orchards, of plundered poultry yards and abducted pigs. The probable mother of a possible child bewails her future offspring 'drawn and quartered' on the rail by the terrible locomotive, and a whole hecatomb of cattle, pigs and sheep, are devoted by imagination to this insatiate Juggernaut. The Engineers who come to spy out the land are met with curses both loud and deep — the laws of property are discussed — the delinquent Member for the County denounced — until a handsome Rodman, by well-timed admiration of Eliza Ann, the rural spokesman's daughter, succeeds in obtaining comfortable quarters for his party, with board, lodging, and washing, at 12s. 6d. per week. The work has commenced; the farmer is offered better prices for his hay and grain than he ever before received: — even milk and vegetables — things he never dreamed of selling — are now sought for; his teams, instead of eating up his substance as formerly in winter, are constantly employed, and his sons are profitably engaged in 'getting out timber' for the contractors; he grows a much larger quantity of oats and potatoes than before — and when the workmen have left, he finds to his astonishment that his old friend the storekeeper is prepared to take all he can spare, to send by the Railroad 'down to town.'

And now some of the 'city folks' come out and take up a water privilege, or erect steam power, and commence manufacturing. Iron is bought, cut into nails, screws and hinges. Cotton is spun and wove, and all the variety of manufacturers introduced, because here motive power, rents and food are cheaper, and labour more easily controlled than in the cities, while transportation and distance have by the Railroad been reduced to a minimum. A town has been built and peopled by the operatives — land rises rapidly in value — the neglected swamp is cleared and the timber is converted into all sorts of wooden 'notions' — tons of vegetables, grains, or grasses, are grown where none grew before — the patient click of the loom, the rushing of the shuttle, the busy hum of the spindle, the thundering of the trip-hammer, and the roaring of steam, are mingled in one continuous sound of active industry. While the physical features of our little hamlet are undergoing such a wonderful transformation, the moral influence of the iron civilizer upon the old inhabitants is bringing a rapid 'change over the spirit of their dreams.' The young men and the maidens, the old men and the matrons, daily collect around the cars: they wonder where so

388

many well-dressed and rich-looking people come from and are going to, &c. — what queer machines those are which they see passing backwards and forwards. They have perhaps an old neighbour whose son had long since wandered off, and now they see him returned, a first class passenger with all the prestige of broadcloth, gold chains, rings, gloves, and a travelled reputation: the damsels rapidly impress upon 'the mind's eye' the shapes of the bonnets, visites, &c., of that superior class of beings who are flying (like angels) over the country, and *drink in* with wide-mouthed admiration, the transcendent splendour and indescribable beauty of 'that 'ere shawl.' All are interested, all are benefited, *cuique suum*. Is he a farmer? he has a practical illustration of the superior cheapness of transportation by increasing the load — the cart is abandoned for the waggon — for he sees the Railroad, notwithstanding the great cost of the cuttings, embankments, tunnels, bridges, engines, cars, and stations, carrying his produce for a less sum than his personal expenses and the feeding of his horses would amount to. Is he a blacksmith? he determines his son shall no longer shoe horses, but build engines. Is he a carpenter? he is proud of his occupation as he surveys the new bridge over the old creek. Even the village tailor gathers 'a wrinkle,' as he criticises the latest effort of Buckmaster or Gibb, whilst the unconscious advertiser is swallowing his coffee. Thus curiosity and emulation are excited and the results are discernible in a general predilection for improved 'modes.' A spirit is engendered which is not confined to dress or equipage, but is rapidly extended to agriculture, roads, and instructive societies, and finally exerts its most powerful influence where it is most needed — in the improved character it gives to the exercise of the franchise. This right is now enjoyed by too large a class, whose chief contact with public affairs has been limited to an occasional chat with ambitious retailers of dry goods, groceries, hardware, and political mysteries — or to a semi-annual sitting in a jury box, unconsciously absorbing all the virtuous indignation of some *nisi prius* wrangler, whose 'familiar face' is shortly after presented to them at the hustings, generously proffering to defend or advocate anything for four dollars per diem and a prospective Judgeship. He is opposed, perhaps, by the public-spirited shopkeeper, who, with mortgages, long credits, tea and tobacco — aided by a 'last call' to all doubtful supporters — incites the noble yeomanry to assert their rights as 'free and independent electors.' If the 'natives' can overcome these prejudices of local associations, or if the lawyer's 'collections' and 'notes' are sufficiently diffuse, ten chances to one the greatest talker is elected, and an improved judicature, instead of an improved country, is the result.

Nothing would be a more powerful antidote to this state of primitive, but not innocuous simplicity, than the transit of Railways through our agricultural districts. The civilizing tendency of the locomotive is one of the modern anomalies, which however inexplicable it may appear to some, is yet so fortunately patent to all, that it is admitted as readily as the action of steam, though the substance be invisible and its secret ways unknown to man. Poverty, indifference, the bigotry or jealousy of religious denominations, local dissensions or political demagogueism may stifle or neutralize the influence of the best intended efforts of an educational system; but that invisible power which has waged successful war with the material elements, will assuredly overcome the prejudices of mental weakness or the designs of mental tyrants. It calls for no cooperation, it waits for no convenient season, but with a restless, rushing, roaring assiduity, it keeps up a constant and unavoidable spirit of enquiry or comparison; and while ministering to the material wants, and appealing to the covetousness of the multitude, it unconsciously, irresistibly, impels them to a more intimate union with their fellow men.

389

Having attempted to illustrate the influence of a Railway upon a district supposed to have culminated, let us proceed to notice some of the general characteristics of the system before we apply the results of our investigations to our own particular wants.

We are not backward in importing improvements or transplanting systems *which we understand:* at the same time, those which are new to us, we have curiosity enough and distrust enough to challenge until their principles are defined — when, with the materials before him, with a particular individuality, each man arrives at his own conclusions as to the practicability of their proposed application to this country. It is to this broad principle of 'common sense,' judgment, or whatever you will, we prefer to appeal rather than to the 'availability' or elasticity of statistics.

Steam has exerted an influence over matter which can only be compared to that which the discovery of Printing has exercised upon mind. These two great discoveries — pillars of cloud and fire which have brought us out of the mental wilderness of the dark and middle ages — have combined to supply the mind with daily food and illustrate the value of time.* Men have now virtually attained antediluvian longevity; ideas are exchanged by

* Steam Printing

lightning — readers and their books travel together but little behind their thoughts — while actors, materials, scenes and scenery are shifted with the rapidity and variety of the kaleidoscope.

The extraordinary expansion of the Railway System, within the last thirty years, is to be ascribed to the improved appreciation of the Value of Time; since it is *now* universally admitted, that distances are virtually shortened in the precise ratio in which the times occupied in passing over them are diminished.

Speed, economy, regularity, safety, and convenience — an array of advantages unequalled — are combined in the Railway System. These we will notice separately.

Speed

The importance of speed in the transport of goods is annually increasing; even now the more valuable descriptions of merchandize take the rail in preference to the slower and cheaper route by canal; and since the cost of transport upon a Railway varies in an inverse proportion with the business of the road, it is annually becoming less, so that economy of time and economy of transport are becoming less and less antagonistical, and are approaching each other so rapidly, as to render the establishment of any line of demarcation exceedingly difficult if not impossible.

390

Economy

Compared with all other land communications, their freighting capabilities may be inferred from the consideration that a horse usually draws from fifteen to thirty hundred weight on a good turnpike or macadamised road (exclusive of vehicle), four to six tons on a plate rail tram road, and fifteen to twenty tons on an edge rail including the waggons; — the friction on a level Railway being only from one-tenth to one-seventh of that upon the roads above mentioned. If this be the effect of the rail alone, it is needless to enlarge upon its power when travelled by an iron horse, with which hunger and thirst are but metaphorical terms, which knows no disease nor fatigue, and to which a thousand miles is but the beginning of a journey, and a thousand tons but an ordinary burthen.

But it is in a more extended sense than the mere *cost* of transport that the economy of the Railway is vindicated. While upon the best roads travelled by horses, the cost and time of transportation increases rapidly with the distance, it is clear that there is a point from whence the transport of certain articles becomes unprofitable or impracticable. Milk, fruits, and vegetables, for immediate use, will not bear ten or twelve hours jolting over fifty miles of the best turnpike to reach a market; while fresh meats, fish, eggs, cattle, pigs, and poultry, lumber, staves, shingles, and fire-wood, and many other necessaries of life, either could not afford the time or the cost of a hundred miles transport by horse-power. The production of these articles, therefore, is very limited in certain districts; but wherever a Railway takes its track their extensive production becomes at once a new element of wealth, and the Locomotive a public benefactor — making 'two blades of grass grow where only one grew before.' Thus the essence of a Railway system is *to increase its own traffic*, adding twenty-five per cent to the value of every farm within fifty miles of the track, doubling that of those near it, and quadrupling the value of timbered lands through which they pass. Railroads are in one respect more economical carriers than canals, in as much as they are both freight and toll receivers, and are therefore content with one profit.

Regularity

The superior speed and safety of Railway travel over the most expeditious water communications are scarcely more important than its extraordinary regularity; to which latter circumstance it is chiefly owing that in every country the Railway has been selected for the transportation of the mails. This monopoly of mails and passengers enables them to transport goods proportionally cheaper — thus becoming powerful rivals to the most favourable water communications. From this principle of regularity, Railways in the winter season have no competitors; and, working the whole year round, without delay of lockage, wind or tide, fog, frost, or rain, they, with a full business and fair 'grades,' can compete with ordinary canals in price, while they can make two trips, to one on the canal, in less than half the time.

Safety

The comparative safety of Railway travel with that upon steamboats is best appreciated by the reflection, that the causes which endanger human life upon the former are limited to collisions or leaving the track — both to be avoided by ordinary care: whereas in the latter, explosion, fire, collision, or wrecking, are attended with imminent risk to all, the only choice often being — the *mode* of death. Explosion of a locomotive boiler, besides being exceedingly rare, is scarcely ever attended with any danger to the lives of the passengers. The remarkable safety of well managed Railways may be further illustrated by the statement of Baron Von Reden, that upon the Railways of Germany only one person in every twelve and a quarter millions of passengers was killed or wounded from defective arrangements of the road, one in every nine millions from his own misconduct, and one in every twenty-five millions from his own negligence. The Germans are undoubtedly a prudent people.

Convenience

The convenience of the Railway System lies chiefly in its adaptation to its peculiar traffic; — artificial navigation is restricted to favourable ground and supplies of water, but modern improvements have enabled the Locomotive to clamber over mountains and penetrate the most remote corners of the land; there is therefore no limit to the number of its auxiliary branches, which can be multiplied and extended until their ramifications give the required facilities to every wharf and every warehouse — to the solitary mill or factory, or to the most neglected districts as an outlet to otherwise worthless products. . . .

392

Transportation*
JOHN McCALLUM

Although the early roads of Ontario received a very bad press, recorded complaints were generally voiced by British travellers of aristocratic origin. As early as 1817 rural residents had expressed mild praise for the serviceability of the roads in their submissions to an investigation conducted by Robert Gourlay. Roads were adequate for the wheat farmer because most produce was either transported to the lake ports by sleigh in the winter or sold to the inland millers. Because time for winter land-clearing was at a premium, the farmer frequently chose the latter course of action despite the higher prices received at the ports.[1]

Road-building was very much the affair of individual farmers, private businessmen, and municipal governments. Especially after 1840, the role of provincial government expenditures was minimal.[2] Farmers and joint stock companies built roads if the anticipated exportable surplus and associated imports were sufficient to justify the cost, while the very *raison d'être* of Ontario towns was based on their ability to tap the agricultural hinterland. Roads, therefore, were much more the result than the cause of the economic opportunity provided by the wheat economy.

A typical example is provided by the village of Oakville which numbered only 300 inhabitants in 1836 and just short of 1000 in 1850. In the 1830s the main concession roads were built by the settlers, secondary roads were opened by statute labour, and only the main Lake Shore Road was built by the provincial government. In the next decade a joint stock company was formed to build a sixty-mile road between Oakville and Fergus. Of a

---

*Chapter 6 from *Unequal Beginnings: Agriculture and Economic Development in Quebec and Ontario until 1870.* Copyright 1980, by University of Toronto Press. Reprinted by permission.

total stock subscription of £7000, £2000 was subscribed by individuals living in the townships through which the road was to pass, £2000 was received from the township council, and £3000 was received from the county council.[3] Such examples are almost as numerous as the towns of mid-century Ontario, and for the province as a whole the great majority of funds for road-building originated at the local level. The government-sponsored colonization roads of the 1850s were the one important exception to this generalization, but they were a fiasco because 'just as the making of these roads was well under way, the good land came to an end.'[4]

The first major canal was the Rideau. Built by the imperial government for military reasons, it was never of much significance for Ontario agriculture. The Welland Canal conferred significant cost savings on farmers to the west, although it was viewed with scepticism by those who feared American competition.[5] For the province as a whole, the most important waterways were the St Lawrence canals and the Erie Canal. The St Lawrence canals were built mainly in the 1840s and their major effect on freight rates was not felt until 1848.[6] By that time the second American Drawback Act, which permitted Canadian produce to pass through the United States in bond, had given Ontario farmers free access to the American route to Britain via the Erie Canal. The St Lawrence canals therefore offered little advantage to the Ontario farmers on shipments to Britain, although, they represented a cost saving on wheat sold in Quebec and the Maritimes.[7]

393

TABLE I — Railways in Quebec and Ontario, 1861 and 1871

| | Mileage opened by January 1861 | | Mileage opened by 1 January 1871 | |
	Quebec	Ontario	Quebec	Ontario
Grand Trunk Mainline	405	465	405	465
Great Western Mainline		229		229
Other	150	658	317	747
Total	555	1352	722	1441

Source: Hind *et al.*, *EIGHTY YEARS' PROGRESS OF BRITISH NORTH AMERICA*, 193-4, and M.L. Bladen, 'Construction of Railways in Canada to the Year 1885,' *Contributions to Canadian Economics*, V (1932), 43-60.

Thus, roads were merely a consequence of more basic factors, and Canadian canals, so crucial to the aspirations of the Montreal merchants, were much less important from the point of view of Ontario farmers. Indeed, it can be argued that the most important development for Ontario farmers was the Erie Canal, for it prevented Montreal from monopolizing the benefits from improvements to the St Lawrence system, and it was a major factor in Ontario's emerging independence from that city. Nevertheless, the combination of the Drawback Act and the St Lawrence canals was undoubtedly a significant factor in the growth of wheat exports during the 1840s.

After 1850 Ontario entered the railway age. In that year the province had no railways, but by 1871 over 1400 miles of track had been opened (Table I). Construction was highly concentrated in the four-year period 1853-56, during which a thousand miles were completed. By the end of the period the province had two major east-west lines, the Grand Trunk and the Great Western. Railways led north from Brockville, Prescott, Port Hope, Cobourg, Toronto (two), Hamilton, Galt, Port Dover, and Port Stanley. Branch lines criss-crossed Ontario west of Toronto.

The coming of the railway increased the potential size of each town's hinterland, but the visions of Ontario railway promoters were generally confined to the territory of their own province. Only in exceptional cases was the trade of the American west a major factor in Ontario-based railway construction. American produce was certainly a key consideration in the construction of the Grand Trunk Railway, but this was an enterprise controlled in Britain and Montreal. Also, the Great Western was designed in part for American traffic, but the value of local freight was considerably greater than the value of foreign freight.[8] The great majority of the other railways of Ontario, making up over half of the province's mileage, depended exclusively on outward shipments of Ontario-produced commodities and inward shipments of goods for consumption in the province. Thus, as in the case of roads, the economic base of the railways was firmly rooted in the Ontario wheat economy.

394

While the stakes had become higher, in many respects the basic nature of the game did not change with the shift from roads to railways. The growth of towns continued to depend on penetration of the agricultural hinterland, and the shift from roads to railways represented merely a technologically based change in the form of that penetration. In both cases the object was to control the imports and exports of the maximum possible territory, and in both cases the energy behind the transportation projects originated in the merchants and municipal governments of the rival towns.

In Toronto both merchants and patricians had become personally committed to building the Northern Railway by 1850,[9] and added to individual commitments were the contributions of local governments. The city of Toronto contributed at least $300,000 to railway projects during the 1850s and 1860s, and smaller bodies such as the Simcoe District council also subscribed funds.[10] In Hamilton and London a group of merchants led by Sir Allan MacNab had obtained a charter for the London and Gore Railroad Company as early as 1834. This company later became the Great Western, and around 1850 it received stock subscriptions of £25,000 each from Oxford County, Middlesex County, Galt, and London. Hamilton bankrupted itself by subscribing £100,000 to the Great Western and £110,000 to local lines.[11] Many other townships, counties, and towns lent or gave money to railways, and funds were also derived directly from the farmers. In the words of Barry Dyster, 'Massive or ambitious funding of financial institutions was rarely attempted [in Toronto], and when it was achieved as in the case of the Bank of Toronto, the major part of the money came from the countryside behind the city. It was to this fertile hinterland that the new finance companies turned as well.'[12]

While the leading merchants and local governments provided the driving force behind railway construction, they nevertheless provided only a relatively small fraction of the money. Railways required capital on a scale that was well beyond the capacity of Canada to provide, and most of this capital was ultimately of external origin. The cost of Canadian railroads and equipment as of 1 January 1861 consisted of the following:[13]

Grand Trunk Railway	$ 56 million
Great Western Railway	23 million
Other Ontario lines	22 million
Other Quebec lines	6 million
Total	$107 million

Apart from government assistance, the Grand Trunk was financed in Britain, and most of the capital for construction of the Great Western originated in the United States. The government of the Province of Canada contributed a total of just over $20 million to these two railways and to the Northern, and in addition it guaranteed $6.5 million in loans to municipalities for railway construction. Including contributions of municipalities that acted on their own credit, the public sector contributed about $30 million to railway construction, although Britain was the ultimate source of most of this as well.[14]

395

Thus, railway construction depended on foreign capital, and foreign capital was forthcoming on the premise that railway-generated agricultural traffic would earn enough foreign exchange to service the debt. It was no accident, therefore, that construction was concentrated in the peak years of the wheat boom, for the traffic of these years fully supported the optimistic expectations on which the supply of foreign capital depended. In its early years the Great Western was a widely reported financial success, declaring dividends of 8 per cent in 1855 and 8.5 per cent in 1856,[15] and in the opinion of Thomas C. Keefer it was this success which allowed the completion of the other Canadian railways:

The great success which attended the early years of the Great Western assisted every other Canadian road, and was doubtless the main instrument in preventing the Grand Trunk from being prematurely abandoned. Whatever loss of prestige or character the province [of Canada] may suffer from the almost universal failure of her railways, as investments, it is clear that in a material sense she has been benefited immensely by the early luck of the Great Western, and by the English infatuation about Grand Trunk; for without these the means for the construction of many miles now in use would not have been raised. The construction of the other lines simultaneously with Grand Trunk was equally opportune, because there would have been little prospect of getting them done after the bankruptcy of that road.[16]

In a double sense, then, Ontario's railway construction flowed from the growth of the wheat economy. On the one hand, this construction was merely a technological extension of the inter-urban competition which had preceded the railway age. On the other hand, the means for this competition, now well beyond the resources of Ontario residents, was forthcoming on the expectation that the wheat boom of the mid-1850s would continue in the future. That it did not was unfortunate for the British and American investors, but Ontario had her railways nevertheless.

In contrast with Ontario railways, most Quebec-based lines were designed to transport goods produced *outside* the province of Quebec. Both the Grand Trunk and the Montreal and Champlain were built in an attempt to strengthen Montreal's position in the competition for the trade of the American and Canadian west. Neither railway had much to do with goods produced in Quebec. Yet, excluding these two railways, Quebec had only 68 miles of track in 1861 and, after the construction of a few short lines connecting the Eastern Townships to the United States, 235 miles in 1871. This compares with close to a thousand miles in Ontario excluding the Grand Trunk. Also, by 1861 Quebec municipalities had borrowed only one-fifth as much as Ontario municipalities from the Municipal Loan Fund,[17] which had been established to assist with the financing of local railways.

These differences in the amount and pattern of railway construction in the two provinces were merely another aspect of the divergent patterns of urban growth, which in turn flowed from differences in the agricultural sector. In Quebec there were fewer towns to connect to each other, and the lower level of trade in agricultural commodities implied lower volumes of potential traffic as well as a weaker basis for urban development. The availability of capital may also have been a factor to the extent that the smaller lines in Ontario depended upon locally generated funds, but the existence of the Municipal Loan Fund suggests that differences in potential traffic were the main factor behind the divergent patterns of railway construction. Both factors, of course, depended ultimately on the productivity of agriculture.

The railways had decisive effects on the rise and fall of Ontario towns. The railway network resolved the conflict between Port Hope and Cobourg in favour of the latter, and it brought stagnation to many of the old wheat ports, particularly those such as Oakville and Port Credit, which were located between Toronto and Hamilton. Oakville was said to have reached its zenith in 1860.[18] Russell D. Smith provides an account of the manner in which 'new towns and villages were created, and existing towns and villages were given new life as industries gravitated towards those places served by the [Great Western] railway.' Towns not located along the railway lost population. Douglas McCalla describes how Hamilton declined as a wholesale centre as the opening of the Grand Trunk west of Toronto provided half of Hamilton's customers with superior access to Toronto.[19] In general Toronto was strengthened by its position as a railway centre. Also, it has been seen that some Quebec towns benefited from their location on a railway line, although such towns were few in number.

In the long run the railways tended to favour the centralization of urban activity. However, their effects in this respect were not great in the years up to 1870, for it has been seen that urban concentration was no greater in 1870 than in 1850 in either province. In these early years railways induced more a reshuffling of the urban population than a marked tendency towards it concentration. More important were the effects of the railways on industrial development. Railways allowed manufacturers to reach wider markets, they broke down the natural protection offered by high transport costs, and they created a demand for railway-related equipment. The point to be emphasized here is that transportation advances followed the same general lines as urban and commercial development. In Ontario development was relatively generalized, and it was based mainly on the local production of wheat and the linkages that flowed from wheat. In Quebec, activity in Montreal was based on production occurring outside the province, and elsewhere in Quebec there was little activity at all.

Notes

1. The information in this paragraph is from Thomas F. McIlwraith, 'The Adequacy of Rural Roads: An Illustration from Upper Canada,' *Canadian Georgrapher* XIV, 4 (1970), 344-60, who based his conclusions on a detailed analysis of York County between 1790 and the 1850s.
2. Between 1791 and 1861 the provincial government spent a total of $3.5 million on roads. To place it in perspective, this sum, covering a period of seventy years, was equal to about one-quarter of the value of the wheat crop of 1851 and to one-sixth of the value of colonial expenditures on canals and other navigation works over the same period. By contrast, in the two decades after the Union of 1841, municipalities and joint stock companies spent $4.4 million on roads, *excluding* all roads made by statute labour or commutation money and all municipal outlays on common roads. H.Y. Hind *et al.*, *Eighty Years' Progress of British North America* (Toronto 1863), 127, 177-8.
3. Hazel C. Mathews, *Oakville and the Sixteen: The History of an Ontario Port* (Toronto 1953), 193.
4. H.A. Innis and A.R.M. Lower, *Select Documents in Canadian Economic History, 1783-1885* (Toronto 1933), 54. George W. Spragge, 'Colonization Roads in Canada West, 1850-1867,' *Ontario History*, XLIX (1957), 1-17, gives a detailed account of the failure of these roads.
5. Hugh G.J. Aitken, *The Welland Canal Company* (Cambridge, Mass. 1954), 121-2; D.G. Creighton, *The Commercial Empire of the St. Lawrence, 1760-1850* (Toronto 1937), 269-71.
6. The freight on a barrel of flour from Hamilton or Toronto to Montreal was about 4 s. in the mid-1820s, 2 to 3 s. in the early 1840s, and 1 s. to 6 d. after 1848. T.W. Acheson, 'The Nature and Structure of York Commerce in the 1820s,' in J.K. Johnson, ed., *Historical Essays on Upper Canada* (Carleton Library no 82, 1975), 184; D.L. Burn, 'Canada and the Repeal of the Corn Laws,' *Cambridge Historical Journal*, II (1928), 270; G.P. de T. Glazebrook, *A History of Transportation in Canada*, 2 vols. (Carleton Library no 11, 1964), I, 93.
7. In the case of the Maritimes, however, a significant and growing volume of Ontario flour arrived there via New York in bond. I.D. Andrews, *Report on the Trade and Commerce of the British North American Colonies and upon the Trade of the Great Lakes and Rivers* (Washington 1853), 435.
8. Russell D. Smith, 'The Early Years of the Great Western Railway, 1833-1857,' *Ontario History*, LX (1968), 222.
9. Barry D. Dyster, 'Toronto, 1840-1860: Making It in a British Protestant Town,' unpublished PHD thesis, University of Toronto, 1970, pp. 306-7.
10. Donald C. Masters, *The Reciprocity Treaty of 1854* (London 1936), 67; Dyster, *ibid.*, 307; Jacob Spelt, *Urban Development in South-Central Ontario* (Carleton Library no 57, 1972), 113.
11. Marjorie Freeman Campbell, *A Mountain and a City: The Story of Hamilton* (Toronto 1966), 110, 120, 134-5; Smith, 'Great Western,' 211.
12. Dyster, 'Toronto,' 292.
13. Hind *et al.*, *Eighty Years' Progress* 195. The total figure of $97.2 million given in this source excludes a number of smaller lines, and it was assumed that the cost per mile for the lines excluded was the same as the average for all other lines.
14. The financing of the Grand Trunk is described in *ibid.*, 197-214; the financing of the Great Western in Smith, 'Great Western,' and in Hind, *ibid.*, 229-36. On government contributions, see *ibid.*, 192, 195, 215-17.
15. Smith, *ibid.*, 222.

16. Cited in Hind *et al.*, *Eighty Years' Progress*, 221.
17. *Ibid.*, 216-17.
18. Spelt, *Urban Development*, 111-12, 115, 135-6; Mathews, *Oakville and the Sixteen*, 333.
19. Smith, 'Great Western,' 225-7; McCalla, 'The Decline of Hamilton as a Wholesale Center.' *Ontario History*, LXV (1973), 247-54.

398

Topic Twelve

Economic Developments in the Atlantic Colonies in the Mid-Nineteenth Century

Very few ties existed between the Atlantic colonies and the Canadas in the mid-nineteenth century. Halifax and Saint John, the leading ports of Nova Scotia and New Brunswick, lay much closer to the great American ports of Boston and New York than to the Canadian harbours on the St. Lawrence; moreover, in winter, ice completely severed what links they did have with Canada. Rather than westward to the interior, the Atlantic colonies — before the building of a rail link with the Canadas — looked eastward to Britain, and southward to the American Atlantic seaboard and the West Indies.

Of the four Atlantic colonies, Nova Scotia was the most significant in the mid-nineteenth century. It had the greatest strategic importance, being located at the entrance to the Gulf of St. Lawrence and on the shipping lanes of the North Atlantic. It had the most balanced economy of the four, with excellent fisheries, good lowland farmland, and supplies of iron and coal. In 1861 Nova Scotia's population of 330,000 exceeded that of any of the other three Atlantic colonies. As a result the business community in Halifax aspired to make their city the regional trading centre of the Maritime region. David Sutherland reviews their metropolitan ambitions in "Halifax Merchants and the Pursuit of Development, 1783-1850."

New Brunswick, like Prince Edward Island (agriculture) and Newfoundland (fisheries), really depended on a single staple industry. The colony had some good farmland in the St. John River Valley, but lumbering remained the mainstay of its economy. The commercial ambitions of the merchants of the leading city in New Brunswick are examined by T.W. Acheson in his, "The Great Merchant and Economic Development in St. John 1820-1850."

For an understanding of the Atlantic region in the mid-nineteenth century students should consult W.S. MacNutt's *The Atlantic Provinces, 1712-1857* (Toronto: McClelland and Stewart, 1965). MacNutt has also written *New Brunswick, A History: 1784-1867* (Toronto: Macmillan, 1963). See also Graeme Wynn, *Timber Colony: A Historical Geography of Early Nineteenth*

Century New Brunswick (Toronto: University of Toronto Press, 1981). William Menzie Whitelaw provides a general overview of all aspects of life in the Atlantic colonies in the mid-nineteenth century in his chapter, "The Atlantic Provinces and Their Neighbors," from *The Maritimes and Canada Before Confederation* (Toronto: Oxford University Press, 1966; first published in 1934), pp. 9-37. Important essays on the Maritime colonies are contained in *Historical Essays on the Atlantic Provinces*, edited by G.A. Rawlyk (Toronto: McClelland and Stewart, 1967). Thomas H. Raddall's *Halifax, Warden of the North* (revised edition; Toronto: McClelland and Stewart, 1971), provides a readable account of that city's past. In "The Relief of the Unemployed Poor in Saint John, Halifax, and St. John's," *Acadiensis* 5(1):32-53, Judith Fingard reviews the early system of poor relief, a topic often ignored. For an understanding of Newfoundland history in this period see: James Hillier and Peter Neary, eds., *Newfoundland in the Nineteenth and Twentieth Centuries: Essays in Interpretation* (Toronto: University of Toronto Press, 1980); and Frederick W. Rowe, *A History of Newfoundland and Labrador* (Toronto: McGraw-Hill Ryerson, 1980). Students should consult the volumes of *Acadiensis* (since 1970) which contain many important articles on Atlantic history. A volume of essays taken from back issues of *Acadiensis* is available: *The Atlantic Provinces Before Confederation* (Fredericton: Acadiensis, 1985).

Halifax Merchants and the Pursuit of Development, 1783-1850*

DAVID SUTHERLAND

The image of the businessman in Canadian history is in a state of flux. Once viewed as the architect of nationhood, more recently he has tended to be portrayed as the agent of continental assimilation.[1] Until now, assessment of entrepreneurial performance has largely concentrated on activities within central Canada. This paper seeks to broaden the geographic scope of the inquiry by analyzing the eighteenth- and early nineteenth-century development strategy of the merchant community in Halifax, Nova Scotia. The inquiry seeks to establish the extent to which this east-coast business élite consciously attempted and in fact succeeded in building a northern regional economy distinct from that of the United States. The analysis focuses on the period between the end of the American Revolution and the coming of free trade.[2]

Any assessment of Halifax's function must begin with acknowledgment of its distinctive geographic characteristics. Although endowed with a large,

*From *Canadian Historical Review*, 59, 1 (1978): 1-17. Reprinted by permission of the author and the University of Toronto Press.

secure, ice-free harbour and situated adjacent to the major transatlantic shipping lanes, the port suffers one crucial liability. Unlike the ports of the St. Lawrence, Halifax lacks river access to the adjoining hinterland. It is trapped on the Atlantic coast, shut off from the resources of the interior by a barrier of rock, swamp, and scrub forest. Communication by sea is interrupted by storms and ice during winter. During the rest of the year, Maritime coastal waters have traditionally played host to an international fishing and commercial fleet competing all too vigorously for control of regional resources and markets. Geography and the presence of external rivals meant that through the first quarter century after its founding in 1749, Halifax functioned as an isolated imperial military garrison, having only minimal commercial contact with the neighbouring region.[3]

The Revolutionary War contributed decisively to a redefinition of Halifax's identity. Loyalist merchants, crowding into the Nova Scotia capital early in the 1780s, became the focus of a lobby demanding implementation of a comprehensive regional development strategy one that envisioned the Maritimes being transformed into a 'new' New England, playing the role of supply base and market for the British Caribbean. Those based in Halifax saw their port emerging as a second Boston, thriving on the West Indies carrying trade and functioning as chief commercial entrepôt within the Maritimes.[4] Implementation of this development programme demanded the elimination of competition from 'old' New England, a task colonial lobbyists believed could be accomplished through the application of mercantilist restriction against American business enterprise. Their aspirations received at least partial support from the British government. While conceding American access to the inshore fisheries of British America under the Treaty of Paris, the London authorities did introduce imperial Orders-in-Council barring American vessels from British Caribbean ports.[5] Thus emboldened, Halifax entrepreneurs embarked during the 1780s on an effort to build their port into a regional commercial metropolis.

401

The development programme achieved only marginal initial success. Given their small population and pioneering economy, the Maritimes could not immediately duplicate the role of New England. Supplies continually had to be imported in large quantities from the United States both for local consumption and for resale to the Caribbean. Halifax merchants found themselves essentially playing the role of middlemen, handling a two-way flow of goods between the island planters and the United States, an arrangement which yielded profits but which left the Maritimes vulnerable to external pressures.[6] Those pressures became manifest early in the 1790s following outbreak of war between Britain and revolutionary France. In order to reduce costs and ease supply shortages in its Caribbean possessions, the British government relaxed restrictions against the entry of American vessels into the island ports.[7] Resurgent American competition in the crucial West Indies carrying trade, combined with their exploitation of the northern fisheries and extensive smuggling operations throughout the Maritimes, severely curtailed commercial enterprise in Halifax. Merchants in the Nova

Scotia capital built up and maintained an extensive network of trade relations with the outport communities, but they entered the nineteenth century without having established anything approaching commercial hegemony over the neighbouring region.[8]

The last phase of the Napoleonic wars proved remarkably fortunate for Halifax. After 1807 hostilities proved increasingly destructive to American commercial interests. At the same time, French curtailment of timber exports from the Baltic created a growing British demand for Maritime and Canadian timber. The resulting expansion of regional trade with both the British Caribbean and Great Britain greatly stimulated the level of commercial activity at Halifax.[9] Trade became even more brisk following the outbreak of war between the United States and Great Britain in 1812. Speculation in prize goods yielded large incomes, while even greater profits were derived from the large-scale illicit trade with New England which persisted throughout the duration of hostilities.[10] Wartime conditions in Halifax were summed up by one local newspaper when it declared in 1814: 'Happy state of Nova Scotia! amongst all this tumult we have lived in peace and security: invaded only by a numerous host of American doubloons and dollars, which have swept away the contents of our stores and shops like a torrent.'[11]

Halifax entrepreneurs regarded this prosperity not as an ephemeral consequence of war but rather as a demonstration of the validity of their long-term development strategy. The profits of war could be sustained into peacetime, they insisted, provided the imperial government moved vigorously to protect colonial interests from the threat of resurgent foreign competition. This was the message reiterated in petition after petition by the Halifax Committee of Trade, an entity established in 1804 to act as a collective voice for the local merchant community.[12] The measure demanded most was exclusion of foreign entrepreneurs from both the British American inshore fisheries and from the West Indies carrying trade. The committee also emphasized the need for continuation of wartime tariff preferences, which assured colonial timber entry into the British market. Another popular request concerned the establishment of Halifax as a permanent 'free port,' open to the receipt of American vessels bringing in goods from New England. The Committee of Trade further urged export of British capital and immigrants to the Maritimes to participate in the work of regional economic and social development.[13] This entire programme was founded on eighteenth-century mercantilist logic.

Halifax's merchant lobby invariably justified their claims to special consideration by warning of the dangers inherent in dependence on trade with foreign powers, especially the United States. Protectionist trade regulations were equated with the preservation of a strong British and colonial merchant marine which, by functioning as a 'nursery for seamen,' provided Britain with an invaluable military reserve. Finally, spokesmen for Halifax's merchant community continually boasted that British America had the potential to develop into a far greater asset to Britain's economic empire than had been lost in the old thirteen colonies.[14]

Despite Committee of Trade rhetoric, many Halifax merchants remained dubious about the postwar era. News of the signing of the Treaty of Ghent, which reached Halifax early in 1815, prompted one local entrepreneur to comment: 'This peace has blasted all our prospects.'[15] In part, anxiety derived from uncertainty over the imperial government's willingness to move decisively against foreign competitors. Disillusionment began to set in as early as 1814 when Britain agreed to a restoration of French fishing rights in Newfoundland waters. An even greater sense of outrage swept the Halifax waterfront in 1818 following the signing of an Anglo-American commercial convention which made it exceedingly difficult to prosecute United States vessels for fishing and smuggling along the coasts of British America.[16]

These reverses were partially offset by the British decision to bar American vessels from its Caribbean ports. At the same time, Halifax and Saint John were established as 'free ports' through which American produce could be exchanged for sugar island commodities. In this way the northern colonies would supposedly be assured of a dominant position in the West Indies carrying trade.[17] American refusal to permit the entry of West Indian goods via the designated free ports destroyed the effectiveness of this arrangement, however. In 1822, responding to vociferous planter demand for direct access to American supplies and markets, the imperial government reversed its policy and offered to negotiate a reciprocal agreement under which American vessels would be granted permanent access to the West Indies carrying trade.[18] This abandonment of a basic component of mercantilism, coming on top of concessions over the fisheries, threatened to render the development strategy of Halifax's merchants utterly obsolete.

Adding to these reverses, Halifax found itself wallowing in the throes of an acute postwar recession featuring slumping exports, falling prices, rising unemployment, a scarcity of both credit and specie, and crop failures. The Nova Scotian capital in peacetime, one contemporary declared, was like 'a town at the close of a fair.'[19] Military demobilization, the resumption of prewar trade flows, economic dislocation in the Caribbean, and resurgent American competition had combined to produce acute commercial stagnation. Desperation drove hundreds of families to the United States, and voices began to be heard calling for Nova Scotia's annexation to the American union.[20] The crisis decimated the Halifax merchant community and brought about the collapse of the Committee of Trade. A core of entrepreneurs, most of them native born or long-term residents, persisted, however, and in 1822, when conditions were worst, they organized the Halifax Chamber of Commerce.[21] This new merchant organization immediately began to lobby for measures designed to stimulate economic recovery.

The Chamber's programme essentially called for the pursuit of old strategic objectives by means of a series of tactical innovations. While still committed to confrontation with American commercial interests, Halifax entrepreneurs resolved to press for a qualified liberalization of mercantilist policy so as to enhance their competitive position. Although not an entirely new departure for these Nova Scotians, their demands in the early 1820s

403

were more comprehensive than ever before.[22] Major emphasis was placed on the need for colonial shippers to be granted parity with their American rivals in terms of the right to trade directly with foreign Europe. Halifax's Chamber of Commerce insisted that major benefits would be derived if local merchants could import a wide range of goods from the European continent. Such an arrangement

> would not only directly encourage the fisheries, by enabling us to fit out our vessels upon equal terms with the Americans, but it would facilitate the sale of our fish in the West Indies, as we could exchange them for the produce of those islands for which we could find a ready sale in the countries from whence we should procure our Hemp, Iron and Sail Cloth...our vessels would have full freights upon three long voyages, instead of returning from the islands in ballast, or bringing articles to this country, with which it is already glutted.[23]

404

The Chamber also requested the establishment of imperial warehouses in Halifax where foreign goods could be stored, duty free, pending their re-export. These facilities, it was claimed, would allow Halifax shippers to 'assort their cargoes from this province, to meet the markets in South America and elsewhere, in the same [manner] as is practiced in the United States.'[24]

As a corollary measure designed to stimulate economic recovery, the Chamber of Commerce urged the London authorities to simplify customs-house regulations to facilitate the transshipment of goods through Halifax to other parts of British America.[25] An appeal went to the Nova Scotian legislature for a subsidy on imported fishery salt as well as for bounties to encourage the production of high quality cured codfish such as was demanded in European and South American markets.[26] Requests were despatched to both the imperial and colonial governments for financial assistance to facilitate building of the Shubenacadie canal, thereby linking Halifax with the Bay of Fundy.[27] Finally, the Chamber lobbied vigorously to convince local legislators of the need for them to grant a corporate charter for a limited-liability bank in Halifax. Such an institution, it was argued, would retain investment capital within the province and provide the volume of commercial credit essential for a revitalization of trade.[28]

It should be emphasized that in pursuing these tactical innovations the Halifax merchants were not abandoning the protectionist system. The Chamber of Commerce adamantly continued to urge that colonial produce and vessels retain a privileged position in trade with Britain and other imperial dependencies. This demand for a redefined mercantilism more conciliatory to colonial interests appeared to gain a measure of recognition in 1825. The London government authorized a major expansion of direct trade between foreign Europe and British America and also agreed to establish bonded warehouses in Halifax and Saint John. These reforms represented, in fact, a concession more to metropolitan than to colonial lobbyists; furthermore, they were widely regarded as heralding a British commitment to a policy of free trade.[29] Most Haligonians chose to overlook these ominous overtures to change, however. Instead, they erupted in rejoicing, convinced that the imperial authorities had revitalized the port's prospects. One local editor declared that Halifax had been 'on the eve of destruction. This has come just in time to save it from ruin.'[30]

The reforms of 1825 did have a positive impact on Halifax trade, leading to a growth in trade with foreign Europe and South America. Even more significant, however, was a simultaneous growth in Halifax's trade with Britain, the British Caribbean, the United States, and adjacent parts of British America. After a decade of postwar commercial stagnation, the port had finally begun to be drawn into the vortex of a general economic boom in Britain and America.[31] By the late 1820s the bustle on the Halifax waterfront was such as to inspire a mood of expansionist optimism among local merchants.[32] Their confidence persisted into the 1830s despite the threat posed by British abolition of slavery within the empire and increased American competition in the West Indies carrying trade. Nova Scotian exports to the Caribbean remained strong, and those to the United States enjoyed marked expansion.[33] Declining sugar prices and a coincidental curtailment of commercial credit created a short-term business panic in Halifax during the mid-1830s.[34] Recovery came quickly, however, and the port emerged relatively unscathed from the general financial panic of 1837. By 1840 provincial trade was running 169 per cent above the levels for 1825.[35] Circumstances were such as to convince most Halifax merchants that, instead of seeking structural change, they should defend the status quo. For over a decade and a half little thought was given to the question of redefining their basic strategy of economic development.

Through the late 1820s and into the 1830s entrepreneurial activity proved extremely vigorous in Halifax. Local merchants became increasingly involved in staples production, particularly with respect to fish and timber. They also acquired an ever growing volume of shipping. Entrepreneurial innovation took the form of ventures into packet service, whaling, and sealing. New financial institutions appeared in the fields of banking and insurance.[36] In response to Halifax merchant initiative, construction began on the Shubenacadie canal, the largest public works project undertaken in Nova Scotia prior to the coming of railways.[37] Halifax capitalists also pioneered with steam navigation. In 1830 they built a steam-powered harbour ferry and that same year joined with Quebec interests to commission construction of an ocean-going steamer for use between the two ports.[38] By 1840 Samuel Cunard, Halifax's leading entrepreneur, had inaugurated a steam packet service running, via Halifax, between Boston and Liverpool. Contemporaries saw Cunard's vessels as the instruments by which the Nova Scotian capital would become 'the focus of Colonial and inter-Colonial trade between the old and our new rising British Empire.' Halifax, its local boosters proclaimed, would now 'become in Peace what it was in the years . . . during the American War.'[39] Samuel Cunard acquired the status of a provincial folk hero, hailed in the local press effusively:

Thy name, great man! to every Patriot dear,
Our children's children from their sires shall hear,
And taught by thee, in future time shall rise
High spirits meet for equal Enterprise.[40]

Entrepreneurial self-assertion was not without limitations, however. Halifax's merchant community displayed little interest in manufacturing. A few individuals invested in pre-industrial manufactories which produced such commodities as sugar, rope, flour, turpentine, nails, and the like.[41] As well, Cunard and others regularly contracted for construction of wooden vessels at shipyards located across the harbour at Dartmouth.[42] Halifax merchants also made one collective venture into the mining and smelting of iron ore deposits in the provincial interior.[43] These initiatives fell short of a commitment to comprehensive industrialization, however. Unlike their New England counterparts, these Halifax merchants were not drawn into investment in the mass production of such commodities as textiles or boots and shoes. Entrepreneurial hesitation in this respect probably stemmed from the lack of a populous, integrated regional market, combined with opposition from the imperial government to any suggestion of protective tariffs to encourage colonial manufacturing.[44] Similarly, Halifax businessmen did not object when the imperial government allowed the British-based General Mining Association to establish monopoly control over Nova Scotia's coal deposits. Cunard, who had ventured into coal mining, sold out his leasehold rights to the GMA.[45] This preference for commercial over industrial ventures was an attitude which Halifax merchants shared with their peers located in the ports of the St. Lawrence.

After a decade and a half of more or less sustained growth, Halifax entered a period of crisis starting early in the 1840s. Within the local business community self-confidence gave way to growing anxiety as hard times became protracted and pervasive. Between 1840 and 1843 Nova Scotian trade declined by 42 per cent.[46] Thereafter, commercial activity remained stagnant, reviving slightly in 1847 only to fall to an all-time low in 1848.[47] Several factors contributed to this commercial disruption. The final phasing out of slavery in the British Caribbean caused severe disruption in the economy of what had been Nova Scotia's chief export market.[48] Local crop failures associated with potato blight further depressed trade. Most decisive of all were the erratic fluctuations between boom and bust conditions within the British and American economies through the 1840s. Sharp contractions in metropolitan demand and credit had a decidedly destructive impact on the Halifax business community, driving many prominent merchants into bankruptcy.[49]

Anxiety might have been less among Halifax entrepreneurs had not hard times coincided with the ascendancy of free trade sentiment in Great Britain. Demands for the abandonment of all remaining mercantilist restraints on foreign competition filled colonial business with a sense of foreboding. Fearful that unqualified free trade would end all hope of eventual economic recovery, Halifax's merchants mounted a vigorous campaign to salvage the legacy of commercial protectionism. The local Chamber of Commerce, which

406

had collapsed during the recession of 1833/34, was revived in 1841 to fight for the retention of imperial preferences on colonial timber exports.[50] The effort failed, however, and by 1846, with the repeal of the Corn Laws, it had become obvious that mercantilism was doomed. Many Halifax merchants believed that as mercantilism collapsed so disappeared their port's prospects for future survival. Their sentiments were echoed by the editor of the Halifax *Times* who declared that the 'life-blood of the country, in commerce, its agriculture, its identity,' were being destroyed, all because a few malcontents and theoreticians had been allowed to exercise their 'desire for change.' Without a return to old truths in the principles of trade and government, the editor predicted that Halifax's business would be reduced 'to the supply of the army and navy stationed within it, and to furnish the interior with a few articles of luxury.'[51]

Anxiety over Halifax's prospects was heightened by an increasing competition within regional trade. Since the end of the Napoleonic Wars, Saint John had been growing as a major commercial rival to the Nova Scotian capital. Assisted by a booming local trade in timber, Saint John merchants had established an hegemony over the Bay of Fundy area, and by the 1840s were threatening further encroachments on Halifax's hinterland by means of coastal steamers and a canal cut through the isthmus separating Nova Scotia from New Brunswick.[52] At the same time the mercantilist regulations which had favoured Halifax over other Nova Scotian ports began to disintegrate. Yarmouth, Liverpool, and other leading outports obtained free-port status and duty-free warehousing facilities, thereby encouraging virtually every coastal community to make similar demands.[53] The decentralization of Maritime commerce associated with these developments threatened Halifax's ambitions to become a dominant regional metropolis.[54]

Hard times, the British retreat from protectionist trade policies, and the coincidental ascendancy of agitation for political reform within Nova Scotia all demoralized and fragmented the Halifax merchant community. Events overwhelmed the recently revived Chamber of Commerce, and it collapsed in the mid 1840s, not to be revived until the mid 1860s.[55] Thus, through the tumultuous late 1840s, Halifax merchants lacked a formally organized collective voice. Nevertheless, individual entrepreneurs remained active in public affairs and contributed to the articulation of an economic strategy appropriate to a post-mercantilist situation. Evidence gleaned from contemporary sources suggests that, by the late 1840s, only a few Halifax merchants clung to protectionist ideals.[56] The majority appeared to have accepted free trade as a regrettable but unavoidable reality, the worst effects of which could be eased through the elimination of legal restraints on trade both within British America and between British America and the United States. Calls for continental free trade derived support from a major trend in Nova Scotian trade evident during the 1840s. Exports to the United States had expanded consistently; for example, by the middle of the decade more provincial fish was going to the American than to the Caribbean market.[57] Accordingly, when Samuel Cunard wrote the provincial authorities in June

1848 to urge reciprocity with the United States, he appeared to be expressing an attitude dominant within the Halifax merchant community.[58]

Acceptance of mercantilism's demise did not mean abandonment of fundamental development aspirations concerning the port of Halifax among local entrepreneurs. Merchants resident in the Nova Scotian capital refused to believe that they were now doomed to function as a minor commercial satellite of Boston or New York. While concerned about the loss of imperial protection, they remained convinced that Halifax could still be established as a major trading entrepôt, dominant within the Maritime region and competitive with ports on the American seaboard. A major factor operating to sustain metropolitan ambitions in Halifax through the difficult 1840s was the prospect of railway construction. Enthusiasm for innovation in overland transportation technology built quickly, and, by late in the decade, plans were being devised to construct lines linking Halifax with the Bay of Fundy, the Northumberland Strait, and even Quebec.[59]

408   Railway boosters claimed that these lines would allow Halifax to overcome the geographic barriers that had so long denied the port ready access to a large hinterland. It was predicted that railways would bring sustained prosperity. One enthusiast declared: 'If we could once open the back country of Canada to our industry, we should enjoy the high advantage of sending our fish and our coal by the Railway even in the depth of winter; and we should have in return the rich products of Canada to export to Europe, and thus keep our commercial marine in full employment.'[60] Besides stimulating the general Maritime economy, railways, it was believed, would focus commercial activity on Halifax. As easternmost Atlantic terminus of a continental rail system, Halifax appeared likely to attract a multiplicity of transatlantic steamship lines and thereby ultimately emerge as the pivot of trade between Europe and North America. In this way steam technology promised to reverse decentralizing trends in regional trade, thereby assuring Halifax of ultimate metropolitan ascendancy.[61]

Aspirations did not lead to immediate achievement. Railway construction in Nova Scotia was deferred until the mid 1850s, and another twenty years passed before a line was constructed between Halifax and Quebec. Delay did nothing, however, to disrupt the railway-oriented development policies embraced by the Halifax merchant community. Sustained by the quarter-century of more or less continual prosperity that followed the difficult 1840s, they felt no need to pursue strategic innovation. Indeed, it appears that in their entire nineteenth-century experience the merchants never really departed from the objective they had established in the aftermath of the American Revolution. Tactics and techniques changed. Protectionist trade regulations were abandoned in favour of free trade allied with railway construction. But ultimate strategy remained the same. Development continued to be defined in terms of establishing Halifax as *the* commercial metropolis of the Maritimes. Moreover, Halifax's entrepreneurs always acted in response to the belief that the Maritime region, while associated with New England, retained an essential identity of its own.

In an effort to preserve both their metropolitan ambitions and a separate regional identity in an era of free trade, Halifax entrepreneurs opted for promotion of ever greater integration between the Maritime and St. Lawrence colonies. In time, the aspiration would come to be associated with a desire to combine commercial with industrial development.[62] Thus it can be seen that the Halifax merchants were moving on a course parallel with their Montreal and Quebec counterparts. Through the first half of the nineteenth century they were leaning toward a joint effort to build a separate northern economic 'empire,' founded initially on commercial enterprise, but with the potential to diversity into industrialization. Ironically, this pursuit of British American integration ultimately led to the destruction of the metropolitan ambitions and separate regional identity which Halifax entrepreneurs had pursued since late in the eighteenth century.[63]

Notes

1. For classic statements of the opposing points of view, see Donald Grant Creighton, *The Empire of the St. Lawrence* (Toronto 1956); R. Tom Naylor, *The History of Canadian Business, 1867-1914*, 2 vols. (Toronto 1975).
2. General studies dealing with Maritime regional economic development include Harold Adams Innis, *The Cod Fisheries: The History of an International Economy* (Toronto 1940); Gerald Sandford Graham, *Sea Power and British North America, 1783-1820: A Study in British Colonial Policy* (Cambridge, Mass. 1941); Andrew Hill Clark, *Acadia: The Geography of Early Nova Scotia to 1760* (Madison, Wisc. 1968); Robin F. Neill, 'National Policy and Regional Development: A Footnote to the Deutsch Report on Maritime Union,' *Journal of Canadian Studies*, IX, 1974, 12-20.
3. Ian Brookes, 'The Physical Geography of the Atlantic Provinces,' in *The Atlantic Provinces*, ed. Alan G. Macpherson (Toronto 1972), 1-45; John Warkentin, 'The Atlantic Region,' in R. Cole Harris and John Warkentin, *Canada before Confederation* (Toronto 1974), 169-231; Arthur Hill Clark, 'Contributions of its Southern Neighbours to the Underdevelopment of the Maritime Provinces Area, 1710-1867 in *The Influence of the United States on Canadian Development: Eleven Case Studies*, ed. Richard A. Preston (Durham, NC 1972), 164-84.
4. William Stewart MacNutt, *The Atlantic Provinces: The Emergences of Colonial Society, 1712-1857* (Toronto 1965), 86-111; Harold Hampden Robertson, 'The Commercial Relationship between Nova Scotia and the British Empire' (unpublished MA thesis, Dalhousie University, 1975), 1-28.
5. Innis, *Cod Fisheries*, 220-227-8; Graham, *Sea Power*, 19-55; Alfred Le Roy Burt, *The United States, Great Britain and British North America from the Revolution to the Establishment of Peace after the War of 1812* (New Haven 1940), 42-70.
6. For reference to proclamations admitting American vessels to Nova Scotian ports see George Frederic Butler, 'Commercial Relations of Nova Scotia with the United States, 1783-1830' (unpublished MA thesis, Dalhousie University, 1934), 3-8. Public Archives of Nova Scotia [PANS], RG 31, folders 31-3, Halifax light duties, 1786, indicates the following destination for vessels departing Halifax (not counting coasting and fishing voyages): Great Britain, 9; British North America, 66; British West Indies, 49; United States, 66; other, 5.
7. Graham, *Sea Power*, 56-73; Robertson, 'Nova Scotia and the British West Indies,' 29-59.
8. David Alexander Sutherland, 'The Merchants of Halifax, 1815-1850: A Commercial Class in Pursuit of Metropolitan Status' (unpublished PHD dissertation, University of Toronto 1975), 13-23.
9. William Stewart MacNutt, *New Brunswick: A History, 1784-1867* (Toronto 1963). PANS, RG 13, vol. 40, indicates a marked quickening of commercial activity in Nova Scotia after 1805:

Date	Country	Imports (tons)	Exports (tons)
1805	Great Britain	4,651	2,902
	British West Indies	4,561	4,853
	British North America	7,610	7,779
	United States	4,442	4,290
	Other	528	252
	Total	21,792	20,076

1811	Great Britain	17,431	16,986
	British West Indies	11,652	13,554
	British North America	17,227	11,864
	United States	1,853	356
	Other	1,988	654
	Total	50,151	43,414

10. Walter Ronald Copp, 'Nova Scotian Trade during the War of 1812,' *Canadian Historical Review*, XVIII, 1937, 141-55. PANS, RG 13, vol. 40, details the extent of wartime boom in Nova Scotia:

Date	Country	*Imports* (tons)	*Exports* (tons)
1812	Great Britain	26,590	27,332
	British West Indies	9,197	11,183
	British North America	8,361	15,514
	United States	4,105	9,925
	Other	1,702	335
	Total	49,955	64,289
1814	Great Britain	25,393	14,476
	British West Indies	14,356	25,867
	British North America	21,803	37,077
	United States	1,011	2,081
	Other	1,924	346
	Total	64,487	79,847

11. *Acadian Recorder*, 14 May 1814.
12. For the establishment of the Committee of Trade and its pre-1815 lobbying efforts see Sutherland, 'Merchants of Halifax,' 32-6, 52-6; and George Frederic Butler, 'The Early Organisation and Influence of Halifax Merchants', Nova Scotia Historical Society, *Collections*, XXV, 1942, 1-16.
13. The merchant programme appears in PANS, RG 1, vol. 304, no 61, William Sabatier to Lewis Wilkins, 22 Feb. 1813; ibid., vol. 304, no 66, Sabatier *et al.* to Lord Bathurst, 8 Oct. 1813; ibid., vol. 226, no 82, Sabatier to Lord Sherbrooke, 8 Nov. 1813; ibid., vol. 305, no 14. Sabatier to Lewis Wilkins, 19 March 1814. Sabatier was chairman of the Halifax Committee of Trade.
14. This point of view was most clearly expressed in [Committee of Trade, Halifax, NS], *Memoir on the Cod and Small Fisheries of Nova-Scotia* ([Halifax, c. 1818]), found in PANS, RG 1, vol. 305, no 113. See also Daniel Cobb Harvey, 'Nova Scotia and the Convention of 1818,' Royal Society of Canada, *Transactions*, 3rd series, XXVII, 1933, sect. II, 57-73.
15. Daniel Cobb Harvey, 'Pre-Agricola John Young, or a Compact Family in Search of Fortune,' Nova Scotia Historical Society, *Collections*, XXXII, 1959, 137, John Young to William Young, 19 Feb. 1815.
16. Sutherland, 'Merchants of Halifax,' 57-68.
17. Gerald Sandford Graham, 'The Origin of Free Ports in British North America,' *Canadian Historical Review*, XXI, 1941, 25-44. The scepticism of some Halifax merchants toward the operation of the free-port system is expressed in Walter C. Hartridge, 'Halifax to Savannah: Letters of Michael Wallace,' *Georgia Historical Quarterly*, XLV, 1961, 173, Michael Wallace to James Wallace, [July or Aug.] 1818.
18. Frank Lee Benns, *The American Struggle for the British West India Carrying Trade, 1815-1830*, Indiana University Studies, X, 56 (Bloomington, Ind. 1923), 83-95.
19. Thomas Chandler Haliburton, *A General Description of Nova Scotia* (Halifax 1823) 171.
20. Sutherland, 'Merchants of Halifax,' 60-8, 94-120.
21. *Free Press* (Halifax), 29 Jan. 1822; Commercial Society, Halifax, NS, *Rules and Regulations of the Commercial Society* (Halifax 1822).
22. The merchant programme can be found in the following petitions: PANS, RG 5, Series P, vol. 120, Richard Tremain *et al.* to Assembly, 25 Feb. 1822; ibid., James Foreman *et al.* to Council, 1 March 1822; PANS, RG 1, vol. 298, no 215, James Fraser *et al.* to Lt-Gov. James Kempt, Council, and Assembly, 19 March 1822.
23. PANS, RG 1, vol. 214½a. 290, merchant memorial dated to Dec. 1824.
24. Ibid.
25. Ibid.; see also Chamber of Commerce annual report, *Acadian Reader* (Halifax), 12 Feb. 1825.
26. PANS, RG 1, vol. 290, no 1, George Grassie *et al.* to Council, 18 Feb. 1823.
27. Chamber of Commerce annual report, *Acadian Recorder*, 12 Feb. 1825. For background on the

canal project see Barbara Grantmyre, 'The Canal that Bisected Nova Scotia,' *Canadian Geographical Journal*, LXXXVIII, 1, 1974, 20-7.
28. PANS, RG 1, vol. 290, no 49, Richard Tremain *et al.* to Council, 5 March 1825. For the generally negative response of the Assembly to this and other merchant proposals involving enactment of provincial legislation see Sutherland, 'Merchants of Halifax,' 123-5, 144-9.
29. Alexander Brady, *William Huskisson and Liberal Reform* (London 1928), 111ff.
30. *Acadian Recorder*, 30 April 1825. For expressions of doubt about the future see *Novascotian* (Halifax), 4 May 1825.
31. PANS, RG 13, vol. 41 gives the following figures for Halifax port traffic:

Date	Country	Imports (£)	Exports (£)
1824	Great Britain	247,774	4,050
	British West Indies	79,820	42,449
	British North America	31,924	21,864
	United States	61,801	11,204
	Other	5,840	14,640
	Total	427,152	94,207
1828	Great Britain	297,010	7,640
	British West Indies	81,409	126,231
	British North America	111,705	80,371
	United States	217,933	5,790
	Other	25,305	26,820
	Total	833,362	246,852

411

32. Sutherland, 'Merchants of Halifax,' 159-73.
33. PRO, CO 217/174, f 193ff gives the following provincial trade statistics:

Date	Country	Imports (£)	Exports (£)
1828	Great Britain	311,100	94,101
	British West Indies	163,548	224,221
	British North America	129,544	179,010
	United States	176,843	13,240
	Other	204,395	39,239
	Total	985,430	549,811
1832	Great Britain	577,285	159,486
	British West Indies	183,465	294,763
	British North America	340,523	339,017
	United States	212,912	87,480
	Other	140,798	34,095
	Total	1,454,983	914,841

34. *Ibid.*

Date	Country	Imports (£)	Exports (£)
1835	Great Britain	220,736	86,720
	British West Indies	212,349	228,498
	British North America	171,646	385,489
	United States	113,520	102,261
	Other	77,031	25,032
	Total	795,282	828,000

35. PANS, RG 2, vol. 45 gives the following Nova Scotian trade statistics:

Date	Country	Imports (£)	Exports (£)
1840	Great Britain	528,168	155,356
	British West Indies	59,935	402,356
	British North America	309,991	405,114
	United States	248,296	116,707
	Other	443,157	59,297
	Total	1,589,547	1,138,830

36. The initial surge of entrepreneurial activity is detailed in the annual reports of the Chamber of Commerce, which appeared in the Halifax weekly press. See, for example, *Halifax Journal*, 6 Feb. 1826; *Royal Gazette* (Halifax), 14 Feb. 1827; *Acadian Recorder*, 9 Feb. 1828. A second surge of business innovation, occurring in the mid to late 1830s, is surveyed in Sutherland, 'Merchants of Halifax,' 284-97.

37. For reports of the organization of the canal company and early progress with construction see *Acadian Recorder*, 6 July 1826; 19 May, 9 June, 20 Oct., 8 Dec. 1827; 23 Feb., 14 June, 18 Oct. 1828. Shortage of capital brought construction to a half in 1831; the project remained moribund for the next quarter century; see *Novascotian*, 22, 29 March 1832.

38. *Acadian Recorder*, 2 Jan. 1830, 3 Sept. 1831. The *Royal William*, built jointly by Quebec and Halifax investors, failed to earn a profit on voyages between the two ports. After less than a year of erratic service the vessel was sold; see *Novascotian*, 22 March 1832, 2 May 1833.

39. Committee report, Society for the Encouragement of Trade and Manufacturers, *Times* (Halifax), 26 March 1839. For background on Cunard's emergence see Hilda Kay Grant, *Samuel Cunard: Pioneer of the Atlantic Steamship* (London 1967).

40. *Novascotian*, 1 Oct. 1840.

41. Halifax merchant investments in local manufacturing prompted the Chamber of Commerce to endorse drawbacks of duties on imported raw materials, but the Chamber's essentially commercial orientation made it hostile to increased duties on imported manufactures. See PANS, RG 1, vol. 298, no 248, Richard Tremain *et al.* to Council, 10 March 1826; ibid., no 251, Richard Tremain *et al.* to Council, 30 March 1826.

42. For references to the activities of Lyle's shipyards in Dartmouth see *Acadian Recorder*, 8 July, 2 Dec., 1826. Unlike Saint John, Halifax failed to develop as a major shipbuilding centre. The lack of a ready local supply of timber encouraged Halifax merchants to commission vessels from builders located in the various provincial outports. This pattern of outport construction on orders from Halifax is noted in John P. Parker, *Cape Breton Ships and Men* (Toronto 1967).

43. Halifax entrepreneurs established the Annapolis Iron Mining Company, capitalized at £20,000, in 1825; see Nova Scotia *Statutes* (1825), c 18. The venture had gone bankrupt by the early 1830s; see 'Rothschild,' *Novascotian*, 5 April 1832.

44. For expressions of imperial hostility to attempts by the Nova Scotian legislature to stimulate local manufacturing by means of tariffs and drawbacks see PRO, CO 217/164, f 34, draft memorandum from Lord Glenelg, 28 Dec. 1837; ibid., f 76, Denis Le Marchant to James Stephen, 11 Dec. 1838. Demand for such protection was concentrated among Halifax artisans, who received support from those merchants with investments in manufacturing; see PANS, RG 5, series P, vol. 123, John E. Fairbanks *et al.* to Assembly, 16 Feb. 1838.

45. Cunard's early involvement with coal mining is detailed in PANS, RG 1 vol. 258, no 96, Samuel Cunard to Benjamin Hawes, undersecretary of state, 18 June 1848. For the entry of the General Mining Association into Nova Scotia see James Stuart Martell, 'Early Coal Mining in Nova Scotia,' *Dalhousie Review*, XXV, 1945/46, 156-72.

46. PANS, RG 2, vol. 46, gives the following Nova Scotian trade statistics:

Date	Country	Imports (£)	Exports (£)
1843	Great Britain	305,312	58,397
	British West Indies	19,846	225,063
	British North America	151,405	306,517
	United States	208,640	83,846
	Other	175,282	36,341
	Total	860,485	710,164

47. *Ibid.* vo. 47, gives these Nova Scotian trade figures:

Date	Country	Imports (£)	Exports (£)
1848	Great Britain	260,399	47,627
	British West Indies	24,347	202,239
	British North America	173,193	96,160
	United States	295,092	150,603
	Other	93,396	37,143
	Total	846,427	533,772

48. Edgar L. Erickson, 'The Introduction of East India Coolies into the British West Indies,' *Journal of Modern History*, VI, 2, 1934, 127-46. Between 1842 and 1843 total trade between Nova Scotia and

412

the British Caribbean declined from £496,949 to £244,909, representing a reduction of 50.72 per cent; see PANS, RG 2, vol. 46.

49. Sutherland, 'Merchants of Halifax,' 329-34, 393-4.

50. Arthur R.M. Lower, 'From Huskisson to Peel: A Study in Mercantilism,' Royal Society of Canada, *Transactions*, 3rd series, XXXI, 1937, sect. II, 51-68. The revival of the Chamber of Commerce is noted in *Times* (Halifax), 30 March 1841.

51. *Times*, 25 July 1843; see also Chamber of Commerce annual report, ibid., 14 March 1843.

52. MacNutt, *New Brunswick*, 277-314. Halifax's sense of competitive rivalry was overtly expressed during an initial burst of enthusiasm for railways; see 'Delta,' *Acadian Recorder*, 30 Aug. 1845; *Acadian Recorder*, 6, 20 Sept., 29 Nov. 1845.

53. The 'free port' question is outlined in Nova Scotia, House of Assembly, *Journals and Proceedings*, 14 April 1838; ibid. (1839/40), Appendices I and II.

54. The threat was more apparent than real. In 1828 Halifax handled 98.33 per cent of Nova Scotia's imports and 42.34 per cent of its exports. In 1852 78.71 per cent of the province's imports and 60.59 per cent of its exports passed through the capital. See trade statistics in PANS, RG 13, vol. 41, and *Novascotian*, extra, 14 Feb. 1854.

55. The Chamber of Commerce never appears in contemporary sources after the issuance of its annual report in March 1843. The re-establishment of a collective organization of Halifax businessmen is detailed in *Sun and Advertiser* (Halifax), 10, 17 May 1865.

56. Several Tory newspapers vigorously attacked the principle of free trade during the late 1840s. See, for example, *Times*, 18 April, 23 May 1848; *British Colonist* (Halifax), 16 Dec. 1848. The campaign appears more rhetorical than substantial, however; the editors saw negotiation of reciprocity with the United States as being more practical than any attempt to revive imperial mercantilism; see *British Colonist*, 23 Nov. 1848; *Church Times* (Halifax), 30 Nov. 1848.

57. *Times*, 2 April 1844. In 1840 the American market accounted for 10.25 per cent of Nova Scotian exports; by 1848 52.49 per cent of provincial exports went to the United States; see PANS, RG 2 vols. 45-7. The trend was subsequently reversed to some extent. In 1852 sales to the United States accounted for only 26.56 per cent of total exports; see *Novascotian*, extra, 14 Feb. 1854.

58. PANS, RG 1, vol. 257, no. 122. Samuel Cunard to Joseph Howe, 19 June 1848.

59. For the initial outburst of enthusiasm for railways in Halifax see *Acadian Recorder*, 15 March, 30 Aug. 1845; *Times*, 9, 10 Sept. 1845; *Novascotian*, 6, 13 Oct. 1845; *Morning Post* (Halifax), 4 Oct. 1845.

60. *Novascotian*, 19 Feb. 1849.

61. In 1849 Nova Scotia's new Liberal cabinet, which had come to power in 1848 with the achievement of responsible government, committed public funds to the construction of a railway between Halifax and Quebec. This decision, taken in defiance of outpost opposition, reflected the fact that all but one of the cabinet members were residents of Halifax; see Assembly debates, *Novascotian*, 23 April, 7, 21 May 1849.

62. Abraham Gesner, *The Industrial Resources of Nova Scotia* (Halifax 1849).

63. The impact of development strategy on the politics of Confederation and Halifax response to the National Policy is discussed in Delphin A. Muise, 'The Federal Election of 1867 in Nova Scotia: An Economic Interpretation,' Nova Scotia Historical Society, *Collections*, XXXVI, 1968, 327-51; and Thomas William Acheson, 'The National Policy and the Industrialization of the Maritimes, 1880-1910,' *Acadiensis*, I, 2, 1972, 3-28.

413

The Great Merchant and Economic Development in St. John 1820-1850*
T.W. ACHESON

One of the liveliest debates in recent Canadian business history has centred on the role of the nineteenth-century merchant in promoting or retarding the development of a locally controlled British North American industrial base. Supporters of the retardation theory usually argue that the colonial

*From *Acadiensis*, 8, 2 (1979): 3-27. Reprinted by permission.

merchant was nurtured in a system based upon the export of raw and semi-finished produce and the import of fully manufactured materials. Dominating the ports and the transportation systems of British North America, he became the principal defender of the economic *status quo*, viewing any substantial re-arrangement of economic relations as a threat to his world. Thus he remained the harbinger of a form of economic colonialism which bound the destiny of British North America and of the forming Dominion of Canada in a subservient relationship to more advanced national economies, particularly those of the United Kingdom and the United States. Opponents of this theory have accepted the primacy of the merchant in the colonial economies but have argued that the gulf separating the merchant from other dynamic elements in the business community was less wide than the retardationists would have us believe. They maintain that the dramatic shift from commercial to industrial emphases and from external to internal markets in the last half of the nineteenth century occurred with the consent and participation of this dominant commercial element.[1]

414

There are several difficulties within this general argument. One of the most basic concerns the definition of "merchant". The meanest cordwainer in the mid-nineteenth century offered his shoes for sale to the general public; conversely, many important shippers and wholesalers owned, in whole or in part, the means to process the basic staple commodities of their region. Even a restricted use of the term leaves a group of businessmen involved in a variety of commercial, financial and transportation functions. In colonial Saint John, for example, "merchant" was a legal status conferred on certain men at the time of their admission to the freedom of the city. Within the hierarchy of occupations which were admissible as freemen, that of merchant was clearly the most important and this importance was reflected in the fees required of those admitted to the status. Although a merchant might also be a sawmill owner, a legal and social line was clearly drawn between merchants possessing a sawmill and sawmill owners by occupation whose status was lower. Moreover, there were a number of commercial functions characteristically performed by merchants, including the importing and wholesaling of produce, the export of fish and wood products, the transport of other people's goods, the purchase of staples produce on other people's accounts, the sale and auction of other people's goods, private banking, and acting as agents or directors for chartered banks, fire, marine and life insurance companies. In village business a single merchant might have exercised most of these functions; the most successful urban merchants were those who focussed their efforts on three or four. In time, the development of competing interests sharply limited the issues on which merchants were able to speak as a class or community. Indeed, on many issues, it is doubtful whether colonial boards of trade and chambers of commerce spoke for anything more than one of several elements within the business community.

Another important question raised by the retardation debate concerns the extent to which "normal" merchant behaviour was modified by the local environment. There can be little doubt but that all merchants in British North America responded to short-term opportunities and that only rarely were they willing to sacrifice these opportunities on the alter of national, colonial or civic interest.[2] Yet, over time, a merchant became attached to the community in which he lived, his response to opportunity conditioned by the idiosyncracies of the local economy, the nature of the relationship between the local and metropolitan economies, and the impact of the economic cycle in reducing the short-term profitability of existing relationships. Any final assessment of the merchant's role in the economic development of British North America will therefore have to wait the completion of a number of case studies of individual communities and firms.[3] The paper which follows is an attempt to explore the role of the merchant in the economic development of colonial Saint John. The city affords an interesting case study both because of its size — in 1840 it was the third largest urban centre in British North America — and because of the central role played by the trade in timber and deals in its economic life.

415

Traditionally the central problem in the study of the economy of Saint John has been to explain the failure of the city to make the necessary adjustments to compensate for the dislocations occasioned by the stagnation of the wood trade following Confederation. Recently, Peter McClelland has put the date of that stagnation back to mid-century, arguing that the shipbuilding industry, the most dynamic element in the provincial economy after 1850, added little to the well-being or growth of that economy.[4] McClelland has highlighted the role of New Brunswick businessmen in this problem by demonstrating the tenacity with which they stood behind the wooden shipbuilding industry, investing perhaps $8 million between 1870 and 1879 in a technology which was effectively obsolete.[5] These businessmen failed to make the transition to metal ships or to establish backward linkages from the shipbuilding industry — particularly those relating to the outfitting of ships and the manufacture of chains and anchors — which could develop in time into significant industries. McClelland has explained this failure in terms of "the absence of alternatives capable of giving to regional growth the sustaining force which timber was losing" after 1850.[6] But even if it is admitted that shipbuilding was unable to play this dynamic role — a thesis that is much more compelling in 1870 than in 1840 — McClelland offers scant evidence to prove that manufacturing and, to a lesser extent, fishing and agriculture, could not have contributed a dynamic element to the regional economy. To support his contention, he is forced to argue that they could not because they did not, an idea grounded in the assumption that by mid-century New Brunswick was backward relative to other colonial economies. To demonstrate this position McClelland offers an output analysis of New Brunswick and Ontario agriculture at the end of the nineteenth century, and points to the inability of some New Brunswick consumer goods producers to compete with central Canadian producers on the central Canadian market in the post-Confederation period. Much of this can be demonstrated for 1890, but it all presumes that what was true at that time must have been true a half-century earlier, and that the absence of a particular resource, say coal, must preclude the development of any industry which employed that resource.

The doubts raised by the ahistorical nature of this analysis are heightened by the persistence with which the provincial business community pursued and supported the wood trade and the wooden ship, even in the face of a technological obsolescence which by 1870 was obvious to all observers. This persistence suggests a commitment to a declining economic base understandable in the small resource-based village economies of much of the province, but more difficult to comprehend in the context of the complex, differentiated economy which existed in Saint John. Indeed, the continuance of these forms of activity and the failure of other kinds of development to occur may have been more the result of human factors than the absence of any particular material resource. Certainly Saint John in the colonial period possessed considerable potential. In 1840 the city was one of the largest urban centres in British North America, with a population of about 27,000. Its merchants possessed a monopoly of the commerce of the Saint John River Valley and its tributaries, a market of nearly 100,000 people. They also dominated the commercial life of the Bay of Fundy counties of New Brunswick and Nova Scotia, containing another 90,000 people.[7] The population of the Saint John River Valley exceeded that of the Home District of Upper Canada, while the city's whole market area compared favourably with that of the Quebec City District of Lower Canada.[8] Shipbuilding had been an important feature of the city's economy for two full generations by 1840 and the St. John industry was clearly the most significant in British North America.[9] In addition, a substantial and diversified manufacturing sector designed to service both the timber trade and the growing consumer market of the area had emerged over the previous two decades, a development reflected in the strong labour movement which had become an important feature of city life in the years following the War of 1812.[10] By 1840 St. John was marked as a growth centre with a distinct advantage over any other community in the Atlantic region. And this is of special significance because nineteenth-century manufacturing growth tended to be cumulative: early leaders generally improved their advantage over other communities as James Gilmour has demonstrated in his study of the spatial evolution of manufacturing in Ontario.[11]

In many ways the 1840s was the most critical decade of the colonial period. It witnessed the collapse of the preferences for colonial timber on the British market, a disaster which St. John businessmen were able to overcome mainly by making the transition from the export of timber to the export of deals. Nonetheless, the trade in wood products reached its largest volume in that period and thereafter stagnated; the economy of the province grew increasingly dependent in the 1850s on the still further processing of wood into ships and their sale on the British market. The abrogation of the Old Colonial System was marked by several short-term economic downturns which severely mauled the wood trades and raised serious doubts about the

416

viability of an economy based upon them. At this point in time any group which persisted in subordinating all other interests to the needs of an already failing industry, it could be argued, can be perceived as contributing to the retardation of the provincial economy at a critical juncture in its history. If, by virtue of their influence within the political framework of the colony and their control of the principal sources of capital, merchants were able to promote or to inhibit certain kinds of development, then their role in determining the economic destiny of the city and its hinterland and was as important as the presence or absence of any specific resource.

The study which follows will test this hypothesis in the context of merchant behaviour in the city of Saint John between 1820 and 1850. It will do so by examining the extent and nature of merchant wealth and the role of leading merchants in promoting or opposing development strategies in the first half of the nineteenth century. A major problem is the sheer size of the city's merchant community. During the colonial period about 800 men held the legal status of merchant and a number of others illegally participated in merchant functions. There were large numbers of transients whose residency in the city was confined to a few years, and even larger numbers of minor businessmen whose sole claim to the status of merchant seems to have been their role as small-scale importers. Their impact on the commercial life of the city was marginal and any attempt to include them in a study of this nature — even if sufficient information were available — could seriously distort its purpose. At the other extreme, the council of the Chamber of Commerce provides a definite group of the influential merchants but these might represent only one faction of important merchants. To overcome both of these difficulties an effort was made to determine which merchants played important roles in the commercial and public life of the city and province over a number of years. The criteria used in the selection included ownership of significant shipping, wharfing and waterfront facilities, directorships of important financial agencies, public esteem and influence as manifested in the press and in public documents, public service and personal wealth. Although the final decision of who to include is both arbitrary and subjective, for the purpose of this study forty leading commercial figures have been identified as "great" merchants. Members of this group comprehended a variety of commercial interests, but all participated in vital shipping and financial concerns of the port and all possessed substantial personal resources. Their influence stemmed not only from this control over most of the city's financial resources, but also from their ability to create a climate of public opinion which identified their interests with the welfare of the community at large,[12] and from their access to the political institutions of the colony.[13] The group included 19 men who held the legal status of merchant, 4 mariners, 2 grocers, 1 fisherman, 1 clerk and 3 who were not freemen of the city.[14]

The great merchants were drawn from all elements within the broader community, but the most numerous were those of Loyalist or pre-Loyalist origins. Several, notably Ezekiel and Thomas Barlow, Noah Disbrow, Ralph

417

Jarvis, John Ward, Stephen Wiggins and John M. and R.D. Wilmot, were scions of important Loyalist merchant families. Several others, such as Nehemiah Merritt, and Thomas and William Leavitt, were children of frugal Loyalist fishermen. Still a third group was the Simonds connection, the principal landed interest in the province, which included the pre-Loyalist, Charles Simonds, and the two fortunate young Loyalists who married his sisters, Thomas Millidge and Henry Gilbert. Equally as important as the natives were the British immigrants. By far the most significant were the Scots, Lauchlan Donaldson, John Duncan, James Kirk, Hugh Johnston, John Robertson and John Wishart, who greatly outnumbered the Protestant Irishmen, John Kinnear and William Parks.[15] All of these immigrants were the offspring of prosperous families and came to the colony as young men of substance, bringing with them at least some capital resources. From positions of comparative advantage in the early nineteenth century, these merchants rode the crest of the timber trade to wealth by the 1840s. Virtually all were involved, to some degree, in the timber trade itself. Frequently they shipped timber which their crews had harvested. More often they bought timber or deals from the producer or took them in trade. Sometimes they would ship them on consignment to the British market. Rarely was the timber merchandising a single activity. Usually it was part of a pattern of business endeavour which included the wholesaling and retailing of British and American imports, coastal shipping, and the purchase, use and sale of sailing vessels.[16]

418

Central to the business activity of all leading merchants was involvement in or ownership of one or more of the three vital elements in city commerce: the banking system, the wharves of the port, and the ships. Most sat on the directorates of at least one of the three local public banks or the local advisory committee of the Bank of British North America.[17] Indeed, given the centrality of credit to the commercial system of the province, it was unthinkable that any substantial local firm would not have easy access to the financial stability which the banks offered, an access ultimately controlled by the bank directors whose committees met twice weekly to approve all loans. Access to the city wharves and water lots on the east side of Saint John harbour, the most valuable mercantile property in the colony, was also critical. The water lots had been leased in perpetuity by the city in return for an annual rental of between £5 and £31, depending on location in the harbour, a merchant received the right to erect improvements on the wharf, to provide free wharfage for his ships and goods, and to charge the legal rates of wharfage to all ships choosing to load or unload at this landing.[18] Possession of this vital harbour resource provided the merchant with both the most geographically advantageous terminal for his sea and river commerce and a modest but continuous income.

The central feature of New Brunswick trade was its de-centralization. Most great merchants were not involved in the timber-harvest or the sawmilling industry. Similarly, although they bought, sold and contracted for the construction of vessels, they rarely participated directly in the shipbuilding industry. The role of most merchants was that of entrepreneur closing the links between the harbours of St. John and Liverpool. Their vehicle was the sailing vessel and by 1841 the port possessed nearly 90,000 tons of shipping, about equally divided between small coasting vessels and those designed for trans-Atlantic crossings.[19] There were great differences in patterns of ownership among the city's major mercantile firms. More than half of the port's tonnage was owned by its great merchants, several of whom possessed sizeable fleets. John Kirk owned 14 vessels totalling over 7,000 tons, Stephen Wiggins 10 vessels of nearly 7,000 tons and John Wishart 9 vessels of 4,500 tons. At the other extreme, a number of merchants actually owned very little shipping, apparently preferring to ship through others. The large firm of Crookshank and Walker, for example, had only a single vessel in 1841. The different ownership patterns reflected the kinds of mercantile specialization that had developed by 1840. The large shipowners were heavily committed to the timber trade, both as merchants and as carriers; Crookshank and Walker were West Indies merchants with strong ties to the coasting trade and played the role of commission merchant and auctioneer. But whatever the area of specialized activity an individual firm might tend to follow, the collective control by the great merchants of the financial structure, harbour facilities, and shipping industry of St. John placed them in the position both to accumulate personal wealth and to play a significant role in determining the kind of economy which might emerge in the city and the colony.

419

Most great merchants built up sizeable fortunes at some point in their careers. And while time and fortune were not always kind to them, the great majority managed to avoid calamitous failures.[20] Any attempt to establish the extent of personal wealth of an individual over time is an exceedingly treacherous enterprise, but it is possible to get a glimpse of the collective resources of the merchant community and to establish with some accuracy the holdings of most merchants at one point in their lives. Something of the size of St. John merchant capital can be glimpsed in the city's fleet. Assuming an average price of £5 a ton, a conservative estimate of the value of vessels registered in St. John in 1841 would be £450,000, and the capital investment of firms such as those of James Kirk or Stephen Wiggins would have been in the order of £30-40,000.[21] All firms had a basic business investment in offices, stores, warehouses, and the harbour-area land or wharves on which they were located. While the size of this investment varied with the scope of the facilities, even a single store in the harbour area was worth £3,000 by mid-century and the larger facilities of many merchants plus the value of stock on hand could multiply that figure five or six times. Yet few merchants committed most of their assets to their mercantile activities. In 1826 the firm of Crookshank and Walker, one of the largest in the city, owned assets valued at more than £50,000 ($200,000). Of this total only 20 per cent was represented by vessels (the firm owned four) and less than 10 per cent by goods on hand.[22] The remainder consisted of investments in property and notes. Johnston withdrew from the firm in 1826 and received the sum of £25,000 from his partner. He also retained ownership of his own firm, H. Johnston & Co., and his total personal assets in that year amounted to over £40,000.[23] Similar stories of substantial capital investment outside the major mercantile operation can be constructed for other great merchants. Nehemiah Merritt died in 1843 possessed of an estate worth about £60,000 ($240,000) exclusive of ships and business stock.[24] In 1864 Stephen Wiggins left more than $700,000 to his heirs, about half of it composed of assets not connected with the firm.[25] And still later, in 1876, "The Lord of the North", John Robertson, passed on $454,000 for the benefit of his children.[26] By 1840 there may have been a dozen merchants each with assets exceeding a quarter of a million American dollars, and a large part of this capital was available for investment beyond the primary enterprises of their holders.

Not surprisingly the most important uses to which the great merchants of St. John devoted their wealth were those designed to further the development strategies which the merchant community deemed essential to its economic well-being. While direction and emphasis of these strategies changed from time to time in response to external circumstances, the broad outline is clearly visible throughout the first half of the nineteenth century. Like their counterparts in most North American ports, St. John merchants emphasized a combination of financial institutions, transportation links, resource exploitation and urban development to enable them to facilitate trans-Atlantic trade and to dominate a hinterland extending for 200 miles around the city. By 1840 their dominance in shipping had turned the Bay of Fundy into a St. John lake and their location had made the entire St. John Valley a satrapy of the city. Their greatest concerns were the development of transportation facilities into the interior and to the north shore of the province and the exploitation of the natural resources found within this natural zone of control. To achieve the first, the merchants pressured for a canal system to open the Grand Lake, some 60 miles from the city. After 1835 they sought to extend the city's control to the North Shore by means of a combined ship-railroad system which would involve construction of short railway lines between Grand Lake and Richibucto and between Shediac and Moncton. To exploit the natural resources of the area, they proposed to develop the sources of water power at the mouth of the St. John River and at the Grand Lake, to mine the coal resources of the Grand Lake area, and to promote the Bay of Fundy and southern whale fisheries.[27]

The most important institutions necessary to the maintenance of this commercial system were financial organizations, notably banks and insurance companies. Banks facilitated the transfer of funds in trans-Atlantic trade and control of the province's major credit agencies gave the leading merchants considerable leverage in their dealings with other parts of New Brunswick society. The Council of New Brunswick had co-operated with the merchant community to charter the first bank in British North America in 1820.[28] But the conservative policies and limited capital resources of the Bank of New Brunswick could not keep pace with the financial needs of merchants in a rapidly expanding colony and by 1836 they had secured royal charters for two more banking institutions, the Commercial and the City banks, over the opposition of the Executive Council of the province.[29] By 1845 the three banks possessed a paid up capital of £250,000 ($1,000,000), most of which was probably held within the city by the merchant community.[30] Through the period 1830-50 banking stock never yielded less than 8 per cent a year and was viewed not only as an excellent security but also a first-class opportunity for speculation. Similar emphasis was placed on the city's two marine insurance companies, and on its fire insurance company. The £50,000 capital of the N.B. Marine Company, the largest of these firms, yielded an annual dividend of 10 to 60% in the 1840s,[31] and more than 80% of the stock of that company was held by city merchants in 1841.[32] The stock of these companies not only yielded an excellent dividend income, but provided the basis for a flourishing speculative trade in stocks.

Nonetheless, the most important single investment made by St. John merchants was in land. It is interesting to speculate on the reasons behind this phenomenon. Land was clearly acquired both incidentally, in payment for debts owed, and because of the high degree of security which it offered. As well, many merchants saw an opportunity to achieve a certain status in the possession of well-known farms and favoured city residences. The nature of the acquisitions reveals several motives on the part of the purchasers: a desire to emulate a landed gentry, to create the security of rental income, to speculate on rising land prices and, in the case of purchases outside New Brunswick, to escape the consequences of the provincial bankruptcy laws in the event of commercial disaster. All merchants maintained one and sometimes two city residences. A large land-holder such as Noah Disbrow owned 12 city lots and 5 houses,[33] while John Robertson paid city taxes on real estate assessed at £25,000 ($100,000) — which almost certainly greatly underestimated its true market value — and held long-term leases, through his brother, on more than 100 city lots.[34] At his death in 1876 Robertson owned city real estate valued at $250,000.[35] Virtually all merchants owned several city lots and most possessed long-term leases on substantial tracts of city land in the harbour area.

Perhaps the most obvious case of land speculation on the part of leading merchants was the development of the suburban lands lying along the Marsh Road area directly north and west of the city. As early as 1819 most of this land had been acquired from the Hazen estate by several merchants — notably Nehemiah Merritt, Stephen Wiggins, Henry Gilbert, Hugh Johnston and Walker Tisdale — as building lots and farms.[36] By mid-century most of the land remained in the hands of the merchant-buyers, who were in the process of subdividing it into township building lots. The same assumptions concerning the development of the interior of the province marked the merchant's land acquisition in the St. John River Valley. Instead of buying up timber land, most merchants deliberately set about to acquire land bordering on the river. Their holdings were marked by a high proportion of intervale land, working farms and tenants, and comprised some of the most valuable agricultural resources in the province. The estate of Hugh

421

Johnston alone contained nearly 12,000 acres of Valley land in 25 separate holdings scattered through Queens, Sunbury, York and Carleton counties in 1835.[37] A number of merchants also acquired extensive holdings in other areas, notably Nova Scotia, Maine, New York and Upper Canada. Nehemiah Merritt, for example, owned three houses at Greenwich & Amos streets in New York City,[38] and he and Walker Tisdale each possessed more than 2,000 acres of land in Northumberland and Durham counties, Upper Canada.[39]

In addition to ownership of lands and financial institutions, the St. John merchant sought security through the public sector of the economy. The debt of the city and the province and the financing of public utilities within the city offered ample opportunity for investment. The city, in particular, had no agency through which it could carry long-term debt contracted for the construction of essential public works and from 1819 onward the merchant came to play an important role as city creditor.[40] By 1842 the municipal funded debt totalled £112,000 of which 40 per cent was held directly by merchants and their families and another 20 per cent by St. John banks and insurance companies.[41] The city's major public utilities were promoted and financed by its merchants. The water company was formed following the cholera epidemic of 1832 and by 1844 had expended £27,000 on the system.[42] The Gas Light Company and Reversing Falls Bridge Company were founded in the 1840s under the inspiration of the same group.[43]

Of all the potential investments in New Brunswick, the one that found least favour with the merchant community was secondary industry. Most merchant investment in this sector was related to the processing of natural resources produced in the province. In the wake of the growing English demand for deals in the mid-1830s several merchants acquired or constructed sawmills in conjunction with their shipping activities. Within the city John Robertson erected a large steam sawmill powered by sawdust and offal,[44] while less impressive operations were conducted by Robert Rankin & Co., Stephen Wiggins, R.D. Wilmot, Thomas and Ezekiel Barlow, and Nehemiah Merritt.[45] Outside the city the Kinnear brothers operated the Wales Stream mill.[46] Several others lent their support to the Portland Mills and Tunnel Company which proposed to cut tunnels through the Reversing Falls gorge to provide water power for a sawmill complex in Portland.[47] The most important industrial undertaking of any merchant before 1850 was the establishment of the Phoenix Foundry by the Barlow brothers in the 1820s. During the first two decades of its existence the firm introduced a number of technical innovations into the city, including construction of the first steamship manufactured entirely in the colony.[48] However, these examples were the exceptions rather than the rule. Most leading merchants had no financial involvement with secondary industry before 1840; those who did, with exception of Robertson and the Barlows, had a very limited investment in the undertakings. There was little investment in the city's major secondary industry — shipbuilding — and most lumber, even in the St. John area, was made in 49 sawmills owned by a different group of men.[49] Quite clearly, comprehensive industrial development stood low on the list of merchant priorities in the period.

422

In view of the rapid pace of industrial growth in the city between 1820 and 1840, the low level of merchant participation is surprising. In 1820, apart from a few shipyards, sawmills, and flour mills, St. John's secondary industry consisted of a wide variety of traditional crafts practiced in dozens of small workshops. Over the course of the next three decades, in response to the needs of a rapidly expanding provincial society, the city and its environs was transformed into an important manufacturing centre. This development occurred along a broad front. Most obvious and most significant was the growth of the shipbuilding and sawmilling industries. But there was also a host of industries producing for provincial consumers. Apart from the enterprises of the master tailors and shoemakers, these included 24 tanneries, 16 flour mills, 4 iron foundries, 2 brass foundries, 12 furniture and 4 soap manufacturers, 8 carriage makers, 2 breweries, a paper mill, and a number of minor industries.[50] The capacity and resources of these firms is perhaps best illustrated in the flour industry which by 1840 represented a capital investment of over £50,000 in mills capable of annually producing more than 150,000 barrels of flour, enough to feed the entire population of the province.[51] The tanners — 4 of whom were capable of generating more than 60 horsepower from their steam engines — made a similar claim for their industry.[52] The Harris Foundry comprised a block of buildings in 1846 with a replacement value of more than £10,000.[53] Most of these firms were developed by local entrepreneurs using their own skills and either their own capital or that of their family or friends.

423

Before 1840 most merchants either held this development at arm's length or viewed it with outright hostility. Wood and fish processing and shipbuilding were regarded as important elements in the commercial system and some merchants were prepared to invest in these undertakings. When local grain and livestock production was expanding in the 1820s, several merchants indicated some support for the tanners in their efforts to exclude the cheap Canadian leather from the province, and even promoted the first steam flour mill to grind local wheat.[54] However, such support was rare. More common was a violent negative reaction. The special objects of the merchants' wrath were the millers and bakers. The latter had long protested because American flour entered the colony with a 5/-a barrel duty while bread entered free.[55] The merchants' reply was to demand the removal of provincial tariffs on both.[56] A clearer indication of the merchants' view of early industrial development is seen in the issues on which they took no position. These included virtually every request for assistance, support or tariff protection by every manufacturing industry and interest in the city between 1820 and 1840. Given the rapid growth of the manufacturing sector during this time, this lack of participation by the merchant community stood in sharp contrast to the support which the manufacturers were able to command in almost every other major segment of urban society.

The principal organization of the merchant community was the Chamber of Commerce and the world which the merchant sought to create and maintain before 1840 is clearly visible through its petitions to the municipal, provincial and imperial governments. The central doctrine in these petitions was the reciprocity of mercantilism and imperial economic preference in return for colonial deference and loyalty in matters economic and political. The merchant identified the prosperity of the colony with his right to buy cheaply and sell dear. To do this he must not only be able to sell colonial produce in a protected imperial market, but to purchase that produce in as free a market as possible. The latter doctrine carried a special significance for colonial producers for the merchant was prepared to use American timber and foodstuffs to keep costs as low as possible in the timber trade. Indeed, on any issue deemed vital to the prosecution of the timber trade the ranks of the great merchants never broke in nearly half a century. Thus woods resources held by the crown and after 1836 by the province must be leased at nominal fees[57]; severe penalties must be imposed on those stealing timber or making lumber, timber, fish and flour of inferior quality[58]; debtors must continue to be imprisoned lest British creditors lose confidence in the colony's will to protect them and cheap justice must be provided to permit the collection of debts[59]; no provincial duties could be imposed on timber, lumber, flour, bread, pork or manufactured tobacco; and provincial tariffs must stand at no more than 5 per cent so that the merchant might keep control of the commerce of the Annapolis Valley of Nova Scotia.[60] Until 1843 imperial regulations permitted the merchant to treat the entire eastern seaboard of the United States and New Brunswick as a single commercial entity for the purposes of the timber trade,[61] and New Brunswick timber makers found their prices set by American competition. Even more significant, in terms of its implications for the fortunes of farmers and millers, was the merchants' bitter and continued opposition to any attempts by either provincial or imperial parliaments to establish or maintain duties on flour or salted provisions, an opposition which finally led lieutenant-governor Sir John Harvey to express doubts as to what extent the St. John Chamber of Commerce "represents the real commercial interests of the province".[62]

By 1840 there is some evidence to suggest that a minority of merchants were prepared to dissent from the Chamber on economic issues not directly related to the timber trade. The flour trade was a case in point. While most fleet owners strongly supported free trade in wheat and flour in order to assure the cheapest provisions for their crews, a number of other great merchants came to see the commercial possibilities of a high tariff on foreign wheat and flour which would enable them to ship wheat from England for processing in St. John mills. And the rapidly expanding domestic market had persuaded a few that not only could greater returns be obtained by importing wheat, rather than flour, but that flour mills offered the best return of all.[63] Nonetheless, until the 1840s the vast majority of merchants still believed that low tariffs were essential.

After 1841 the assumptions upon which the merchants' system had been built were undermined by external factors. The first major jolt was the dramatic recession of 1841 occasioned by the collapse of the British timber market. As the ripples of this unusually severe crisis spread through the local economy, the layers of provincial society collapsed hierarchically, beginning with the ships labourers, passing into the minor shopkeepers and journeymen craftsmen, then into the ranks of the master crasftsmen, shipbuilders, traders, contractors, small merchants, and lawyers,[64] finally claiming its victims among even the most stalwart with the bankruptcies of leading merchants such as James Hanford, Alex Yeats and J. & H. Kinnear in 1843.[65] Just as the economy was recovering from the recession in 1843, the British Government began its gradual dismantlement of the mercantilist structure with the regulations prohibiting the import of Maine-produced timber into the United Kingdom under the preferential trariff.[66] In the short run the regulations produced no significant impact on the timber trade other than to limit the merchants' choice of producers. The long-run effect of the tariff declension between 1843 and 1849 was a sharp decline in the quantity and value of timber shipped from St. John, and a corresponding increase in the export of lumber and deals.[67]

The rapid change and threat of change in the early 1840s produced a crisis   *425*
of confidence in the mercantile assumptions which had dominated the economy of New Brunswick since Napoleonic times. The producer, whether shoemaker, farmer, sawmill owner or founder, had existed in a gray area of semi-protection since the creation of the colony. Although the combination of imperial protective tariffs and provincial revenue duties had been sufficient to keep most local produce competitive with that from the United States, British produce entered the colony burdened only by the small revenue tariff. Provincial duties on British manufactures, for example, were fixed at 2½ per cent while those levied on American were 10 per cent.[68] The proposed elimination of the imperial tariff threatened to visit further disaster on an already badly demoralized artisan community. Hundreds of St. John artisans and mechanics had abandoned the city during the recession of 1841-2 and the exodus continued through 1842 and 1843 as economic prospects for the colony dimmed. By 1843 the city was divided by acrimonious debate between those prepared to follow the mother country into free trade, and those who argued that the wealth of colony was being dissipated on imported produce to the detriment of the producing classes. These protectionist views were strengthened by the emergence of a significant mechanics' revolt against what was perceived as the tyranny of the merchants. Out of the thriving mechanics community which had developed in the 1830s was formed, late in 1843, the Provincial Association, which brought together representatives of every major group of producers in the province.[69] The Association advocated protection and promotion of the interests of farmers, fishers, mechanics and manufacturers, through the use of duties, bounties, model farms and mechanics fairs. Among other things it urged the imposition of a substantial tariff on cordage and canvas, coupled with the payment of a bounty to farmers to grow hemp and flax.[70]

By 1844 the debate between free traders and protectionist had been transferred from the meeting hall to the Legislative Assembly, where the protectionists succeeded in imposing a compromise on the merchant interests after six close divisions in the House. Provincial duties were raised to 25 per cent on clocks, 20 per cent on wooden ware and chairs, 15 per cent on furniture and agricultural implements, 10 per cent on castings, cut nails and brick, and specific duties were imposed on cattle, oxen, horses and apples. At the same time any product required for the building of ships or the provisioning of crews, including flour, was placed on the free list. The debate over the most hotly contested duties, those on footwear and clothing, ended in a tie when a 10 per cent duty was imposed on footwear (a 5 per cent proposal was narrowly defeated) and clothing was admitted under a 4 per cent tariff.[71]

The compromise was only a temporary truce. Led by the St. John Chamber of Commerce, the free traders counterattacked at the 1845 sitting of the Assembly. Winning the support of several farmers who had voted with the protectionists the previous year, the free traders succeeded in reducing the tariff schedule to its 1843 levels, cutting some duties by as much as 60 per cent.[72] In response, one outraged protectionist leader vented his spleen in the columns of *The Morning News* on the "Free Trade Chamber of Commerce" of St. John, those "few selfish individuals" who were prepared to impose "this vicious system of one-sided free trade" on the "productive classes . . . the bone and sinew of the country".[73] However, this setback was temporary. Much to the chagrin of leading reformers like George Fenety, protection became a basic political issue during the 1840s and 50s, one that cut across the constitutional issues so dear to the hearts of reformers.[74] The Revenue Bill of the province was prepared each year by a select committee of the Assembly which acted on resolutions passed at each sitting of the Legislature. In 1847 the House, by a 21-10 majority, accepted the principle that "in enacting a Revenue Bill, the principle of protection to home industry, irrespective of revenue, should be recognized by levying duties on those productions and manufactures of foreign countries which the people of this province are capable of producing and manufacturing themselves".[75] The thrust of this resolution was directed against American produce and the Revenue Bill of that year introduced differential duties on British and foreign manufacturers. After 1850, however, the protectionists on the select committee were able to develop a policy of modest protection for a number of local industries. This included a 15 per cent tariff on footwear, leather, furniture, machinery, iron castings (stoves, ranges, boilers, furnaces, grates), most agricultural implements, wagons and sleighs, veneers, cigars, hats and pianos.

The merchant community of St. John was ill-prepared to meet the threat posed by the rise of the Provincial Association. By 1843 it was still recovering from the blows dealt it by the collapse of 1841-2 and it perceived the major threat to its security among the British free traders rather than in a diverse group of local protectionists. While the Chamber of Commerce traditionally had been the principal vehicle of merchant views, by 1843 it had come to represent the great fleet owners in their struggle against the threats to the protected status of the colonial timber trade. The Chamber's initial reaction to the Provincial Association and its proposals to divert provincial resources from the timber trade into agriculture and manufacturing was negative. In strongly worded petitions to the provincial and imperial authorities it reiterated support for traditional mercantilist policies in the timber trade and for a maximum 5 per cent duty on all provincial imports.[76] Yet, while the majority apparently accepted the Chamber of Commerce position, a significant minority came out in support of the Provincial Association and its policies of economic diversification and protective tariffs.[77] Among the heretics were R.D. Wilmot, William Parks, the Jarvises, Henry Gilbert, John Walker, Noah Disbrow, Charles Ward and Walker Tisdale.[78] The principal spokesman for the movement in St. John in the mid-1840s was R.D. Wilmot. When the Provincial Association entered the political arena with its platform of the "new New Brunswick", Wilmot was returned to the House of Assembly where he replaced his cousin, Lemuel Allan Wilmot, as the province's leading protectionist. Meanwhile, in an effort to restore a semblance of unity to the divided merchant community, the Chamber of Commerce was re-organized in the spring of 1845 and the membership of its new directorate reflected the attempts made to provide representation from a wide range of merchant opinions and interests.[79] At the final crisis of mercantilism, in 1849, the Chamber played an important part in the organization of the New Brunswick Colonial Association which brought together the city's most distinguished citizens in an effort to define the province's role in the new economic order.[80] The early programme of the Association clearly represented an attempt to reconcile all viewpoints and included a proposal urging the encouragement of home industry.[81] These efforts muted but could not entirely conceal the tensions between merchant free traders and protectionists.

427

By 1850 the Colonial Association had dropped its proposal for the encouragement of home industry and offered reciprocity in trade and navigation with the United States as the sole panacea for the province's economic ills.[82] And in the House of Assembly the merchants and their supporters were able to impose a compromise on the protectionists the effect of which was to create two economic systems. The artisan and manufacturer were granted a moderate tariff on material not required in the prosecution of the wood trades, while virtually everything necessary to the lumber industry, the timber trade, the building of wooden ships, and the victualling of crews was admitted free to the New Brunswick market. The latter included mill engines, anchors, chain, canvas, cordage, tackle, felt, sails, spikes, cotton ways, and iron bolts, bars, plates and sheating, as well as rigging, tin and copper plate, sheathing paper, grain, flour, meal, bread, meats, fruit and vegetables.[83] In effect, every backward linkage that the rapidly growing shipbuilding and shipping industry might have provided to the provincial economy was discouraged by provincial policy. Ship builders were encouraged to import all materials required in the building process, other than wood. Merchants were rewarded both with the transportation costs of the building materials and with cheap vessels which they sold in the United

Kingdom. It was a policy which permitted the application of a limited range of skills and the use of a small capital to produce a product which was competitive on the British market. Unfortunately such a policy conferred only limited benefits on the provincial economy and did not provide the flexibility or profit margins that gave the ship builder either the capital resources or the incentive to undertake any extensive technological innovation. More important it did not allow the development of substantial industries, dependent on these backward linkages, which might have promoted these changes.

Nonetheless, the activities of the Provincial Association remained an important theme in city politics into the 1850s. Of the 37 great merchants still living in St. John after 1842, 16 lent their support to at least some significant part of the protectionist programme and 12 of these consistently supported its general objective.[84] Not surprisingly, the merchants split on the issue of protection in terms of the emphasis which their business activities gave to the timber trade. Those with the most significant trading concerns — like John Ward, John Wishart and John Robertson — remained largely divorced from the concerns of other elements within the broader community. They were, as well, the major shipowners and their focus remained on the trans-Atlantic community. They did not, necessarily, oppose the protectionist impulse *per se*, but they did fear its emphasis on economic self-sufficiency, its inefficiencies, and, particularly, the stated goal of protectionists to transfer resources out of the timber industry and into manufacturing, agriculture and fishing.[85] Yet, while leading merchants opposed protectionist policies where they threatened to make the New Brunswick shipping industry uncompetitive on international runs by imposing substantial tariffs on flour, bread and pork, a number were prepared to accept the new order. Although it is difficult to generalize about them, they tended to include men whose principal activities had centred on the merchandising activities of the wholesaler and those whose interests were more concerned with New Brunswick than the trans-Atlantic community. While they were men of substance, none could match the personal fortunes amassed by the more substantial timber merchants, particularly those with heavy investments in ships. At his death in 1853, Noah Disbrow left over $80,000 (£20,800) to be divided among his 6 daughters and 2 sons,[86] and three years later Munson Jarvis' brother, William, a prominent dockside merchant left $50,000.[87] The next year William Parks placed a value of £17,484 (about $70,000) on the assets of his firm.[88] By comparison, Stephen Wiggins' share of the firm of Stephen Wiggins & Son was valued at $389,000 in 1863, most of which would have been in shipping.[89] Over the course of the 1850s, however, a minority of the great merchants did play an increasingly important role in the industrial development of the city through promotion of enterprises as diverse as woollen mills and coal oil refineries. As their industrial interests grew, their involvement in the staples' trade became less significant. Several had been or became agents for the transfer of resources from the staples to the manufacturing sector of the provincial economy in an attempt to create a more balanced economy. The Barlow brothers have been mentioned already in con-

428

nection with the secondary iron industry. The hardware merchant, William Henry Scovil, established his cut nail factory in the early 1840s, while the wholesale grocer, William Parks, ended his career in the 1860s as proprietor of one of the first cotton mills in British North America.

Those who identified most closely with the community were generally most willing to commit capital to its internal development; those with strong British ties and alternatives were usually much less willing to make this commitment. The former characteristic is reflected in the relatively high proportion of merchants of Loyalist origins who supported the Provincial Association and its objectives. In essence, they viewed St. John as the central element in a limited regional economy, in preference to its position in the larger metropolitan economy. It was merchants who had developed these more limited horizons and who saw their future in terms of local enterprise who came to the support of the manufacturers and artisans of the city, the group largely responsible for the not inconsiderable manufacturing development of the period from 1820 to 1850. The manufacturers and artisans were drawn from different origins, participated at different levels of civic society, and enjoyed a distinctly inferior status to their mercantile counterparts. Their special interests and ideas received serious consideration by the leaders of the community only during periods of economic crisis, such as the 1840s and 1870s. Even then the producers were able to achieve a position of influence only in alliance with a portion of the merchant community. When merchants closed ranks, they were able to establish the goals of the community at large and these goals were almost always designed to further the integration of the region into a larger trading complex in which the region was subordinated to the interests of a metropolitan community. So long as the imperial economic system was possible, the merchants used their capital and their great influence to maintain and further that system, largely ignoring the interests of farmers, manufacturers and other producers in the province. Nowhere was this more evident than in the crucial area of credit. Not only did they use the financial institutions in the city to direct the available credit to their own commercial purposes, but they successfully thwarted every effort by producers to obtain their own banking facilities.

The great merchants certainly organized and financed the commercial and financial super-structure needed for the conduct of the timber trade in a major sea port and they played important roles in providing capital for the exploitation of the natural resources of the region and for the construction of public works and utilities within the city. A minority, distinguished by their wholesaling concerns and native origins, began to participate in some fashion in the development of a more diversified urban economy. But the majority of great merchants retained a commitment to an unmodified staples economy. In the early nineteenth century it was this group which produced the dominant economic class, the institutions and myths — particularly that of commerce as the great creator of prosperity — which formed the community of St. John. Throughout the period they were able to mould the economy to their essentially interregional export-oriented needs. In so doing,

429

they exploited the province's natural resources of timber and stimulated the development of major sawmilling and shipbuilding industries both of which produced significant short-term benefits for the economy. Ancillary benefits were derived from the provision of shipping, credit facilities and insurance services.

The manufacturing sector of the New Brunswick economy did grow rapidly in the 1850s and 60s. Gordon Bertram has demonstrated that in 1871 the *per capita* output of the province's manufacturing industries rivalled that of Ontario and Quebec and was nearly twice that of Nova Scotia.[90] Nearly half of the industrial output of New Brunswick was produced in and around the city of St. John.[91] McClelland suggests that there was an average annual growth of one per cent in New Brunswick's deal and lumber exports during the period.[92] Not surprisingly, the largest components of the province's industrial output were sawmill products and wooden ships (44% for the province and 38% for the city).[93] Apart from these traditional staples, however, virtually every industry which had received even a modest degree of protection in the previous generation flourished. Foundry products, footwear and clothing all exceeded shipbuilding in value, while furniture and carriage making, boiler making, saw and file manufacture, and tin and sheet iron output and leather making all played significant roles in the local economy.[94] Some backward linkages from shipbuilding, which earlier tariff policies had done so little to encourage, were also able to develop by the later 1860s. The most obvious example was the small rope making industry functioning in the city and there can be little doubt that at least some of the foundry activity was stimulated by the market created by the ship builders.[95]

Yet the outlines of the earlier emphases were still visible in the city's industrial stucture. There was, apparently, no industry capable of producing the chain, anchors, and canvas used in the shipbuilding industry, nor to provide the machinery employed in the province's 565 sawmills.[96] Although steam engines had been constructed in St. John in the 1840s, there was no engine building firm in the province by 1870.[97] A similar situation existed in the basic food industries. The ancient flour industry had been virtually eliminated and only a miniscule meat curing industry survived.[98] There were no distilleries and only four small breweries.[99] The debate over the virtues of the ordered pastoral life as opposed to the disordered and transient nature of the timber industry was a recurring theme in nineteenth-century New Brunswick. The debate came to be couched in such explicit moral terms that it is difficult to make any assessment from it of the economic viability of provincial agriculture in the period, or to determine the extent to which the agricultural development of the province was effected by the timber trade.[100] The rapidity of agricultural development between 1840 and 1870 would seem to indicate that there was some truth to the charges of the timber critics; at the very least, the combination of rewards which the trade could offer to the rural inhabitants coupled with the refusal of the provincial legislature to provide any protection for the nascent colonial agriculture, severely retarded the development of a substantial agriculture in the early nineteenth century.[101]

The retardation was of vital importance to the health of the colonial economy. New Brunswick ran a perennial deficit in its current account and in most years the entire trade imbalance resulted from the substantial imports of foodstuffs for use within the province. The most prominent example of this phenomenon was American wheat and flour, but it was reflected, as well, in large imports of rye flour, Indian meal, pork, beef, lamb, butter, potatoes, vegetables, fruit and even oats. The proportion of agricultural products ranged from just over 20% of the province's total imports in 1840 to just under 40% in 1855.[102] Wheat and flour imports alone exceeded the value of timber exports by 1852 and by 1855 the 170,000 barrels of flour and 110,000 bushels of wheat, worth £334,000 in all, rivalled the £380,000 in deals shipped from the province.[103] New Brunswick agricultural conditions were not particularly suited to the production of wheat, although the doubling of output following the National Policy of 1879 indicates that a much larger production than occurred up to Confederation was possible.[104] But it is more difficult to explain the import of most other foodstuffs which could be produced domestically. Given the fact that substantial quantities of these products were grown in the province in the 1840s, that the land for producing more was readily available, and that there was a substantial local demand for these foodstuffs which could not be met by local producers, it seems probable that the incentives offered by the timber trade, and the refusal of the province to afford even nominal protection to local producers were the major factors in inhibiting the growth of a more substantial agricultural sector before 1850.

In the final analysis there is no simple answer to the question of merchant responsibility for economic growth or retardation in St. John and New Brunswick. While they agreed on the validity of the concept of economic growth, merchants rarely spoke with a single voice when the subject of a specific development strategy was raised. Most were prepared to permit, and some to support a strategy which included the development of certain kinds of secondary industry. These efforts were generally successful although this success was due more to the efforts of the city's artisans than to its merchants. Merchant endeavours were particularly aimed at supporting and preserving the traditional timber staple and its milling, shipping, and shipbuilding ancilliaries. The manufacture of producers' goods used in any of these activities, including mill engines and machinery, shipbuilding materials, and domestic foodstuffs needed for ship crews, woods workers and mill labourers, were afforded no encouragement. In effect two economic systems based upon mutually exclusive values were the result of the synthesis which emerged from the conflict of the 1840s. The most obvious victim of that synthesis was the shipbuilding industry, potentially the most dynamic element in the provincial economy, which was locked into the more conservative timber-trade economy. Thus a city containing a number of secondary iron and steel firms, which for decades had possessed the capabi-

431

lity of manufacturing complete steamships and engines, and a labour force skilled at working in both wood and iron was unable to manufacture metal ships or even to make any substantial adjustment in the face of technologial changes which were gradually eroding this vital industry. In the course of 1860s and 70s the ship builders built and the timber merchants bought and sold ships in the traditional way simply because they could not perceive the industry apart from the timber trade or from the lumber which was basic to both building and trade. While the timber merchants were not alone able to shape the provincial economy to their perceptions, they provided an effective and powerful leadership to substantial interests in the province which identified with the traditional timber trade. By 1871 the economy was becoming increasingly diversified and self-sufficient and the dynamic elements in this development were to be found in secondary industry and in agriculture, but the influence of the great merchants delayed this development by two critical decades. In this sense they contributed to the retardation of a viable industrial base in the city.

432

Notes

1. The literature of this debate has been explored by L.R. MacDonald in "Merchants against Industry: An Idea and Its Origins", *Canadian Historical Review*, LVI (1975), pp. 263-81.
2. A point most recently made by Professor Gerald Tulchinsky in *The River Barons* (Toronto, 1977), p. 234.
3. Nonetheless, a good beginning has been made with Tulchinsky's examination of the Montreal business community at mid-century, and in David Sutherland's study of the business strategies of Halifax merchants in the colonial period. Tulchinsky, *op. cit.*; David Sutherland, "Halifax Merchants and the Pursuit of Development 1783-1850", *CHR*, LIX (1978), pp. 1-17.
4. Peter D. McClelland, "The New Brunswick Economy in the Nineteenth Century" (PhD thesis, Harvard University, 1966), pp. 3-4. McClelland argues that shipbuilding may have added no more than 2.6% to the gross regional product (p. 189) and that it had few significant backward or forward linkages.
5. *Ibid.*, pp. 229-30.
6. *Ibid.*, p. 4.
7. New Brunswick, *Journal of the House of Assembly*, 1841, pp. xvii-xxx; Canada, *Census of 1871*, IV, p. 125.
8. Canada, *Census of 1871*, IV, p. 128.
9. The early development of this industry is discussed by Lewis R. Fischer in "From Barques to Barges: Shipping Industry of Saint John, N.B. 1820-1914" (unpublished paper read to the Atlantic Canada Studies Conference, Fredericton, 1978).
10. Eugene A. Forsey, *The Canadian Labour Movement 1812-1902* (Ottawa, Canadian Historical Association, 1974), pp. 3-4; J. Richard Rice, "A History of Organized Labour in Saint John, New Brunswick 1813-1890" (MA thesis, U.N.B., 1968), ch. 1.
11. James M. Gilmour, *Spatial Evolution of Manufacturing: Southern Ontario 1851-1891* (Toronto, 1972).
12. For the extent to which they succeeded in this goal see the testimonials to the merchants delivered by George Fenety and Henry Chubb, the city's most respected and influential newspaper editors in the 1840s. See *The Commercial News and General Advertiser* (St. John), 10 September 1839, and *The New Brunswick Courier* (St. John), 10 February 1843.
13. This thesis is argued by Stewart MacNutt in his "Politics of the Timber Trade in Colonial New Brunswick 1825-40", *CHR*, XXX (1949), pp. 47-65.
14. This group includes L.H. Deveber, Thomas Barlow, Ezekiel Barlow, Jr., Issac Bedell, Robert W. Crookshank, Noah Disbrow, Jr., Lauchlan Donaldson, John Duncan, Henry Gilbert, James T. Hanford, John Hammond, David Hatfield, James Hendricks, Ralph M. Jarvis, Hugh Johnston, Sr., Hon. Hugh Johnston, Jr., John H. Kinnear, James Kirk, Thomas Leavitt, William H. Leavitt, Nehemiah

Merritt, Thomas Millidge, D.L. McLaughlin, Thomas E. Millidge, William Parks, John Pollok, Robert Rankin, E.D.W. Ratchford, Hon. John Robertson, W.H. Scovil, Hon. Charles Simonds, Walker Tisdale, John V. Thurgar, John Walker, John Ward, Jr., Charles Ward, Stephen Wiggins, John M. Wilmot, R.D. Wilmot, John Wishart.

15. David Macmillan explores the early development of the St. John Scottish community in ''The New Men in Action: Scottish Mercantile and Shipping Operations in North American Colonies 1760-1825'', *Canadian Business History: Selected Studies, 1497-1971* (Toronto, 1972), pp. 82-99.

16. A good description of these activities if found in Graeme Wynn, "Industry, Entrepreneurship and Opportunity in the New Brunswick Timber Trade" in Lewis R. Fischer and Eric W. Sager, eds., *The Enterprising Canadians: Entrepreneurs and Economic Development in Eastern Canada, 1820-1914* (St. John's, Memorial University of Newfoundland, 1979).

17. Reports revealing the directors and the financial state of affairs of each bank were published annually in *Journal of the House of Assembly*.

18. Schedule of Real Estate Belonging to St. John, Wharf Leases in Perpetuity, Records of the Executive Council, REX/PA, Miscellaneous, Provincial Archives of New Brunswick [hereafter PANB].

19. This description of the St. John fleet, containing information on the date of acquisition, size and ownership of each vessel, is found in "Customs House Account, Returns of Shipping, Port of Saint John, New Brunswick", *Journal of the House of Assembly*, 1842, cclvii-cclxvii.

20. Two notable failures were the firms John M. Wilmot, in 1837 and James Hanford, Alex Yeats and J. & H. Kinnear, in 1843. *The New Brunswick Courier*, 4 March, 18, 25 November 1843; A.R.M. Lower, *Great Britain's Woodyard* (Toronto, 1973), p. 151.

21. Prices for New Brunswick-built vessels fluctuated between £5 and £12 a ton throughout the 1830s and 1840s.

22. Account Book I, pp. 5-10, Hugh Johnston Papers, New Brunswick Museum [hereafter NBM].

23. Schedule of Real and Personal Effects, May 1826, *ibid.*

24. Last will and testament of Nehemiah Merritt, Records of the Court of Probate, City and County of St. John, Book G, pp. 131 ff., PANB. The totals include estimates of property values.

25. Stephen Wiggins, 1864, RG 7, RS 71, PANB.

26. John Robertson, 1876, *ibid.*

27. New Brunswick, Records of the Legislative Assembly [RLE], 1834, Petitions, vol. 2, no. 41; 1836, Petitions, vol. 5, nos. 70, 75, 81; 1834, Petitions, vol. 6, no. 130, PANB.

28. James Hannay, *History of New Brunswick* (St. John, 1909), II, pp. 428-9.

29. NB, RLE, 1836, Petitions, vol. 5, no. 64, PANB; Hannay, pp. 430-2.

30. These estimates are drawn from Bank of New Brunswick dividend payments, newspaper accounts of bank stock sales, and wills. There was no public statement disclosing the ownership of bank stock in colonial New Brunswick.

31. The annual reports of the N.B. Marine Insurance Company between 1830 and 1850 may be found in the appendices of the Journals of the New Brunswick House of Assembly.

32. New Brunswick, *Journal of the House of Assembly*, 1842, Appendix — Returns of Incorporated Companies, The N.B. Marine Insurance Company.

33. Records of the Court of Probate, City and County of St. John, Book H, pp. 454 ff., PANB.

34. John Robertson to Common Council, 10 October 1849, St. John Common Council Supporting Papers, vol. 20, St. John Manuscripts, PANB; Saint John Schedule (etc.), 1842, REX/PA, Miscellaneous, PANB.

35. John Robertson, 1876, RG 7, RS 71, PANB.

36. Extract of Cash Received for Land Sold 1814-1821, Hon. William F. Hazen Papers, Daybook and Journal 1814-34, NBM.

37. Inventory of Estate of Hugh Johnston, 1 May 1835, Hugh Johnston Papers, Account Book I, NBM.

38. Probate Records, Book G, p. 131, PANB.

39. *Ibid.*, Book I, p. 267.

40. The city debt rose from £4413 in 1822 to £115,366 in 1845. Minutes of the Common Council, vol. V, 5 April 1822; vol. XVII, 10 September 1845, Common Clerk's Office, Saint John City Hall.

41. Common Council Supporting Papers, vol. VI, 7/8-12/13 September 1842, Saint John Manuscripts, PANB.

42. NB, RLE, 1844, Petitions, vol. 7, no. 181, PANB.

43. *The New Brunswick Courier*, 27 March 1843.

44. *The New Brunswick Courier*, 11 September 1852.

45. *The Morning News* (St. John), 23 April 1841.

46. *The New Brunswick Courier*, 25 November 1843.

47. NB, RLE, 1834, Petitions, vol. 2, no. 41; 1836, Petitions, vol. 5, no. 75; 1839, Petitions, vol. 2, no. 43, PANB.

48. Common Council Minutes, vol. XV, 23 December 1840, 14 January 1841, Common Clerk's Office, St. John City Hall.

49. The most important of these was probably George Bond who held the lease for the tidal-powered

433

Carleton mills, the most significant power source in the St. John area.

50. NB, RLE, 1840, Petitions, vol. 4, no. 122; 1843, Petitions, vol. 6, no. 149; 1850, Petitions, vol. 17, no. 357; 1850, Petitions, no. 414; 1836, Petitions, vol. 5, no. 112, PANB; *The New Brunswick Courier*, 12 October 1850, 5 July 1851.

51. NB, RLE, 1840, Petitions, vol. 4, no. 122, PANB.

52. *Ibid.*, 1845, Petitions, vol. 9, no. 298.

53. *The New Brunswick Courier*, 27 June 1846.

54. NB, RLE, 1834, Petitions, vol. 4, no. 91; 1828, Petitions, vol. 2, no. 43, PANB.

55. *Ibid.*, 1835, Petitions, vol. 4, no. 124; 1842, Petitions, vol. 3, no. 54.

56. *Ibid.*, 1833, Petitions, vol. 3, no. 102; 1840, Petitions, vol. 4, no. 121; 1842, Petitions, vol. 12, no.237; 1851, Petitions, vol. 15, no. 457; *The New Brunswick Courier*, 4 February 1843.

57. W.S. MacNutt, "Politics of the Timber Trade in Colonial New Brunswick 1825-40", pp. 47-65; Graeme Wynn, "Administration in Adversity: The Deputy Surveyors and Control of the New Brunswick Crown Forests Before 1844", *Acadiensis*, VII (Autumn 1977), pp. 49-65.

58. NB, RLE, 1839, Petitions, vol. 3, no. 80; 1824, D, Petitions, no. 6, PANB.

59. *Ibid.*, 1831, F. Petitions, vol. 2, no. 10.

60. *Ibid.*, 1850, Petitions, vol. 6, no. 138; *The New Brunswick Courier*, 24 February 1849.

61. *The New Brunswick Courier*, 20 January 1844.

62. Sir John Harvey to Lord Glenelg, 15 May 1838, CO 188/59, ff. 733-42, but also see Petition of St. John Merchants, 17 February 1834, CO 188/49, ff. 169-71; Sir John Harvey to Lord John Russell, 4 September 1840, CO 188/69, ff. 152-3; Sir William Colebrooke to Stanley, 29 March 1842, CO 188/75, ff. 341-5. Both Harvey and Colebrooke feared the economic and social consequences of an over-specialized staples economy.

63. NB, RLE, 1840, Petitions, vol. 4, no. 122, PANB. Among the dissenters were N. Merritt, R. Rankin, John Walker, D. Wilmot, I. Bedell, Wm. Parks.

64. *The New Brunswick Courier*, 4 March, 3 June, 15 July, 7 October 1843.

65. *Ibid.*, 4 March, 18, 25, November 1843.

66. NB, RLE, 1843, Petitions, vol. 9, no. 244, PANB.

67. Between 1840 and 1849 the value of timber exports from New Brunswick declined from £271,000 to £179,000; that of deals and boards increased from £180,000 to £266,000. New Brunswick, *Journal of the House of Assembly*, 1841, 1850, Customs House Returns.

68. *Ibid.*, 1842, Appendix, p. cclxxiv.

69. *The New Brunswick Courier*, 4 January 1844.

70. *Ibid.*, 10 February 1844.

71. New Brunswick, *Journal of the House of Assembly*, 1844, pp. 152-7.

72. *The Morning News*, 24 March 1845. The defectors included Barbarie from Restigouche, Earle from Queens, Hanington and Palmer from Westmorland. See New Brunswick, *Journal of the House of Assembly*, 1845, pp. 219-21.

73. *The Morning News*, 19 March 1845.

74. Editor and publisher of *The Morning News* and later Queens Printer under the Liberals, Fenety was unsympathetic to the views of the protectionists. G.E. Fenety, *Political Notes and Observations* (Fredericton, 1867), I, chs. V, XXI. On the other hand both Lemual Allan Wilmot and Samuel Leonard Tilley supported the protectionist position.

75. New Brunswick, *Journal of the House of Assembly*, 1847, pp. 190-1.

76. *The New Brunswick Courier*, 4 February 1844.

77. *Ibid.*, 10 February 1844.

78. NB, RLE, 1843, Petitions, vol. 6, no. 143, PANB.

79. *The Morning News*, 2 April, 16 April, 6 May, 7 May 1845; 25 February 1846.

80. *The New Brunswick Courier*, 28 June, 4 August 1849.

81. *Ibid.*, 15 September 1849.

82. *Ibid.*, 8 June 1850.

83. The evolution of New Brunswick policy between 1837 and 1860 is illustrated through the following commodities:

	1837		1842		1844	1845	1848		1855	1859
	Brit.	For.	Brit.	For.			Brit.	For.		
Wagons	2.5%	10%	2.5%	10%	10%	4%	4%	30%	15%	15%
Footwear	2.5%	5%	2.5%	10%	10%	7.5%	4%	30%	15%	15%
Agricultural Implements	Free	Free	Free	Free	10%	4%	4%	15%	15%	15%

Stoves	2.5%	10%	2.5%	10%	10%	7.5%	4%	15%	15%	15%
Chain	2.5%	10%	2.5%	10%	Free	Free	Free	Free	1%	1%
Canvas	Free	Free	Free	Free	Free	Free	Free	Free	1%	1%
Cordage	Free	Free	Free	Free	Free	Free	Free	Free	1%	1%
Mill Engines	Free	10%	Free	10%	Free	Free	Free	Free	10%	12.5%
Meat	Free	Free	Free	Free	Free	Free	Free	Free	Free	Free
Bread Flour	Free	Free	Free	Free	Free	4%	4%	10%	Free	Free

Source: Statutes of New Brunswick, 7 William IV, c.1.; 5 Victoria, c.1.; 7 Victoria, c.1.; 8 Victoria, c.2.; 11 Victoria, c.1.; 18 Victoria, c.1.

84. NB, RLE, 1850, Petitions, vol. 6, no. 416, PANB.
85. *Ibid.*, 10 February 1843, 23 February 1850.
86. Noah Disbrow, 1853, RG 7, RS 71, PANB.
87. William Jarvis, 1856, *ibid.*
88. Partnership Agreements, William Parks Papers, F #3, NBM. This figure does not include Park's personal estate.
89. Stephen Wiggins, 1853, RG 7, RS 71, PNB.
90. Gordon W. Bertram, "Historical Statistics on Growth and Structure in Manufacturing in Canada 1870-1957", in J. Henripen and A. Asimakopulas, eds., *Canadian Political Science Association Conference on Statistics 1962 & 1963* (Toronto, 1964), p. 122. The figures for Ontario, Quebec, New Brunswick and Nova Scotia were $69.60, $62.60, $59.80, $30.70.
91. St. John County output totalled $8,312,627; that of the province was $17,367,687. Canada, *Census of 1871*, vol. III, Table LIV.
92. McClelland, p. 124.
93. *Ibid.*, Tables XXII, XXXIX.
94. The shipbuilding industry produced vessels to a value of $538,042 and employed 647 men. Foundry output, including fittings, nails, and tacks, was $786,000 (507 employees); clothing $826,660 (1033 employees); footwear $539,230 (565 employees). Canada, *Census of 1871*, vol. III, Tables, XXI, XXXII, XXIII, XXIV, XXXVI, XXXVI, XXXIX, XLV, LI, LII, LIII.
95. *Ibid.*, Table L.
96. The number of sawmills in the province had declined in the 1860s. There were 609 Water-powered and 80 steam-powered sawmills in 1861. Canada, *Census of 1871*, vol. IV, pp. 336-43.
97. Canada, *Census of 1871*, vol. III, Table XLVI.
98. *Ibid.*, Tables XXI, XXXVII.
99. *Ibid.*, Table XXXV.
100. Soil maps would seem to indicate that the agricultural potential of the province is limited. However, since the arable area comprises several million acres of land, this source is only useful as an indicator of the upper limits of agricultural growth. In the short run the province possessed a considerable potential as the rapid growth of mid-century reveals.
101. Acreage of cultivated land increased from 435,861 in 1840 to 1,171,157 in 1870 at a rate much more rapid than that of population growth. Consequently the number of cultivated acres *per capita* rose from 2.7 to 4.6. In the single decade of the 1860s the number of farmers in the province rose by nearly 30%; the population by 13%. Canada, *Census of 1871*, vol. III, pp. 90-1; vol. IV, pp. 129, 336-43.
102. New Brunswick, *Journal of the House of Assembly*, 1841, pp. cclxxvi-cclxxvii; 1856, pp. clxiii-clxvi.
103. Flour and wheat to the value of £169,000 was imported in 1854. This compared with exports of 134,000 tons of timber valued at £165,000. Two years later the respective values of the two commodities was £286,000 and £160,000, and in 1855 imported flour and wheat totalled £377,000, a value rivalling that of the provinces lumber output (£437,000). See New Brunswick, *Journal of the House of Assembly*, 1853, 1855, 1856, Customs House Returns.
104. Canada, *Census of 1881*, vol. III, pp. 42-3, 120-1, 158-9. New Brunswick wheat output rose from 204,911 bushels in 1871 to 521,956 in 1881.

435

Topic Thirteen
The Pacific Coast

436 Europeans first visited Canada's Pacific coast in the 1770s. Approximately one generation later the Nor'Westers, operating out of Montreal reached the Fraser and Columbia river-basins. Large-scale white settlements began after the Gold Rush on the Fraser River in the late 1850s. As L.F.S. Upton points out in "Contact and Conflict on the Atlantic and Pacific Coasts of Canada," the Indian groups on the Atlantic had centuries to make the adjustment that the Pacific Coast peoples were obliged to make in decades.

The Hudson's Bay Company, after its union with the North West Company in 1821, established fur trading operations all along the Pacific Coast. The demarcation in 1846 of the boundary between British and American territory obliged the Company to leave Oregon. Three years later Vancouver Island became a crown colony, and the lower Fraser River on the mainland was opened as a commercial highway. In 1858 the discovery of gold on the Fraser River opened up the mainland, leading Britain to establish the separate colony of British Columbia that same year, to offset the domination of American prospectors. James Douglas, the Governor of Vancouver Island, became governor of the new mainland colony as well, firmly planting British institutions there, making New Westminster (founded by day labourers and speculators from Upper Canada and Nova Scotia) the new capital. In 1866 the two colonies were joined under the title of British Columbia. Barry Gough offers an interpretative sketch of early British Columbia in his "The Character of the British Columbia Frontier."

An essential work for an appreciation of early European contact on the Pacific Coast is Warren L. Cook's *Flood Tide of Empire: Spain and the Pacific Northwest, 1543-1819* (New Haven: Yale University Press, 1973), a study of Spanish ties with the Pacific Coast. Christon Archer has written two articles on the same subject in *BC Studies*, "The Transient Presence: A Re-appraisal of Spanish Attitudes Toward the Northwest Coast in the Eighteenth Century," no. 18 (1973): 3-32; and "Retreat from the North: Spain's Withdrawal from Nootka Sound, 1793-1795," no. 37 (1978): 19-36; see also his,

"Cannibalism in the Early History of the Northwest Coast: Enduring Myths and Neglected Realities," *Canadian Historical Review*, 61 (1980): 453-479. Iris Higbie Wilson has translated and edited José Mariano Moziño, *Noticias de Nutka: An Account of Nootka Sound in 1792* (Seattle: University of Washington Press, 1970). Philip Drucker reviews the Pacific Coast Indian societies in *Cultures of the North Pacific Coast* (Scranton, Pennsylvania: Chandler Publishing Company, 1965).

The history of the Indians' involvement in the fur trade in the area is covered in Wilson Duff's, *The Indian History of British Columbia* (Victoria: Provincial Museum of British Columbia, 1964). More recent studies are: Robin Fisher's, *Contact and Conflict: Indian-European Relations in British Columbia, 1774-1890* (Vancouver: University of British Columbia Press, 1977); and Theodore J. Karamanski, *Fur Trade and Exploration: Opening the Far Northwest 1821-1852* (Vancouver: University of British Columbia Press, 1983).

Barry Gough has written on the maritime history of the Pacific Coast: *437* *Distant Dominion: Britain and the Northwest Coast of North America, 1579-1809* (Vancouver: University of British Columbia Press, 1980). W. Kaye Lamb has edited the journals of George Vancouver's expedition, 1791-1795, in four volumes, *The Voyage of George Vancouver, 1791-1795* (London: The Hakluyt Society, 1984). For the later period see Barry Gough, *The Royal Navy and the Northwest Coast of North America, 1810-1914: A Study of British Maritime Ascendancy* (Vancouver: University of British Columbia Press, 1971) and his *Gunboat Frontier: British Maritime Authority and Northwest Coast Indians, 1846-90* (Vancouver: University of British Columbia Press, 1984).

For an overview of developments on the mainland, see R. Cole Harris's, "British Columbia" in *Canada Before Confederation*, edited by R. Cole Harris and John Warkentin (Toronto: Oxford, 1974), pp. 289-311. The standard, but now rather dated, history of the area is Margaret A. Ormsby's *British Columbia: A History* (Toronto: Macmillan, 1958). George Woodcock provides a readable sketch of an early British Columbian journalist and politician in his *Amor de Cosmos: Journalist and Reformer* (Toronto: Oxford University Press, 1975). W. Peter Ward and Robert A.J. McDonald, eds., *British Columbia: Historical Readings* (Vancouver: Douglas and McIntyre Ltd., 1981), contains several valuable essays on early British Columbia history.

Contact and Conflict on the Atlantic and Pacific Coasts of Canada*

L. F. S. UPTON

The contact years on the Atlantic coast were spread out over centuries, on the Pacific coast over decades.[1] European fishermen were probably in touch with the Micmacs of Acadia as early as 1500; a handful of French colonists was established there by 1650; British settlers arrived in 1750, but the area was not extensively populated by outsiders until the 1780s. Before contact, the number of Micmacs has been estimated at anywhere from 16 000 upwards, but after 1600 the population hovered around the 3000 mark and stayed remarkably constant until recent years.[2] The Micmacs, alone among Canadian Indians, fought for their lands, holding the British at bay for almost fifty years with the support of France, which had conceded Acadia to Britain in 1713 but refused to allow its new owners quiet enjoyment of the land. The collapse of French power in America ended Micmac resistance.[3] At about the same time that the Micmacs were adjusting to the reality of British control, the Indians of the west coast — upwards of 50 000 in number — were receiving their first visits from Europeans, more than 250 years after the Micmacs had first entertained such strangers. The newcomers came to trade, and they traded under a number of flags. However, the west coast of the nineteenth century did not become the scene of great power rivalry on the same scale as had the Atlantic coast in the eighteenth. International disputes were settled by compromise and it was in the interest of no party to enlist the Indians in a war on its behalf.[4] The west coast Indians thus avoided entrapment in European power politics. Some ninety years elapsed between the appearance of the first white navigators and the first push of white settlement; not as long a period of grace as the Micmacs enjoyed, but longer than was granted many Indian peoples.

The contrast between these two histories is vast, for they occur in different times and places, hundreds of years and thousands of miles apart. Time made a difference to the principal actors involved. The nineteenth-century European was not the same as his seventeenth-century predecessor. The Micmac of 1600 was patently different from, say, the Haida of 1800. The accommodations that whites and Indians made to each other were of necessity affected by these differences. The boreal forest of eastern Canada was not the same as the rain forest of the west coast, nor could it support the same standard of life. But through these disparate histories run several themes that do, nevertheless, bind the two together. The process of contact followed a course that was largely determined by

*From *Acadiensis,* 9 (1980): 3–13. Copyright by University of New Brunswick Department of History. Reprinted by permission.

the coastal nature of the land and its accessibility by sea. Consequently, the shape of that experience was markedly different from what it was elsewhere in Canada, where the whites approached the Indian residents either overland or by seasonal river navigation. The contact experiences on the east and west coasts of Canada have more in common with each other than they do with similar events in any of the interior regions.

The first and most obvious similarity was the coastal environment — the ocean, the inlets, the rivers, the evergreen forests — that played a critical part in determining the life of the Indians and would, one day, mould the life of the whites who supplanted them. Drucker's description of the resources available to the west coast Indian applies also to the Micmacs: "From the sea and river, fish . . . could be taken in abundance. Some of the fish appeared only seasonally, but were easy to preserve. The sea also provided a tremendous quantity of edible mollusks . . . . More spectacular was the marine game; hair seal, sea lion, sea otter, porpoise and even whale. On shore, land game too abounded. Vegetable foods were less plentiful, although many species of wild berries were abundant in their season".[5] However, the Micmacs did not develop as complex a material culture on this basis as did the west coast Indians, for the western environment was milder and supported a more sedentary life. The Micmacs had no straight grained cedar ready for the splitting and had to content themselves with simple shelters of bark stripped from their trees. Nor did they develop a complex society with the stratification and ceremonial found on the west coast.[6] Their basic unit remained a band that was little more than an extended family, for they were forced to hunt game in late winter each year, and the hunt could best be pursued by small groups. But it was for only two months of each year — February and March — that the coasts and rivers failed them. When those lean weeks were over, they came together in increasing numbers and from April to October lived on the coast — usually at the mouth of a river at the head of a bay — at village sites to which they regularly returned. In the autumn they began to move inland along the rivers, taking fish and waterfowl as they dispersed themselves into smaller units to prepare for the winter hunt.[7]

It was this hunt that prevented the development of Micmac society along west coast lines; that diffused authority among numerous band chiefs; that simplified their ceremonial and limited their material possessions to what was portable. But it would be wrong to depict the Micmacs as a people endlessly wandering the forests in search of food, for they had the resources to be sedentary for at least half of each year. It would also be wrong to ignore the fact that the natural development of their social life was distorted by European intrusions a full 250 years before those same influences went to work on the west coast.

When Europeans came to these coastal people, they came from over the seas. Of course, all Europeans came to North America from over the seas, but not all the Indians who met them perceived this fact. The stereotype European on the coasts would be very different from the one encountered

439

on the inland fringes of settlement. Europeans travelled in boats. The people in these boats were male, were still domiciled in their country of origin, were in America for a predictably short time, and were employees answerable to an authority they had to recognise since they would be returning home in a matter of weeks. Their boats were their homes in America and they had no need to establish settlements. They did not approach the new land in the possessive way pioneers adopted in the interior. They had the advantage of a demonstrably superior technology in their ships, which enabled them to travel distances that the Indians could not comprehend; but this advantage was offset by the fact that, since they had come to the Indians (and not vice versa), they were regarded as suppliants from distressed as well as distant lands.[8]

Throughout the sixteenth century Europeans made landfall in North America for shelter, repairs and recuperation. There were probably several hundred landfalls a year in Acadia by mid-century.[9] Trade was an incidental, for the fishery was the important economic activity; trade goods were simply the surplus hardware of the fishing industry. Trade for fur and hides became organized in the seventeenth century, but its cycle remained geared to the fishing seasons. Europeans knew the location of the summer villages and knew where the Indians would be each year. Therefore there was no need to establish land posts in order to concentrate the Indians for the convenience of traders. The few whites who tried permanent posts had difficulty competing with the ship-borne traders who found their profit not only in furs but also in fish.[10] On the west coast, there were differences in detail. Europeans opened trade not as an offshoot of an established industry but as a thing in itself. They came with specialised trade goods in a few large, specialised ships, and anticipated a lucrative market for their furs in China. The difference was partly that of the passage of time: of 150 years' experience of trading with the Indians; of superior navigation; of global trade. The Hudson's Bay Company founded land-based posts, but these were developing a maritime pattern of trade until cut short by the great divide of 1846.[11] The basics were the same as in the sixteenth centuries: no desire for acquiring land, no incentive for settlement, no motive to displace Indian suppliers. The coming together of Europeans and Indian interests along a narrow range of mutual interest was shown by the argot of Micmac, Basque and French spoken along the shores of Acadia by 1600, and in the Chinook mixture that had achieved the same status along the west coast by 1850.[12] Any European impulse to remove or annihilate or acculturate the Indians was stifled in these coastal areas.

The evergreen forests that provided the Indians with their material culture bespoke a soil too poor to attract European families; the fish that provided the staple of life could be harvested from boats offshore; the furs that justified the new trade could perfectly well be acquired by the Indians. The process of contact began to lengthen out into a routine of trade conducted by European men and an Indian society. This type of restricted white contact had some benefits for the host people, who might profit from a new efficiency. A fowling piece loaded with shot would kill half a dozen ducks that before had had to be taken one at a time; a metal cooking pot made a band more mobile in the winter hunt; an iron hatchet made a warrior more lethal. But what was done with the extra leisure thus gained? In the case of the Micmacs, the routine of life was destroyed by the need to hunt for furs at all times of year to pay for trade goods.[13] On the west coast, the more efficient European tools led to an efflorescence of art and ceremonial, but the desire to buy the new goods brought on increased hostility with inland tribes.[14]

Occasional contacts with the whites promoted change even though no European was domiciled on Indian land; occasional contact also brought disease and a rapid loss of population. The decline was not only physical but spiritual as well, for the close alliance between the spirits and health in native belief alienated the Indians from their traditional spiritual supports.[15] There was a large but unknowable decline in the Micmac population in the sixteenth century; certainly by 1600 they were aware of being the survivors of a people vastly shrunken in numbers.[16] The proportionate loss on the west coast was probably not as large but Duff, for example, gives a figure for the whole of British Columbia of 70 000 in 1835 and 28 000 fifty years later.[17] In both areas, however, the Indians had enough time to absorb these terrible losses before settlement was upon them. If the settler had been paramount, and not the sea-borne trader, these losses would have gravely weakened the Indian societies.

441

The spread of new disease was the first result of the Europeans' visits to the east coast; then came trade goods; then the missionaries. The priests who came to Acadia presented a direct challenge to spiritual beliefs already undermined by disease, and the newcomers were listened to, since it was assumed that they might provide an explanation of the changes that were occurring. These missionaries had to live on the charity of the Indians for they had no white settlements to turn to: they could not restore their faith in the sanctuary of a colonial church, nor attend to the familiar spiritual needs of fellow-Europeans. Consequently the early missionaries had to understand and in large measure accept the Micmac way of life. There were no "praying villages" where the Indians could be grouped in facsimiles of European society in the name of an assimilation that would paradoxically save them from the vices of Europeans. The purely spiritual impact of the missionaries was further diluted when they acted as highly pragmatic war chiefs leading resistance to Britain in the eighteenth century.[18] There was, of necessity, compromise and a synthesis of ideas and ceremonial evolved into a form of Micmac Christianity that the people could identify with and cleave to as peculiarly their own without doing total violence to their traditional beliefs. This Christianity, being French in origin and militant in practice, continued to form a line of demarcation between Micmacs and English colonists long after the wars were over.

There was no missionary activity on the west coast in the first sixty years of contact. Again, this is partly a matter of timing. The missionary impulse had declined somewhat or diverted itself to other areas of the world. But where there were settlers in nineteenth-century Canada there were also missionaries, no longer going before but with them. The absence of one meant the absence of the other, and this had not been the case in the seventeenth century. The delay in settlement imposed by the trader also delayed those who would destroy the Indian's spiritual world in hopes of his salvation. When settlers arrived on the coast, so did the missionary and so did the "praying village".[19] But at least there had been an intermission during which the Indians had learned to cope with one facet of European culture at a time.

The delay in the settlement of the two coasts was not entirely due to the prominence of the trader: it was also because the areas took a long time to fit into European imperial strategies. Acadia, as it developed in the seventeenth century, was overshadowed by Boston just as mid-nineteenth century British Columbia lived in the shadow of San Francisco and Portland. The southern coasts were staked out first, for there lay natural harbours together with the fertile hinterlands that the more northerly coasts lacked. The English fishing industry, when it required land bases, found them in New England and provided that area with settlers.[20] The French put a few dozen colonists in Acadia and reserved their major effort for the inland area of the upper St. Lawrence safe from marauding navies on the Atlantic shore. Neither France nor Britain had any role for Acadia to play until France constructed the fortress town of Louisburg in the eighteenth century to cover the exposed flank of Canada. The British, eventually, countered with their military town of Halifax. On the west coast, the New Caledonia department of the Hudson's Bay Company was very much a holding operation against Russians and Americans; in terms of the strategy of trade, its function was to guard the southwestern flank of the Mackenzie Valley.[21] Neither coastal area was regarded as of much intrinsic value, but each found a role as protector of distant and far richer territories.

The changes that took place and led to white settlement were fortuitous as in neither case were they based on the inherent capacity of the land to support white families. The founding of Halifax was a military decision backed by £600 000 of public money poured into a neglected corner of the empire in the space of six years. Here indeed was a Nova Scotia "gold rush" of immense proportions, drawing in profit seekers of all descriptions. When the rush passed, it left an exhausted, weak and purposeless colony behind it, but it also left some settlers. The British Columbia gold rushes had the same effect on that colony, and left the same languor in their wake. Nova Scotia was snatched from obscurity by a second fortuitous event, the independence of the United States and the expulsion of 30 000 Americans to the last habitable coastal possession Britain held on the Atlantic.[22] British Columbia waited for a railway, and when that came had to wait all over again for the boom decade that began the twentieth century before settlers came in large numbers.[23] These sudden influxes of population put the Indians in a new light and did so almost instantaneously. The Micmacs had long been enemies of the English, but their defeat had not been a matter of priority. But once Halifax was founded, its military value depended on the British having a firm grip on its landward approaches and the Indians could not be permitted to endanger it any more than could the French. The British moved in families to back up their military forces. In British Columbia the gold rush was quickly followed by the whole paraphernalia of colonial rule, a matter previously of no priority at all: the issuing of land grants, the establishment and enforcement of British law, the creation of volunteer forces for *ad hoc* services against the Indians. Within a year the old inhabitants of the area had passed from being partners in trade to being obstacles to progress.[24]

The events that overwhelmed the Indians followed from the coastal nature of the two areas. When the blow fell, it fell swiftly. Halifax was to be the North Atlantic summer base of the Royal Navy and such it became. The movement of people and material in such quantity and with such rapidity could only have been accomplished by sea transport, and only the quest for naval supremacy could have justified the vast expense. The rapidity of events in British Columbia would also have been impossible without sea access. If gold had been found at Bow River in 1857, for example, the difficulty of getting there would have diffused the impact on the local Indians and left them with some measure of control over the situation. Against the mobility and carrying capacity of European shipping, the coastal Indians had no defence.

Throughout the contact period the coastal Indians were peculiarly vulnerable to sea power. For one thing, control of the sea determined which group of Europeans would ultimately displace them. Even in the late seventeenth century, English shipping dominated the coastal waters of Acadia and made possible the repeated attacks on Port Royal that finally gave the area to Britain. Naval power made it practical to supply land forces over great distances, whether at Halifax or New Westminster. Just as the Royal Navy was the guarantor that Nova Scotia would be British, so too was it the guarantor of a *British* Columbia. The navy was not only for use in great power conflicts; it also had a role to play in "pacifying" the natives. Land-locked Indians might meet white invaders on terms of near military equality, but those on the coast had to be prepared to face floating batteries of cannon and small but well trained landing parties of professional fighters. When the Micmacs attacked a trading post on the Miramichi River, HMS *Viper* proceeded to the spot (under French colours), put out a long-boat (under American colours, for this was during the American Revolution), seized sixteen Indians and carried them off to its next port-of-call, Quebec City. Revolutionary efforts to organise a coalition of Micmacs and Malecites to fight the British disintegrated as another warship, HMS *Vulture* made her leisurely progress up the Saint John River.[25] On the west coast there was a name for this sort of thing: "forest diplomacy". The Royal Navy collaborated with the Hudson's Bay Company and, later,

443

the colonial governments, to keep the Indians in line. When three British deserters were murdered by members of the Newitty tribe near Fort
Rupert in 1850, a corvette was sent to the scene to apprehend the murderers.
A landing party drove the Indians out of their village and set it on fire. A
second expedition returned the following year and again "stormed and
burned" the camp. Royal Navy ships were sent on similar missions against
the Indians until the 1880s.[26]

The coastal Indians were not without their own means of naval action.
The sea-going canoes of the west coast are well known, and the Micmacs
had sea-going capability at least from the beginning of the seventeenth
century. The Micmac canoe was small and not a craft for the open sea;
some may have crossed the narrow waters from Cape Breton to Newfoundland, but if they did, it was more by accident than design. However,
the desire for sea travel was so strong that among the first European
artifacts acquired were shallops (longboats) and the Micmacs were adept at
handling them in their own sea fishery. These boats, oar propelled or
under sail, would have the same range and carrying capacity as the largest
Haida canoe and enabled the Micmacs to ply the coastal waters and
short stretches of open sea. A Micmac settlement at St. George's Bay,
Newfoundland, dates from the 1720s and is the only example of Indian
overseas expansion: it was made possible by the shallop.[27]

Interior Indians defended their hunting grounds, coastal Indians their
fishing sites and shoreline. When Micmacs seized a number of English
fishing boats at Cape Sable in 1715 and held the crews to ransom, they
justified their action by stating that "ye Lands are theirs and they can
make Warr & peace when they please".[28] The shallop was frequently used
against the British, and a formidable enemy it was, especially if the victim
were a two-man fishing dory. A shallop could be mounted with swivel
guns and a crew of well-armed Indians formed a highly mobile strike
force. The British fishing station at Canso fell to amphibious attack in
1720; in July 1722 Micmacs captured eighteen vessels in one coastal sweep
and it required two naval sloops to defeat them. The British took counter-
measures, hiring Wampanoags in whaleboats to terrorize the Micmacs.
But the fisheries were never entirely safe; on at least one occasion a boat
was seized off Newfoundland and sailed back to Cape Breton.[29] Micmac
resistance through the seizure of boats and the killing or capturing of their
crews can be paralleled by similar incidents on the west coast. The Indians
of Clayoquot Sound captured an English ship, the *Kingfisher*, in 1864 and
murdered its crew. Two warships (one aptly named the *Devastation*) were
sent to take the murderers and, in a coastal sweep, killed thirteen Indians
and destroyed nine villages and sixty-four canoes by shellfire.[30] The
British did not waste cannonballs on the flimsy bark wigwams of the
Micmacs, but the west coast longhouses were fixed installations worthy of
their floating batteries.

As the period of trade passed, through the medium of sea power, to the
period of settlement, it is noteworthy that neither coast was acquired from

the Indians by treaty. The interior of British North America was eventually covered by treaties of land cession made in accordance with the royal proclamation of 1763, the coasts never. Inland, the process of consultation, gift-giving and promise-making was regularly performed and recorded with legal formality by government agents. With the slight exception of Governor Douglas's private treaties covering a small portion of Vancouver Island — treaties that formed no precedent for the public acquisition of Indian land — similar procedures never took place on the coasts.[31]

Is this more than just coincidence? The British claimed the land of Acadia by right of cession from France and made no enquiry into the nature of that title. That transfer took place fifty years before the proclamation, but Cape Breton and Prince Edward Island were newly-acquired territories in 1763 and Indian rights there were simply ignored. The British government made no attempt to enlighten the ignorance of successive colonial administrations, and the Indians concerned were too few to be of any account. On the west coast, the poverty of the crown colony and the refusal of the imperial government to expend the British taxpayer's money led to the straightforward seizure of Indian land, a necessity that became a virtue overnight and has remained the law ever since. Such resistance as there was in the early days was put down by naval demonstrations and land forces. It could be argued that the military factors that made it the better part of wisdom to treat with the inland Indians did not apply on coastlines within the range of naval guns, where the British enjoyed as much mobility as the Indians and could bring their forces to bear at will. One warship was worth a dozen forlornly stockaded posts, isolated and incommunicado in the forest wilderness.

445

Land cession treaties in the interior were not simply tokens of a change in ownership; they were the bench marks of a revolution in the use of an area's resources. This change could be plotted, it could be made visible. Not so on the coasts: the forest and the sea would still dominate. When the whites did come to settle and live off the resources of the coastal lands, they found that they had to live within the same bounds as had the Indians. Elsewhere the deciduous trees could be levelled and the prairie grasses ploughed for farmsteads, but not on the coasts. True, the settler's axe rang out, but the farmer remained peripheral to the coastal societies which were as dependent on the forest and the fishery as ever the Indians had been. Europeans replaced Indians as the workforce that exploited these resources. On the prairies, by contrast, settled farmers replaced mobile buffalo hunters as the new people brought a new economy with them. On the coasts, employment remained largely seasonal and therefore casual; periods of intense activity alternated with idleness in a cycle unknown to the pioneer farmer. The transition from Indian to settler economy was to an extent masked by an identity of resources.

The first effect of this identity was to increase tension. Both natives and whites prized the same areas because they prized the same resources. "Indian gardens" in Nova Scotia — cleared sites of traditional camps —

were in the best locations for whites as well; the fishing spots best for one were best for the other; control of the rivers took an additional importance as whites floated logs on them or powered sawmills at the expense of the fish runs. Similarly on the west coast, the prime points of white interest exactly corresponded to the Indians'. In the long run, the Indians of the coasts might have been expected to adapt to a white economy that had a basis familiar to them. While the Micmacs were too few to be important as a labour force, they were to be found in the forest industry of New Brunswick and were especially valued as log drivers on the rivers. They shot porpoises and sold the oil commercially; they fished for profit. They worked in wood and sold their wares to the settlers: barrels, axe handles, and, later, hockey sticks and pit props. Their woven baskets found a steady market, and not just among tourists. They were employed as railway construction workers and stevedores. But they were always marginal workers, and in an economy that was itself increasingly marginal there was little chance for steady employment.[32] On the west coast, Indian labour was the basis of the economy in the first generation of white settlement. The scope of employment was similar: in the forest, on the docks, in the fisheries. Traditional artifacts continued to be made, largely for collectors. New industries such as fish canning employed seasonal labour, more successfully on the west coast than the east. The Indian in a sawmill is a far remove from the artisan who built a longhouse; but possibly not as distant from his ancestor as the buffalo hunter with a hoe in his hand.[33]

446

How far did the coastal fact influence the course of Indian-white relations? The sea-borne approach of Europeans imposed different terms of contact than that of overland settlers, and different terms of power too. The prolonged gap between first contact and significant settlement was not unique to the coasts, for it was the common lot of the prairie Indians. But there the power factor was missing and the whites had no choice but to maintain a minimal presence for two hundred years. On the coasts, the ability to proceed to rapid conquest and rapid settlement lay with the Europeans, if they chose to exercise it. Only with the building of the Canadian Pacific Railway did whites have an equivalent power on the prairies. This power — of mass movement and effective communication with established centres — was not exercised on the coasts until many years had passed. The topography of the two coasts was of prime importance. Being unable to bend the environment to their will, whites directed their colonising efforts to parts of the continent that were more amenable to their ways of family life. Only accident forced settlers on the coastal lands, and then they had to live on the same terms as the Indians.

Notes

1. The standard work on the Micmacs is by the anthropologists W. D. and R. S. Wallis, *The Micmac Indians of Eastern Canada* (Minneapolis, 1955). Alfred G. Bailey, *The Conflict of European and Eastern*

Algonkian Culture 1504–1700 (2nd ed., Toronto, 1969) is an excellent account of the early contact period. The years that follow are examined in L. F. S. Upton, *Micmacs and Colonists: Indian-White Relations in the Maritime Provinces, 1713–1867* (Vancouver, 1979). The best histories of contact along the Pacific coast are Wilson Duff, *The Indian History of British Columbia* (Victoria, 1964) and Robin Fisher, *Contact & Conflict: Indian-European Relations in British Columbia, 1713–1867* (Vancouver, 1977), to whom I am indebted for the title of this article.

2. For speculations about the size of pre-contact populations, see Virginia P. Miller "Aboriginal Micmac Population: A Review of the Evidence", *Ethnohistory* 23 (1976), pp. 117–27.

3. Olive P. Dickason, *Louisburg and the Indians: A Study is Imperial Race Relations, 1713–1760* (Ottawa, 1976).

4. John S. Galbraith, *The Hudson's Bay Company as an Imperial Factor 1821–1869* (Toronto, 1957).

5. Philip Drucker, *Indians of the Northwest Coast* (New York, 1963), p. 3.

6. Wallis, *Micmac Indians*, chs. IV, XI.

7. Bernard G. Hoffman. "The Historical Ethnography of the Micmac of the Sixteenth and Seventeenth Centuries" (PhD thesis, University of California at Berkeley, 1955), pp. 129–32.

8. "For if France . . . is a little terrestrial paradise, art thou sensible to leave it? And why abandon wives, children, relations and friends? Why risk thy life and thy property?" Chrestien Le Clerq, *New Relation of Gaspesia*, edited by W. F. Ganong (Toronto, 1910), pp. 104–5.

9. Bernard G. Hoffman, *Cabot to Cartier* (Toronto, 1961), *passim*.

10. Nicolas Denys, *The Description and Natural History of the Coasts of North America (Acadia)*, edited by W. F. Ganong (Toronto, 1908), pp. 445–6.

11. For example, Galbraith, *Imperial Factor*, pp. 135–7.

12. Marc Lescarbot, *Nova Francia: A description of Acadia*, edited by H. P. Biggar (London, 1928), p. 183; Melville Jacobs, ed., *Texts in Chinook Jargon* (Seattle, 1936).

13. Denys, *Acadia*, p. 442; Calvin Martin, "The European Impact on the Culture of a Northeastern Algonquin Tribe: An Ecological Interpretation", *William and Mary Quarterly*, new ser., 31 (1975), pp. 3–26.

14. Fisher, *Contact*, pp. 20–1.

15. A thesis ably argued in Calvin Martin, *Keepers of the Game: Indian-Animal Relationships and the Fur Trade* (Berkeley, 1978). This book received the 1979 Beveridge Prize of the American Historical Association for the best work on the history of the United States, Canada or Latin America. Anthropologists have criticised it severely.

16. In 1611, Chief Membertou remembered that he had seen Indians, "as thickly planted there as the hairs upon his head". Reuben G. Thwaites, ed., *The Jesuit Relations and Allied Documents* (Cleveland, 1886), I, p. 177.

17. Duff, *Indian History*, p. 39.

18. Micheline Dumont Johnson, *Apôtres ou Agitateurs: La France missionaire en Acadie* (Trois Rivières, 1970).

19. Jean Usher, *William Duncan of Metlakatla* (Ottawa, 1974); Fisher, *Contact*, pp. 132–4.

20. George Rawlyk, *Nova Scotia's Massachusetts* (Montreal, 1973), pp. xiii–xiv.

21. Galbraith, *Imperial Factor*, pp. 9–11.

22. W. S. MacNutt, The *Atlantic Provinces, 1712–1857* (Toronto, 1965), pp. 89–95.

23. M. A. Ormsby, *British Columbia: A History* (Toronto, 1958), pp. 343, 357–9.

24. The swiftness of the transition is emphasised in Fisher, *Contact*, pp. 104–6.

25. Upton, *Micmacs and Colonists*, pp. 75–7.

26. Barry M. Gough, *The Royal Navy and the Northwest Coast of North America* (Vancouver, 1971), pp. 90–3; Gough, "Official Uses of Violence against Northwest Coast Indians in Colonial British Columbia", in James W. Scott, ed., *Pacific Northwest Themes: Historical Essays in Honor of Keith A. Murray* (Bellingham, Washington, 1978), pp. 43–69.

27. The first Micmacs that Marc Lescarbot saw in 1606 were sailing a shallop with great skill. Lescarbot, *Nova Francia*, p. 84: Ralph T. Pastore, "Micmac Colonization of Newfoundland" (paper presented at the annual meeting of the Canadian Historical Association, 1977); Upton, *Micmacs and Colonists*, pp. 1, 64, 157–8.

28. Upton, *Micmacs and Colonists*, p. 40.

29. W.A.B. Douglas, "The Royal Navy and the Canso Station" (typescript): Rawlyk, *Nova Scotia*, pp. 126–32; Upton, *Micmacs and Colonists*, pp. 40–5.

30. Fisher, *Contact*, pp. 168–9.

31. Peter A. Cumming and Neil H. Mickenberg, eds., *Native Rights in Canada* (2nd ed., Toronto, 1972), chs. 12, 17.

32. Philip K. Bock, *The Micmac Indians of Restigouche* (Ottawa, 1966), pp. 42–54; William C. Sayres, ed., *Sammy Louis: The Life History of a Young Micmac* (New Haven, 1966); Upton, *Micmacs and Colonists*, pp. 129–30, 173–4.

447

33. Although the differences were great enough. As Rolf Knight puts it in his *Indians at Work, an Informal History of Native Labour in British Columbia* (Vancouver, 1978), p. 16: "Only the most unregenerate romantic can . . . find no major difference between the occasional tree felling of aboriginal times and . . . commercial logging". See *passim* for Indian adaptations to a white economy: H. B. Hawthorn, C. S. Belshaw and S. N. Jamieson, *The Indians of British Columbia: A Study of Contemporary Social Adjustment* (Toronto, 1958); James Spradley and James Sewid, *Guests Never Leave Hungry: The Autobiography of James Sewid, a Kwakiutl Indian* (Montreal, 1972).

The Character of the British Columbia Frontier*
BARRY M. GOUGH

448

Chief among the concerns of historians studying the founding of new societies has been the concept of the frontier, and in the writing of the history of Canada, the United States, South Africa, Australia and New Zealand, among others, the frontier has been a substantial theme.[1] "Frontier" itself has been variously defined — from the outer fringe of metropolitan influence, to the actual geographical area of control, to a zone to be occupied, to a border between states.[2] Usually such definitions tend to be Eurocentric and agrarian, describing the process of the founding of the new society in question in terms of the expanding society's change in new conditions, its occupations of lands suitable for agriculture, and its evolving legal systems. Often such historical inquiry neglects two essential ingredients: the contact of cultures and races within the zone of influence and the geographical features of the zone itself. By doing so, such studies frequently do violence to the important result of how the aboriginal society already occupying the land and exploiting its resources responded and changed in the face of new circumstances. And such research neglects the role of environment in the historical process.

Our study of the formative years of British Columbia history must, however, concern itself with the frontier, though an enlarged, more encompassing perspective is required than hitherto offered by historians of British Columbia.[3] Such an inquiry cannot be hagiographical in nature but must analyse the institutions and forces whereby British Columbia changed from Indian territory to fur trade realm, then to colony and finally to province all within a brief span of forty years. During the years 1846 to 1871 an imperial tide lapped the shores of the Northwest Coast and in doing so changed the character of human occupation, and it brought with it at the flood new political, legal and social institutions whose legacies are still apparent. This process forms a "frontier" and for the purposes of this paper "frontier" will be taken to mean the zone of influence of imperial administration emanating from London and from the colonial capitals of Victoria and New Westminster. Also for the purposes of this essay "frontier process"

*From *BC Studies*, 32 (1976/77): 28-40. Reprinted by permission.

will be taken to mean the methods by which Europeans extended their jurisdiction, occupied land, managed a resource base, developed an Indian policy,
and established sites for the exploitation of the sea coast and the interior
land mass. The first section of this essay examines environmental determinants, the second explores British and American influences, and the third
provides a summary of the character of the British Columbia frontier and
its legacies.

I

From the earliest European contact with the Northwest Coast, explorers
understood that the nature of the environment would determine the type
of human occupation in that locale. The European reconnaissance of British
Columbia in the late eighteenth century revealed that the environment was
generally devoid of level land suitable for agriculture. Rather they found
a mountainous terrain bordering the Pacific, a land whose scale was impressive, whose physical landscape was varied. Rugged off-shore islands,
inshore channels and inlets, coastal mountains and lowlands, river deltas,
interior plateaus and narrow river valleys testified to the lack of level land
at low elevation. Yet the sea and land provided resources for exploitation
— sea otter and beaver, salmon, timber and spars — and from the very beginning of European contact with this portion of the Northwest Coast the exporting of primary resources formed the central feature of white-Indian trade
relations. Moreover, the potential resource wealth of the region brought international rivalry among Russia, Spain, Britain and the United States, and
by 1846 the present boundaries of British Columbia had been largely determined in this first rush for spoils.[4]

449

The British Columbia frontier properly dates from 1846 for it was in that
year that British sovereignty over the region was determined by Anglo-
American treaty, presumptuously without any compliance on the part of
the Indians who now found that they had new political institutions with
which to deal. That treaty had, the British government hoped, secured a
great fur-trading preserve north of the boundary for the Hudson's Bay Company. The Oregon Boundary dispute had underscored the conflict between
fur trade and settlement on the Pacific slope: its resolution had left the
Americans with lands more suitable for agricultural settlement, and it gave
the British the rich fur preserve of the north.[5] Moreover, the dispute resulted
in the retreat of the Hudson's Bay Company and its agricultural subsidiary,
the Puget's Sound Agricultural Company, north from its Oregon holdings;
and in the process the Company developed new sites of occupation and its
agricultural subsidiary farmed some of the best lands available in Vancouver
Island, then virtually the sole lands known to be suitable for settlement.
Other lands might be available, but in some areas such as Cowichan the
Indians were known to be hostile[6] and in others the availability of scarce
land suitable for tillage was not discovered until the Vancouver Island Ex-

ploration Expedition of 1864. Perhaps in the end it was the mountainous, non-agrarian character of the British Columbia frontier that saved the area from American squatter settlement. Now the Hudson's Bay Company's dominance of the Pacific slope had to be confined within new political boundaries.[7]

Within this area the Hudson's Bay Company had already established a commercial network of posts, trails and shipping routes. In 1843 Fort Victoria had been built as the focal point of Company seaborne commerce, and subsequently Forts Rupert and Nanaimo had been established to mine and market steamer coal. Forts Hope and Yale had been built to provide new transportation links north of the forty-ninth parallel.[8] Fort Langley acquired new importance on the lower Fraser while Port Simpson at the entrance to Portland Inlet became the focal point for northern trade extending to the Queen Charlotte Islands, Alaska and the continental interior.

450

The patterns of resource exploitation, of corporate dominance, and of cluster settlement in and around forts had begun to appear long before miners searched tributaries of the Fraser River in 1858 for gold. The gold seekers, too, had to face environmental realities; the weather and climate were different than in some areas of California they had mined previously. Though on the lower reaches of the Fraser miners could use the "rocker" or "cradle," on the upper Fraser they were obliged to tunnel into the pay-channel lying below the creekbed. In the dry diggings they engaged in sluicing, using quicksilver brought from California. But again, the environment determined that gold extraction would necessitate expensive hydraulic equipment and substantial financial outlay. These features influenced the early demise of the individual miners' rush of 1858-9 and the rise of companies such as the Van Winkle Company that prospered into the 1870s.[9] And not least among the geographical influences was the isolation of the area from California, the eastern seaboard of North America, Europe and Asia — an isolation that determined costs of transportation, slowness of communication, modes of travel, and, for the early settlers, political and social perspectives. Not least, it influenced the character of official response, whether from the imperial or colonial capitals, when a threat to sovereignty within or on the border of British territory seemed real or when "troubles" with Indians in British or adjacent territories threatened the peaceful repose of the settler communities.

Environmental determinants also meant that governments had to put a premium on encouraging means of transportation. Coastal and river navigation had to be made safer by surveys and markers. River channels had to be widened and cleared of debris. New wagon roads beyond the headwaters of sternwheeler navigation had to be built and these required large government outlays that in some cases had to be recovered by a tolls system. And new way stations and administrative systems for a growing colonial bureaucracy had to be built to serve a governmental network that now, in the early 1860s, encompassed the Cariboo within its zone of influence.

By this time also the "heartland" of the region was the Georgia Strait area with its administrative and political leadership extending over a network of rivers and roads into the cordillera.[10] The Cariboo rush of the 1860s and the growth of lumbering on Vancouver Island extended commercial links inland and on the seaboard, and until the Canadian Pacific Railway reached Pacific tidewater and the Panama Canal shortened links with the Atlantic Victoria remained the focus of the region. Vancouver City, important in the diversification of economic activities, was a latter-day corruption on this frontier. A functional unity based around the Fraser — Britain's Columbia, if you will — already existed by 1871.

II

Tempting as it might be to argue that the character of the British Columbia frontier was shaped by environmental realities, such a conclusion would exclude any study of the type of persons who came to British Columbia in its formative years and the form of government and authority emerging as a result of their migration. No sooner had the British government acquired sovereignty to Vancouver Island and continental territory north of the 49th parallel than it set about to establish means of countering the frontier tendencies of Americans.[11] Vancouver Island was established as a colony proper in 1849 to counter the threat of American squatter settlement, and the Hudson's Bay Company was assigned the task of developing a colony under strict regulations. Such a policy intended, at once, to encourage British immigration and to safeguard the interests of the Indians. The Colonial Office exhibited naivety on both counts, but it is important to note here that from the very beginning of settlement, the patterns of land occupation were government-directed.[12] Land by pre-emption was not available at first. Indian land title was alienated only in a few cases. The result was a different type of society than that emerging in adjacent American history.[13]

The second phase of government desires to protect British territory from American interest occurred only a few years later, in 1850 and 1851, when Victoria's political jurisdiction was extended to the Queen Charlotte Islands. London elevated the territory into a colonial territory administered by the Governor of Vancouver Island as a separate Lieutenant-Governorship, and the reason for this was that London intended to protect sovereignty there from "marauders without title."[14] In an age of American filibustering, Britain could take no chances. Gunboats were sent and signs erected in the islands, but the gold of the islands that had attracted five or six American ships out of San Francisco proved insufficient for economical exploitation and the environment proved unattractive to settlers. Nonetheless, an additional territory had been added to the formal British Empire's jurisdiction.

Two similar extensions of the imperial frontier subsequently occurred: first in New Caledonia with the establishment of the Colony of British Columbia in 1858, the second in the Stikine Territory in 1862 when a reorganization of British Columbia's boundaries allowed for the extension of imperial jurisdiction north to 60° North latitude (except to the Alaskan panhandle) and west to include the Queen Charlotte Islands.[15] The union of the colonies of Vancouver Island and British Columbia in 1866 was a natural successor to the administrative growth and consolidation that had gone on since 1849. In short, the means of formal control had been extended within a territory already British in sovereignty, and in every case the government's actions were motivated by a desire to pre-empt American squatter settlement and to protect the interests of the Crown.

Yet at the very same time, what Professor John S. Galbraith has rightly called "the imperial factor" — the Hudson's Bay Company — was fighting a rearguard action change.[16] The Company gave little encouragement to settlement on Vancouver Island. It sought to monopolize gold extraction from the Queen Charlotte Islands. It endeavoured to control means of transportation to the Fraser gold districts. It acted in a similar way during the Stikine rush of 1862. In each case it sought to exploit the resources of British Columbia in its own way as best it could, and it did so in an age when metropolitan and colonial critics of monopoly and of chartered companies — in others words, advocates of free trade — were making themselves heard in London. Indeed, from the very beginning of colonization on Vancouver Island, critics of the restrictive nature of Company control (particularly in land alienation and transportation control) objected to the domineering manner of the Company.[17] The Colonial Office's desire to end the Company's control on Vancouver Island was well advanced by the mid-1850s, and in 1856 the first legislative assembly met in Victoria — the first representative political institution in the Colony. In the following year a British parliamentary inquiry pointed to the end of Company monopoly in New Caledonia, and the Colonial Office was seeking ways of phasing out Company control on the mainland at the very time news reached London of the great rush to the Fraser in 1858. The result this time was a Crown Colony: a formal jurisdiction in which the colonial governor was answerable to London within rather confined limits. Now the governor was solely an imperial representative, and in a series of political moves initiated the Hudson's Bay Company's imperium came to an end. In its place London's authority held sway, more paternalistic than the Company regime and more anxious as time progressed to make the colonies on the Pacific seaboard not only united but self-sufficient and members of a British North American confederation.

By creating British Columbia as a colony proper, the imperial government could increase British executive control because, as the preamble to the 1851 act stated, "it is desirable to make some temporary provision for the Civil Government of such territories, until permanent settlements shall be thereupon established, and the number of Colonists increased...."[18] Self-government was deliberately withheld because the Secretary of State for the Colonies, Sir Edward Bulwer Lytton, thought "the grand principle of free institutions" should not be risked "among settlers so wild, so miscellaneous, perhaps so transitory, and in a form of society so crude."[19] The Undersecretary of State for the Colonies, Herman Merivale, believed that

452

only by providing security for settlers and affording the appropriate political climate could a responsible government free from the factiousness of American politics be fostered.[20] Moreover, central authority would provide trusteeship over the Indians, and prevent "cruelties and horrors that had been perpetrated in the early days of our colonies" and in the western United States.[21] In these respects, the British government devised a form of government that they thought suitable for the circumstances: it was arbitrary government, they admitted, but one in which there could be a relaxation of executive powers with the changing circumstances.[22]

This metropolitan form of control allowed the governor, James Douglas, and the first chief justice, Matthew Begbie, to establish a uniform judicial system throughout the colony. Californians, who formed the large majority of migrants into this frontier, by and large came to respect British law on this far western frontier. The reason for this, Begbie argued, was that the populace had willingly submitted to the powers of the executive — powers which, no matter how contrary to their wishes, were clearly and directly expressed.[23] At the same time Douglas devised a licence scheme (based on a system used in New South Wales in 1851 and the Colony of Victoria, Australia, in 1854) for miners that enabled the government to raise revenue for administration and public works, to keep a record of the number of adventurers entering the gold region, and to provide salaries for law enforcement officers and gold commissioners. Douglas attempted to establish a boat licence whereby the public were to observe the Company's exclusive rights of trade with the Indians, its rights of sole navigation to the mining region and elsewhere within its territories, and its requirement that all non-Company trading vessels possess licences issued by the Company. The Colonial Office declared this proclamation invalid because the Company's monopoly extended only to British trade with the Indians and instructed Douglas that it be removed. However, in the four-month interval that it was in force it alienated miners who rightly saw the governor acting for the private interests of the Company rather than the public interests of the Crown.[24] Another measure of the colonial government to regulate the activities of miners within their jurisdiction, the establishing of mining boards, provided the miners with regulation over the matters they were most concerned with — the size of claims and sluices and the rules for working and holding them. These boards provided a vent for miners' complaints and thus aided the British in their local administration.

In Indian relations as well, the executive exercised the initiative. Its principal aim was to prevent whites and Indians from taking the law into their own hands. Interracial conflict did occur during this critical phase of British Columbia's government, but a show of force was made by the governor, who took pains to explain to persons of both races that British law allowed for the protection of all men regardless of race. He appointed prominent members of Indian tribes as magistrates to keep order among the Indians and appointed justices of the peace at various places on the Fraser River to whom whites and Indians alike could apply for redress of grievance. The

453

governor's diplomacy among Indian peoples was important but the forbearance of the Indians themselves[25] allowed for the peaceful resolution of difference so uncharacteristic of race relations in adjacent American territory.

Certainly Californians who entered British territory objected to the domineering influence of the Company and Crown in British Columbia, but they came to respect the strong role of the executive. They found the boat licence "outrageous." They objected to the tolls of roads. They disliked mining licenses. But they came to respect in British Columbia, as in New South Wales, Western Australia and Victoria, the type of frontier government emanating from an empire that had once ruled their own country. They found the colonial government well managed, void of the graft and corruption of California politics, and contributory to the common good of the populace and the growth of the economy.[26]

There were, however, exceptions to the willingness of Californians to submit to British regulations. Case studies show that some Americans with not a little bravado attempted to violate British regulations in the Fraser River. Others attempted to continue the feuding of California mining camps in British territory. Still others of a criminal nature continued their careers north of the border. Many of them were opposed to British regulations *per se;* they were spirited gold seekers willing to "twist the Lion's tail" if they got the chance.[27] They were individuals bent on fortune, and they did not form a group which might combine to subvert British authority as officials in Victoria and London feared. The United States Consular resident in Victoria, John Nugent, did attempt to marshal American complaints against the colonial government and courts with a view to fostering an annexation movement. But Douglas, in his own defence, prepared a lengthy memorandum for the British government in which he documented how American citizens in British Columbia were treated in a comparable manner to British citizens in California. Subsequently in Washington, D.C., General Lewis Cass, the United States Secretary of State, acknowledged that the regulations prevailing in British Columbia respecting the rights of foreign miners were in fact more liberal than those in force in California. As for Nugent, he was branded as a subversive by British colonial officials who believed that he intended to provoke a filibuster under the guise of protecting Americans from misrule. No such action occurred, Nugent returned to San Francisco, and the only organized American political protest against British rule in the region — a protest by and large the work of one man and without the support of the press — came to an end.[28]

The Nugent case and those of various Americans opposing British law and order tended to underscore the fears of British officials that Americans would indeed subvert the government unless checked by a strong executive authority. It has tended to glorify Douglas and Begbie as guardians of constitutional rights at the expense of ignoring how both had their critics within the ranks of British and Canadian colonists who did not believe that their rights as Englishmen were being protected by an arbitrary government. The birth of the *British Colonist,* a Victoria newspaper, came precisely from this political quarter, and for many years political factions took as their main point of contention the role of the executive in colonial government. The 1858 rush, therefore, had brought important American influences into British territory: influences that authorities feared, and influences which they used to establish strong, centralized administrations to prevent Americans from undermining legal authority.

The British Columbia frontier, then, was a British imperial frontier — a counterfrontier, so to speak, projected from London and Victoria in response to influences and pressures from neighbouring frontiers, particularly from Oregon in the case of Vancouver Island and California in the case of British Columbia. The frontier process occurred in a zone already occupied and exploited by the Hudson's Bay Company, and for a time (particularly on Vancouver Island and for a brief moment in British Columbia) a type of double-image executive authority existed whereby the interest of Company and Crown were often inseparable and often confused. The imperial government, however, forced the clarification of responsibilities between the two. Indeed, the 1858 rush afforded the Colonial Office the opportunity of pressing for full imperial jurisdiction in New Caledonia.[29]

455

This imperial extension of control allowed for the opening up of the colonies by new transportation routes and by settlement of lands hitherto controlled by the Company. These measures were undertaken by government in response to fears that large numbers of Americans and other foreign land or gold seekers might squat on British territory, establish a popular government and drumhead court, invoke their own crude legal remedies for existing lawlessness, and treat Indians in a violent and inhuman way. These inter-related forces — squatter settlement, the filibuster, and lawlessness — became in their own ways material determinants on the British Columbia frontier. They forced colonial and imperial governments to establish regulations, introduce judicial systems, and provide military aid in support of the civil power in order that similar developments could be avoided in British territory.[30] It was precisely the American frontiersman's propensity to manage his own political affairs (in Frederick Jackson Turner's words, "to preserve order, even in the absence of legal authority"[31]) which most disturbed governors of Vancouver Island and British Columbia and a succession of British Colonial Secretaries and Undersecretaries during the course of the timespan considered by this essay. Officials wanted a self-sufficient territory free from American lawlessness, and they responded in a fairly regular and predictable way in the founding of the Colony of Vancouver Island, in the extension of jurisdiction to the Queen Charlotte Islands, in the constituting of the gold colony of British Columbia, and in the extention of boundaries in the Stikine. Government's concerns for securing the boundaries of British Columbia adjacent to the Alaska Panhandle and the Yukon as well as in the San Juan archipelago were merely extensions of government's attempts to secure the outer fringes of the imperial frontier.

In this way the British Columbia frontier was markedly similar to that of the rest of Canada. It was structured, to employ the words of the Canadian economic historians Easterbook and Aitken, in "the interests of a unity threatened by United States' penetration." The American frontier, by contrast, with its security against outside intervention, constituted an expansive, emerging force which greatly accelerated the rate of economic advance."[32] The structured unity of the British Columbia frontier was provided by London, erected on foundations supplied by the Hudson's Bay Company, and made secure by the material means which the British government was able to provide in the form of ships of the Royal Navy and men of the Royal Marines and Royal Engineers. London provided the finance, the manpower, and, not least, the psychological support rendered by the world's pre-eminent nation and empire that made the British Columbia frontier an imperial frontier.

But such metropolitan dominance on this western North American frontier also meant that arbitrary government enjoyed a lingering death; responsible government did not appear until British Columbia joined the Canadian confederation in 1871. Myths of suspected American takeovers continued for some time.[33] The founding fathers of the new colonies, Douglas and Begbie, were lionized at the expense of others such as Richard Blanshard and Amor de Cosmos who fought for more democratic causes. Above all, metropolitan influence tended to reinforce colonial perspectives whereby things British were, as a colonist wrote enthusiastically, "burnished and made the most of!!!"[34] In these ways the metropolitan origins of the British Columbia frontier did much to define the uniqueness of that province in relation to adjacent American states, and, for that matter, to other provinces in Canada or to certain Commonwealth countries. The unique environment of the Pacific slope meant obviously that the founding of a new society in the area now known as British Columbia would be influenced by geographical features, particularly in land occupation, resource extraction and spatial functions of hinterland and metropolis; but the British role in the extension of political jurisdiction and sovereignty, a role undertaken to counter American influences, also shaped the character of the political society emerging in this most distant west.

456

Notes

1. For reviews on the literature on Canadian frontiers, see J.M.S. Careless, "Frontierism, Metropolitanism, and Canadian History," *Canadian Historical Review*, XXXV, I (March 1954), 1-21, and Michael Cross, *The Frontier Thesis and the Canadas: the Debate on the Impact of the Canadian Environment* (Toronto, 1970), pp. 1-7 and pp. 186-88.
2. The typology provided by the frontier thesis of Frederick Jackson Turner as given in his "Significance of the Frontier in American History" (1893) and his *Significance of Sections in American History* (New York, 1932) has long been discredited by American historians. Nonetheless, American frontier experiences still invite comparative studies with adjacent Canadian territories and other former British Empire countries. See the guidelines offered by Paul Sharp, "Three Frontiers: Some Comparative Studies of Canadian, American, and Australian Settlement," *Pacific Historical Review*, XXIV (November 1955), 369-77. The best interpretive work on comparative frontiers in Robin W. Winks,

The Myth of the American Frontier: Its Relevance to America, Canada and Australia (Leicester: The Sir George Watson Lectures, 1971). These suggestive inquiries invite further empirical research.

3. See, for instance, the narrow constitutional approach provided by W.N. Sage in "The Gold Colony of British Columbia," *Canadian Historical Review*, II (1921), 340-59.

4. R.W. Van Alstyne, "International Rivalries in the Pacific Northwest," *Oregon Historical Quarterly*, XLVI (1945), 185-218.

5. The outcome of the dispute also gave both nations access to ports in the lower straits area separating Vancouver Island and the mainland and freedom of navigation there. Norman Graebner, *Empire on the Pacific* (New York, 1955).

6. Eden Colville to Sir John Pelly, 15 October 1849, in E.E. Rich (ed.), *London Correspondence Inward from Eden Colville, 1849-1852* (London: Hudson's Bay Record Society, vol. XIX, 1956), p. 5.

7. Not that the Company could not trade in American territory, but the United States government undertook to indemnify the Company for loss of their property in Oregon, and American politicians were anxious that the removal of the Company be effected as soon as possible. John S. Galbraith, *The Hudson's Bay Company as an Imperial Factor, 1821-1868* (Berkeley and Los Angeles, 1957), ch. 13.

8. The new routes through the Similkameen Country were developed, in part to provide security for Company brigades so that they would not have to travel through the Cayuse Territory where an Indian War was in progress in the late 1840s. Gloria Griffin Cline, *Peter Skene Ogden and the Hudson's Bay Company* (Norman, Oklahoma, 1974)

9. H.A. Innis and A.R.M. Lower, eds., *Select Documents in Canadian Economic History, 1783-1885* (Toronto, 1933), pp. 771-77, 780-90, and W.J. Trimble, *The Mining Advance into the Inland Empire* (Madison, Wisconsin, 1914).

10. J. Lewis Robinson and Walter G. Hardwick, *British Columbia: One Hundred Years of Geographical Change* (Vancouver, 1973), p. 12.

11. W.P. Morrell, *Colonial Policy in the Age of Peel and Russell* (Oxford, 1930), pp. 444-46.

12. Land alienation was partially based on the theories of Edward Gibson Wakefield, whereby land was fixed at the "sufficient price" of £1 per acre. Land prices later were reduced in efforts to encourage colonization.

13. The bailiff system attempted to introduce established society and deferential relationships into the Vancouver Island colony. Partially successful (though in a very small way), it tended to encourage the idea of a landed gentry in the Victoria area.

14. James Doublas to Earl Grey, 29 January 1852, C.O. 305/3, Public Record Office, London; Lord Malmesbury to Admiralty, 23 June 1852, Admiralty Correspondence, I, Provincial Archives of British Columbia, Victoria.

15. W.E. Ireland, "Evolution of the Boundaries of British Columbia," *British Columbia Historical Quarterly*, III (October 1939), 263-82.

16. Galbraith, *Hudson's Bay Company*, passim.

17. Governor Douglas' identification with the Company was so strong that independent colonists tried to short-circuit imperial communications by sending delegations and petitions to London. During the Parliamentary Inquiry into the Company's affairs in 1857 the same critics were able to make their complaints known to the government.

18. Great Britain, Statutes at Large, 21 and 22 *Vic.*, c. 99.

19. Great Britain, *Hansard's Parliamentary Debates*, 3rd ser., 151 (1858), 1102.

20. These views are set forth in E. Bulwer Lytton to Colonel Moody, 29 October 1858, C.O. 60/3. See also Merivale's article in *The Edinburgh Review*, CVII (April 1858), 295-321.

21. Hansard, 3d ser., 151 (1858), 2102.

22. *Ibid.*, 1769.

23. M.B. Begbie, "Journey into the Interior of British Columbia," *Journal of the Royal Geographical Society*, 3, (1861), 248.

24. F.W. Howay in F.W. Howay, W.N. Sage and H.F. Angus, *British Columbia and the United States* (Toronto and New Haven, 1942), p. 147.

25. Indians have argued that the peace on the frontier was owing to their forbearance and willingness to allow whites "to use that country on equal terms with ourselves." One tribe, the Couteau, "saved the country from war when the Indians were about to combine and drive out the Whites." Evidence of Chief John Tedlenitsa of the Couteau tribe, in deputation to Sir Wilfrid Laurier, 27 April 1916, in Borden Papers, MG 26 H 1(a), vol. 38, pp. 16394-5, Public Archives of Canada.

26. W.E. Ireland, ed., "Gold Rush Days in Victoria, 1858-1859," *British Columbia Historical Quarterly*, XII (July 1948), 241. Also, Rodman W. Paul, "'Old Californians' in British Gold Fields," *Huntington Library Quarterly*, XVII (1954).

27. Barry M. Gough, "Keeping British Columbia British: The Law-and-Order Question on a Gold Mining Frontier," *ibid.*, XXXVIII (1975), 269-80.

28. R.L. Reid, "John Nugent: The Impertinent Envoy," *British Columbia Historical Quarterly*, VIII (1944), 53-76.

457

29. John S. Galbraith, "Bulwer-Lytton's Ultimatum," *The Beaver,* Outfit 268 (Spring 1958), 20-24.
30. On the question of military support for the civil power, see Barry M. Gough, "'Turbulent Frontiers' and British Expansion: Governor James Douglas, The Royal Navy and the British Columbia
Gold Rushes," *Pacific Historical Review,* XLI (1972), 15-32.
31. Turner's statement is quoted in H.C. Allen, *Bush and Backwoods: A Comparison of the Frontier in
Australian and the United States* (East Lansing, Mich., 1959), p. 101.
32. W.T. Easterbrook and H.G.J. Aitken, *Canadian Economic History* (Toronto, 1958), p. 356.
33. W.N. Sage, "The Annexationist Movement in British Columbia," *Proceedings and Transactions of
the Royal Society of Canada,* ser. 3, vol. 21 (1927), sec. II, 97-110.
34. Quoted in M.A. Ormsby, *British Columbia: A History* (Toronto, 1958), p. 107.

Topic Fourteen
Why Was Confederation Accepted?

Union of British North America had been considered as far back as 1790, but never achieved. A renewed interest arose in the 1850s when increased tension between British North America and the United States, and the emerging political deadlock in the Canadas, made the option of a larger colonial union attractive. While union did not come about at this time, these preliminary discussions — as Donald Creighton points out in ''The United States and Canadian Confederation'' — served as a ''dress-rehearsal'' for what actually would occur five or six years later.

In the mid-1860s the right conditions prevailed for the politicians of the Canadas, New Brunswick and Nova Scotia to bring about Confederation. The details of union were worked out at two important conferences in 1864. At the Charlottetown conference, the delegates agreed in principle on a number of the important features of the eventual federation: the regional representation of the upper house (Senate), and ''representation by popula-tion'' in the lower house (House of Commons). They also arrived at the nature of the division of powers between provincial and federal governments. A second conference at Quebec — October 1864, only one month later, finalized these understandings in the Seventy-two Resolutions. Between 1864 and 1867, the politicians worked to convince their respective colonial assemblies to adopt Confederation.

In Canada West, support for the proposals was widespread. Confedera-tion was seen as a solution to the perennial problem of political deadlock. Moreover, an economic union would work to the advantage of the Canada West, as the largest province and the most commercially advanced. Union would also provide increased protection of the inland province at a time of an acute American military threat. Canada West would also benefit from the eventual expansion of the new nation across the continent, particularly into the North West.

Elsewhere, however, the Confederation idea met with great opposition. The two islands, Newfoundland and Prince Edward Island — which looked eastward, not westward — rejected it. Nova Scotia, too, opposed the scheme, and only Tupper kept the issue alive. In New Brunswick sentiments were decidedly mixed. In Canada East, as Jean-Charles Bonenfant describes in "The French Canadians and the Birth of Confederation," the anti-Confederate Rouge Party under Antoine-Aimé Dorion, strongly opposed Confederation.

In light of such opposition to Confederation, several questions come to mind: why was there such urgency to establish a British North American federation? To what extent did the haste to form the union contribute to regional divisions and misunderstandings?

Many excellent books exist on the subject of British North American federation. A good starting point is Donald Creighton's *The Road to Confederation* (Toronto: Macmillan, 1964). W.L. Morton's *The Critical Years, 1857-1873* (Toronto: McClelland and Stewart, 1968), is also extremely useful. A lively account of the confederation movement in the Canadas and the Atlantic region is P.B. Waite's *The Life and Times of Confederation, 1864-1867* (Toronto: University of Toronto Press, 1962). P.B. Waite has edited the original debates in the United Canadas in *The Confederation Debates in the Province of Canada, 1865* (Toronto: University of Toronto Press, 1967). *Confederation*, edited by Ramsay Cook (Toronto: University of Toronto Press, 1967) contains important articles on the subject, including the essay on New Brunswick by Alfred G. Bailey, "The Basis and Persistence of Opposition to Confederation in New Brunswick." A full account of the Maritime colonies' position toward federation appears in William Menzie Whitelaw's *The Maritimes and Canada Before Confederation* (Toronto: Oxford University Press, 1966; first published in 1934). J.M.S. Careless's *Brown of the Globe* (Toronto: Macmillan, 1963) Volume 2 and Donald Creighton's *John A. Macdonald:* Volume 1 *The Young Politician* (Toronto: Macmillan, 1952) review the ideas and the important role of these leading figures in the Confederation movement. A recent article on the background to Confederation is Ged Martin's "Launching Canadian Confederation: Means to Ends, 1836-1864," *The Historical Journal*, 27, 3 (1984): 575-602.

460

The United States and Canadian Confederation*
D. G. CREIGHTON

In the next decade both the United States and Canada will face an impressive succession of important centenaries. On April 12, 1961, it will be a hundred years since the Confederate bombardment opened upon Fort Sumter

*From *Canadian Historical Review*, 39 (1958): 209-222. Reprinted by permission of the University of Toronto Press. Originally given as a lecture at the University of Chicago, February, 1958.

in Charleston harbour. On June 22, 1964, it will be a century since a coalition Government of Reformers and Liberal-Conservatives took office in the Province of Canada with the declared intention of establishing a general federal union of the whole of British North America. Between these two events — the Civil War in the United States and the federation of British North America — there exists an interesting relationship which I should like to explore with you tonight. It is an important, but also a complex, imprecise, and ambiguous relationship; and it seems to me that there might be more enlightenment in approaching its analysis circuitously than directly. These two famous dates and the national dramas which they recall and commemorate will therefore, for the moment, be set aside; and we can go back a little in time. There is an earlier episode in Canadian history, which could be most appropriately examined on this occasion, for its centenary will be reached, though certainly not enthusiastically celebrated, during the summer of 1958. It is an episode much less well known than the foundation of the coalition Government and the declaration of the coalition Government's purpose in June of 1864; but, for all that, it has its own real significance. And an examination of it may throw some light upon the curious relationship between the American Civil War and the federal union of British North America, upon the influence of the United States on Canadian Confederation.

461

In the summer of 1858 — it was in August, to be precise — the government of the Province of Canada came to a momentous decision. It was, in itself, an important decision, and it was much more important simply because it was the Province of Canada which had reached it. In 1858, the province was only a little over fifteen years old, for it had been formed in 1841 by the union of the two older and smaller provinces of Upper and Lower Canada; but already, in size, ambition, political consequence, and political influence, it was clearly the "empire province" of British North America. From the Gulf of St. Lawrence, it extended westward along the whole long line of the great river and the Great Lakes. On the south, its limit was the international boundary between British North America and the United States; to the north, its frontier was that highly uncertain, vaguely defined line which bounded Rupert's Land, the chartered territories of the Hudson's Bay Company. The other British provinces — Nova Scotia, New Brunswick, Prince Edward Island, and Newfoundland in the east, and Vancouver Island and British Columbia in the far west — were undeniably dwarfed in importance by the Province of Canada. Canada was more prosperous than any of them. Canada was more populous than all of them put together.

It was all true, as the other colonies somewhat enviously admitted; but it was also true that the "empire province" was a socially turbulent and politically agitated community, and that the division between its French-speaking and English-speaking citizens had created a cultural cleavage far more serious than existed elsewhere in the North American Empire. The other northern provinces regarded Canada with a measure of doubt and distrust. The eyebrows of sober Nova Scotians, in particular, were lifted often in pained disapproval at its erratic course. It was always in the throes of some political crisis or other; its citizens were invariably at each other's throats; and it had the highly reprehensible habit of breaking its word in cheerful disregard of the interest of the rest of British North America. Its whole record, in fact, was simply deplorable. And yet, the unwelcome but inescapable fact was that Canada counted. However violent its actions and however incomprehensible its purposes, they had to be taken seriously. And once again, during the agitated summer of 1858, the Canadian government had given the other provincial administrations considerable food for thought. On August 16, when, after a long and turbulent session, the Governor, Sir Edmund Head, finally prorogued the session of the Canadian legislature, he made a brief formal announcement of the policy which his new Government intended to follow. "I propose in the course of the recess," he told the Houses, "to communicate with Her Majesty's Government, and with the Governments of the sister Colonies, on another matter of very great importance. I am desirous of inviting them to discuss with us the principles on which a bond of a federal character, uniting the Provinces of British North America, may perhaps hereafter be practicable."

What happened? What had persuaded this most important of British American governments to adopt, as its declared policy, the plan of a British American federal union? Long before this, of course, British governors and high commissioners, colonial statesmen, authors, and public speakers had been talking and writing about federal union; but until Governor Head made his famous announcement on the afternoon of August 16, 1858, the whole question had remained almost entirely academic. Why did George E. Cartier and John A. Macdonald, the leaders of the Canadian Administration, decided to commit themselves to an ambitious policy which no other British American government had ventured to espouse before? Nearly six years later, on June 22, 1864, another Canadian Government, as we have already seen, was to make another open profession of faith in a federal plan and, after an interval, was to succeed in carrying it out. Yet these two general declarations of purpose are very similar; and at first sight, the occasion, if not the cause of both of them seem very much alike. Each appears to have arisen out of the chronic weakness and instability of Canadian politics.

The fact was that the Canadian union of 1841 had been formal, not real. In theory, the province was a unitary state; in fact, it was an unacknowledged federal system. Its two sections, Canada East and Canada West, the one largely French and the other overwhelmingly English, were united economically by the St. Lawrence transport system and divided socially by their two contrasting cultural inheritances. They had found it impossible to live apart as the separate provinces of Upper and Lower Canada; they were finding it almost equally difficult to live together as the two divisions of a single government. It was true, of course, that the Union Act had itself helped to make these difficulties almost insuperable. By its terms, Canada East and Canada West had been given equal representation in the provincial legislature, irrespective of population; and this political equality tended to harden the sectional division of the province and to exacerbate its inevitable cultural misunderstandings. The cabinet and several of the important departments of government were organized on a sectional basis. Much of the legislation that was passed had to be sectional in character; and the political parties, although they tried, of course, to win a following in both French- and English-speaking Canada, had an irresistible tendency to become strong in one section of the province and correspondingly weak in the other. They tended also, as a natural consequence, to reach a level of approximate political equality; and thus the public affairs of the province were characterized both by a permanent state of sectional conflict and a persistent condition of political instability.

During the summer of 1858 this chronic political unsettlement reached a sudden, sharp crisis; and it was this crisis which provided the occasion for the Cartier-Macdonald Government's dramatic announcement of its adoption of the federal plan. Earlier in the session, the Assembly had been discussing the constitutional problem which lay at the root of its sectional difficulties. The Assembly was always discussing the constitutional problem. It was always anxiously reviewing a number of contradictory proposals for constitutional reform — including federal schemes — which, it was argued, would remove the province from the inveterate embarrassments of sectionalism; and this painfully familiar exercise was barely over, when there occurred an episode which was, in effect, a preposterous, almost ludicrous, illustration of the political stalemate which everybody was so anxious to end. It origins were simple and absurdly characteristic of the province's real nature. The political crisis of the summer of 1858 arose out of the endless and agonizing problem of deciding where the capital of this politically united but sectionally divided province was to be.

463

Ever since the union in 1841, this question had been arousing the most acrimonious dissention. Originally, the seat of government had been fixed at Kingston in Canada West; it had then been transferred to Montreal, in Canada East — a distinctly unfortunate removal, as it turned out, for a few years later, in 1849, the enraged Montreal Conservatives burnt the Parliament Buildings to the ground. For some time after this disgrace, the attempt to find a permanent capital was tacitly abandoned; and the seat of government alternated, at intervals, between Quebec, which was the old capital of Lower Canada, and Toronto, which was the old capital of the upper province. Every few years, the cabinet ministers and a small army of civil servants, together with great masses of official records, government furniture, and personal effects, were laboriously transported, up or down the river valley, in trains and steamships, to their new political headquarters. It is hardly surprising that everybody in politics found these fairly regularly recurring removals an intolerable nuisance; and in 1857 John A. Macdonald had hit upon what was thought to be a most ingenious method of securing permanence. Queen Victoria was invited to name a permanent capital for the united province; and Queen Victoria, duly but privately advised from

Canada, decided in favour of a little backwoods town, some distance up the Ottawa River, once called Bytown and now Ottawa.

Ottawa had the advantage of a location on the west bank of the river which formed the boundary between the two sections of the province; but it was definitely in Canada West. Still more obviously, it was neither Quebec nor Montreal; and the French-Canadians in the legislature, even though the great majority of them were members of the Conservative party which had referred the problem to the Queen for final decision, regarded the choice of Ottawa with the darkest disapproval. It was always possible, on a question of such enormous sectional prestige, to persuade some of them, at least momentarily, to forswear their Conservative allegiance; and this was exactly what happened on July 28, 1858. An address to the Queen on the subject of the capital was under consideration. An amendment, declaring flatly that Ottawa ought not to be the permanent seat of government was deliberately moved by the opposition. A small, but sufficient bloc of French-Canadian votes changed sides, and the Government was defeated on this issue.

Macdonald and Cartier decided to resign; and George Brown, the leader of the Liberal Opposition, accepted the Governor's invitation to form a new Government. What followed is of considerable interest in the law and custom of parliamentary institutions in the British Commonwealth. The political crisis of the summer of 1858 anticipates, in some measure, though the circumstances were widely different, the much more famous Canadian constitutional crisis of the summer of 1926 and even finds a faint echo in the speculations and discussions which went on for some time in Canada after the general election of June, 1957. Our concern here, however, is not with constitutional issues as such, but with the political instability which resulted in part from the defective constitution of the Province of Canada. Rapidly it became apparent that Brown and his associate French-Canadian leader,, Dorion, were in a much more precarious position in the Assembly than their predecessors, Macdonald and Cartier, had ever been. The French-Canadian opponents of Ottawa as the Canadian capital would quickly, if sheepishly, return to the Conservative fold; and, by the law as it then stood, George Brown, Dorion, and the other new ministers would be obliged, on accepting office under the Crown, to resign their seats in parliament and to seek re-election. With numbers so seriously reduced in such an evenly divided Assembly, the new Government would not be able to meet the inevitable want-of-confidence motion; and Brown, with failure staring him in the face, requested the Governor to grant him a dissolution of Parliament. The request was declined; and on August 4, after having held office for only two days, the Brown-Dorion Administration, "Her Majestys most ephemeral government," as the Conservatives derisively called it, was obliged to resign, and Macdonald and Cartier were back in power once more.

The crisis had not lasted a long time; it had begun on July 28, and it ended, with the installation of the old ministers, on August 6. Yet this sort of period of fewer than ten days had provided an almost grotesque illustration of the political instability and futility which was sectionalism's evil gift to the Province of Canada. The Conservative ministers did not, of course, admit that the episode had taught them a lesson — their own triumphant return to office precluded any such embarrassing avowal; but, at the same time, their subsequent actions proved only too clearly that they had now decided to escape, if possible, from the existing state of affairs. Up to this time, it had been the Liberals or Reformers, not the Conservatives, who had kept suggesting solutions for the sectional problem — who had kept pointing out possible exits from the constitutional impasse in which the province found itself. Now, for the first time, the Conservatives took their stand also upon a new policy. For a colony such as Canada, whose two sections could not afford to be separated and did not want to be too closely united, what could be more suitable than a federal form of government? On August 7, the day after the Ministry was formed, Cartier briefly alluded to the new policy, and on August 16, when he prorogued Parliament, Head formally committed his cabinet to the federal scheme.

465

II

Undoubtedly the political crisis of the summer of 1858 had precipitated the Canadian Conservatives' adoption of the plan of a general British North American federal union. A way out of the political deadlock of sectionalism had been proved to be peremptorily necessary; and a federal union was surely the solution best calculated to preserve the essential character of the Province of Canada. Yet what kind of a federal union? Why had Macdonald and Cartier declared themselves in favour of a comprehensive scheme which would embrace not only all the Maritime Provinces but also, at some future date, the enormous territories of the British north-west? Why had they not been content with the project of converting Canada into a federation of two provinces? This second, smaller plan, which was actually adopted a year later by the Reform party as its policy, was a much more manageable enterprise. It could have been carried out by Canada herself, at her own convenience, and without the slightest reference to the other colonies. Yet this was not the plan which the Conservative party adopted. Instead it had accepted a vastly more ambitious, vastly more difficult undertaking, which could only be completed with the concurrence of four other colonial governments. Why? The urgent necessity of finding a solution for sectional problems is not a satisfactory explanation, for the sectional problem could have been solved just as effectively, and much more expeditiously, by "applying the federal principle," as contemporaries called it, to the Province of Canada alone. What were the other purposes and intentions which lay behind Macdonald's decision? Why had he and his colleagues conceived the grandiose design of a transcontinental British North American federation?

Now it is quite obvious that Canada, in contrast with the Maritime Provinces, had always held to a tradition of western empire. The Maritime Provinces — New Brunswick, Prince Edward Island, and, above all, Nova Scotia and Newfoundland — had grown up in a world in which the three words, "ships, colonies, and commerce" formed the indissoluble principles, the virtual "holy trinity," of empire. The dominion in which, on the whole, they had been so comfortably adjusted, was an oceanic dominion; but the empire which Canada had sought to achieve through the centuries had been essentially continental in character. From the days of the French explorers onward, all the political and commercial leaders of the community of the St. Lawrence valley had tried to make the Great River and its Great Lakes the basis of an enormous inland empire. The peace treaty of 1783, which cut a line, at that time artificial and almost meaningless, through the centre of this vast region, had transferred its south-west sector to the United States; and it was these tragic losses on their left flank which helped to impel the Montreal fur traders, the real westerners of the period, into the territories north-west of Lake Superior. Here, in a region which could still be made good for the British Empire, the great trader-explorers of the North West Company, Alexander Mackenzie, David Thompson, and Simon Fraser, drove the fur trade across the prairies and through the mountains to the ocean. They clinched the claims of Cook and Vancouver; they helped to give British North America its wide open window on the Pacific. But the terrible struggle with the Hudson's Bay Company, of which these western exploring enterprises were only a part, had exhausted the North West Company; and in 1821 it virtually capitulated to its great rival. From then on, the Hudson's Bay Company held the north-west quarter of the continent in trust for the future Kingdom of Canada; and for a generation the provinces on the St. Lawrence almost forgot their traditional western empire.

Then, fairly suddenly and without much warning, Canadian interest in the region beyond Lake Superior began to revive. The date of the revival is highly significant, for it began just about eighteen months before the Conservatives adopted their federal scheme in the summer of 1858; and this near coincidence in time suggests that, in matters other than its sectional and constitutional problems, the Province of Canada was reaching a species of crisis in its development. It had, in fact, come nearly to the limit of its possibilities of expansion in the circumstances of the moment, and this at the very time when the rule of the Hudson's Bay Company in the north-west was becoming increasingly uncertain and precarious. There was no longer an agricultural frontier in Canada West, for the good lands south of the Precambrian Shield had all been occupied. There was no real prospect of acquiring the bulk of the trade of the international North American west, for the St. Lawrence was obviously losing in its struggle with the American Atlantic ports. The expansive energies of Canada were being held back in frustration and defeat; but far to the north-west, beyond Lake Superior, was an immense and empty territory which lay waiting for both agricultural settlement and commercial exploitation. Why should not the Province of Canada acquire these lands for its own and British North America's good? Why should it not take over from a moribund seventeenth-

466

century commercial company whose chartered claims were fraudulent, whose rule was baneful, and whose feeble authority was quite incapable of protecting the north-west from encroachment?

Macdonald and his colleagues looked both eagerly and dubiously upon the domain of the Hudson's Bay Company. They were both fascinated and frightened by the thought of acquiring Rupert's Land and the North-west Territories. Inside Canada itself, the popular impulses towards its annexation were very strong; and their strength was powerfully increased by pressures in the same direction which came from outside through both the United Kingdom and the United States. There was no doubt at all that Great Britain was anxious to make new arrangements which would enable her to cut her commitments and reduce her contingent liabilities in North America. In 1857, two years before the Hudson's Bay Company's trading licence was to expire, the British government sponsored a parliamentary committee to consider the state and prospects of Rupert's Land; and although the committee's report made simply a guarded and general recommendation in favour of Canadian settlements in suitable parts of the Red and Saskatchewan valleys, it was quite plain that the imperial government was eager to have Canada take over the responsibility for the north-west.

467

Yet even this was not all. To the spur of British encouragement was added the stimulus of American rivalry. Canada was determined, sooner or later, to acquire Rupert's Land; the United Kingdom was anxious to arrange a secure British North American future for Rupert's Land; and finally, for both British and Canadians, the irrepressible fear that the United States might succeed in forestalling them lent an additional urgency to their plans for Canadian expansion. This fear was, of course, simply a new western variant of a much older fear, which went back as far as 1775 when, nearly a year before they declared their independence, the Thirteen Colonies launched an attack on Quebec. The armed occupation of Quebec in 1775-6 and the repeated American invasions of the War of 1812 had bred in the British colonies the unshakeable conviction that the United States was the one real threat to their survival on the North American continent. The events which had occurred in the forty years since the Peace of Ghent had, in the main, confirmed rather than qualified this view. At every moment of trouble in British North America, on every occasion of dispute between the United Kingdom and the United States, the threat of American intervention or American attack returned. Only two years before, in 1856, the Crimean War had brought a brief renewal of the old danger. The Nova Scotian, Joseph Howe, with some encouragement and assistance from J.F.T. Crampton, the British Minister at Washington, attempted to secure recruits for the Crimea from among the currently unemployed in the republic. This childishly inept and foolhardy venture was discovered in due course; it was described, a little grandiloquently, by the American Administration as "an act of usurpation against the sovereign rights of the United States." Crampton's recall was demanded; the American newspapers fulminated in indignation. And all this occurred, as similar dangers had occurred so often in the past, when the size of the British garrisons in the northern colonies had been sharply reduced and when Great Britain's hands were tied with a war in Europe.

The fear was an old one, frequently renewed. And now it had taken on a new shape and found a fresh expression. The survival of the existing colonies in a continent dominated by the United States was still not entirely certain; but far more uncertain was British North America's acquisition of the north-west and its expansion to the Pacific Ocean. Would the transcontinental dominion, of which people were already dreaming, ever become a triumphant reality? The Convention of 1818 and the Washington Treaty of 1856 had settled the international boundary, at least on paper; but might not the hard, solid facts of human occupation determine it ultimately in a quite different fashion? There were only three tiny British American communities in the whole north-west — at Red River, on Vancouver Island, and on the mainland of British Columbia; and the tide of American frontier settlement, the network of the American communication systems, were creeping steadily closer to them with every year that passed. Minnesota became a state in 1858, Oregon was to follow in 1859. Hudson Bay had ceased to be the sole centre of the Hudson's Bay Company's transport system; and the Red River settlement was becoming an economic outpost of St. Paul, just as the Pacific colonies were becoming economic outposts of San Francisco.

468

All this was part of the speculations of informed Canadians in the summer of 1858. All this was inevitably present in the minds of Macdonald and his fellow ministers when they decided to adopt the policy of a general British North American federation. The sectional crisis in the Province of Canada had led them to the idea of federal union; but the shape and scope which they gave to their federal plan had been determined with a view to British North America as a whole. They were eager, not only to reconstruct the constitution of a province, but also to lay the foundations of a nation; and they were convinced that this was the only way in which a transcontinental nation in the northern half of North America could be built. Union with the Maritime Provinces was essential to secure the future nation's Atlantic frontage; but union with the Maritime Provinces was almost equally necessary to provide a base broad and strong enough to support the acquisition of the northwest. Alone, the Province of Canada might not have been sufficiently powerful to bear the responsibility; and even if she had been willing to try, the basic division between her French- and English-speaking citizens would almost certainly have prevented her from making the attempt. Even if only a part of Rupert's Land and the North-west Territories had been added to the united province, the addition would simply have emphasized the already existing preponderance of Canada West. It would probably have forced the adoption of representation by population and led to the abandonment of sectional equality in the provincial legislature. It would, in the eyes of French Canadians, have seriously threatened their distinctive culture; and the union might have broken apart in fear and anger.

British North American federation would prevent all this. British North

American federation could transform a provincial crisis into a national triumph. It would provide a framework in which French-Canadian culture would be given the protection of provincial status and in which Rupert's Land and the North-west Territories could be gradually organized as they developed. Only in this fashion, in all probability, could a transcontinental nation be created; and the potential strength of transcontinental nationhood would perhaps alone suffice to ensure the survival of British North America.

III

As one looks back, over the intervening century, at the events of the summer of 1858, one cannot help but be impressed by their prophetic significance in Canadian history. As one regards those three years from 1856 to 1859, one feels almost a sense of astonishment at the closeness of their resemblance to another, much more famous three years which began with the formation of the coalition Government in 1864 and ended with Canadian Confederation in 1867. It is almost as if the period from 1856 to 1859 could be looked upon as a preliminary experiment, a species of dress rehearsal, for successful federal union. Many of the actors have already taken their positions on the stage; some of those with star parts are already clearly discernible. And, as one reads over the letters and memoranda in which the Canadians tried to explain their federal plan to the British Colonial Office during the autumn of 1858, one gets the distinct impression that the dialogue is taking shape and that some of the very best lines have already been written. The situations in the years 1856-9 seem vaguely to anticipate those of 1864-7; and the two plots have an odd family relationship as if, at least, they had been contrived by the same author. The scenery in both cases is identical — a few small, underpopulated, staple-producing provinces, set in the howling wilderness of half a continent, with somewhere in the background, lurking menacingly in the shadow, that sinister villain of all Canadian dramas, the United States.

469

And yet the dress rehearsal of 1856-9 was not the immediate prelude to a real production. The famous announcement of the summer of 1858 had no direct consequences, while the declared purpose of the summer of 1864 was achieved three years later in Canadian Confederation. How is the success of the one and the failure of the other to be explained? The two episodes lie before us, implying contrasts, inviting comparisons; and one is inevitably tempted to use that method, regarded so fondly by sociologists in general and logical positivists in particular, and, in my opinion at least, so properly distrusted by historians. If we embark on an exercise in the comparative method, we shall probably not discover a general law about movements towards federal union, or even, to narrow the field very sharply indeed, about Canadian movements towards federal union. We may discover that the apparent resemblance between these two examples of the same historical species is a superficial resemblance, observable only from the outside; and that, on closer examination from the inside, the two episodes will turn out to be two separate and quite distinct cases.

One important contrast emerges immediately when one compares the purely parliamentary events of July and August, 1858, with those of June, 1864. The rapidly changing political situation of the summer of 1858 certainly provided a much better illustration of the governmental instability which sectionalism had brought to the Province of Canada. The constitutional crisis of 1858 was far more dramatic than that of 1864. And yet — and this, surely, is the important point — its parliamentary consequences were a good deal less significant. The federal plan of 1858 was adopted by a Conservative Administration; but it was a coalition Government of Conservatives and Reformers, commanding a large majority in the House and formed with the express purpose of attempting constitutional reform, which, in June, 1864, announced that it would seek a federal union of the whole of British North America. There was a good deal of truth in the charge of one of the officials in the Colonial Office that in 1858 the Confederation issue was still in ''a crude state of party politics.'' By 1864 it had been lifted out of the crude state of party politics; and both parties, and all but a small minority of the House, had agreed to end a situation from which everybody had suffered.

The agreement of the Canadian parties was not the only new factor in the situation. The attitude of the United Kingdom had altered in an important and striking fashion in the short period of six years. It was true, of course, that Great Britain's major objectives in the north remained fundamentally much the same. Labouchere and Bulwer-Lytton, the Colonial Secretaries of the late 1850s did not differ materially in purpose from Cardwell and Carnarvon who held office at the time of Canadian Confederation. All of them wished equally to cut British commitments in North America; all of them hoped to persuade the colonies in general, and the Province of Canada in particular, to assume a larger part of the responsibility of government in the new world. Here they were agreed; but Cardwell and Carnarvon realized, as Bulwer-Lytton most emphatically did not, that a British North American federal union would be of immense assistance in achieving these purely imperial objectives. The temperamental Bulwer-Lytton, who, one sometimes suspects, carried the melodrama of his romances into the conduct of the Colonial Office, was at one and the same time hotly insistent that Canada should take over Rupert's Land and the North-west Territories, and coldly discouraging to the plan of federal union. It was Cardwell and Carnarvon, not Bulwer-Lytton, who understood the essential connections between the west and Confederation. It was Cardwell and Carnarvon who sensibly realized that if Great Britain wished to get rid of some of the burdens in North America, she must help to found a British American state which was strong enough to bear them. From the moment when the new Confederation scheme was first broached in 1864, Cardwell, and later Carnarvon, supported it with conviction and vigour.

British encouragement was much stronger in 1864 than it had been in

1858. And so also, in the eyes of Canadians, was pressure from the United States. The increasing weight of this negative influence, of which British Americans were becoming more and more anxiously conscious during the early 1860s, is attributable largely to the American Civil War. The danger of the encroachment of American settlement and exploitation on the tiny British outposts in the northwest was much as it had been a few years before; it may, indeed, have been developing a little more slowly, as a result, in part, of the republic's concentration on its own desperate domestic struggle. But there was no real reason for assurance here; and there was much cause for disquiet elsewhere. The special peril which threatened Rupert's Land and the new colonies on the Pacific coast might not have increased very noticeably; but the general danger facing British North America as a whole was greater than any of its citizens then living could remember its ever having been before. It is here, perhaps, that we touch upon one of the greatest, if not the greatest of the differences between the situation of 1858 and that of 1864. The Crimean enlistment controversy of 1856 had produced a short, sharp explosion of American annoyance; but the Civil War led to a steady and ominous deterioration of the relations between the United Kingdom and the United States.

471

British North America was inevitably involved in this mounting antagonism, either directly through the breaches of neutrality which the United States alleged she had committed, or indirectly through the controversies which arose between the United Kingdom and the republic. The *Trent* incident, which led John A. Macdonald to propose a militia force of one hundred thousand men for Canada alone, provoked the first of these angry quarrels; but the *Trent* incident, for all its seriousness, occurred early, when the hands of the North were more than full and when the outcome of the struggle was still far from certain. In June, 1864, when the Canadian coalition Government was formed and when the battle of Gettysburg was nearly a year in the past, the situation had greatly changed. It had changed still more by the autumn of the same year, when a handful of Confederate soldiers launched, from the Province of Canada, their stupid and ineffective raid upon the town of St. Albans in Vermont. By that time the United States was ready and eager for reprisals. It announced the abrogation of the Reciprocity Treaty with British North America; it threatened — and, in the circumstances, no more sinister threat could have been imagined — to suspend the Rush-Bagot agreement limiting naval armaments on the Great Lakes.

It is easy to exaggerate the influence of the American Civil War upon the movement for Canadian Confederation. It is easy, in particular, to overestimate the effects of the St. Albans Raid. The coalition Government of June, 1864, was formed and its purpose declared in direct response to a domestic, not an international, crisis. The Quebec Conference, which laid the bases of the federal constitution, met nine days before the St. Albans Raid occurred and the British government's favourable attitude to Confederation had been decided upon even earlier. The American Civil War did not inspire the Canadian desire for constitutional reform or the British wish for retrenchment; but it did help to give both amplitude and urgency to the Anglo-Canadian plans for achieving their objectives. For both Canadians and British it was not enough to do a little constitutional tinkering and make a few budget cuts. They had to build a nation. And their nation had to be built in the midst of a great war which had convulsed the North American continent and threatened to embroil the English-speaking world.

The French Canadians and the Birth of Confederation *

JEAN-CHARLES BONENFANT

472

Translated by Grace Maurice

At the time of the birth of Confederation, the French Canadians formed a homogeneous group of almost a million inhabitants, representing not quite a third of the total population of the four provinces that were to form the Dominion of Canada. There were nearly 900 000 of them in Quebec, and already some 150 000 in Ontario, New Brunswick, and Nova Scotia, though the latter exercised very little influence. The French Canadians of Lower Canada were nearly all Roman Catholics and the great majority of them lived in the country. Especially since 1840, they had developed their scholastic and municipal institutions; they had numerous newspapers and possessed an embryonic literature as illustrated by the Quebec literary school of 1860. What would be their reactions when faced with the events which would take place from June 1864 to 1 July 1867, and which would constitute the genesis of Confederation?

Before 1864

For a century, theoretical projects to unite the British North American colonies in a federal union had been widely propounded. In general the French Canadians had known very little of these projects, which came for the most part from their political opponents, and, to the French Canadians they often signified legislative union. However, as early as 1847, *Le Canadien* wrote, on 8 September, that "they (the French Canadians) confidently anticipate a greater freedom of action in a federation." In 1858, a French Canadian, Joseph-Charles Taché, published the last and one of the most complete of the theoretical schemes of federalism, entitled *Des provinces de l'Amérique du Nord et d'une union fédérale*, a slightly

Canadian Historical Association Booklet No. 21. Copyright 1966 by the Canadian Historical Association. Reprinted by permission.

revised version of thirty-three articles which he had written in his newspaper, *Le Courrier du Canada*, the preceding year. At the time of the debate on the Quebec Resolutions, in the 1865 session, the member for Lévis, Dr. Joseph S. Blanchet, quoted Taché abundantly in order to declare, with a little friendly exaggeration, that "in the division of powers between the local governments and the central government, the plan of the conference was almost word for word the work of Monsieur Taché." It was also in 1858 that Joseph-Edouard Cauchon edited in brochure form some articles which he had written in his *Journal de Québec*. As the federal system became less and less a theoretical one for the inhabitants of the British North American colonies, the French Canadians became interested in it, but they were not really called upon to make up their minds until the question became the object of political decision.

Political Federalism 473

Federalism began to become a political possibility in August 1858, when Alexander T. Galt demanded acceptance of his project of confederation before he would enter the Cartier-Macdonald ministry. George-Etienne Cartier was then converted to the idea of confederation, an important development considering the authority that he exerted over a large number of his French-speaking compatriots. However, the mother country did not take the project seriously, and only with the political crisis of June 1864 did federalism really cease to be an academic problem. Under the patriarchal direction of Sir Etienne-Paschal Taché who had agreed to come out of retirement in the preceding March to become premier of a Conservative government of which John A. Macdonald and George-Etienne Cartier were the real chiefs, a kind of sacred union was formed, due to the entry into the ministry of the Upper Canadian Liberal leader George Brown and some of his colleagues. The only important group which remained outside the coalition were the Liberals of Lower Canada, the "Rouges", to whom must be added some French-Canadian Conservatives who broke away from their party on this occasion, and an English-Canadian Conservative of stature, Christopher Dunkin. These Liberals were French Canadians except for a few, including two leading figures, Luther Hamilton Holton and Lucius Seth Huntington. The serious opposition to Confederation in the united Canadas, then, was that of the French-speaking Liberals of Lower Canada, led by Antoine-Aimé Dorion, and next to him his younger brother, Jean-Baptiste Eric, the impetuous and radical *enfant terrible*, who died suddenly on 1 November 1866, and so was spared the sorrow of witnessing the realization of Confederation.

The first act of the opponents of Confederation was to attack the coalition and to ridicule the Conservatives for becoming the friends of Brown, whom they had heretofore denounced as the greatest enemy of the French-Canadian Catholics. The struggle did not become clearly defined, however, until after the government had entered into relations with the other colonies at Charlottetown at the beginning of September 1864, and especially after the plan of federalism had been enunciated in the Quebec Resolutions at the conclusion of the Quebec Conference which was held in October. From the social point of view in particular, the latter event was steeped in the French atmosphere of the city, but the deliberations were carried on exclusively in English and with all the pragmatism of the British. Of the thirty-three delegates who met at Quebec, only four were French-Canadian: Etienne-Paschal Taché, who presided over the conference; George-Etienne Cartier, Jean-Charles Chapais and Hector Langevin. Cartier himself seems to have been rather silent during the conference, though he must have put forward his ideas inside the cabinet of the united Canadas, which prepared the propositions which John A. Macdonald then submitted to the delegates.

474 Dorion's Manifesto

By the beginning of November, although there had been no official announcement, numerous speeches and newspaper articles had made known the essential elements of the propositions adopted by the Quebec Conference, and, on 7 November, Antoine-Aimé Dorion considered it necessary to denounce them in a manifesto addressed to his constituents in the county of Hochelaga. The text of this manifesto, together with the speech which Dorion made during the winter of 1865 in the Canadian legislature at the time of the debate on the Quebec Resolutions, and the *Manifeste des vingt* of 1866, constitute a basic documentation of the struggle against Confederation in Lower Canada.

Dorion wondered, first, what independence the provinces would retain "if they were deprived of the right to regulate their own criminal and commercial laws, and if they could modify their civil and municipal laws, laws concerning public instruction and other similar questions, only with the approval of the central government?" Theoretically Dorion was correct, for if the rights of reservation and disallowance which were written into the constitution had worked as John A. Macdonald desired at the outset, it would have been a veritable legislative union that had been created. In Dorion's eyes, the necessity of settling the problem of representation by population in the united Canada was not a sufficient reason for creating a Confederation. He argued that it would have been better to grant some extra members in the assembly to Upper Canada, while preserving the equality between Upper and Lower Canada in the Legislative Council. In Dorion's opinion, the entry of the Maritime provinces into Confederation would only increase the financial drain on Upper and Lower Canada, without any compensating commercial advantages. The defense of the country would become more difficult when New Brunswick and its 500 miles of frontier with the United States were added. The Legislative Council, that is to say, the Senate, "composed of a fixed number of members appointed for life by the Crown, could impede the wishes of public opinion and paralyze all progressive legislation." And Dorion concluded with the argument which, until 1867, remained the most serious of those formulated by the opponents of Confederation when he said, "In whatever manner one views the proposed changes, there is one point on which there can be no difference of opinion, and that is that when we are concerned with nothing less than the remaking of the constitution, and the creation of new foundations for the political edifice, the people whose interest and posterity are affected should be consulted." Although the government never succeeded in defending its attitude adequately, it was never to permit the people to express their opinion. The government claimed that it did not fear a popular consultation, but that it was unnecessary because in a number of elections the government candidates had been successful

After Dorion's manifesto, at the end of 1864 and the beginning of 1865, the people formed ranks for battle. Meetings were held, especially in the counties of Rouville, Verchères, Iberville, Laprairie, Drummond and Arthabaska, Jacques Cartier, Chambly, Bagot and Saint-Hyacinthe. On 7 January 1865, *Le Pays* asserted that the people were waking up in earnest and that soon the movement would embrace all of Lower Canada.

475

Since the present ministry [added *Le Pays*] does not intend to ask the people for their opinion on the constitutional changes which it is preparing for us, the people must take the initiative and prove that they are not inclined to sign this sort of death sentence without examining it very closely. Therefore, let the mayors of each village, let the prefects of each county, all set to work, and let Lower Canada, by means of public assemblies, pronounce its opinion on the plan of Confederation which is to be submitted to her representatives in Parliament in the very near future.

The assembly held at Verchères on 27 December was regarded by *Le Pays* in its edition of 29 December as "a perfect anti-Confederate triumph." The newspaper published the resolutions of the meeting, one of which was a very good summation of the arguments of the participants who were opposed to Confederation:

1. Because the new system would be expensive and complicated; 2. Because it would imperil the institutions and the religious faith, as well as the autonomy, of the French-Canadian nationality, guaranteed by solemn treaties and Imperial statutes; 3. Because it would impose on this province pecuniary obligations which were incumbent exclusively and by law on the other provinces of British North America, and very onerous material sacrifices, such as direct taxation, without procuring in return in this region any real or tangible benefit; 4. Because it would very probably instigate, sooner or later, throughout the said provinces, and particularly in this region, civil troubles and perhaps very serious ones.

Thus public opinion had been awakened when, at the beginning of February, the Upper and Lower Houses of the united Canadas began to study the Quebec Resolutions.

Debate on the Quebec Resolutions

Even though Premier Taché sat in the Legislative Council, it was in the lower chamber that the principal speeches were made to praise the project as well as to fight it. Among the French Canadians, the most fervent partisans of Confederation were George-Etienne Cartier and Hector Langevin, both members of the Cabinet, and Joseph-Edouard Cauchon, who was a backbencher, but who exercised considerable influence over his fellow citizens through his newspaper, the *Journal de Québec*.

Antoine-Aimé Dorion, by virtue of his position as leader of the opposition, intervened several times, but on 16 February, he made his greatest speech, which may be regarded as the summation of the arguments of the French-Canadian adversaries of Confederation. Once again he took up the arguments of his manifesto and he defended himself successfully against the charge of having recently been in favour of a federal solution, as the Conservatives charged, when he declared that he was only "in favour of a Confederation of the two provinces of Upper and Lower Canada, but a real Confederation, giving greater powers to the local governments, and only a delegated authority to the central government." As for the problem of defense, to which was linked the construction of the inter-colonial railroad uniting Canada with the Maritime provinces, Dorion considered it impossible to regulate by means of Confederation. "What it would be better for Canada to do," he added, "would be to remain peaceful, and not give our neighbours any pretext for war." Dorion claimed also that the British railway magnates, desiring to restore the state of their finances, were the secret artisans of Confederation. He ended his speech with the words: "I greatly fear that the day when this Confederation is adopted will be a dark day for Lower Canada . . . I consider it one of the worst measures which could be submitted to us and, if it happens that it is adopted, without the sanction of the people of this province, the country will have more than one occasion to regret it." Eric Dorion added almost nothing to the arguments of his brother, though his style was more dramatic. After showing that the coalition of June 1864, and the project of Confederation which resulted from it, were only a manoeuvre of the Conservative party to remain in power, he repeated over and over again, "I am opposed to the project of Confederation because . . . "

Among the other French-Canadian opponents of Confederation were Henri-Elzéar Taschereau, Conservative representative from Beauce, who broke with his party on this occasion because, he said, he was not convinced that the proposed constitution contained "in itself sufficient guarantees for the protection of our rights" and Joseph-Xavier Perrault, member for Richelieu, who in a very long speech, after more serious arguments, took the time to revive memories of the persecutions against the Irish, the expulsion of the Acadians, the constitutional struggles of Lower Canada, and made the assertion that on the island of Mauritius, England had not respected the clauses of the treaty which ceded that colony to her — all this

476

to prove that the new constitution was a threat to the French Canadians.

Several votes were taken. The most revealing was that of 10 March, when the government proposal was approved by 91 votes to 33. The vote may be analyzed as follows: in Upper Canada, 54 in favour of the measure, 8 opposed; in Lower Canada, 37 in favour, 25 opposed; among the French Canadians, 26 in favour, 22 opposed. A proposal to appeal to the people before submitting the project to the Imperial parliament was rejected by 84 to 35, the great majority of the latter being French-Canadian members. The Liberal newspaper *Le Pays* wrote on 14 March that the night of 10 March, the night of the most important vote, had seen "the most iniquitous act, the most degrading act, which parliamentary government had witnessed since the treason of the Irish deputies who sold their country to England for positions, honours, and gold." In an obviously different tone, the Conservative newspaper *La Minerve* had written on 11 March: "The vote in the Canadian legislature marked an important date in the history of Canada . . . The union of the colonies is the consecration of our political and national existence and the guarantee of our future."

477

In the Legislative Council on 20 February, the Quebec Resolutions had been approved by 45 votes to 15, the latter including 8 councillors from Lower Canada. Seven of these had been elected and consequently could claim to express the sentiments of a fairly large group of public opinion. The French-Canadian voters of Lower Canada could not express their views on the project of Confederation before it was adopted, but the fact remains that a large number of their representatives in both houses were opposed to it.

From the approval of the Quebec Resolutions by the Canadian parliament to their study at the London Conference in December 1866, the plan of Confederation continued to be the object of political discussions between its partisans and its adversaries. At the beginning of March 1865, it suffered a severe blow when the government of New Brunswick, which favoured Confederation, was defeated in a provincial general election. In spite of the affirmations of Cartier and his supporters, the project seemed to have broken down and during the autumn of 1865, many people, including newspaper editors, wondered whether it might not be necessary to replace the plan for the wider union with one for the federation of the two Canadas only. However, new elections were held in New Brunswick in 1866, which returned the Confederation party to power. This made possible the London Conference in December of the same year, and finally, in 1867, the drafting and the adoption of the British North America Act.

The Session of 1866

During this waiting period, various problems deriving from Confederation, of particular interest to the French Canadians, were discussed, and solutions were found for them during the last session of the assembly of the united Canadas in the summer of 1866. The most important debate concerned the resolutions providing for the constitutions of the future provinces of Quebec and Ontario. John A. Macdonald did not want an Upper House in Ontario, but Cartier demanded one for Quebec. The government had some difficulty in explaining this anomaly. According to Cartier, Lower Canada wanted "to give more dignity to legislative institutions" but there were further reasons for the creation of a Legislative Council. In reality, the Council was thought necessary to protect the Anglo-Saxon minority against possible legislative action by the Lower House.

At the birth of Confederation, the English and Protestant Canadians of Quebec did not wish to risk their position. They represented nearly a quarter of the population, but their real power was more considerable than their number, for, in the cities of Quebec and Montreal, they were the masters of industry, commerce, and finance, and they dominated the Eastern Townships. They were afraid that, under the new constitution, they would lose their privileged position, and that they would henceforth be at the mercy of the French-Canadian Catholic majority in the future local legislature. Their leader, Alexander T. Galt, tried to reassure them in a speech made on 23 November 1864 in the city of Sherbrooke, for which he was the member in the Legislative assembly. He rejected the idea that the French Canadians could one day deprive their compatriots of a substantial representation in the legislative assembly, but even so, he had the prudence to have twelve privileged electoral districts constituted, which could not be interfered with without the consent of an absolute majority of the members who would represent them.

Galt also tried to ensure better protection for the schools of the Protestant minority in Quebec. In 1866 he was unsuccessful in his attempt to have the Legislative Assembly adopt a measure to this effect, and he resigned from the government, but, as a delegate to the London Conference, he obtained approximately what he wanted in the final text of the British North America Act.

The problem of education for minorities at the time of Confederation, it should be remembered, was always presented from the religious viewpoint and never from the linguistic. That was no disadvantage to the Anglo-Saxon minority of Quebec which was then identical with the Protestant minority. In the other provinces the French-Canadian population belonged to the Catholic minority, and it was only as such that it was protected. George-Etienne Cartier went so far as to say in 1866: "Upper Canada is inhabited by only one race; the same is not true of Lower Canada." Hector Langevin had made the same point in 1865: "Upper Canada has a homogeneous population professing different religions." In fact, there were nearly 75 000 French-speaking Canadians in Upper Canada, but for their compatriots of Lower Canada they were only a sort of avant-garde whose future was viewed as quite hazy. As for the Acadians, it is revealing that, during the debate on the Quebec Resolutions in the Canadian legislature, their expulsion was mentioned only twice. It was solely as Catholics that they received a meagre protection, and furthermore they were to be deprived of this protection on the morrow of Confederation. In reality, the struggle surrounding the problems of education, before as after Confederation, brought two different philosophies face to face: that of the Catholics who favoured separate schools, and that of the Protestants who, in spite of appearances, more easily accepted schools which were for all practical purposes public schools, in which the question of a specific religion was not seriously raised.

The Final Opposition

A final assault against the project of Confederation was launched at the end of October 1866 by the drafting and publication of a manifesto signed by twenty members of the Legislative Assembly and sent to the Colonial Secretary, Lord Carnarvon. Coming after more than two years of struggle, when the die was definitely cast, the manifesto did not present any new arguments. It summed up events from the first official step towards Confederation, taken by Cartier, Ross, and Galt in 1859, to the decision which had just been made by Nova Scotia, New Brunswick, and the Canadas to send delegates to London to establish the Union. The signatories concluded:

479

> We have striven to prove that the initiative for the project of Confederation, and all the subsequent steps to have it adopted, are due to exigencies of the parties and not to a spontaneous and general desire of the people to make radical changes in their institutions or in their political relations.

Lord Carnarvon was unmoved by the protests which were presented to him. During the debates in the House of Lords and the House of Commons on the proposed British North America Act, the problem of the opposition which had been manifested in Nova Scotia was raised, but that of the Liberals of Lower Canada was not. Lord Carnarvon contented himself with declaring on 22 February that in the case of Upper and Lower Canada, the delegates in London had the most complete powers. For the British government, the approval of the Quebec Resolutions in 1865 constituted a definite acquiescence on the part of the two sections of united Canada. The manifesto received considerable attention in the newspapers of Lower Canada, but it left the mother country indifferent.

The First of July 1867

During the winter of 1866–67, Lower Canadians attentively followed the events which were taking place in London, even though the newspapers were often several weeks late in reporting the news, because the newly-inaugurated transatlantic telegraph provided very little information about the conference. In the spring, the text of the act, which Queen Victoria had sanctioned on 29 March, was sent to Canada and was immediately translated into rather inelegant French. On the first of July, which was a

Monday, Confederation was born, and the day was marked by great public rejoicing in the new province of Quebec. Of course its Liberal opponents accepted the new regime without enthusiasm, but it is probable that the following lines from the editorial of the *Courrier du Canada* represented more than the partisan sentiments of a Conservative newspaper:

One hundred and six years, eight months and eighteen days ago yesterday, M. de Vaudreuil, the last of the French governors of New France, concluded a capitulation which delivered forever to his secular enemies "the most beautiful, the most French, and the most neglected" of the colonies that France possessed . . . Who would have been able to foresee, we shall not say a hundred years ago, fifty or twenty-five years ago, but seven or eight years ago, who would have been able to foresee that Lower Canada, the cradle of the French-Canadian nationality, would be, in the very near future and without ceasing to be a colony of England, governed by a French-Canadian Catholic?

The Causes of Confederation

480

Even if the opposition to Confederation in Lower Canada was considerable, it cannot be assumed that the new regime had been brutally imposed on the population. Both profound causes and immediate motives led a good proportion of the French Canadians to be favourable to it.

In the birth of Confederation, several causes were intermingled, but they can be conveniently classified in this way: the economic exigencies of the time; the necessity of constructing the Intercolonial and of re-financing the railway system already in existence; fear of the United States and at the same time, to a degree, a desire to imitate them; the needs of defense; the birth in the different colonies of a common national sentiment; the consent of the mother country; and finally the desire of the Canadian government to be free of the difficulties which had for some time paralysed the working of its political institutions.

The transformation of the economy of Great Britain in the middle of the nineteenth century considerably damaged the commerce of the colonies. A grave crisis followed and some of the discontented English Canadians even advocated annexation to the United States. Less bound to business and industry, the French Canadians generally remained outside this movement. The Reciprocity Treaty, signed in 1854, brought a temporary prosperity to the colonies, a prosperity which became even greater during the American Civil War from 1860 to 1865, when Canadian exports increased and agriculture profited. However, the Canadians feared that the treaty would be abrogated and this in fact happened in 1866. The partisans of Confederation claimed that the problems associated with the termination of Reciprocity would be corrected by the increase in commerce between the reunited colonies. Facing the economic difficulties of the time, aggravated by poor harvests, particularly in 1864, and foreseeing the greater hardship which the end of reciprocity would bring, Canadians had seen a certain degree of salvation in the new system. The French Canadians shared this hope. When in a speech to the Legislative Assembly on 9 March 1865, Eric Dorion drew a somber picture of the farmer in the fields of Lower Canada, he was obviously exaggerating, as any opponent of the government would, but all the same his testimony revealed a recurring situation which led the people to look for a new solution, a solution such as Confederation.

Most of the French Canadians, except for some of their leaders like Cartier, were not so bound to financial and railway interests that the necessity of building the Intercolonial influenced them directly to favour Confederation, but, even so, on 1 August 1867, the Conservative newspaper *Le Courrier de Saint-Hyacinthe* wrote:

There is no doubt . . . that the Intercolonial Railway will bring wealth to the part of the country through which it runs. Its first effect will be to stimulate commerce and to favour colonization greatly. The counties of Temiscouata and Rimouski which it crosses are very fertile, the immigrant will find good land there, and abundant facilities for communication with the centres of commerce.

Moreover, the construction of the Intercolonial was only one important aspect of two other factors: the fear of the United States and the necessities of defense.

481

Rightly or wrongly, between 1860 and 1870, the French Canadians feared annexation to the United States and viewed Confederation as the only way to prevent this. While it is true that English-Canadian politicians and newspapers sometimes invoked this argument, few attached as much importance to it as the French Canadians. Several of their political leaders and several of their newspapers presented the alternative: "Confederation or annexation." At that time, all Canadians had serious reasons to fear the United States, and particularly the northern states who emerged victorious from the Civil War. England had shown sympathy towards the southern states and it would have been normal for the North to take its vengeance on the British colonies of North America. Besides, the fear of the United States took a concrete form in the Fenian menace, which the politicians did not fail to exploit. In 1866, the Fenians, Irish fanatics who had been organizing in the United States and had taken advantage of the Civil War to acquire military training, attacked New Brunswick at Campobello, Upper Canada on the Niagara peninsula, and Lower Canada at Frelighsburg. On 28 June 1866, on the occasion of the feast of Saint-Jean-Baptiste, *Le Canadien* published a poem by Arthur Cassegrain entitled "The Fenian Invasion" in which he launched the appeal:

Aux armes! fils de Jean-Baptiste
Entendez le canon! . . .
Que votre patron vous assiste!
Pensez à Carillon.

Moreover, the general problem of the defense of Canada was one of the important influences on the birth of Confederation in French Canada as well as elsewhere. Their politicians had made this a debating point and on 13 February 1865, *La Minerve* wrote: "It is to assure ourselves a force and sufficient means of defense that we desire a union of all the provinces destined to march under the same flag in case of war."

Several politicians and newspapers also emphasized that, at the time of Confederation, a new country was being born. The French Canadians do not seem to have been preoccupied with this idea except in so far as it concerned their survival as a group, or the possibility that union would permit them to avoid annexation. In opposing the new regime, the French-Canadian Liberals claimed, of course, that it endangered the survival of French Canada, but the *Journal de Québec* seems to have represented a large part of public opinion when it wrote on 17 December 1864:

> We want to be a nation one day, and as that is our necessary destiny and the goal to which we aspire, we prefer the political condition of which we will be a vital element, and in which we will still be in existence, rather than to be thrown into the midst of an immense people, like a drop of water lost in the ocean, where in a few years we would lose our language, our laws, and even the memory of our glorious origins.

It should be added that, at the birth of Confederation, French Canadians were happy that legal recognition was given to the use of their language in parliament and in the courts, where French had previously had only *de facto* recognition.

Finally, an examination of the causes which led to Confederation reveals that action was precipitated by the desire to escape from the political difficulties of the united province. The Union of 1840, by creating equal representation in the Lower House for Upper and Lower Canada, became eventually unjust to the Anglo-Saxon element and made representation by population one of the most important themes of political life in the united Canadas. This problem was one of the principal causes of ministerial instability and to resolve it, federalism seemed the best solution. This was what Cartier understood, and this is what he succeeded in making a large portion of the population understand. *La Minerve* summed up the situation on 16 July 1864 when it wrote:

> Representation by population in Confederation is a completely different question from representation by population in the existing Union, since in the first case is is a safeguard and guarantee of independence and in the second case it is an infallible means to servitude and degradation.

Several days before, *La Minerve* had underlined the fact that Lower Canada could not be an obstacle to Confederation and consequently could not oppose another factor which determined the course of events, the will of London. The Conservative newspaper wrote:

> For a long time, people in England have been talking of uniting all the British possessions in America under the same legislative government. When a general movement towards Confederation develops and when this movement is perfectly motivated, can we allow ourselves to stand in the way like an insuperable barrier, at the risk of bringing about their ruin and our own?

The Catholic Clergy

"Without Cartier and the Catholic clergy of Quebec, it would have been impossible to accomplish the union of 1867," wrote the journalist and historian, Sir John Willison. The Conservative party which advocated Confederation was of course on better terms with the Catholic clergy than was the Liberal Party which opposed it. The bishops and curés still exercised an influence over the electorate in political matters which they were not to lose until the victory of Laurier in 1896. Moreover, much importance was attached to the opinion of the clergy. Cartier declared in the House during the winter of 1865:

> I will say that the opinion of the clergy is favourable to Confederation . . . In general, the clergy are the enemy of all political dissension and if they support this project, it is because they see in Confederation a solution to the difficulties which have existed for so long.

Perhaps not all the bishops and curés were as favourable to Confederation as Cartier said. At least, this is what the Liberals claimed, but as they had never been on very good terms with the Catholic church, it was difficult for them to boast of interpreting the sentiments of its representatives.

However, it can be affirmed that from June 1864 to the spring of 1867, the Catholic clergy, while generally favouring the Confederation project, refused to commit themselves and even felt some fear of facing the unknown. But after the new political system had been adopted by the British parliament, the five bishops of Lower Canada published pastoral letters in which they left their flock little liberty to vote against the constitution. For them, of course, it was the recognition of a *fait accompli*, the traditional acceptance by the Catholic hierarchy of established power and authority, but it was also an almost morbid fear of annexation to the United States, and a consequence of the game of bipartisanship. In effect, not to approve Confederation would have been the same as allying themselves with its opponents, who for the most part were Liberals who had broken with the clergy. Thus the bishops were only expressing publicly sentiments which they had already held for a long time, and which the public knew. The Conservatives shamelessly took advantage of this, especially during the elections which followed Confederation; the Liberals suffered from it and allowed their anger to burst forth violently in the autumn of 1867.

The French-Canadian bishop who seems to have shown the greatest enthusiasm for Confederation was Monseigneur Charles Larocque, who became bishop of Saint-Hyacinthe in March 1866. In his pastoral letter of 18 June 1867, after saying that "In our opinion, Confederation does not appear to be a danger to be feared at all," he wrote:

> Republican institutions do not suit us any better than they suit the great people from whom we are descended, the French. And the fate which would be awaiting us, if God suffered us at same future date to enter the great American republic, would be exactly comparable to that of so many tributaries which come to be swallowed up in the great, deep St. Lawrence, where they disappear without leaving the slightest trace of their existence.

After listening to such remarks, it was rather difficult for anyone who was accustomed to obeying his bishop to oppose Confederation and to vote in favour of its opponents.

483

George-Etienne Cartier

Without a doubt, the great artisan of Confederation in Lower Canada, the one who succeeded in channeling all the latent forces, was George-Etienne Cartier. He was not a theorist and, if he made himself the apostle of Confederation, it was not to bring about the triumph of the system. It was because he believed that it was the only way out of the situation, favourable to Lower Canada but unjust to Upper Canada, which had been created by equal representation, and perhaps also because he was to some extent associated with railway interests. To these motives may be added the natural desire of a politician to play a role on a higher stage, and an almost morbid fear of the United States and their republican institutions. In the great speech which Cartier made on 7 February 1865 in favour of the Quebec resolutions, he declared: "The question is reduced to this: we must either have a British North American federation or else be absorbed into the American federation." When Cartier feared annexation, it was not only because it would mark a change of allegiance, but also because of something more important: Cartier, as a monarchist and a Conservative, feared republican institutions. Cartier has sometimes been criticized for not ensuring sufficiently the protection of his compatriots, and particularly for forgetting the French minorities living outside Quebec, but we must not judge a politician in the light of events which have occurred in the intervening century and which he could not have foreseen. In the sometimes difficult circumstances in which he found himself, at grips with an artful colleague like John A. Macdonald, Cartier sought concrete solutions. At the most, one can reproach him, like many other politicians after him, for having had a conception of federalism that was too simplified and too optimistic. He expressed it in 1865 in these words:

484

> Under the federal system, which leaves to the central government the great questions of general interest in which racial differences are not concerned, it will not be possible that the rights of race and religion fail to be appreciated.

The Elections of 1867

In attempting to understand the attitude of the French Canadians at the time of the birth of Confederation, it is necessary finally to see what happened in Quebec when the first elections were held, at the beginning of September, to elect members to the House of Commons and to the Legislative Assembly of Quebec. The Conservatives tried to transform the vote into a sort of plebiscite in favour of Confederation. At least it was easy for them to claim that their Liberal opponents, who were opposed to the new regime, were hardly likely to make it function. In another connection, as we have seen, after the new system had been adopted by the British parliament, the bishops sent out the pastoral letters in which they left their flock little liberty to vote against Confederation. The Liberals, directed by Antoine-Aimé Dorion, formed an organization not to fight against Confederation, but to "neutralize the effects of the new system." This was the Reform Association of Lower Canada, which consisted of moderate Liberals, as opposed to the young radical Liberals, often annexationists, who followed Médéric Lanctôt. As often happened at the time, the arguments of the two principal groups of opponents crystallized into two brochures, entitled, respectively, *La Confédération, couronnement de dix années de mauvaise administration* and *La Confédération, c'est le salut du Bas-Canada*.

The federal election ended in a resounding victory for the Conservatives and consequently for the supporters of Confederation. In the whole country they won 101 seats out of 181, and in Quebec, 45 out of 65. The Conservatives were also victorious in the elections for the Legislative Assembly.

The First Session

The first session of the new federal Parliament opened on 7 November and, at the very beginning, a minor incident seemed to indicate that the French Canadians who feared Confederation and claimed that it would not easily permit the realization of Canadian duality, were right. After Macdonald and Cartier had proposed James Cockburn, a Conservative member from Ontario, and a Father of Confederation, as speaker, the member from Montcalm, Joseph Dufresne, opposed this choice "because Cockburn did not understand the two languages which were to be on equal footing in the House of Commons." *La Minerve* itself, while favourable to the government, did not hesitate to write: "Perhaps it was wise to present openly the rights of the French Canadian minority in Confederation as soon as Parliament opened." This was the beginning of the difficulties which French-speaking Canadians would often meet in their attempts to participate freely in political life at the federal level, difficulties which would impel them to develop the autonomy of the province of which they would be masters because they constituted the majority.

For the moment, they felt a certain pride in possessing their own institutions. When the Lieutenant-Governor, Sir Narcisse Belleau, opened the first session of the provincial legislature on 28 December 1867, he could declare:

485

The constitution has entrusted you with great interests but has imposed serious obligations on you, concerning the administration of justice, public instruction, the patronage of science, the humanities, and the arts, the exploitation of public property, including our vast forests and our mines that are so important, the development of our social resources, immigration, colonization, the police, and in general, civil law and property law.

For better or for worse, the die was cast, and the legislative machinery of Confederation began to function.

Conclusion

Although we have no mathematical proof, it seems likely that the majority of French Canadians were favourable to Confederation during its formative stages from 1864 to 1867, and while they possessed most of the characteristics which, since the principle of nationality had developed, had led people in Europe to dream of independence, nevertheless it can be affirmed that at this time, even though the French Canadians wanted to preserve their identity, they never seriously thought of independence as a solution.

On the other hand, it appears that they understood that the political system created by the Union of 1840, even if it had become on the whole favourable to them, had to be altered because the English-speaking Canadians of Upper Canada could not agree indefinitely to a refusal of representation by population. At the time there was certainly a strong temptation towards annexation to the United States, or at least the impression that this annexation would be inevitable some day, and that, after all, it would serve no purpose to fight against geographical, economic, and political imperatives, but George-Etienne Cartier and the Catholic clergy succeeded in convincing the population of the dangers which annexation would entail for them. Besides, they could believe that annexation was inevitable without wishing to take definite steps which would facilitate it.

486

While accepting federalism as inevitable, the French Canadians did not have a very advanced theoretical vision of it, and they would have been incapable of discussing most of the problems it poses today. They did not even suspect these problems. It could not be expected, for example, that they could imagine all the furore that lay in Paragraph 13 of Section 92 on property and civil rights. They could not have suspected that judicial interpretation would give this article such importance. They could not know all that was hidden in the words "public lands, timber and woods" of Paragraph 5 of Section 92.

The French Canadians were forced to make the best of pragmatic solutions and to foresee as well as possible the difficulties these would create. Events must not be judged in the light of later developments, with an insight which contemporaries could not possess. The French Canadians seem to have understood fairly well the powers it was necessary to entrust to the provinces so that Quebec could remain master of its institutions at the time. They thought that provincial power would be so much developed, especially in the case of Quebec, that they gave little thought to the possibility of a genuine Canadian duality at the federal level. However, it must not be forgotten that Confederation was accomplished at a time when Canada was an Anglo-Saxon colony and when the best government was the one which interfered to the least possible degree in the life of its people. It was therefore much less serious a hundred years ago that the federal government was almost completely Anglo-Saxon, because Canada had no international status, the state did not intervene in economic life, and there were, as yet, practically no social security measures.

However, the French Canadians of Lower Canada can be reproached for not really understanding the situation of the French minorities in Upper Canada and the maritime provinces, who from a political point of view, were not represented. At the time, the problems of education were much more centred on religion than on language and thus the protection which was claimed for the minorities depended on the former rather than on the latter.

A majority of French Canadians favoured Confederation a hundred years ago because it was the only realistic solution which presented itself to them, and even those who opposed it were content to say that it was premature but did not offer an alternative solution. Confederation was achieved because the English Canadians needed to have the French Canadians in it, and the French could not then become independent. The great majority of nations have been formed, not by people who desired intensely to live together, but rather by people who could not live separately. *487*

Topic Fifteen
The Nature of the Confederation Agreement

Ever since the passage of the British North America Act in the British Parliament in 1867, its true meaning has been heatedly discussed. For more than just historical interest it is important to examine exactly what the document means. What kind of federal union was agreed upon in the Charlottetown, Quebec, and London meetings? Was it a union as Macdonald wished, with a strong central and weak provincial governments? or one, as Cartier had argued, in which significant provincial rights were guaranteed and protected?

Perhaps the most important sections of the British North America Act are its clauses dealing with the division of legislative powers: sections 91 to 95. Do the powers given the federal government in 1867 indicate a superior authority over the provinces? One of the strongest statements ever made in favour of the federal authority appears in the Rowell-Sirois Report of 1940. It plainly states, "for various reasons, the builders of the new nation planned a federation comprised of a central government with authority over matters of general and common interest and provincial governments with authority over matters of local concern."

In his "Act or Pact: Another Look at Confederation," George Stanley takes an opposing stand. He suggests that the agreements at Charlottetown, Quebec, and London were really first a compact between French- and English-speaking Canadians, and then by extension a compact between the provinces, or a treaty between the various colonies who agreed to establish a federal union. What are the implications of this interpretation? How does the compact theory strengthen the hands of the provinces? The final reading comprises sections 91–95, on the distribution of Legislative powers, of the British North America Act itself.

One of the most important secondary studies is Ramsay Cook's "Provincial Autonomy, Minority Rights and the Compact Theory," a report prepared in 1965 for the Royal Commission on Bilingualism and Biculturalism and published separately by the Queen's Printer in 1969. It also contains a number of bibliographical references on the subject. Donald V. S. Smiley had edited the original version of *The Rowell-Sirois Report* (Toronto: McClelland and Stewart, 1963; first published in 1940). A general discussion of the major issues is contained in "Part II: The Constitution" in R. M. Dawson's *The Government of Canada* (Toronto: University of Toronto Press, 1947, and subsequent revisions). The various bibliographical suggestions given in Topic Fourteen, "Why Was Confederation Accepted?" might also be consulted.

The Nature of Confederation*
THE ROWELL-SIROIS REPORT

Principal Objectives 489

Confederation was conceived as the solution for a number of political and economic difficulties and, therefore, had both political and economic aims. Politically, it was designed to establish a new nation to meet the changed conditions of British policy and to brace the scattered provinces against possible American aggression. Economically, it was intended to foster a national economy which would relieve dependence upon a few industries and lessen exposure to the effects of the economic policies pursued by the United States and Great Britain.

Political union was expected to promote strength as against the external world. The triumphant Northern States appeared a threat to territorial integrity. Other interests needed protection too. Nova Scotia felt her deep-sea fishery interests threatened, and the special institutions and culture of Lower Canada would not long have survived absorption of the colonies by the United States. Political union was designed to defend navigation rights on the St. Lawrence and its canals, and fishing rights at sea. A single united authority could use both these and access to its extended internal market as bargaining counters for advantages in international trade. A stable political authority would restore the public credit, so badly damaged by the accumulation of debt and political dissension. In the money markets of the world, the credit of the whole would be greater than that of the parts and would provide a broader base for the government expenditures necessary to attain new and difficult economic objectives.

Federal union was a plan whereby, through mutual concession, cultural and local loyalties could be preserved and reconciled with the political strength and solidarity of the whole. These separate loyalties were strong and their existence was keenly realized. They existed not only in Canada but also in the Maritimes where they had helped to frustrate projects for

*From *The Rowell-Sirois Report*, edited by Donald V. Smiley. Copyright 1963 by Macmillan of Canada. Reprinted by permission of Gage Publishing Limited.

Maritime legislative union. Mutual concession required the English-speaking elements of Lower Canada to relinquish their integral union with the English-speaking people of Upper Canada while the French-speaking Canadians abandoned their objections to a superior political authority in whose councils they would be in a minority. In compensation, the broad questions of trade and commerce which so intimately concerned the English-speaking people of Lower Canada were to be given to the federal authority, thus securing the benefits of single control in these matters of general interest while French-speaking Canada was to be secured in sole control of the cherished values it so tenaciously held. Equally, this solution offered security for the historic traditions firmly rooted in the Maritimes.

Economically, the first objectives of Confederation were to establish a free-trade area comprising the five old provinces and to develop interprovincial transportation facilities. The resources and industries of the several provinces, it was thought, would prove complementary to each other, and would increase prosperity and self-sufficiency. To make this a reality, the Intercolonial Railway was to link the Maritime Province with the St. Lawrence Valley and to give Canada winter access to the sea.

Another great economic objective of Confederation, to be realized as soon as circumstances permitted, was the opening up of the Northwest and the inclusion of the Pacific province. For the Province of Canada, in particular, this westward expansion was to provide an escape from a *cul-de-sac* and the threatened economic stagnation. New frontiers and new resources would provide opportunities for settlement and development. It was recognized as an immense undertaking for which no specific detailed plan could be made under the urgencies and limitations of the moment.

This project had to await the acquisition of the lands of the Hudson's Bay Company. It required the building of a transcontinental railway. This, in turn, depended upon attracting new capital and capital, at that time, had become shy of Canadian ventures. Collective effort and resources on a scale which only government could secure were necessary and, at the same time, conditional on the restoration of the public credit.

Although these plans were necessarily vague in 1867, they were nevertheless resolutely held. The new political framework was designed to give the Federal Government ample powers for the prodigious task of opening up the West. The Federal Government was intended to give a vigorous lead in the development of the new national transcontinental economy and in matters relating to that development there was to be no doubt, such as had recently arisen in the United States, about its authority.

There were some among the Fathers of Confederation who favoured a unitary state as an instrument for realizing these plans. As is well known, John A. Macdonald had a strong preference for a unitary state and Galt accepted the federal scheme with reluctance and hoped it might later coalesce into a legislative union.[1] But legislative union was not acceptable to the French-speaking Canadians or to the Maritime Provinces. Furthermore, municipal institutions had not yet been established in the Maritimes,

490

and they were still in the early stages of development in Lower Canada. The centralization of all governmental powers under one government was, therefore, impracticable from an administrative point of view. The distractions of local administration might well have diverted some of the energies of the central government from its larger creative tasks. Thus, for various reasons, the builders of the new nation planned a federation comprised of a central government with authority over matters of general and common interest and provincial governments with authority over matters of local concern.

The Division of Legislative Powers

The British North America Act was the final embodiment of their scheme. The acknowledged necessity of a federal type of union was recognized by the preamble to the Act which recited the desire of the Provinces of Canada, Nova Scotia and New Brunswick "to be federally united into One Dominion". The vital core of a federal constitution is the division of legislative powers between the central authority and the component states or provinces. This division represents the compromise between the forces which make union possible and those which inhibit the formation of a closer union. It marks the limits of what can be done by common agreement and the extent to which the separate states must be permitted to differ and work out their own destinies. In sections 91 to 95 of the British North America Act, the main lines of this division were set forth.

491

In section 92, certain classes of subjects were enumerated and the provinces were given exclusive power to make laws in relation to matters coming within these classes of subjects. These classes included such things as the administration of justice, municipal institutions, the establishment and maintenance of prisons, hospitals, asylums and charitable institutions and control over the public lands of the province. The provinces were also given control over local works and undertakings. But an exception reserved international and interprovincial lines of transport and communication to the Dominion and authorized the Dominion to take legislative power over any local work at any time by declaring it to be for the general advantage of Canada or for the advantage of two or more provinces. A power of direct taxation to raise revenue for provincial purposes was given, although it was thought that expanding revenues from the public lands would make it generally unnecessary for the provinces to exercise this power.[2]

The classes of subjects in section 92 included two of vague and general reference, viz., "Property and Civil Rights in the Province" and "Generally all Matters of a merely local or private Nature in the Province". Section 93 gave the provinces control over education, subject to certain clauses designed to protect the rights of Roman Catholic and Protestant religious minorities. By section 95, the Dominion and the provinces were given concurrent powers over agriculture and immigration, federal legislation to prevail in case of conflict.

The opening paragraph of section 91 gave the Dominion power "to make Laws for the Peace, Order and good Government of Canada, in relation to all Matters not coming within the Classes of Subjects by this Act assigned exclusively to the Legislatures of the Provinces". That is to say, the residue of powers not expressly given to the provinces was reserved to the Dominion. The section then proceeded with a specific enumeration of twenty-nine classes of subjects, illustrating but not restricting the scope of the general words used earlier in the section.

This enumeration included such classes of subjects as defence, criminal law, naturalization and aliens, and the postal system. It also included regulation of trade and commerce, fisheries, banking, currency and coinage, commercial paper, weights and measures, bankruptcy and insolvency and certain other topics of primarily economic reference. It also gave the Dominion unlimited powers of taxation. The concluding paragraph of section 91 provided against these enumerated topics being "deemed to come within the Class of Matters of a local or private Nature comprised in the Enumeration of the Classes of Subjects" assigned to the provinces by section 92. An exception to section 92 gave the Dominion control over all interprovincial and international transportation and communications.

492

The Problem of Interpreting the Division of Legislative Powers

No amount of care in phrasing the division of powers in a federal scheme will prevent difficulty when the division comes to be applied to the variety and complexity of social relationships. The different aspects of life in a society are not insulated from one another in such a way as to make possible a mechanical application of the division of powers. There is nothing in human affairs which corresponds to the neat logical divisions found in the constitution. Therefore, attempts to exercise the powers allotted by the constitution frequently raise questions as to its meaning in relation to particular circumstances.

The British North America Act has not escaped this difficulty. Manifestly, it would be difficult for the Dominion to make any law for the "Peace, Order and good Government of Canada" without affecting, in some way, one or other of the specific subjects in relation to which the provinces were given exclusive powers. On the other hand, laws made by the provinces under the heads of jurisdiction given by section 92 would frequently have direct implications for the "Peace, Order and good Government of Canada" or would bear in some unexpected way upon the enumerated classes of subjects in section 91 over which the Dominion was given exclusive power. The implications and sometimes the express provisions of legislation would seem to cross the line which, in theory, divided the spheres of legislation assigned to the provinces and the Dominion. In a variety of circumstances, the problem of what amounted to an invasion of the field of one by the other would raise difficult questions of interpretation.

The task of interpretation was complicated by the existence, in sections 91 and 92, of several general descriptions of the ambit of legislative power given to the Dominion and the provinces which lacked a clear, legal meaning. "Peace, Order and good Government", "Regulation of Trade and Commerce", "Property and Civil Rights in the Province" do not convey precise signification. Since 1867, the Privy Council has had the last word on the meaning of the British North America Act and has laid down rules of construction for determining when section 91 was to have primacy over section 92. By a process of textual criticism, it has given some concreteness to the general phrases just mentioned. In this way, it has elucidated the legal meaning of the constitution and imparted greater certainty to the division of powers than could have existed when the Act first came into operation. This legal meaning is binding on all other courts and on the Dominion and provincial legislatures.

The British North America Act was a statute of the British Parliament and the Privy Council brought to its task of elucidation an elaborate set of rules binding on the courts in their interpretation of all statutes. These rules required the Privy Council to consider the literal meaning of the words used without any conjectures as to the intentions of those who framed the Quebec and London Resolutions. The Privy Council as a court was not free to consider historical evidence about intentions but was bound to restrict itself to a consideration of what may be called, by contrast, legal evidence — the intention actually expressed by the words used in the Act.[3] Much controversy, past and present, has centred on the question whether the intention which the Privy Council has found to be expressed in the Act accords with the actual intention of the Fathers; in short, whether we now have the constitution which they intended to give us.

493

Some are satisfied that the Privy Council has merely made explicit what the Fathers intended. Others dismiss the controversy on the ground that we cannot now know what they intended. Others, again, hold that the constitution today is vastly different from what its framers meant it to be and seek to support their contentions from certain historical evidence. In an account of the forces behind Confederation and of the nature of the constitution established in 1867, it is important to note the historical arguments which form the basis of many current criticisms of the Privy Council.[4] For purposes of record, we summarize these arguments here but we do not accept them as conclusive upon certain points, some of them of considerable importance. The critics of the Privy Council do not appear to have fully substantiated their case but, at the same time, they do marshall an impressive mass of historical evidence in support of their general conclusions and their arguments cannot be dismissed as mere hypotheses. Confederation being relatively close to us in time, and the records of its achievement being relatively ample, it is argued we have no reason to assume that it is inherently impossible to determine now the intentions of the Fathers, although it may well be admitted that it is difficult to establish with conclusive finality the meaning of some of the phrases which they employed. The historical case presented by the critics of the Privy Council has not been accepted by all authorities but it merits the attention and consideration of serious students of the problem.

Historical Interpretation of the Intentions of the Fathers — Arguments Supporting a Broad View of Dominion Powers

Some historians urge that the Fathers intended to give wide, sweeping powers to the Dominion and to restrict the provinces to a narrow range of functions, in the exercise of which they were to be subject to the control and supervision of the Dominion.[5] They claim that the general phrases in section 91, "Peace, Order and good Government" and "Regulation of Trade and Commerce", to which the Privy Council has given a restricted meaning were intended to have a broad interpretation and that the general phrase, "Property and Civil Rights in the Province", in section 92, to which the Privy Council has given an extended meaning, was intended by the framers to have a much more limited interpretation.

Some of the leading figures among the framers of the federal scheme evidently intended the general government, as it was called, to have broad and far-reaching powers. John A. Macdonald explained that "all the great questions which affect the general interests of the Confederacy as a whole, are confided to the Federal Parliament."[6] Galt declared that among the subjects given to the general government would be found "all that could in any way be considered of a public and general character".[7] Lord Carnarvon, the Colonial Secretary, introducing the scheme to the House of Lords said it proposed to give to the central authority "those high functions and almost sovereign powers by which general principles and uniformity of legislation may be secured in those questions that are of common import to all the provinces".[8]

Some of the opponents of the scheme criticized it on much the same grounds. A. A. Dorion claimed that it "gives all the powers to the Central Government, and reserves for the local governments the smallest possible amount of freedom of action,"[9] and J. B. E. Dorion opposed the scheme "because we are offered local parliaments which will be simply nonentities, with a mere semblance of power on questions of minor importance".[10]

Supporters of this historical interpretation urge that this view of the relative importance of the Dominion and provincial governments in the new scheme is borne out by various sections of the constitution. They point to the power of the Dominion to appoint the Lieutenant-Governors of the provinces and emphasize the fact that while the provinces were given power to amend the provincial constitutions, they were forbidden to alter in any way the office of Lieutenant-Governor. They contend that the

494

intention to give the Dominion a dominating position is confirmed by the power to reserve and disallow provincial legislation which was given to the Dominion.

In support of this general position, they place great importance on the opening paragraph of section 91 which gave the Dominion power to make laws for the "Peace, Order and good Government of Canada" in relation to all matters not exclusively assigned to the provincial legislatures. This phrase had acquired a wide, though not very precise, significance in the legislative history of the British Empire before 1867.[11] "Peace, order and good government", and the variation, "peace, welfare and good government" were the phrases habitually used by the British colonial authorities in vesting colonial legislatures with the full range of their legislative powers.

In conferring these powers on colonial legislatures, it was not customary to enumerate specific powers; it was customary merely to grant, in one or other of these well-worn phrases, the entire measure of jurisdiction deemed compatible with imperial control. As imperial control in the internal affairs of the colonies was mainly exercised through the power of disallowance, these phrases carried complete internal legislative competence. In fact, they are the title-deeds of the legislatures of the self-governing Dominions, not again added to by imperial legislation until the Statute of Westminster. The exponents of this historical interpretation, emphasizing the breadth of Dominion powers, infer from the insertion of this phrase in section 91, that the framers must have intended its full historic meaning to prevail saving only the powers expressly given to the provinces in section 92.

495

It is similarly urged that the Fathers meant an extended signification to be given to the phrase "Regulation of Trade and Commerce", in section 91. At the time of Confederation, Canada was just beginning to emerge from the commercial into the industrial age. The distinguishing feature of the commercial age was its pre-occupation with exchange, the trading of raw or crudely processed products on a world-wide scale. This required an extended organization, interprovincial and international in its scope. It was a delicate system, for its life-lines were everywhere exposed. Prosperity depended on its maintenance and its maintenance and development, in turn, depended on the sympathetic consideration, if not the positive assistance, of governments. Nothing showed this more clearly than the British imperial trading organization of the 18th and early 19th centuries. British North American statesmen had lived with this system and had seen what control over extended trading relationships by a single government could achieve. Trade and commerce, because of their nature and scope, were inevitably public matters of great import and it is argued that the phrase "the regulation of trade and commerce" had a very wide significance both historically and in the current usage of the Confederation period.

In addition, it is contended, they must have been acutely aware of the confusion which arises when control over such matters is parcelled out among several governments. During the fifty years in which the Provinces of Upper and Lower Canada maintained their separate existence, the control of the St. Lawrence and its commerce had been divided between two distinct and independent governments. This division led to conflicts between Upper and Lower Canada and to bitter struggles between the commercial and agrarian parties in each.[12] Upper Canada had disagreed with Lower Canada and the commercial interests in Montreal had quarrelled with the leaders of the Patriot party over many economic matters of common concern to the whole St. Lawrence Valley.

The impossibility of arriving quickly at a vigorous common policy in these matters had hampered Canada in its bid for the trade of the mid-continent. The frustrations engendered by divided authority formed part of the living memory of public men at the time of Confederation and this appeal to history for a broad interpretation of Dominion powers argues that the Fathers, who wanted to create a robust national economy, must have intended the control of such matters to be placed in the hands of a single government.

In support of this thesis, they draw attention to the reluctance among the commercial element in Montreal to give up the Union of 1841 which had established a common government to deal with these economic matters. The confederation plan asked them to abandon this union and one of the tasks of the advocates of a wider union was to convince them that the establishment again of two provinces in the St. Lawrence Valley would not mean a return to the old confusions. John Rose assured them that they had nothing to fear because the general legislature would have control over the post office, trade, commerce, navigation: — "all the great and important interests . . . that effect the minority in Lower Canada . . . ".[13] Galt reiterated that "the interests of trade and commerce . . . would be taken out of the category of local questions . . .".[14] Cartier, stating that he could understand the concern of the commercial minority of Lower Canada lest there should be a return of the old difficulties, said these fears were groundless because "it would be for the General Government to deal with our commercial matters".[15] On the basis of these statements, supporters of this historical interpretation argue that the words "Regulation of Trade and Commerce", were intended to transfer a wide range of economic matters to the control of the central authority.[16]

A historical interpretation which would magnify the scope of Dominion powers by attaching a limited special meaning to the phrase, "Property and Civil Rights in the Province" has also been urged. This phrase has had a long history in British North America, rising out of the relationships of French and English in the valley of the St. Lawrence. British statesmanship sought a solution of this racial problem which would preserve to French Canada the institutions which were vital to its way of life. The Quebec Act of 1774 secured "His Majesty's Canadian subjects within the Province of Quebec" in the enjoyment of their property and civil rights and provided that "in all matters of controversy relative to property and civil rights,

496

resort shall be had to the laws of Canada as the rule for the decision of the same".

In the constitutional and legislative enactments of both Upper and Lower Canada, there were a number of references to the law "relating to property and civil rights". In these references, the phrase was used to signify either the common law of England or the French customary law. That is to say, it denoted the set of laws and customs which were at once the expression and support of the distinctive ways of life of the French-speaking and English-speaking Canadians. The phrase found its way into sections 92 and 94 of the British North America Act.

Supporters of a broad view of federal power argue that the sole purpose of introducing the phrase "Property and Civil Rights in the Province" into section 92 was to protect the unique institutions and ways of life of the Province of Quebec. They lay strong emphasis on section 94 which contemplates certain conditions under which the federal authority may secure unrestricted power to make uniform laws "relative to Property and Civil Rights in Ontario, Nova Scotia and New Brunswick". To them, this section suggests that the phrase had reference only to matters on which these three provinces were in fundamental agreement and that regional differences of interest were not involved. Ontario, Nova Scotia and New Brunswick, with their acceptance of the English common law, were in agreement on precisely those matters in which each differed so completely from Quebec. Thus it is argued that the inclusion of this phrase in section 92 was not designed to express genuinely local as against national interests nor to fix the spheres of the different levels of government but rather to protect regional interests only in so far as they were specifically cultural in character.

497

This historical interpretation, therefore, maintains that the phrase, "Property and Civil Rights in the Province", as used in section 92, was intended to cover only what was necessary for this limited but important purpose of safeguarding the cultural autonomy of Quebec. It appeals to statements of British officials prior to the passing of the Quebec Act of 1774 and to the instructions of the British Government to the Governors of Quebec after 1774 as showing what were long understood to be the essential laws for safeguarding the fundamental institutions and ways of life of Quebec. These instructions to the Governors repeatedly commanded that the Canadians were to enjoy the "benefit and use of their own Laws, Usages and Customs in all Controversies respecting Titles of Land, and the Tenure, Descent . . . of Real Estates, and the distribution of the personal property of Persons dying intestate . . .".[17] Accordingly, the phrase in question would include matters of civil law concerning the relations of citizen and citizen, such as ownership, transfer and various dealings in property, inheritance and succession by will, rights arising from personal status, such as minority and capacity to make contracts, and from the intimate domestic relations of the family. It would include a variety of other matters of private law but it would not include a number of matters inextricably bound up with the public law such as nation-wide regulation of industry and trade. Still less could it include social insurance which had formed no part of either French or English law and the idea of which was unknown to those who framed the British North America Act. In this way, it is sought to infer from historical evidence an intention to give the phrase "Property and Civil Rights in the Province" a much more restricted meaning than that given to it by the Privy Council.

Historical Interpretation of the Intentions of the Fathers — Arguments Supporting a Broad View of Provincial Powers

These historical arguments as to the intentions of the Fathers of Confederation and the meaning assigned by them to general phrases such as "Peace, Order and good Government", "Regulation of Trade and Commerce" and "Property and Civil Rights in the Province" have not gone without challenge on historical grounds.[18] For example, it is urged that the expression "property and civil rights" has always had a very wide meaning in our constitutional history.

By Royal Edict in 1663, Louis XIV of France created a sovereign Council at Quebec giving it the power "de connaître de toutes causes civiles et criminelles, pour juger souverainement et en dernier ressort selon les lois et ordonnances de notre royaume",[19] which ruled New France at the time of the conquest.

The Royal Proclamation of George III of England in October, 1763, which proposed to introduce the English common law into the conquered territory in North America was naturally resented as a grave injustice by the people of Quebec. The Quebec Act of 1774 which was passed to meet this grievance, repealed the proclamation of October, 1763. Section 8 of the Act declared that "His Majesty's Canadian Subjects, within the province of Quebec . . . may also hold and enjoy their Property and Possessions, together with all Customs and Usages relative thereto, and all other their Civil Rights, in as large, ample, and beneficial Manner, as if the said Proclamation . . . had not been made" and then continued to provide, as quoted above, that the laws of Canada should provide the rule of decision in controversies "relative to Property and Civil Rights". This section of the Quebec Act has never been repealed.

The French law in its entirety was in force in New France at the time of the conquest and the people of Quebec desired to retain it. This was the ground of their objection to the Proclamation of 1763 and the Quebec Act was passed to meet this grievance. On the basis of these facts, it is argued that the Quebec Act was intended to meet the grievance fully and that the expression, "Property and Civil Rights", as used in the Act, was intended to comprise the entire French civil law and not merely certain selected portions of it. The only thing which is important for understanding the

498

scope of the Act is the purpose for which it was passed. The statements of British officials and the instructions of the British Government to colonial governors merely reveal their opinions. They do not give clues to the meaning of phrases used in the Quebec Act.

This argument attributes a very wide meaning to the expression "Property and Civil Rights" as used in the Quebec Act, and holds that when used in later statutes, the expression bears the same extended meaning unless an express limitation is introduced. No express limitation on the meaning of the phrase occurs in the British North America Act and therefore it is concluded that the broad meaning given to it by the Privy Council is in accordance with its original historical meaning.[20]

The Limitations of the Historical Arguments

All the historical interpretations go far afield for their arguments. There is no final certainty as to what the framers meant by the use of these phrases. The records of the time have not preserved all their opinions on all points. Clear statements of the views of some on particular points have come down to us; of the views of others, nothing is known.[21]

All that is certainly known is that the framers had large plans for the new Dominion and they proposed a strong central government with ample financial powers to carry the program through. The financial settlement which gave the Dominion the unrestricted taxing power, and the exclusive use of the most important revenue sources of the time (nearly four-fifths of the former provincial revenues were given to the new Dominion Government) is the most significant evidence of the leading role cast for the new Federal Government and of the responsibilities which it was expected to assume. In the provisions for reservation and disallowance of provincial legislation, the Fathers gave the Dominion legal power to supervise and control the legislatures of the provinces. At the same time, it was agreed that the state should be federal with exclusive spheres of power reserved to both the provinces and the Dominion. But the exact meanings intended to be given to the general words used in outlining these exclusive spheres of legislative power remain a matter for speculation.

There is no doubt that some of the framers had wanted a legislative union. Those who expected to be members of the new Federal Government naturally wanted a large stage on which to exhibit their capacity as statesmen.[22] But whatever their intentions, they could not overcome the limitations imposed by physical conditions. They could not ignore the social forces rooted in the history of the colonies any more than they could presume to bind the future indefinitely to the past.

There is a further limitation inherent in all historical interpretation of political constitutions which are to govern the distant future. The framers of the constitution could not foresee the revolutionary economic and social changes that have since taken place and therefore could have no intention at all concerning them. Whatever powers Confederation was intended to

499

confer on the Dominion, these intentions cannot provide answers for many of the questions which agitate us now for the simple reason that the conditions out of which present difficulties arise were not even remotely considered as possibilities. The intentions of the founders cannot, except by chance, provide solutions for problems of which they never dreamed.

Notes

1. *Speech on the Proposed Union of the British North American Provinces*, delivered at Sherbrooke on Nov. 23, 1864, p. 22.
2. Speech by Galt, *Confederation Debates*, p. 68.
3. In interpreting the British North America Act, "the question is not what may be supposed to have been intended but what has been said." Lord Sankey in *Edwards* v. *Attorney General of Canada* [1930] A.C. 124 at p. 137.
4. *E.g.*, C. H. Cahan, *The British North America Act*, 1867, an address delivered before the Canadian Club of Toronto, September 15, 1937; *cf. Report pursuant to Resolution of the Senate to the Honourable the Speaker, by the Parliamentory Counsel relating to the Enactment of the British North America Act*, Ottawa, 1939.
5. For historical interpretations in general supporting this view, see Appendix 2 — D. G. Creighton. *British North America at Confederation*; R. G. Trotter, *Canadian Federation* (Toronto, 1934); "The Coming of Confederation." *Cambridge History of the British Empire*, Vol. VI, pp. 438–62; Chester Martin, "British Policy in Canadian Federation." *Canadian Historical Review*, Vol. XIII, pp. 3–19; W. M. Whitelaw. *The Maritimes and Canada before Confederation*, (Toronto, 1934); W. P. M. Kennedy, *Essays in Constitutional Law*, p. 85*ff*; V. C. MacDonald, "Judicial Interpretation of the Canadian Constitution", *University of Toronto Law Journal*, Vol. I. No. 2, p. 260*ff*. For careful description of the Quebec Conference see W. M. Whitelaw, "Reconstructing the Quebec Conference", *Canadian Historical Review*, Vol. XIX, pp. 123–37.
6. *Confederation Debates*, p. 40. See also pp. 30, 33, 41.
7. *Speech on the Proposed Union*, p. 10.
8. Quoted by V. C. MacDonald, "Judicial Interpretations of the Canadian Constitution" (1936), *University of Toronto Law Journal*, p. 263.
9. *Confederation Debates*, p. 250.
10. *Ibid.*, p. 859.
11. C. H. Cahan, *op. cit.*
12. These conflicts are examined in detail in D. G. Creighton, *The Commercial Empire of the St. Lawrence, 1760–1850.*
13. *Confederation Debates*, p. 409.
14. *Speech on the Proposed Union*, p. 20.
15. *Confederation Debates*, p. 61.
16. See Appendix 2 to *The Rowell-Sirois Report* — D. G. Creighton, *British North America at Confederation*, pp. 50–52.
17. W. P. M. Kennedy, *Statutes, Treaties and Documents*, p. 156.
18. P. B. Mignault (formerly Mr. Justice Mignault of the Supreme Court of Canada), "Nos Problèmes Constitutionnels" (1928), 16 *Revue du Droit*, p. 577; V. Evan Gray, "The O'Connor Report on the British North America Act" (1939), 17 *Canadian Bar Review* 309.
19. "to deal with all civil and criminal cases, to judge finally and in the last resort according to the laws and ordinances of our kingdom".
20. For this argument, see P. B. Mignault, *op. cit.*
21. The agreement reached by delegates to the Quebec Conference is acknowledged to have been a compromise and it is unlikely that the delegates, in the subsequent discussions, always distinguished clearly between the compromise and their own conception of what Confederation should have been. For a clear statement of the difficulties attending historical interpretation, see V. Evan Gray "The O'Connor Report on the British North America Act", (1939), 309 at pp. 315–8.
22. John A. Macdonald probably had the possibility of a great future in mind when he said, "We are all mere petty provincial politicians at present; perhaps by and by some of us will rise to the level of national statemen." Quoted by A. R. M. Lower in "Sir John A. Macdonald", (1939), 19 *Dalhousie Review*, p. 86.

Act or Pact:
Another Look at Confederation*
GEORGE F. G. STANLEY

I

There are probably few Canadian historians, and even fewer political scientists, who have not, at some time or another, taken a second glance at the British North America Act of 1867; few of them, too, who have not lectured to their students upon the facts underlying the federal union of which the Act is the legislative expression, and commented upon the nature and essence of Canadian federalism. It is because of the generality of interest in the British North America Act that I have yielded to the temptation, not to present to you, as my presidential address, a detailed paper upon some narrow aspect of the historical researches which have absorbed my time during the last two or three years, but to offer for your consideration a few general comments upon a subject which has both a wide and topical interest at the present time. My approach is, of course, that of the historian. I am concerned, not with what our constitution is or ought to be — that I leave to my scientifically political brethren — but with how it became what it is.

501

To my mind the principal factor — I do not suggest it as the sole factor but as one of the most important — in determining the course of Canadian constitutional development, has been the existence, within Canada, of two competing ethnic, cultural groups. The Earl of Durham, in his famous *Report*, chose to refer to them as "two nations warring in the bosom of a single state".[1] Were he writing in today's idiom, he might have preferred to substitute the word "co-existing" for "warring". Certainly "warring" is too strong and too inaccurate a word to describe what has been simply the political struggle on the part of the English-speaking population for supremacy, and on the part of the French-speaking population for survival. This struggle has dominated the whole story of Canadian politics. It probably accounts for the prepossession of Canadian historians with political and constitutional history. The struggle is one which still continues, and the issues are still the same; supremacy as against survival, or to use the contemporary terms, centralization as against provincial autonomy.

And yet, perhaps, if the word "warring" is unsuitable as a general description of Anglo-French relations within the bosom of this country, Canada, at times it has not been without some aptness; for the bitterness and misunderstandings which have frequently accompanied our relations have cut, on occasions, close to the bone. That civil strife in Canada has

*From *Canadian Historical Association Report*, 1956, 1–25. Copyright by the Canadian Historical Association. Reprinted by permission.

never degenerated into civil war has been due, in part at least, to the recognition by both peoples of the necessity of some *modus vivendi* and the recognition by each of the rights of the other. The recognition and definition of these rights is the basis of the entente, understanding, pact, compact, call it what you will, which is the foundation of our political unity. Without such an entente there would have been, and would be no Canada as we know it today. Much has been written, both in the French and English languages about this pact; some of it narrow and legalistic; more of it unhistorical; much of it purely polemical. If we attempt to look upon this pact or entente as a legal contract, freely entered into by two parties and intended by them to be legally enforceable in a court of law, our vision will be so limited as to be distorted; for a pact or compact is not a contract in the legal sense. It is a gentleman's agreement, an understanding based upon mutual consent, with a moral rather than a juridical sanction. The Anglo-French understanding which alone has made government possible within the boundaries of the larger Canada has become sanctified by time and continued acceptance, until today it is looked upon by many as a convention of our constitution. It is my immediate purpose, this evening, to trace for you the origin and growth of this convention, and to discuss some of its implications in the development of our constitution.

502

II

It was the cession of Canada to Great Britain in 1763, that initiated the problem of which our bi-racial pact in Canada became the ultimate solution. It brought within an English, Protestant empire, a French, Catholic colony. How the one could successfully incorporate the other was the question which confronted British statesmen following the Treaty of Paris. Previous experience with Acadia offered little in the way of guidance; the expulsion of the inhabitants of the new colony was neither a humane nor a politically satisfying solution. The easy answer seemed to be assimilation; the King's new subjects might even be induced to abandon their heretical ways before they were swamped by British immigration to Canada. Assimilation was the object and essence of the Proclamation issued on October 7, 1763, over the sign manual of George III.[2] It was also the object of the long commission and letter of instructions issued the first British Governor of Canada, James Murray.[3] But assimilation, particularly a half-hearted assimilation, proved unsuccessful. Its one effect was to stiffen the heart and mind of the French-speaking population, and to give strength and cohesion to its determination to survive as a cultural and as a political group. Ten years of criminations and recriminations between the King's old and new subjects resulted in a victory for the latter. In 1774, the Quebec Act[4] definitely removed the anti-French, anti-Catholic bias of earlier policy. It cleared the way for French Canadians to accept government appointments; it guaranteed to the French those civil laws and religious privileges which, to this time, had either been denied, neglected, or merely tolerated. In brief, the Quebec Act placed the French Canadians, the King's new subjects, on a basis of political and religious equality with the English and Anglo-Americans, the so-called old subjects. The Act did not father the French fact in Canada; what it did do was to provide it with a juridical foundation. An English-Canadian historian, Professor A. L. Burt, has written "the Quebec Act embodied a new sovereign principle of the British Empire: the liberty of non-English peoples to be themselves";[5] a French Canadian, Etienne Parent, has called the Act, "a true social contract between us and England . . . the consecration of our natural right".[6] The Quebec Act, it might be noted in passing, was never repealed by the British Parliament; some of its provisions have been nullified by subsequent legislation, but it still stands, honoured by French Canadians as the Magna Charta of their national rights and privileges.

From the standpoint of the French Canadians, the guarantees afforded by the Quebec Act had come none too soon. Within several shot-riddled years, the whole demographic premise upon which the British Government had made the concessions embodied in the Act, that of a continuing predominance of the French-speaking population, had been altered by the coming of the United Empire Loyalists. From one-twentieth of the total population, the English-speaking inhabitants of the old province of Quebec increased, in a few months, to one-seventh. Co-existence, or perhaps I should say co-habitation, became more difficult than ever. The constitution of 1774 became an anachronism. It brought neither understanding nor prosperity to the province. It was, in truth, satisfactory neither to the French nor to the English-speaking population; both of whom could unite their voices upon two demands only, political separation from each other and a greater share in the management of their own local affairs. The Loyalists had been accustomed to and demanded elective, representative institutions on the British parliamentary model; many French Canadians, imbued with the pro-English ideas of Voltaire and the Encyclopaedists, or perhaps only with those of Pierre du Calvet, likewise demanded the political freedom denied them by the constitution of 1774. Some there were in London who wondered what the effect of the changes would be: some who argued that the establishment of a "separate and local" legislature "under any form or model which can be adopted for the purpose" would lead inevitably "to habitual Notions of a distinct interest", and "to the existence of a virtual independence" and then, "naturally to prepare the way for an entire separation, whenever other circumstances shall bring it forward".[7] But the British government believed that it knew what the situation required: the old province of Quebec should be divided into two new, separate and distinct provinces on an ethnic basis, with the Ottawa river as the line of division: and each province should be provided with a new constitution generally assimilated to that of Great Britain, including an elective assembly as well as appointed legislative and executive councils. On June 19, 1791, Canada's second constitution by British parliamentary enactment received the royal assent and became law.[8]

Few British politicians, or Anglo-Canadians for that matter, fully appreciated what impact the Constitutional Act would have upon the problem of

503

reconciling the French and English-speaking inhabitants of the two Canadas. Grenville seems to have had some vague ideas when he wrote to Lord Dorchester, sending him a draft copy of the new constitution, that "a considerable degree of attention is due to the prejudices and habits of the French Inhabitants who compose so large a proportion of the community, and every degree of caution should be used to continue to them the enjoyment of those civil and religious rights which were secured to them by the Capitulation of the Province, or have since been granted by the liberal and enlightened spirit of the British Government."[9] So too did William Pitt, when he answered Fox's objections to dividing the old province, that any effort to unite the two peoples within a single political entity governed by a single legislature, would lead only to "a perpetual scene of factious discord."[10] But Grenville, when he wrote about the rights of the French Canadians, was thinking only of how the British Government might distract their attention away from what Frenchmen, and French women too, were doing and saying in the streets of the Paris of the Revolution. And William Pitt beclouded his argument with Fox by talking airly and unrealistically about how the French Canadians, novices in the art of parliamentary government, would be so impressed with the success attending the working of the new English-type constitution in the neighbouring province, that they would strive to enjoy its fullest benefits by uniting with English-speaking Canada. Race, religion, laws and traditions would, one after the other, be discarded, as Lower Canadians sought the Holy Grail of political success and economic prosperity. The very fact of splitting Quebec into two provinces, Upper and Lower Canada, of which Fox (and the English-speaking minority in Lower Canada) had complained, would, in the end, be the means of bringing about ultimate unity. Edmund Burke spoke in a similar vein. It was a strange kind of reasoning. Granting the sincerity of their convictions, one may only conclude that they were ignorant of Canada, that they had misread its history, and that they misunderstood the whole concept of nationality.[11]

Far from encouraging the French to abandon their own consciousness of identity, the effect of the Constitutional Act of 1791 was to give renewed vigour to the idea of French Canadian separateness. It provided the French fact with a geographical as well as a political buttress. If the Quebec Act of 1774 guaranteed the survival of the French Canadians, the Constitutional Act of 1791 guaranteed the survival of French Canada. The Act of 1791 was the logical, if not the inevitable sequel to the Act of 1774. It was, in the words of Canon Groulx, "a renewed consecration of the French fact in Canada."[12]

This is not the place to discuss the internal defects of the Constitution of 1791. They are familiar to every student of our history. And yet I wonder, sometimes, whether there has not been too much inclination on the part of Canadians to treat the Act of 1791 as a kind of constitutional whipping boy; whether in trying to be political scientists, we cease to be historians. Do we not sometimes fall into the error of confusing the regime with its institutions? Do we not, all too frequently, look upon the history of Canada in isolation, forgetting that these years are, at the same time, the years of Conservative ascendancy in Great Britain, the years of the anti-liberal restrictive legislation inspired by the excesses of the French Revolution? Is it wholly without significance, when considering the constitutional developments of Canada between 1791 and 1840, to recall that only three weeks before the passage of the Act the same British government which sponsored it issued the first of the decrees against sedition; and that in 1830, only seven years before blood was shed on the banks of the Richelieu, and near Gallow's Hill, the Duke of Wellington had cried that he would never bring forward any measure of parliamentary reform, and that "as long as he held any station in the Government of the country, he should always feel it his duty to resist any such measure when proposed by others."[13] I do not mean to imply that the Constitution of 1791 was without fault. I simply suggest that, taking conditions as they were, there could be no answer during these years to the dilemma of how to reconcile imperial centralization and colonial autonomy. There could be no accommodation between a reactionary, metropolitan Toryism and a revolutionary provincial democracy, within the rigid framework of the constitution. Under other circumstances the Constitution of 1791 might have worked moderately well; under the circumstances such as they were, it collapsed in fire and bloodshed.

505

The immediate sequel to the rebellions in Upper and Lower Canada was the suppression of the ill-fated constitution and the appointment of a special commissioner, the Earl of Durham, to inquire into the political situation and make recommendations regarding "the Form and Administration of the Civil Government" to be granted to the two Canadas. In his Report, dated January 31, 1839, Durham exposed the weakness of the previous regime, and recommended the concession of effective self-government to the Canadians. But if Durham favoured self-government (or what is known in our history as responsible government) it was only for a government dominated by English-speaking people. Essentially an Imperialist and a centralizer, Durham was the effective advocate of the supremacy of things English. He toyed with the idea of a federal union of the British North American provinces, but cast it aside when he realized that it would inevitably give the French Canadians of Lower Canada control over their own local affairs; instead, he recommended that Upper and Lower Canada be joined together in an indissoluble union with one government and one legislature. "I believe", he wrote, "that tranquillity can only be restored by subjecting the Province to the vigorous rule of an English majority; and that the only efficacious government would be that formed by a legislative union".[14] It was the old policy of assimilation all over again.

In 1840 the British Parliament performed the marriage ceremony. The two Canadian provinces, dissimilar in numbers, as well as in origin, faith, language and tradition, were united by the Act of Union.[15] The new constitution did not, however, follow strictly to the letter the recommendations which Durham had penned the year before. The union was not a thorough-going, punitive, Anglicizing union such as the Earl had contemplated. The demographic situation would not permit it. The fact was that the English-speaking populations of the two provinces combined did not enjoy what Durham mistakenly believed to be the case, "a clear English majority".[16] A legislative union pure and simple, instead of overwhelming the French Canadians, would have had the opposite results; it would have given them unquestioned control of the legislature of the united province, and this state of affairs, even though it might endure only a few years, was regarded as intolerable. The only way to defeat the French majority would be to crib, cabin and confine it to Lower Canada; and this could best be done by preserving as distinct, political entities the two provinces which it had been proposed to obliterate and by giving each of them equal representation in the new legislature. Since the English-speaking representatives from Upper Canada could always hope to find a few compatriots among the representatives of Lower Canada, together they would outnumber the delegates of French origin. The new constitution was thus, in effect, a vague, unintended, and undefined form of federalism, with the provinces of Upper and Lower Canada continuing in existence under the names of Canada West and Canada East, despite their union in one political entity called the Province of Canada. *Nil facit error nominis, cum de corpore constat*, the name does not affect the substance so long as its identity is manifest, is a maxim familiar to every lawyer.

But British policy in the end defeated itself. By denying French Canadians the temporary advantage of representation according to population, the British authorities not only strengthened French determination to hold securely every privilege gained in 1774 and 1791, they unwittingly provided them with the very means of holding these privileges, when as expected, the numbers of the French-speaking population fell below those of their English-speaking rivals. Equality of representation for the two provinces which were the political and geographical expressions of the two racial groups, was a sword which cut both ways.

The federal nature of the new constitution became more and more apparent as the years passed. Voting and acting as a political unit, the French Canadians were too large and too significant a *bloc* to be ignored. Government by one province alone, Canada West, was impossible; the collaboration of Canada East was not only desirable, it was a political necessity. And this collaboration could only be obtained upon French Canada's own terms. Sir Charles Bagot recognized this fact when, in 1842, he finally took Louis LaFontaine, the French Canadian leader, into his ministry along with his English-speaking colleague, Robert Baldwin. Sir Charles wrote to an infuriated Colonial Secretary in London:

I knew . . . that I could not hope to succeed with the French Canadians as a Race . . . and not as a mere party in the House, unless I could secure the services of men who possessed their confidence, and who would bring to my assistance, not only their own talents, and some votes in the House of Assembly, but the goodwill and attachment of their race, and that I could not obtain such services unless I was willing to place the individuals in a position in my Council which would prevent them from feeling themselves a hopeless minority against a suspicious and adverse majority.[17]

Bagot congratulated himself that he had "satisfied" the French Canadians that the Union was "capable of being administered for their happiness and advantage, and have consequently disarmed their opposition to it". He had, however, done a great deal more. He had established the first of the dual ministries with their premiers and their attorneys-general from both Canada East and Canada West; he had pointed the way to the development of the principle of the double-majority; he had given official sanction to the federal idea implicit in the Act of 1840. The two old provinces of Upper and Lower Canada might have ceased to exist in law, but they did exist in fact and in practice, and continued to exist throughout the whole of the Union period. There was real truth in John A. Macdonald's statement in 1865, "although we now sit in one Parliament, supposed constitutionally to represent the people without regard to sections or localities, yet we know, as a matter of fact, that since the union in 1841, we have had a Federal Union."[18] There was a wide gap between intention and reality. In spite of Bagot's precedent, the original idea behind the Union died hard. Metcalfe tried to win French support by appealing not to a race but simply to individuals of French origin. He failed. In the end Lord Elgin gave the *coup de grâce* to Durham's policy of denationalization and assimilation. He reverted to Sir Charles Bagot's policy, and in so doing restored the principle that an Anglo-French entente or understanding was the *sine qua non* of the successful operation of the Canadian political system. It is a principle which has lasted to the present day. Not only did Lord Elgin recall Baldwin and LaFontaine to his ministry, he also set the seal of approval upon the bi-national character of the regime by obtaining from the British authorities the abrogation of Article XLI of the Act of Union declaring English to be the one language of official record. And then, at the opening of the legislative session in January 1849, he read the speech from the throne both in French and in English.[19]

The Union did not, however, enjoy a long or peaceful life. Fundamentally the explanation for its early demise is to be found in the internal contradiction upon which it was based, for it was neither frankly federal nor unequivocally unitary. The union, indeed, managed to survive its twenty-five harried years only by applying the principles of disunion. The heavy hammer blows which finally brought about its end were those wielded by the French-baiting, Catholic-hating Clear Grits of Canada West and their francophobe journalist leader, George Brown. *No Popery* and *No French Domination* were the constant Grit refrain; to which was added, once Canada West had passed the neighbouring province in population, the more positive and more politically dangerous slogan, *Rep. by Pop.* Representation by population was a denial of the political understanding upon which LaFontaine and Canada East had agreed to collaborate with

507

Baldwin and Canada West in the administration of the United Province. It meant the end of the principle of equality, the collapse of the federal concept, the exposure of Lower Canada to the rule of a hostile, alien majority, the overthrow of the entente which had alone made government possible. As the new slogan gained adherents so too did the idea that the premise upon which Anglo-French collaboration was based, namely the mutual acceptance of equality of status, was a vital and fundamental principle of the constitution; that it constituted, if not an unbreakable pact, at least a gentleman's agreement between the two racial groups which went to make up the population. In 1849 LaFontaine had replied to Papineau:

It is on the basis of the principle of looking upon the Act of Union as a confederation of two provinces . . . that I hereby emphatically declare that never I will consent to one of the sections of the Province having, in this House, a greater number of members than the other, whatever the numbers of its population may be.[20]

Hincks, Cartier and Macdonald all spoke in a similar vein. In April 1861, during one of the periodic debates on representation by population, Macdonald uttered what may possibly be the first statement in English of what we today speak of as the Compact theory of Confederation, when he said "The Union was a distinct bargain, a solemn contract".[21] This was no slip of the tongue. In 1865, during the Confederation debates, he again referred to "The Treaty of Union" between Lower and Upper Canadians.[22]

III

There is no need for me to discuss the various factors leading to Confederation — the threat of American imperialism, the fear of the westward expansion of the United States, the necessity for improved railway communications, the political impasse in Canada; all of this is familiar ground to generations of Canadian students. Nor is it necessary for me to chronicle the erratic course of the ambulatory conference of 1864 or to follow its members, bottle by bottle, as they travelled through the Maritimes and Canada, dispensing good will and self-congratulatory speeches to all who were prepared to listen to them. However, I do wish to direct your attention, for a moment, to the fundamental problem which faced the delegates who met at Charlottetown and at Quebec, that of reconciling the conflicting interests of the two racial groups and of the conflicting principles of centralization and provincial autonomy. Broadly speaking — and there are, of course, exceptions to this general statement — the English-speaking representatives, pragmatists, suspicious of ideas and generalizations, preoccupied with economic and political interests and secure in their every increasing majority over the French Canadians, were disposed to favour a strong central government, if not actually a legislative union; the French Canadians, empiricists, uneasy, apprehensive, and deeply concerned with the survival of their culture, were by religion and by history in favour of a constitution which would, at the very least, secure them such guarantees as they had already extracted from the British government during the hundred years which had gone before. No French Canadian, intent upon preserving his national identity or bettering his political future could ever agree to a legislative union. Only federalism would permit the two, distinct, and separate, cultures to co-exist side by side within the bosom of a single state. Federalism, not a half-way, hesitant, ill-defined, semi-unitary federalism like that which had evolved out of the Act of Union, but an honest, whole-hearted, clearly-stated, precise federalism was the only solution acceptable to the French Canadian leaders. Thus, the one group was, at heart, for unity and fusion; the other for diversity and co-operation; the one was dominated by economic fact and the other, philosophical principle.

The fundamental opposition of these two divergent points of view does not, unfortunately, appear in the documentary fragments of the conferences which we possess; it does, however, emerge clearly in a letter written by Sir Arthur Gordon, Lieutenant-Governor of New Brunswick, following his visit to Charlottetown and his conversations with Cartier, Brown and Galt. In a lengthy despatch to the Colonial Office outlining the details of the union scheme as the Canadians had put it up to the Maritimers, Gordon wrote:

509

> With regard to the important question of the attributes to be assigned to the respective Legislatures and Governments, there was a very great divergence of opinion. The aim of Lower Canada is a local independence as complete as circumstances will permit, and the peculiarities of race, religion and habits which distinguish its people render their desire respectable and natural.[23]

It was at Quebec that the new constitution took form and shape. To the old capital of New France came delegates from the six provinces, the four seaboard provinces of Nova Scotia, Newfoundland, Prince Edward Island and New Brunswick, and the two provinces of Canada, which, if they did not have a juridical basis, had, at least, as I have pointed out, a factual foundation. This gathering at Quebec was the first and only constituent body in the whole of our constitutional history. All previous constitutions had been drafted, considered, and passed, by an outside authority; in 1864 the thirty-three representatives of the British North American provinces met, with the blessing and approval of the British Government, to do what had hitherto always been done for them.

The constitution which they adopted in the form of seventy-two Resolutions had already been prepared in draft form before the Canadian delegates had ever disembarked at Charlottetown. In many respects it bore a striking resemblance to an outline plan which had appeared over the name of Joseph Charles Taché in *Le Courrier du Canada* in 1857, and which had been published as a book in the following year.[24] In summary form, what the Quebec Conference decided was that the new union should be federal in character; that its central parliament should comprise two houses, the

upper based on representation by provinces, and the lower upon representation by population; that the powers of the central government should be
of a general character and those of the provincial legislatures of a local
nature. These powers were carefully enumerated, but the legislative residuum
was given to the central parliament. The French and English languages
were to enjoy equal status in the central parliament and courts and in the
legislature and courts of the province of Lower Canada.

George Cartier, generally, was satisfied with what had been achieved.
He felt that even though he had been obliged to yield much to the
demands of Macdonald and Brown and other advocates of a strong central
government, he had, nevertheless, succeeded in preserving the rights and
privileges of his own people and of the province in which they lived.[25] He
had, moreover, succeeded in maintaining the fundamental principle of the
entente between the two racial groups in Canada, equality of race, equality
of religion, equality of language, equality of laws. Even George Brown, the
old francophobe, had gone as far as to admit to the Canadian legislature
"whether we ask for parliamentary reform for Canada alone, or in union
with the Maritime Provinces, the French Canadians must have their views
consulted as well as us (sic). This scheme can be carried and no scheme can
be that has not the support of both sections of the province."[26] The new
constitution might not be designed to be the most efficient, but it would,
at least, be just.

The next step was as easy as it was logical. Since both races were equal,
a decision taken, an agreement arrived at by the equal partners on the
fundamental character of the new constitution, could not be changed
without the consent of each. It was, in fact a treaty, a compact binding
upon both parties. This was a view which scarcely roused a dissenting
voice in the Canada of 1865. Not one of the Canadians who fathered the
resolutions at Quebec failed to stress the unalterable character of the
agreement they had made. Macdonald said, "these resolutions were in the
nature of a treaty, and if not adopted in their entirety, the proceedings
would have to be commenced de novo".[27] McGee, in his high-pitched but
not unmusical voice, cried:

And that there may be no doubt about our position in regard to that document we say,
question it you may, reject it you may, or accept it you may, but alter it you may not.
(Hear, hear.) It is beyond your power, or our power, to alter it. There is not a sentence —
ay, or even a word — you can alter without desiring to throw out the document . . . . On
this point, I repeat after all my hon. friends who have already spoken, for one party to alter
a treaty is, of course, to destroy it.[28]

Taché, Cartier, McDougall, Brown, all of them described the Quebec
Resolutions as a "treaty" or as a "pact", and argued for adoption without
amendment.[29]

It is easy for the lawyer or the political scientist, three generations later,
to reply that in 1865 there was no treaty really made at all, that the
Compromise of Quebec could not possess the attributes of a treaty or of a
legal contract. Nevertheless the historical fact remains that the men who

used these terms were the men who drafted the Resolutions; they chose their words with deliberation; many of them were lawyers, they knew what they were saying. They were not, every one of them, trying to becloud the issue before the legislature or to confuse the legislators. I have found no evidence which would lead me to question their sincerity or to believe that they disbelieved their own assertions. In strict law it is probably true that the terms they used to describe the Quebec Resolutions were not all that could be desired in the way of legalistic exactitude; but to my mind these terms adequately expressed the ideas which the Fathers of the Confederate Resolutions wished to convey to their listeners and to posterity, for they spoke to both. The idea of a compact between races was not a new one in 1865; it had already become a vital thing in our history. It influenced both the political thinking and the political vocabulary of the day; and it was already on the way to become a tradition and a convention of our constitution.

511

The idea of a compact as I have outlined it was essentially, in its origin, a racial concept. But the meeting of the maritime delegates with those of Canada at Charlottetown and at Quebec introduced a new interpretation which has had mighty impact upon the course of our later history, namely, the idea of a compact between the politico-geographic areas which go to make up Canada. Even before the conferences it had become the common practice to identify the racial groups with the areas from which they came. When thinking of French Canadians or of Anglo-Canadians, it was all too simple to speak of them in geographical terms, as Lower Canada and Upper Canada. It was a confusion of mind and speech of which we in our own day and generation are all too frequently guilty. Almost without thought "Quebec" and "French Canadians", or "Ontario" and "Anglo-Canadians", became synonymous terms in the mouths of Canadians of both tongues. It is, of course, a slipshod way of thinking as well as of speaking, for there are French Canadians in Ontario and English Canadians in Quebec; and in many ways it has been unfortunate, for it has limited to Quebec language rights which might, under happier circumstances, have been accorded French Canadians in other parts of the country. That English did not suffer the same fate in Quebec as did the French tongue in other provinces, was due in part to the effective role of English-speaking Quebeckers, like McGee and Galt, in the drafting of the federative act, as well as to a greater appreciation on the part of French Canadians of the need for toleration. However, the point which I really wish to make is this; once Canadians (as distinct from Maritimers) began to identify provinces with specific linguistic groups, the idea of a pact between races was transformed into the idea of a pact between provinces. And the Compromise of Quebec became a compact between the provinces which participated in the conference. I have no need to labour this point. It emerges in all clarity from a careful reading of the speeches to be found in Confederation Debates of 1865.

However, the compact idea, was still, in 1865, peculiarly a Canadian one.

It was not shared by the delegates of the several Maritime colonies who had journeyed to Quebec. From what I have seen of the debates in the legislatures and the speeches reported in the press of Nova Scotia and New Brunswick, the words so familiar in Canada, words like "pact", "treaty" or "compact" were rarely used in reference to what had been decided upon at Charlottetown or Quebec. There was never any idea in the minds of the Maritime representatives that the Seventy-Two Resolutions were sacrosanct. Thus, when Nova Scotia and New Brunswick resolved in 1866 to renew the negotiations for a federal union with Canada, they sent their representatives to London with full authority to make any changes and to conclude any new arrangement they might see fit. In the case of Nova Scotia, Sir Charles Tupper, an ardent exponent of federation on the basis of the Quebec Scheme, accepted without comment a proposal that the Quebec Resolutions should be abandoned and a new confederate agreement drawn up in conjunction with the other provinces concerned.[30] This distinction between the Canadian and Maritime approaches to the Quebec Resolutions was brought out when the Canadian and Maritime representatives met in conference in London in December 1866. Macdonald, Galt and McDougall, all agreed that the Canadians, at least, were bound to adhere to the details of the Quebec scheme. Jonathan McCully and J. W. Ritchie of Nova Scotia took the view that, as far as Nova Scotians were concerned, they were bound by nothing. Said John A. Macdonald in reply, "The Maritime delegates are differently situated from us. Our Legislature passed an address to the Queen praying for an Act of Union, on the basis of the Quebec Resolutions. We replied to enquiries in our last Session of Parliament that we did not feel at liberty ourselves to vary those resolutions".[31] W. P. Howland, another Canadian delegate, added, "We place ourselves in a false position in every departure from the Quebec scheme".[32]

In the end, the terms of the agreement drafted and adopted at the Westminster Palace Hotel in London in December 1866, were substantially those which had previously been discussed and accepted at Quebec. A great deal has, I know, been made of the London Resolutions as a new departure and as an effective denial of the idea of a binding pact having been concluded at Quebec; but a detailed comparison of the two sets of resolutions reveals no really substantial points of difference. The outline is similar; the wording in many instances is unchanged. Such alterations as were made, appear to have been either of a minor nature intended to clarify an ambiguity or inserted to strengthen, rather than to weaken the bi-racial, bi-cultural aspect of the pact. Certainly the people of the day who were most concerned viewed the revised resolutions after this fashion. On January 5th, 1867 the editor of *The Morning Freeman* of St. John, N.B., wrote, "If the Quebec Scheme has been modified in any important particulars they are profoundly ignorant of what the modifications are".[33] Two months later he wrote again while the British North America Bill was before Parliament:

512

We ask any reasonable, intelligent man of any party to take up that Bill, compare it with the original Quebec Scheme, and discover, if he can, anything that could possibly have occupied honest, earnest men, for even a week, no matter what the particular objections to the few changes that have been made . . . . Could not all these matters have been settled as well and as much to the satisfaction of the public by letter, at an expense of a few shillings postage . . . as by this large and most costly delegation?[34]

The London Resolution of 1866 were, in a word, little if anything more than an edited version of the Quebec Resolutions of 1864; the contractual nature of the pact remained unaffected.

The British seemed to like the idea of a provincial compact. Both the Colonial Secretary, Lord Carnarvon and his undersecretary. the Honourable Charles Adderley, accepted it as an accurate description of what was intended and what was achieved. Mr. Adderley, who introduced the Bill based on the resolutions into the British House of Commons, urged upon the members, in words which might have come straight from the mouth of Macdonald or Cartier, that no change or alteration should be made in the terms of the Bill:

513

The House may ask what occasion there can be for our interfering in a question of this description. It will, however, I think, be manifest, upon reflection, that, as the arrangement is a matter of mutual concession on the part of the Provinces, there must be some external authority to give sanction to the compact into which they have entered . . . . If, again, federation has in this case specially been a matter of most delicate mutual treaty and compact between the provinces — if it has been a matter of mutual concession and compromise — it is clearly necessary that there should be a third party *ab extra* to give sanction to the treaty made between them. Such seems to me to be the office we have to perform in regard to this Bill.[35]

Lord Carnarvon, in the House of Lords, said:

the Quebec Resolutions, with some slight changes, form the basis of a measure that I have now the honour to submit to Parliament. To those resolutions all the British Provinces in North America were, as I have said, consenting parties, and the measure founded upon them must be accepted as a treaty of union.[36]

Later in the same speech Carnarvon, after pointing out that a legislative union was "impracticable", because of Lower Canada's jealousy and pride in "her ancestral customs and traditions" and her willingness to enter Confederation "only upon the distinct understanding that she retains them", stated emphatically that the terms of the British North America Bill were "of the nature of a treaty of union, every single clause in which had been debated over and over again, and had been submitted to the closest scrutiny, and, in fact each of them represented a compromise between the different interests involved." "There might be alterations where they are not material", he continued, "and do not go to the essence of the measure . . . . But it will be my duty to resist the alteration of anything which is in the nature of a compromise between the Provinces, as an amendment of that nature, if carried, would be fatal to the measure."[37]

The legalist will, of course, reply that the intervention of the Colonial

Office and the passing of the Bill as an Act of the British Parliament in effect destroyed the compactual — I prefer to avoid the word "contractual" with its juridical connotation — basis of the historical process of confederation. Perhaps it does; to the lawyer. But to the historian the simple fact remains that the officers of the Colonial Office accepted without question the assessment of the situation given them by the colonial delegates. To them the Bill was in the nature of a colonial treaty, even if such a treaty were not to be found in the classifications usually given in the text books of international law. In consequence they were prepared to leave the colonial delegates alone, to let them make their own arrangements, thresh out their own differences, draft their own agreement. Neither Lord Carnarvon nor the members of his office entered the negotiations or took part in them until the Quebec Resolutions had undergone the revision or editing to which I have referred. When they did, it was at the specific request of the delegates, with the object of acting in an advisory capacity only. Perhaps the British role is best expressed in the suggestion that the Colonial Secretary acted in the capacity of a notary reducing to proper legal terms an understanding already arrived at by the parties concerned. That certainly was the role in which Carnarvon saw himself. The British North America Act was, therefore, not the work of the British authorities, nor the expression of ideas of the British Colonial Office; it was, in essence, simply the recognition in law of the agreement arrived at originally in Quebec and clarified later in London, by the representatives of the provinces of Nova Scotia, New Brunswick, and Canada with its two divisions, Canada East and Canada West.

514

The British North America Act passed through its necessary readings in the House of Commons and in the House of Lords without change or alteration; on March 28, 1867, it received the Royal Assent. By royal proclamation it came into effect on the first day of July following. The new constitution was, without question, a statute of the British Parliament, and as such possessed the attributes of an ordinary statute. But it was a statute distinctly unlike any other previously passed by the Parliament at Westminster. The Quebec Act of 1774, the Constitutional Act of 1791, the Act of Union of 1840, all of them had been devised, drafted, and enacted, without reference to the people of the provinces concerned. Individuals and groups of individuals had been consulted, it is true; but the work was done and the responsibility was taken by the Imperial authorities. The British North America Act, however, was, to all intents and purposes, the work of the several self-governing, quasi-sovereign colonies themselves. The Colonial Office did no more than put the words into proper form and the British Parliament no more than give them legislative sanction. The British North America Act was, therefore, to use the words of an early Canadian jurist, "a simple ratification by the Mother Country of the agreement entered into by the provinces, which in confirming its provisions rendered them obligatory by giving them the authority of an Imperial Act".[38]

IV

But the legal supplementing of the interprovincial pact, both by the Canadian and British governments, did not mean that the problems of the coexistence of the two contending races within the bosom of a single state had been solved. Agreement there could be on broad lines of how to divide authority between the central and provincial governments, but disagreement on the details of the division was inherent in the very nature of a federal constitution, and particularly in Canada where federal union in the mouth of a Lower Canadian usually meant "the independence of his Province from English and Protestant influences"[39] and in that of the Upper Canadian, a preference for a strong central government.[40] Ministers and Prime Ministers might pay lip service to the doctrine of a Pact;[41] they might honestly believe in its validity; they could shelve but could not shed their centralizing proclivities. There was never any underhand conspiracy to destroy the Anglo-French entente: but there was an openhanded effort to add to the powers of the central governmet at the expense of those of the provinces. I need only mention the names of Macdonald, Mowat and Mercier to recall to mind the early trials of strength of the two opposing points of view. Fortunately the arbiter was there, the courts: the controversies which opposing points of view engendered were resolvable by due process of law. The powers of federal parliament and those of the provincial legislatures had, in 1867, been carefully tabulated. All that was necessary was to apply the tabulation to each specific dispute.

515

Although Canadian judges were at first disposed to take the view that the British North America Act was something more than a simple British statute,[42] the judges of the Privy Council preferred to base their judgments upon the principle that the courts should always "treat the provisions of the Act . . . by the same methods of construction and exposition which they apply to other statutes".[43] These rules or methods are well known: the meaning of a statute is primarily to be gathered from the words of the statute itself, and not from what the legislature may be supposed to have intended;[44] if the words of a statute are ambiguous, recourse must be had to the context and scheme of the Act;[45] if there are seemingly conflicting provisions in a statute, the conflicting provisions must be read together and, if possible, a reasonable reconciliation effected:[46] and, the "parliamentary history" of a statute may not be referred to for the purpose of explaining its meaning, although "historical knowledge" of the circumstances surrounding the passing thereof may, on occasion, be used as an aid in construing the statute.[47] This one concession to the historical approach did not, however, mean very much. Rarely, if ever, did references to the Quebec and London Resolutions ever have a controlling or determining effect upon the decisions handed down by the Judicial Committee of the Privy Council. Judges and lawyers are bound by precedent and rule; they cannot shake off the shackles of a rigid legalism to enjoy the freedom of historical speculation.

The remarkable thing is that the courts have, nevertheless, rarely misunderstood the meaning of the union. This is, indeed, a tribute to the skill with which the Resolutions of 1866 were transformed into legal parlance by the lawyers of the Colonial Office. And perhaps it is just as well that the lawyers have not been prepared to take readily to the historian's approach; for nothing could be more frustrating to the legal mind than the effort to determine the "intentions" of the Fathers of Confederation. Including, as they did, Fathers favouring a unitary state and others aiming at a wide degree of provincial autonomy, to try to determine the common denominator of their joint intentions from their speeches and their public statements before and after 1867 would produce only a series of irreconcilable contradictions.[48] The one sure guide as to what the Fathers really agreed to agree upon, was the language of their resolutions, or better still, the language of the British North America Act itself. And in construing this Act in the way they have, the judges probably arrived at a more accurate interpretation than have the multitude of critics who have so emphatically disagreed with them.

516

There have been many and severe critics of the judgments laid down by the courts. Within the last twenty years in particular it has been the common sport of constitutional lawyers in Canada to criticize, cavil and poke fun at the *dicta* of the judges of the Privy Council and their decisions in Canadian cases. Canadian historians and political scientists have followed the legal party line with condemnations of "the judicial revolution" said to have been accomplished by Lord Watson and Lord Haldane, and the alleged willful nullification of the true intentions of the Fathers of Confederation.[49] The explanation of these attacks on the part of lawyers, professional and lay, court and class-room alike, may be found in the impact of the Great Depression of the 1930's upon the economy of the country and the inability of governments, provincial and federal, to deal with it. It is natural for the human mind to seek simple solutions and to find scapegoats for their ills.[50] If, by the simple process of an Act of Parliament, full employment can be secured and that Act of Parliament is unconstitutional, then change the constitution and the problem is solved. No provincial jurisdiction, no acknowledged right or privilege, no historic pact should be allowed to stand in the way of such an easy solution for the economic problems of the day. Facts, not principles should be the decisive determinants of history. Unfortunately, however, neither the causes nor the solution of the Great Depression were as simple as all that. The economic crisis of the 1930's was the result of a multiplicity of factors, external as well as internal, and a change in the interpretation of the British North America Act or in the Act itself would have given rise to as many new problems as it might have solved of the old. In any event, it is no part of the task of the judges to try to make the constitution fit the constantly changing facts of economic and political history.

Here is the criticism in its simplest terms. Proceeding from the basic premise that the fundamental intentions of the Fathers of Confederation were to limit strictly the powers of the provincial legislatures and give the central government a real, effective, and dominating position in the federal scheme, the critics of the courts contend that the tabulated or enumerated powers given to the federal parliament by Section 91 are, in fact, not specially allocated powers, but rather illustrations of an overriding general jurisdiction embodied in the well-known words "And it shall be lawful for the Queen, by and with the Advice and Consent of the Senate and the House of Commons, to make Laws for the Peace, Order and Good Government of Canada . . . ."[51] They argue that the enumerated powers which follow later in the wording of the same section are not in addition to this general power, but flow from it and are examples of it. The critics take the view that the courts, by attaching a "primacy" to the enumerated powers, have altered the balance of Sections 91 and 92, and have, in consequence, distorted the aims and objects of the founding fathers and given greater authority to the provincial legislators than it was ever intended that they should have. The cumulative effect of judicial decisions over the years has been to establish a union in which the sovereign provincial legislatures, in effect, possess a field of jurisdiction so great, and the federal parliament a field so restricted, as to alter the whole purpose of the original federative Act.

517

It is not for me, at this point, to discuss the syntax of the controversial sections of the British North America Act. As I said at the beginning, my approach is, of necessity, historical. And, the pre-parliamentary history of the Act appears to me to confirm the interpretation of the criticized rather than that of the critics. From the date of the publication of the first practical scheme of confederation, framers of federal constitutions in Canada have followed the procedure, not of enumerating only the subject matters upon which one party to the federation may legislate and giving all the rest (the residuum of powers) to the other, but rather of tabulating or enumerating the legislative powers of *both* parties. The scheme advanced by Joseph Charles Taché, in 1857, upon which the later Canadian scheme is sometimes said to have been based, followed this course. Taché allocated to the federal parliament "Commerce, including laws of a purely commercial nature, such as laws relating to banks and other financial institutions, of a general character; moneys, weights and measures; customs duties, including the establishment of a uniform tariff and the collection of the revenues which it produces; large public works and navigation, such as canals, railways, telegraph lines, harbour works, coastal lighthouses; postal service as a whole both inside and outside the country; the organization of the militia as a whole; criminal justice including all offences beyond the level of the jurisdiction of police magistrates and justices of the peace". All the rest "dealing with civil laws, education, public welfare, the establishment of public lands, agriculture, police, urban and rural, highways, in fact everything relating to family life in each province, would remain under the exclusive control of the respective government of each province as an inherent right".[52] The draft scheme of

1864, presented by the Canadians to the Maritime delegates at Charlotte-town, likewise included a series of enumerated powers to be allocated to the federal and provincial legislatures. According to this scheme the "Federal Legislature" was to be given "the control of — Trade, Currency, Banking, General Taxation, Interest and Usury Laws, Insolvency and Bankruptcy, Weights and Measures, Navigation of Rivers and Lakes, Lighthouses, Sea Fisheries, Patent and Copyright Laws, Telegraphs, Natu-ralization, Marriage and Divorce, Postal Service, Militia and Defence, Criminal Law, Intercolonial Works". The local legislatures were "to be entrusted with the care of — Education (with the exception of Universi-ties), Inland Fisheries, Control of Public Lands, Immigration, Mines and Minerals, Prisons, Hospitals and Charities, Agriculture, Roads and Bridges, Registration of Titles, Municipal Laws".[53]

518

When the delegates finally convened at Quebec to settle the details of the federation which they had agreed upon at Charlottetown, these lists of items were thoroughly discussed between the 21st and 25th of October. The simplest method of proceeding would have been, once it had been decided to concede the residuum of powers to the federal parliament, to define only those powers which would belong exclusively to the provinces. This course was, in fact, suggested. "Enumerate for Local Governments their powers, and give all the rest to General Government, but do not enumerate both", said J. M. Johnston of New Brunswick; William Henry of Nova Scotia echoed this view, "We should not define powers of General Legislature. I would ask Lower Canada not to fight for a shadow. Give a clause to give general powers (except such as given to Local Legislatures) to Federal Legislature. Anything beyond that is hampering the case with difficulties".[54] But the Conference did not agree. From Henry's remark we may infer that Cartier and his colleagues were determined to follow the plan of specifying in detail the powers of *both* the federal parliament and the provincial legislatures. Accordingly, sections 29 and 43 of the Quebec Resolutions contained an enumeration of the powers of each party to the federation. Section 29 read: "The General Parliament shall have power to make laws for the peace, welfare and good government of the Federated Provinces (saving the sovereignty of England), and especially laws respecting the following subjects", and then listed thirty-seven specific matters upon which the federal parliament would be free to legislate. Section 43 outlined eighteen matters over which the provinces would have exclusive jurisdic-tion, ending with what may be regarded as a provincial residuum of powers: "generally all matters of a private or local nature, not assigned to the General Parliament".[55] From the evidence afforded by Joseph Pope, it would appear that the delegates at no time seriously attempted to define the scope of the enumerated items or their possible overlapping, beyond George Brown's suggestion that "the courts of each Province should decide what is Local and what General Government jurisdiction, with appeal to the Appeal or Superior Court".[56] The same procedure was followed at London. Sections 28 and 41 of the London Resolutions are almost identical (with one or two small exceptions) with their counterparts in the resolutions of Quebec.

The evolution of these two sets of resolutions through the various drafts of the British North America Bill supports the view that the Fathers intended that primacy should attend the enumerated heads. Section 36 of the first "Rough Draft" of the Bill prepared by the Canadian and Maritime delegates themselves, read simply that "The Parliament shall have power to make laws respecting the following subjects" and then listed thirty-seven, one of which was the power to pass laws for the "peace, welfare and good government of the Confederation respecting all matters of a general character, not specially and exclusively herein reserved for the Legislatures [of the provinces]".[57] This was altered in the draft prepared by the Imperial Government's draftsman and dated January 23, 1867, which adopted a wording which, with only insignificant changes, was to be that of section 91 of the British North America Act.[58] Thus, only in the final stages, after the Imperial authorities had been invited to put the bill into final shape, were the introductory words of Section 91, as we know them, interpolated, apparently for the purpose of lessening the possibility of overlapping jurisdiction. The colonial delegates had believed the enumerated powers to be mutually exclusive; only agriculture and immigration, which had been included among the powers assigned to both federal and provincial legislatures, seemed to provide any real problems, and these were to be obviated by giving federal legislation in respect to these matters precedence over that of the provinces. While there is no documentary evidence directly bearing on this point, it seems more than likely that the British draftsman pointed out the possibility of further overlapping and therefore revised the first draft of the Bill in such a way as to ensure, syntactically, the unquestioned paramountcy of the enumerated federal powers, upon which the delegates, ever since 1864, had placed so much emphasis.

519

That some of these conclusions may appear to be based upon circumstantial historical evidence is a valid criticism; but historians, no more than lawyers, are not to be debarred from using circumstantial evidence. The majority of the problems of historical synthesis are really problems of probability.

V

But to return to the question of the Confederative pact. Despite the frequency with which Canadian political leaders have reiterated the existence of the pact, despite the legal support afforded the concept of the pact by the highest court of appeal — as late as the 1930's, the Privy Council referred to the British North America Act as a "contract", a "compact" and a "treaty" founded on the Quebec and London Resolutions[59] — the pact concept was never universally understood or wholly accepted by each and all of the provinces of Canada. Indeed the popularity of the pact idea seems to vary in some provinces in inverse ratio to their fiscal need. The concept of the pact was slow to be accepted in the Maritimes. In the early years after Confederation, there was still strong opposition to the very fact of union, and the pact upon which it was based was never very popular. In 1869 the Saint John *Morning Freeman* criticized the idea of a pact of confederation, denying that there was any continuity between the pre- and post-confederation provinces.[60] From time to time, various provinces have supported the doctrine of the pact, including New Brunswick, Alberta and British Columbia; but their support has not been marked by unanimity or consistency. Only in Ontario and Quebec has the concept remained undiminished in strength and popularity, at least in political circles, if not always in legal and academic. The Ontario-Quebec axis has transcended both time and political parties. The original alliance of Mowat and Mercier, has carried on through that of Whitney and Gouin, Ferguson and Taschereau, and Drew and Duplessis. It has always been the principal buttress of provincial autonomy.

520

The explanation why the pact idea has remained most vigorous in the two central provinces is to be found in their history. We need only recall the point I have established earlier this evening, the fact that the pact was, in its origin, an entente between the two racial groups of Old Canada, between the two provinces which were each the focus of a distinctive culture. Only in the two provinces of Old Canada did the racial struggle play any real part in our history; only in the two provinces of Old Canada did this struggle have any real meaning. The Maritimers of 1864 were not concerned with racial problems; their interest in federal union was largely financial, in the recovery of a passing age of sea-going prosperity. The western provinces, with the exception of British Columbia which found its own version of a compact in the terms of union in 1871, were the offspring of the federal loins; their interest in federal union was in their maintenance and subsistence. But in Upper and Lower Canada federation was the solution of the politico-racial contest for supremacy and survival, which had marked their joint history since the day Vaudreuil and Amherst signed the Capitulation of Montreal. The concept of a pact of federation was thus peculiarly a Canadian one (I use Canadian in the sense in which it was used in 1864, and in which it is still used in some parts of the Maritimes today); it still remains peculiarly Canadian. Duality of culture as the central feature of the constitutional problem has a meaning and a reality to the people of the two provinces of Old Canada which it cannot have to those of the other provinces. That is why neither Ontario nor Quebec has departed in its provincial policy from the strict interpretation of the federal basis of the constitution, or from the concept of a federative pact. The identification of the racial pact, which was a very real thing in the 1850s and 1860s with the compromise arrived at by the several provinces in 1864 and 1866, has tended to obscure the racial aspect of the bargain and to deprive it of some of its strength. The Canadian delegates to Quebec and London were thoroughly convinced that their bargain was a treaty or a pact; however, this conviction was always weaker among the Maritimers than among the Canadians, and especially the French Canadians, whose principal concern as a vital minority, has been and must be the survival of their culture and the pact which is the constitutional assurance of that survival.

It is the racial aspect of the pact of Confederation which gives the pact its historicity and confirms its continued usage. If the population of Canada were one in race, language, and religion, our federation would be marked by flexibility; amendment would be a comparatively easy matter where there was agreement upon fundamental issues. Since history has given us a dual culture, with its diversities of race and language, we must maintain a precarious balance between the two groups; and our constitution is rigid and inflexible. That is what I meant, when I said at the outset, that the historic pact of the Union has become, by acceptance and usage, a necessary convention of our constitution. It will continue to be such so long as the minority group retains its numbers and its will to survive.

521

Notes

1. Sir Reginald Coupland, *The Durham Report, an abridged version with an introduction and notes* (Oxford, 1945), p. 15. For an unabridged edition see that published by Methuen & Co. Limited, London, 1902; or Sir Charles Lucas, *Lord Durham's Report on the Affairs of British North America*, Oxford, 1912, vol. II.
2. A. Shortt and A. G. Doughty, *Documents Relating to the Constitutional History of Canada, 1759–1791* (Ottawa, 1918), I, 163 ff.
3. *Ibid.*, 173 ff, 181 ff.
4. *Ibid.*, 570 ff; 14 Geo. III, c. 83.
5. A. L. Burt, *The Old Province of Quebec* (Toronto and Minneapolis, 1933) p. 200.
6. Quoted in L. Groulx, *Histoire du Canada français depuis la découverte* (Montréal, 1952), III, 75.
7. Shortt and Doughty, *Documents*, II, p. 983; Discussion of Petitions and Counter Petitions re Change of Government in Canada, enclosed in Grenville to Dorchester, Oct. 20, 1789.
8. *Ibid.*, II, p. 1031 ff.
9. *Ibid.*, II, p. 988; Grenville to Dorchester, Oct. 20, 1789.
10. *The Annual Register or a View of the History, Politics and Literature for the Year 1791* (London, 1795), p. 111. Charles James Fox had criticized the proposed division of the old province on the grounds that "the French and English Canadians would be completely distinguished from each other. But he considered such a measure big with mischief; and maintained that the wisest policy would be to form the two descriptions of people into one body, and endeavour to annihilate all national distinctions". (*Annual Register*, 1791, 110).
11. W. P. M. Kennedy, *The Constitution of Canada, 1534–1937, an introduction to its development, law and custom* (Oxford, 1938), p. 86.
12. Groulx, *Histoire du Canada français*, III, 133.
13. Quoted in J. A. R. Marriott, *England Since Waterloo* (London, 1936), p. 88.
14. Coupland, *The Durham Report*, p. 161.
15. W. P. M. Kennedy, *Documents of the Canadian Constitution, 1759–1915* (Toronto, 1918), pp. 536–550; 3 & 4 Victoria, c. 35.
16. Coupland, *The Durham Report*, p. 161.
17. K. N. Bell and W. P. Morrell, *Select Documents on British Colonial Policy, 1830–1860* (Oxford, 1928), pp. 62–71: Bagot to Stanley, Sep. 26, 1842.
18. *Parliamentary Debates on the Subject of the Confederation of the British North American Provinces* (Quebec, 1865), p. 30.
19. Kennedy, *The Constitution of Canada*, p. 257.
20. Quoted in Groulx, *Histoire du Canada français*, IV, p. 21.
21. *The Leader*, Toronto, April 30, 1861. *La Minerve* (April 25, 1861) praised Macdonald for his stand against *Rep by Pop*: "Soyons francs! est-ce qu'il ne faut pas un grand courage, une grande force d'âme et beaucoup d'honnêteté pour agir ainsi? Mettez donc cette conduite ferme et sincère en parallèle avec la lâche conduite d'un de ses adversaires, et dites où est l'homme d'état, où est l'allié naturel des Bas Canadiens?"
22. *Confederation Debates*, p. 28.

23. Public Archives of Canada, New Brunswick, C.O. 189, vol. 9: Gordon to Cardwell, confidential, Sep. 22, 1864. This letter is reproduced, in part, in W. F. O'Connor, *Report pursuant to Resolution of the Senate to the Honourable the Speaker by the Parliamentary Counsel* (Ottawa, 1939), Annex 2, pp. 84–6. Large sections of the original letter were, however, omitted in the printed version. The quotation given here is one of the omitted portions.

24. J. C. Taché, *Des provinces de l'Amérique du Nord et d'une union fédérale* (Québec, 1858).

25. "Objection had been taken to the scheme now under consideration, because of the words, 'new nationality'. Now, when we were united together, if union were attained, we would form a political nationality with which neither the national origin, nor the religion of any individual would interfere. It was lamented by some that we had this diversity of races, and hopes were expressed that this distinctive feature would cease. The idea of unity of races was utopian — it was impossible. . . . We could not do away with the distinctions of race. We could not legislate for the disappearance of the French Canadians from American soil, but British and French Canadians alike could appreciate and understand their position relative to each other". (Cartier, Feb. 7, 1865, *Confederation Debates*, p. 60). Subsequently, in answer to the criticisms of A. A. Dorion, Cartier said, "I have always had the interests of Lower Canada at heart and have guarded them more seduously than the hon. member for Hochelaga and his partisans have ever done." (*Confederation Debates*, p. 714). Hector Langevin, the Solicitor-General, took the same view. He said, "We are considering the establishment of a Confederacy — with a Central Parliament and local parliaments. The Central or Federal Parliament will have the control of all measures of a general character . . ., but all matters of local interest, all that relates to the affairs and rights of the different sections of the Confederacy, will be reserved for the control of the local parliaments. . . . It will be the duty of the Central Government to see that the country prospers, but it will not be its duty to attack our religion, our institutions, or our nationality, which . . . will be amply protected." (*Confederation Debates*, pp. 367–8. See also pp. 373, 392.)

26. *Confederation Debates*, p. 87.

27. *Ibid.*, p. 16. Macdonald repeated this idea several times throughout his speech; see pp. 31–2.

28. *Ibid.*, p. 136.

29. *Ibid.*, pp. 83, 88, 714, 720. See also Chapter II in Sir George Ross, *The Senate of Canada, its Constitution Powers and Duties Historically Considered* (Toronto 1914.)

30. *Nova Scotia Parliamentary Debates, 1866. 3rd Session, 23rd Assembly.* See debate, April 3, 1866. Quotations from these debates will be found in O'Connor, *Report*, Annex 2, pp. 67–71.

31. Joseph Pope, *Confederation: being a series of hitherto unpublished documents bearing on the British North America Act* (Toronto, 1895), p. 121.

32. *Ibid.*, p. 122.

33. *The Morning Freeman*, Saint John, N.B., Jan. 5, 1867.

34. *Ibid.*, March 7, 1867.

35. Quoted in O'Connor, *Report*, Annex 4, p. 149.

36. Sir R. Herbert, *Speeches on Canadian Affairs by Henry Howard Molyneux, fourth Earl of Carnarvon* (London, 1902), p. 92.

37. *Ibid.*, pp. 110, 130.

38. Hon. Justice T. J. J. Loranger, *Letters upon the Interpretation of the Federal Constitution known as the British North America Act 1867* (Quebec, 1884), p. 63.

39. O'Connor, *Report*, Annex 2, p. 83: Gordon to Cardwell, Sep. 12, 1864. After visiting Charlottetown during the meeting of the provincial delegates and receiving daily reports from the New Brunswick delegation, Lieutenant-Governor Gordon wrote to the Colonial Secretary:

A "Federal Union" in the mouth of a Lower Canadian usually means the independence of his Province from English and Protestant influences. In the mouth of an inhabitant of the Maritime Provinces it means the retention of the machinery of the existing local Executive Government, the expenditure within each Province of the revenue raised from it, except a quota to be paid towards Federal expenses, and the preservation of the existing Legislatures in their integrity, with the somewhat cumbrous addition of a central Parliament to which the consideration of some few topics of general interest is to be confided under restraints prompted by a jealous care for the maintenance of Provincial independence.

40. *Confederation Debates*, p. 29.

41. See, for instance, statements by Sir Wilfrid Laurier (*House of Commons Debates, Canada*, Jan. 28, 1907, p. 2199); Robert Borden (*Ibid.*, Jan. 28, 1907, p. 2199); Ernest Lapointe (*Ibid.*, Feb. 18, 1925, pp. 297–300); Arthur Meighen (*Ibid.*, Feb. 19, 1925, p. 335) and Richard B. Bennett (*Ibid.*, Feb. 24, 1930, p. 24).

42. See Strong J. in *St. Catharines Milling and Lumber Co. v. The Queen* (1887), 13, S.C.R., p. 606. For a criticism of this point of view see W. H. P. Clement, *The Law of the Canadian Constitution* (Toronto, 1916), p. 364; and V. C. Macdonald "Constitutional Interpretation and Extrinsic Evidence" (*The Canadian Bar Review*, Feb. 1939, XVII, 2).

43. *Bank of Toronto v. Lambe* (1887), 12 App. Cas., p. 579.

44. *Brophy v. Attorney-General for Manitoba* (1895), A.C., p. 216.

45. *Attorney-General for Ontario v. Attorney-General for Canada* (1912), A.C., p. 583.

46. *Citizens Insurance Company of Canada, v. Parsons* (1881), 7 App. Cas., p. 109.

47. *Edwards v. Attorney-General for Canada* (1930), A.C., p. 134.

48. See, for instance, the conflicting points of view of Sir John A. Macdonald and Sir Oliver Mowat after Confederation, although both of them had been delegates to the Quebec Conference. It is equally difficult to reconcile some of the statements of men like Galt and Macdonald, who hoped that federal union might develop into a legislative union, and those of Cartier and Langevin who upheld provincial rights, all of whom were "Fathers of Confederation."

49. The most complete criticism from a legal standpoint is to be found in O'Connor, *Report*. See also N. M. Rogers, "The Compact Theory of Confederation", (*Proceedings of the Canadian Political Science Association*, 1931), pp. 205–30; F. R. Scott, *Canada Today, a Study of her National Interests and National Policy* (Toronto, 1938) pp. 75–8; A. R. M. Lower, *Colony to Nation, a History of Canada* (Toronto, 1946), pp. 328–9. For views contrary to those of O'Connor, see V. E. Gray "The O'Connor Report on the British North America Act, 1867" (*The Canadian Bar Review*, May, 1939, XVII, 5, pp. 309–337).

50. L. Richer, *Notre Problème Politique* (Montreal, n.d.), pp. 20–1.

51. O'Connor, *Report*, Annex 1, pp. 18–51.

52. J. C. Taché, *op. cit.*, p. 148.

53. Gordon to Cardwell, confidential, Sep. 22, 1864, (*cf. supra*, note 23).

54. Pope, *Confederation Documents*, p. 87.

55. Copies of the Quebec and London Resolutions will be found in Pope, *Confederation Documents*, pp. 38–52, 98–110; in O'Connor, *Report*, Annex 4, pp. 49–66, and in *British North America Act and Amendments 1867–1948*, (Ottawa, 1948), pp. 39–58.

56. Pope, *Confederation Documents*, p. 85.

57. *Ibid.*, pp. 130–2.

58. *Ibid.*, pp. 152–4.

59. *Attorney-General for Australia v. Colonial Sugar Co.* (1914) A.C., p. 253; *In re the Regulation and Control of Aeronautics in Canada* (1932) A.C., p. 70; *Attorney-General for Canada v. Attorney-General for Ontario and others* (1937) A.C., p. 351.

60. *The Morning Freeman*, Saint John, N.B., Nov. 25, 1869.

The British North America Act*

VI. — DISTRIBUTION OF LEGISLATIVE POWERS.

Powers of the Parliament.

Legislative Authority of Parliament of Canada

91. It shall be lawful for the Queen, by and with the Advice and Consent of the Senate and House of Commons, to make Laws for the Peace, Order, and good Government of Canada, in relation to all Matters not coming within the Classes of Subjects by this Act assigned exclusively to the Legislatures of the Provinces; and for greater Certainty, but not so as to restrict the Generality of the foregoing Terms of this Section, it is hereby declared that (notwithstanding anything in this Act) the exclusive Legislative Authority of the Parliament of Canada extends to all Matters coming within the Classes of Subjects next herein-after enumerated; that is to say, —

1. The amendment from time to time of the Constitution of Canada, except as regards matters coming within the classes of subjects by this Act assigned exclusively to the Legislatures of the provinces, or as regards rights or privileges by this or any other Constitutional Act granted or secured to the Legislature or the Government of a province, or to any class of persons with respect to schools or as regards the use of the English or the French language or as regards the requirements that there shall be a session of the Parliament of Canada at least once each year, and that no House of Commons shall continue for more than five years from the day of the return of the Writs for choosing the House: provided, however, that a House of Commons may in time of real or apprehended war, invasion or insurrection be continued by the Parliament of Canada if such continuation is not opposed by the votes of more than one-third of the members of such house (39)

1A. The Public Debt and Property. (40)
2. The Regulation of Trade and Commerce.

---

(39) Added by the *British North America (No. 2) Act, 1949*, 13 Geo VI, c.81 (U.K.).
(40) Re-numbered by the *British North America (No. 2) Act*, 1949.

*From *A Consolidation of the British North American Acts, 1867–1975*, edited by Elmer A. Driedger. Copyright 1976 by Supply and Services Canada. Reprinted by permission.

2.A. Unemployment insurance. (41)
3. The raising of Money by any Mode or System of Taxation.
4. The borrowing of Money on the Public Credit.
5. Postal Service.
6. The Census and Statistics.
7. Militia, Military and Naval Service, and Defence.
8. The fixing of and providing for the Salaries and Allowances of Civil and other Officers of the Government of Canada.
9. Beacons, Buoys, Lighthouses, and Sable Island.
10. Navigation and Shipping.
11. Quarantine and the Establishment and Maintenance of Marine Hospitals.
12. Sea Coasts and Inland Fisheries.
13. Ferries between a Province and any British or Foreign Country or between Two Provinces.
14. Currency and Coinage.
15. Banking, Incorporation of Banks, and the Issue of Paper Money.
16. Savings Banks.
17. Weights and Measures.
18. Bills of Exchange and Promissory Notes.
19. Interest.
20. Legal Tender.
21. Bankruptcy and Insolvency.
22. Patents of Invention and Discovery.
23. Copyrights.
24. Indians, and Lands reserved for the Indians.
25. Naturalization and Aliens.
26. Marriage and Divorce.
27. The Criminal Law, except the Constitution of Courts of Criminal Jurisdiction, but including the Procedure in Criminal Matters.
28. The Establishment, Maintenance, and Management of Penitentiaries.
29. Such Classes of Subjects as are expressly excepted in the Enumeration of the Classes of Subjects by this Act assigned exclusively to the Legislatures of the Provinces.

And any Matter coming within any of the Classes of Subjects enumerated in this Section shall not be deemed to come within the Class of Matters of a local or private Nature comprised in

525

---

(41) Added by the *British North America Act*, 1940, 3–4 Geo VI, c.36 (U.K.).

the Enumeration of the Classes of Subjects by this Act assigned exclusively to the Legislatures of the Provinces. (42)

Exclusive Powers of Provincial Legislatures.

Subjects of exclusive Provincial Legislation. **92.** In each Province the Legislature may exclusively make Laws in relation to Matters coming within the Classes of Subject next herein-after enumerated; that is to say, —

1. The Amendment from Time to Time, notwithstanding anything in this Act, of the Constitution of the Prov-

---

(42) Legislative authority has been conferred on Parliament by other Acts as follows:
  1. The *British North America Act, 1871,* 34–35 Vict., c. 28 (U.K.).

  2. The Parliament of Canada, may from time to time establish new Provinces in any territories forming for the time being part of the Dominion of Canada, but not included in any Province thereof, and may, at the time of such establishment, make provision for the constitution and administration of any such Province, and for the passing of laws for the peace, order, and good government of such Province, and for its representation in the said Parliament.

  3. The Parliament of Canada may from time to time, with the consent of the Legislature of any Province of the said Dominion, increase, diminish, or otherwise alter the limits of such Province, upon such terms and conditions as may be agreed to by the said Legislature, and may, with the like consent, make provision respecting the effect and operation of any such increase or diminution or alteration of territory in relation to any Province affected thereby.

  4. The Parliament of Canada may from time to time make provision for the administration peace, order, and good government of any territory not for the time being included in any Province.

  5. The following Acts passed by the said Parliament of Canada, and intituled respectively, — "An Act for the temporary government of Rupert's Land and the North Western Territory when united with Canada"; and "An Act to amend and continue to Act thirty-two and thirty-three Victoria, chapter three, and to establish and provide for the government of "the Province of Manitoba," shall be and be deemed to have been valid and effectual for all purposes whatsoever from the date at which they respectively received the assent, in the Queen's name, of the Governor General of the said Dominion of Canada.

  6. Except as provided by the third section of this Act, it shall not be competent for the Parliament of Canada to alter the provisions of the last-mentioned Act of the said Parliament in so far as it relates to the Province of Manitoba, or of any other Act hereafter establishing new Provinces in the said Dominion, subject always to the right of the Legislature of the Province of Manitoba to alter from time to time the provisions of any law respecting the qualification of electors and members of the Legislative Assembly, and to make laws respecting elections in the said Province.

  The *Rupert's Land Act 1868,* 31–32 Vict., c. 105 (U.K.) (repealed by the *Statute Law Revision Act, 1893,* 56–57, Vict., c. 14 (U.K.)) had previously conferred similar authority in relation to *Rupert's Land* and the North-Western Territory upon admission of those areas.

  2. *The British North America Act, 1886,* 49–50 Vict., c. 35, (U.K.).

  1. The Parliament of Canada may from time to time make provision for the representation in the Senate and House of Commons of Canada, or in either of them, of any territories which for the time being form part of the Dominion of Canada, but are not included in any province thereof.

  3. The *Statute of Westminster, 1931,* 22 Geo. V, c. 4, (U.K.).

  3. It is hereby declared and enacted that the Parliament of a Dominion has full power to make laws having extra-territorial operation.

ince, except as regards the Office of Lieutenant Governor.

2. Direct Taxation within the Province in order to the raising of a Revenue for Provincial Purposes.

3. The borrowing of Money on the sole Credit of the Province.

4. The Establishment and Tenure of Provincial Offices and the Appointment and Payment of Provincial Officers.

5. The Management and Sale of the Public Lands belonging to the Province and of the Timber and Wood thereon.

6. The Establishment, Maintenance, and Management of Public and Reformatory Prisons in and for the Province.

527

7. The Establishment, Maintenance, and Management of Hospitals, Asylums, Charities, and Eleemosynary Institutions in and for the Province, other than Marine Hospitals.

8. Municipal Institutions in the Province.

9. Shop, Saloon, Tavern, Auctioneer, and other Licences in order to the raising of a Revenue for Provincial, Local, or Municipal Purposes.

10. Local Works and Undertakings other than such as are of the following Classes: —

    (a) Lines of Steam or other Ships, Railways, Canals, Telegraphs, and other Works and Undertakings connecting the Province with any other or others of the Provinces, or extending beyond the Limits of the Province;
    (b) Lines of Steam Ships between the Province and any British or Foreign Country;
    (c) Such Works as, although wholly situate within the Province, are before or after their Execution declared by the Parliament of Canada to be for the general Advantage of Canada or for the Advantage of Two or more of the Provinces.

11. The Incorporation of Companies with Provincial Objects.

12. The Solemnization of Marriage in the Province.

13. Property and Civil Rights in the Province.

14. The Administration of Justice in the Province, including the Constitution, Maintenance, and Organization of Provincial Courts, both of Civil and of Criminal Jurisdiction, and including Procedure in Civil Matters in those Courts.

15. The Imposition of Punishment by Fine, Penalty, or Imprisonment for enforcing any Law of the Province made in relation to any Matter coming within any of the Classes of Subjects enumerated in this Section.

16. Generally all Matters of a merely local or private Nature in the Province.

Education.

528

Legislation respecting Education

93. In and for each Province the Legislature may exclusively make Laws in relation to Education, subject and according to the following Provisions:

(1) Nothing in any such Law shall prejudicially affect any Right or Privilege with respect to Denominational Schools which any Class of Persons have by Law in the Province at the Union.

(2) All the Powers, Privileges, and Duties at the Union by law conferred and imposed in Upper Canada on the Separate Schools and School Trustees of the Queen's Roman Catholic Subjects shall be and the same are hereby extended to the Dissentient Schools of the Queen's Protestant and Roman Catholic Subjects in Quebec:

(3) Where in any Province a System of Separate or Dissentient Schools exists by Law at the Union or is thereafter established by the Legislature of the Province, an Appeal shall lie to the Governor General in Council from any Act or Decision of any Provincial Authority affecting any Right or Privilege of the Protestant or Roman Catholic Minority of the Queen's Subjects in relation to Education:

(4) In case any such Provincial Law as from Time to Time seems to the Governor General in Council requisite for the due Execution of the Provisions of this Section is not made, or in case any Decision of the Governor General in Council on any Appeal under this Section is not duly executed by the proper Provincial Authority

in that Behalf, then and in every such Case, and as far only as the Circumstances of each Case require, the Parliament of Canada may make remedial Laws for the due Execution of the Provisions of this Section and of any Decision of the Governor General in Council under this Section.(43)

(43) Altered for Manitoba by section 22 of the *Manitoba Act,* 33 Vict., c. 3 (Canada), (confirmed by the *British North America Act, 1871*). which reads as follows:

22. In and for the Province, the said Legislature may exclusively make Laws in relation to Education, subject and according to the following provisions:

(1) Nothing in any such Law shall prejudicially affect any right or privilege with respect to Denominational Schools which any class of persons have by Law or practice in the Province at the Union:

(2) An appeal shall lie to the Governor General in Council from any Act or decision of the Legislature of the Province, or of any Provincial Authority, affecting any right or privilege, of the Protestant or Roman Catholic minority of the Queen's subjects in relation to Education:

529

(3) In case any such Provincial Law, as from time to time seems to the Governor General in Council requisite for the due execution of the provisions of this section is not made, or in case any decision of the Governor General in Council on any appeal under this section is not duly executed by the proper Provincial Authority in that behalf, then, and in every such case, and as far only as the circumstances of each case require, the Parliament of Canada may make remedial Laws for the due execution of the provision of this section, and of any decision of the Governor General in Council under this section.

Altered for Alberta by section 17 of *The Alberta Act,* 4–5 Edw. VII, c. 3 which reads as follows:

17. Section 93 of The British North America Act, 1867, shall apply to the said province, with the substitution for paragraph (1) of the said section 93 of the following paragraph:

(1) Nothing in any such law shall prejudicially affect any right or privilege with respect to separate schools which any class of persons have at the date of the passing of this Act, under the terms of chapters 29 and 30 of the Ordinances of the Northwest Territories, passed in the year 1901, or with respect to religious instruction in any public or separate school provided for in the said ordinances.

(2) In the appropriation by the Legislature or distribution by the Government of the province of any moneys for the support of schools organized and carried on in accordance with the said chapter 29 or any Act passed in amendment thereof, or in substitution therefor, there shall be no discrimination against schools of any class described in the said chapter 29.

(3) Where the expression "by law" is employed in paragraph 3 of the said section 93, it shall be held to mean the law as set out in the said chapters 29 and 30, and where the expression "at the Union" is employed, in the said paragraph 3, it whall be held to mean the date at which this Act comes into force.

Altered for Saskatchewan by section 17 of *The Saskatchewan Act,* 4–5 Edw. VII, c. 42, which reads as follows:

17. Section 93 of the British North America Act, 1867, shall apply to the said province, with the substitution for paragraph (1) of the said section 93, of the following paragraph:

(1) Nothing in any such law shall prejudicially affect any right or privilege with respect to separate schools which any class of persons have at the date of the passing of this Act, under the terms of chapters 29 and 30 of the Ordinances of the Northwest Territories, passed in the year 1901, or with respect to religious instruction in any public or separate school as provided for in the said ordinances.

(2) In the appropriation by the Legislature or distribution by the Government of the

Uniformity of Laws in Ontario, Nova Scotia and New Brunswick

Legislation for Uniformity of Laws in Three Provinces.

94. Notwithstanding anything in this Act, the Parliament of Canada may make Provision for the Uniformity of all or any of the Laws relative to Property and Civil Rights in Ontario, Nova Scotia, and New Brunswick, and of the Procedure of all or any of the Courts in Those Three Provinces, and from and after the passing of any Act in the Behalf the Power of the Parliament of Canada to make Laws in relation to any Matter comprised in any such Act shall, notwithstanding anything in this Act, be unrestricted; but any Act of the Parliament of Canada making Provision for such Uniformity shall not have effect in any Province unless and until it is adopted and enacted as Law by the Legislature thereof.

530

Old Age Pensions.

Legislation respecting old age pensions and supplementary benefits

94.A. The Parliament of Canada may make laws in relation to old age pensions and supplementary benefits, including survivors and disability benefits irrespective of age, but no such law shall affect the operation of any law present or future of a provincial legislature in relation to any such matter.(44)

---

province of any moneys for the support of schools organized and carried on in accordance with the said chapter 29, or any Act passed in amendment thereof or in substitution therefor, there shall be no discrimination against schools of any class described in the said chapter 29.

(3) Where the expression "by law" is employed in paragraph (3) of the said section 93, it shall be held to mean the law as set out in the said chapters 29 and 30; and where the expression "at the Union" is employed in the said paragraph (3), it shall be held to mean the date at which this Act comes into force.

Altered by Term 17 of the Terms of Union of Newfoundland with Canada (confirmed by the *British North America Act 1949*, 12–13 Geo. VI, c. 22. (UK.)), which reads as follows:

17. In lieu of section ninety-three of the British North America Act, 1867, the following term shall apply in respect of the Province of Newfoundland:

In and for the Province of Newfoundland the Legislature shall have exclusive authority to make laws in relation to education, but the Legislature will not have authority to make laws prejudicially affecting any right or privilege with respect to denominational schools, common (amalgamated) schools, or denominational colleges, that any class or classes of persons have by law in Newfoundland at the date of Union, and out of public funds of the Province of Newfoundland, provided for education.

(a) all such schools shall receive their share of such funds in accordance with scales determined on a non-discriminatory basis from time to time by the Legislature for all schools then being conducted under authority of the Legislature; and

(b) all such colleges shall receive their share of any grant from time to time voted for all colleges then being conducted under authority of the Legislature, such grant being distributed on a non-discriminatory basis.

(44) Added by the *British North America Act, 1964* 12–13, Eliz II, c. 73 (U.K.). Originally enacted by the *British North America Act, 1951* 14–15 Geo. VI, c. 32 (U.K.), as follows:

94.A. It is hereby declared that the Parliament of Canada may from time to time make laws in relation to old age pensions in Canada, but no law made by the Parliament of Canada in relation to old age pensions shall affect the operation of any law present or future of a Provincial Legislature in relation to old age pensions.

Agriculture and Immigration.

95. In each province the Legislature may make Laws in relation to Agriculture in the Province, and to Immigration into the Province; and it is hereby declared that the Parliament of Canada may from Time to Time make Laws in relation to Agriculture in all or any of the Provinces, and to Immigration into all or any of the Provinces; and any Law of the Legislature of a Province relative to Agriculture or to Immigration shall have effect in and for the Province as long and as far only as it is not repugnant to any Act of the Parliament of Canada.

Concurrent Powers of Legislation respecting Agriculture, etc.

531